Holocaust Survivors in Postwar Germany, 1945–1957

Stranded in Germany after the Second World War, 300,000 Holocaust survivors began to rebuild their lives while awaiting emigration. Brought together by their shared persecution, Jewish displaced persons forged a vibrant community, redefining Jewish identity after Auschwitz. Asserting their dignity as Jews, they practiced Jewish rituals, created new families, embraced Zionism, agitated against British policies in Palestine, and tried to force Germans to acknowledge their responsibility for wartime crimes. In *Holocaust Survivors in Postwar Germany, 1945–1957*, Margarete Myers Feinstein uses survivor memoirs and interviews, allowing the reader to "hear" the survivors' voices, to focus on the personal aspects of the transition to normalcy. Unlike previous political histories, this study emphasizes Jewish identity and cultural life after the war.

Margarete Myers Feinstein is Research Scholar at the University of California, Los Angeles. Interested in questions of identity and legacies of the Nazi regime, she has focused her research on postwar German national identity and Jewish displaced persons. She is the author of *State Symbols: The Quest for Legitimacy in the Federal Republic of Germany and the German Democratic Republic, 1949–1959*, as well as numerous articles.

Holocaust Survivors in Postwar Germany, 1945–1957

MARGARETE MYERS FEINSTEIN

University of California, Los Angeles

CAMBRIDGE UNIVERSITY PRESS
Cambridge, New York, Melbourne, Madrid, Cape Town, Singapore,
São Paulo, Delhi, Dubai, Tokyo

Cambridge University Press
32 Avenue of the Americas, New York, NY 10013-2473, USA

www.cambridge.org
Information on this title: www.cambridge.org/9780521429580

First published 2010

Printed in the United States of America

A catalog record for this publication is available from the British Library.

Library of Congress Cataloging in Publication data
Feinstein, Margarete Myers, 1962–
Holocaust survivors in postwar Germany, 1945–1957 / Margarete Myers Feinstein.
    p.   cm.
Includes bibliographical references and index.
ISBN 978-0-521-42958-0 (hardback)
1. Jews – Germany – History – 1945–1990.   2. Holocaust survivors – Germany –
History – 20th century.   3. Holocaust survivors – Germany – Social conditions –
20th century   4. Holocaust survivors – Germany – Social life and customs – 20th century
5. Holocaust survivors – Germany – Politics and government – 20th century
6. Holocaust survivors – Germany – Psychology.   7. Jews – Germany – Identity.
8. Jewish children – Germany – History – 20th century.   9. Refugee children –
Germany – History – 20th century.   10. Refugees, Jewish – Germany – History –
20th century.   11. Germany – Ethnic relations – History – 20th century.
12. Refugee camps – Germany – History – 20th century.   I. Title.
DS134.26.F45 2009
940.53′18140943–dc22   2009015827

ISBN 978-0-521-42958-0 Hardback

Contents

Acknowledgments

In the fall of 1982 two events brought me to the study of Jewish displaced persons. As a junior at Reed College, I had the fortunate experience of taking a class on the Holocaust from Steven Aschheim. Also at that time, my mother lent me a copy of Lea Fleischmann's memoir, *Dies ist nicht mein Land*, and I discovered that Jewish survivors had lived in displaced persons (DP) camps on German soil until the late 1950s. Realizing that the history of the Holocaust did not end with the liberation of the concentration camps in 1944–1945, I wrote my senior history thesis about Jewish DPs. Naively, I thought that I had finished with the topic. I went on to research Nazi maternity homes and then postwar German national identity and state symbols. But I kept coming back to the DPs. There was more to their story that I needed to understand and to tell.

It is with pleasure that I acknowledge the assistance that I received for this project. Grants from the American Philosophical Society and from Indiana University financed vital archival research. The UCLA Center for Jewish Studies; the UCLA Center for the Study of Women; and the Center for the Study of the Holocaust, Genocide, and Human Rights at Claremont-McKenna College provided me with important institutional support during the final stages of research and writing.

Numerous archivists assisted me in my research, and I am thankful to them all. Here I recognize those who went above and beyond the call of duty: Michlean Amir (United States Holocaust Memorial Museum Archives), Crispin Brooks (USC Shoah Foundation Institute), Johannes Ibel (Archiv KZ-Gedenkstätte Flossenbürg), Yehudit Kleiman (Yad Vashem), Shelley Lightburn (United Nations), Lee Rotbart (Central Zionist Archives), Christa Scheitinger (Stadtarchiv Neunburg v.W.), Amy Schmidt (National Archives at College Park, MD), and Vincent Slatt (United States Holocaust Memorial Museum Library). This book is the richer for the resources to which these professionals so expertly guided me.

I am greatly indebted to William W. Hagen, who has been my advisor and mentor from the time of my doctoral studies at the University of California at Davis. He taught me to trust my scholarly judgment. I will be forever grateful for his guidance and encouragement as I searched to find my own voice as an historian. He has that rare ability to teach students while simultaneously learning from them and allowing them room to grow.

Colleagues have generously given their time and expertise to assist me with this project. Doris Bergen first suggested that my material about DPs merited treatment as a book. She has generously served as a sounding board, reading various drafts, offering suggestions and insights, and sharing her enthusiasm for historical inquiry. Jonathan Petropoulos has provided invaluable support and sage advice at critical junctures. Special thanks also go to Beth Cohen, Jay Geller, Judith Gerson, Laura Hilton, Avinoam Patt, Karen Remmler, and Emily Rosenbaum for commenting on draft chapters, contributing their knowledge, and helping me refine my arguments and prose. For their guidance and encouragement at various points in the project, I am grateful to Bianca Adams, Arthur Brenner, Michael Brenner, Elizabeth Clement, Louise Collins, Alex d'Erizans, Helga Embacher, Ronald Granieri, Atina Grossmann, Ursula Heckner-Hagen, Miriam Isaacs, Irene Kacandes, Betsy Lucal, Devin Pendas, Susanne Rolinek, Monica Tetzlaff, Leslie Walker, and Laurie Anne Whitcomb-Norden. All of these scholars have contributed to the strengths of this work; the remaining shortcomings are my own responsibility.

To those former DPs who gave of their time and of themselves to talk with me about their experiences, I offer my profound gratitude. I also thank those survivors whom I never met but whose memoirs and videotaped interviews provided me with invaluable information. I hope they find that I have done justice to their experiences.

Contrary to Virginia Woolf's assertion that a woman writer needs a room of her own, I have found that the dining room table suffices as long as one has a tremendously tolerant and supportive family. I am blessed with such a family. Everyone pitched in to keep the household running, and we were fortunate to have the help of Teresa Gonzalez and Maritza Aburto. Niece Deena cheerfully scanned documents written in a language she couldn't read, stepson Aaron researched tuberculosis treatments from the 1940s, and his brother Ari made trips to the library on my behalf. Eliana and Renata have lived with this project their entire lives. They carefully avoided Imma's papers and computer and were very patient when I was preoccupied. My husband Morley served as rabbinic advisor, editor, and Rock of Gibraltar. Without his love and support, this book would not have been possible. We are still rejoicing, though, at the return of the dining room table to its original purpose.

Holocaust Survivors in Postwar Germany, 1945–1957

Introduction

At the conclusion of Steven Spielberg's film *Schindler's List*, a Soviet officer on horseback arrives at the gates of the labor camp and tells the surviving Jews that they are free to go. Looking at one another in confusion, the survivors hesitate and then slowly shuffle through the gates. Through cinematic magic, they are suddenly striding across the hills of Israel fifty years later. For Hollywood, the Holocaust ended with the arrival of Allied troops and the defeat of Nazi Germany. For the 300,000 Jewish survivors who became displaced persons (DPs), liberation occurred only after they left Europe. Their transition to life in freedom took place in DP camps and in German towns. Temporarily living amid their former persecutors, these survivors reclaimed their Jewish heritage, began creating new families, and sought to define Jewish identity after Auschwitz.

The story of how nearly 300,000 Jewish survivors arrived in Germany is one of inconceivable loss, postwar persecution, and extraordinary determination. In 1944, Soviet forces pushed into Poland and began liberating the few remaining survivors of the concentration camps whom the Nazis had left behind. When the Nazis retreated, they forced the majority of prisoners on death marches into Germany. On January 27, 1945, the Red Army liberated Auschwitz. As the Soviets advanced, there emerged other Jews who had survived hiding in the forests, or fighting with the partisans, or passing as Christians with Aryan papers. As soon as they were physically able, these survivors returned to their hometowns to search for their families. Most Jews chose to rebuild their lives in their country of origin. An unknown number who had survived on Aryan papers retained their assumed identities and lived on as non-Jews. Particularly those survivors with leftist political leanings, such as communists and Bundists, remained to build a socialist future that they hoped would eradicate antisemitism and permit Jewish citizens to live in peace. Hungarian Jews in particular returned to their homes in large numbers.

Polish and Lithuanian Jews returned home burdened by memories of neighbors and fellow nationals who had collaborated with the Nazi persecution of the

Jews. Met with the physical ruin of their communities and the realization that few Jews remained alive, they contemplated their future. Often their Christian neighbors reacted with hostility to their return, muttering sentiments along the lines of "What! You're still alive? We thought Hitler had taken care of the Jews." Those Eastern Europeans who had profited from the plundering of Jews and who now occupied their homes and businesses did not intend to lose their booty. Some survivors who returned home were murdered by those who sought to retain ill-gotten Jewish property.

Under such circumstances, tens of thousands of these survivors sought a way out of Europe. Beginning in spring 1945, some Jews followed the path laid out by former Jewish partisans under the leadership of Abba Kovner of Vilna and headed south through Romania to Palestine. Political instability in the Balkans forced Brichah, the organization for the illegal movement of Jews out of Eastern Europe, to find new routes. Divided by the victorious Allies into American, British, French, and Soviet zones of occupation, the western zones of Germany became major reception areas for Jews fleeing Eastern Europe.

By summer 1945, Jews who had survived in hiding, survivors of the concentration camps, and former partisans hoping to get passage to a new life in Palestine or the United States began entering Germany. For logistical reasons the vast majority entered the American Zone of occupied Germany, although a sizeable minority resided in the British Zone, particularly in the Belsen DP camp. Once in Germany, these survivors joined 18,000 to 20,000 German Jews and approximately 60,000 other Jews who had survived liberation there and were now in displaced persons assembly centers (DP camps).[1] Later, in 1946–1947, nearly 200,000 "infiltrees," mostly Polish Jews who had survived the war in Soviet exile under debilitating conditions, would join these DPs. They made the dangerous, illegal journey to Germany, viewing it as a way station to a better life elsewhere. So it was that without a national homeland, their communities decimated, and their families murdered, Jewish DPs began rebuilding their lives in the land of their persecutors. From 1945 to 1957, Jewish survivors in Germany established families; engaged in meaningful religious practices; and began to integrate their prewar, wartime, and postwar lives.

It was rare for anyone over forty years old to survive the harsh conditions of the concentration camps or for anyone under sixteen to avoid selection to the gas chambers. That so many survivors were in late adolescence affected not only the sexual and reproductive activities in the DP camps but also religious and political beliefs and activities. Because the survivors were in Germany, seemingly mundane aspects of DP life (clothing, sports, and romance) became invested

---

[1] Approximately 80,000 Jews were liberated from concentration camps in Germany, but thousands continued to die of disease and complications related to starvation. Others repatriated, at least temporarily, immediately after liberation in their search for family. By summer 1945 approximately 60,000 Jewish camp survivors were alive in Germany. The German Jews mentioned survived outside of the camps in hiding or as "privileged" Jews in mixed marriages or of "half-Jewish" parentage. See Hagit Lavsky, *New Beginnings: Holocaust Survivors in Bergen-Belsen and the British Zone in Germany, 1945–1950* (Detroit, MI: Wayne State University Press, 2002), pp. 28–29.

with symbolic meaning. Meanwhile, the presence of DPs in their country not only contributed to German feelings of victimization but also allowed Germans to transfer their discontent with Allied military government authorities onto the weaker DPs. The interactions of Jews and Germans shed light on issues of rehabilitation, revenge, and reconciliation in the aftermath of genocide.

Jewish DPs were a self-selected group who refused to repatriate to their countries of origin. Few of them could imagine remaining in Europe, let alone Germany. They could not put down roots in what they called "blood-soaked soil." Germans still evoked fear, and their refusal to accept responsibility for wartime crimes reinforced Jewish suspicion of them. The DPs' future lay elsewhere – in a new Jewish home in Palestine or with relatives outside of Europe. Opportunities for emigration were initially few. Britain restricted Jewish entry into Palestine in order to placate Arabs as both Jews and Arabs challenged Britain's mandate. The United States maintained immigration quotas that favored non-Jews, and countries of the British Commonwealth had immigration schemes designed to attract labor in areas for which few Jewish survivors qualified. Even if one could acquire a visa to a host country, there remained much paperwork for individuals who had no birth certificates or other documentation required by modern bureaucracies. There were also medical exams, and a spot on a lung in a chest x-ray could delay emigration, sometimes indefinitely. Finally, in 1948, Israel declared its independence and the United States relaxed its immigration laws. As a result DPs flowed out of Germany, and by 1950 most Jewish DP camps had closed. A few ill and rudderless survivors remained in the Baviarian DP camp of Föhrenwald until its closure in 1957.

Most scholarship on DPs has approached the topic from the perspective of political history. Early studies emphasized the Cold War and international politics, minimizing the political autonomy of the survivors and focusing instead on international politics, Allied policymakers, and Zionists from the *Yishuv* (Jewish community in Palestine).[2] Even those historians who credited the DPs with influencing international public opinion concerning the creation of the State of Israel tended to emphasize the leadership role of the Yishuv in organizing the DPs.[3] In Israel, the "new historians," such as Tom Segev, Idith Zertal, and Yosef Grodzinsky, have argued that Zionists manipulated and exploited survivors for their own political purposes.[4] The voices of the survivors are muted

---

[2] See Leonard Dinnerstein, *America and the Survivors of the Holocaust* (New York: Columbia University Press, 1982); Wolfgang Jacobmeyer, *Vom Zwangsarbeiter zum Heimatlosen Ausländer* (Göttingen: Vandenhoeck und Ruprecht, 1985); Angelika Königseder and Juliane Wetzel, *Lebensmut im Wartesaal* (Frankfurt a.M.: Fischer Taschenbuch Verlag, 1994); Michael Marrus, *The Unwanted* (New York: Oxford University Press, 1985).

[3] See Zeev Tzahor, "Holocaust Survivors as a Political Factor," *Middle Eastern Studies* 24 (1988): 432–444; Abram L. Sacher, *Redemption of the Unwanted* (New York: St. Martin's Press, 1983); Idith Zertal, *From Catastrophe to Power: Holocaust Survivors and the Emergence of Israel* (Berkeley: University of California Press, 1998).

[4] Tom Segev, *The Seventh Million: The Israelis and the Holocaust* (New York: Hill and Wang, 1993); Idith Zertal, *Israel's Holocaust and the Politics of Nationhood* (Cambridge: Cambridge University Press, 2005) and *From Catastrophe to Power*; Yosef Grodzinsky, *In the Shadow of the Holocaust* (Monroe, ME: Common Courage Press, 2004).

in these histories, and DPs remain without agency.[5] Important recent studies that focus on the internal politics of the DP community have demonstrated that survivors had very clearly defined interests and argued vigorously on their own behalf, refuting the suggestions of DP passivity and victimization.[6]

Historians of postwar Germany have also concentrated on political history, either the policies of the occupying governments or state founding in the German Democratic Republic and the Federal Republic of Germany. After 1985, scholars began exploring issues of social history, gender, and popular culture in postwar Germany. They analyzed the ways that Germans had developed a narrative of their own victimization, and some noted the role German perceptions of DPs played in that process.[7] An interest in local histories of the period led some historians to write about DP camps as a forgotten episode in the recent German past.[8] The results primarily described DP organizational life and, concentrating on the large DP camps, tended to treat them as relatively isolated from local Germans. More recently, historians of the Jewish community in Germany have emphasized the important role DPs played in developing postwar Jewish organizations.[9] Sociologists are examining questions of Jewish identity, but they have focused more on post-1989 developments than on the immediate

[5] On the "new history" and its approach to the DPs, see Yechiam Weitz, "Dialectical versus Unequivocal: Israeli Historiography's Treatment of the Yishuv and Zionist Movement Attitudes toward the Holocaust," in *Making Israel*, edited by Benny Morris (Ann Arbor: University of Michigan Press, 2007), pp. 278–298, esp. pp. 286–287 and 293; Derek J. Penslar, *Israel in History: The Jewish State in Comparative Perspective* (London: Routledge, 2007), pp. 37–38.

[6] Lavsky, *New Beginnings*; Zeev Mankowitz, *Life between Memory and Hope: The Survivors of the Holocaust in Occupied Germany* (Cambridge: Cambridge University Press, 2002). Mankowitz's book concentrates on the American Zone.

[7] Robert G. Moeller, *War Stories: The Search for a Usable Past in the Federal Republic of Germany* (Berkeley: University of California Press, 2001); Maria Höhn, *GIs and Fräuleins: The German-American Encounter in 1950s West Germany* (Chapel Hill: The University of North Carolina Press, 2002); Elizabeth Heineman, "The Hour of the Woman," *American Historical Review* 101:2 (April 1996): 354–395; Atina Grossmann, *Jews, Germans, and Allies: Close Encounters in Occupied Germany* (Princeton, NJ: Princeton University Press, 2007).

[8] Susanne Dietrich and Julia Schulze Wessel, *Zwischen Selbstorganisation und Stigmatisierung: Die Lebenswirklichkeit jüdischer Displaced Persons und die neue Gestalt des Antisemitismus in der deutschen Nachkriegsgesellschaft*, Veröffentlichungen des Stadtarchivs Stuttgart, vol. 75 (Stuttgart: Klett-Cotta, 1998); Angelika Eder, *Flüchtige Heimat: Jüdische Displaced Persons in Landsberg am Lech, 1945 bis 1950*, Miscellanea Bavarica Monacensia, vol. 170 (Munich: UNI-Druck, 1998); Angelika Königseder and Juliane Wetzel, *Lebensmut im Wartesaal: Die jüdischen DPs (Displaced Persons) im Nachkriegsdeutschland* (Frankfurt: Fischer Taschenbuch, 1994); Ulrich Müller, *Fremde in der Nachkriegszeit: Displaced Persons – zwangsverschleppte Personen – in Stuttgart und Württemberg-Baden, 1945–1951*, Veröffentlichungen des Stadtarchivs Stuttgart, vol. 49 (Stuttgart: Klett-Cotta, 1990); Frank Stern, "The Historic Triangle: Occupiers, Germans and Jews in Postwar Germany," *Tel Aviver Jahrbuch für deutsche Geschichte* 19 (1990): pp. 47–76; Juliane Wetzel, *Jüdisches Leben in München, 1945–1951: Durchgangsstation oder Wiederaufbau?*, Miscellanea Bavarica Monacensia, vol. 135 (Munich: UNI-Druck, 1987).

[9] Jay Howard Geller, *Jews in Post-Holocaust Germany, 1945–1953* (Cambridge: Cambridge University Press, 2005); Michael Brenner, *After the Holocaust: Rebuilding Jewish Lives in Postwar Germany* (Princeton, NJ: Princeton University Press, 1997).

postwar period.[10] Historians are now investigating the "second history" of the Nazi regime, namely, the efforts of Germans to confront their Nazi past. In these histories, Jewish–German relations are often connected to generational interests and shifts.[11] Finally, historians are beginning to recognize the multicultural aspects of postwar German experiences and to incorporate Jews and ethnic German expellees into the larger narrative of German history.

This book examines the internal life of the DP communities in both the American and British Zones of occupied Germany while firmly placing the DPs within the context of postwar Germany.[12] A fundamental premise is that location had an impact on DPs, that residence in Germany affected DPs as they attempted to make the transition to life after the Holocaust. The interaction of Jewish DPs with the German landscape and people had a tremendous influence on the meanings DPs attributed to their actions and to their identity. For instance, farming a plot of land requisitioned from a former Nazi had important psychological, emotional, and political significance for survivors of the Holocaust. Giving birth to children in Germany with German medical personnel in attendance simultaneously evoked the trauma of the fate of mothers and children during the Holocaust and led to feelings of DP triumph and revenge. DP efforts to force Germans to acknowledge responsibility for wartime crimes often resulted in the opposite effect, and yet the attempts helped to foster DP pride and to restore their sense of agency.

Social and cultural activities served as mechanisms for the development of ethnic identity and gender roles. Religious rituals assumed importance as a means of performing and creating Jewish identity and community. Secular and Orthodox alike came to understand the Holocaust as part of the cycle of Jewish history and to claim their place among the generations. Through sharing their memories of their wartime persecution, survivors of different backgrounds and experiences created social memories of the Holocaust and forged a common identity. Schools, newspapers, kibbutzim, and mourning academies helped to create a DP memory community and to promote new communal ties. The obligation to honor the dead led DPs to insist on the cooperation of

---

[10] For example, Lynn Rappaport, *Jews in Germany after the Holocaust: Memory, Identity, and Jewish-German Relations* (Cambridge: Cambridge University Press, 1997); Anson Rabinbach and Jack Zipes, eds., *Germans and Jews since the Holocaust: The Changing Situation in West Germany* (New York: Holmes and Meier, 1986).

[11] Norbert Frei, *1945 und Wir: Das Dritte Reich im Bewußtsein der Deutschen* (Munich: Verlag C. H. Beck, 2005), p. 27; Peter Reichel, *Vergangenheitsbewältigung in Deutschland: Die Auseinandersetzung mit der NS-Diktatur von 1945 bis heute* (Munich: Verlag C. H. Beck, 2001), p. 9. On early postwar German attempts to confront the past, see also Anthony D. Kauders, *Democratization and the Jews: Munich, 1945–1965* (Lincoln: The University of Nebraska Press for the Vital Sassoon International Center for the Study of Antisemitism, The Hebrew University of Jerusalem, 2004).

[12] With the exception of Hagit Lavsky's book and a collection of essays on the Belsen DP camp, scholars have focused on the American Zone of occupied Germany, where most DPs resided. Lavsky, *New Beginnings*; Jo Reilly, et al., eds., *Belsen in History and Memory* (London: Frank Cass, 1997).

Allied and German authorities in reburials and to demand, in the name of the
dead, open immigration to Palestine. DP theatrical performances transformed
the Holocaust narrative into one of Jewish resistance and created new endings
through imagined family reunions and a Jewish future in Palestine. Rejecting
the notion of Jewish passivity, DPs emphasized the strong, revenge-seeking
new Zionist man and his female equivalents: the partisan girl and the new
Zionist mother. Despite their nightmares, fears, and uncertain future, Jewish
DPs sought to re-imagine themselves not as victims of Nazism but as survivors of the great catastrophe. As DPs in occupied Germany, Jewish survivors
of the Holocaust demanded respect and demonstrated their determination to
reclaim control over their lives.

The study of Jewish DPs reveals much about non-Jewish German behavior
and opens a window onto immediate postwar German responses to defeat,
occupation, and Jews. Just as DPs reacted to living among Germans, Germans
responded to the presence of Jewish DPs. Confronted with bombed-out cities,
a devastated infrastructure, millions of men detained as prisoners of war, and
housing and food shortages, Germans concentrated on their own experiences
of trauma and victimization. They had little sympathy for the foreign nationals
in their midst, believing that they should return to their countries of origin and
cease to be a burden on German communities. Germans portrayed Jewish DPs
as criminal outsiders unfairly protected and coddled by the occupying Allied
forces. Rather than attributing their misery to failed German policies of military
aggression, Germans could blame Jewish DPs for postwar criminality and housing shortages. Jewish DPs were relatively powerless targets of German dissatisfaction with defeat and occupation. By castigating Jewish DPs, Germans found
a safe way to criticize Allied occupation forces for their failure to maintain law
and order and for their requisitioning of German property. The emphasis on the
supposed immorality and criminality of Jewish DPs enabled some Germans to
attempt to salve their consciences with the belief that the Jews had been at least
partially responsible for their own persecution.[13]

Although it is tempting to explain all such lack of empathy toward Jewish
survivors as the enduring influence of Nazism, German expressions of
antisemitism after 1945 frequently reflected continuity with the pre-Nazi past.
Germans had made similar complaints against Eastern European Jews in the
aftermath of the First World War.[14] Even the tensions between Jewish DPs and
German Jews reflected these older stereotypes of Western and Eastern European
Jews.[15] Where remnants of the Nazi ideal of the *Volksgemeinschaft* (national
community) did become apparent was when Germans welcomed ethnic German
expellees from the East while attempting to exclude Jewish DPs.

[13] In 1949 one-fifth of Germans polled agreed that Jews shared responsibility for their persecution.
Reichel, *Vergangenheitsbewältigung*, p. 85.
[14] See Steven E. Aschheim, *Brothers and Strangers: The East European Jew in German and German
Jewish Consciousness, 1800–1923* (Madison: The University of Wisconsin Press, 1982), p. 230.
[15] Kauders, *Democratization and the Jews*, pp. 51–52.

Despite general hostility toward Jewish DPs and the unwillingness of the majority of Germans to acknowledge any moral or material obligation toward DPs, there were signs of a new beginning in German Christian–Jewish dialogue. Many relationships between non-Jewish Germans and Jewish DPs were born of opportunism and economic necessity, yet some genuine friendships occurred. Germans missing their former German-Jewish friends and colleagues were often open to new relationships with Jewish DPs. Non-Jewish German concentration camp survivors viewed Jewish survivors as fellow persecutees. Anti-Nazis expressed their rejection of the Nazi regime through friendships with Jews. Some Germans reached out with kindness to their DP neighbors, and some German women converted to Judaism and married DPs. By 1950, a few prominent politicians, cultural figures, and clergy were speaking out about German responsibility for the crimes committed against the Jews. While these were small steps toward Christian–Jewish dialogue in immediate postwar Germany, they helped to create the basis for the more widespread engagement of the late 1950s.

The study of interactions between Germans and Jews and the internal life of DP communities required the use of previously underutilized sources. Many Jewish–German interactions occurred in small towns and villages; local German archives contain important materials. This book begins to mine these rich resources. DP organizations generated a tremendous number of Yiddish-language documents, recording their efforts both to govern the DPs and to represent their interests to the outside world. In addition to those documents related to organizational and political matters, I examined religious and cultural records.

In the past, sources have been an obstacle to the study of the private lives of DPs. The records most commonly used by historians to document their work on DPs, reports written by military and United Nations Relief and Rehabilitation Administration (UNRRA) personnel, frequently ignored domestic life.[16] Often women and children were mentioned only when their marriages and births were registered. Social workers, psychologists, and other observers recorded their interpretations of DP attitudes and living conditions in reports and journals, but often they imposed their own preconceived ideas onto the DPs. Thus, they often tell us more about the attitudes of the observers than of the DPs themselves.[17] The study of domestic life and identity construction requires the use of new sources, such as memoirs and oral history interviews.

Personal narratives illuminate the meanings behind DP behavior, helping us to understand the significance of religious rituals after the Holocaust

---

[16] Jo Reilly, "Cleaner, Carer and Occasional Dance Partner? Writing Women Back into the Liberation of Bergen-Belsen," in *Belsen in History and Memory*, p. 158.

[17] Paul Friedman, "The Road Back for the DP's: Healing the Psychological Scars of Nazism," *Commentary* 6 (December 1948): 502–10; Koppel Pinson, "Jewish Life in Liberated Germany: A Study of the Jewish DPs," *Jewish Social Studies* 9 (1947): 101–26; Edward A. Shils, "Social and Psychological Aspects of Displacement and Repatriation," *Journal of Social Issues* 2 (August 1946): 3–18.

and to explain attitudes toward revenge and questions of gender and ethnic identity. I have supplemented the written record of DP documents with diaries, memoirs, and oral history interviews. In addition to conducting my own interviews of former DPs, I studied several hundred videotaped interviews at the Visual History Archive of the University of Southern California Shoah Foundation Institute for Visual History and Education.

It is essential to treat personal narratives of the Holocaust with great care. Scholars have discussed the difficulties that survivors have articulating their memories and that their audiences have comprehending them; researchers have warned against the temptation of infusing meaning into survivors' suffering.[18] Memories of the DP experience, however, are usually less traumatic than those of the Holocaust. While the ability to communicate the trauma of the Holocaust is limited by what is "tellable" by the survivor and "hearable" by the reader or interviewer,[19] memories of the DP period are easier to convey. Like all historical documents, however, DP narratives need to be analyzed by taking into account their manner of creation, the purpose for which they were created, and the intended audience. An awareness of the conditions in which the recounted memory was encoded and in which it was retrieved as well as how the gender of the survivor shaped the memory can help the historian gauge its usefulness for historical evidence.[20]

In the cases of a few survivors, I was able to compare earlier and later interviews and interviews with memoirs. The central memories remained constant with slight variations in the details that the survivor remembered or chose to share at a particular time. Historian Christopher Browning has also discovered that survivor memories are more stable and less alterable over time than one might expect, affirming their usefulness as historical documents, particularly when no other records exist.[21] Memory studies also show that individual

---

[18] For discussions of the intricacies involved in interpreting survivor narratives and in using them as historical evidence, see Geoffrey H. Hartman, "Learning from Survivors: The Yale Testimony Project," *Holocaust and Genocide Studies*, 9 (Fall 1995): 192–207; Lawrence Langer, *Holocaust Testimonies: The Ruins of Memory* (New Haven, CT: Yale University Press, 1991); Efraim Sicher, ed., *Breaking Crystal: Writing and Memory after Auschwitz* (Urbana: University of Illinois Press, 1998); James E. Young, *Writing and Rewriting the Holocaust: Narrative and the Consequences of Interpretation* (Bloomington: Indiana University Press, 1990).

[19] Henry Greenspan, *On Listening to Holocaust Survivors: Recounting Life and History* (Westport, CT: Praeger, 1998), pp. 20, 30–31.

[20] On the encoding and retrieval of memories, see Daniel L. Schacter, *Searching for Memory: The Brain, the Mind, and the Past* (New York: Basic Books, 1996), pp. 45–46, 60, and 71. On gender, see Elizabeth R. Baer and Myrna Goldenberg, eds., *Experience and Expression: Women, the Nazis, and the Holocaust* (Detroit, MI: Wayne State University Press, 2003); Marlene E. Heinemann, *Gender and Destiny: Women Writers and the Holocaust* (New York: Greenwood Press, 1986); Sara R. Horowitz, "Gender, Genocide, and Jewish Memory," *Prooftexts: A Journal of Jewish Literary History* 20 (Winter/Spring 2000): 158–190; R. Ruth Linden, *Making Stories, Making Selves: Feminist Reflections on the Holocaust* (Columbus: Ohio State University Press, 1993); Jill Ker Conway, *When Memory Speaks: Reflections on Autobiography* (New York: Alfred A. Kopf, 1998).

[21] Christopher Browning, *Collected Memories: Holocaust History and Post-War Testimony* (Madison: University of Wisconsin Press, 2003), p. 47.

memories are surprisingly consistent over time. When one has access to a large number of personal narratives, they can help isolate core memories and screen out any distortions. Neuroscientist Daniel Schacter has argued that videotaped interviews with Holocaust survivors "can help to ensure that forgetting and distortion – which can infiltrate any individual rememberer's story – are counteracted by the overwhelming truths that emerge from core elements that are shared by numerous rememberers."[22] Carefully read and analyzed, DP personal narratives can provide important information about events as well as about the meanings survivors have given to them.

In order to provide a sense of how survivors' options were shaped by their interactions with others, the book begins with an overview of DP relations with Allied personnel, international relief workers, and Germans. It proceeds thematically in a roughly chronological fashion to illuminate the steps by which survivors rebuilt their lives: mourning the dead, redefining Jewish manhood and womanhood, caring for children, shaping Jewish identities, and leaving Germany. The survivors' immediate need to mourn and to commemorate the dead leads us to investigate Jewish identity and the role of religious rituals. Commemorative events also exposed German attempts to evade responsibility for the deaths. As survivors recovered their physical strength and secondary sex characteristics, they strove to attain new gender ideals and to create new Jewish families. Children, both those who survived the Holocaust and those born in its aftermath, represented hope for the continuity of Jewish generations. DPs placed a tremendous value on Jewish children and frequently came into conflict with relief workers over what constituted the best interests of the children. In the educational programs of the schools and kibbutzim, in holiday observances, and in the cultural activities of the newspapers and theaters, survivors sought to understand their past and to put it into a narrative framework that linked Jewish history with their personal experiences of persecution, their existence in the DP camps, and their dreams of a Jewish future in Palestine. Through their courts of honor, DPs asserted their Jewish values and their distinctiveness as a people. DP political organizations consistently demanded free immigration to Palestine as the solution to their displacement. A Jewish state in Israel represented a new home and a new family to the survivors.

What emerges from this study is a picture of Jews not torn from their roots but continuing to draw strength from them and committing themselves to building lives in the spirit of their childhood homes; that they undertook this project of renewal on German soil added to their urgency. Reestablishing Jewish life and families in full view of their former oppressors gave DPs a sense of satisfaction and revenge. At the same time, the unwillingness of Germans to accept responsibility for Nazi crimes increased Jewish anxiety about their security and their future. Germans forced to participate in commemorations for Holocaust victims considered themselves freed from guilt and without need to confront the past. Paradoxically, the Jewish presence in Germany facilitated

[22] Schacter, *Searching for Memory*, p. 305.

German forgetting of wartime crimes and contributed to the growing myth of German victimhood as Germans and Jews competed for housing, food, and the good will of the Allies.

Within the DP camps Jewish survivors reminisced about their prewar homes, shared their experiences of the war years, and dreamed of a future away from Europe. Here they learned to integrate their Shoah experiences into their life narratives. They also had their first indications that outsiders did not want to hear about what had happened. Well-meaning Allied relief workers told them to forget about their experiences and to focus on the future, that it was not healthy to dwell on the past. And yet, for the few years that many survivors spent in the DP camps, they engaged in an instinctual group therapy before entering a world that, unwilling to listen, forced them into a silence that lasted for decades. This book seeks to reclaim a portion of that silenced past.

I

Bamidbar

In the Wilderness

Jews, Germans, and Allies had all assumed that the displaced persons would quickly leave Germany. Jewish survivors anticipated easily reuniting with relatives abroad or emigrating to Palestine. Allies and Germans had expected them to repatriate to their countries of origin. In fact, more than seven million DPs did repatriate by September 1945, but Jewish DPs either refused to repatriate or else they returned to Germany soon after repatriation, leaving behind what had become for them the graveyard of Eastern Europe. When the DPs found virtually all avenues of emigration closed to them, their stay on German soil became indefinite and tensions emerged between Jews, Germans, and Allies. This chapter provides an overview of these relationships since they fundamentally shaped the options available to the DPs and provided the context in which DPs reclaimed control over their lives and reestablished Jewish community life after the Holocaust. Increasingly, DPs felt embattled on all sides, reinforcing their desire to leave Europe.

In their fantasies of liberation, survivors of the Shoah had imagined the world lifting them up, embracing them, and punishing their oppressors. They identified with their liberators and saw themselves joined in their common battle against the Germans. Their imaginings had not taken into consideration the logistical and political realities facing the United States, Great Britain, and the Soviet Union. Unable to emigrate, they believed themselves to be living in the wilderness, awaiting entry to the Promised Land.[1] Forced to remain behind barbed wire, inadequately housed and fed, while Germans continued to live in their homes eating fresh meat, fruits, and vegetables, DPs protested their treatment. After years during which an assertion of their rights would have meant death, DPs now vocally demanded improved living conditions and freedom to travel in search of family members. They refused to accept anything less than acquiescence

---

[1] DPs repeatedly used the Biblical phrase "bamidbar" (in the wilderness) to refer to their plight. It was also the name of the Föhrenwald DP newspaper.

to their demands, making them unpopular with many United Nations Relief and Rehabilitation Administration (UNRRA) and military officials alike.[2] Their disdain for authority, tendency toward emotional outbursts, and disregard for regulations reinforced stereotypes that Allied personnel had already formed about what sort of people would have survived the Nazi onslaught.

Once the Allies had become aware of the extent of Nazi persecution of the Jews, they made assumptions about those who had managed to survive. They believed that only the most cunning and amoral could have escaped death, possibly even through collaboration. The dehumanization of the concentration camps would have left the survivors uncivilized and selfish. Partisans were to be feared for their lawlessness and disregard for authority. Even Jewish leaders abroad shared the dismal evaluation of the survivors, believing that Jewish intellectuals and community leaders had all been murdered and that the survivors were the dregs of the prewar communities. Even before the war Zionist leaders in Palestine had a negative view of Jews living in the Diaspora, assuming that the best had already made *aliyah* (immigration to Palestine/Israel).[3] These attitudes dismayed and frustrated survivors, who had viewed their liberators as allies against the Nazis. DPs were unprepared for the Allies' different priorities and frames of reference.

When the Allies defeated Germany, they divided it into American, British, French, and Soviet zones of occupation. The capital city of Berlin was divided into four sectors. Eight or nine million forced laborers, concentration camp inmates, and other foreigners displaced by war came under their control.[4] Of these, approximately 60,000 were Jewish concentration camp survivors. An additional 18,000 German Jews had survived in Germany as privileged Jews (either "half-Jews" or married to non-Jews) or in hiding, and another 9,000 German Jews returned from concentration camps outside of Germany (especially Theresienstadt).[5] There were few Jews in the French Zone of occupation,

---

[2] Major Harold E. Gould, 39th Infantry Regiment, to Commanding Officer, 39th Infantry Regiment, "DP Camp Fohrenwald [sic]," 5 May 1946, p. 6; Report on DP Camp Foehrenwald; The Public Safety Branch: Records Relating to Displaced Persons Camps 1945–49; Civil Affairs Division (CAD); Office of the Military Government United States (OMGUS), Record Group (RG) 260; United States National Archives at College Park, MD (NACP).

[3] Eva Fogelman, "Coping with the Psychological Aftermath of Extreme Trauma," in *Life Reborn: Jewish Displaced Persons 1945–1951, Conference Proceedings*, ed. Menachem Z. Rosensaft (Washington, DC: United States Holocaust Memorial Museum, 2001), pp. 89–90.

[4] Statistics for the chaotic, immediate postwar period are not particularly accurate, so these are generally acceptable rough numbers. See Leonard Dinnerstein, *America and the Survivors of the Holocaust* (New York: Columbia University Press, 1982), p. 276. Hagit Lavsky uses the lower estimate of 6 million DPs in Germany at war's end with 2 million remaining in western Germany by the end of summer 1945 and 900,000 remaining by December 1945. See Hagit Lavsky, *New Beginnings: Holocaust Survivors in Bergen-Belsen and the British Zone in Germany, 1945–1950* (Detroit, MI: Wayne State University Press, 2002), p. 17. Zeev Mankowitz estimates 9 million DPs liberated in Germany with more than 1.5 million remaining in occupied Germany, Austria, and Italy in August 1945. Zeev Mankowitz, *Life between Memory and Hope: The Survivors of the Holocaust in Occupied Germany* (Cambridge: Cambridge University Press, 2002), pp. 11–12.

[5] Statistics for this period are rough estimates. Thousands of survivors died in the weeks following liberation and others moved from place to place, meaning that they either were not counted

and the Soviets quickly repatriated the surviving Jews in their zone or required their absorption into the local German communities, so that officially there were no DPs in Soviet-occupied Germany. In northern Germany under British control, a significant number of survivors lived in the Belsen DP camp. The vast majority of Jewish survivors were liberated in Bavaria and came under American occupation.

Military commanders concerned with establishing order in the areas under their control were intent on keeping civilians off of the roads, reestablishing law and order, and preventing epidemics. They also wanted to protect Germans from marauding survivors and at the same time shield survivors from German attacks. This translated into keeping concentration camp inmates separated from Germans, often requiring liberated prisoners to remain within concentration camps, behind barbed wire, and under Allied guards. UNRRA workers focused on repatriating the displaced to their countries of origin, but the increasing unwillingness of Jewish DPs to return to Eastern Europe frustrated their efforts. Particularly in the British and American Zones, where most Jewish DPs resided, Allied military men, chaplains, social workers, physicians, nurses, and academics viewed the DPs as a problem that needed to be managed and solved.

Aid workers had difficulties relating to their wards not only because of the DPs' Holocaust experiences but also because of cultural differences. Often relief workers and DPs had no language in common, and assimilated British and American Jews often had difficulty creating bonds with coreligionists from more traditional backgrounds.[6] Some even fell victim to the notion that DPs were unfamiliar with acceptable standards of behavior. A survivor recalled a Hebrew Immigrant Aid Society (HIAS) worker at a transit camp preparing those with U.S. visas for life in their new country: "She picked up a fork and she said, 'Do you know what this is?' Like in Europe you never saw a fork! We were outraged. We thought, 'what do they think we are? Animals or something?' Even my two-year-old ... she was already eating with a fork and knife."[7] Cultural differences and preconceptions interfered with relations between DPs and others, even under the best of circumstances.

---

at all or were counted more than once. For a good discussion of these figures see Lavsky, *New Beginnings*, pp. 27–29.

[6] The UNRRA director of Feldafing, in a humorous vein, requested "oh Lord, please send me a Deputy Director, an Assistant Supply Officer and a Stenographer, with a knowledge of Kosher Salami preferred." In response, the acting regional director wrote that "Your infinite forbearance and longsuffering draw the mind to ... Job, who also had certain difficulties with his flocks. He had, however, the advantage of a fair knowledge of Hebrew, as well as possibly some Yiddish." Edwin S. Richeson, Director, Team 109, to Miss Mastousva, Mr. Deane, Mr. Winslow, "Oh, Lord, Give me Help," 31 October 1945, and Roger G. Mastrude to Director, Team 109, "The Divine Condescension," [no date], United States Holocaust Memorial Museum Archive (USHMM), Samuel Zisman Papers, RG-19.047.02*09; Hadassah Rosensaft, *Yesterday: My Story* (Washington, DC: United States Holocaust Memorial Museum, 2004), p. 82.

[7] Ethel Kleinman, "Videotaped interview, by the University of Southern California Shoah Foundation Institute for Visual History and Education," Interview Code (IC) 36783, Segments

One should remember that Allied personnel represented cross sections of their national populations in which antisemitism was not uncommon. For every Allied soldier who felt compassion for Jewish victims of persecution there was another who believed Jews were Christ killers, criminals, or communists. Even sympathetic individuals could not always escape the antisemitic stereotypes of their upbringing. For example, International Relief Organization (IRO) worker Kathryn Hulme wrote of Jewish DPs:

From the moment of my first encounter with their contrary, critical and demanding leaders, I had the feeling that I was dealing not with people but with phoenixes. The wild way they used up their energies, which their thin wiry bodies seemed incapable of generating in the first place, was alarming to behold. Their smoldering eyes looked like burnt holes but they missed absolutely nothing, as if the flames that had passed through them had only sharpened their sight. Their voices were unmusical and hoarse from violent expostulation and their hands moved continuously in manual dialogue of a derisory nature.[8]

Despite her admiration for these Jews who had arisen from the ashes of the Holocaust, Hulme's description of their physical and linguistic characteristics as well as their contrariness reflects negative Jewish stereotypes.

Traumatized by wartime bombings and mass rape, often homeless and hungry amid the rubble, defeated Germans created narratives of the war and occupation that portrayed Germans as victims. As victims themselves, focused on their own struggle for survival in the chaos of political and economic collapse, they felt little responsibility for the Holocaust survivors in their midst.[9] Germans justified the past treatment of concentration camp inmates by rationalizing that the prisoners were criminals, and that made their release even more frightening. Fearful that the survivors would inflict harm on themselves and their communities and suffering their own deprivations, Germans resented demands that they provide housing or clothing to the survivors. They grew impatient with the living reminders of German crimes and their competition for scarce resources. Wartime bombings had led to housing shortages that were aggravated by the increasing numbers of DPs and ethnic Germans expelled from Eastern Europe. Material conditions were miserable and millions of German men were dead or in Allied, particularly Soviet, prisoner of war camps. Germans simply wanted the survivors and all that they represented to go away.

Although only a minority of Germans were rabid antisemites, many shared the more moderate, respectable antisemitism of the Allies. Indeed, Allied soldiers often felt they had more in common with the well-mannered Germans than

102–103, Visual History Archive (VHA) [on-line at subscribing institutions]; www.usc.edu/vhi.VHA.

[8] Kathryn Hulme, *The Wild Place* (Boston: Little, Brown, 1953), pp. 212–213.

[9] See Robert G. Moeller, *War Stories: The Search for a Usable Past in the Federal Republic of Germany* (Berkeley: University of California Press, 2001), p. 13; Atina Grossmann, *Jews, Germans, and Allies: Close Encounters in Occupied Germany* (Princeton: Princeton University Press, 2007), p. 34.

with their unruly DP wards. Despite prohibitions on fraternization, military personnel formed cordial relations with local Germans and grew sympathetic to their views of the postwar situation. This development, promoted by the emerging Cold War and Allied decisions to rebuild West Germany as a bulwark against communism, left DPs feeling betrayed.

FROM LIBERATION TO THE HARRISON REPORT

Allied planners had prepared for the humanitarian crisis, creating UNRRA to handle the temporary care of the displaced and their repatriation. They were not prepared for the scope of the problem, nor were they prepared for a significant number of DPs, particularly Polish Jews, to refuse repatriation to their countries of origin out of fear of antisemitic violence and an unwillingness to settle amid the ruins of their former lives. UNRRA did not have enough personnel to supply the teams needed to cope with the situation in Germany. Communication problems between the military and UNRRA also delayed the deployment of personnel.[10] Even once UNRRA personnel arrived, they could find that UNRRA Headquarters had failed to make arrangements for their staff, causing delays in the transfer from military to UNRRA authorities.[11] In order to concentrate its efforts in repatriation, UNRRA left military authorities in overall charge of DPs. Initial plans to turn over DP operations to UNRRA by October 1945 were delayed.

Because of military concerns about civilian personnel in a war zone, nongovernmental organizations, such as the American Jewish Joint Distribution Committee (JDC) and an offshoot of the Central British Fund, the Jewish Committee for Relief Abroad (JCRA), were prevented from entering Germany until summer 1945. In June 1945, the first JDC team entered Buchenwald, but it was not until August 4 that another team was admitted to Munich in the U.S. Zone without supplies. The British admitted another JDC team without equipment to Belsen in early July.[12] The first team of the JCRA's operational arm, the Jewish Relief Unit (JRU), arrived in Belsen only in August 1945.[13]

The first contact with world Jewry, therefore, came from Jewish soldiers and chaplains serving in the Allied armies. These individuals, often acting on their own initiative and with no resources, provided tremendous humanitarian assistance in the immediate aftermath of the war. Among them were Jewish Brigade soldiers, men from the Jewish community in Palestine (*Yishuv*) who had volunteered to serve with the British Army and had helped with the liberation of Italy. Although the Jewish Brigade had been in contact with former partisans

[10] Muriel Knox Doherty, letters dated 10 June 1945 and 10 July 1945, in *Letters from Belsen: An Australian nurse's experiences with the survivors of war*, eds. Judith Cornell and R. Lynette Russell (St. Leonards, NSW Australia: Allen & Unwin, 2000), esp. pp. 7 and 16.

[11] Doherty, letter dated 16 July 1945, in *Letters from Belsen*, p. 33.

[12] Lavsky, *New Beginnings*, p. 107.

[13] Neil Belton, *The Good Listener: Helen Bamber, A Life Against Cruelty* (New York: Pantheon Books, 1998), p. 72.

from Eastern Europe while stationed in Italy, it was only in late June 1945 that
a delegation of Brigade soldiers entered southern Germany.[14] Twenty-seven
emissaries (*shlichim*) from the Yishuv, nominated by political parties and
appointed by the Jewish Agency for Palestine according to a party key, arrived
in the American Zone of Germany in December 1945.[15] It was not until March
1946 that a representative of the Jewish Agency for Palestine entered the British
Zone.[16] The delayed arrival of Jewish aid workers fueled the DPs' sense that the
world had neglected them and necessitated their activism on their own behalf.
Thus, early DP organizations founded by survivors with the assistance of military chaplains, particularly Rabbi Abraham Klausner in the American Zone,
reflected genuine DP sentiment, free from most outside influences.

Initially Allied governments refused to acknowledge Jews as a distinct
category and treated them according to their national citizenship. In practice
this policy resulted in German Jews being treated as enemy nationals, receiving
the lower food rations given to Germans and dependent on German officials
for housing and aid. Non-German Jews were threatened with repatriation.
Although General Dwight D. Eisenhower, the Commanding General of the
Supreme Headquarters of the Allied Expeditionary Forces in Europe (SHAEF),
had ordered on June 20, 1945 that special camps be established for stateless
victims of Nazi persecution and nonrepatriables, General George S. Patton of
the U.S. Third Army ordered all liberated persons in the Munich area to be sent
to repatriation centers. The orders were rescinded a few days later.[17] Patton had
great contempt for DPs and insisted on keeping them behind barbed wire and
under guard.

In the British Zone, German Jews and Jews living outside of DP camps were
also at the mercy of local German authorities for their housing and rations.
Within the DP camps of both zones, Jewish DPs found themselves victimized
by antisemitic Poles and other Eastern Europeans. In the Belsen DP camp, the
British classified Jews by their country of citizenship despite Jewish DPs having
formed a separate Jewish committee. The British refusal to give Jews a separate status was motivated out of a sense of fairness and out of a realization
that the acknowledgment of Jews as a distinct category in Belsen would have
implications for Zionist demands for a Jewish homeland in Palestine. Thus, the
non-Jewish Poles dominated the early camp government.

Immediately upon liberation Jewish survivors had begun organizing to
represent Jewish interests before the military and UNRRA. In the American Zone
leaders emerged from the predominantly Lithuanian underground movements
in Dachau's subcamps. With the assistance of Rabbi Klausner, they were able to

[14] Yoav Gelber, "Jewish Soldiers and *She-erit Hapletah*," in *She'erit Hapletah 1944–1948: Rehabilitation and Political Struggle*, eds. Yisrael Gutman and Avital Saf (Jerusalem: Yad Vashem, 1990), p. 74.
[15] Irit Keynan, "The Yishuv's Mission in Germany, August 1945-May 1946," in *She'erit Hapletah*, eds. Gutman and Saf, p. 239.
[16] Lavsky, *New Beginnings*, p. 104.
[17] Herbert Agar, *The Saving Remnant* (New York: Viking Press, 1960), p. 182.

bring together leaders from various camps and to establish a regional committee for Bavaria in July 1945.[18] In Belsen, Polish Jews whose wartime leadership skills had won the confidence of camp inmates formed a committee in April 1945. By June the Belsen committee had established contact with Jews outside of the camp and began to represent them as well.[19] The committees demanded improved living conditions in the DP camps and speedy immigration to Palestine. To help administer the DP camps, UNRRA turned to the camp committees in autumn 1945. DPs elected their representatives who now assumed much responsibility for sanitation, police, education, and cultural work. Although the American and British military governments worked with the Central Committees, they only granted official recognition to the Central Committee of Liberated Jews in the American Zone in September 1946 and to the Central Jewish Committee in the British Zone in April 1947.

Until the formation of all-Jewish camps, Jewish survivors frequently faced hostility from antisemites among the general DP population. Former concentration camp inmates were in camps with former Ukrainian guards and Polish kapos. It was not until Polish DP police burned a synagogue during Hanukkah 1945 that British authorities permitted a separate Jewish police force.[20] In Lübeck UNRRA officials hesitated to grant DP status to Hungarian Jews who were targets of anti-semitic actions and to allow them to move in with Polish Jews because of the political implications; they permitted the move only when the British military government approved it.[21] In a predominantly Polish camp in the American Zone, a female survivor felt threatened by the men, including Polish American soldiers, who disapproved of her friendship with an African American GI. She felt safe

---

[18] See Zeev Mankowitz, "The Formation of *She'erit Hapleita*: November 1944–July 1945," *Yad Vashem Studies* 20 (1990): 337–370.

[19] Lavsky, *New Beginnings*, Chapter 4.

[20] Raphael Olievsky, "Protest Meeting against Vandalism to the Synagogue" (in Yiddish), [December 1945], Yad Vashem Archives (YV) O-70/7. For other instances of Polish DP attacks on Jews, see Norbert Wollheim, "Betrifft: Überfall von Mitgliedern des Central Jewish Committee in Bergen-Belsen durch polnische Polizei," 19 February, 1946, YV O-70/7; Norbert Wollheim, "Bericht: Zusammenstoß zwischen jüdischer Polizei und polnischen Banditen im jüdischen Lager von Bergen-Belsen," 24 March 1946, YV O-70/7; Jewish Telegraphic Agency Wire report, "Eight Jews Stabbed, One Shot by Polish DP's at Bergen-Belsen Camp; Situation Tense," 17 May 1946, USHMM, Hadassah Rosensaft Papers, RG-08.002*10; H. J. Wachtel, Director UNRRA Team 560, to Sam Zisman, District Director, "Report of Polish Activities in Reference to Jewish Residents," 22 February 1946, Zisman Papers, RG-19.047.02*19. Also in 1946, Polish DPs murdered a Jewish survivor in his home in Planegg. Their threats forced the remaining family members to flee to Belsen in the British Zone and to change their names. David Piotrkowski, "Videotaped interview," VHA, IC 20081, Segs. 30–31.

[21] Norbert Wollheim, "Auseinandersetzung mit der Militärregierung und der UNRRA in Lübeck hinsichtlich der Behandlung ungarischer Juden," 13 March 1946, YV O-70/63; Norbert Wollheim, "Behandlung ungarischer Juden als D.P.s," 8 April 1946, YV O-70/63. Also in Lübeck, survivors called themselves "Jewish DPs of former Polish citizenship" to avoid collective punishment for crimes committed by Polish DPs and to avoid forcible repatriation by denying any commonality with Poles. Norbert Wollheim, "Behandlung von Juden früherer polnischer Staatsangehörigkeit als Polen," 8 April 1946, YV O-70/63.

only when the chaplain facilitated her move to the predominantly Jewish camp
of Landsberg.[22] She recalled that at Landsberg "We weren't scared. We were very
safe, because everybody had the same background. … We had all lost all of our
families and we had all suffered the same way, maybe in different camps, but the
same way and so we had so much in common."[23] Only among other Jews did
many survivors feel truly safe.

Reports of poor conditions in the DP camps and demands by American Jewish
leaders for an investigation prompted President Harry Truman to send Earl G.
Harrison, former U.S. Commissioner of Immigration and representative to the
Intergovernmental Committee on Refugees, on a fact-finding tour of the DP
camps in July 1945, with special attention to the plight of Jewish DPs. Although
critical of UNRRA's inefficiency and its emphasis on repatriation, Harrison saved
his most blistering critique for the military. He objected to restrictions on the
movement of DPs outside of camps and the posting of armed guards. Military
government officers charged with getting the German communities working
again were reluctant to inconvenience Germans; they felt they had to get along
with the Germans for the long run while the DPs were a temporary problem.
Harrison urged the creation of separate Jewish camps so that the special needs of
Jewish survivors could be met. The solution to the Jewish DP problem, Harrison
argued, was the quick evacuation to Palestine of all Jews who wished it.[24]

Scathed by the report, General Eisenhower issued a series of directives to
implement Harrison's suggestions. Jewish DPs would be housed in all-Jewish
camps; German housing would be requisitioned for DP needs; DP rations would
be increased; German Jews would be treated as DPs, giving them Allied protection and access to improved rations; DPs would be hired over Germans; and an
advisor on Jewish affairs was to be added to the general's staff. In November 1945
General Joseph T. McNarney took over as SHAEF commander and continued
Eisenhower's policies regarding Jewish DPs. Despite inspections to ensure that
officers in the field were complying with the directives, military government officers (MGOs) and soldiers often failed to implement them or remained unaware
of them. British Jews called on the British military government to implement
similar measures in the British Zone, and in December 1945 the British, too,
began segregating Jewish DPs from others and allowing preferential treatment
for German Jews; however, it was not until spring 1946 that a Jewish advisor
took office and only in June 1946 did Belsen become an all-Jewish camp.[25]

REHABILITATION: CLEANLINESS, MORALITY, AND FOOD

In the postwar period, many Allied personnel viewed cleanliness as a sign of
morality and the restoration of social order. Much of the early conflict between

---

[22] Hilda Mantelmacher, interview by the author, tape recording, Harrisburg, PA, 31 March 1996.
[23] Mantelmacher, interview.
[24] Earl G. Harrison, "Report of Earl G. Harrison," *Department of State Bulletin* 13 (September 30,
     1945): 456–463.
[25] Lavsky, *New Beginnings*, p. 99.

DPs and Allied authorities centered on hygiene and the material conditions of the DP camps. DP demands for better living conditions antagonized many of the army and UNRRA officials assigned to their care. Many Allied officials believed that the DPs were unappreciative and irrational in their demands. Harsh conditions made it difficult for DPs to maintain cleanliness or to preserve modesty, leading Allied personnel to unwarranted conclusions about the DPs' capacity for rehabilitation.

DP camps were often located in former German military or workers' barracks and had all the grim features of barracks life. Other centers were in stables and garages, while a few were located in former hospitals, hotels, apartment blocks, and summer resorts.[26] As late as July 1945 some Holocaust survivors were still housed in former Nazi concentration camps. Living conditions varied between camps, but most required unrelated individuals to share sleeping quarters and facilities. A garage at a former Luftwaffe base was converted into a DP camp and 1,800 DPs shared three toilets.[27] The Landsberg DP camp had large blocks in which DPs attempted to create private space by hanging blankets between the beds. Entire blocks shared bathroom facilities, with men and women trying to avoid being at the showers at the same time.[28] A former workers' community for I. G. Farben, Föhrenwald had a more home-like environment and yet even here multiple families shared an apartment house with one bathroom.[29] Such overcrowding made personal and household cleanliness difficult, let alone privacy and intimacy.

The lack of soap and cleaning supplies also affected sanitation in the DP camps. Major Irving Heymont, commander of the Landsberg DP camp, wrote, "A severe handicap is the complete lack of toilet paper. It seems that an Army unit here some time ago put up posters in the latrines stressing the importance of clean latrines. They made a serious mistake by having the posters printed on thin paper. The posters were all gone in a few hours. The latrines are continually clogged because of the newspapers the people use."[30] The Army assumed that the DPs needed posters to instruct them that clean toilets were desirable and yet did not provide the DPs with the proper materials. Heymont understood that the lack of toilet paper was a major problem, but less sympathetic officials would see the filth as a failing of the DPs. Heymont's letters and UNRRA, JDC, and JRCA reports also discuss the persistent lack of cleaning

---

[26] Koppel S. Pinson, "Jewish Life in Liberated Germany: A Study of the Jewish DP's," *Jewish Social Studies* 9 (April 1947): 105.

[27] Ira A. Hirschman, *The Embers Still Burn* (New York: Simon and Schuster, 1949), p. 90.

[28] Mantelmacher, interview.

[29] Jacob Biber, *Risen from the Ashes: A Story of the Jewish Displaced Persons in the Aftermath of World War II* (San Bernardino, CA: Borgo Press, 1990), pp. 18 and 91; Mantelmacher also spent time in Föhrenwald, where she shared a room with 11 other boys and girls in a house with one bathroom. Mantelmacher, interview.

[30] Irving Heymont, *Among the Survivors of the Holocaust – 1945: The Landsberg DP Camp Letters of Major Irving Heymont, United States Army* (Cincinnati, OH: American Jewish Archives, 1982), p. 23.

supplies such as garbage cans, brushes, and brooms.[31] Heymont effectively hid his Jewish background from his military comrades and from the DPs.[32] It is likely, however, that his ability to look beyond the surface situation and to find sympathy for the DPs stemmed from his repressed Jewish identity.

Outside observers recognized the lack of hygiene among the DPs but often attributed it to psychological causes or moral failings. The hygienic problems served as evidence of the obstacles facing the DPs in their path to rehabilitation and normalization. In 1946 sociologist Edward Shils published his findings after visiting the DP camps. Shils argued that the survivors suffered from regression due to the loss of support and affection resulting from the destruction of their families and communities. Shils maintained that these regressive tendencies "manifested themselves in the deterioration of hygienic standards – men went unwashed and unshaven for quite long periods, took no interest in the upkeep of their dwellings, disregarded ordinary sanitary procedures."[33] Although Shils acknowledged that regression had been reinforced by material deprivation, he did not place much weight on the living conditions as an explanation for lack of hygiene.

A young British psychiatrist studying DP behavior also neglected to account for the effect of material deprivation. He arrived at Belsen and observed hospital patients in order to identify psychiatric problems. He excitedly informed a DP dentist working in the hospital, Hadassah Bimko (later Rosensaft), that he had identified his first patient, a girl who combed her hair with a broken comb while looking in a broken mirror. Bimko knew the girl. Surprised that the girl had been identified as a psychiatric case, Bimko asked why he had found her behavior peculiar. Later Rosensaft recalled, "he repeated his observation. I said that he should give the girl a whole comb and a whole mirror; if she refused, then he had a patient."[34] Rather than understanding the girl's efforts to maintain her appearance within the restrictions of camp life, the eager psychiatrist had applied the standards of normal society to her and mistakenly concluded that she suffered psychic injury. Camp conditions forced DPs to improvise and to make do with what they had, but that led to behaviors that Allied personnel misconstrued as abnormal.

Shils also assumed that the DPs would share his definition of "ordinary sanitary procedures." Only a few, such as the sympathetic commander of the Landsberg DP camp, recognized that many of the survivors had not known

---

[31] Heymont, *Among the Survivors*, pp. 22 and 71; Helen Matouskova, Field Supervisor to S. B. Zisman, District Director, UNRRA District 5, "Field Supervisor's Report – Team 311, Landsberg," 4 February 1946, p. 3, United Nations Archives (UN), Series S-0436, Box 42, File 6; A. G. Brotman and Harry Viteles, "Survey on Conditions of Jews in the British Zone of Germany in March 1946," page 5, YV O-70/6.

[32] Colonel Irving Heymont (remarks at the Conference on Vu ahin, Le'an, Where Shall We Go? Jewish Holocaust Survivors and the Search for Belonging, 1945–1952, at the Joseph and Rebecca Meyerhoff Center for Jewish Studies, University of Maryland, 21 February 1999).

[33] Edward A. Shils, "Displacement and Repatriation," *Journal of Social Issues* (August 1946): 5.

[34] Rosensaft, *Yesterday*, p. 58.

modern sanitation in their prewar communities before and thus had different standards than the American observers.[35] Even in more advanced Western Europe, many prewar housing complexes lacked indoor plumbing. Some of the conflicts about hygiene may have owed as much if not more to inadequate facilities and differences in standards as to regression. In addition, many DPs initially viewed their stay in the camps as temporary and did not see fit to expend precious energy on cleaning and maintaining their dwellings. Only as winter 1945 approached and the chances for emigration remained slim did the DPs begin to respond to Army and UNRRA demands for improved household cleanliness. Even then, winter conditions worked against sanitation efforts. In Landsberg unheated bathrooms without window frames led to broken water pipes and stopped up lavatories.[36] Showers operated only three times each week.[37] In 1946 the influx of Jews from Eastern Europe into the DP camps in the American Zone along with continuing supply problems hindered cleanliness efforts.[38]

Housekeeping was part of rehabilitation efforts, and much of the responsibility for housecleaning fell on the women. Like most males of their generation, Jewish men were unaccustomed to performing their own housework and preferred to leave it undone or to hire domestic labor. By 1947 the JDC had recognized that DP women bore the burden of dealing with poor living conditions and child rearing and assigned some women workers to train female DPs on how to cope with the situation.[39] Jewish relief workers at the Belsen DP camp offered courses in handicrafts to women DPs, so that they might have the opportunity "of using their leisure profitably and to express themselves in those occupations by producing useful and beautiful articles for their homes."[40] Rehabilitation of the DPs was to include productive labor and the civilized touches of home decorating. The beautification of the physical environment was intended to contribute to the re-socialization of the survivors, instructing women in their proper domestic roles.

Just as the overcrowded conditions made hygiene difficult, they also interfered with attempts to restore individual and familial privacy. Newlywed couples had to share sleeping quarters with others. Men and women slept on the same dormitory floors with only sheets or blankets as walls between them. DPs willingly made room for additional survivors rather than turn them

---

[35] Heymont, *Among the Survivors*, p. 23.

[36] Luretta A. Usner, "Report," p. 3, attached to Usner to Field Supervisor (Helen Matouskova), "Inspection of Landsberg Landkreis," 14 March 1946, UN S-0436, Box 42, File 6.

[37] Major General Arthur A. White, 71st Infantry Division, "Inspection of DP Camp," 22 & 23 December 1945, p. 1, UN, S-0436, Box 42, File 6.

[38] Appalling conditions in Föhrenwald DP camp are described in Harold E. Gould, Major, 39th Infantry Regiment, to Commanding Officer, 39th Infantry Regiment, "DP Camp Fohrenwald [sic]" 5 May 1946, pp. 3–4.

[39] Yehuda Bauer, *Out of The Ashes* (New York: Pergamon Press, 1989), p. 223.

[40] J. Weingreen, "Survey of Educational Work in Bergen-Belsen, July 30th to September 10th, 1946," p. 5, YV O-70/28.

away from the shelter of the DP camp.[41] Privacy and modesty were secondary considerations when the well-being of others was in question. Wartime experiences and postwar living conditions tended to make earlier notions of modesty obsolete. An American chaplain noted that Jewish women had lost their sense of shame and would continue undressing or dressing when his duties brought him into their barracks.[42] When overcrowding at the Landsberg DP camp resulted in co-ed housing, it was the Army that worried about segregating the sexes, not the DPs.[43] In Föhrenwald, a young female DP felt comfortable sharing a room with teenage Jewish boys. Cramped conditions in the ghettos had prepared her for such close quarters with others, and in the DP camp "we would take a blanket and we put [it over] a string in the middle of the room. We would just go change clothes under the blanket, and the boys would never take it off or something like that. Today I'm sure they would, but they would never do it."[44] Among DP men there was an understanding that Jewish women were to be treated with a certain amount of circumspection. DPs valued privacy as an aspect of normal living, but they had no false modesty when circumstances forced them into close proximity. Allied officials often interpreted these arrangements as evidence of "moral irregularities."[45]

Military officers in charge of the DPs in the early months after liberation were often insensitive to the special consideration DPs needed. Accustomed to working with individuals familiar with military discipline and conditioned to taking orders, military officers viewed the solutions to DP demands in military terms. When faced with complaints about a shortage of bed space at Landsberg, Lieutenant General W. B. Smith observed that bunk beds could solve the problem. UNRRA workers informed him that DPs refused to use bunk beds since they felt degraded by the reminder of the concentration camps. Smith reported unsympathetically, "I pointed out that American soldiers used double-decked bunks and directed that the bunks be double-decked."[46] During his visit, Smith questioned whether "We are coddling these DPs too much."[47]

A British officer had a similar reaction to complaints about the DP diet. Rabbi Isaac Levy, Senior Jewish Chaplain to the British Liberation Army, expressed frustration over the military officers' inability to understand the inadequacy of the diet provided to DPs. "I talk of food and they feel that I am speaking from bias. The diet is not good enough and the people can't eat the

[41] Heymont, *Among the Survivors*, p. 45; Mantelmacher, interview.
[42] Brenner, *After the Holocaust*, p. 13.
[43] Heymont, *Among the Survivors*, p. 45; "Inspection of DP Camp."
[44] Mantelmacher, interview.
[45] Representatives of the JDC and JRCA suspected that such reports were exaggerated. Brotman and Viteles, "Survey on Conditions of Jews."
[46] Smith, to Lieutenant General Frederick E. Morgan, Chief, European Regional Office, UNRRA, "Conditions at Displaced Persons Center in Landsberg, [copy]," 7 December 1945, p. 2, Zisman Papers, RG-19.047.02*16.
[47] Assistant District Medical Officer, UNRRA, to Chief Medical Officer, UNRRA, U.S. Zone, "Inspection at Landsberg, Team 311, December 6, 1945," p. 1, UN, S-0425, Box 43, File 6.

food and the Brigadier tells me that he hates bully beef but has had to eat it for five years. Is that an answer? Has he or any of them ever known what hunger is?"[48] Military men often did not understand that DPs were civilians recovering from starvation and brutalization.

Just as the authorities viewed DP attitudes toward privacy as abnormal, so too did they treat DP demands for improved rations. Disputes over food pitted the DPs against the officials in charge of their care. Even though the caloric intake was theoretically sufficient for sustaining the DPs, the nutritional value of the food was often negligible.[49] A regulation issued in October 1945 by U.S. Army Headquarters that DPs be fed only from military supplies, not from local German sources, meant that DPs would not have access to vitamin-rich fresh meat, eggs, vegetables, and fruit.[50] The Landsberg UNRRA director reported that the diet of canned foods was "monotonous and inadequate."[51] The canned meat was often only 30 percent meat and the remainder largely potatoes. Combined with the prohibition against use of local fresh foodstuffs, the diet was heavily based on bread and potatoes. One survivor recalled, "Even when I was pregnant I never got an egg, never got any vitamins, never got milk. ... They just gave us bread and soup and maybe coffee."[52] DPs were vocal in their demands for improved nutrition.

While some observers understood that the rations were inadequate for a population recovering from starvation, others dismissed the DP demands as rooted in psychological factors.[53] Shils reported, "Although most of the DPs experienced an elevation in standard of living in the DP camps, their cantankerousness over food increased with their reiterated demands for affection."[54] A psychiatrist, Paul Friedman, sent by the JDC to study the mental health of Jewish DPs, reported similar findings:

[T]heir demands are often not justified by physical necessity so much as by a fear of losing out, of being rejected, a fear that others might get more than they ... it is also essential if only for their own sake, that they learn to come to practical terms with

---

48 Isaac Levy, *Witness to Evil: Bergen-Belsen 1945* (London: Peter Halban, 1995), p. 35.

49 On the importance of the calorie for U.S. policymakers, see Nick Cullather, "The Foreign Policy of the Calorie," *American Historical Review* 112 (April 2007): 337–354. For the effects on DP diet, see Margarete L. Myers, "Jewish Displaced Persons: Reconstructing Individual and Community in the US Zone of Occupied Germany," *Leo Baeck Year Book* 42 (1997): 316.

50 See Zorach Warhaftig, "Jews in the Camps in Germany and Austria: Report Based on Observations Made During a Trip, October 12–November 27, 1945," in *American Jewish Archives, Cincinnati: The Papers of the World Jewish Congress, 1945–1950*, ed. Abraham J. Peck, Archives of the Holocaust, vol. 9 (New York: Routledge, 1990), p. 122; George Vida, *From Doom to Dawn: A Jewish Chaplain's Story of Displaced Persons* (New York: J. David, 1967), pp. 64–65.

51 A. C. Glassgold, report dated 16 November 1945, UN S-0436, Box 42, File 6.

52 Mantelmacher, interview.

53 An otherwise sympathetic UNRRA nurse wrote, "They were not sufficiently mentally fit, as yet, to appreciate the fact that their diet was highly nutritious." Doherty, letter dated 29 July 1945, in *Letters from Belsen*, p. 62.

54 Shils, "Displacement and Repatriation," p. 10.

the world outside the barbed wire. Too many of the field workers who first came into contact with DP's did not understand this. They either acceded to the demands or made promises that they were unable to carry out.[55]

Given the monotony and negligible nutritional value of much of the DP diet, the suggestion that DPs had been coddled and were irrational in their demands is simplistic at best and insensitive at worst.

There were psychological aspects to the desire for food, although not exactly what Shils and Friedman suggested. DPs had a greater understanding than their observers that food was essential for survival. In a typical account one DP mother obsessively urged her children to eat because "People can have everything taken from them except what's in their stomachs."[56] After years of starvation the DPs did not take for granted that there would be another meal for them. As for their fear of losing out, DPs believed that their persecution at the hands of Germans entitled them to receive better treatment than the Germans. DPs were quite aware that despite the lower caloric value of German rations, Germans had access to fresh foods and a more varied diet. Eight out of ten Germans in the American Zone supplemented their rations with food from their own gardens or with food from friends or relatives living on farms.[57] The majority of Germans were eating much more than their allotted rations, yet no one suggested that their demands for greater quantities of food were irrational. The DPs simply believed that they should eat as well as their former tormentors. In the quest for better and more food, DPs turned to the black market.

THE QUESTION OF JEWISH CRIMINALITY

Black market activities were a source of conflict between DPs and the authorities. While it is true that there were those DPs who engaged in black market activities as a game to pass the time,[58] and others who sought to accumulate portable wealth for use when they were resettled, most of the Jews involved in the black market limited their activities to small-scale bartering for fresh food.[59] Germans and Allies classified German barter as the more acceptable "gray" market but DP trade as profiteering from the illegal "black" market.[60] German public opinion attributed most of the criminal and black

[55] Paul Friedman, "Road Back for DP's: Healing the Psychological Scars of Nazism." *Commentary* 6 (1948): 503.

[56] Lea Fleischmann, *Dies ist nicht mein Land: Eine Jüdin verläßt die Bundesrepublik* (Hamburg: Hoffmann und Campe, 1980), p. 27. See also Frederika in Julie Heifetz, *Too Young to Remember* (Detroit, MI: Wayne State University Press, 1989), p. 122.

[57] Anna J. and Richard L. Merritt, eds., *Public Opinion in Occupied Germany* (Urbana: University of Illinois Press, 1970), pp. 17–18.

[58] Marie Syrkin, *The State of the Jews* (Washington, DC: New Republic Books, 1980), p. 47.

[59] Heymont, *Among the Survivors*, p. 63.

[60] Laura J. Hilton, "The Struggle to Re-establish Law and Order: An Examination of the Participation of Displaced Persons in Economic Crimes in Postwar Germany," paper presented at the annual meeting of the German Studies Association, San Diego, CA, October 2007, p. 6.

market activities to the DPs, especially Jewish DPs. Local military officials, observing the contrast between their unruly wards and the obedient Germans, were inclined to agree. Although mass searches rarely substantiated the reports that led to them, the Jewish centers were the most frequent targets of the raids conducted on DP camps.[61]

For centuries antisemitic stereotypes had depicted Jews as conniving, economic exploiters of non-Jews. During the First World War German encounters with Eastern European Jews had reinforced the stereotype of Jews as profiteering and immoral.[62] The Nazis had emphasized the criminality of Jews in their efforts to make their antisemitic campaign more palatable to the German public.[63] Although the black market in Germany started during the war years,[64] Germans tended to blame DPs for postwar economic turmoil. Thus German accusations against Jewish DPs as black market operators could be expressions of antisemitism. This antisemitism did not necessarily represent remnants of Nazism but was rather a sign of continuity with pre-Nazi attitudes toward Eastern Jews. At the same time, German assertions that the DPs were primarily responsible for economic crimes reinforced the developing postwar myth of German victimization. German complaints about the black market also served as indirect criticism of the Allied occupation, suggesting its ineffectiveness in guaranteeing Germans a higher standard of living and in maintaining law and order.

Allied soldiers also focused on Jewish DP criminality. By 1946 most Allied troops were fresh recruits, that is, not war veterans, who admired the cooperative Germans and were perplexed or annoyed by the demanding DPs. They were sympathetic to the attitudes of the Germans and susceptible to antisemitic stereotypes of Jews as economic parasites. Although Jewish DPs accounted for 3 percent of the population of the American Zone, only 1.5 percent of those convicted for black market crimes were Jewish DPs. U.S. military government statistics showed that in March 1948 only 3.3 percent of black market crimes involved DPs.[65] Jewish DPs would have been an even smaller percentage. Despite the fact that DPs in general, and Jewish DPs in particular, were *not* major players in the black market, military soldiers and constabulary troops continued to focus their attention on DPs. The military's treatment of Jewish DPs perpetuated the myth of Jewish black market activity, feeding German rumor mills that blamed Jewish DPs for much of Germany's economic woes and justifying German shopkeepers' exploitation of

---

[61] Abraham S. Hyman, "Displaced Persons," *American Jewish Year Book* 50 (1948–49): 469; Julia Schulze Wessel, "Zur Reformulierung des Antisemitismus in der deutschen Nachkriegsgesellschaft: Eine Analyse deutscher Polizeiakten aus der Zeit von 1945 bis 1948," in *Zwischen Selbstorganisation und Stigmatisierung*, p. 136.

[62] Steven E. Aschheim, *Brothers and Strangers: The East European Jew in German and German Jewish Consciousness, 1800–1923* (Madison: University of Wisconsin Press, 1982), p.145.

[63] Michael Berkowitz, *The Crime of My Very Existence: Nazism and the Myth of Jewish Criminality* (Berkeley: University of California Press, 2007), p. 29.

[64] Berkowitz, *Crime of Existence*, p. 150.

[65] Hilton, "Struggle to Re-establish Law and Order," p. 7.

their Jewish customers. The DP leadership, not without justification, protested, "The smear campaign against the Jews is only a trick to distract attention from the [German] sources. And besides the black market activity by Jews would end if the provisioning of the Jewish camps were satisfactory."[66]

Dependent on rations provided by UNRRA and Jewish welfare organizations, the DPs frequently had unmet needs. Food and clothing were often inadequate. In order to acquire the goods that they needed, the survivors "made a little business," usually through simple barter.[67] Cigarettes were the real currency in postwar Germany, and DPs traded theirs for farm goods and textiles. More entrepreneurial sorts could trade cigarettes to Germans for whisky and then sell the alcohol to U.S. soldiers for dollars. Some of the larger operators crossed the border into Switzerland and converted their proceeds into easily transportable diamonds and into merchandise, such as Swiss chocolate, for further business transactions.[68] Others used their access to Allied supplies or partnered with well-placed Germans to purchase goods from German factories to stock stores that then sold to Germans.[69] Jewish DP officials frequently looked the other way from the small-time barter, although they deplored profiteering for harming the reputation of Jews.

Allied officials tended not to differentiate between those bartering for items needed for personal use and those engaged in profiteering. Possession of even small amounts of contraband could result in harsh treatment and severe penalties. For example, civilians in Germany were not allowed to possess foreign currency. An exemption was made for DPs, but that was not publicized to prevent DPs from becoming carriers of German-owned foreign exchange. Zealous American enforcers in Greater Hesse applied the prohibition to DPs and imprisoned Jews and confiscated their Polish zloty, even when they could prove the money was legitimately acquired, such as through the sale of family property. Jewish DPs who received ten dollars from a sympathetic GI were also imprisoned under this law. Although the military government in Bavaria honored the exemption of DPs from the foreign currency control as long as the DP could demonstrate the money was legitimately his or hers, the burden of proof on the DP must have been great.[70]

---

[66] Samuel Gringauz, "Di greste lager-einhajt," *Jidisze Cajtung*, 22 November 1946, p. 3. Josef Rosensaft, Chairman of the Belsen Committee, also pointed out that German rumors of Jewish black market activity were designed to harm Jewish prestige and to divert attention from the real centers of black market activity. A raid on Belsen resulting from German rumors had found little of consequence. Rosensaft to Brigadier Kensington, Chief, PWDP Division, "Growth of Antisemitism and Nazism in the British Zone of Germany," 16 July 1948, p. 1, Rosensaft Papers, RG-08.002*04.

[67] The UNRRA Director for Belsen reported that a psychologist had informed him that the number of mental cases would increase if the survivors did not have the outlet that business provided. R. G. Morren, "Birds Eye View of Hohne Assembly Centre," 10 February 1947, p. 4, UN S-0429, Box 5, File 1.

[68] Zoltan Marek, "Videotaped interview," VHA, IC 1767, Seg. 115.

[69] Oscar-Asher Rosenberg, "Videotaped interview," VHA, IC 26785, Segs. 94–99.

[70] J. H. Whiting to UNRRA District Offices, "Foreign Exchange Control," 29 July 1946, p. 1, UN S-0425, Box 62, File 9; Major Abraham S. Hyman to Rabbi Philip S. Bernstein, "Study

Military authorities and German police often deemed the possession of items not distributed by UNRRA to DPs or a surplus of rationed items as proof of black market activity. In Föhrenwald, the DP court protested: "Such a position … is completely untenable and can lead to terrible consequences. For example, it would even affect cherries and other fruit that UNRRA does not provide to the camp residents and that one or another camp resident has bought for his own use. … At present there is still no prohibition on possessing money."[71] At the same time, DP police did occasionally bring charges against suspected black marketeers. For the small-time operators, their punishment consisted of the confiscation of goods that were then turned over to the camp magazine.[72] One survivor recalled, "To the Americans [the black market] was a big crime. We didn't consider it a crime. It was just a business."[73] DPs had very different attitudes from Allied military forces toward economic crimes.

Lady Rose L. Henriques led the JRU at the Belsen DP camp. In a report dated November 20, 1945, she criticized British policy that turned acts of economic necessity into crimes. Rather than being arrested for violent crimes such as rape, burglary, or murder, Jewish DPs were accused of being in possession of food, money, and/or cigarettes; being without papers; being out on the streets at night; and bartering jewelry and other possessions. She writes, "if a trinket will provide a warm garment, it would be a fool who would face the German winter with a ring on his finger and no underwear."[74] Henriques points out that Germans were not arrested for having food in their possession or in their homes and that the British gave some DPs cigarettes and outside the camps it was British troops who sold their cigarettes to DPs. Allied policies also criminalized efforts to procure kosher meat.[75] With German supplies of fresh produce and meat off limits to DPs, survivors were initially forced to purchase cattle on the black market for kosher slaughter until the Allies modified their policy to permit kosher slaughter in designated locations.

Jewish DPs were disproportionately harassed during military police and constabulary actions against black marketeering. Military officials suggested that fences be put around the camps and that DPs be subjected to spot checks on the clothes that they possessed.[76] None suggested that German towns be

on Maintenance of Law and Order Among Jewish Displaced Persons," pp. 6–7, University of Rochester Archive (URA), Philip S. Bernstein Papers, Box 1, Item 61.

71 Adam Wilk to Lagerverwaltung Foehrenwald, "Zustaendigkeitshalber weitergeleitet," YIVO, RG 294.2, MK 483, Microfilm reel 55, Folder 760.

72 Föhrenwald Court, "Protokol," 19 July 1946, YIVO, RG 294.2, MK 483, Microfilm reel 55, Folder 761.

73 Harry Aftel, "Videotaped interview," VHA, IC 11817, Seg. 21.

74 "Copy of a Report from Rose L. Henriques," November 20, 1945, Lady Rose L. Henriques Archive, Wiener Library, London (Microfilm reel 15, United States Holocaust Memorial Museum).

75 White, "Inspection of DP Camp," p. 2, UN S-0436, Box 42, File 6.

76 Even though American investigators found no evidence of centralized black market activities at Feldafing, they recommended fencing off the camp area and posting military guards at the gates.

cordoned off or that permanent road checks of Germans be conducted.[77] Antisemitic attitudes existed among military personnel, and often units charged with cracking down on the black market listened to German opinions that the DP camps, particularly the Jewish ones, were the centers of illicit activity.[78] In the British Zone, a raid on the Belsen DP camp discovered little illicit economic activity. Later, the targeted black market ring was broken, implicating British personnel. A Jewish Relief Unit worker remembered that the "highest of the brass" were in the black market.[79] Often military police would detain Jewish suspects but not their German counterparts. DPs complained of the disparity; yet, when caught by authorities, DPs refused to provide the names of their German trading partners.[80] Some DPs may have protected these Germans out of friendship, but most likely they wanted to protect their sources of goods.

In the American Zone, military police would search Jewish-looking suspects but leave Germans unmolested. In one raid on a Munich restaurant known for illicit activity, MPs lined up the Jewish customers and searched them; whenever they found a packet of cigarettes, the MPs tossed it to the Germans, who remained seated at their tables. Years later, survivors' memories of military raids on DP camps continued to arouse indignation: not over the nature of the soldiers' jobs, but over their rude treatment of the DPs.[81] DPs felt humiliated when they were subjected to body searches simply for being DPs while Germans walked away without being stopped.[82]

Guenter Borg, Documents Section, to Major Peter Vacca, Branch Chief of Intelligence, Office of Military Government for Bavaria, "Investigation of Black Market Conditions," 7 December 1945, p. 3, UN S-0435, Box 14, File 8; Lieutenant David S. Buttler, CAC Supply Branch, to Lieutenant Colonel Bender, Chief of Supply Section E-201, "D.P. Camp Landsberg/Lech," 29 November 1945, p. 3, UN S-0425, Box 43, File 6.

[77] The British commander of the Belsen DP camp recognized the military's unfair focus on Jewish DP crime. He suggested that German police better enforce regulations against the illegal use of vehicles and gasoline to prevent Germans from participating in the black market. (DPs referred to the camp as Belsen to keep fresh the connection to the concentration camp Bergen-Belsen, but the British called it Hohne.) A. C. Clarke to Relief Detachement Celle, "Black Market Activities at HOHNE Camp," 8 December 1948, YV O-70/6.

[78] E. E. Farber to Chief of Constabulary, Bamberg, "2nd Lt. William D. MacNaughton, 2nd Constabulary Squadron," 23 July 1946, UN S-0425, Box 18, File 2; Robert L. Taylor to C.D.L. Fraser, "Polish Camp. Schwabish Gmund. Bismark Kazerne. Team 166," 9 April 1946, UN S-0425, Box 62, File 9; Brian Arthur Libby, *Policing Germany: The United States Constabulary, 1946–1952* (Ph.D. diss., Purdue University, 1977), p. 78.

[79] Lily Schwarzschild, "Videotaped interview," VHA, IC 33592, Seg. 136.

[80] Major Paul L. Steers found this surprising. PLS, Director, Office of Military Government for Landkreis Wolfratshausen, to Commanding General, Third U.S. Army, "DP Camp Föhrenwald (Jewish – 5,000)," 9 May 1946, p. 2; Report on DP Camp Foehrenwald; The Public Safety Branch: Records Relating to Displaced Persons Camps 1945–49; CAD; OMGUS, RG 260; NACP.

[81] Michael Bokor, "Videotaped interview," VHA, IC 11058, Seg. 88; Frumie Cohen, "Videotaped interview," VHA, IC 47312, Seg. 18; Berthold Zarwyn, "Videotaped interview," VHA, IC 41186, Seg. 21.

[82] R. W. Collins, Chief, UNRRA Department of Social Services, to Civil Affairs Division, "Incident in Gersfeld Camp," 8 June 1947, UN S-0425, Box 43, File 4.

Under such circumstances, Jewish DP police enjoyed bringing German criminality to the notice of Allied officials. Although only DPs in the camps fell under their jurisdiction, on occasion DP police arrested Germans for loitering and entering camps for the purposes of engaging in black market activity.[83] Even though the Germans had to be released quickly, the DP police had made their statement concerning German participation in the black market. A triumph for the Belsen Jewish DP police came when they discovered that a German policeman and a chain gang under orders from a local mayor were responsible for the theft of UNRRA building materials from the camp.[84] In these small but dramatic ways, Jewish DP police attempted to challenge the stereotype of Jewish criminality, emphasizing their commitment to law and order while demonstrating the criminal behavior of Germans. Even some German police officials and American public safety officers acknowledged that German police published misleading statistics about the number of non-Germans, especially DPs, suspected of crimes. The chief of the Rural Police of Upper Bavaria had reason to believe that German farmers were selling cattle on the black market and then reporting them as stolen, blaming DPs for the alleged thefts.[85]

Indicative of the prejudice concerning DP criminality, punishments meted out to DPs were often not commensurate with the crime or comparable to the sentences handed down to non-DPs. The U.S. Army imprisoned one DP for several months for trading an Army shirt for cigarettes, while the American soldier who headed the Landsberg black market operations received a three-month sentence but was allowed to keep his profits.[86] In another case, two soldiers testified against a DP with whom they had exchanged cigarettes for cognac. The DP was sentenced to six months in jail. When counsel reminded the judge that if such a transaction had taken place, then the witnesses for the prosecution were also guilty, the judge replied that he had no authority to punish the soldiers.[87] UNRRA efforts to have the military investigate what appeared to be entrapment met with no response.[88] The material conditions of the camps forced many Jewish DPs to supplement their rations through barter and this brought them into conflict with the authorities' attempts to eliminate the black market. Since a conviction of black marketeering

---

[83] For example, see H. Frank Brull, UNRRA Security Officer, to Officer in Charge, "Siedlung Camp Riot," 3 April 1946, Zisman Papers, RG-19.047.02*19.

[84] H. Mitlehner to Public Safety Officer (Celle), "Disposal of Scrap Building Material at HOHNE Camp," 22 May 1947, UN S-0429, Box 5, File 1.

[85] Leo Steingut, CAD Field Representative, to Chief, Public Safety Branch, OMG for Bavaria, "Monthly Statistical Reports," 14 December 1948; Public Welfare: (d2) Refugees, Expellees, DPs; General Records of Public Welfare and Displaced Persons 1946–50; CAD; OMGUS, RG 260, Entry A2 B3 C1; NACP.

[86] Dinnerstein, *America and the Survivors*, p. 51. UNRRA teams complained of sentences disproportionate to the crimes; see, for example, E.S.S., "Area Team 1005 Monthly Report – May," 19 June 1947, UN S-0425, Box 43, File 4.

[87] E. E. Farber, UNRRA Director, to M.O. Talent, Legal Officer, "Discipline of Enlisted Men," 9 August 1946, UN S-0425, Box 19, File 10.

[88] Paul Winter, UNRRA Legal Officer, to Captain M. G. Karsner, Office of Military Government for Bavaria, "Black Market Entrapment," 26 November 1946, UN S-0425, Box 19, File 10.

would make a DP ineligible for emigration, DPs resented this criminalization of activities they saw as necessary for life. Army and UNRRA personnel, meanwhile, often attributed DP black market activities to antisocial attitudes.[89]

Other behavior deemed criminal stemmed from the DPs' enjoyment in identifying themselves with the victorious Allies. Occasionally this led to misunderstandings resulting in the imprisonment of DPs for impersonating military government personnel. Immediately following liberation, sympathetic Allied officers often engaged survivors as translators and liaisons to local survivors. They were given titles and sometimes parts of American uniforms to distinguish themselves. DPs and German Jews selected for these positions often believed they held official office; however, these informal arrangements were not recognized by regular military. DPs could be prosecuted and jailed for misrepresenting themselves as members of the military government. In one such case, a survivor was sentenced to six months in jail and a 5,000 RM fine for impersonating an officer of the military government when he had only been on the staff of a city commander who had since returned to the United States.[90] Survivors considered themselves members of the Allies and were bewildered when that view was not reciprocated.

Occasionally UNRRA issued clothing made from undyed yardage of military stores, and some DPs found themselves accused of improper use of military clothing.[91] Military officials were suspicious of DP police who wore American helmet liners painted white with the letters "DP" marked in front and who saluted American officers, since these appeared to be pretensions to equality with the U.S. Military Police.[92] DP police received military gloves when they completed an American training course, but U.S. MPs often accused them of misappropriation of American uniforms and suggested that the DP police carry cards indicating that they were permitted to wear the gloves. The misuse of military uniforms was a serious matter since criminal gangs could use military garb to evade authorities and to perpetrate crimes. The eagerness of survivors to be of service to their liberators and to dress like them conflicted with the military's need to maintain proper channels of command and to distinguish itself from civilians. Thus, without criminal intent, and often wearing items issued to them either by the military or UNRRA, DPs inadvertently committed crimes.

---

[89] Although she recognized that DPs felt justified in looting from Germans, the UNRRA nurse connected the behavior to "a lowering of moral standards" that she believed took place in the concentration camps. Doherty, letter dated 29 July 1946, in *Letters from Belsen*, p. 67.

[90] The Jewish Committee of Bad-Wörishofen [German] to an unnamed general, 14 December 1945, YIVO, RG 294.2, MK 483, Microfilm reel 2, Folder 27. For a similar case of a Yugoslav Jewish DP, see Otto Schonstein to Parole Board, Legal Division, Military Government Office for Greater Hesse, 11 November 1946, UN S-0425, Box 18, File 2.

[91] Director, UNRRA Team 311, to Major Rein, Military Government Landsberg, "Arrest of Camp Landsberg DP's," 26 November 1945, UN S-0425, Box 43, File 6; Buttler to Bender, "D.P. Camp Landsberg/Lech," p. 2.

[92] Gould to Commanding Officer, "DP Camp Fohrenwald [sic]" 5 May 1946, p. 1.

Other Jewish DPs knowingly engaged in criminal activities for profit and for revenge. Some DPs pimped German women, both to acquire wealth and to exact a type of sexual revenge on Germans by facilitating the degradation of German womanhood.[93] Other Jews owned taverns at which German women and GIs met and socialized, contributing to what Germans considered the sexual deviance and national decline brought on by the occupation.[94] Although some Jewish barkeeps refused to serve African American soldiers, others welcomed them along with white German women customers. Miscegenation scandalized Germans and white Americans alike. They often viewed Jews as promoters of these racial transgressions, contributing to the image of Jews as criminals even though these businesses were legitimate.

In their determined quest to leave Europe, Holocaust survivors crossed borders illegally; used forged documents; and falsified their ages, occupations, countries of origin, and medical conditions in order to qualify for visas to a new homeland. With the help of sympathetic American soldiers, DP drivers in Bavaria used trucks from the auto pool to transport DPs illegally across borders at night on the first stage their journey from the DP camps to ports in Italy and France, where ships bound for Palestine awaited them. While perhaps understandable, and to the DPs forgivable, many Germans and some Allied personnel viewed this behavior as further evidence of Jewish lawlessness.[95]

DPs engaged in illegal activity in support of the Jewish community in Palestine and later Israel. Because they considered themselves to be still at war against both unrepentant Germans and the British Mandate in Palestine, DPs believed their cause warranted violating Allied and German laws that stood in their way. Especially when it came to flouting British restrictions on immigration and exports to Palestine, DPs felt justified in ignoring what they considered unjust laws. Former partisans stole or purchased weapons and ammunition for shipment to Palestine to aid the Haganah (the future Israel Defense Forces) in its preparations for the Israeli War for Independence.[96] DP leaders purchased on the black market commodities needed in Palestine and shipped them disguised as personal items of legal immigrants.

In July 1949 Israeli agents stole machinery from a German gunpowder factory in the American Zone. Pursued by American authorities, the Israelis turned for help to Josef Rosensaft, chairman of the Belsen Camp Committee.

[93] Samuel Pisar, *Of Blood and Hope* (New York: Macmillan, 1980), p. 93; Zwi Rosenwein, "Videotaped interview," VHA, IC 1598, Seg. 150.

[94] Maria Höhn, *GIs and Fräuleins: The German-American Encounter in 1950s West Germany* (Chapel Hill: University of North Carolina Press, 2002), pp. 113–115.

[95] Berkowitz, *Crime of Existence*, pp. 151–153. Confusion existed about whether or not Jewish infiltrees were criminals. A U.S. Provost Marshall sentenced one survivor, smuggled across the border into Germany and captured by German police, to six months' imprisonment. The Jewish officer apparently felt the need to show the Germans in his courtroom that he could be strict with a Jewish defendant. After three months a new Provost Marshall arrived and released the survivor. David Ackerman, "Videotaped interview," VHA, IC 2416, Segs. 68–78.

[96] Faye Schulman, *A Partisan's Memoir: Woman of the Holocaust* (Toronto: Second Story Press, 1995), p. 222.

He bribed German customs officials to allow the machinery to come to Belsen and then arranged with the German company that handled the transportation of property for DP immigrants to Israel to provide a small ship. Later, American authorities looking for the machinery and smuggled weapons stopped the *Dromit*, the ship originally intended to carry the machinery. Finding no contraband, the Americans turned the ship over to British authorities. After a lengthy investigation that revealed no major wrongdoing in this case,[97] the British paid the Belsen Committee compensation for the spoiled foodstuffs that had constituted the majority of the *Dromit*'s cargo.[98] Rosensaft turned the money over to Youth Aliyah in Israel.[99] The occupation forces were correct in suspecting DP involvement in the transport of the stolen machinery, and they remained rightly suspicious that DPs were engaged in illegal projects in support of Israel. For the DPs, they were engaged in guerilla warfare in defense of their de facto homeland, Israel.

Jewish survivors rejected notions that they were criminal. Although the DP leadership and others believed that black market activity and other crimes demeaned Jewish DPs,[100] many survivors felt German crimes outweighed whatever they might be doing.[101] For example, a Belsen DP and her friends, hungry for fresh food, stole and ate a chicken: "After going through what we'd been through, you think 'why shouldn't I? They have taken everything, all my life.' And yet you don't think about that person who's probably an innocent farmer. But we enjoyed that chicken!"[102] Since Germans had robbed Europe's Jews of all of their possessions, DPs justified acquiring German property through trade or even theft as partial payment on the stolen goods.[103] Some Jewish DPs sought to demonstrate their moral superiority by refraining from acts of vengeance, while others inflicted their own style of justice, whether through economic prowess or physical assault. Some Jewish survivors satisfied

---

[97] DPs were permitted to take household goods. Disagreement arose between British officials and DP leaders as to whether machinery personally owned and used by DPs could be included as household items or whether they required export licenses. Rosensaft pleaded ignorance of British restrictions on exports. British Civil Police Unit, "Statement of Witness Josef Rosensaft," 14 November 1949, Rosensaft Papers, RG-08.002*03; "S.S. Dromit Delayed at Bremen," World Jewish Affairs News and Feature Service, 6 April 1950, p. 1, Rosensaft Papers, RG-08.002*09.

[98] J. S. Hill, Senior Finance Officer, to Josef Rosensaft, "Goods Seized ex S.S. DROMIT," 5 June 1950, Rosensaft Papers, RG-08.002*03.

[99] Rosensaft, *Yesterday*, pp. 121–122.

[100] Landsberg leaders campaigned against the black market with slogans such as "Trading helps the Germans and only blackens the Jewish name." Pinson, "Jewish Life in Liberated Germany," p. 123, fn. 23.

[101] Sociologist Lynn Rapaport demonstrates that collective memories of the Holocaust facilitated postwar Jewish ethnic identity by defining Jews as morally pure and Germans as impure, as murderers and antisemites. Lynn Rapaport, *Jews in Germany after the Holocaust: Memory, Identity, and Jewish-German Relations* (Cambridge: Cambridge University Press, 1997), pp. 18 and 45.

[102] Ilona Naylor, "Videotaped interview," VHA, IC 45981, Seg. 219.

[103] Mankowitz, *Life between Memory and Hope*, pp. 240–241; Alex Gringauz, "Videotaped interview," VHA, IC 24880, Seg. 18.

their thirst for vengeance by seeing Germans humiliated, what Zeev Mankowitz calls "symbolic revenge."[104] Realizing that killing ten Germans would not be much of an exchange for what had happened to Europe's Jews, DP Abraham Marber said, "I prefer to see them really grovel."[105] Most DPs felt that Germans deserved whatever ill befell them.[106]

For the survivors, the war in Europe would not end until their departure from Germany, and in their minds that was connected with the battle to create a Jewish homeland in Palestine. Jewish DPs remained mobilized for self-defense against the Germans and for the conflict in Palestine. They used the necessities of war to excuse their abrogation of Allied and German laws. DPs resented the restrictions the Allies and Germans attempted to impose on their activities. Meanwhile, Allied and German authorities labeled DPs as criminal and were frustrated by a population that seemed to write its own rules.

LIVING WITH THE GERMANS

In the immediate aftermath of liberation, before the establishment of DP camps, many survivors sought shelter in German villages and on German farms. Oftentimes the DPs remained for weeks until they were able to leave in search of family or decided to move to a DP camp, where they could receive supplemental rations and be among fellow survivors. A significant number, however, decided to remain among the Germans, trying to establish as normal a life as possible. Later, when DP camps could not accommodate Jewish infiltrees, those DPs sought housing in German communities as well. These arrangements brought Jews and non-Jewish Germans into close contact, resulting in friction, coexistence, and occasionally friendship.

When newly liberated concentration camp inmates approached Germans, the Germans often reacted with fear. Already disoriented by military defeat and postwar chaos, these mostly elderly or female Germans did not know what treatment to expect from the emaciated, filthy, lice-ridden survivors. Historian Steven Aschheim described the encounter between Germans and Polish Jews during the First World War when "the fright at seeing poor and seemingly degenerate figures made it easy to transfer incipient compassion into a more manageable stereotypical judgment. It is never easy to identify with people living in dehumanized conditions."[107] How much more difficult for post-1945

---

[104] Charles Sternbach, "Videotaped interview," VHA, IC 8981, Segs. 102–104; Mankowitz, *Life between Memory and Hope*, p. 239.

[105] Abraham Marber, "Videotaped interview," VHA, IC 46992, Seg. 318.

[106] A DP involved in a traffic accident felt no remorse for the death of a German bicyclist struck by his car: "At that time, five and a half months after the liberation that a German was killed just by accident didn't bother me. Now it does bother me." Abraham Besser, "Videotaped interview," VHA, IC 19988, Seg. 146; other examples include Helen Goldring, "Videotaped interview," VHA, IC 5590, Seg. 135; Zula Schibuk, "Videotaped interview," VHA, IC 37065, Segs. 189–192.

[107] Aschheim, *Brothers and Strangers*, p. 144.

Germans to empathize with Jewish survivors. Not only were the survivors in more dehumanized condition than the Jews of the First World War, but the Germans were also struggling with their unbearable, long-held suspicions or knowledge of Nazi crimes and their own shame of complicity.[108]

Survivors occasionally reacted with anger to German fear, such as one woman who shouted, "we are not the ones who are harming children or stealing other people's properties. You look at your own people."[109] While Jewish DPs did not engage in excesses to the extent of Soviet or other non-Jewish DPs, Germans did have reason to be wary of them. Years of persecution had left survivors with poor impulse control and they could be prone to violent outbursts, although usually with provocation. On occasion an antisemitic comment or personal insult directed toward a Jew prompted a violent reaction. One week after liberation, Moshe Mangel wanted to trade his concentration camp uniform for civilian clothing. He approached a German woman who had her husband's suits and asked for one. She hurled an insult at him and the next thing that he knew, he had kicked her down some stairs and taken the suit. "I never did this in my life, but when she said, 'God punish the riff-raff!' it reminded me what they did to us."[110] Mangel had reacted instinctively, without conscious thought, and in retrospect he was shocked by his actions but unrepentant. Despite their fears of potentially volatile DPs, some Germans did not always refrain from provocative comments.

It was not only Germans who attempted to keep their distance from "the other." Jewish survivors often blamed all Germans for the atrocities committed against them, seeing their parents' murderers in every German face.[111] A group of DPs refused to interact with the German women who housed and cared for them in the weeks immediately following liberation. "We didn't speak to them. … We hated to look at them. We didn't want to look at them because we knew, we said, all the Germans are guilty and that's that."[112] Another survivor recalled not wanting to talk to Germans: "[W]e knew what kind of people they were."[113] Forced out of necessity to live among Germans, these DPs sought to minimize contact, refusing to engage with Germans on a social level.

With an understandable distrust of Germans, DPs had difficulty knowing how to respond to or to interpret German acts of kindness. The most distrusting viewed friendly overtures as some sort of trick, such as the young woman who rejected an invitation to Sunday dinner because she felt she was being asked to deny her Jewishness.[114] Instead of interpreting the invitation as

---

[108] Frei, *1945 und Wir*, p. 149.
[109] Julia Skalina, "Videotaped interview," VHA, IC 33759, Segs. 164–165.
[110] Moshe Mangel, "Videotaped interview," VHA, IC 4423, Segs. 119–120.
[111] Emanuel Moss, "Videotaped interview," VHA, IC 11264, Seg. 59; Nicholas Friedman, "Videotaped interview," VHA, IC 39581, Seg. 19; Freda Narev, "Videotaped interview," VHA, IC 38341, Seg. 17.
[112] Mary Wishnic, "Videotaped interview," VHA, IC 18706, Seg. 66.
[113] Miriam Goldstein, "Videotaped interview," VHA, IC 73, Seg. 43.
[114] Margaret Rosenberg, "Videotaped interview," VHA, IC 14650, Seg. 121.

a German's desire to share her family's best food with an impoverished victim of German aggression, possibly as a gesture of atonement, the survivor found antisemitic motives within it. Not able to believe the sincerity of German compassion for Jews, some survivors attributed German pleasantness to their fears of how the Jews would treat them or of upsetting the Allied authorities.[115] There were, however, survivors who believed that the Germans who took them in were genuinely kind,[116] and there were also DPs who wanted to believe in the sincerity of those who gave them shelter but had doubts. In Wöbbelin, U.S. troops ordered a woman and her two teenaged sons to take three newly liberated survivors into their home. One of those DPs commented, "They were nice. They had to be nice. Maybe they were nice. You know you can't blame everybody."[117] Here was the awareness that Germans had incentives to be nice, that the Allies required decent treatment of survivors, that befriending a Jew could help one before a denazification tribunal. At the same time, there was the hope that German kindness had been genuine and the determination to acknowledge that not all Germans had been involved in the crimes against the Jews.

The Allied housing policies often forced Jews into contact with Germans they knew to be hostile. The Allies favored requisitioning rooms, hotels, houses, and apartments from Nazis. The theory was to inconvenience Nazis rather than other Germans as a form of punishment and to reeducate them by forcing them into contact with Jews. When it came to Jews being assigned rooms in Nazi homes, neither the German families nor the Jews appreciated the policy. One DP recalled that the German family "hated us" but housed and fed them as required. "Poor us, we had enough of Nazis!"[118] Forced to live among people who hated them and who had worked with the murderers of their families seemed a cruelty to the DPs.

At the same time, German residents and property owners suffered hostility from their boarders and tenants. Some Germans complained of physical attacks from the DPs assigned to their homes, and other suffered surliness and animosity. A woman with two children whose husband had been arrested for being a Nazi was required to house a group of Jewish DPs. Sharing the kitchen with the DPs, the woman was aware of their greater rations and their access to luxury goods, such as coffee. She and her children would eat their leftovers. Recalled one DP, "they didn't deserve it, but you're a human being, right?"[119] The DPs' contemptuous attitude toward the German woman and schadenfreude over her situation may be

[115] Roza Chlevicki, "Videotaped interview," VHA, IC 22056, Seg. 69; Abram Erlich, "Videotaped interview," VHA, IC 21971, Seg. 117; Saul Nitzberg, "Videotaped interview," VHA, IC 44064, Seg. 38; George (Gedali) Fliger, "Videotaped interview," VHA, IC 13799, Seg. 82.

[116] Mary Balzam, "Videotaped interview," VHA, IC 37216, Segs. 71–82; Fanny Elbaum, "Videotaped interview," VHA, IC 46146, Segs. 149–152; Victor Silver, "Videotaped interview," VHA, IC 5189, Seg. 105.

[117] Adam Sulkowicz, "Videotaped interview," VHA, IC 32285, Seg. 15.

[118] Ilse Levy-Koster, "Videotaped interview," VHA, IC 10384, Seg. 92.

[119] Rose Berkenwald, VHA, IC 9081, Seg. 97.

understandable given her husband's Nazi party affiliation and the survivors' years of suffering. At the same time, it was unlikely that their presence in the German woman's house helped reeducate her and her children regarding their attitudes toward Jews. When the DPs finally left the home on their way to America, one of them deliberately broke the family's fancy clock. The act of vandalism sought to inflict symbolic damage on the Nazi family that still lived in their well-appointed rooms while the DPs could never recover their destroyed homes and families.

While deliberate destruction of property was not all that common, Jewish DPs frequently allowed requisitioned German property to fall into disrepair. Behind the neglect was a feeling that Germans should suffer too.[120] In addition to the decline of their property, German landlords lost rental income when their hotels, vacation homes, and apartment buildings were requisitioned. Not surprisingly, German communities sought to restrict the number of Jewish DPs living there and tried to give them the least desirable housing, hoping that the Jews would move on to the larger, self-contained DP camps. Many Jewish survivors did move to the larger camps, but a significant number of DPs wanted to establish as normal an existence as possible and rejected camp life. Other DPs, arriving after a camp reached maximum capacity, would have no choice but to find housing in a German town.

Germans faced their own housing shortage and often feared that DPs were criminals. They did not encourage Jews to stay. In the village of Cham, in Oberpfalz near the Czech border, Germans sought to impose a curfew on Jewish DPs.[121] In November 1945 the Jewish community of Tirschenreuth consisted of 130 Jews, 30 of whom had no apartments and were forced to live in unacceptable conditions. Lying near the Czech border, Tirschenreuth also saw 50 border crossers on average each day, compounding the problem.[122] Local German officials in Moosburg refused to register Jews and to provide them with housing. Jews were sleeping on floors in substandard housing. The survivors appealed to the Central Committee of Liberated Jews in Munich for help. After a representative of the Central Committee joined local Jewish leaders in lengthy negotiations with the mayor, city inspector, housing commissioner, and the police chief, German officials promised to requisition decent housing for the Jews and to move Jews from the unacceptable apartments into the better ones.[123] Even where local authorities cooperated with military government regulations, homeowners refused entry to Jews assigned to their quarters or removed property from the DPs' rooms, from furniture to lightswitches.[124]

[120] Eva Lehner, VHA, IC 30032, Seg. 23.
[121] Central Committee to the Jewish Committee of Cham (in German), 12 December 1945, YIVO, RG 294.2, MK 483, Microfilm reel 2, Folder 27.
[122] Jüdisches Komitee Tirschenreuth to Jüdisches Zentralkomitee in Bayern, 14 November 1945, YIVO, RG 294.2, MK 483, Microfilm reel 2, Folder 16.
[123] Kinas, "Prezes Szwimer endert di bacijung fun dajcze amtn cu jidn in Moosburg," *Landsberger Lager Cajtung*, 30 August 1946, p. 13.
[124] A. C. Glassgold, Director, UNRRA Team 311, to Captain Toms, Commanding Officer Company I, Landsberg, "Antisemitic Incidents," 7 March 1946, Zisman Papers, RG-19.047.02*16; Pola Suss, "Videotaped interview," VHA, IC 25284, Seg. 97.

The attitude of the local military government officers greatly affected the treatment of so-called free-living Jews. Shortly after liberation a U.S. military government officer wrote from Mannheim, "There are some [MGOs] that believe their job is to assist the Germans in the reconstruction and rehabilitation of their country. These feel that their job is to make the DP as uncomfortable as possible. And I might say they succeed. Here one of our brilliant officers had the MPs raiding homes and taking DPs out of their homes and leading them to the camp."[125] In Schwabmünchen, the arrival of a new commander in October 1945 led to a worsening of conditions for Jews in the town. The Jews no longer received supplementary rations for former concentration-camp inmates, and the new commander indicated that he wanted the Jews to move into a camp. Taking their cue from the MGO, local Germans began evicting Jews from furnished quarters and insulting Jewish residents.[126]

In December 1945, British occupation authorities ordered free-living Jewish DPs to be treated as Germans and subject to German administration, affecting housing assignments and rations.[127] Near Belsen, in the community of Celle, the local officer, Major Leytham, ordered the Housing Office not to issue apartments to Jews without his express permission, denied the assignment of a room for use as a synagogue, and refused to lift the curfew so that Jews could celebrate the Passover Seder as a community.[128] In Landsberg, an American officer, in violation of U.S. policy, ordered the Housing Office not to issue billets to Jews. When a visiting colonel discovered this breach of policy, he ordered it countermanded and recommended the removal of the offending officer from Landsberg on the grounds that he was anti-DP and antisemitic.[129] In both cases Jewish appeals to higher authorities found sympathetic responses, reassuring DPs that even if local officers treated them poorly, they could still depend on Allied protection in the long run.

Since MGOs anticipated the occupation of Germany lasting longer than DP residence there, they often felt their interests best served by accommodating the Germans. The British were especially forthright in acknowledging early on that their priority was the rehabilitation of Germany, of which the removal of DPs was part.[130] In the American Zone, Major General White of the 71st Infantry Division couched his desire to forcibly remove free-living Jews from

[125] Albert Hutler, letter dated 15 May 1945, USHMM, Albert Hutler Letters, RG-19.028.

[126] "Notiz über die Verhältnisse und Beziehungen zu den im Kreis Schabmünchen wohnenden jüdischen Ex-Häftlingen," 1 December 1945, YIVO, RG 294.2, MK 483, Microfilm reel 2, Folder 16.

[127] Major Hudson to Chief Rabbi, 17 December 1945, YV O-70/64; Norbert Wollheim, "Bericht: Neue Richtlinien hinsichtlich Stellung und Behandlung der D.P.'s in der britischen Zone," 14 June 1946, YV O-70/6.

[128] Jewish Committee of Celle to Central Jewish Committee and attached documents, 19 April 1946, YV O-70/64.

[129] Colonel O. A. Nelson to Brigadier General Walter J. Muller, 10 December 1945, p. 2, Zisman Papers, RG-19.047.02*16.

[130] Wollheim, "Bericht: Neue Richtlinien."

his district in terms of the difficulty "of caring for these people satisfactorily in conformity with the policies of General Eisenhower."[131] His main concern, however, was the possibility of "trouble" if the Jews remained as they were because the local German population wanted the Jews to be removed. For their part, the survivors wanted to remain in the area where they had been liberated, where they were among their friends and where they could live a relatively normal domestic life. They also did not want to satisfy the local Germans' desire to see them leave.[132] DPs believed that the well-being of the victors, of whom they considered themselves a part, should be put ahead of the desires of the defeated Germans. Friction among Jews, Germans, and Allies would only increase, and conditions for free-living Jews would deteriorate in 1946 with the arrival of more Jews from Eastern Europe that put further strains on German communities and dashed the expectation of a speedy removal of Jewish DPs.

The influx of ethnic German expellees and Jewish infiltrees heightened tensions, particularly in Bavaria, where most of these people arrived in need of housing, food, clothing, and medical care. In Bavaria, 625,058 expellees settled between January and August 31, 1946.[133] Local communities perceived the expellees and DPs as threats to their standard of living and maintenance of law and order. Some Germans viewed all outsiders as undesirable.[134] Other Germans, however, favored the expellees as fellow-countrymen and German speakers over the more foreign DPs, demonstrating the lingering ideal of Volksgemeinschaft. Attachment to Volksgemeinschaft can be seen in the reactions to the housing crisis when local Germans included newly arrived ethnic Germans from the East within their circle of obligation but excluded Jewish DPs who had lived among them since the war's end. Expellees with their stories of brutalization and their impact on the strained economies of German towns contributed to the image of German suffering that dominated

---

[131] Major General Arthur A. White, to Commanding General, XX Corps, US Army, "Care of Jewish Displaced Persons," 29 October 1945, UN S-0425, Box 10, File 7.

[132] Lieutenant Jack M. Sauter to G-2 71st Infantry Division, "Report on Jewish DP's in Turkheim and Vicinity," 19 October 1945, UN S-0425, Box 10, File 7; R. Stuchen, JDC Senior Field Representative, to Colonel Foster, 19 October 1945, UN S-0425, Box 10, File 7.

[133] In the period covered by the report, Germany received 1,247,831 expellees from Eastern Europe. There were also more than 300,000 non-Bavarian evacuees from other parts of Germany and additional non-Jewish refugees from Silesia and the Soviet Zone of Germany adding to the burden. Office of Military Government for Bavaria, "After Action, Report, Refugee Section, 1 August through 31 August," 9 September 1946, pp. 1–2; Refugees and Expellees; General Records of Public Welfare and Displaced Persons 1946–50; CAD; OMGUS, RG 260, Entry A2 B3 C1; NACP.

[134] Gertrud Altman and her roommate, Roman Bieniek, assaulted a Jewish family living in their building. Police reported that Bieniek said, "Too bad you eternal Jews are still alive, but the Nazis will come again soon and then you will be done in." Earlier Altman and Bieniek had persecuted a Sudeten German family, throwing their firewood into the street. Newspaper clipping, "Jüdische Familie schwer misshandelt" [byline Scharzenbach/Saale]; Bayr. Hilfswerk/Jewish Agency; General Records of Public Welfare and Displaced Persons 1946–50; CAD; OMGUS, RG 260, Entry A2 B3 C1; NACP.

postwar West German public memory.[135] Meanwhile, the increasing number of Jews unsettled the notion that German–Jewish relations were only temporary. Without the promise of temporariness, resentment came out into the open in the form of window breaking, antisemitic posters, and physical assaults.[136]

Whether military officers received insufficient training in DP matters or they, too, were becoming impatient with the difficulties DPs represented, UNRRA officials reported increasing numbers of cases of military authorities improperly evicting DPs from their residences.[137] Local U.S. Army troops did not implement directives to give preference to persecutees over Germans, and the cooperation with German police strengthened the impression of an alliance between Germans and Americans.[138] DPs could not even count on the protection of American MPs, although in early 1946 there were signs that the military was beginning to take seriously the abuse of military authority against DPs.[139] Despite their supposedly protected status, DPs remained insecure, dependent on the personalities and whims of Allied officials and the attitudes of local Germans.

[135] Moeller, *War Stories*, pp. 32–37.

[136] On New Year's Eve 1946/1947 Germans threw rocks through the windows of Jewish apartments in Dieburg, a town south of Frankfurt a.M., and through the mess hall window where DPs were holding their party in Bad Salzschlirf, northeast of Frankfurt, near Fulda. The window-breaking campaign lasted a week in Dieburg, and in Bad Salzschlirf it was accompanied by antisemitic and anti-American handbills stating "Long live Hitler, the German nation does not stop hating Jews because they are our misfortune, Heil Hitler," and "Down and out with the Jews, Americans and KPD Bigwigs, Heil Hitler, and soon the sun will shine for us." On January 10, 1947 Germans attacked a Jewish bicyclist in Wetzlar, north of Frankfurt. A German policeman in civilian clothes witnessed the incident but did not assist the injured boy. A passing Jewish Agency worker intervened and called MPs. P. Trouchaud, Director, UNRRA, Area Team 1021, "Relations between the Jewish population and the German Population of Dieburg," [copy], 6 January 1947, UN S-0425, Box 12, File 3; J. Ned H. Burford, Director, Fulda Assembly Centres, to Lieutenant Colonel Howard R. Cross, Commanding Officer, Fulda Military Government Detachment, "Terroristic Activities at Bad Salschlirf [sic] Jewish Camp," 2 January 1947, UN S-0425, Box 12, File 3; M. Shapiro, JAFP Wetzlar, to M. Petitjean, Director, Wetzlar, "Jewish DP Beaten by Germans," 14 January 1947, UN S-0425, Box 12, File 3.

[137] For example, on a Sunday night in January 1947, a U.S. military captain, in violation of military directives, ordered the immediate eviction of 300 Jewish survivors from their apartments near the Landsberg prison, where they had been living since May 1945. W. J. Korn, UNRRA, Director Landsberg, to E. E. Farber, Area Director, Area Team 1065, "Unauthorized Movement of DP Persecutees," 26 January 1947; Carl C. Caole, to Commanding General, 1st Division, U.S. Army, "Eviction of D.Ps. at Landsberg," 5 February 1947, Zisman Papers, RG-19.049.02*23.

[138] Frank Stern, *The Whitewashing of the Yellow Badge: Antisemitism and Philosemitism in Postwar Germany*, trans. William Templer (Oxford: Pergamon Press, 1992), p. 75.

[139] For example, on December 26, 1946, an MP pistol-whipped a Wetzlar DP without provocation. The military sentenced the MP to six months' hard labor and forfeiture of pay. The severe sentence reassured UNRRA personnel that the military was confronting the abuse of military authority against DPs. Michael Petitjean, Director, Weszlar, to Area Director, Hersfeld, "Incident between Jewish DPs and MP's," 26 December 1946, UN S-0425, Box 12, File 3; Jean M. Fisher, UNRRA Protective Division, memorandum to P. B. Edwards, UNRRA Zone Director, "Incident between Jewish DP's and MP's at Wetzlar," 15 February, 1947, UN S-0425, Box 12, File 3; H. Frank Brull, Senior Protective Officer, to Chief Protective Officer, U.S. Zone,

By 1947 German officials were becoming even more confident in asserting the priority of Germans over DPs.[140] German bureaucrats used red tape to
delay assisting Jews with food and housing issues without getting into trouble
with American officials.[141] Conditions for Jewish DPs in Straubing became
so untenable in early 1947 that the military launched an investigation into
UNRRA complaints about the Straubing Military Government and the actions
of German officials there.[142] Many Straubing Jews lived in apartments or
private rooms that had been requisitioned from Nazis. Under the direction of
the Housing Office administrator, Herr Schaller, household items and furnishings were removed from two DP homes while the DPs were out of town. One
of these victims left town again only to return to find that the Housing Office
had moved a recently released Nazi into her apartment.[143] Schaller harassed
local Jews with lists of items that they were ordered to turn over to the original
owners by arbitrary deadlines, and he would have removed stoves and lighting
fixtures had UNRRA not intervened.[144]

The local MGO condoned the Housing Office's activities to the point that
local former Nazis felt comfortable enough to threaten those in possession of
what had been their property, hinting at support from American authorities.[145]
In one case a German landlord harassed Jews assigned private rooms in his
home, restricting kitchen and bathroom access, and occasionally threatening
physical violence.[146] When one of the Jews complained to authorities, Schaller

Heidelberg, "Incident between Jewish DP's and MP's," 7 February 1947, UN S-0425, Box 12,
    File 3.
[140] Clearly hoping to evict infiltrees from German buildings, in 1947 the Länderrat wanted to
    know if DPs who entered the U.S. Zone after December 13, 1945 had the right to dwell in
    requisitioned houses. They did. Harry S. Messec to Chief of Staff, "Clarification with Regard to
    Groups of Persons Entitled to Occupy Housing Space Requisitioned by US Army for UNRRA,"
    9 November 1947, DP Camps: Welfare Problems; PW & DP Br.; (National Archives Microfiche
    3/173-2/1, 2 of 4); CAD; OMGUS, RG 260; NACP.
[141] Stern, *Whitewashing of the Yellow Badge*, pp. 97 and 99.
[142] James E. Flannery, Field Operations, UNRRA District 3, to Director, UNRRA, U.S. Zone, Third
    Army, "Straubing Military Government Relationship with Displaced Persons," 15 March 1947,
    UN S-0425, Box 43, File 3.
[143] Ernst Dannemann, AJDC, summary of the case of Mrs. Alma Klüger, 21 February 1947, UN
    S-0425, Box 43, File 3.
[144] William R. Trigg III, Field Observer, UNNRA, Area Team 1046, "A Narrative Account of the
    Actions of the German Habitation Office and the Counter-Measures Taken to Date by AJDC and
    UNRRA, Straubing," 21 February 1947, UN S-0425, Box 43, File 3; Elise Kemser, "Statement
    on 11-2-47," 13 February 1947, UN S-0425, Box 43, File 3; A. Michalowicz, "Statement," 19
    February 1947, UN S-0425, Box 43, File 3. In 1946 JDC and JCRA representatives took note of
    German Jews in the British Zone reporting removal without notice of their furniture by the Nazi
    families. Brotman and Viteles, "Survey on Conditions of Jews," p. 5.
[145] Thomas Angermeier to Maria Schmidt, 1 February 1947, UN S-0425, Box 43, File 3; Dannemann,
    summary of the case of Mrs. Alma Klüger.
[146] [Isaak] Rotmensch to Bavarian Ministry of Home Office, Commissioner of the State for racial
    religious and political persecutes, "Second Complaint against the Dentist Kratzer," 12 February
    1947, UN S-0425, Box 43, File 3; Chaim Majteles to Commissioner of the State for political,

threatened him with eviction. Locals also harassed German maids who worked for Jews, signifying the growing acceptance of antisemitism in the town.[147] While the situation in Straubing may have been worse because of the confluence of a hostile city official and an either unsympathetic or disinterested MGO, additional communities sought the removal of DPs.

In July 1947 the city council of Weilheim, a town in the Bavarian Alps between Munich and Garmisch-Partenkirchen, requested that military government officials move Jewish DPs from the city to a camp. In making their appeal the German officials noted that ethnic German expellees were living in crowded conditions and were beginning to turn toward communism. An outbreak of contagious diseases also threatened. The Germans argued that this situation could be rectified by moving the Jewish DPs, who had come voluntarily to Germany, had occupied rooms and buildings in the town for two years, and were participating in the black market, buying stolen goods.[148] The town leaders played on the fears of the military government: communism, epidemic, and crime.[149] If the situation of the expellees was accurately reported, it was clearly unacceptable: Ninety-six were living in a cattle auction hall and another 56 families in a gymnasium. However, rather than ask that these more recent arrivals be moved to another town or camp with more suitable housing, the city council viewed itself as responsible for the ethnic Germans in opposition to the interests of Jewish DPs who had resided in the town since the war's end.[150] The Jews were supposed to be temporary residents and thus did not merit the protection of town authorities.

Archival records most likely emphasize acrimonious relations since documents were generated when authorities were called in to mediate. More cordial relations between Germans and Jews are occasionally mentioned in survivor personal narratives. Former DP Abraham Secemski recalled that relations with Germans in town were initially strained. When German efforts to persuade American troops to resettle DPs from the town hotel to Feldafing

religious and racial persecutes, "Complaint against the dentist, Mr. Kratzer," undated, UN S-0425, Box 43, File 3.

[147] Jan Malicki, "Certification," 6 February 1947, UN S-0425, Box 43, File 3; [Isaak] Rotmensch to Jewish Commissioner of the State for political and racial persecutes [sic], "Accusation against the Dentist Kratzer," 6 December 1946, UN S-0425, Box 43, File 3.

[148] Dr. Machon, 1st Buergermeister, to Major Brown, Director, Liaison and Security Office, Weilheim, 19 July 1947, Zisman Papers, RG-19.047.02*23.

[149] The Union of Evacuated House-Owners and Tenants of Lampertheim made similar claims in their efforts to have DPs removed from their requisitioned residences. Harry S. Messec, "Survey of German Housing in Lampertheim," 10 December 1947, DP Camps: Welfare Problems; PW & DP Br. (National Archives Microfiche 3/173–2/1, 2 of 4); CAD; OMGUS, RG 260; NACP; Margarete Kraus to Military Government of Wiesbaden, 25 April 1948, DP Camps: Welfare Problems; PW & DP Br.; (National Archives Microfiche 3/173–2/1, 1 of 4); CAD; OMGUS, RG 260; NACP.

[150] Six out of ten Germans considered expellees to be German citizens and almost half believed Germany should support them, whereas only 15 percent of Germans were willing to accept responsibility for the DPs. ICD Opinion Surveys, "German Reactions to Expellees and DPs," Report No. 81, 3 December 1947, pp. 1 and 8; Correspondence regarding Displaced Persons;

failed, townspeople realized that they could not be rid of the Jewish DPs. As a result "we learned how to live with each other. As a matter of fact we made a lot of friends between the local population. And some not so good. We had fights, yes. [If] we ever found out who was in the S.S., we took care of that. We didn't kill him, but we gave him a lesson that was of their own medicine."[151] Here was one case in which the realization that the Jews would not be quickly gone actually led to improved, although not always tranquil, relations.

On the individual level, Jews and Germans often accommodated one another as a way to get through everyday life with the minimum of conflict. DPs who lived outside of the major camps could not avoid Germans. Some camp dwellers found employment or sought entertainment outside of the camps and, as former DP Jack Novin commented, "once you left camp you had no choice but to meet them." Although he suspected most of the German doctors and nurses with whom he worked at the Feldafing hospital of being Nazis, Novin became friendly with them, dining at their homes and joining them on ski weekends. "I got along well. You had no choice. You couldn't ignore them. You depended on them."[152] Rather than warmth and companionship, Novin seems to have viewed these self-described friendships as necessary for smoothing his way through life in postwar Germany. Another observer noted that Jewish DPs would speak of their hatred of Germans in one breath and then of their "dear neighbors, the Müllers" in the next, "for even the greatest hatred cannot live in complete isolation when you have to go on living where the torment took place."[153] Living among the Germans gave DPs the opportunity to learn that not all Germans had supported the Nazi regime and that there were some "good Germans" among them.

Non-Jewish German concentration camp survivors often took an interest in Jewish DPs. In addition to important political figures, such as Kurt Schumacher of the Social Democratic Party, there were other German survivors who spoke out in the immediate postwar years in favor of reparations for DPs.[154] Such Germans were lauded in DP newspapers that also reported the difficulties these Germans sometimes had returning to their previous lives.[155]

Sometimes the contact from shared living quarters and proximity within villages could lead to peaceful coexistence and other times it led to something approaching friendship. For example, a German man, the former

---

The Public Health and the Public Welfare Branches: Subject Files of the Medical Affairs Section 1945–49; CAD; OMGUS, RG 260; NACP.

[151] Abraham Secemski, "Videotaped interview," VHA, IC 38093, Seg. 179.

[152] Jack Novin, "Videotaped interview," VHA IC 24267, Seg. 17.

[153] Julius Posner, *In Deutschland 1945–1956* (Jerusalem, 1947), p. 115, quoted in Michael Brenner, *After the Holocaust: Rebuilding Jewish Lives in Postwar Germany* (Princeton, NJ: Princeton University Press, 1997), p. 52.

[154] Michael Brenner, "Impressionen jüdischen Lebens in der Oberpfalz nach 1945," in *Die Juden in der Oberpfalz*, eds. Michael Brenner and Renate Höpfinger (Munich: Oldenbourg Wissenschaftsverlag, 2009), p. 234.

[155] Leib Courland, "A Visit with Dr. Karl Kreide" (in Yiddish), *Unzer Weg*, 25 September 1946, p. 6.

husband of a German Jew, found his Jewish DP neighbor bleeding profusely after a miscarriage. "I shall always cherish his memory as one who saved my life. Despite many Germans and because of one of them, I was two times a survivor."[156] The two families became so close that the German neighbors attended the circumcision of the DP's son. A number of DP men found romance with German women, and some of those relationships resulted in marriage. One DP discovered that it was not unpleasant to discuss with his German girl-friend the difficult relationship between Jews and Germans.[157] Although pleasant relations did evolve, often (although not always) the bonds ended when the DPs left Germany. Describing these relationships, Jewish survivors often seemed somewhat detached, describing the Germans as more emotionally invested in the friendships. We cannot determine here whether those were accurate assessments or wishful thinking; however, it does suggest the limited possibilities for a genuine friendship of equals between DPs and Germans in the immediate postwar years.

Despite efforts to get along, these free-living Jews often experienced discrimination in German-owned shops and struggled to obtain ration cards from German authorities. Germans received rations with lower caloric value than those allotted to DPs, and thus Germans did not want to sell limited supplies to Jews. German shopkeepers turned away one young DP woman, telling her "You get your food through the Americans."[158] In Ulm three Jewish DP families relied on a Jewish girl with "Aryan" looks to purchase their food since farmers at the market refused to sell to Jews.[159] Some DPs faced abuse from their German landlords. Living outside of the DP camps provided survivors with a semblance of normal living, but they remained aware that they were unwanted and vulnerable to capricious treatment by Germans and Allies alike.

INFILTREES AND THE ANGLO-AMERICAN COMMITTEE OF INQUIRY

Cordial relations between Germans and DPs often depended on the temporary nature of their arrangements.[160] In 1945 both groups had anticipated the speedy departure of the Jewish DPs. Germans assumed that the Jews would repatriate to their countries of origin and would no longer occupy housing or otherwise disrupt the German return to normalcy. Humbled by defeat, Germans feared angering the DPs' protectors, the Allies, and initially tolerated the DP presence. For their part, Jewish survivors had anticipated the world

---

[156] Rachela Walshaw in Rachela and Sam Walshaw, *From Out of the Firestorm: A Memoir of the Holocaust* (New York: Shapolsky Publishers, 1991), pp. 142–143. See also Sara Tuvel Bernstein, *The Seamstress: A Memoir of Survival* (New York: Berkley Books, 1997), p. 311; Regina Tauber, interview by the author, audio recording, Los Angeles, CA, 4 June 2007.

[157] Brenner, "Impressionen jüdischen Lebens," p. 240.

[158] Ruth Stern, "Videotaped interview," VHA, IC 34333, Seg. 117.

[159] Ida Chait, "Videotaped interview," VHA, IC 30112, Seg. 26.

[160] Atina Grossmann argues that the temporariness of these relationships facilitated "'a departure from violence' and active hatred." *Jews, Germans, and Allies*, pp. 215–217.

lifting them up and taking them in to new homes either in Palestine or abroad. When the temporary arrangement threatened to become permanent, tensions mounted. Instead of disappearing, Jewish DPs were increasing in number, especially in the American Zone. This unexpected development angered Germans and frustrated Allied military government personnel. What could be tolerated in the short term became insufferable, as prospects for the resolution of the DP problem remained dim.

In 1946 opportunities for emigration remained few for the Jewish DPs, and their numbers were swelling with "infiltrees" from Eastern Europe. As the Cold War divisions intensified, the Western Allies shifted their policy to the reconstruction of Germany. Suspicion that communists were among the infiltrees and impatience with Jewish DPs' refusal to contribute to the German economy influenced Allied officers' treatment of DPs.[161] Germans, emboldened by the changing Allied position, faced with the influx of ethnic Germans expelled from Eastern Europe, and frustrated by the indefinite stay of the DPs, became more open in their hostility toward the survivors. Searching for a way to remove Jewish DPs from Germany, the Anglo-Americans investigated the Jewish DP question in relation to Palestine, raising the hopes of DPs and Germans alike that the crisis could be resolved soon. The refusal of the British government to issue the 100,000 immigration certificates to Palestine recommended by the Anglo-American Committee of Inquiry dashed those hopes, adding fuel to the fire in Germany.

Jews liberated in Eastern Europe had been making their way into occupied Germany since the summer of 1945 aided by Brichah (Flight), an organization founded by former partisans but joined by increasing numbers of Allied soldiers; Jewish Brigade soldiers; and UNRRA, JDC, and JCRA personnel. Initially treated as posthostility refugees, the "infiltrees" did not qualify for UNRRA or military assistance. Jews who were registered for the DP camps shared their rations and overcrowded quarters with the new arrivals. Allied officials worried about the health consequences of unregistered people who did not receive medical exams and who strained the sanitation facilities of the camps. The need to provide for those who did not have ration cards also would encourage black market operations.

By December 1945 UNRRA accepted responsibility to aid those who had suffered "internal displacement" because of the war, and the fact that their external displacement occurred after the war was considered immaterial. Jews were automatically assumed to qualify for this status unless there was definite proof to the contrary. Non-Jews had to prove that they qualified.[162] In January 1946 the U.S. Army established transit camps in Berlin to house these people. Arrivals in Munich needing assignment to a DP camp frequently went to the Central Committee of Liberated Jews' headquarters in the Deutsches Museum,

---

[161] Victor Cavendish Bentinck to Foreign Office, Telegram No. 56, 9 January 1946, Public Record Office (PRO), Foreign Office (FO) 945/655 (microfilm, USHMM).

[162] George Woodbridge, *UNRRA: The History of the United Nations Relief and Rehabilitation Administration*, vol. 2 (New York: Columbia University Press, 1950), p. 510.

where an UNRRA team ran a DP Transient and Information Center.[163] Although UNRRA accepted responsibility for infiltrees, in northern Germany the British refused to permit the registration of new DPs beginning in July 1946. Since the British army controlled the food supply, UNRRA in practice was forced to carry out British policy. Infiltrees continued to reach Belsen, but they put a considerable strain on the camp population that had to share their normal rations of 1,550 calories per day with the unregistered newcomers.[164]

The infiltration of these Jews lessened some lower echelon officials' sympathy for Jewish DPs. One officer pointed out to Landsberg DPs that the overcrowding they complained about was the fault of "their own people coming into the area voluntarily and often illegally."[165] At a press conference on January 2, 1946 by General Frederick E. Morgan, the head of UNRRA's European operations suggested that the infiltrees did not deserve sympathy. During an informal discussion after the official briefing, the British general made reference to the infiltrees as "well-dressed, well fed, rosy-cheeked and [having] plenty of money" and probably aided by "some secret Jewish organization." The purpose of the influx, he claimed, was to force the British hand and permit increased immigration to Palestine. "He was not convinced by 'all the talk' about pogroms in Poland."[166] Despite the furor that his comments generated, Jewish organizations refrained from demanding Morgan's resignation because of warnings that any such action would strain Army–DP relations.[167] The U.S. military appeared to concur with the British assessment that arriving infiltrees had not personally experienced persecution in postwar Poland but had simply heard about violence in the next village. One British officer suggested that the U.S. military was hesitant to speak out because "they were scared of touching the Jewish problem since the Earl Harrison Report."[168]

Morgan was correct that many of these Jews made the trip with the assistance of Brichah and that Brichah organizers intended to overburden the DP camps to create an international climate of opinion that would force Britain to open the gates of Palestine to Jews. However, he was incorrect to discount the pogroms and violent antisemitism in Poland. Britain's own embassy in Poland reported repeatedly of the hostile atmosphere Jewish survivors faced when they returned to their former homes and denied that Zionist propaganda was responsible for the exodus.[169] The high profile of Jewish-born communists in the postwar Polish government aroused antisemitic sentiment, and Poles also feared that

[163] Susan Pettiss, Deputy Director, UNRRA, Team 108, to Sam Zisman, UNRRA Regional Director, "Infiltree Group," 11 January 1946, Zisman Papers, RG-19.047.02*08.

[164] [illegible signature] to Mr. Crawford, General Department, Control Office for Germany & Austria, 13 September 1946, PRO, FO 945/655.

[165] Colonel O.A. Nelson to Brigadier General Walter J. Muller, 10 December 1945, p. 1, UN S-0436, Box 42, File 6.

[166] Sidney B. Fay, "Displaced Persons in Europe," *Current History* (March 1946): 204.

[167] Yehuda Bauer, *Flight and Rescue: Brichah* (New York: Random House, 1970), p. 197.

[168] W. J. Hasler, "Statement by General Morgan," 4 January 1946, PRO, FO 945/655.

[169] V. Cavendish Bentinck to Ernest Bevin, Secretary of State for Foreign Affairs, 18 December 1945, PRO, FO 945/655; [signature illegible], British Embassy, Warsaw, to Christopher Warner, Foreign Office, letter dated 20 February 1946, p. 2, PRO, FO 945/655. The U.S. Embassy in Warsaw also

returning Jews would reclaim their property. Former partisan Abe Tauber made certain to display his rifle prominently when he returned to his father's farm, quite aware that he would not be warmly received by his former townspeople. Tauber then helped Jewish Red Army soldiers to smuggle Jews from Stettin into Berlin before he and his wife decided to become infiltrees themselves.[170]

Morgan's comments came just before the Anglo-American Committee of Inquiry began its fact-finding tour of Europe. Charged with investigating the DP problem and its relationship to Palestine, the committee members, composed of twelve American and British appointees, represented neutral, Zionist, and anti-Zionist perspectives. In early February 1946, teams of committee members visited DP camps. Polls of the DPs recorded their determination to reach Palestine, with 80 percent in the British Zone and 90 percent or more in the camps of the American Zone indicating Palestine as their first choice for immigration.[171] Although Zionist activists may have been able to inflate some of the numbers in a limited number of locations, the committee was impressed by the genuine desire of the majority for the opening of the gates to Palestine.[172]

The Anglo-American Committee also traveled to Austria, Poland, Egypt, and Palestine. In its unanimous report, the committee did not urge the creation of a Jewish state but did call for the issuance of 100,000 certificates of immigration to Palestine. Despite Foreign Minister Ernest Bevin's statement that he would abide by the recommendations of a unanimous report, the British government did not implement the recommendations.[173] The hopes that the committee had raised were now dashed. DP frustration with the lack of emigration opportunities likely contributed to the tensions that erupted in the spring and summer of 1946.

TENSIONS EXPLODE: STUTTGART, LANDSBERG, AND WOLFRATSHAUSEN

As the Allies began transferring more power to local German authorities, tensions mounted between DPs and Germans. German police harassed DPs, Jewish and

attributed Jewish flight from Poland to rising antisemitism. Lane to Mr. Muccio, Telegram no. 174, 15 July 1946; Situation in Poland; PW & DP Br. (National Archives Microfiche 3/174–2/19, 2 of 2); CAD; OMGUS, RG 260; NACP.

[170] Abe Tauber, interview by the author, audio recording, Los Angeles, CA, 4 June 2007. More on Tauber's experiences as a partisan can be found in Abraham Tauber, "Videotaped interview," VHA, IC 26589.

[171] "Information on Jews in British Zone as Required in War Office Telegram SUGRA 374 of 26 Jan to BERCOMB," [February 1946?], p. 3, PRO, FO 945/590; Harry Lerner, letter dated 7 February 1946, USHMM, Harry and Clare Lerner Papers, RG-19.029*01.

[172] Harry Lerner, letters dated 5 February 1946 and 7 February 1946, Lerner Papers, RG-19.029*01.

[173] For more on the Anglo-American Committee of Inquiry, see Abram L. Sachar, *The Redemption of the Unwanted: From the Liberation of the Death Camps to the Founding of Israel* (New York: St. Martin's/MAREK, 1983), pp. 201–205; Arieh J. Kochavi, *Post-Holocaust Politics: Britain, the*

non-Jewish alike, using unnecessary force and confiscating property without just cause.[174] Small incidents demonstrating German animosity toward Jewish DPs also increased DP anxiety.[175] The deterioration of relations between DPs and Germans coincided with the arrival of new Allied troops who were more sympathetic to the Germans. One UNRRA worker despaired, "Do all the boys go home praising the German Frauleins – the efficiency and cleanliness of the Germans? Do they speak of D.P.'s as though they were a lower form of society – 'Why don't they go home?' They are all a bunch of thieves anyway.'"[176] Conflicts between military and UNRRA personnel contributed to the rising tensions. With emboldened Germans, unsympathetic soldiers, and beleaguered DPs, the stage was set for tragedy in the spring and early summer of 1946. The details of these incidents and their aftermath provide insight into the mental frameworks of the competing communities, with each group exculpating itself and pointing accusatory fingers at the others.

An American intelligence officer noted that antisemitism was on the rise once again in Germany. In Straubing, a city on the Danube east of Regensburg and not far from the Czech border, locals blamed the town's 400–500 Jewish DPs for the black market, even though of 250 such cases from January to April 1946, only 3 Jews were charged with black market crimes and 2 of them were acquitted. On March 22 two Jewish boys were killed in an automobile accident. The Straubing lumber merchant refused to release the wood necessary for the caskets, even after ordered to do so by the MGO. In Oberramingen on March 28, a minor altercation between Germans and Jewish DPs escalated when Germans surrounded the schoolhouse where forty DPs lived. U.S. troops and German Rural Police had to disperse the crowd and arrested the town's mayor and a farmer.[177] Armed Poles terrorized Jewish DPs at the Neu-Freimann (Munich) Siedlung camp after Jewish survivors denounced a Polish kapo to American authorities in February 1946. American guards briefly protected

United States, and Jewish Refugees, 1945–1948 (Chapel Hill: University of North Carolina Press, 2001), pp. 102–110. Kochavi demonstrates that Bevin was more willing to support the committee's recommendations than previously believed.

[174] L. G. Wielezynski, UNRRA Field Supervisor, to Samuel Zisman, Director, UNRRA, District 5, "Aggravation of Attitude of Germans toward Displaced Persons," 10 April 1946, Zisman Papers, RG-19.047.02*01; Henry Ortner, Director, UNRRA, Team 109, to Samuel Zisman, District Director, 15 April 1946, and Henry Ortner to District Director thru Field Supervisor Matouskova, "Injustice Done to Moschek Milstein," 20 June 1946, Zisman Papers, RG-19.047.02*09.

[175] Jews reported desecrations of Jewish cemeteries almost monthly, although military officials frequently attributed the damage to poor maintenance and harmless adolescent pranks. In March 1946 Bavarian villagers in Oberammingen physically assaulted two Jewish bicyclists, and in April several Jewish buildings in Frankfurt were covered in antisemitic graffiti. On the anniversary of Kristallnacht 1946, the lone German Jewish returnee to Herford found his car torched and house damaged. Brenner, *After the Holocaust*, pp. 52–53.

[176] Anonymous, letter dated March 1946, USHMM, Greta Fischer Papers, RG-19.034*03.

[177] Major Peter Vacca, Intelligence Officer for Land Bavaria, "Periodic Report for Week Ending 24 hours 3 April 1946," 5 April 1946, pp. 8–11, UN S-0425, Box 44, File 7.

the camp, but after their removal in March Polish DPs fired on Jews on two separate occasions. The second time, on March 26, 1946, led to a riot in which one U.S. soldier and one Jewish DP were wounded.[178] The failure of military forces to protect the DPs increased Jewish insecurities about their vulnerability to antisemitic attacks.

Tensions had been mounting in the Landsberg area since at least February 12, 1946, when an antisemitic drawing appeared on the front gate of a building housing 200 Jewish DP children in nearby Greifenberg. Only two days later someone fired shots at the local UNRRA director as he traveled the road between Greifenberg and Landsberg.[179] The same UNRRA officer reported that Jews living outside the center had encountered discrimination and that a local pastor had given an antisemitic sermon.[180] Military government investigators dismissed the complaints as unfounded, but DPs gave them credence. When Jews and German police confronted one another in Stuttgart in late March, DPs throughout the American Zone found confirmation of their worst fears.

Stuttgart

In Stuttgart a streetcar line ran through the DP center that consisted of a few city blocks of apartment buildings. The streetcar brought undesirable elements to the DP center, contributing to its image as a center of black market activity, and German streetcar personnel accused foreigners and Polish DPs of assault on numerous occasions. "Foreigner" and "Polish" were code words for Jewish DPs. Jewish DPs reportedly carried heavy suitcases onto the streetcars, raising suspicion of black market activities. In March Stuttgart police received reports from Germans living adjacent to the DP center concerning illegal slaughter of animals and DP possession of excessive food ration cards and German currency.[181]

In the early morning of March 29, 1946, 216 armed German police accompanied by police dogs raided the apartment blocks that constituted the Stuttgart DP camp. Wearing their wartime issue uniforms, including spiked helmets and leather boots, the German police banged on doors and shouted at the Jewish DPs to get out of their apartments. Since February 6, 1946 Stuttgart's UNRRA director, Harry Lerner, had required MPs arriving at the camp to work

---

[178] H. Frank Brull, UNRRA Security Officer, memorandum for the Officer in Charge, "Siedlung Camp Riot," 3 April 1946, Zisman Papers, RG-19.047.02*19; Wachtel to Zisman, "Report of Polish Activities."

[179] A. C. Glassgold, Director, UNRRA, Team 311, to Captain Toms, Commanding Officer, 3rd Battalion, 5th Infantry 9th Division Landsberg, "Acts against Security," 20 February 1946, Zisman Papers, RG-19.047.02*16.

[180] A. C. Glassgold, Director, UNRRA, Team 311, to Captain Toms, Commanding Officer Company I, Landsberg, "Antisemitic Incidents," 7 March 1946, Zisman Papers, RG-19.047.02*16.

[181] "Exhibit B," dated Stuttgart, 1.4.1946, attached to Colonel Edward G. Farrand's memorandum to Commanding General, Third U.S. Army, "Investigation of Camp No. 664, Stuttgart," 11 April 1946, UN S-0425, Box 44, File 7.

with Jewish DP police, and when conducting searches "they will fulfill their mission without working with the German Police," and as a result DPs did not believe German police had any right to be present in the camp.[182] For the DPs it seemed to be a repeat of wartime actions in the ghettos, but this time they would not comply. One fifteen-year-old girl grabbed a frying pan before leaving her room. Later she recalled, "This time we were not going to let them get away with it, and we started beating them up."[183] DPs pelted the German police with bottles and flowerpots. When a German policeman began beating a DP with his nightstick, a crowd advanced to free him. At that point, feeling threatened by the crowd, the police began to fire as they retreated. One DP died from a gunshot to the head. Only the night before he had been reunited with his wife and daughters. Three others were wounded.[184]

Although the military government had authorized the raid, no American officer had been put in charge of the mission. The eight MPs who initially accompanied the Germans had been told that they were to protect American soldiers and, not knowing what to do when the Germans began forcing DPs from their residences, they left. In violation of military policy, UNRRA officials were not notified in advance of the raid and as a result they were not on hand to help maintain calm. As would become common practice in such cases, particularly involving Jewish UNRRA personnel, the military declared the UNRRA director unsuitable, forcing his reassignment.[185] At the same time, two military government officers were reprimanded, as were five military officers for their failures in the incident. The military chose to keep these disciplinary actions secret.[186] In the future, only unarmed German police would be allowed into Soviet or Jewish centers, and then only as individuals in the company of U.S. military personnel for the purposes of identifying persons involved in criminal acts committed outside of the camps.[187]

---

[182] Lerner attached his notice to the order by General Keyes permitting German police to assist MPs inside DP camps. "Exhibit D" attached to Farrand to Commanding General, "Investigation"; Jay Howard Geller, *Jews in Post-Holocaust Germany, 1945–1953* (Cambridge: Cambridge University Press, 2005), p. 40.

[183] Lillian Le Bental, "Videotaped interview," VHA, IC 3710, Segs. 61–62.

[184] For the events of the raid see David Clearfield, Deputy Director, "Report of Incident at UNRRA DP Center 502," 29 March 1946, USHMM, UNRRA Records Relating to a Riot (UNRRA Records), RG-19.030; Statements of witnesses Jean Nyskovsky and Salek Weinstock, 29 March 1946, UNRRA Records, RG-19.030; Harry V. Lerner, Director, UNRRA, Team 502, to Staff Association, UNRRA, "Public Action for Riot in DP Center, Stuttgart," 11 May 1946, UNRRA Records, RG-19.030; Harry Lerner, letter dated 4 April 1946, Lerner Papers, RG 19.029*01; Harry Lerner to his parents, letter dated 21 May 1946, Lerner Papers, RG 19.029*01.

[185] The investigating officer noted the director's youth and stated, "Mr. Lerner, a Jew himself, is not temperamentally suited to the position." Farrand to Commanding General, "Investigation," p. 3.

[186] General McNarney, USFET to AGWAR for WARCOS, Ref. No. S-4348, 23 May 1946; Maintenance of Law and Order; The Prisoner of War and Displaced Persons Branch: Records Relating to DP's in Germany and Other Countries 1945–49; CAD; OMGUS, RG 260; NACP.

[187] McNarney, UFSET to AGWAR for Chief of Staff, S-6132, 22 June 1946, Maintenance of Law and Order; The Prisoner of War and Displaced Persons Branch: Records Relating to DP's in Germany and Other Countries 1945–49; CAD; OMGUS, RG 260; NACP.

The incident at Stuttgart proved to the DPs that antisemitism was still a threat in Germany and that they were not safe as Germans regained authority. German police were armed, while DP police were not, at least not officially. U.S. military protection could not be relied on at a time when U.S. policy had shifted to rebuild Germany.[188] While the DPs viewed the incident as evidence of German antisemitism, however, a German police official saw it as proof of Jewish disregard for law enforcement. In a telephone conversation monitored by U.S. censors, the official commented to a German reporter, "There has never been a police force in Germany, that would allow its employees to be beaten up and trampled upon, without doing something. This only gives the Nazis another opportunity to further their propaganda."[189] In this version, the German police were the victims of assault by criminal Jews. Jewish resistance to German authority became evidence of Jewish lawlessness to the glee of antisemites.[190]

Landsberg

One month later, in Landsberg, rumors that German police had kidnapped two young guards from a DP kibbutz sparked a riot. Although it was later thought that the guards had voluntarily left their posts to go in search of relatives, the suggestion that their disappearance was due to foul play seemed reasonable to local DPs. In addition to minor local incidents, the events in Stuttgart and the April 1946 murder in Regensburg of a fourteen-year-old Jewish boy heightened DP anxiety. Under these circumstances, DPs were prepared to believe that they were under a real threat of German violence.

On April 27, 1946, in retaliation for the alleged kidnappings, Landsberg DPs attacked Germans and set a bus on fire. Nineteen Germans were injured in the rioting. Eight were hospitalized, and all but four were released from the hospital by May 7, 1946.[191] Bavarian officials initially claimed that two Germans were

[188] DPs had planned to commemorate the seventh day of death, marking the end of the family of the deceased's sitting of shiva (intensive period of mourning), with a demonstration in Munich. Military authorities prohibited such a gathering but allowed DPs to carry out the observance within the DP camps. Alex E. Squadrilli, Deputy Director, UNRRA U.S. Zone, to Deputy Chief of Staff USFET, "Memorandum Regarding the Proposed Jewish Demonstrations of 4 April 1946," 9 April 1946, UN S-0425, Box 44, File 7.
[189] U.S. Civil Censorship (Germany), telephone call from Chefreporter of DANA to Herr Meyer, Rechtsanwalt Polizei Stuttgart, 8 April 1946; Maintenance of Law and Order; The Prisoner of War and Displaced Persons Branch: Records Relating to DP's in Germany and Other Countries 1945–49; CAD; OMGUS, RG 260; NACP.
[190] The German police report emphasized the restraint of the police and the organized resistance of the DPs and decried the impression in the world "as if the Stuttgarters had made themselves guilty of a great offense representing a relapse into the time of the Nazi regime." The report scrupulously refers to the DPs as Poles, not Jews. Weber, "Second Report about the Occurrences during the Search Action in Upper Reinsbergstrasse on 29 March 1946," [translation] 1 April 1946, esp. p. 12, attached as "Exhibit C" to Farrand to Commanding General, "Investigation."
[191] Lieutenant B. Streim, Medical Officer to Mr. Glassgold, "Visit to German Hospital April 26 and 29 Examine Germans Who Were Assaulted," 29 April 1946, Zisman Papers, RG-19.047.02*16; Lieutenant Streim to Glassgold "Condition of German Patients Involved in Sundays Disturbance," 7 May 1946, Zisman Papers, RG-19.047.02*16.

killed,[192] but this appears not to have been the case. UNRRA officials recognized that the reasonable and sensitive manner of Major Thurston of the 9th Division helped to calm matters just as the attitude of Landsberg Military Governor Captain Mott threatened to inflame the situation.[193] A month earlier Mott had abruptly, and with profanity, ceased to cooperate with UNRRA in housing DPs in town to ease overcrowding in the camp.[194] The MGO's aggressive attitude toward DPs may also have contributed to the DPs' sense of vulnerability to German attack, fuelling their reaction to the rumors. Also, on the day of the riot, Germans were participating in the first postwar election, representing the restoration of local German authority, while the DPs' status remained stagnant in the camps.

In the end, twenty DPs were arrested and tried for their actions during the riot. Interestingly, the charges had more to do with resisting arrest and throwing stones at U.S. military personnel than with attacks on Germans. It became a cause celebre with a U.S. congressman offering to provide legal counsel to the accused.[195] When nineteen convictions and one acquittal were handed down, the DPs reacted calmly. They were shocked by the length of the sentences (as much as two years for some of the convicted) but reassured that the trial had been fair and that the boys, whose disappearance had led to the incident, were in fact safe.[196] The DP leadership pleaded for clemency. The Advisor to the Theater Commander on Jewish Affairs, Rabbi Philip S. Bernstein, intervened and four of the DPs were paroled under his supervision. Another seven who had served approximately three-months imprisonment were paroled in July and another six were paroled three months later.[197]

On April 30, 1946, just three days after the Landsberg incident, MPs executed a violent raid on the Jewish center in Cham, a town in Oberpfalz. A drunken soldier had a scuffle with three DPs that resulted in the raid. Earlier in the day MPs had been called to aid German police when three DPs refused to show them their identity papers. This earlier incident appeared to have annoyed the

---

[192] General McNarney, USFET to AGWAR, Ref. No. S-3105, 2 May 1946, p. 2; Maintenance of Law and Order; The Prisoner of War and Displaced Persons Branch: Records Relating to DP's in Germany and Other Countries 1945–49; CAD; OMGUS, RG 260; NACP.

[193] Helen Matouskova, UNRRA Field Supervisor, to S. B. Zisman, District Director, "Incident at Landsberg, 28 April 1946," 29 April 1946, Zisman Papers, RG-19.047.02*16. When Thurston suggested that groups of five or more be dispersed, Mott said they would be arrested. Upon Thurston's suggestion that MPs shoot into the air in a time of crisis, Mott wanted them to shoot to kill. "Testimony of Walter Korn," p. 2, Zisman Papers, RG-19.047.02*16.

[194] J. Gevov, Billeting Officer, to Director, Team 311, Landsberg, 26 March 1946, Zisman Papers, RG-19.047.02*16.

[195] General McNarney, USFET to AGWAR, Ref. No. S-4016, 16 May 1946, p. 2; Maintenance of Law and Order; The Prisoner of War and Displaced Persons Branch: Records Relating to DP's in Germany and Other Countries 1945–49; CAD; OMGUS, RG 260; NACP.

[196] General McNarney, USFET to AGWAR, Ref. No. S-6038, 21 June 1946; Maintenance of Law and Order; The Prisoner of War and Displaced Persons Branch: Records Relating to DP's in Germany and Other Countries 1945–49; CAD; OMGUS, RG 260; NACP.

[197] Office of Military Government for Germany (U.S.) Public Relations Office, "For Simultaneous Release at 1700 Hours, 21 December 1946," UN S-0425, Box 19, File 10.

MPs, so that when they conducted the raid they violently broke down doors and assaulted DPs. One DP was shot three times in his legs and hospitalized. One woman suffered a miscarriage as a result of the raid. A third DP, Gutman, was arrested and convicted in a military court of assaulting the drunken soldier. The soldier at one point denied being struck by the DPs but changed his story. Gutman and the three DPs who had encountered the soldier all maintained that Gutman had not been present. Gutman was not allowed to present his case in court and his conviction was appealed.[198] DPs blamed German women for inciting American military personnel to attack Jews in the weeks preceding the raid and accused the MPs of demanding money and jewelry.[199] Indeed, DPs and some Germans in other locations also blamed the mistreatment of Jews on GI fraternization with German women.[200] Increasingly DPs throughout the American Zone felt that their special relationship with Allied troops was being replaced by a new alliance between occupation troops and Germans against the DPs. UNRRA and Jewish relief workers appeared to be their only defenders. UNRRA personnel shared this perception.[201]

Wolfratshausen

Tensions between Germans and the military on one side and UNRRA and DPs on the other were also mounting in the Wolfratshausen area. On May 4, 1946, the first significant physical confrontation in the town between Jews and Germans took place at the local cinema when, according to the local MGO Major Paul L. Steers, Jewish DPs "rushed" the door, causing a German policeman to strike a DP with his truncheon. A second rush occurred and approximately 300 DPs attacked the police officers. The two policemen

---

[198] O. A. Mintzer to Leo W. Schwarz, "Incident at Cham, week of 5 May," 11 May 1946, UN S-0436, Box 52, File 2. Mintzer mistakenly dates the events as occurring on 2 May; Joseph Levine, AJDC Regensburg, to A. C. Dunn, UNRRA, Director, Regensburg, "Incident in Cham and conviction of Gutman, Moses," 15 June 1946, UN S-0436, Box 52, File 2; Chaim Diamand, "Reisebericht für den Ausschuss des Central Komitees Regensburg," 4 May 1946, YIVO, RG 294.2, MK 483, Microfilm reel 63, Folder 888.

[199] F. A. King, Director, UNRRA, Team 187, to UNRRA District Headquarters, Regensburg, "Report on Incident between Jews and Military on the Night of 30th of April 1946," 7 May 1946, and attached Statements of Ernest Nebel (Leader of the Jewish Community of Cham), Samuel Stern, Jozef Sturm, Fella Mosler, UN S-0436, Box 52, File 2.

[200] Rudy Kennedy and five other DPs lived in a Frankfurt building. The owner's daughter dated a local U.S. commander. Kennedy believed the officer ordered the raid to empty the building for the girlfriend's father. In Stuttgart a DP approached U.S. soldiers and their girlfriends to ask for a cigarette. A soldier threw a cigarette on the ground, stepped on it, and told the DP he could have it. The DP's wife recalled, "We went through a concentration camp but we didn't know such primitives, such low-class people." Kennedy, "Videotaped interview," VHA, IC 35935, Segs. 343–350; Rose Epstein, "Videotaped interview," VHA, IC 31413, Seg. 140. Also, Leib Courland, "A Visit with Dr. Karl Kreide" (in Yiddish), *Unzer Weg*, 25 September 1946, p. 6.

[201] "All Directors were certain that were UNRRA not in the picture defending lawful treatment of Allied Nationals in Germany, nobody would defend them from violence and injustice." Wielezynski to Zisman, "Aggravation of Attitude," Zisman Papers, RG-19.047.02*01.

suffered facial injuries, and a small amount of property damage occurred. Steers used the occasion of the incident to complain about noncooperation from the Föhrenwald UNRRA team and its director, Henry Cohen. Among Steers's concerns were military training in the camp, the bartering of clothing for food, and DPs wearing GI clothing.[202] The fate of Henry Cohen demonstrates the conflict between military and UNRRA objectives and explains the Föhrenwald DPs' growing sense of abandonment by the U.S. military in summer 1946.

Forceful in his advocacy on behalf of the DPs under his care, Cohen aroused animosity and suspicion among soldiers and military government officers. An officer from the 39th Infantry Regiment accused Cohen of "allowing his sympathies toward the DP's to interfere with or dominate his judgment; in other words he is not suited to the job and his presence in the camp is undesirable."[203] The officer called for his removal and suggested Mr. Frum as his replacement. Edouard Frum would also be removed later in 1946 as unsuitable after he championed the work of the Föhrenwald DP court.

The UNRRA team argued in Cohen's defense that relations with the Army were the result of fundamental differences between military discipline and rehabilitation work: "[T]hat is the conflict between a method of authoritarian discipline, on the one hand, which has obedience, docility, and outward conformity as its aim; and, on the other hand, a method of discussion, of persuasion, of education, of foregoing of quick results for humane consideration."[204] The team expressed frustration with the lack of military support for their work and with what they considered unrealistic expectations for the control of the DP population and unwarranted interference with the internal administration of the camp.

The DP leadership praised UNRRA director Cohen for his compassion and understanding, saying, "He stood side by side with us and spoke from the heart the pure, naked truth. Because of this and similar 'sins' his superiors sought to remove him from us. Our public protest of 2,000 voices unfortunately did not help and we must part from him."[205] Cohen's departure removed a thorn from the side of the local military government, but it did not calm the local situation. If anything, it left the UNRRA team and DPs feeling isolated in a hostile environment.

Two days after Cohen's announcement of his ouster there was an incident that further eroded the relations between DPs and the U.S. military. On May 22, 1946

[202] PLS, Director, Office of Military Government for Landkreis Wolfratshausen, to Commanding General, Third U.S. Army, "DP Camp Föhrenwald (Jewish – 5,000)," 9 May 1946; Report on DP Camp Foehrenwald; The Public Safety Branch: Records Relating to Displaced Persons Camps 1945–49; CAD; OMGUS, RG 260; NACP.

[203] Major Harold E. Gould, 39th Infantry Regiment, to Commanding Officer, 39th Infantry Regiment, "DP Camp Fohrenwald [sic]," 5 May 1946, p. 6; Report on DP Camp Foehrenwald; The Public Safety Branch: Records Relating to Displaced Persons Camps 1945–49; CAD; OMGUS, RG 260; NACP.

[204] Staff of Team 106 to Sam Zisman, Director, UNRRA, District 5, "Declaration," 20 May 1946, p. 1, Zisman Papers, RG-19.047.03*04.

[205] "On the departure of Director H. Cohen" (in Yiddish), *Bamidbar,* 7 July 1946, p. 5.

two U.S. soldiers from the 39th Infantry Regiment visited a German woman in Wolfratshausen. When she told them that she was having trouble with a Jewish DP who lived in the building the two drunken soldiers entered an apartment housing DPs in the building and accosted them. One soldier pistol-whipped two Jewish DPs before the German woman was able to disarm him of his knife and gun, since he had attacked the wrong DP.[206]

Rumors reached the Föhrenwald DP camp that a Jew had been murdered in town. Another rumor said that a carload of Germans had kidnapped a Jew. DPs formed a mob and headed toward town. They were turned around, but not before beating some local German mayors who happened to be driving nearby.[207] Military government officials and German authorities pinned the blame for the situation on UNRRA even though it was the quick work of Cohen and his team that returned the DPs to the camp and to their quarters.[208] An investigator from Munich stated that the riot and the beating of DPs by soldiers were "coincidents [sic]" and likened it to the Landsberg situation, where "two kidnapped D.P.s had just taken a train."[209] The investigator thus denied that the DPs in either case had reacted to real or perceived threats to members of their community, portraying DPs as a threat to public order and liable to unleash violence without provocation.

In Wolfratshausen, everyday contact continued to result in situations that, although commonplace, assumed heightened significance because of the German–Jewish dynamic. For example, on June 6, 1946 a bartender beat a drunken, obnoxious Föhrenwald resident. A DP witness reported to DP police that the German beat the DP until he fell to the ground and then kicked him on the ground before returning to the pub. The bartender admitted to German police only to slapping the DP with his open hand.[210] The Wolfratshausen Military Government Security Officer reported the incident in a memo with the subject heading "Report of Jewish incident."[211] The language of this report highlighted Jewish aggression in contrast to the reasonableness of Germans and prompted two UNRRA field supervisors to protest the antisemitic attitude of the officer and to recommend his removal.[212] In the Wolfratshausen area,

---

[206] E. Ostry, Principal Welfare Officer, UNRRA, Team 106, to H. Cohen, Director, UNRRA, Team 106, "Statements Submitted by the Following Regarding the Incident at Obermarkt Strasse, Wolfratshausen on Wednesday, 22nd of May 1946, about 7.30 PM," 23 May 1946, Zisman Papers, RG-19.047.02*07.

[207] Henry Cohen, Director, UNRRA, Team 106, "Reconstruction of Events," Zisman Papers, RG-19.047.02*07.

[208] H. Frank Brull, Protective Officer, UNRRA, District 5, to Director, District 5, "Interim Report on Wolfratshausen Beatings," 24 May 1946, Zisman Papers, RG-19.047.02*07.

[209] Brull, to Director, District 5, "Interim Report on Wolfratshausen Beatings."

[210] D.P. Police Föhrenwald, "Protokoll: Franz Bross; Niederschrift aufgenommen am Landpolizeihauptposten Wolfratshausen," 6 June 1946, YIVO, RG 294.2, MK 483, Microfilm reel 55, Folder 743.

[211] Captain Jesse L. Ott, Public Safety Officer, to Director, Office of Military Government for Bavaria, "Report of Jewish Incident," 15 June 1946, Zisman Papers, RG-19.047.02*07.

[212] Helen Matouskova to S. B. Zisman, District Director, UNRRA, District 5, "Report on Incident in Wolfratshausen," 12 July 1946, Zisman Papers, RG-19.047.02*07; Carl Atkin to

UNRRA and DPs were on one side while Germans and military officials were on the other. These alliances influenced the responses later that summer to the murder of an innocent DP by German police.

On July 24, 1946 a German policeman fatally shot an innocent DP outside the Föhrenwald DP camp. DPs, UNRRA, and the U.S. military government gave differing accounts of the incident, highlighting the profound tensions in Wolfratshausen during the summer of 1946. The facts on which all agreed are that two German police officers approached an automobile carrying DPs. As other DPs moved toward the car, one (or both) of the police officers fired a gun, wounding one DP and killing another, Yitzhak (Isak) Feldberg. UNRRA workers managed to dissuade the DPs from leaving the camp despite the DP sentiment that "in Stuttgart, the people stood up against the German police and that the same was going to be done here."[213] Remarkably, there were no further incidents that night following the shooting death of an innocent, well-liked DP who left behind a pregnant widow.

The DP and UNRRA versions of events reported that the German policemen overreacted when witnesses began to move toward the scene and discharged their weapons out of fear.[214] The DP camp newspaper reported, "One thing is clear to us. The innocent victim fell only because the weapon was in the hand of Germans, and they are accustomed to shooting at us."[215] Perhaps not surprisingly given the local military government's strained relationship with the DP camp, its report accepted the policemen's claim that three or four DPs had attempted to disarm them when they were checking a car for black market goods. According to this version of events, it was during the struggle that each policeman fired two shots. The report did acknowledge that the two victims were innocent passersby not involved in the altercation.[216]

The military government did not appear concerned that German police were operating so close to a DP camp and stopping DPs. UNRRA Acting Field Supervisor Carl Atkin criticized the German police, arguing that DPs were outside of their jurisdiction. Atkin continued, "A state of war still exists. The peace treaty has not yet been written. Under present conditions, I firmly believe that if DP police can police communities of five thousand people without arms, the German police can do the same."[217] UNRRA officials distrusted Germans and military government officers distrusted DPs.

S. B. Zisman, "Recommendation Relating to Attached Report," 29 July 1946, Zisman Papers, RG-19.047.02*07.

[213] "Statement made by Miss Ethel Ostry, Principal Welfare Officer at Fahrenwald [sic]," 25 July 1946, p. 1, Zisman Papers, RG-19.047.02*07.

[214] Edouard Frum, Acting Director, UNRRA, Team 106, to Field Supervisor, UNRRA, 5th District, "Incidents which Occurred on the 24th and 25th of July 1946," 27 July 1946, Zisman Papers, RG-19.047.02*07.

[215] "What Really Happened in Föhrenwald" (in Yiddish), *Bamidbar* 14 August 1946, p. 4.

[216] McNarney, USFET to AGWAR for WDSCA, Ref. No. S-8274, 31 July 1946; Maintenance of Law and Order; The Prisoner of War and Displaced Persons Branch: Records Relating to DP's in Germany and Other Countries 1945–49; CAD; OMGUS, RG 260; NACP.

[217] Carl Atkin to S. B. Zisman, District Director, UNNRA, District 5, "Incident at Fohrenwald, 24 July 1946," 26 July 1946, Zisman Papers, RG-19.047.02*07.

Feldberg's funeral led to another incident, this time between DPs and U.S. soldiers. Acting UNRRA camp director Edouard Frum obtained authorization for the coffin and sixteen people to leave the camp the following day on a truck for the cemetery in Gauting. An officer of the military police gave permission for camp residents to accompany the coffin beyond the gates but apparently neglected to inform the platoon from the 39th Infantry responsible for guarding the road. When more camp residents than expected pushed through the gates, the Chairman of the Jewish Committee and several UNRRA workers decided that it would be better for the group to return to camp. With the assistance of DP police, they began pushing the crowd toward the camp. In the chaos platoon soldiers were ordered to move the crowd into the camp. The DPs, thinking they had permission to leave the camp, became confused and angry when soldiers attempted to turn them back. In the commotion two soldiers used their bayonets, wounding six DPs.[218]

While UNRRA accounts highlighted the cooperation of the DP leadership and the understandable confusion of the DPs in a potentially explosive situation, the military government's version of events emphasized the threat of violence represented by DPs and their disrespect for American military personnel. Its account charged that DPs "surged through the camp gate about sixteen abreast."[219] It also maintained that military police had formed a line 50 yards from the camp but that DPs pushed through and surrounded it. At this point, the platoon commander "ordered his men to dismount from their trucks, fix bayonets and form a riot line." The DPs attempted to break through the line, hitting and spitting on the soldiers. The troops then forced the DPs back. The military government acknowledged that some DP police assisted the soldiers and MPs. The report also mentioned that DPs called the soldiers "SS," "Gestapo," and "Swine."

Military officers distrusted DP intentions. If we recall that local military observers had been concerned by military training within the DP camp, it could explain the soldiers' fears at seeing a crowd of "sixteen abreast." Aware of longstanding tensions between DPs and local Germans, a coordinated revenge attack on the German community would not have stretched the imagination, although camp residents had remained relatively calm after Feldberg's murder. If UNRRA versions are to be believed, then the military police were kept abreast of the situation but neglected to inform the platoon, indicating a communications problem on the American side. The DPs also had reason

---

[218] Edouard Frum, Acting Director, UNRRA, Team 106, to Field Supervisor, UNRRA, District 5, "Incidents which Occurred on the 24th and 25th of July 1946," 27 July 1946, Zisman Papers, RG-19.047.02*07; Carl Atkin to S. B. Zisman, District Director, UNNRA, District 5, "Incident at Fohrenwald, 25 July 1946," 27 July 1946, Zisman Papers, RG-19.047.02*07.

[219] McNarney to AGWAR for WDSCA, Ref. No. S-8274, p. 2. This report puts the date of the funeral at July 26 instead of July 25, as in the UNRRA account. This appears to be an error. Not only would it have been too long after the death for a Jewish burial, but also July 26, 1946 was a Friday. It is highly unlikely that the DPs would have organized a funeral procession to begin late in the afternoon when they would have had to return before sundown for the beginning of the Sabbath.

to resent the soldiers. It had been soldiers of the 39th Infantry Regiment who attacked Jewish DPs in the May 22, 1946 Wolfratshausen incident. Its officers had targeted for removal the popular UNRRA director, Henry Cohen. The sight of 39th Infantry soldiers with fixed bayonets would not have calmed DP nerves. Acting UNRRA camp director Frum pointed out the deleterious effect the events had on the rehabilitation work of the UNRRA team and mentioned that DP bitterness had been increased by false reports about them in the press and on the radio.[220]

The lengthening stay of Holocaust survivors in Germany strained not only German–Jewish relations but also relations between the survivors and the Allies. As Allied policy turned toward the reconstruction of the German economy and the creation of a German bulwark against the communist East, the DPs were an unwanted reminder of the past conflict. Their refusal to participate in the reconstruction of Germany thwarted Allied goals. Military officials resented the manpower and material resources needed to manage the DP situation. Most of the troops had not participated in the liberation of the concentration camps and did not feel responsible for the care of the survivors. They felt more comfortable with the less traumatized and more cooperative Germans.

DPs were increasingly frustrated by the limited options available to them. Their hopes that the recommendations of the Anglo-American Committee of Inquiry would lead to their imminent emigration from Germany were dashed. As conflict increased in Palestine, such as the British mass arrests of Jews on June 29, 1946 and the bombing of British headquarters at the King David Hotel on July 22, 1946 by the extremist Irgun (the fighting arm of the Revisionist Party), British resolve stiffened. In August 1946 the British began deporting illegal immigrants to Palestine to detention camps on Cyprus.

With speedy immigration to Palestine no longer an option, DPs increasingly turned their attention to organizing social and cultural life in the DP camps, recognizing that their stay would be indefinite. They also remained on guard against any German aggression and continued to press their demands for decent treatment from the Allied authorities. As the incidents in Stuttgart, Landsberg, and Wolfratshausen indicated, DPs were willing to defend themselves against any and all threats, whether they came from Germans or Allies. What they viewed as self-defense, however, confirmed the DPs as violent and irrational in the minds of many Germans and Allied personnel.

CRISIS POINT AND THE BATTLE FOR PALESTINE

Even had the 100,000 certificates recommended by the Anglo-American Committee of Inquiry been issued immediately, events ensured that they would

---

[220] Frum to Field Supervisor, "Incidents which Occurred on the 24th and 25th of July 1946," pp. 2–3. Reaction of the DPs to grossly distorted reports in both U.S. military and German newspapers can be found in "What Really Happened in Föhrenwald."

have been insufficient. In 1946 the Soviet Union began repatriating half a million Polish Jews who had survived the war years in Soviet exile. They returned to discover the extent of the destruction of their communities and families. Confronted with antisemitism and pogroms, nearly half of them, too, decided to leave Europe. On July 4, 1946 the Kielce pogrom left forty-one Jews dead and many others wounded. A massive exodus of Polish Jews ensued. In April, May, and June 1946 the influx of Jewish refugees into the American Zone (excluding Berlin and Bremen) averaged 8,616 per month, but in July 16,733 arrived that month alone, and in August and September an average of 24,327 per month entered the American Zone.[221] Their movement westward was inadvertently aided by the expulsion of ethnic Germans from Eastern Europe. Surreptitiously Jews were able to board the transports carrying ethnic Germans to Germany.

British authorities were determined to deter the influx of these infiltrees to their zone, refusing to grant them DP status and the accompanying extra rations, housing consideration, and protection.[222] They treated Jews who entered on German expellee transports as German refugees, dispersing them to German communities and requiring them to register locally for German rations and housing. Jewish relief workers protested a policy that forced non–German-speaking Jews into isolation and into areas without synagogues or other Jewish communal resources.[223] More than 4,000 infiltrees did manage to enter the Belsen DP camp, where camp leaders gave them identity cards left behind by those who had departed illegally for Palestine or shared rations out of those provided to the camp's legal residents.

The strain that unregistered infiltrees placed on DP resources was such that the Belsen Camp Committee and its chairman, Josef Rosensaft, successfully moved more than 2,000 of them out of the camp and into German communities. In January 1947 there were 1,868 unregistered infiltrees remaining in Belsen, and Rosensaft did not believe that they could be moved. Many were old or infirm Orthodox Jews whose needs could not be met outside of the camp. The younger families among them wanted their children to benefit from the Belsen schools and refused to leave. British authorities refused to grant these people DP status. Rosensaft proposed that, in exchange for the British granting the 1,868 infiltrees the status of refugees who would receive German rations in the camp and be the financial responsibility of the Germans, he would ensure that no further infiltrees would be admitted to the camp.[224] Rosensaft appeared to

---

[221] American Joint Distribution Committee, "Jewish Population in U.S. Zone of Occupation in Germany," 30 September 1946, p. 10, Zisman Papers, RG-19.047.03*03.

[222] For a fuller discussion of infiltrees in the British Zone and its political implications, see Kochavi, *Post-Holocaust Politics*, pp. 43–59.

[223] One British officer wrote, "the Jews are averse to being split up … as they rightly consider that they can wield more influence if they remain banded together." A. C. Todd, PW & DP Division, Zonal Executive Offices, to R. S. Crawford, Control Office for Germany and Austria, letter dated 19 November 1946, PRO, FO 945/723; E. G. Lowenthal, "Report on Jewish Refugees (Infiltrees)," 5 December 1946, PRO, FO 945/723.

[224] Josef Rosensaft to Colonel Robert H. Solomon, Jewish Advisor in British Zone, 31 January 1947, PRO, FO 945/723.

be motivated by concern for the camp residents, but the British suspected that he could make political capital out of winning rations for infiltrees.[225]

In the American Zone military officials worried about the consequences of a massive influx of Jewish refugees. Initially they housed infiltrees in separate, newly established camps, although some found their way into existing Jewish camps. Realizing that it would be politically impossible to close the borders to the refugees, General McNarney proposed transferring them into occupied Italy. This proposal was abandoned after it ran into British opposition since the British viewed it as encouraging the flow of refugees and putting them closer to the embarkation points for illegal immigration to Palestine. In March 1947, General Lucius Clay took over from McNarney as the American Military Governor for Germany. His solution was to order that infiltrees arriving in the American Zone of Germany after April 21, 1947 would not be permitted into the DP camps and would not receive rations from American supplies.[226] This policy was similar to that already implemented by the British. The result was to put the burden of support on Jewish organizations, particularly the JDC. Because the border remained open, Jewish infiltrees continued to enter the American Zone. The willingness of American military authorities to facilitate their movement into Italy and France from whence they could continue on to Palestine meant that Brichah continued to plot its routes through the American Zone.[227] Meanwhile, the closure of the DP camps to new registrants meant that many infiltrees had to find housing in German communities. Germans complained that the occupation forces needed to do more to stop the "illegal" immigration of foreigners.[228]

If the Americans were impatient with the DP problem, the British were even more so. Jewish extremists in Palestine continued to attack British installations, and the numbers of illegal immigrants attempting to reach Palestine rose steadily. In February 1947, Bevin announced that he was turning over the question of Palestine to the United Nations. On May 13, 1947 the United Nations Special Committee on Palestine (UNSCOP) was established to examine alternatives to the British mandate in Palestine. Two events highlighted the connection between the DPs in Germany and Jews in Palestine.

In May 1947 four members of Irgun crossed from the American Zone into the British Zone with the intent of blowing up railways and British troop trains. Apprehended, the four were sentenced to death. DPs in the American

225 Dean, CONFOLK to Brownjohn, Berlin, "Jewish Illegal Infiltrees Hohne Camp," J. W. L. Ivimy, Foreign Office (German Section) to Brigadier A. G. Kenchington, Chief, PW & DP Division (Berlin), letter dated 11 February, 1947, PRO, FO 945/723.

226 S. R. Mickelsen, "Denial of United Nations Care and Treatment to New Applicants after 21 April 47," 21 April 1947, DP Camps: Welfare Problems; PW & DP Br.; (National Archives Microfiche 3/173–2/1, 2 of 4); CAD; OMGUS, RG 260; NACP.

227 See Kochavi, *Post-Holocaust Politics*, pp. 134–146.

228 See Wolfgang Eibl, Bezirks-Inspektor Landpolizei Niederbayern/Oberpfalz, to Mr. Kolb, CIC Deggendorf, "Wochenbericht zum Donnerstag," 10 July 1946; Police Reports – 1946; Public Safety Reports – Deggendorf Res Liaison and Security Office 1945–48; Records of the Field Operations Division; OMGUS, RG 260, Entry Bavaria; NACP.

Zone created a commission to advocate for a commutation of the sentence, and they appealed to the Central Jewish Committee in the British Zone to do the same.[229] Josef Rosensaft interceded on behalf of the young men, arguing that it was wrong to execute Jews on German soil.[230] Two of the men were released and the others had their sentences commuted to twenty years in prison.[231] The fight against the British in Palestine was threatening to spill over onto a new front in Germany.

While UNSCOP members were in Palestine, the drama of the *Exodus 1947* was enacted. On July 11, 1947 the ship *Exodus 1947* set sail from France to Palestine with 4,500 illegal immigrants aboard. Hopeful of reaching Palestine, the passengers were aware that since August 1946 the British had intercepted the majority of ships and transferred their passengers to detention camps on British-controlled Cyprus. The British had hoped that the harsh conditions on Cyprus would deter DPs from making future such trips. While British policy did discourage some DPs, especially those with young children, there were many others who volunteered for the dangerous voyage.[232] Zionist activists adapted to the British strategy by resisting British sailors and capturing world headlines. The *Exodus* passengers understood that they would likely end up in a confrontation with the British and land in Cyprus, but the British changed the rules of the game.[233]

British destroyers intercepted the *Exodus*. The ensuing battle left two Jews and one American crewman dead and more than 100 wounded. Frustrated that the detention centers on Cyprus were not deterring the immigrants, British Foreign Minister Ernest Bevin determined to make an example of this ship and ordered its passengers returned to their port of embarkation. The French government agreed to accept only those passengers who disembarked voluntarily. One hundred and thirty pregnant women, elderly, and sick left the deportation ships during the three weeks they were anchored off of France. On August 21, the British government announced that the remaining passengers would be returned to Germany. And so it was that in Hamburg on September 8, the refugees were forced from the ships and taken to special

---

[229] Moshe Halperin to Josef Rosensaft, 14 December 1947, YV O-70/20.

[230] Rosensaft, *Yesterday*, pp. 117–118.

[231] In 1949 Jewish DPs were leaving Germany at a rapid rate and two new German states were created. Fearful that the remaining two prisoners would be left without advocates, Revisionist leaders in Munich appealed to Rosensaft to secure the release of the remaining two Irgun prisoners. In 1950 the British agreed to release the prisoners to Israel. Moshe Halperin to Josef Rosensaft, 11 July 1949, YV O-70/20; G. Ingham to H. G. Van Dam, "Abraham HUBERT and Jacob REDLICH," 21 April 1950, YV O-70/20.

[232] See Chapter 6 for more on DPs' fears of Cyprus.

[233] Idith Zertal's account of the *Exodus 1947* portrays the passengers as "captives" of Zionist agents, asserting that they were unaware of the possible dangers. It does not consider that most DPs had personal experience with illegal border crossings and were well informed about the fate of previous illegal transports and conditions on Cyprus, nor does it sufficiently take into account that noone anticipated that the British would return the passengers to Germany. Idith Zertal, *Israel's*

detention centers.[234] They were denied DP status and when immigration from the British Zone to Palestine began in 1947, the British excluded them.

DPs across Germany protested British treatment of the *Exodus* passengers. In the British Zone, anonymous DPs sent a message of support to the detained illegal immigrants, denouncing the British for "cold-blooded crimes that have no equal in the history of the recent past."[235] Objectively there could be no comparison between British and Nazi actions, yet some DPs perceived British aggressiveness in preventing Jewish immigration to Palestine as more painful than wartime persecution because it was a betrayal by an ally in the fight against Nazism. The Central Jewish Committee alluded to that alliance in its declaration of protest: "[T]hose who overcame Dunkirk and conquered El-Alamein have not been shy in their brutality and inhumanity, making unarmed old men, women and children the victims of their belligerence." [236] The committee contrasted British rowdiness to the discipline of the fearful Jews, further emphasizing the out-of-control nature of British policy and the deserving character of the Jews. DPs declared their solidarity with the imprisoned passengers and managed to provide material assistance to them. DP leaders also succeeded in helping some *Exodus* Jews to escape from their prison camps and smuggling them to Palestine.

In early August, while the detention ships carrying the *Exodus* passengers were still in French waters, a subcommittee of UNSCOP arrived in the American Zone of Germany to study the conditions of the DPs. Tours of the DP camps and a meeting with Rabbi Philip S. Bernstein impressed upon the commissioners the need for speedy immigration and the Jews' desire for Palestine. At the end of August 1947, UNSCOP advised the U.N. to end the British mandate in Palestine. The majority report recommended the partition of Palestine into a Jewish and an Arab state. The minority report called for Jewish immigration but, instead of two independent states, called for a federation of a Jewish area and an Arab sector. On November 29, 1947 the United Nations voted to partition Palestine into Jewish and Arab states, and the British began their withdrawal from Palestine. Jewish DPs celebrated, anticipating a speedy end to their sojourn on German soil.

Once again, however, expectations were not met. The outbreak of war on the creation of the Jewish state impeded immigration. Israel gave priority to those DPs who could contribute to the war effort, while the Allies attempted to prevent potential military combatants from leaving Germany for Israel. With tens of thousands of DPs still on German soil in 1949, vandalism of Jewish cemeteries increased as German antisemites sought to encourage the DPs' departure. By

Holocaust and the Politics of Nationhood (Cambridge: Cambridge University Press, 2005), pp. 44–48.

[234] Kochavi, *Post-Holocaust Politics*, pp. 266–274; Sachar, *Redemption of the Unwanted*, p. 186.

[235] Ajere Chavejrim, "Brider un szwester mapilim fun Ekzodus 1947!" [no date], YV O-70/14.

[236] "Erklärung des Central Committee of Liberated Jews in the British Zone of Germany zum Beginn der Landungsoperation der "EXODUS"-Flüchtlinge am 8. September 1947 in Hamburg," 8 September 1947, YV O-70/14.

the end of 1951 the vast majority of DPs did indeed leave Germany for new homes elsewhere, but Föhrenwald continued to house Jewish DPs until 1957. A minority of Eastern European survivors remained in Germany, joining the local Jewish *Gemeinden* (communities) and participating in the construction of a permanent Jewish presence in Germany.

CONCLUSION

Mistaken expectations characterized the initial postwar relationships among Jews, Allies, and Germans. Jewish survivors anticipated an alliance with their liberators but discovered that even the most sympathetic of them harbored prejudices about what sort of person would have survived Nazi genocide. Volatile DP behaviors, characteristic of what is now known as post-traumatic stress syndrome, and differing standards of hygiene and modesty reinforced Allied assumptions that DPs were the damaged dregs of European Jewry. Jewish DPs were too demanding and not suitably deferential to outside authorities for the MGOs' tastes. Military officers expected DPs to live according to military standards of discipline, housing, and food. When UNRRA, JDC, and JRU workers attempted to explain that traumatized, malnourished civilians needed a different approach, military officials dismissed them as softhearted do-gooders coddling the DPs. Military discipline conflicted with the project of rehabilitation, and DPs were caught in the middle.

DPs expected Germans to acknowledge their crimes against the Jews, but postwar conditions facilitated the Germans' reversal of the categories of victims and persecutors. Even though the black market had begun in the final years of the war, Germans blamed Jewish DPs for it and transformed themselves into victims of Jewish avarice. The arrival of millions of ethnic German expellees and their tales of expropriation, rape, hunger, and physical assault further contributed to postwar collective memories of German victimization and increased German impatience with Eastern European Jews, whom they saw as undeserving competitors for housing and resources. Emboldened by friendships with local MGOs and by the transfer of authority to local German officials, Germans increasingly demanded the eviction of Jews from their midst by late 1946.

Jewish DPs rejected antisemitic stereotypes of Jewish criminality in postwar Germany. They fought back by exposing German black marketers, accusing Germans of diverting attention from their own criminal activities. The issue of Jewish criminality was significant for DPs because of its antisemitic overtones and because it threatened their alliance with the occupation forces. Fears over the growing alliance between Allies and Germans along with the increasing assertiveness of German police contributed to violent clashes in the summer of 1946.

Jews, Germans, and Americans agreed that the solution to the DP problem lay in the rapid emigration of Jews from Germany. Germans did not care where the Jewish DPs went as long as they left Germany quickly. Most Jewish DPs emphasized their desire for a Jewish home in Palestine, although many planned to join relatives in other locations. President Harry S Truman also favored opening the gates of Palestine to Jewish immigration and exerted pressure on the British. The British government, worried about maintaining control over its mandate in Palestine, wanted DPs to immigrate to other parts of the world, repatriate, or settle in Germany. As conditions in Palestine deteriorated and the costs of maintaining the mandate and the DPs became more burdensome, however, British authorities turned over the question of Palestine to the U.N. and began permitting the immigration of Jews from Belsen to Palestine in 1947. DP pressure played a role in those international developments.

Despite their dependence on international aid and despite living among their former persecutors, DPs defiantly demanded control over their lives and asserted their rights as Jews. They seemed determined to disprove the image of Jews as passive victims. In the next chapter, we will see how they took their first steps to reclaim their heritage and to confront Germans with the evidence both of German crimes and of Jewish survival.

2

The Living and the Dead

Liberation brought joy, relief, and tremendous sorrow. Without the constant struggle for survival to numb their emotions, survivors were free to feel the enormity of their losses for the first time. All survivors were mourners. Although they held out hope for the survival of some family members, everyone had witnessed the murder of family and friends. None of the dead had been permitted proper burial according to Jewish traditions, and none of the mourners had been permitted the solace of proper mourning. Even as survivors began the search for surviving family members, they sought ways to commemorate and honor the dead. In doing so, they affirmed their Jewish heritage, connected themselves to the spirit of the resistance fighters and partisans, and called for confrontation with the Germans and with the British in Palestine.

Magnifying the pain of loss was the knowledge that their loved ones had died horrible deaths and that their bodies had been treated without care. Many of the dead were heaped indiscriminately into mass graves. Others were cremated, an abomination according to Jewish tradition since it would prohibit the resurrection of the deceased at the dawn of the messianic age. Death march victims had been left in fields and forests to be preyed upon by passing animals. Jewish law and tradition placed great emphasis on the loving care due a deceased body and on its interment, in its entirety, in a marked grave. It would not be possible for the vast majority of survivors to find their family members, give them proper burial, and observe the rituals of mourning, such as remaining at home for seven days after burial. Instead they recited mourner's prayers and created new ways of honoring Jewish dead through secular mourning academies, re-creation of death marches, and reburials of death march victims.

Commemorating the dead through Jewish rituals fulfilled survivors' personal needs to maintain a bond with their deceased loved ones and to honor them in ways they would have wanted. These acts required the gathering of Jews for prayer, since Jewish mourners' prayers may only be recited aloud in the presence of a *minyan* (traditionally a quorum of ten adult Jewish men). Mourning the dead required the formation of a Jewish community. Within that community the observances demonstrated that despite the tremendous losses, the Jewish people still lived.

DPs created opportunities for survivors of particular towns and regions to meet and to share their stories of life before the war and during the German occupation. Through these ceremonies, DPs formed collective memories of the Holocaust and learned to integrate them into their own life narratives. Within the Jewish community commemorations provided opportunities for the living to interpret the desires of the dead. Consistently the message was "leave us here and go lead Jewish lives in the Land of Israel." DPs connected the battle for aliyah to Palestine with the struggle of the partisans and ghetto resistance fighters. Through their commemorations of the Warsaw Ghetto Uprising, DPs retroactively allied themselves with the wartime resistance and legitimated their own postwar militancy.

When Jewish DPs sought to perform their commemorative ceremonies outside the confines of the DP camps, they involved Allies and Germans in these activities. In order to stage reenactments of death marches or to rebury victims, DPs had to win the cooperation of authorities who often had different priorities from theirs. The survivors' force of will in this regard was remarkable and indicated the survivors' determination to be treated with dignity and to promote Jewish values regardless of the obstacles.

Because of their location in Germany, Jewish DP mourning took on added meanings and significance. To the outside world, the DPs designed the commemorative events to say, "We are here! The Jewish people lives. We were innocent victims. Germans are guilty of the crimes against us. We are victors and allies of Germany's occupiers." As we will see, Germans understood the message but rejected it.

The dead had tremendous influence on the living. They were omnipresent in both private and public spheres. DPs dedicated themselves to acting in the name of the dead. Political and religious leaders alike called on DPs to honor the memory of the dead by leading Jewish lives. At the same time that most DPs rededicated themselves to Jewish life, however, there were those survivors for whom the losses were too overwhelming and for whom there could be no solace. We turn to them first.

THE SUICIDES

In order to survive, Nazi victims had had to suppress their grief for murdered loved ones. Many had remained dry-eyed as they focused on the task of making it alive through one more moment, through one more day. Once liberation freed them from the constant fight for survival, they were able to absorb the realization that their families were gone, murdered. For some, the grief and loneliness were too much to bear. One American soldier in charge of five prisoners of war and DP camps recalled that every morning there were "3, 4, 6 suicides." He especially remembered the hanging death of a Polish Jew who had wrapped a belt around his neck and jumped from the third tier of the bunk bed.[1] A former DP recalled

---

[1] James Hayes, "Videotaped interview, by the University of Southern California Shoah Foundation Institute for Visual History and Education," Interview Code (IC) 93, Segments 35–37.

that in an Austrian hospital immediately following liberation one to two patients committed suicide each night.[2] Despite religious prohibitions against suicide and having survived the Nazi onslaught, they now chose their own moment and means of death.

DP suicides did not leave behind notes to explain their decision to take their lives. Some survivors suspect that among those who died in the immediate aftermath were those who chose to no longer make the effort to survive. They did not actively take their lives, but they did not actively try to preserve them either. As one survivor remarked, "People couldn't handle liberation ... they lay down and died."[3] Leon Zelman, a survivor in Austria, echoed this notion that survivors found liberation disorienting and lacked a certain amount of will. He reported that many survivors faced depression when confronted with their aloneness in the world and "due to years of subordinating ourselves to orders that had to be followed or else face death, our will was not particularly pronounced. There was a temptation to let oneself go; suicide was a solution that seemed to suggest itself. It was chosen by many in our surroundings. Even I thought more than once about this way out."[4] To proceed in a strange and hostile world without family left some survivors feeling that the sorrow was too difficult to bear.

The absence of family is a recurring theme in discussions of survivor suicides. At night in the Feldafing DP camp, fourteen-year-old Bill Gluck would dream that he was home with his family in normal times. "I used to sit up and scream and sweat. And then I realize where I am. And those were the few times that I wished somebody would shoot me in the head. When out of that world I find myself in this world."[5] In his dreams he was loved and safe with his family. Upon waking, the reality of a world without his family, a world that had stood by while Germans murdered his family, left him wishing for death. DP Sara Ostrzega-Greening also contemplated suicide because of the "unbearable silence" of the dead and the absence of children and elderly. Instead, she dedicated herself to study "in memory of darkness."[6] The enormity of the survivors' losses and the vicious methods that led to their loved ones' deaths may have driven some of these survivors to suicide.

The rush of suicides immediately following liberation subsided. The number picked up again by fall 1945 in response to the lack of emigration opportunities. Jacob Biber, founder of the Föhrenwald DP school, observed, "a general malaise was growing as we realized how indifferent the world was to our tragedy. Soon we began seeing men and women who had survived the worst tragedies imaginable during the war years suddenly killing themselves, often

[2] Ivan Deutsch, "Videotaped interview," VHA, IC 33391, Seg. 55.
[3] Sidonia Lax, "Videotaped interview," VHA, IC 9, Seg. 24.
[4] Leon Zelman, *After Survival: One Man's Mission in the Cause of Memory* (New York: Holmes & Meier, 1998), p. 120. Zelman credited his rescue from depression to a Viennese physician who "resolved to play the role of a stern father." *After Survival*, p. 121.
[5] Bill Gluck, "Videotaped interview," VHA, IC 29159, Seg. 169.
[6] Sarah Ostrzega-Greening, "Videotaped interview," VHA, IC 7021, Segs. 72–75.

by hanging. ... We felt like so much surplus junk, human garbage which the governments of the world wished would somehow go away."[7] The DP leadership recognized this problem and issued an SOS to stimulate a reaction from the Allies. In the October 19, 1945 issue of the central Jewish DP newspaper, S. Grinberg warned, "Our lives consist of a gruesome, terrifying yesterday, a bitter and hard today, and a hopeless tomorrow. It is therefore no wonder that the despairing people, the people who lived through the concentration camps, that it now happens – suicides."[8] The horrors and losses of the past became overwhelming for some who saw no way out of their predicament. They could not bring back their dead and they saw no future on their own.

In other cases, the inability to reunite with living family members motivated suicides. Representatives of Jewish relief organizations reported in March 1946, "There was a young mother in Dortmund who lost her child in a concentration camp – who attempted suicide because she was frustrated in her efforts to join her husband in England."[9] Depressed and alone, some survivors did not have the inner resources to cope with such frustrations. Livia Bitton-Jackson recalls the case of David, a young Zionist survivor who chose to wait for permission to immigrate to the United States in order to join his brother there. In early winter 1951, David finally had his interview with the military's Criminal Investigation Division officer. With the Korean War raging, U.S. officials wanted to be certain that no communist sympathizers or agents were allowed to immigrate. Asked if he would fight in the U.S. Army should he be drafted, David answered yes. The officer then asked if he would fight against Israel. Although the interpreter, Bitton-Jackson herself, urged him to say yes, David said he would not shoot a fellow Jew. His file was stamped "Unfit for U.S. Immigration." That night David hung himself.[10] Unwilling to betray his loyalty to the Jewish people despite his desperate longing to reunite with his brother, this young man took his own life. The survivors' constant awareness of their dead family and the apparent indifference of the international community to their needs contributed to their frustration, depression, and even suicide.

The issue of DP suicides has received little attention. Because the suicides often left no explanations, we can only infer a correlation between overwhelming loss, the denial of immigration for family reunion, and suicide. The sense of loneliness that beset the survivors after liberation as well as the disappointment that the world had not embraced them with open arms was too much for some to endure. Unable to reunite with their deceased loved ones and often frustrated in attempts to join relatives abroad, these few survivors chose to take their own lives.

---

[7] Jacob Biber, *Risen from the Ashes: A Story of the Jewish Displaced Persons in the Aftermath of World War II* (San Bernadino, CA: The Borgo Press, 1990), p. 22.

[8] S. Grinberg, "S.O.S. Call" (in Yiddish), *Unzer Welt*, 19 October 1945, p. 2.

[9] A. G. Brotman and Harry Viteles, "Survey on Conditions of Jews in the British Zone in March 1946," p. 15, Yad Vashem (YV), O-70/6.

[10] Livia Bitton-Jackson, *My Bridges of Hope: Searching for Live and Love after Auschwitz* (New York: Simon & Schuster, 1999), p. 239.

MOURNER'S PRAYER

The majority of DPs found comfort in Jewish rituals of mourning and burial. Spontaneously Jewish survivors joined together to say memorial prayers for their deceased loved ones, creating communities of mourners. Even less religiously observant Jews sought to honor their parents' memories in this way, reaffirming their Jewish identity. Mourning the dead and providing proper burials were often the first communal religious acts after liberation. Ernst Landau's transport was liberated near Feldafing by U.S. soldiers who immediately brought their Jewish chaplain to meet with the survivors. In an open field, the few rabbis who were in the transport together with the chaplain led an estimated 1,500 survivors in their first religious service in freedom. With no *kippot* to cover their heads for worship, these survivors improvised: "We put the jacket of the concentration camp uniform on or just put our hand on our head."[11] Since everyone had lost most of their families, they first recited a memorial prayer for the dead, *El Malei Rachamim.*[12] Those who knew that their parents, spouses, children, or siblings had been murdered or no longer had hopes that they had survived said the mourners' *Kaddish.*[13] Landau recalls, "it was the most moving religious service I have ever experienced."[14] *Kaddish* touched an emotional chord in the survivors; virtually all were in mourning for their parents.

A prayer in praise of God, *Kaddish* does not mention death, but reaffirms the faith of the living, and provides a sense of continuity between the ages. One scholar has observed that "[*Kaddish*] transfers, subliminally, the fixed, inner gaze of the mourner from the departed to the living, from crisis to peace, from despair to hope, from isolation to community."[15] Traditionally recited in a public congregation, or minyan,[16] the prayer often had a consoling effect, demonstrating to the mourner that he was not alone and building a sense of community.[17]

[11] Ernest Landau, "The First Days of Freedom," in Michael Brenner, *After the Holocaust: Rebuilding Jewish Lives in Postwar Germany*, trans. Barbara Harshav (Princeton, NJ: Princeton University Press, 1997), p. 82.

[12] This prayer asks that the deceased be raised to heaven and to eternal peace beneath God's protective wing. At the moment in the prayer at which the deceased's name is said, some survivors inserted "for the souls of our brothers the Jewish people, the holy and pure, who fell at the hands of murderers, whose blood was spilled in Auschwitz, in Majdanek, in Treblinka and the other camps of destruction in Europe, who were slain, burned, and slaughtered, and who were buried alive with extreme cruelty for the sanctification of the Divine Name." Joseph Sher, Interview by John Menszer, audio file, http://www.holocaustsurvivors.org, accessed 11 July 2006.

[13] According to tradition, only those in mourning or commemorating the *Yahrzeit* (anniversary of death) for an immediate family member stand for the *Kaddish*.

[14] Landau, "First Days", in Brenner, *After the Holocaust*, p. 82.

[15] Maurice Lamm, *The Jewish Way in Death and Mourning* (New York: Jonathan David Publishers, 1969), pp. 154–155.

[16] Although today the Reform and Conservative movements permit women to be counted toward the minyan, the DPs would not have done so in the 1940s.

[17] In traditional Judaism, women are not obligated to recite *Kaddish* since it would interfere with their household duties. Rachela Walshaw's first thought upon hearing of her brother's survival was that

Despite his anger at God at the time, Elie Wiesel helped to organize a minyan to say *Kaddish* after the liberation of Buchenwald: "That Kaddish at once a glorification of God's name and a protest against His creation, still echoes in my ears." Praise and protest mingled in the hearts of the worshipers. The communal nature of the minyan finds expression in Wiesel's language. He writes not of his personal feelings about this *Kaddish* but of the collective experience: "It was a thanksgiving for having spared *us*, but it was also an outcry. 'Why did You not spare so many others?' There were no joyous embraces, no shouts or songs to mark *our* happiness, for that word was meaningless to *us*. *We* were not happy. (emphasis added)"[18] With liberation the struggle for mere survival had ended, and mourning could begin. Even while some raged against God, they offered the prayer of *Kaddish*, honoring the memory of their dead and forming a Jewish community of mourners.

Bergen-Belsen survivor Pearl Benisch recalled an impromptu address at a Belsen DP camp assembly by Rivkah Horowitz, the leader of the Beth Jacob school, an ultra-Orthodox girls movement affiliated with Agudat Israel. While endorsing the Zionist program of the Jewish Camp Committee, Horowitz exhorted the survivors to live for more than immigration to Palestine:

God has chosen us to live. Why us? We don't know, but we know that we were chosen, chosen to continue the chain of Jewish heritage by living a pure and moral life, by following in our parents' footsteps and embodying their creed. ... Dear sisters and brothers, we were left in this world to say a collective *Kaddish* for all those who are gone, to sanctify Hashem's Name and theirs by continuing to live as they did. In spite of all our enemies, we are here, alive! *Am Yisrael chai*! Our nation is destined to live.[19]

Horowitz appealed to the memories of the dead parents to inspire the survivors to lead devout lives; this type of rhetoric would be used repeatedly by the religious parties to try to win support for their programs. She also connected the recitation of *Kaddish* to the survivors' duty to remember their parents and to maintain Jewish traditions and life. Through mourning rituals the Jewish nation could demonstrate its continued existence and vitality.

The shared experiences of loss and need to commemorate led survivors to join together to recite the mourners' prayer. Benisch describes the reaction of the assembled DPs to Horowitz's words, "Echoing her note of determined hope, the whole assembly rose, and a spontaneous *Kaddish* reverberated from the walls. There was not a dry eye in the audience, but neither was there a despairing heart."[20] The mourners' prayer united Jewish survivors, whether Orthodox or secular, in their sorrow and offered consolation. The persistence

"my father's wish had come true. Someone had survived to say Kaddish for him." *From Out of the Firestorm: A Memoir of the Holocaust* (New York: Shapolsky Publishers, 1991), p. 128.

[18] Elie Wiesel, *All Rivers Run to the Sea: Memoirs* (New York: Alfred A. Knopf, 1995), p. 96.

[19] Rivkah Horowitz, quoted in Pearl Benisch, *To Vanquish the Dragon* (New York: Feldheim Publishers, 1991), p. 417.

[20] Benisch, *Vanquish the Dragon*, p. 417.

of religious ritual expressed the survivors' determination to create a vibrant
Jewish community.

PROPER BURIAL

The centrality of *Kaddish* in survivors' worship was only part of the survivors'
obligation to the dead. Proper burial was also an immediate concern. Death
march victims had often been hastily buried in shallow graves by German
villagers hoping to avoid being held responsible for the deaths. Liberating troops
quickly buried the corpses they found in mass graves, frequently forcing former
concentration camp guards and local Nazis to do the physical labor. While the
humbling of the once proud guards had an appeal to survivors, their uncaring
handling of the corpses was still an affront to their victims. According to Jewish
tradition corpses were to be accorded the utmost respect until burial, in order
to preserve the dignity of the dead. Likewise, it was traditionally considered a
great privilege to assist in the preparation and burial of the body.[21] Certainly the
vanquished guards did not ensure the dignity of the dead; as non-Jews their very
handling of the body was a violation of Jewish law.[22]

After liberation, tens of thousands of Jews continued to die of epidemics as
well as gastrointestinal illness caused by eating foods that their starved bodies
were unprepared to digest. No longer at the mercy of their tormentors, survivors
did their best to bury the dead with dignity and according to Jewish tradition.
At Bergen-Belsen, a group of Beth Jacob teachers and students, themselves still
recovering from typhus, dug a shallow grave for one of their comrades. Benisch
observed their efforts: "The girls filled the grave and recited *Kaddish* for their
friend. A *minyan* or so of girls, barely alive themselves, glorified God's Name, pro-
claiming their gratitude for having the merit at last, for the first time in the Valley
of Death, to bring their friend to a *kever Yisrael* [Jewish grave], to provide a Jew
with a dignified Jewish burial."[23] Unable to bury those who had been murdered by
the Nazis and those who had been cremated, these survivors found meaning in the
revival of Jewish observance. In the women's camp, there were no men to create
the requisite minyan, so these devout women took on the duty for themselves.

Survivors were determined to provide Jewish interment for unburied concentration camp inmates and for death march victims. Many DP leaders began
their community service by tending to the needs of the dead. For example, eight
days after liberation, the man who would become the president of the Jewish
community of Neunburg vorm Wald oversaw the burial of 220 victims of
Nazism at the town's cemetery (Figure 1).[24] U.S. soldiers ordered the town's

---

[21] Lamm, *Death and Mourning*, p. 239.
[22] Only Jews are to handle the casket, and Jewish law prohibits the use of anonymous gravediggers.
See Lamm, *Death and Mourning*, p. 59.
[23] Benisch, *Vanquish the Dragon*, p. 407.
[24] "Kurzer Bericht über den Werdegang der Jüdischen Gemeinde Neunburg v. Wald vom Tage der
Befreiung am 23. 4. 1945," no date, YV M-1/P-65.

FIGURE 1. Citizens of Neunburg vorm Wald, Germany, in April 1945 carry death march victims to the town cemetery for reburial. *Credit*: U.S. Army Signal Corps, courtesy of Harry S Truman Library

residents, mostly women and elderly, to don their best clothing and to carry the bodies to their burial site. Because of the health hazard presented by exposed corpses, military officials readily assisted these early efforts.

The continuing deaths after liberation led to the formation of traditional burial societies as one of the first Jewish institutions in postwar Germany.[25] Composed of DP rabbis, the Rabbinic Council in the American Zone of occupation reported in October 1945, "We have also done our brotherly duty for our

[25] Landau, "The First Days of Freedom," in Brenner, *After the Holocaust*, p. 84.

martyrs beginning with fencing in the cemeteries and erecting memorial stones for our tortured brothers and sisters."[26] A German Jewish survivor who went to Lübeck after his liberation became active in the Jewish community there. "Our first task was to bury the dead in the old Jewish cemetery. We buried them in a special section of the cemetery; I think there were sixty to a hundred who had died soon after the Liberation."[27] In assuming this responsibility, these leaders were performing one of the greatest duties in Judaism, caring for the abandoned dead. That these acts occurred on German soil heightened their significance. In the land of their persecutors, survivors performed Jewish rituals, affirming Jewish values and the continuity of tradition.

Not surprisingly, survivors were very sensitive to the condition of Jewish cemeteries. In the postwar period German antisemitism mainly manifested itself in the desecration of cemeteries.[28] Jewish communities, intent on fulfilling their duty to the dead, demanded repairs to desecrated cemeteries and the construction of fences to protect them. Allied policy required local German communities to finance restoration efforts, giving Germans a financial, if not moral, incentive to guard against cemetery desecration.[29]

Attacks on cemeteries and other antisemitic violence increased with the transfer of authority to Germans.[30] A new phase of rising antisemitism began in 1947.[31] Belsen's Central Jewish Committee reported the desecration of thirty-eight Jewish cemeteries in the British Zone in the period from January 1, 1947 to June 30, 1948.[32] With the founding of the Federal Republic of Germany in 1949, reports of cemetery vandalism increased. Allied investigators frequently downplayed these incidents, either citing insufficient evidence

---

[26] "Council Meeting of Jews in Bavaria" (in Yiddish), *Unzer Weg*, 19 October 1945, p. 4.

[27] Norbert Wollheim, "Jewish Autonomy in the British Zone," in Brenner, *After the Holocaust*, p. 96.

[28] Norbert Wollheim, "An alle Jüdischen Gemeinden und Komitees in der Britischen Zone Deutschlands: Betrifft: Antisemitismus," 4 March 1948, YV O-70/13; Hagit Lavsky, *New Beginnings: Holocaust Survivors in Bergen-Belsen and the British Zone in Germany, 1945–1950* (Detroit, MI: Wayne State University Press, 2002), p. 130.

[29] Ralph A. Kennedy, Assistant Adjutant General, "Conditions of Jewish Cemeteries," 9 July 1948, p. 1; Displaced Persons; General Records of Amberg Resident Liaison and Security Office 1945–49; Records of the Field Operations Division; Office of the Military Government United States (OMGUS), RG 260, Entry Bavaria; National Archives at College Park (NACP); Norbert Wollheim, "Bericht! Unterhandlungen im Zusammenhang mit der Zerstörung des Jüdischen Friedhofs in Lübeck-Moisling," 9 April 1947, p. 2, YV O-70/63.

[30] In Berlin the failure to restore Jewish cemetaries indicated a continuation of Nazi ideas of proper burial. The Nazi notion that individual burial was for the racially pure while mass graves sufficed for others had been turned upside down during the final battle for Berlin and its aftermath when Germans were buried in mass graves and fallen Soviet soldiers were given individual graves. Monica A. Black, "Reburying and Rebuilding: Reflecting on Proper Burial in Berlin after 'Zero Hour,'" pp. 69–90, in *Between Mass Death and Individual Loss: The Place of the Dead in Twentieth-Century Germany*, eds. Alon Confino, Paul Betts, and Dirk Schumann (New York: Berghahn Books, 2008).

[31] Frank Stern, *The Whitewashing of the Yellow Badge: Antisemitism and Philosemitism in Postwar Germany* (Oxford: Pergamon Press, 1992), pp. 140 and 142.

[32] Josef Rosensaft to Brigadier M.G. Kenchington, 10 August 1948, YV O-70/7.

of human agency in the destruction of tombstones or attributing vandalism to juvenile pranksters. They dismissed Jewish concerns as disproportionate to the situation, referring in one case to "bitter resentment in emotionally-sensitive quarters" and in another to "propaganda not truth."[33] The rising tensions of the Cold War encouraged American and British officials to rebuild West Germany as an ally against the communist East. They were not about to jeopardize their newfound friendship with West Germans over some broken Jewish gravemarkers.

CALENDAR OF REMEMBRANCE

While (re)burials sought to provide corporeal dignity to the dead, liturgy provided the survivors with regular temporal opportunities to remember and honor deceased parents and close relatives. The memorial service, *Yizkor*, "based on the firm belief that the living, by acts of piety and goodness, can redeem the dead,"[34] was recited on four major holidays: Yom Kippur, Passover, Shavuot, and Sukkot. Additionally, mourners would recite *Kaddish* on the *Yahrzeit* or anniversary of the deceased's passing. Since many survivors did not know the dates, they improvised. In the process they began to observe the Yahrzeit not only for individuals but also for entire communities. Through the observance of *Yizkor* and Yahrzeit, DPs confirmed their membership in the Jewish community even as they wrestled with questions about God and faith. For some survivors, participation in these ritual observances helped to reconcile them to Judaism. Memorial events allowed for the construction of social memories of the Holocaust and entered new dates onto the Jewish calendar for collective commemoration.

Yizkor

DP camp religious offices made certain to notify DPs of the dates for the *Yizkor* service. Recitation of the memorial prayer played a major role in many survivors' experience. Bertha Ferderber-Salz admits, "In the synagogue I can visualize the unforgettable figures who were cruelly torn from me, especially during the memorial prayer (*Yizkor*), when they appear before me as clearly and tangibly as if they had come back to life and followed me to the house of prayer. I admit that I go to synagogue, not to pray or listen to the cantor's devotions, but solely in order to meet my dear ones once more. Only there can I bring them to mind as they were in their lifetimes."[35] For Ferderber-Salz, the synagogue became a

---

[33] R.C. Martindale, Director, Intelligence Division, "Inspection of Jewish Cemeteries," 30 June 1948, pp. 2 and 8; Displaced Persons; General Records of Amberg Resident Liaison and Security Office 1945–49; Records of the Field Operations Division; OMGUS, RG 260, Entry Bavaria; NACP; Rosensaft to Kenchington, 10 August, 1948, YV O-70/7; Smedley to Easterman, 2 March 1950, p. 2, YV O-70/8.

[34] Lamm, *Death and Mourning*, p. 196.

[35] Bertha Ferderber-Salz, *And the Sun Kept Shining* (New York: Holocaust Library, 1980), p. 229.

place not so much of worship but of reunion with her murdered family. *Yizkor* provided a link between the living and the dead. It served to connect the survivor with the prewar world.[36]

For some the connection to the past was unbearably painful. One survivor reported that on Jewish holidays she was devastatingly reminded of her lost loved ones, "It was more than I could stand. For a long time I couldn't practice Judaism again as I previously had. But I forced myself to go to the synagogue for *Yizkor*, the service for the dead, three times a year and at the high holy days and that helped me gradually to resume practicing Judaism again almost as I had previously."[37] Here, the ritual obligation to remember the dead helped facilitate a survivor's reconciliation to her religious heritage, her decline in religious observance temporary. Even those whose faith had been shaken by their wartime experiences sought to honor the dead as they would have wished it. As we will see in Chapter 5, parents' values and religious observance influenced many survivors in their continuing performance of Jewish ritual after the Shoah.

Yahrzeit

Other dates for commemorating the dead were more difficult to determine. The primary purpose of Yahrzeit was to commemorate the Hebrew date of a parent, sibling, spouse, or child's death, although it could be observed for any relative or friend. It was observed with the lighting of a memorial candle and with the recitation of *Kaddish* at the synagogue. With families torn apart by Nazi persecution and with the fate of so many unknown, it was impossible for many survivors to determine the exact dates of their parents' deaths. Rabbinic texts permitted those unable to remember or to determine the date of a parent's death to choose the date of the Yahrzeit.[38] Some chose the date of their parents' deportation to concentration camps as the date of death. Others commemorated their deceased parents on Tisha b'Av, the day for commemorating the destruction of the Temples in Jerusalem. This day was a traditional one for visiting family graves and, as the saddest date in the Hebrew calendar, it seemed fitting. As we will see in the section on the Day of Liberation, the DPs attempted to create a unified day of mourning to combat the proliferation of days of mourning. Later the State of Israel created a national holiday, *Yom HaShoah*, which in essence is a national Yahrzeit and is now observed by Jewish communities around the world in recognition that there are families for whom no survivors remain to remember them.[39]

---

[36] See also Gabriel N. Finder, "Yizkor! Commemoration of the Dead by Jewish Displaced Persons in Postwar Germany," pp. 232–258, in *Between Mass Death and Individual Loss*.

[37] Anonymous Polish female survivor, quoted in Brenner, *Faith and Doubt*, p. 61.

[38] Rabbi Katriel Tchorsh, responsum on whether all Jews are obliged to recite Kaddish for the Holocaust Victims, quoted in *Rabbinic Responsa of the Holocaust Era*, ed. Robert Kirschner (New York: Schocken Books, 1985), pp. 172 and 176 n. 8.

[39] See Tchorsh, responsum on whether all Jews are obliged to recite Kaddish, in *Rabbinic Responsa of the Holocaust Era*, pp. 165–176.

The lack of graves, known dates of death, and even surviving family members created the need for innovation. In 1947 Chaim Nachum Mermelsztajn began *Kolel Kiddush Hashem*, an organization to create a memory book for the six million martyrs and to provide religious commemoration for the dead. Kolel Kiddush Hashem encouraged the study of the Mishna (oral law) to benefit the deceased souls and promised to light Yahrzeit candles in the Diaspora and Israel. The Landsberg Camp Committee gave its approval to Mermelsztajn's project in November 1947. The Central Committee followed with its recognition in January 1948. Faced with the unprecedented destruction of Jewish families and communities, Jewish DPs found new ways to fulfill their obligations to the dead.

Mourning Academies

DPs created a new form of commemoration, mourning academies (*troyer akademyen*), in which to remember the destroyed communities of Eastern Europe and to share memories of their prewar homes and their wartime destruction. DP mourning academies convened for the observance of a communal Yahrzeit on the date of the liquidation of a ghetto or of a major Nazi action in a particular ghetto or community. Modeled after secular, prewar literary evenings commemorating a deceased Yiddish author,[40] mourning academies brought together survivors from a particular town or region to exchange stories of life under the Nazis and of the liquidation of the ghettos. They created social memories of the Holocaust and of shared persecution, binding together Jews who had different wartime experiences.

Announced in posters and in newspapers, these gatherings brought together survivors of particular regions or cities on the dates of major Nazi actions and ghetto liquidations.[41] For example, the August 1946 mourning academy for survivors of Ostrog-Wolyn drew attendees from Munich, Neu-Freimann, Föhrenwald, Starnberg, Eschwege, Windsheim, Bayreuth, Bad Reichenhall, and other camps to commemorate "the first mass slaughter of Jews" in the area of Ostrog-Wolyn.[42] Another such academy held in the Landsberg DP camp on October 29, 1946 marked the fifth Yahrzeit of the October Action in the Kovno

[40] At these events, participants would read selected passages by the honored author. Sholem Aleichem had requested that his Yahrzeit be observed with readings of his writings and thus may have begun this tradition. Miriam Isaacs, "Historicizing Trauma, Rituals of Mourning: The Case of Jewish DPs" (paper presented at the Conference on Birth of a Refugee Nation: Displaced Persons in Post-War Europe, 1945–1951, at the Remarque Institute, New York University, April 20, 2001), pp. 6–7.

[41] See, for example, "Attention Lodwifaler Jews" (in Yiddish), *Unzer Weg*, 30 August 1946, p. 7; "Remember that Day!" (in Yiddish), *Unzer Weg*, 15 November 1946, p. 12; "Jizkor!" and "Achtung Tomaszower un Sopnicer jidn!" in *Jidisze Cajtung*, 29 November 1946, p. 2; and "Achtung Zetler!," *Undzer Hofenung*, 2 May 1947, p. 8.

[42] "Trojer-cusamenfor fun di Ostroger jidn in Munchen," *Landsberger Lager Cajtung*, 30 August 1946, p. 13.

Ghetto that coincided with the liquidation of Lithuanian Jewry. All Lithuanian Jews in the American Zone were invited to "participate in the academy with memories and creative presentations about the Jewish tragedy in Lithuania."[43]

The formats of the commemorations were similar. Prior to the mourning academy, participants would visit a nearby cemetery containing Jewish victims of the Holocaust. Despite their secular origin, DP mourning academies usually included recitations of the religious memorial service and *Kaddish*. The secular aspects included speeches about life under German occupation, the liquidation of the ghettos, and often the behavior of the surrounding non-Jewish population. Often there were dramatic or musical performances.[44] The academies invariably ended with the singing of the Zionist anthem, "Hatikvah." For example, the October 1946 remembrance of Lithuanian Jewry began with a memorial service at the mass graves of Dachau, where many survivors of the Kovno ghetto perished (Figure 2). It was followed by the mourning academy in the Landsberg DP camp, at which survivors spoke about life in the Lithuanian ghettos and about the liquidation.[45] What the newspaper did not report was that the day before a group of DPs attempted to hold a memorial service at a nearby cemetery belonging to the camp, but it was disrupted by military police who had been warned of a demonstration outside of the camp. Later General McBride of the 9th Division apologized to the Landsberg Camp Committee for the misunderstanding.[46]

Newspapers helped to publicize not only the mourning academies but also the wartime events that had led to the communities' destruction.[47] On the occasion of the anniversary of the liquidation of Lida, the Föhrenwald newpaper published a lengthy article about the Belarussian community of Lida under German occupation until its liquidation. It reported that twenty-two Jewish DPs gathered to commemorate the liquidation and decided to appeal to Lidar Jews in the United States and Palestine to plant trees through the Jewish National Fund in Palestine "as a memorial for our fallen nearest and dearest."[48] The article educated readers about life in Lida under the occupation and connected the memories of the dead to a living memorial in Palestine. The trees took the place of gravesites to signify

---

[43] Organizer Komitet, "Achtung Jidn Fun Lite!!!" 22 October 1946, YV M-1/P-10 II.

[44] Ch. Gnieslow, "Di antsztejung un di likwidacje fun Lodzer getto," *Dos Fraje Wort*, 6 September 1946, p. 5; "Akademie cu der likwidacje fun Wilner geto," *Dos Fraje Wort*, 25 September 1946, p. 3; "Ajndruksfule trojer-akademje in Dachau," *Jidisze Cajtung*, 22 November 1946, p. 9.

[45] "Yizkor for Lithuanian Jewry" (in Yiddish), *Unzer Weg*, 15 November 1946, p. 6.

[46] W. J. Korn, Director, UNRRA, Team 311, to Carl Atkin, Deputy Director, Jewish Affairs, "Ban of Religious Ceremony, Brief Report of Today's Events in Landsberg," 28 October 1946, United States Holocaust Memorial Museum Archive (USHMM), Samuel Zisman Papers, RG-19.047.02*23; H. L. McBride, Major General, U.S. Army, to Samuel Zisman, UNRRA District Director, 29 October 1946, Zisman Papers, RG-19.047.02*23. Interestingly, both Korn and Atkin would become targets of military investigations and accusations of abuse of office. These charges were not uncommon against UNRRA officials, who were deemed too sympathetic to the DPs.

[47] For example, "Bjalistoker getto," *Dos Fraje Wort*, 23 August 1946; Jacob Oleski, "Elul 5701 in Kovno Ghetto" (in Yiddish), *Unzer Weg*, 25 September 1946, p.5; "Ajndruksfule trojer-akademje in Dachau," *Jidisze Cajtung*, 22 November 1946, p. 9.

[48] Z. Kalmanowicz, "Der churbn fun der jidiszer Lide," *Bamidbar*, 4 June 1946, p.8.

FIGURE 2. DP police from the Lechfeld DP camp carry a wreath to a memorial to Jewish victims at the Dachau concentration camp, 1950. *Credit*: United State Holocaust Memorial Museum (USHMM), courtesy of George Gerzon (Gerzon Trzcina)

that the deceased had left their mark on this earth. The newspaper article magnified the effect of the mourning academy beyond its twenty-two participants. Through this sharing of memories, the survivors formed a collective memory of the Shoah and found ways both to narrate their experiences and to incorporate them into their personal and communal histories.

DP mourning academies helped to establish common ground among DPs of different socio-economic backgrounds and wartime experiences. Mourning academies created a venue in which the survivors could express their loss and find comfort with others whose families had shared a common fate. They could reminisce about the neighborhoods of their youth and discover friends in common. Mourning academies provided a forum in which nonobservant Jews and observant Jews could meet in shared grief and remembrance. Because these were secular events, men and women could both participate and sit together. Participants need not have been present in the town or region at the time of the ghetto liquidations to participate in these academies. Thus they provided a forum in which those who had survived the war years in the Soviet Union and who had arrived later in the DP camps could share their grief with others from their hometown and become integrated into the preexisting DP society. The speeches about conditions in the ghettos, Nazi methods, and the role of the local population enabled survivors to integrate their own personal experiences within the larger narrative framework of the Holocaust. They also informed those who were in hiding or in exile about the conditions in which their family members had struggled and died.

While most mourning academies took place within the DP camps, occasionally they entered into German towns and villages. One mourning academy, held in April 1946 on the anniversary of the murder of the last concentration camp inmate on a death march from Ganacker-Platting to Eggenfelden, took the character of a demonstration and reenactment of the death march. Representatives of the military government of Landau, the denazified local *Landrat* (a German district official), and mayors accompanied the procession of twenty-five trucks from Eggenfelden to Landau, Ganacker, Platting, Arnstdorf, and back. Approximately 1,000 people participated. A survivor report proudly noted that Jewish DP police had kept the peace without the assistance of American or German police. They rode motorcycles and there were no reports of disturbances.[49] Jewish respectability and restraint had been demonstrated to the vanquished Germans. The procession was simultaneously a commemoration for those who died on the death march, an accusation of German guilt, and a celebration of survival for those who this time paraded through the German streets in triumphant alliance with the victors of the war.

DPs in the Mittenwald DP camp reenacted the death march from Dachau to Tyrol in May 1946. They held a major assembly in Mittenwald attended by American officials and German dignitaries. Through their respectable attire of suits and dresses, DPs demonstrated their own dignity as well as that due to the dead. Banners carried in the procession called on the British government to allow Jewish immigration to Palestine.[50] The commemoration of the dead was tied to the political demands of the living.

Mourning academies could also serve to emphasize within the Jewish community the importance of Jewish resistance and the strength of survivors. In 1947 three DP communities chose to hold mourning academies in honor of the Warsaw ghetto resistance fighters. At the Bamberg academy, a Warsaw ghetto fighter spoke about the meaning of the fight in the ghetto and others spoke about aspects of the battle and the high moral niveau of the fighters. The academy closed with the singing of "Hatikvah."[51] The fighters were presented as role models to the DPs, and the singing of the Zionist anthem suggested that the new battle for survival would be waged in Palestine. The community in Wetzlar, north of Frankfurt am Main, also held a mourning academy in honor of the Warsaw ghetto fighters. The speakers emphasized the necessity of continuing the fight in Palestine. One also spoke about the unity of the ghetto fighters and the need to put aside political differences to build a new home in Palestine.[52] The survivors' original ideal of unity received new life in this academy. The community in Ziegenheim, also northeast of Frankfurt, declared a day of mourning in honor of the Warsaw ghetto uprising. All offices and workplaces were closed and at noon a rally of all organizations with their flags and the entire camp population began at the memorial to the fallen six million. Following the rally, a mourning academy was held in the theater.[53] The Warsaw ghetto uprising had become a symbol of Jewish strength that all survivors could embrace.

---

[49] Chaim Diamond, "Bericht über die Trauer-Akademie am 28. April 1946 in der Gemeinde Eggenfelden," 5 May 1946, YIVO Institute for Jewish Research (YIVO), RG 294.2, MK 483, Microfilm reel 63, Folder 888.
[50] See, USHMM, Photo Archive, W/S #20090.
[51] "Jorcajt-akademje cum warszewer geto-ojfsztand," *Undzer Hofenung*, 2 May 1947, p. 5.
[52] "Trojer-akademje in Wetzlar," *Undzer Hofenung*, 2 May 1947, p. 5.
[53] "Di anthilung fun a denkmol in lager Cigenhain," *Undzer Hofenung*, 13 May 1947, p. 7.

This valorization was not a foregone conclusion. During the war Germans had responded to Jewish resistance with harsh retribution, and many Jews in the ghettos feared that resistance fighters would only bring harm to the Jewish community. After the war, tensions had existed between the concentration camp survivors and partisans over who had suffered more or had been more heroic, despite early expressions of admiration by all for the self-sacrifice of both the partisans and resistance fighters.[54] If the fighters had died a "beautiful death," then the corollary seemed to be that the concentration camp victims had died an "unsightly" one.[55] Thus the survivors' need to honor the martyred dead came into conflict with the desire to extol the heroism of the resistance fighters.[56]

DPs resolved the apparent tension between heroic and ignoble death by asserting the commonalities between the victims of the concentration camps and the resistance fighters and partisans. They decided after the fact that the Jewish community had all supported the resistance fighters, who had expressed the will of the Jewish people. By late 1946 DP newspapers began to offer a framework for reconciling partisans and others. They presented the partisans as having emerged from the same communities as the concentration camp inmates, having shared the same losses, and having faced their own terrorization at the hands of Germans and other antisemites.[57] One author reminded partisans that everyone had lost a loved one in the concentration camps but not everyone had had the opportunity or connections to escape to the woods, implying that they would have wanted to join the partisans had they been able to do so. He also bluntly pointed out to concentration camp survivors that they must "understand that the heroes of the ghetto uprising in Warsaw have more dignity in the eyes of the outside world than the victims of the concentration camp."[58] Partisans needed to honor the deaths of the concentration camp victims, and camp survivors needed to acknowledge the value of the resistance fighters' deaths, if only because the international community did. Reconciling the two groups necessitated interpreting ghetto fighters and partisans as expressions of the will of the Jewish community. This interpretation required survivors to forget their wartime opposition to the resistance fighters. DP newspapers participated in this process of reconciliation by emphasizing the commonality of experiences between partisans and camp survivors.

---

[54] "Yizkor!" *Unzer Weg*, 12 October 1945, p.1.

[55] Idith Zertal, *Israel's Holocaust and the Politics of Nationhood* (Cambridge: Cambridge University Press, 2005), p. 26.

[56] Israeli "new historian" Idith Zertal argues that Zionists needed to separate the heroes from the Diaspora Jews, and they accomplished this "by cloaking the rebels in the mantle of Zionism and transforming them into Palmach fighters, accidentally snared in the spheres of Diaspora; and conversely, by rejecting the conduct of the Jewish masses and their elderly leaders, the heads of the Judenrat, for failing to stand up and rebel." Zertal, *Israel's Holocaust*, pp. 30f. and 32.

[57] "Kacetler un partizaner," *Landsberger Lager Cajtung*, 9 October 1946, p. 9; Jicchok Sutin, "Der 16-joriker heldisz-jidiszer partizan," *Landsberger Lager Cajtung*, 16 October 1946; "Der emes wegen jidisze partizaner," *Jidisze Cajtung*, 15 November 1946, p. 7.

[58] "Kacetler un partizaner," *Landsberger Lager Cajtung*, 9 October 1946, p. 9.

DP theatrical productions valorized Jewish resistance fighters, often in ways that emphasized their connection to the Jewish community. For example, the 1945 Belsen KZ-Theater production of *Partisans* ended with the head of the ghetto's Judenrat joining the partisans. The message was that the partisans expressed the will of the entire Jewish people, even those cautious community leaders who initially feared the reprisals that resistance could, and did, bring down on the Jewish community. In the 1948 DP film *Lang ist der Weg* (Long is the Road), the hero escapes from a transport and joins the partisans, while his parents continue to a concentration camp where the father is murdered. The hero-partisan is a son of the Jewish people whom circumstance and physical strength granted the opportunity to fight. Before the war he was the assimilated son of traditional parents with no obvious political orientation. By the time he reaches the DP camps, he is preparing for a future in Palestine. His transformation into a Zionist hero is complete. Within the DP community, concentration camp survivors came to see partisans and resistance fighters as their alter egos who had expressed their will to resist when they had been unable to do so themselves.[59]

Zionists readily embraced the mythology of the Jewish warrior sacrificing all for honor. Members of Zionist youth groups learned about the heroic fighters of their movement in order to identify with their histories and to be inspired to emulate their deeds. The socialist Zionist party Poale Zion praised the partisans and front soldiers of the veterans' organization Pachach for "staying true to the tradition of the Maccabees" and for "taking their place in the ranks of the pioneering movement."[60] While this portrayal preserved an avant-guard role for the partisans, it linked them to ancient Jewish rebels, creating a heroic Jewish tradition.

By 1947 a significant number of Jewish DPs were those who had spent the war years in Soviet exile. They were neither concentration camp survivors nor partisans. They could honor the memory of the martyrs in the concentration camps and extol the heroes of the uprising. They could imagine that they would have been resistance fighters had they had the opportunity. The mourning academies for the Warsaw uprising honored not only the fallen individuals but also the Zionist vision of the proud, combative Jew; they served to rewrite the past, replacing passive martyrdom with heroic resistance.

When the survivors arrived in Israel they had already embraced the ghetto uprisings as examples of Zionist heroism. With the entire Jewish community recast as Zionists and resistance fighters at heart, they shared in the Zionist interpretation of wartime resistance as connected to the battle for Jewish survival and demands for a Jewish state. The survivors had transformed themselves into exceptions to the stereotype of the passive, victimized Jew

[59] Zeev W. Mankowitz reaches a similar conclusion in *Life between Memory and Hope: The Survivors of the Holocaust in Occupied Germany* (Cambridge: Cambridge University Press, 2002), pp. 211–212.

[60] "Rezolucjes fun cusamenfor," *Landsberger Lager Cajtung*, 21 June 1946, p. 11.

of the Diaspora.[61] In the mourning academies for the Warsaw uprising, DPs honored the dead and established their own retroactive connection to the resistance, easing the "burden of victimhood."[62] The integration of different wartime experiences through the memories shared in the mourning academies helped to create a collective memory of the Holocaust that included resistance and an affirmation of Zionism.

Day of Liberation

DP leaders attempted to simplify the calendar of mourning with the creation of liberation celebrations. The day of liberation became a date on which to recall those who had died and to rededicate oneself to building Jewish life in freedom. In the British Zone, April 15, the date of Belsen's liberation, became the date of community observance. In the American Zone, the Central Committee selected a Hebrew date, the 14th of Iyar. Although the Central Committee had hoped that this new holiday would reduce the number of memorial observances, DPs continued to gather in mourning academies to commemorate the liquidation of particular towns or regions. Liberation Day ceremonies served a slightly different function, however. Liberation Day brought together all DPs regardless of place of origin, and although Liberation Day ceremonies provided the opportunity to mourn, they also consciously demonstrated survival, victory, and dedication to building Jewish life in a Jewish homeland.

For those DPs liberated in Germany, they could return to the site of their liberation for communal ceremonies. The structure of these events contained many of the features of the mourning academies: visits to cemeteries and mass graves, memorial prayers, speeches, and the singing of "Hatikvah." Unlike the mourning academies that focused on a particular region of origin, Liberation Day events focused on the more broadly shared sites of persecution and liberation. They fostered a greater Jewish national character bringing together Polish, Lithuanian, and Hungarian Jews and emphasizing their common experience of Nazi persecution. Also, mourning academies tended to be insular affairs, while Liberation Day ceremonies often went out into the German communities when participants reenacted death marches. Liberation Day events commemorated the dead, but they also demonstrated the victory of the survivors over

---

[61] Even if we accept Zertal's argument that Israeli Zionists distinguished between the heroic rebels and the passive Jewish masses, it does not follow that survivors who immigrated to Israel and condemned non-Zionist interpretations of the Warsaw ghetto uprising "bore witness to the coercive, engulfing ideologic pressure exerted over newcomers by the prevailing Israeli discourse of the first years of statehood." In fact, this process of interpretation had already occurred within the DP camps years prior to Israeli statehood and was part of an internal discussion among survivors themselves. Even though they did not necessarily accept that the resistance fighters were a different type of Jew from the masses of European Jewry, the survivors had already internalized the Zionist precept that the uprisings were connected to the fight of the Jewish people for survival and to their demand for a Jewish homeland. Zertal, *Israel's Holocaust*, pp. 40–41.

[62] Mankowitz, *Life between Memory and Hope*, p. 209.

their German oppressors and demanded an end to the DPs' suffering by open immigration to Palestine.

At Belsen the first anniversary of liberation coincided with the beginning of Passover on April 15, 1946. Jewish DPs marked the occasion by unveiling a monument to the 30,000 Jewish victims of Bergen-Belsen with inscriptions in English and Hebrew. Thousands participated in a parade holding banners and flags. A DP speaker insisted that the international community could have saved more Jewish lives. The event concluded with a traditional commemorative prayer service. An UNRRA nurse noted the stark contrast between the somber tone of the Jewish ceremonies and the festive nature of the Polish observances of the day.[63]

The Jewish commemoration had political implications. British authorities objected to the stone monument in honor of Jewish victims, since they wanted to emphasize the "international character" of Belsen's former inmates. To acknowledge the Jews as a distinct group would undermine the British position that the Jews did not have a right to a homeland in Palestine. For the Belsen Central Committee commemoration was key to its bid for recognition and for the Jewish national struggle.[64]

In the American Zone the Central Committee urged the observance of a "Unified Day of Remembrance and Liberation" that would simultaneously recall the dead and commemorate the survival of the Jewish people. It selected the date of 14 Iyar on the Hebrew calendar, which coincided with May 15, 1946. The 14th of Iyar had religious significance as the Second Passover, the day on which those who were unable to observe the Passover Seder one month earlier could rectify that omission. Its significance as a day of returning to God, of liberation from Pharaoh's oppression, or rededicating oneself to Jewish life might have influenced the decision. But American rabbis rejected this date for commemoration because it is prohibited to mourn on that day.[65] The 14th of Iyar failed to become an international day of Jewish commemoration, but it had great resonance within the DP community.

Newspapers published photos and articles reporting the commemoration ceremonies for those who did not attend and emphasized the significance and meaning of the day for those who did. On the first anniversary of liberation, the Landsberg newspaper printed photos of graves and memorial services. Captions identified two women visiting graves of the "martyrs of Muehldorf," the exhumation of sixty-seven death march victims by former SS personnel, the transfer of the coffins to the cemetery where concentration camp survivors spoke, and a second memorial service in nearby Gauting.[66]

---

[63] "Belsen Liberation Anniversary Marked by Ceremonies," extract from UNRRA Regional Office, 4 May 1946, in Muriel Knox Doherty, *Letters from Belsen 1945: An Australian nurse's experiences with the survivors of war*, eds. Judith Cornell and R. Lynette Russell (St. Leonards, NSW Australia: Allen & Unwin, 2000), pp. 205–206.

[64] Lavsky, *New Beginnings*, p. 120.

[65] For an insightful discussion of the Day of Remembrance and Liberation, see Mankowitz, *Life Between Memory and Hope*, Chapter 9.

[66] *Unterwegs (Feldafinger Magazin)*, 4 June 1946, entire.

In other localities, survivors retraced the routes of death marches. Germans lined the streets under orders of American military government officers to watch the processions. DP organizers reported with pride that Jewish DP police had kept the peace and that the DPs had behaved with dignity. The processions demonstrated the respectability of the survivors and by extension that of the dead. Simultaneously, the march of the DPs recalled their persecution at the hands of the Germans and enacted their victory over them. The survivors were still there to prove the continuity of the Jewish people and to remind the Germans of Nazi crimes. At the same time, the German populace did not join as mourners and rejected the accusatory note of the reenactments. The original death march had disrupted their peaceful communities, but its origins and, thus they concluded, the responsibility for it lay elsewhere. The town residents did not feel responsible for the crimes of the Nazi regime and likely resented the order to show their respects.[67]

Commemorations of liberation could also serve to promote images of Jewish strength and survival. In Föhrenwald the first anniversary of liberation coincided with the second conference of Jewish fighters and with the visit of American literary figures H. Leivik and Israel Efros and the Yiddish singer Emma Shaver. The Jewish veterans' organization *(Histadrut Lochmim Ivrim)* organized the camp's academy in honor of the liberation with the participation of the American guests. The conference of partisans and front soldiers drew approximately 100 delegates from 19 cities, representing more than 2,000 organized partisans and soldiers. The local DP newspaper reported that those in attendance were buoyed "by the courageous and proud words spoken by the Jewish veterans and the honored guests in their greetings on the occasion of the anniversary of liberation."[68] References to veterans, partisans, and ghetto fighters helped to redefine the image of the Holocaust experience from passive victimization to heroic resistance and victory. In Munich the day concluded with Emma Shaver's concert, producing the desired effect of transitioning from mourning to celebration. The blending of sorrow and joy was a standard feature of DP commemorations that always emphasized the need for the survivors to rebuild Jewish lives and form community as a tribute to the dead.

The second anniversary of liberation found the survivors frustrated by their extended stay on German soil. In 1947 the Belsen festivities began with the "traditional march" to the mass graves in the old camp. Twenty DP police, demonstrating Jewish discipline and strength, led the procession followed by four children from the secular and religious schools, representing the Jewish future. The participation of Zionist and ultra-Orthodox organizations demonstrated the unity of the DPs. At the memorial unveiled the previous year, leaders of the

---

[67] Liberating troops had forced local Germans to tour concentration camps. Harold Marcuse noted that these compulsory viewings were "more likely to arouse feelings of bitterness and disgrace than impart a lesson in civic obligation and democratic behavior." *Legacies of Dachau: The Uses and Abuses of a Concentration Camp, 1933–2001* (Cambridge: Cambridge University Press, 2001), p. 56.

[68] "2-te Konferenc fun jidisze kemfer," *Bamidbar*, 4 June 1946, p. 9.

Central Jewish Committee spoke, as did the Jewish Agency representative and a British general. The ceremony ended with the singing of "Hatikvah." In keeping with the combination of mourning and celebration that liberation brought forth, that evening 2,000 people attended a party. Prior to the party, Rosensaft spoke at a plenary session of the Central Jewish Committee. He referred to the failure to secure certificates to Palestine but "called for unity and collective labor. He mentioned the systematic desecration of cemeteries by the Nazis and continuing even to today's second liberation day. In expectation of a general solution and regulation of our problem, two years after liberation we are still sentenced to live in a camp. This situation should unite us without distinction of parties and opinions in order to show the outside world that we stand unweakened and unshaken in the fight for our basic rights."[69] The celebration of the second anniversary of liberation was marred by the fact that the DPs were still in Germany. Frustration over the lack of emigration opportunities threatened to fragment the DPs, but in Belsen unity prevailed.

The Day of Remembrance and Liberation in the American Zone also was the occasion for demands for DP emigration. At a ceremony commemorating the second anniversary of the liberation of concentration camps in Mittenwald, Arie Reter, a member of the Central Committee, called in English on the American Army to help end the tragedy of the Jewish people. "We swear on the bodies of our brothers that we will not rest until we have erected a monument to their memory – a free Jewish Land of Israel."[70] Unlike the stone memorials survivors dedicated at various sites in Germany, the ultimate monument would be the living memorial of a Jewish state.

When Israel was founded on the 5th of Iyar, the Day of Remembrance and Liberation no longer fit the Jewish calendar. If the State of Israel was to be the answer to the tribulations of the Diaspora as epitomized by the Holocaust, then commemoration needed to precede the celebration of independence. Israel created Yom HaShoah on 27 Nisan as the day to remember the victims of the Holocaust. It occurs twelve days after the start of Passover, seven days before Israel's memorial day for fallen soldiers, and eight days before Independence Day. In Europe Holocaust commemorations take place on January 27th, the anniversary of the liberation of Auschwitz. The DPs' attempts to link remembrance with the conclusion of the war did not succeed in the long run, but they played a significant role on the DP calendar for the time that the DP camps existed. It served their need to dedicate themselves to a Jewish future in memory of the dead and to perform their victory over Germans.

While *Kaddish* and *Yizkor* encouraged mourners to join a community for the purpose of prayer, the grief and experiences remained personal. Through Liberation Day ceremonies and mourning academies, survivors could speak about the past, recount experiences, and create shared memories. As sociologist Eviatar Zerubavel writes, collective memory "involves the integration of various

[69] Central Jewish Committee Sekretariat, "Rundschreiben Nr. 25/10," YV O-70/13.
[70] "In tog fun frejd un trojer," *Undzer Hofenung*, 13 May 1947, p. 3.

different personal pasts into a single common past that all members of a particular community come to remember collectively."[71] Commemorative events help to create and reinforce these collective memories by bringing together individuals for the shared experience of remembrance. The association of the academies and Liberation Day with a particular date on the calendar ensured that members of the community would remember together on an annual basis. Newspaper reports detailing the speeches and performances of the commemorative events widened the memory community beyond the actual participants.

EXHUMATION AND REBURIAL

As part of their efforts to commemorate the dead, DPs attempted to provide Jewish burials for concentration camp and death march victims who lay in mass graves throughout the German countryside. Often the survivors placed monuments on the graves and dedicated them with religious ceremonies. Occasionally, the dead were exhumed and reburied. DPs had to win the cooperation of military government or local German officials to acquire the manpower, equipment, and/or land necessary for exhumation and reburial. The ability to accomplish these tasks in the face of Allied and German recalcitrance only highlighted the survivors' determination to exercise their agency. Reburials also provided opportunities for DPs to exert their moral claims against their German persecutors. As Katherine Verdery noted in her study of postsocialist reburials, "Assessing blame and demanding accountability can occur at many sites, one of them being dead bodies."[72] Survivors intended for the parades of Jewish victims accompanied by Allied and denazified German dignitaries to demonstrate Jewish innocence and German culpability. Instead the reburials provided a window into postwar tensions between Germans and Jews and the very different ways in which the two communities understood their past and present experiences. The reburials encouraged German forgetting and denial but succeeded both in strengthening Jewish self-esteem and in fostering Jewish community.

Allied commanders overwhelmed with the problems of maintaining order, feeding and clothing civilians, and reconstructing the German infrastructure often had little patience for DP requests. In June 1945, Wolf Weil entered Germany illegally after searching for surviving family in Krakow and was immediately asked to take a leadership role in the Jewish community of Hof. His first task was to secure the burial of more than 100 death march victims whose bodies still lay in the surrounding forests. The local American commander refused to permit the burial of the dead, yet Weil would not be intimidated. With obvious satisfaction, he states, "I finally carried out everything, and [the American commander] himself was even present. Today, the memorial stone,

[71] Eviatar Zerubavel, "Social Memories: Steps to a Sociology of the Past," *Qualitative Sociology* 19 (1996): 294.

[72] Katherine Verdery, *The Political Lives of Dead Bodies: Reburial and Postsocialist Change* (New York: Columbia University Press, 1999), p. 38.

with the inscription that 142 concentration camp inmates are buried here, is still standing."[73] Jewish DPs persevered even when confronted by obstacles.

Some survivors did succeed in gaining the cooperation of local Germans in honoring the dead. In either the fall of 1945 or early spring of 1946, DPs discovered another mass grave in Neunburg vorm Wald. Since they found Jewish prayers and *tefillin* (phylacteries) in the corpses' pockets, the survivors wanted to give them a Jewish burial. The mayor granted DPs permission to rebury some Jewish remains in a corner of the town cemetery. Exhuming the forty to fifty bodies themselves, the Jews transported the corpses on blankets to the new burial site.[74] A participant in the reburial recalled, "We were very glad we did something, a good deed. People would fall apart in the ditches or the animals would eat them up, but they have a Jewish burial. So very important to me. ... We did our duty to get them out."[75] Fulfilling one's obligation to the dead brought satisfaction. The first thing that the well-known German-Jewish journalist, Karl Marx, did on his return to Düsseldorf was to demand that the city council put up a memorial plaque to the murdered Jews. In 1946 the city complied. Marx's widow recalls, "It was the first act that gave us a little satisfaction, a tiny consolation."[76] The reassertion of the dignity of the dead was a source of pride for the living. Where exhumation was not possible or desirable, survivors enclosed mass gravesites so that they could be preserved and memorials constructed.[77] The ability to perform the essential tasks of Jewish burial symbolized the continued expression of Jewish values and community.[78]

Mass Graves at Dachau and Belsen

Mass graves presented many challenges in postwar Germany as survivors, Germans, and Allies asserted their rights to the land and the dead. At Dachau, city officials demonstrated their desire to forget the dead and to reclaim the land for their own purposes. Some 20,000 dead were buried on a hill near Dachau concentration camp called the Leiten or Leitenberg. After a 1945 plan to create a memorial on the Leitenberg was abandoned, the graves were unattended. Dachau city officials knowingly misrepresented the number of dead and built a road over some mass graves. They later returned a body from the mass graves to an Italian widow, despite the impossibility of determining the identity of the body and despite health regulations prohibiting such actions.

---

[73] Wolf Weil, "A Schindler Jew in the Bavarian Province," in Brenner, *After the Holocaust*, pp. 155–156.

[74] Sher, interview by John Menszer.

[75] Joseph Sher, "Videotaped interview," VHA, IC 29094, Seg. 48.

[76] Lilli Marx, "The Renewal of the German-Jewish Press," in Brenner, *After the Holocaust*, p. 126.

[77] Alexander Contract, "Videotaped interview," VHA, IC 36559, Seg. 60; Marie Syrkin, "Mass Graves and Mass Synagogues," in *The State of the Jews* (Washington, DC: New Republic Books, 1980), esp. pp. 51–52.

[78] "Council Meeting of Jews in Bavaria" (in Yiddish), *Unzer Weg* 19 October 1945, p.4; Religiezes Amt bajm Regjonal Komitet to Joint-Rel. Amt Munich, 4 February 1948, YIVO, RG 294.2, MK 483, Microfilm reel 63, Folder 887.

The situation on the Leitenberg finally came to the attention of higher authorities when new bodies were discovered outside of the known mass gravesite and a French commission deplored the conditions of the graves. In the midst of the controversy, German officials "rediscovered" a map created by the company retained in 1945 to design a memorial. The map showed numerous gravesites not then under protection. A commission composed of Bavarian government ministers who were former concentration camp inmates, local German officials, representatives of the Dachau survivors' organization, U.S. military government officials, and French representatives studied the problem.[79] The discussions revealed the tensions between those who wanted the Leitenberg to remain available for economic use and those who wanted to rope off the site as sacral land. The desire to use the land for present purposes regardless of the dead buried there was not limited to Dachau city leaders. Farmers in Bavaria, anxious to return land to cultivation, leveled mass graves, even ones marked with crosses.[80]

While the desire to limit the amount of land set aside for memorialization can seem callous, it is also understandable that locals wanted to preserve their rights to the land and its meaning. As one scholar has noted, in Poland the tensions between Poles who use Treblinka for recreation and survivors who view it as sacred space "illuminate the difficulties that societies face in preserving landscapes that have multiple meanings for past and present generations."[81] The presence of corpses on the Leitenberg tipped the balance to the side of sacralization.

In the process of the public debates, however, German officials tried to discredit the survivors.[82] Many of Dachau's victims had been non-Jewish Germans, but the Nazis had marginalized them so completely as communists, socialists, and criminals that even after the war the stigma remained and could be revived. The situation of the graves at Leitenberg revealed the general postwar German desire to ignore the crimes committed in the concentration camps and the sense of victimization Germans felt when forced by Allies and survivors to confront them.[83]

At Belsen, the British emphasis on the international character of the victims and a certain naiveté led to conflict with Jewish survivors. In 1948 construction of an international memorial to the victims of Belsen involved planting fir trees in such a fashion that they blocked the preexisting Jewish memorial and eliminated the open space on which Jewish Belseners had commemorated Liberation Day in 1946 and 1947. Workers removed stones that survivors had placed on

[79] "Minutes of Second Meeting of the Joint OLCB – Bavarian Government Commission for Investigation of the Dachau Mass Graves," 4 October 1949; Dead Bodies; General Records of the Public Health Branch, 1947–49; Records of the Civil Administration Division (CAD); OMGUS, RG 260, Entry A2 B3 C1; NACP.

[80] "Minutes of Second Meeting of the Joint OLCB – Bavarian Government Commission," p. 4.

[81] Janet Jacobs, "From the Profane to the Sacred: Ritual and Mourning at Sites of Terror and Violence," *Journal for the Scientific Study of Religion* 43:3 (2004): 314.

[82] For more on the Leitenberg affair, see Marcuse, *Legacies of Dachau*, pp. 142–151 and 189–198.

[83] Marcuse, *Legacies of Dachau*, p. 198.

the sites where their relatives had been killed, outraging the survivors. Plans to plant flowers and shrubs atop the mass graves also offended Jewish sensibilities, since such ornamentation was contrary to Jewish tradition. An investigation into Jewish DP leader Josef Rosensaft's complaints resulted in modifications to the plan and the restoration of the open area around the Jewish memorial.[84] The advocacy of the Central Jewish Committee was essential for preserving the Jewish character of the site and guaranteeing observance of Jewish burial traditions.

In 1950 the World Jewish Congress attempted to gain Jewish oversight for the Belsen graves, but the British insisted on the international character of the site and the transfer of authority to German officials.[85] That same year British authorities requested Rosensaft's acquiescence to the transfer of two Jewish graves that were inconveniently located near the fields where British troops played soccer. One military government officer suggested that Rosensaft accept the recommendation "so that you should be given the opportunity of helping to avoid any future embarrassment both to yourselves and to the British Troops using the playing fields."[86] Apparently, misaimed British soccer balls would be an embarrassment to Jewish DPs. Rosensaft's reply was not in the records but, two years later, German officials in charge of the Belsen cemeteries requested permission to move the same two bodies to a larger grave in order to simplify maintenance. Rosensaft, now empowered by the Jewish Agency to negotiate with German, British, and other authorities concerning the international cemetery of Bergen-Belsen,[87] replied that the gravesite had been used to bury those who died in the nearby barracks that had served as a hospital in the immediate aftermath of the war. He cautioned, "The fact that there exist only two tombstones should not induce you to believe that only two people have been buried there."[88] The normal assumption that each body had a tombstone did not apply to Nazi victims. That British and German authorities made this assumption demonstrates their lack of understanding of the situation in Belsen and other sites of mass murder. Rosensaft also indicated that "extremely serious religious problems" would be involved in any exhumation. Jewish law ordinarily prohibited exhumation except for reburial in Israel.

Later, Rosensaft led a ten-year legal battle to prevent the French Mission for the Search of Victims of War from exhuming bodies at Belsen. In the mid-1950s the French developed new forensic techniques that aided them in identifying the remains of French nationals. In 1955 they exhumed bodies from the Leitenberg to repatriate them to France. In 1958 the French wanted to locate the 139 French nationals who had been murdered in Belsen and return them to France as well. In

---

[84] [Gibson?], Regional Governmental Officer, Land Niedersachsen, "Belsen Memorial," 9 March 1948, YV O-70/8.

[85] Basil Marsden Smedley, Foreign Office to A.L. Easterman, World Jewish Congress, 2 March 1950 [German translation], YV O-70/8.

[86] W. D. Symington to Rosensaft, "Transfer of Jewish Graves," 21 July 1950, YV O-70/30.

[87] N. Goldmann to Josef Rosensaft, 24 March 1952, YV O-70/19.

[88] Josef Rosensaft to W.A. Symington, 7 May 1952, YV O-70/8.

order to identify the remains of the French nationals, tens of thousands of other bodies would be disturbed. The Jewish Belsen survivors argued that the unlikely possibility of locating the French corpses did not justify the desecration of the other bodies. In 1969 an international arbitration commission decided against exhumation.[89] Rosensaft and the Jewish Belseners had successfully defended the dignity of their dead and reminded the world of the enormity of the crimes perpetrated against them.

The Mass Grave in Floß and German Forgetting

In addition to mass graves at former concentration camps, death march victims had often been buried in shallow graves throughout the German countryside, particularly in Bavaria. Since these graves were in danger of being forgotten or plowed under, DPs sought to move the corpses to proper cemeteries. The efforts of DP representatives in the Bavarian community of Tirschenreuth to secure the close cooperation of military government and German officials resulted in a noteworthy event. The reinterment of thirty-nine victims of a death march from Buchenwald was a ceremonial occasion that spoke to the rehabilitation of the survivors and their will to determine their future.[90] The victims had been murdered on April 13, 1945 and were subsequently buried in six mass graves. Two of the graves were ploughed up even though the German landowner had known that Jews were buried there. The Jewish Committee of Tirschenreuth had long sought the reburial of these victims, but it was only when the local MGO, Captain Lyle Mariels, became involved that the reburial took place. An orphan raised in a foster home in a predominantly Jewish neighborhood in Portland, Oregon, Mariels was a champion of the disadvantaged and sympathetic to Jewish concerns.[91]

On August 19, 1946, under orders from Captain Mariels, ninety-eight former Nazis exhumed the bodies.[92] The coffins had an honor guard of American M.P.s and Jewish DP policemen during the night, in keeping with Jewish tradition that the deceased be attended until burial as well as a safeguard against antisemitic vandals.[93] On the morning of August 20, a funeral procession including representatives of the regional military government, local UNRRA workers, the Landrat, mayors of the surrounding towns, as well as members of neighboring

---

[89] Hadassah Rosensaft, *Yesterday: My Story* (Washington, DC: United States Holocaust Memorial Museum, 2004), p. 134.

[90] The following description is based on Alfred Slomnicki, "Bericht über die Beerdigung von 39 Juden am 20. 8. 1946 in Floss," 25 August 1946, YV M-1/P-74. A brief mention of the reburial in Floß is also found in Jewish Community Tirschenreuth, "Kulturbericht für Monat August 1946," 4 September 1946, YIVO RG 294.2, MK 483, Microfilm reel 70, Folder 1012.

[91] Ray Mariels (nephew of Lyle Mariels), telephone interview by the author, 26 April 2006.

[92] "Germans Exhume Jews: Known Nazis Forced to Dig Up Bodies for Reburial," *New York Times*, 20 August 1946.

[93] According to Jewish law, once the body is exhumed, it is to be treated with the same respect as was due on the day of death. See Lamm, *Death and Mourning*, pp. 71–74.

Jewish committees drove through a number of towns along a 60-kilometer stretch to the Jewish cemetery in the hamlet of Floß.

The Tirschenreuth Community called it a burial "with military honors."[94] Americans, Jews, and Germans appeared to be united in their respect for the dead. By riding in Mariels's car the leaders of the Tirschenreuth Jewish community emphasized the especially close alliance of the Jews and Americans. Leading the procession were three Jewish DP policemen displaying the Zionist flag. The coffins, carried on an UNRRA truck, were decorated with flowers and wreaths. Captain Mariels had ordered that shops along the route be closed and that German residents line the streets with their heads bared. In Tirschenreuth and Floß a band accompanied the procession.

This event was a departure from prewar Jewish traditions. Reinterment is generally discouraged in Jewish law and practice; however, the circumstance of the mass graves created legally permissible reasons for reburial. Rabbi Ephraim Oshry of Kovno ruled that whoever moved the body of a Holocaust victim to a Jewish cemetery did so for the deceased's honor and therefore performed a great service.[95] Both the floral decorations and the musical accompaniment of the funeral procession were contrary to Jewish funeral practices.[96] It may have been that the organizers were secular Jews who had adopted non-Jewish funereal rites, but it is also likely that they were motivated by the desire to speak in a symbolic form comprehensible to Germans. The report of the Tirschenreuth Jewish Committee expressed great satisfaction with the effects of the flowers and music, commenting that, "The procession made an exceptionally deep impression on the entire German population."[97] Indeed, the procession appears to have been designed with the Germans in mind.

As the vice president of the Tirschenreuth Jewish Committee stated at the graveside later that day, "Our procession ... today has once again brought sharply before the eyes of the German population of this district how the Hitler regime dealt with innocent people. It is a belated honor, a belated rehabilitation for the Jews who did no wrong and were forced to give up their lives simply for their faith, for holding fast to the traditions of their fathers. But it is the survivors' tribute for that silent martyrdom, that silent heroism; it is an admonition to Germany to acknowledge finally the infamy of the past and finally to find the path to true tolerance."[98] The Jewish Committee of Tirschenreuth sought to honor the dead in a way that would be comprehensible to the German

---

[94] "Kuturbericht für Monat August 1946."

[95] See Irving J. Rosenbaum, *The Holocaust and Halakhah* (New York: Ktav Publishing, 1976), p. 144.

[96] Traditionally, funerals are to be simple, "without excessive show." Memorial gifts of charity or of religious objects to the synagogue are considered more appropriate and enduring than flowers. See Michael Asheri, *Living Jewish: The Lore and Law of the Practicing Jew*, 2nd edition (New York: Everest House, 1978), p. 110; Lamm, *Death and Mourning*, p. 75.

[97] Slomnicki, "Bericht," YV M-1/P-74.

[98] Josef Kohs, "Rede des 2. Vorsitzenden des Jüdischen Komitees Tirschenreuth Josef Kohs Gehalten anläßlich der Bestattung von 39 KZ-Häftlingen in Floß," 20 August 1946, YV M-1/P-74.

population and that would instruct them in the innocence of the dead and in German culpability for their deaths.

The ultimate goal was to lead Germans onto the paths of remorse and tolerance, but in reality reburials create a community of mourners that excludes others. Verdery states that "a (re)burial creates an audience of 'mourners' all of whom think they have some relation to the dead person,"[99] and in the case of death march victims all Jews, regardless of national origin and wartime experiences, identified themselves as mourners. But even though the Jewish organizers spoke to the German observers, they did not perceive the Germans as mourners. They spoke to them as perpetrators. The Germans also understood themselves to be outside the community of mourners and resented the accusations made against them. While the survivors succeeded in fulfilling their religious obligations to the dead, their hopes of making a lasting impression on the people of the Bavarian region of Oberpfalz went unrealized.

In the spring of 1950, the International Tracing Service made inquiries about the origin of the mass grave in Floß. On March 3, 1950, Mayor Lehner replied that thirty-one or thirty-two former Jewish concentration camp inmates had died on a march. They were reburied on August 20, 1946 in a mass grave in the Jewish cemetery in Floß. It was not known if they were foreigners or Germans, but they had been previously buried in Poppenreuth II and Lengenfeld II (in the Tirschenreuth area). Only two months later, on May 2, 1950, in response to a request for further information, Lehner wrote that the reburial had dealt with precisely thirty-one dead but "more details cannot be provided since the transfer was conducted by the Jewish successor organization. There are no documents here! Even the day of the burial is unknown. Possibly the Jewish Cultural Community of Tirschenreuth [isr. Kultusgemeinde Tirschenreuth] has more data."[100] The official's displeasure at having to deal with the mass grave was evident.

Mayor Lehner's reply emphasized how little the grave meant to the people of Floß. First the date of the burial was forgotten. The town had no documents concerning the event. Indeed, even the Landrat who participated in the procession did not mention it in his weekly report.[101] Perhaps the Jewish community in Tirschenreuth knew more. If we need more evidence of the willful ignorance in the response, the International Tracing Service discovered that a survivor who had participated in the reburial resided in Floß. Oskar Rosenberg must have

99 Vedery, *Political Lives*, p. 108.

100 Lehner to Schrem, reference no. L9, Archiv KZ-Gedenkstätte Flossenbürg (AGFl), Signatur A290.

101 Otto Freundl, "Politischer Wochenbericht 16.8. bis 22.8.1946," Staatsarchiv Amberg (StAA), OMGBy 9/73–3/29. To complicate matters, military government records mistakenly identify Flossenbürg as the location of the cemetery. Flossenbürg was the destination of the death march, and since Floß was such a small community, it is not surprising that someone would type the nearby and more notorious place name of Flossenbürg. See Lieutenant Colonel R. M. Connolly, to Major Emmerick, 15 August 1946; Refugees; General Records of Tirschenreuth Resident Liaison and Security Office, 1945–49; Records of Field Operations Division; OMGUS, RG 260, Entry Bavaria; NACP; Military Government Liaison & Security Office Det. D-277, "Historical Report for the Month of August 1946," StAA, OMGBy 9/73–3/25.

been known to all in the small community of Floß as a Jewish survivor. The last of the Jewish DPs to remain in Floß after 1949, he had established a very successful business with the assistance of a German insider at the lumberyard.[102] It took outside prompting to motivate Floß officials to interview him. As it was, Rosenberg could only recall the general outlines of the event, identifying the dead as having been previously buried in the proximity of Tirschenreuth. And the town continued its forgetting.[103]

Not remembering the origins of the mass grave, the residents of Floß then invented a new explanation for it. In April 1945 Allied bombers had attacked a train near Floß carrying prisoners from Flossenbürg concentration camp, resulting in some dead.[104] With the true origin of the mass grave no longer known, the assumption grew that the grave contained the remains of those killed by Allied bombs. The terror of the bombings engraved the event in German memories unlike the peaceful, and forgettable, funeral procession the following year. Also, such an origin helped to exculpate the local community. Yes, the dead were concentration camp victims, but they were killed by the Allies in an accident of war not by Nazi genocidal policies. At one point it was even suggested that the dead were Soviet prisoners, not Jews at all.[105] By rewriting the history of the mass grave in the Jewish cemetery, the residents of Floß were able to distance themselves from genocide. Floß had had an active Nazi party presence since 1923 and was the hometown of the last commandant of Auschwitz.[106] Thus, in the period of denazification, the population of Floß had reason to minimize its connection to German mistreatment of the Jews. The residents also erased the shame-inducing memory of the funeral procession that both highlighted the alliance of U.S. occupation forces with Jews and humbled German officials who followed behind the coffins. Jewish and American hopes that the procession would educate the German public and lead to German remorse and repentance resulted instead in German humiliation and forgetting.

Settling Scores in Neunburg vorm Wald

Approximately one month after the dead were reburied in Floß, a Jewish DP in Neunburg vorm Wald, 35 miles south of Floß, reported that his German girlfriend had told him about a mass grave of death march victims in nearby woods. On Saturday, September 28, 1946, the local MGO, Capt. Dudley Field, ordered U.S. Army Constabulary Troops to guard the site in preparation for

---

[102] Oskar-Asher Rosenberg, "Videotaped interview," VHA, IC 26785, Segs. 94–99.
[103] Perhaps it is more than coincidence that passengers on a train from Weiden to Floß began a blood libel rumor in 1947. See Stern, *Whitewashing*, 145.
[104] A survivor of a train bombed in Floß by Americans put the date in March 1945. Once the Americans realized it was a prison transport, they took out the engine and left the passengers alone. Julius Lefkowitz, "Videotaped interview," VHA, IC 18772, Segs. 18–19.
[105] Johannes Ibel, letter to author, 28 December 2005.
[106] Renate Höpfinger, "Die jüdische Gemeinde von Floß," in *Die Juden in der Oberpfalz*, eds. Michael Brenner and Renate Höpfinger (Munich: Oldenbourg Wissenschaftsverlag, 2009), p. 100.

an exhumation.[107] On Monday, September 30, twelve former Nazis, under orders of the mayor on behalf of the military government,[108] began opening the grave. When they discovered more bodies than anticipated, another twenty former Nazis were ordered to the site. Public Safety Officer for the Military Government Lieutenant Honour ordered the town's residents to view the decomposed remains that very afternoon.[109] The former Nazis were ordered to return to the gravesite the next morning. On Tuesday, October 1, 1946, assaults occurred against German civilians. Jewish displaced persons rounded up local men, including many shopkeepers, to prepare the exhumed bodies for burial. While approximately 90 Germans cleaned the badly decomposed bodies of debris, another 100 or so Germans were forced to search for additional graves.[110] Germans complained that they were repeatedly kicked and beaten with sticks by Jews, Poles, and American soldiers.[111]

The violent confrontation during the exhumation of death march victims in Neunburg vorm Wald opens another window onto the triangular relations of Germans, Americans, and Jews. By autumn 1946 tensions were rising between residents of Neunburg vorm Wald and Jewish DPs. The Germans viewed themselves as being generous hosts to Jewish DPs who were not sufficiently grateful for their treatment. The director of the *Landpolizei* lauded the humane treatment local residents had shown death march prisoners even at the risk of their own safety. He also offered an example of German humanitarianism and Jewish ingratitude: The dentist Dr. Birk had offered free dental service to any survivor who had requested it but, he falsely reported, the dentist was repaid with fatal injuries during the exhumation.[112] In addition to supposed ingratitude, local

---

[107] Captain Charles W. Lutman, "Report of Incident," to Commanding Officer, 8th Constabulary Squadron (Attn S-2), 9 October 1946, p. 1; Troops and German National Incidents; The Public Safety Branch: Records Relating to Displaced Persons Camps 1945–49; CAD; OMGUS, RG 260; NACP.

[108] Mayor of Neunburg vorm Wald to Josef Elsner, 29 September 1946, AGFl, Signatur A963.

[109] F. Reichold (Bezirks-Inspektor, Landpolizei), record of telephone conversation with Mr. Eick of the Neunburg vorm Wald Military Government, 30 September 1946, AGFl, Signatur A963.

[110] Lutman, "Report of Incident," (Attn S-2), 9 October 1946, p. 2. At the end of the war in Schwarzenfeld, 20 kilometers northeast of Neunburg v.W., American soldiers ordered residents to wash and clothe corpses that were exhumed three days after their initial burial. It is not clear whether the constabulary troops issued similar orders in 1946 for Neunburgers to cleanse the bodies or whether Germans made the charge based on remembered reports of the Schwarzenfeld reburial. On Schwarzenfeld, see Katrin Greiser, "Die Todesmärsche von Buchenwald: Räumung des Lagerkomplexes im Frühjahr 1945 und Spuren der Erinnerung" (Ph.D. diss., Universität Lüneburg, 2007), p. 339, http://kirke.ub.uni-lueneburg.de/volltexte/2007/414/pdf/Dissertation.pdf, accessed 1 January 2008.

[111] Inspector of Rural Police Böck, Report (Copy), 4 October 1946; Troops and German National Incidents; The Public Safety Branch: Records Relating to Displaced Persons Camps 1945–49; CAD; OMGUS, RG 260; NACP.

[112] Freiherr von Godin, "Excesses against the German Population on Occasion of the Digging Out of Corpses in the Forest near Neunburg v.W.," to Office of Military Government for Bavaria, Ref. Nr. 547/46 Crim. Dept., 5 October 1946; Troops and German National Incidents; The Public Safety Branch: Records Relating to Displaced Persons Camps 1945–49; CAD; OMGUS, RG 260; NACP.

Germans blamed the Jews for black market activity, viewing them as destroyers of the German economy.[113]

As for the exhumation itself, Germans were outraged that leading citizens who had not been Nazi party members or who had been cleared by a denazification tribunal were among those forced to exhume bodies and to search the woods for additional graves. These complaints implied that while major Nazi figures bore responsibility for crimes committed in Germany's name, exonerated small-time Nazis and fellow-travelers should have been exempted. In this view, U.S. Army Constabulary troopers had failed to uphold the rules of denazification. Postwar Germans often felt themselves to be the victims of inequitable denazification rules,[114] and the irregularities at the gravesite confirmed their sentiments.

A second major complaint was that the U.S. soldiers had not implemented sanitary procedures for the exhumation. Germans used shovels until the bodies were revealed and then they were required to use their bare hands for the rest of the work. Witnesses contrasted this experience to the first exhumation and reburial in Neunburg vorm Wald on April 29, 1945. At that time, Nazis exhumed the bodies, but with the young men still at war, local women were among the pallbearers. Those who had participated then had mixed reactions to their experience. A few accepted responsibility for crimes that had been committed in their name, but many felt victimized, forced into gruesome labor because of someone else's criminal behavior.[115] It is also quite likely that the townspeople considered themselves absolved of guilt through their participation in the reburial of April 1945, heightening their sense of victimization at being forced to repeat their roles in 1946.[116] Thus, even before the physical assaults that took place on October 1, 1946, the local populace had felt victimized by the requirement to view the badly decomposed remains the day before.

For Jewish DPs the picture looked somewhat different. Those who had been in Neunburg vorm Wald since fall 1945 could recall the local mayor granting them permission to rebury some Jewish remains in a corner of the town cemetery. Exhuming the bodies themselves, the Jews transported them on blankets to the new burial site.[117] But by late summer 1946, Jewish survivors fleeing pogroms in Eastern Europe were crossing the Czech border into Germany. They had not experienced the kindnesses of Neunburg vorm Wald. The president of the DP community, Mr. Neumann, blamed many of these newcomers for the violence. In addition, many of the Jewish DPs found themselves facing discrimination from local shopkeepers. Grocers refused service to DPs on the grounds that UNRRA was supposed to provide their rations. If they had the means to

---

[113] Mayor Ettl, "Angelegenheit der Unruhen und Massnahmen gegen jüdische Bevölkerung," to Philipp Auerbach, Bavarian State Commissioner for Victims of Fascism, 15 October 1946, AGFl, Signatur A965.

[114] Norbert Frei, *1945 und Wir* (Munich: Verlag C.H. Beck, 2005), p. 68.

[115] Todd Richissin, "The Road to Neunburg," *The Sun* (Baltimore, MD), 1 May 2005.

[116] On exhumation as a cathartic event, see Greiser, "Die Todesmärsche von Buchenwald," p. 346.

[117] Joseph Sher, interview by John Menszer.

purchase something in the grocery, then Germans thought it must be ill-gotten gain from the black market. The barber required Jews to provide their own soap and towels, an antisemitic insult.[118] These everyday offenses certainly help to explain why DPs dragooned so many shopkeepers into exhuming bodies and why those Germans who may not have been official Nazi party members but who had discriminated against Jews would have been targeted by DPs. It was not only the crimes of the Holocaust that the DPs sought to punish, but also the poor treatment of Jews in the postwar period.

The image of the benevolent German attacked by the ungrateful Jew is further challenged by the fate of Dr. Birk, the dentist. Dr. Birk had been a small-time Nazi party member who had probably been denounced. Rosa Hastreiter, a city employee, testified that a young Jewish boy had repeatedly kicked Dr. Birk as he knelt by a coffin at the exhumation site. The boy punctuated each kick with, "one for my father, one for my mother, one for my brother, one for my sister," at which point Dr. Birk turned around and asked, "didn't you also have a grandmother once?"[119] One must consider whether Dr. Birk's free dental service to survivors was simply a ploy to gain character witnesses for denazification purposes. And contrary to the report of the Landpolizei, Dr. Birk did not die of his wounds but continued to practice dentistry in Neunburg vorm Wald, dying in 1968.

Desire for revenge, both for Nazi crimes of the Holocaust and for the indignities of antisemitic treatment by local Germans afterwards, motivated the survivors in their physical assaults on these particular German men. The ferocity of the attacks can be attributed to the participation of Jews new to the area who felt little compunction to get along with local residents, as well as to the behavior of U.S. soldiers that signaled a willingness to tolerate mistreatment of Germans. Now we must turn our attention to the U.S. Army Constabulary Troopers who were charged with maintaining order in Neunburg vorm Wald during the exhumation and reburial.

A partial explanation for the troopers' dereliction of duty can be found in the history of the constabulary itself. Its mission was to provide police services in occupied Germany, including securing the borders, quelling insurgency, and fighting the black market. The U. S. Army Constabulary School opened in March 1946, and in July 1946 the constabulary assumed its responsibilities. Thus, the constabulary had only been fully operational for three months before the Neunburg vorm Wald incident.

Although the military's goal was to create an elite force, redeployments depleted units.[120] Many of the soldiers were on their first overseas tour of duty, serving in remote locations with little supervision. As one military historian has

---

[118] Ettl, "Angelegenheit der Unruhen," to Auerbach, 15 October 1946.

[119] Rosa Hastreiter, quoted by archivist Christa Scheitinger, letter to author, 27 July 2006.

[120] The constabulary suffered a 100 percent personnel turnover rate in 1946 and 1947. Kendall D. Gott, *Mobility, Vigilance, and Justice: The U.S. Army Constabulary in Germany, 1946–1953* (Ft. Leavenworth, KS: Combat Studies Institute Press, 2005), p. 15.

observed, "Discipline posed a critical threat to the constabulary's effectiveness from day one of its operations."[121] Indeed, indiscipline rates among the constabulary were higher than among other troops.[122] The alliance of the troopers with the Jewish DPs was not a foregone conclusion, however, since the constabulary's anti–black market activity frequently targeted Jews and created an antisemitic atmosphere concerning assumptions about Jewish criminality.[123]

In Neunburg vorm Wald, lax supervision of the soldiers combined with rapidly changing conditions contributed to the indiscipline. The 8th Constabulary Squadron's commander, Captain Lutman, visited the exhumation site only once, on Tuesday morning before the assaults occurred, snapping a few photographs before leaving.[124] Neunburgers complained about American soldiers taking pictures of their grisly work, something reminiscent of trophy photographs taken during the war. Thus the commander's visit apparently did little to reinforce discipline among his troops while it increased the Germans' sense of mistreatment.

The inexperience of local military government officers also contributed to the confusion and later chaos. Uncertain of what course to take, the military government officer, Captain Field, and the public safety officer, Lieutenant Honour, both consulted with headquarters in Regensburg. It was after one such consultation on Monday, September 30, that Lieutenant Honour decided to order the town to view the remains by that afternoon. Loudspeakers notified the civilians that their presence at the exhumation site was obligatory. The hurried nature of the order and the fact that most Neunburgers had already witnessed at least one prior exhumation only increased German resentment of their treatment. Forced viewings of corpses left Germans feeling unjustly accused of collective guilt.[125] The behavior of the constabulary troopers, detaining some men without cause and placing them under guard while forcing others to view the bodies repeatedly, foreshadowed the abuse that was to come the next day.

Perhaps in an attempt to discredit the Landrat who had been responsible for lodging complaints in Regensburg against his men, Captain Lutman reported, "this Landrat has upon several cases proven himself to be uncooperative and in my opinion is very pro-Nazi."[126] The poor working relationship between Lutman and the Landrat possibly reflected wider feelings of distrust between the American forces and the local population, contributing to the constabulary soldiers' hostility and the breakdown in discipline. It certainly

---

[121] Robert Cameron, "There and Back Again: Constabulary Training and Organization, 1946–1950," in *Armed Diplomacy: Two Centuries of American Campaigning* (Ft. Leavenworth, KS: Combat Studies Institute Press, 2003), p. 125.

[122] Cameron, "There and Back," in *Armed Diplomacy*, p. 128.

[123] Brian Arthur Libby, *Policing Germany: The United States Constabulary, 1946–1952* (Ph.D. diss., Purdue University, 1977), p. 8.

[124] Lutman, "Report of Incident," (Attn S-2), 9 October 1946, p. 2.

[125] Frei, *1945 und Wir*, p. 147.

[126] Captain Charles W. Lutman, "Report of Incident," to Commanding Officer, 8th Constabulary Squadron (Attn S-3), 9 October 1946, p. 1; Troops and German National Incidents; The Public

explains why the Landrat did not immediately report the incident to Lutman but went instead to the regional government in Regensburg. The fiction of the military government working with the mayor, maintained by the mayor issuing orders on behalf of the military government, was exposed by the mayor's absence from the exhumation site except when the Americans ordered him to be present.

Lutman went on to observe that "after talking to the Landrat it is the opinion of the undersigned that the people are angry about having to dig these dead Jews up and view the remains and, knowing that higher Headquarters is interested figure it is a good chance to get a little revenge and exaggerating their own stories."[127] Again this passage could have been intended to exculpate his men, but it also contains truth. The Germans were resentful and did exaggerate the wounds they received that day. At the same time, the town had been terrorized and the victims had the right to demand justice.

In an apparent attempt to discredit further the exhumation and reburial in Neunburg vorm Wald, the Landpolizei inspector reported that the presumption that the corpses were concentration camp inmates had come from the testimony of "a Neunburg Jew."[128] In fact, the military government officers reported that a number of Jewish survivors of the death march had taken this position. It is clear that the inspector found this testimony insufficient. Recent research by historian Omer Bartov shows that Jewish survivor testimonies were often discounted as unreliable in German courts, so Inspector Böck's misgivings were not uncommon.[129]

Casting further doubt on the Jewishness of the dead, Böck described the original grave as deep, straw and stones placed between the layers of bodies, and the corpses neatly interred. Since the SS would not have taken the time to bury their victims in such a fashion, the reader begins to doubt. Next Böck reported that "One of the dead wore army top-boots, another breeches, another a field-jacket and a gray army-pullover. The parts of uniforms were in a good state and looked pretty new. One of the dead wore mountainshoes...several others wore army lace-up boots. At one a soldier's newspaper (German) has been found. At another one a dictionary English-French, and at another a notebook with pencil has been found. Who took this [sic] items couldn't be stated hitherto."[130] The implication is that these were soldiers, partisans, spies, or a combination thereof that died in combat. Their deaths, therefore, were legitimate within the rules of

Safety Branch: Records Relating to Displaced Persons Camps 1945–49; CAD; OMGUS, RG 260; NACP.

[127] Lutman, "Report of Incident," (Attn S-3), p. 2.

[128] Böck, Report (Copy), 4 October 1946, p. 1.

[129] Omer Bartov, "Guilt and Accountability in the Postwar Courtroom: The Holocaust in Czortków and Buczacz, East Galicia as Seen in West German Legal Discourse," in "Repairing the Past: Confronting the Legacies of Slavery, Genocide and Caste," Yale University, October 27–29, 2005, http://yale.edu/glc/justice/bartov.pdf, accessed 5 July 2007.

[130] Böck, Report (Copy), 4 October 1946, p. 2.

warfare, and they had been buried accordingly. Or so the police inspector and his anonymous sources would like us to believe.

The complete absence of physical evidence undercuts the inspector's efforts to cast doubt on the origin of the corpses. He does not identify the source/s for these assertions nor does he explain why they should be given credence.[131] There is no mention of weapons being found. Although bodies were reportedly wearing pieces of uniforms, not one is described as being in full uniform. The lack of specificity concerning the national origin of the uniforms is also of interest.[132] There is nothing reported that would compel a further investigation into the identity of those in the grave. No evidence is given that would encourage Allied personnel to seek to retrieve their own dead or that would warrant a further German investigation and exhumation. The report contains just enough innuendo to create confusion and to cast doubt on the Jewishness of the victims in the mass grave without stating an alternate identity that could be verified or disproved.[133]

U.S. military government documents do not question the identity of the dead. Neunburg DPs held a Jewish funeral service for the dead on Thursday, October 3, 1945, attesting to their belief in the Jewishness of the dead. Photos of the exhumed bodies show striped concentration camp uniforms and articles of civilian clothing.[134] The inspector and his informants undoubtedly hoped to discredit both the Americans and the Jewish DPs with their insinuations concerning the deceased. By suggesting that the dead were military combatants, the townspeople could distance themselves from the taint of genocide and could portray themselves as unjustly painted with the brush of collective guilt and as the victims of Jewish and American hostility.

The injustice of the occupation also seems to have driven German interpretations of events. Just as Jewish DPs sought to identify themselves with the occupying powers, so too did the Germans associate Jews with the occupation. While the Jewish DPs had complaints about the German population, the Germans had their own complaints about the occupation. Powerless to confront the American military government, Neunburgers took their frustration out on the weaker Jewish DPs. Mayor Ettl defended the antisemitic practices of local shopkeepers to the Bavarian State Commissioner for the Victims of Fascism, Philip Auerbach. Shopkeepers were allowed to differentiate between customers if they so wished, he argued. He charged that Jews had no business

---

[131] If the grave was indeed as orderly as reported, then it is possible that the dead were buried by liberating American forces as they passed through the area. There is at least one example in the Neunburg v. Wald area of U.S. soldiers taking the initiative to bury the dead. Richissin, "Road to Neunburg."

[132] If individuals were wearing pieces of uniforms, perhaps they were POWs or partisans. Finally, despite the indiscipline of the constabulary troopers, it is unlikely that they would not have noticed that the deceased were military combatants had that been the case.

[133] My thanks to Doris L. Bergen for this insight into the ambiguity of the document.

[134] Photographs reproduced in Claudia Rester, "Die Todesmärsche von Flossenbürg und ihre Auswirkungen auf Neunburg v.W." (Facharbeit, 1987), p. 24, in Stadtarchiv Neunburg v.W.

in local grocery stores since UNRRA catered to their needs. If they had money with which to purchase something, then it must be the product of black market activity. On the surface, Ettl appears to be repeating old antisemitic stereotypes of Jewish avariciousness and economic exploitation. As a non-Nazi, Ettl may have felt free to express such opinions, since, as historian Anthony Kauders has argued, "personal 'innocence' licensed people to cultivate prejudices they had accepted a long time ago."[135] But beneath the traditional antisemitism there is a subtext that reveals animosity toward the occupation. Jews received goods from UNRRA and were under the jurisdiction of Allied authorities who failed to control the black market. Germans resented the Jews' proximity to the authorities and their easy access to luxury items such as coffee and cigarettes that gave them an unfair advantage (so the Germans believed) in barter exchange and the black market. From this perspective, Germans played by the rules of occupation and suffered, while Jews benefited from their close relations with the occupying powers.

Tensions may also have been raised by the gender ratio in the two communities. Early in the war the population of Neunburg numbered around 2,300, but by May 1945 that number had increased to 4,480, of whom 1,160 were German wartime evacuees and 820 were former concentration camp inmates.[136] Neunburg v.W. had lost 158 men in the war;[137] others were still in prisoner of war camps, leaving German women with limited options for partners among German men. The DP who reported the mass grave had learned about it from his German girlfriend. He was not alone in finding female companionship among the local population.

In 1946 Neunburg had a population of 181 Jewish DPs: 114 men, 49 women, and 18 children.[138] Even if all of the Jewish women paired with a Jewish man, that left 65 young men without a female mate. Even if not all 65 were interested in women or romance, it still left a sizeable number potentially seeking available German women. Neunburg v. W. reportedly saw a number of Jewish–German romances that led to marriage.[139] Germans uncomfortable with outsiders keeping company with "their" women may have felt that Jewish men had an unfair advantage because of their access to American luxury items that would appeal to the women and make the Jewish men attractive mates.

Neunburgers also resented the material aid that they had been forced to provide the survivors. Local women had trained as Red Cross aides, and U.S.

---

[135] Anthony D. Kauders, *Democratization and the Jews* (Lincoln: University of Nebraska Press for the Vidal Sassoon International Center for the Study of Antisemitism, the Hebrew University of Jerusalem, 2004), p. 111.

[136] "Vor 28 Jahren wehte auf dem Neunburger Kirchturm die weiße Fahne," *Neunburger Anzeiger*, Easter edition 1973.

[137] Thomas Rettelbach, "Die Beleiterscheinungen des Zuges der Häftlinge des Konzentrationslagers Flossenbürg durch Neunburg vorm Wald im April 1945" (Facharbeit, Regental-Gymnasium Nittenau, 1988), p.3, in Stadtarchiv Neunburg v.W.

[138] "Population in Oberpfalz," YIVO RG 294.2, MK 483, Microfilm reel 63, Folder 888.

[139] Rettelbach, "Beleiterscheinungen des Zuges der Häftlinge," p. 16.

military forces put them to work nursing the liberated concentration camp inmates. Physically exhausted from the labor and often ill treated by their patients, the women were also expected to cook food for the patients. Finally, a local woman proposed that healthy survivors be recruited to cook for the others, and the Americans agreed. This freed the townswomen to cook for the German prisoners of war at a nearby camp.

Without adequate clothing and supplies for the liberated survivors, the soldiers in the area looked the other way or even provided escorts on June 16, 1945, when French and Polish former prisoners of war along with some former concentration camp inmates plundered Neunburg and other towns. The action followed certain rules of engagement. Homes of Red Cross nurses, concentration camp survivors, and Americans were spared. Known Nazis and Nazi sympathizers were targeted. The most sought-after items: men's suits and underwear. Citizens reported to the town that, among other things, 154 suits, 96 trousers, and 62 heavy jackets had been taken. Clearly the survivors were not plundering for luxury items or great personal gain. Still, the presence of thieving strangers, often in the company of armed occupation soldiers, unnerved the villagers and they experienced it as an unwarranted attack.

Significantly, the day of the raid was the same day that the Americans finally removed the wartime mayor from office and arrested him as a Nazi.[140] Hans Ettl, a former member of the Bavarian Peoples Party, was then appointed mayor, a post he later won in election on January 27, 1946. Denazification had been accompanied by officially sanctioned lawlessness. Later the Landrat, Erich Braun, announced that Germans were to voluntarily hand over items for distribution to DPs so that further looting could be avoided. The Germans kept careful records of every item handed over. Decades later, the Neunburger newspaper included itemized lists and the value of the donated goods in its articles commemorating the war's end.[141] Clearly local German resentment toward the American forces and their DP dependents seethed below the surface.

The Tirschenreuth-Floß and Neunburg v.W. exhumations and reburials in 1946 appear on the surface to be different in their impact on the German population and yet upon closer examination are remarkably similar. The orderliness of the Tirschenreuth-Floß events can be attributed to the careful planning and leadership of Captain Mariels and the Jewish Committee of Tirschenreuth. The mayhem committed in Neunburg vorm Wald can be ascribed to the rising tensions in the town between Jews and Germans, as well as to the poor planning and leadership of the American officers. The initial failure to secure sufficient German labor to open the grave along with the last-minute orders for

[140] Gunther Wiesneth, "Das Ende des Zweiten Weltkrieges in Neunburg vorm Wald" (Facharbeit, Robert-Schumann-Gymnasium Cham, n.d.), p. 209, in Stadtarchiv Neunburg v.W.
[141] "Vor 28 Jahren wehte auf dem Neunburger Kirchturm die weiße Fahne," *Neunburger Anzeiger*, Easter edition 1973; "So erlebte Neunburg vorm Wald das Ende des 2. Weltkriegs," *Neunburger Anzeiger*, 19/20 April 1975.

the assembly of the civilian population created a chaotic situation that allowed emotions to overflow, ultimately culminating in the beatings.

For the Jews, these reburials provided opportunities for revenge. In the Tirschenreuth-Floß case, it took the nonviolent form of humiliation. The former Nazis forced to exhume the mass grave performed their disgrace. The German population was humbled as, under orders from the occupation forces, it paid respects to the concentration camp inmates it had feared and reviled. Revenge took a more physical form in Neunburg vorm Wald as DPs took out their rage and frustration on former Nazis and on those they deemed antisemites. The obverse side of revenge was the restoration of dignity to the Jewish dead. Both through the performance of Jewish ritual and through the required German respects paid to the dead, the DPs sought to reclaim their honor.

What is striking is that both events, designed to reeducate Germans and to restore the dignity of Jewish victims of Nazism, provided opportunities for German forgetting and denial. Some Germans referred to an "expiatory burial" (*Sühnebegräbnis*) or an act of atonement (*Sühnemassnahme*), demonstrating their belief that participation in an exhumation or reburial removed all guilt from them, making it unnecessary to work through the past.[142] Through reburials Germans transformed themselves into suffering victims of the cruel occupiers and brutal foreigners, reclaiming some of the moral superiority that war, crimes, and defeat had discredited.[143] Feeling unjustly painted with the brush of collective guilt, they could shove aside the question of their personal guilt.[144] The alliance of postwar German officials with the U.S. military government was revealed as superficial in these cases. In Floß and in Neunburg vorm Wald there were those who sought to portray the dead as the victims of war, not victims of genocidal German policies. In these versions, neither the residents of Floß nor of Neunburg v. W. bore direct responsibility for the loss of life. In their efforts to deflect responsibility for Nazi crimes, the villagers of Floß found a plausible alternative history to the mass grave in their town that placed the blame on Allied bombers, while some former Nazis forced to exhume a grave in Neunburg v. W. sought to deny the innocence of the dead by implying that they were in fact combatants. In both cases, German officials exhibited exasperation with American authorities. Since their positions depended on cooperation with the military government officers, these German officials ultimately repressed their resentment. Local populations found it easier to take out their frustration on Jewish DPs than to confront the occupation forces directly.

The breakdown in order that occurred in Neunburg v. W. led the U.S. military government to launch a full-scale investigation that resulted in criminal prosecutions of DPs and a soldier, disciplinary actions against soldiers and military

[142] Greiser, "Die Todesmärsche von Buchenwald," p. 357.

[143] Alex d'Erizans, "The Stranger Within: German Confrontation with Nazism amidst Catastrophe and Fragmentation in Hanover, 1945–48" (paper presented at the German Studies Association Annual Meeting, Pittsburgh, PA, September 29, 2006), p. 14.

[144] Frei, *1945 und Wir*, p. 154.

government officers, and a change in regulations concerning exhumations and reinterments. After Neunburg vorm Wald, the military government declared that "the procedure of forcing German civilians to view the remains of disinterred bodies no longer has any educational or disciplinary value and may well result in adverse criticism of United States policies and practices."[145] Reburials would henceforth be conducted only under the supervision of Land Offices of Military Government.

The residents of Neunburg v.W. did receive justice in the U.S. military government courts with the convictions of a DP and disciplinary action against U.S. soldiers, which may have helped to restore the honor of American democracy. Meanwhile, the mayor of Neunburg vorm Wald had learned the lesson that, officially at least, Jews had to be accorded fair treatment. On the same day that he defended the antisemitic practices of local shopkeepers to the Bavarian State Commissioner for the Victims of Fascism, Mayor Ettl ordered Neunburger shopkeepers to treat politically and racially persecuted customers the same as the general population.[146] The philosemitism that would characterize postwar German officialdom got a turbulent start in Neunburg vorm Wald.

IN THE NAME OF THE DEAD

Public commemorations provided DPs with opportunities for eulogies and speeches. DP political and religious leaders took to the podiums, and they spoke in the name of the dead. The message was consistent: The dead wanted the survivors to rebuild Jewish life, but this was no longer possible in Europe. Only in a Jewish homeland, they said, could Jewish life flourish (Figure 3).

Yizkor provided opportunities for commemorative words. On Yom Kippur 1945, DP leader Samuel Gringauz spoke at Landsberg. He altered the traditional notion of martyrdom for the sanctification of God's name to the sanctification of the nation. "All of you, Jewish children and women, Jewish rabbis and Jewish leaders, Jewish workers and Jewish intellectuals, all of you fell to sanctify the nation. You have fallen because our dream for our own home was not realized – because the world did not want to recognize our holy right to our own home in our own land. And for this you fell to sanctify the Land."[147] Their blood did not sanctify the European lands where it was spilled but rather the Jewish home in the Land of Israel. A new, secular model of martyrdom had replaced the traditional one. The lesson of the Holocaust, according to Gringauz, was that only a Jewish state could protect the Jewish people from genocide.

While the survivors had designed the reburial procession from Tirschenreuth to Floß to speak to a German audience, the ceremony at the graveside was for

---

[145] Brigadier General C. K. Gailey, "Exhumation of Bodies of Nazi Victims," AG 333.5, December 1946; Troops and German National Incidents; The Public Safety Branch: Records Relating to Displaced Persons Camps 1945–49; CAD; OMGUS, RG 260; NACP.

[146] Ettl, "Anglegenheit der Unruhen," to Auerbach, 15 October 1946; "Bekanntmachung: Behandlung von politisch und rassisch Verfolgten," 15 October 1946, AGFl, Signatur A965.

[147] Samuel Gringauz, "Jizker," *Landsberger Lager Cajtung*, 8 October 1945, p. 3.

FIGURE 3. Jewish DPs commemorate the death march from Dachau to Tyrol and protest British immigration policy to Palestine at the Mittenwald DP camp, May 4, 1947. *Credit*: USHMM, courtesy of Aviva Kempner

the 800 survivors who had accompanied the coffins. The coffins were placed in the ground and a minute of silence was observed for the six million Jewish dead. A cantor from Hof sang the memorial prayer for the dead, *El Malei Rachamim*. Various officials offered words of empathy and solace. An elderly Jew, a rarity among the survivors, led the assembled mourners and dignitaries in *Kaddish*. The singing of the Zionist anthem, "Hatikvah," which concluded the service, followed the mourner's prayer. The combination of the mourner's prayer with the Zionist song echoed the speech that had been offered by the vice president of the Tirschenreuth Jewish Community:

For us the death of these Jews shall be a warning and reminder, a guidepost and a guiding principle for the future of a new Judaism, for the future of our children. We want to identify our errors through the sorrows of the past and to learn from our mistakes. We know that only those nations are respected who have their own land; that only those nations are respected who are strong enough to defend their security and freedom with their own land, and to earn the respect that every nation is due. ... Let us now take our leave from our brothers with the vow, never to remain in Europe, the part of the earth where our fathers experienced so many and unheard of persecutions, the part of the world that is soaked through and through with Jewish blood, dampened millions of times by Jewish tears. Let us be a true union of brothers forged together by the fire of destruction, strong in faith in our own strength, and let us put all of our dreams and efforts, all of our talents to use in building our own land, our own home, so that we can erect on our own soil, our own ground, a secure future for our children and children's children ...[148]

The connection between the dead of Europe and the need for an independent homeland in Palestine was made explicit in this speech and demonstrated symbolically in the juxtaposition of *Kaddish* and "Hatikvah," the future anthem of

[148] Kohs, "Rede," YV M-1/P-74.

the State of Israel. Religious observance created a space for the performance of this ethnic identity and its political expression, Zionism.

Throughout the DP community, commemorations of the dead led to expressions of Zionism. On the occasion of the first anniversary of liberation, DPs at St. Ottilien published a one-time newspaper. Under the heading "Yizkor!" it proclaimed, "we vow to bind the spilled, innocent blood of our brothers and sisters with the eternal ideal of the Jewish people to create a free home in the Land of Israel."[149] As historian Zeev Mankowitz noted, "the creation of a Jewish state in the Land of Israel was taken to be the last will and testament bequeathed by the dead to the living. ... It signified the only real hope for the rescue and rehabilitation of the little that remained of European Jewry and, in the longer term, the promise of the Jewish future."[150] The sacrifice of the dead would not have been in vain if the survivors guaranteed the Jewish future by building the Jewish homeland.

Postwar Zionist politicians frequently pointed to the murdered Jews of Europe as evidence for the need for a Jewish state, but religious leaders also made similar connections.[151] The rabbi at a mourning academy in Dachau said, "May we who have made so many sacrifices soon inherit and possess our land."[152] In an announcement for the memorial service on the last day of Passover 1948, the Belsen DP rabbinate encouraged survivors to attend in order to commemorate not only "our dear parents, children, sisters, brothers who were murdered in the sanctification of God's Name by Nazi butchers," but also "the heroic fighters, the holy ones who daily fall in the Holy Land at the hands of various enemies, who want, God forbid, to deliver a death blow to the Yishuv and simultaneously the entire Jewish people."[153] In that crucial time between the U.N. vote for the partition of Palestine in November 1947 and the declaration of the State of Israel in May 1948, Jewish soldiers were engaged in frequent battles. The DPs understood their hopes for emigration depended on the soldiers' victory. For many DPs the fate of the Yishuv was the fate of the entire Jewish people. The announcement concluded, "Let us gather in order to pray to God in the image of the spilled blood of our sacrifices, so that we may be worthy of the merit of the holy deceased for final victory and complete redemption, may it be speedily in our day, Amen." The identification of European DPs with Jews in Palestine was expressed in this call to prayer, as was the connection between the Holocaust and the Zionist future.

Whatever the political convictions of Nazi victims had been in life, in death they were Zionists. While DPs protested any attempt to appropriate the dead for

---

[149] "Yizkor!" *St. Ottiliener Sztime*, 1 May 1946; YIVO RG 294.2, MK 483, Microfilm reel 113, Folder 1554.

[150] Mankowitz, *Life Between Memory and Hope*, p. 69.

[151] Gershon Greenberg, "From *Hurban* to Redemption: Orthodox Jewish Thought in the Munich Area, 1945–1948," *Simon Wiesenthal Center Annual* 6 (1989): 102.

[152] "Ajndruksfule trojer-akademje in Dachau," *Jidisze Cajtung*, 22 November 1946, p. 9.

[153] Bergen-Belsen Rabbinate, "Remember What Amalek Did to You" (in Yiddish), Intermediary days of Passover 5708 [April 1948], YV O-70/29.

a particular political party,[154] there was tacit agreement that the dead supported the movement of the survivors to the Land of Israel. Since dead people do not speak, it is easy for the living to put words in their mouths.[155] Yet the message must be a plausible one for it to resonate with the living. The vast majority of DPs, including DP Bundists who advocated life in the Diaspora, believed it necessary to leave Europe. While the Bundists considered Palestine one option among many, the message that DP leaders placed into the mouths of the dead was not so very different. Even many ultra-Orthodox Jews who had believed that a mass movement of Jews to the Land of Israel should occur only under the Messiah now argued that only in the Land of Israel could a Torah-based life be fully realized and joined with Zionists in demanding emmigration to Palestine.[156] No one objected to the Zionist interpretation of the will of the dead.[157] In death Jewish victims joined their voices into an eternal chorus for reconstructing Jewish life in a Jewish homeland.

CONCLUSION

Ritual observances for the dead had both personal and social significance for the survivors. The presence of deceased family members that was especially felt during *Yizkor* and rituals for commemorating the dead helped to revive the survivors' commitment to Jewish traditions. Participating in Jewish mourning rituals expressed the survivors' Jewish identity and reinforced it, linking DPs to their past and creating a promise to continue the Jewish people into the future. They later affirmed this through their Jewish weddings and the circumcisions of their sons.

Memorial services forged communities out of grieving individuals, providing opportunities to participate in common rituals and prayers. Mourning academies and the Day of Liberation ceremonies filled the calendar with regular dates on which to share memories of prewar and wartime experiences, creating social memories of the Holocaust that informed DP identity and integrated Jews of disparate backgrounds and experiences into a memory community. Public commemorations served the survivors' needs on a number of levels. Reburials on German soil evoked feelings of satisfaction that they had fulfilled Jewish obligations to the dead, restoring their dignity. Through reburials and commemorative events DPs reminded the occupying powers of their alliance against the common enemy of Nazism and of the Allies' moral obligation to aid the DPs' immigration to Palestine. In the British Zone, the connection to Palestine provoked the British and increased tensions between authorities and DPs. The messages given to the

---

[154] A mourning academy organized by Poale-Zion (C.S.) drew a protest that no party could lay claim to the victims. Letter to editors, *Landsberger Lager Cajtung*, 26 July 1946, p. 6.

[155] Verdery, *Political Lives*, p. 29.

[156] "1-te landes-konferenc fun Poalej-Agudas-Jisroel in Dajczland," *Jidisze Cajtung*, 24 January 1947, p. 8.

[157] Zertal rightly points out that Israel defined the dead millions "post factum (and unverifiably) as potential Zionists." That the survivors themselves made this claim suggests that the Israelis were

Germans were both accusatory (you murdered our comrades and persecuted us) and defiant (we are here).

Germans resented the accusations of guilt. Their forced participation in exhumations and reburials paradoxically facilitated their quest for absolution and contributed to the forgetting and denial of German crimes. The alliance of DPs and Allies made visible at commemorative events allowed Germans to displace their hostility toward the occupying powers onto the DPs. This may have been what Federal Republic President Theodor Heuss had in mind when he denounced the desecrations of Jewish cemeteries in 1949 as attempts to undermine West German democracy. Heuss, the West German moral conscience of the postwar period, did not believe the vandalism was aimed at Jews since there were so few in Germany. He argued that cemetery desecrations were "the conscious political hooliganism of persons who wish to endanger this state, and its position among the nations – a state where very few Jews are as yet active."[158] In fact, these attacks on Jewish cemeteries occurred at the moment when immigration opportunities finally existed so that German Jews and Jewish DPs had the opportunity to decide whether to emigrate or to remain in Germany.

Ironically for those who sought to drive the remaining Jews from Germany, some survivors argued that they needed to remain in Germany to fulfill their obligations to the dead and to commemorate the Holocaust.[159] For most survivors, however, the vandalism confirmed that Germans had not changed and fueled their anxiety about Jewish security in Germany. The Jewish dead continued to remind both Germans and Jews of the recent past, accusing the former and cautioning the latter not to remain on the blood-soaked soil.

---

not too far out of line when putting Zionist words into the mouths of the dead. Zertal, *Israel's Holocaust*, p. 61.

[158] Quoted in Stern, *Whitewashing*, p. 333.

[159] Lavsky, *New Beginnings*, p. 130.

3

The New Jewish Man and Woman

The reconstruction of Jewish life involved not only honoring the dead but also a reappraisal of what it meant to be Jewish men and Jewish women after Auschwitz. Nazi policies had upset Jewish gender roles and family relations even before the death camps went into operation. Men, deprived of jobs, humiliated, and physically assaulted, were unable to protect their families; women assumed previously masculine duties; women and girls became more vulnerable to sexual exploitation; children became both a source of support and a hindrance to their parents.[1] The physical ravages of years of persecution robbed Jewish bodies, especially female ones, of their secondary sex characteristics. Emaciated women lost the fat in their breasts and ceased menstruating. Jewish men were shaved of their beards and often experienced impotence. With the return of physical health, survivors rediscovered (or younger survivors discovered for the first time) their bodies' sex. Even as DP camp conditions and the desire for normalcy encouraged a restoration of prewar gendered divisions of labor, the experiences of persecution and the belief that they must remain mobilized for defense against the Germans and for war against the British in Palestine led DPs to adopt militant models of masculinity and femininity.

In the DP camps survivors formed a temporary society in which they shaped their ideas of gender, drawing on their individual and collective memories of prewar gender expectations, the lessons of the Holocaust, and the gender norms of the Allied officials who managed the DP camps. Living among their former tormentors forced DPs to consider the place of revenge in their reconstructed gender roles. Jewish men and women experienced strong desires to exact retribution from Germans. Although many did not act on those violent impulses, most DPs accepted that Jewish men had the duty to fight on behalf of the Jewish people, both in its defense and in revenge. The Zionist image of the physically

[1] See Renée Fodor, "The Impact of the Nazi Occupation of Poland on the Jewish Mother-Child Relationship," *YIVO Annual of Jewish Social Science*, 11 (1956/1957): 270–285; Marion Kaplan, *Between Dignity and Despair: Jewish Life in Nazi Germany* (New York: Oxford University Press, 1998); Dalia Ofer and Lenore J. Weitzman eds., *Women in the Holocaust* (New Haven, CT: Yale University Press, 1998).

strong and combative male dominated the DPs' sense of masculinity. In the immediate postliberation period DPs also considered Jewish women capable of fighting on behalf of the Jewish people, adopting a glorified image of sexually independent female partisans. What the survivors now viewed as the passivity of the ghetto Jew was replaced with the fighting heroism of resistance fighters, partisans, and Jewish Brigade soldiers from Palestine.

Once their physical health returned, DPs initially engaged in high levels of sexual activity, shocking aid workers and military personnel alike with what they interpreted as promiscuity. Soon, though, stable couples formed within the DP community, and rabbinic authorities encouraged marriage. Reproduction served as a form of revenge, an assertion of Jewish survival, but it also aroused survivors' fears. It brought back memories of German atrocities against Jewish mothers and children. Pregnancy and childbirth brought many Jewish women and infants into contact with German medical personnel, where they were victimized once again by lack of empathy, incompetence, and possibly even murderous intent.

DPs welcomed the arrival of children as symbols of continuity and the survival of the Jewish people. Baby boys provided opportunities for performing the ritual of circumcision that created community and transmitted Jewish culture. The demands of childrearing and memories of childhood family life encouraged the return to prewar gendered divisions of labor. The poor physical state of many new mothers frequently forced them to rely on German nannies. The hiring of German servants allowed Jewish DPs to attain a sense of social status, and it provided opportunities for limited reconciliation between Germans and Jews on an individual basis. The model for the new Zionist *mamele* drew on the prewar ideal of self-sacrificing motherhood, but this postwar version not only protected and cared for her children, she raised them with a nationalist consciousness, preparing her sons for future battle.

DISCOVERING THE BODY HAS A SEX

The reconstruction of gender began with the body. Women and men knew from the prewar era that they had been born female or male, but the conditions of German occupation had deprived them of some of the physical signifiers of their gender. Women suffered from the shaving of their hair, the loss of their feminine roundness and softness, and amenorrhea. Erna Rubinstein described her first bath after liberation, "I touched my breasts and found only two small raisins sticking out. I had a difficult time recognizing my body, even though I could feel it, I could touch it. It seemed like the body of a stranger. My recollection was from a long time ago, and I remembered my body full and rounded, though not fat, my head covered with long blond hair."[2] Without breasts and hair it was difficult

[2] Erna F. Rubinstein, *After the Holocaust: The Long Road to Freedom* (North Haven, CT: Archon Books, 1995), pp. 20–21.

for female survivors to recognize themselves as women.[3] Eva Torres recalled, "I was very, very skinny and [had] no hair because they shaved us again. I looked like a boy. I don't know what my husband saw in me."[4] Unable to see themselves as sexual beings, women survivors were unprepared for sexual advances from the first men they encountered, the liberating troops.

Alone or in small groups of women without community or male protection, women survivors were easy prey for Allied military personnel seeking sexual adventure or reward. The Soviet Army pursued a policy of rape that victimized not only enemy nationals but also occasionally survivors of the concentration camps and of the forests.[5] The western military commanders did not condone rape and maintained greater control over their troops, so instances of rape by western Allied soldiers were less common. Even so, misunderstandings often led to terror for the women survivors. Soldiers in all Allied armies frequently expected sexual rewards in exchange for a ride to the next town, a gift of food, or an evening out. Women survivors often did not realize that the soldiers would expect such payment until after they had accepted the proffered assistance.[6]

The Holocaust had disrupted the survivors' adolescence. Survivors tended to be between fifteen and twenty-five years old. Most women older than twenty-six years of age had been either mothers of young children or too old to work and were sent to the gas chambers.[7] This meant that most female survivors had been teenagers at the outbreak of the war. Many lost their adolescence in the ghettos and concentration camps.[8] Without the usual experiences of first courtships, many of the women DPs failed to recognize the implications of their own friendly behavior and did not anticipate the sexual demands of the men they

---

[3] Objections to exhibiting women's hair from Auschwitz at the U.S. Holocaust Memorial Museum came mostly from women: "perhaps because men do not feel about hair the same way women do. Men are used to shaving daily, while for a woman the shaving of her head is a violation of her womanhood." Hadassah Rosensaft, *Yesterday: My Story* (Washington, DC: United States Holocaust Memorial Museum, 2004), p. 197. See also Pascale Bos, "Women and the Holocaust: Analyzing Gender Difference," in *Experience and Expression: Women, the Nazis, and the Holocaust*, eds. Elizabeth R. Baer and Myrna Goldenberg (Detroit, MI: Wayne State University Press, 2003), pp. 33–34.

[4] Eva Torres, "Videotaped interview, by the University of Southern California Shoah Foundation Institute for Visual History and Education," Interview Code [IC] 6094, Segment [Seg.] 49, Visual History Archive [VHA] [on-line at subscribing institutions]; www.usc.edu/vhi.VHA.

[5] One survivor remembered the Russian soldiers saying, "We are your liberators. You have to thank us that we liberated you. You have to go to sleep with us. Go sleep with him!" Tamara Freitag, "Videotaped interview," VHA, IC 4182, Seg. 70. See also Ruth Krol, "Videotaped interview," VHA IC 7273, Seg. 128, and Georgia M. Gabor, *My Destiny: Survivor of the Holocaust* (Arcadia, CA: Amen Publishing, 1981), pp. 142–144.

[6] Gabor, *My Destiny*, pp. 142–144; Helen Farkas, *Remember the Holocaust* (Santa Barbara, CA: Fithian Press, 1995), p. 111; Fanya Gottesfeld Heller, *Strange and Unexpected Love: A Teenage Girl's Holocaust Memoirs* (Hoboken, NJ: KTAV Publishing, 1993), p. 272; Sara Zyskind, *Stolen Years* (Minneapolis, MN: Lerner Publication Group, 1981), p. 262.

[7] Hilda Mantelmacher, interview by the author, tape recording, Harrisburg, PA, 31 March 1996.

[8] Alicia Appleman-Jurman, *Alicia: My Story* (New York: Bantam Books, 1988), p. 302; Rubinstein, *After the Holocaust*, p. 96.

[9] Rubinstein, *After the Holocaust*, p. 95.

encountered.[9] The unexpected advances from men they had welcomed as liberators terrorized these women, who were very aware of their dependence on the
good will of Allied troops.

Although the experiences of the concentration camps had instilled in
survivors a distrust of doctors, the loss of menses and the accompanying fear of
infertility compelled women survivors to seek medical assistance even when it
meant seeing a German physician.[10] Some had their fears of infertility confirmed,
but most were reassured that with proper nutrition their menstrual cycles would
resume.[11] At least one DP physician, a survivor of the Kovno ghetto, recognized
the connection between "acute psychological trauma" and ghetto amenorrhea.[12]
Without the stress of persecution and with improved rations, many DP women
welcomed the return of menses. For women survivors, menstruation was significant to their femaleness.

While menstruation was a defining physical trait for women, the ability to
achieve an erection appears to have served a similar function for men. Medical
personnel reported that former concentration camp inmates showed evidence of
severe loss or disturbances of sexual function.[13] Men were often traumatized by
their loss of sex drive, impotence, and their emaciated physiques. Rumors circulated that Jewish men were no longer able to "function as men" due to experiments in the concentration camps.[14] Some Jewish men concerned about their
fertility sought out German medical advice despite fear and feelings of shame.[15]
One psychoanalyst touring the camps observed, "Until liberation, when the
death threat was finally lifted, most of the men were impotent."[16] In the case of
male impotence, sexual activity could represent a restoration of the survivor's
masculinity. Bert Linder reported that he had not engaged in any sexual activity
during his time in the concentration camps. His first postwar sexual encounter
occurred at the same time that his appearance (hair, weight, clothing) became
more like that of other civilians.[17] Roman Halter told an interviewer of his bartering Ovaltine for the services of a prostitute. "He described his experiences

[10] Helen Waterford, *Commitment to the Dead* (Frederick, CO: Renaissance House, 1987), p. 97.
     See also Rubinstein, *After the Holocaust*, p. 84; Eva Slomovits, "Videotaped interview," VHA, IC
     24130, Seg. 211.
[11] See Appleman-Jurman, *Alicia*, p. 356; Gabor, *My Destiny*, p. 177. See also Ruth Minsky Sender,
     To Life (New York: Macmillan Publishing, 1988), p. 51.
[12] See J. Nochimowski, "Die Ghettoamenorrhoe," *Medizinische Klinik: Wochenschrift für Klinik
     und Praxis* 41 (August 1946), Yad Vashem (YV), M-1/P-53.
[13] Leib Szfman and W.M. Schmidt, "Jewish Health and Medical Work in Europe" *Jewish Social
     Service Quarterly* 25 (June 1949): 425.
[14] Jacob Biber, *Risen from the Ashes: A Story of the Jewish Displaced Persons in the Aftermath
     of World War II* (San Bernardino, CA: Borgo Press, 1990), p. 36; Atina Grossmann, "Victims,
     Villains, and Survivors: Gendered Perceptions and Self-Perceptions of Jewish Displaced Persons in
     Occupied Postwar Germany," *Journal of the History of Sexuality* 11 (January/April 2002): 305.
[15] Jane Borenstein, "Videotaped interview," VHA, IC 10534, Segs. 105–108.
[16] Paul Friedman, "The Road Back for the DP's: Healing the Psychological Scars of Nazism"
     Commentary 6 (December 1948): 506.
[17] Bert Linder, *Condemned without Judgment* (New York: S.P.I. Books, 1995), p. 272.

with her, with mesmerizing frankness, as though wishing to convey the physical state he was then in – what it felt like to be safe at last, his body discovering that it had a sex."[18] The sexual act represented his physical survival and the reassertion of his masculinity.[19]

The re-growth of hair served to signify masculinity as well as femininity. In occupied Europe the Nazis attacked Jewish men wearing traditional beards and *payes* (side curls) and tried to force them to shave by threatening unemployment for bearded men.[20] Men and women had been shaved in the concentration camps. After the war, Orthodox men regrew their beards and payes, marking their returning masculinity and their adherence to Jewish law. Women DPs, who as concentration camp inmates had been particularly traumatized by the shaving of their hair, wore kerchiefs over their heads until their hair grew long enough for feminine styling. Short hair represented masculinity and contributed to female survivors feeling less like women in the initial period following liberation.

Clothing the body also became a way for women and men to highlight their newfound sense of masculinity and femininity. Women were eager to acquire brassieres, feeling embarrassed and exposed without them.[21] Skilled seamstresses remade inmate uniforms and mattress covers into jumpers and summer frocks. Tailors cut military blankets and refashioned them into flannel suits.[22] As supplies arrived from international Jewish organizations, Orthodox men once again donned *kitteln* (prayer robes) and traditional headcoverings, and Orthodox women who agreed to wear a wig after marriage received dowries with funds from American Hassidic Jews.[23]

Many secular survivors adopted the military fashion of pants tucked into riding boots and military-styled jackets. A few men did so in unconscious imitation of the aggressively masculine Nazis.[24] Most, however, adopted the fashion in a deliberate attempt to distinguish themselves from Germans and to identify with the victorious Allies and partisans. Some DPs proudly wore uniforms given them by their liberators.[25] One male survivor stitched his prisoner number and

[18] Neil Belton, *The Good Listener: Helen Bamber, A Life against Cruelty* (New York: Pantheon Books, 1998), p. 138.

[19] During the war, a partisan-man asking a woman for sex would say "Let me check if I am alive." Nechama Tec, *Resilience and Courage: Women, Men, and the Holocaust* (New Haven, CT: Yale University Press, 2003), p. 320.

[20] Lucjan Dobroszycki, ed., *The Chronicle of the Lodz Ghetto, 1941–1944* (New Haven, CT: Yale University Press, 1984), pp. 61 and 206; *The Warsaw Diary of Chaim A. Kaplan*, ed. Abraham I. Katsh (New York: Collier Books, 1973), pp. 320 and 331.

[21] Anna Rozen, "Videotaped interview," VHA, IC 5256, Seg. 77.

[22] A girl wearing a skirt made from the Union Jack was reprimanded. Muriel Knox Doherty, letter dated August 1945, *Letters from Belsen 1945: An Australian Nurse's Experiences with the Survivors of War*, eds. Judith Cornell and R. Lynette Russell (St. Leonards NSW, Australia: Allen & Unwin, 2000), p. 74; Rabbi Isaac Levy, "Videotaped interview," VHA, IC 8610, Segs. 43–44.

[23] Biber, *Risen from Ashes*, 34.

[24] Samuel Pisar, *Of Blood and Hope* (New York: MacMillan Publishing, 1979), pp. 93, 109–111.

[25] Abraham Besser, "Videotaped interview," VHA, IC 19988, Seg. 135.

yellow triangle onto the blue Eisenhower jacket that U.S. troops had given him, so that "any Nazis I might meet could appreciate the dramatic reversal in our relationship."[26] The alliance of the survivors with their American liberators, the triumph of the victims over the former persecutors, became visible in this way. Simon Schochet, a survivor in Feldafing, noted that women also wore the boots but added touches of fur to their coats to "suggest a more feminine militancy."[27] Unlike American or German women, some DP women initially did not wear make-up. Their ideal was the "partisan girl" or the Russian woman soldier, described by Schochet as "plain, tough and heroic, in marked contrast to the lithe and carefully-groomed American nurses or officers' wives with whom they can scarcely align themselves."[28] Through their clothing, the DPs performed the gender roles of the new Zionist man and the partisan girl.

THE NEW ZIONIST MAN

The identification with partisans and Allied soldiers helped to alleviate the feelings of powerlessness and emasculation that victimization had evoked, but it also indicated the survivors' new belief that Jewish survival depended on physical strength and self-defense.[29] Many survivors rejected the traditional martyrdom of *Kiddush ha-Shem* (Sanctification of God's Name), which they viewed as passive and weak. The lessons of the Holocaust had reinforced and spread the prewar Zionist ideal of the so-called new Jewish man. From the Zionist movement's inception, it had been concerned with reshaping the Jewish male's body. Instead of the slender, pale scholars of Orthodoxy, the Zionist movement sought to create strong, robust men engaged in "productive" labor.[30] Secular DPs (who formed the overwhelming majority of the DP population) adopted this image of masculinity for themselves.

DP theatrical productions emphasizing the heroism of Jewish partisans helped to make this type of Jewish man appear more prevalent than he was in reality. Reviewers of the professional production of Moshe Pinczewski's play "Ich leb" noted that the play glorified the heroic partisan over passive Kiddush haShem.[31] Numerous professional and amateur theatrical productions glorified the partisan

---

[26] Quoted in Grossmann, "Victims, Villians, and Survivors," p. 311.

[27] Simon Schochet, *Feldafing* (Vancouver: November House, 1983), p. 164.

[28] Schochet, *Feldafing*, pp. 164–5.

[29] Abraham J. Peck, "Jewish Survivors of the Holocaust in Germany: Revolutionary Vanguard or Remnants of a Destroyed People?" *Tel Aviver Jahrbuch für deutsche Geschichte* 19 (1990): 33.

[30] Billie Melman, "Re-Generation and the Construction of Gender in Peace and War – Palestine Jews, 1900–1918" in *Borderlines: Genders and Identities in War and Peace, 1870–1930*, ed. Billie Melman (New York: Routledge, 1998), p. 125; Paula E. Hyman, "Gender and the Shaping of Modern Jewish Identities" *Jewish Social Studies* 8 (2002): 157. See also Daniel Boyarin, *Unheroic Conduct: The Rise of Heterosexuality and the Invention of the Jewish Male* (Berkeley: University of California Press, 1997), pp. 33–36.

[31] B.H., "Ich leb," *Jidisze Cajtung*, November 1946, YV M-1/P-85; "Ich leb," 15 November 1946, unknown newspaper, YV M-1/P-85.

FIGURE 4. Soccer teams parade through the streets of the Foehrenwald DP camp, no date. *Credit*: USHMM, courtesy of YIVO Institute

and Palestinian Jewish soldier.[32] Holiday celebrations connected the Maccabees and other Jewish fighters of old with contemporary partisans, and newspapers ran stories about heroic Jewish fighters against the Nazis.[33] In the DP kibbutzim, sports clubs, and Zionist youth groups, survivors furthered the development of the new Zionist man by engaging in physical activities designed to improve health, prepare for battle in Palestine, and promote manual labor (Figure 4). Their drills and competitions, mistakenly attributed by some observers to Nazi influences, demonstrated to the Germans and to the world that these Jewish men were prepared for physical confrontation.[34] DPs were quick to defend themselves against German threats, as demonstrated by their resistance to a raid by German police in Stuttgart and by the Landsberg DP riot in response to rumors that Germans had killed two young DPs.

DP policemen also represented the strong Jewish male protector of the Jewish people. They physically defended Jewish interests and symbolically proclaimed Jewish authority and respectability.[35] Chaim Haftarczyk joined the Föhrenwald fire department and then the police force so that he could walk on the street

---

[32] Among others were "Partisan" in Belsen and a similar skit in Leipheim and the film *Lang ist der Weg*. Palestinian Jewish soldiers and Zionist activists were lionized in "Blood and Fire" in Feldafing and a play performed in Föhrenwald by a drama circle.

[33] For example, Mieter, "Di kamfn fun jidisze partizaner in di Garbower welder," *Undzer Hofenung*, 31 January 1947; J. Miler, "Pruwn fun an ojfsztand in Tremblinke," *Undzer Hofenung*, 31 January 1947.

[34] The JDC's Koppel Pinson attributed the DPs' interest in drills, marching, and uniforms as evidence of totalitarian methods adopted from the Nazis. "Jewish Life in Liberated Germany: A Study of the Jewish DP's," *Jewish Social Studies* 9 (April 1947): 113–114. Zeev W. Mankowitz deftly refutes Pinson's interpretation in *Life between Memory and Hope: The Survivors of the Holocaust in Occupied Germany* (Cambridge: Cambridge University Press, 2002), p. 143.

[35] Michael Berkowitz, *The Crime of My Very Existence: Nazism and the Myth of Jewish Criminality* (Berkeley: University of California Press, 2007), pp. 214–219.

with pride, unlike the days of the ghetto.[36] Other men joined the DP police as a
productive alternative to the black market and took pride in their professional
training (provided by the Allies) and uniforms.[37] In Feldafing the police force
began as a militia intended to defend the DPs from Germans.[38] In Belsen the
Jewish DP police force, long demanded by Jewish DPs, came into being after
Polish DPs attacked the camp synagogue during Hanukkah 1945. Former partisans formed the core of the Belsen force.[39] Belsen was not an all-Jewish camp
until June 1946, and prior to that Jewish DP police searched for non-Jewish
kapos and collaborators there and in the nearby Hungarian DP camp. They
forced confessions from suspected Nazi collaborators and turned the suspects
over to British authorities for trial.[40] The Allies recruited some DP police to aid
in war crimes investigations, allowing Jewish men to exact legal revenge.[41]

In their defense of the Jewish community, DP police could not be intimidated
by Germans or Allies. In one case, DP police at the Ansbach DP camp reportedly
detained an American soldier accused of raping a DP woman. Despite the camp
being surrounded by U.S. troops, the Ansbach Camp Committee agreed to hand
over the soldier only when assured that he would stand before a court martial.[42]
Jewish men would not permit abuse of a member of the Jewish community, no
matter how powerful the perpetrator might be. DP police also played an important role in military preparations for the battle over Palestine. Despite Allied
prohibitions, DP police trained for military combat and aided the smuggling
of arms to Palestine.[43] Unlike the Jewish police in the wartime ghettos, whom
survivors often viewed as collaborators, DP police followed the Jewish community's code of justice.

The most controversial characteristic of the new Jewish man, and the new
Jewish woman, was the right to seek revenge for the crimes committed against
the Jewish people. In its most violent form, revenge consisted of murdering former SS men, other Nazis, and collaborators.[44] Only a minority of DPs committed violent acts of retribution, and they were overwhelmingly aimed at

[36] Chaim Haftarczyk, "Videotaped interview," VHA, IC 19219, Segs. 14–16.

[37] Beny Yankowitz, "Videotaped interview," VHA, IC 27365, Segs. 79–80; Bill Gluck, "Videotapted
interview," VHA, IC 29159, Segs. 184–187; Ned Aron, "Videotaped interview," IC 7724, Segs.
176–178.

[38] Adam Goldman, "Videotaped interview," VHA, IC 15582, Segs. 92–94; Frieda Reinstein,
"Videotaped interview," VHA, IC 46129, Segs. 93–94.

[39] Hagit Lavsky, *New Beginnings: Holocaust Survivors in Bergen-Belsen and the British Zone in
Germany, 1945–1950* (Detroit, MI: Wayne State University Press, 2002), p. 119; David Zyferman,
"Videotaped interview," VHA, IC 29351, Segs. 101–102; Zoltan Marek, "Videotaped interview,"
VHA, IC 1767, Segs. 112–113.

[40] Zoltan Marek, "Videotaped interview," VHA, IC 1767, Segs. 118–120.

[41] Mendel Flaster, "Videotaped interview," VHA, IC 9963, Seg. 34.

[42] George Gelberman, "Videotaped interview," VHA, IC 44139, Seg. 15.

[43] Samuel Silbiger Falsehaber, "Videotaped interview," VHA, IC 28336, Segs. 96–100; Frieda
Reinstein, "Videotaped interview," VHA, IC 46129, Segs. 93–95.

[44] Ernest Landau, in Michael Brenner, *After the Holocaust: Rebuilding Jewish Lives in Postwar
Germany*, trans. Barbara Harshav (Princeton, NJ: Princeton University Press, 1997), pp. 80–81;
Linder, *Condemned without Judgment*, p. 257; Ludvig Sendery, "Videotaped interview," VHA,

individuals suspected of particular crimes. One unusual case (in that the victim was an innocent, noncombatant German) involved Abram F., an eighteen-year-old resident of the Föhrenwald youth block when he was interviewed by JDC psychiatric consultant Becky Althoff. Orphaned at fifteen, Abram joined and then deserted the Soviet Army, hid in the woods, and then was captured and sent to a concentration camp. After liberation Abram felt the need to "quiet the inner surge, as he puts it, within himself" and murdered a German man in cold blood. "He said after he saw the lacerated corpse he felt better and went home."[45] At the time of the interview he had been in Föhrenwald for nine months and exhibited normal behavior, even working for the police. Engaged to a "pleasant young Jewish girl," Abram observed a few of the religious holidays and planned to emmigrate to Palestine. Althoff concluded that despite his lack of remorse, "he feels that because the man was a German he was in part responsible for the death of his family, the severe sufferings and deprivations which he himself endured," Abram F. did not pose a threat to society and would do well in Palestine given adequate work.[46] While Abram was untroubled by his act of vengeance, other survivors found themselves tormented after their initial bloodlust was sated.

The majority of survivors, both men and women, remembered the teachings of their parents and resisted the temptation to attack others physically. Beating up a German was "hardly repayment"[47] for what the Jews had suffered, and murder raised too many moral issues. Raised in a traditional yet Zionist home, Jacob Biber wrestled with the conflicting messages. As a child he was taught to forgive. "I have asked myself 'did this teaching make me a weakling? Was I a weakling for not trying to avenge the spilled blood of my family?' ... But shooting down Germans would make me no better than they were. ... There was no forgiveness in my heart ... for any of the killers. But after the war I could not find it in my heart to seek revenge."[48] Biber had absorbed enough of the new Zionist masculinity to question whether he was right to restrain his impulse for vengeance, but like other DPs he refused to take action that he felt would put him on the same moral plane as Germans.[49]

There were political as well as moral reasons to avoid violence. Revenge murders distracted the Jewish man's energies from the task of creating a Jewish state in Palestine. They involved fighting past enemies when the Zionists needed to focus on those enemies in the present (the British and Arabs). The Avengers, a group of former partisans intent on taking revenge, encountered the tension

---

IC 18001, Segs. 120–124; Charles Sternbach, "Videotaped interview," VHA, IC 8981, Segs. 102–104.

[45] Becky Althoff, "Report on Abram F." attached to "Semi-monthly Report," June 21, 1946, p. 1, United States Holocaust Memorial Museum (USHMM), Henry Holland Collection, RG-10.146*01.

[46] Althoff, "Report on Abram F." attached to "Semi-monthly Report," p. 2.

[47] Alex Gringauz, "Videotaped interview," VHA, IC 24880, Seg. 18.

[48] Biber, *Risen from Ashes*, p. 79. See also, Pisar, *Of Blood and Hope*, p. 89.

[49] See Otto Berets, "Videotaped interview," VHA, IC 8739, Seg. 45.

between vengeance and building Israel, between looking back and looking forward, when they met with Jewish Brigade soldiers from Palestine. Despite opposition from the Palestinian Jews, they continued with their plans.[50] Most DPs would take satisfaction in symbolic revenge, separating themselves from the Germans, and taking vengeance in the creation of a Jewish state.[51]

Survivors found destruction of German property or its acquisition through "organizing" or black market activities less problematic forms of vengeance.[52] Since Germans had stolen all of the DPs' possessions, they felt justified in taking from the Germans. Others enjoyed the humiliation of the defeated Germans. Alex Gringauz took pleasure in watching Germans "demeaning themselves" by following U.S. soldiers so that they could pounce on the cigarette butts that they dropped.[53] Others pimped German women, earning a profit and at the same time contributing to the German sense of victimization and military concerns about Jewish criminality and venereal disease.[54]

Revenge through sexual relations with German women also occurred.[55] Few Jewish DPs committed rape against German women, but those who did were motivated by revenge.[56] More commonly, Jewish men bartered their rations for sex. Years of Nazi propaganda celebrating the German woman as the feminine ideal and denigrating the Eastern European man as a beast had encouraged this form of "revenge and desire to taste the forbidden fruit."[57] At the very least such sexual contact turned the Nazi racial order upside down, demonstrating its defeat. This sense of revenge and conquest undoubtedly accompanied a host of emotions. For Samuel Pisar, there may have been tender feelings for his

---

[50] Joseph Harmatz, *From the Wings: A Long Journey, 1940–1960* (Sussex, England: The Book Guild, 1998), pp. 116–117.

[51] Mankowitz, *Life between Memory and Hope*, pp. 239–242. Shamai Davidson makes a similar point about the survivors viewing their rebirth in an unsullied homeland as an act of revenge and triumph over the Nazis. "Surviving During the Holocaust and Afterwards: The Post-Liberation Experience," in *Holding on to Humanity – The Message of Holocaust Survivors: The Shamai Davidson Papers*, ed. Israel W. Charny (New York: New York University Press, 1992), p. 74.

[52] Berel Lang discussed the "displacement effect" of revenge appearing in guises other than violence in "Holocaust Memory and Revenge: The Presence of the Past," *Jewish Social Studies* 2 (Winter 1996): 1–20. For examples of such activities see Linder, *Condemned without Judgment*, p. 263; Pisar, *Of Blood and Hope*, p. 90. Women also participated in looting. See Anita Lasker-Wallfisch, *Inherit the Truth* (New York: St. Martin's Press, 1996), pp. 108–109; Regina Feldman, "Videotaped interview," VHA, IC 20671, Seg. 25.

[53] Gringauz, "Videotaped interview," VHA, IC 24880, Seg. 18.

[54] Pisar, *Of Blood and Hope*, p. 93; Zwi Rosenwein, "Videotaped interview," VHA, IC 1598, Seg. 150.

[55] The gender imbalance within the DP population may have prompted some Jewish men to look outside the Jewish community for female companionship. Mankowitz, *Life between Memory and Hope*, p. 19. A few Jewish men found romantic love with German women. Biber, *Risen from Ashes*, pp. 22–25.

[56] See Judith Tydor Baumel, *Kibbutz Buchenwald: Survivors and Pioneers*, trans. Dena Ordan (New Brunswick, NJ: Rutgers University Press, 1997), pp. 20–21.

[57] Schochet, *Feldafing*, pp. 161–162; Lucy S. Dawidowicz, *From that Time and Place: A Memoir, 1938–1947* (New York: W. W. Norton, 1989), p. 302; Davidson, "Surviving During the Holocaust and Afterwards," p. 72.

German partner or a "tinge of racial revenge" or "simply the first stirrings of manhood," but he was mostly "grateful that she was so alive."[58] Untouched by the years of deprivation and persecution that had afflicted Jewish women and men, the German woman represented life. Sex with her affirmed his new life as a free man.

Many DPs viewed sexual relations between Jewish men and German women with disapproval, viewing them as "coarse" and "undignified."[59] While some men found instances of rape and the frequenting of prostitutes morally repugnant, others also considered romantic liaisons between Jews and Germans to be a form of betrayal, even treason.[60] In a proposal to the First Congress of Liberated Jews, religious delegates asked that "in the name of faithful Jewry, treat those Jews who marry German women as traitors and exclude them from the Sherit Hapleita/the remainder of Jewry in Europe."[61] Fraternization between Jewish survivors and Germans also concerned the members of Kibbutz Buchenwald, who agreed in June 1945 to expel any member guilty of "intimate relations" with a German woman.[62] DP newspapers and rabbis also called for the expulsion of Jews who consorted with German women.[63]

Part of the repugnance to Jewish–German liaisons stemmed from the Jewish DPs' association of all Germans with the Nazi murderers of their families, and part of it was the fear of losing what remained of European Jewry to assimilation. In this respect, DP leaders intended the expulsions of a few individuals to serve as deterrents to the further formation of Jewish–German couples. The community feared that sexual revenge could backfire with Jewish men being seduced away from the Jewish community. Not only would the men be lost to the Jewish community but also their offspring. The fear that Hitler could achieve a posthumous victory underlay the condemnations.

Only former kapos were as vilified as these sexual transgressors, signifying that DPs experienced these forms of betrayal as essentially similar despite the differences. Fear of Jewish male collaboration in Jewish annihilation forms the common denominator between kapos and postwar sex with German women. By paying attention to these extraordinary betrayals by a limited number of individuals, survivors could avoid the question of Jewish men's inability to protect their families

---

[58] Pisar, *Of Blood and Hope*, p. 92.

[59] Josef Warscher, "From Buchenwald to Stuttgart," in Brenner, *After the Holocaust*, p. 112. Another Buchenwald survivor described the activities of those who snuck out of camp contrary to the camp commandant's order: "Some sightsee; others go to 'organize' something to barter: eggs, salami, onions, salt, etc. Others seek a woman. ... But this is not freedom." Avraham Ahuria, Personal Diary, 25 April 1945, quoted in *Kibbutz Buchenwald*, p. 21.

[60] In contrast to the mostly Eastern European DPs, German Jews were more accepting of mixed marriages. Brenner, *After the Holocaust*, pp. 48–49.

[61] "Die Konferenz beschliesst," YIVO microfilm read at YV, JM/10263, Folder 44.

[62] "Homecoming in Israel: Journal of Kibbutz Buchenwald," in *The Root and the Bough*, ed. Leo W. Schwarz (New York: Rinehart, 1949), p. 316.

[63] "Resolution of the Central Rabbinate at the 2nd Congress of the She'erit Hapletah in the British Zone" (in Yiddish), 22 July 1947, YV O-70/29; *Undzer Moment*, quoted in Brenner, *After the Holocaust*, p. 49.

and communities during the war. Survivors' personal narratives are fraught with tension between feelings of anger and disappointment at their fathers' wartime helplessness on the one hand and their love and desire to honor their fathers' memories on the other.[64] Adding to feelings of disloyalty was the promotion of the ideal of the new Zionist man, an implicit critique of the older generation's failings. It was easier to condemn the sexual activity of some survivors with German women than to confront the reality of near annihilation and the inability of Jewish men to prevent it. This avoidance suggests a Jewish parallel to Dagmar Herzog's argument that postwar German debates about sexual propriety resulted in "the displacement of the discourse of morality away from murder and onto sex."[65] DPs' preoccupation with sexual propriety could mask an inability to cope with the reality of near extermination and its implications for Jewish masculinity.

THE PARTISAN GIRL[66]

While the ideal of the Zionist man had preceded the Holocaust even if it acquired more adherents in the aftermath, Jews responded to the Holocaust by creating a new type of Jewish femininity. Before the war, Zionists and Orthodox alike had seen women in their maternal role and blamed them for the decline of Jewish culture and religion, respectively.[67] The good Jewish woman was to use her maternal role to preserve Jewish values and transmit them to her children. While the Zionists' "new" Jewish male was permitted to kill in revenge, women had been prohibited from such killing.[68] The partisan girl marked a departure from this image of Jewish womanhood. She had fought and killed on behalf of the Jewish people during the war. After liberation, women were members of the Avengers, former partisans who sought to take revenge against Germans in the postwar period.[69] Women participated in the veterans' organizations and prepared for battle in Palestine. The image of the independent, sexually free, and vengeful woman partisan resonated with many young female survivors (Figure 5).

Jewish women took satisfaction in physical revenge on Germans. In one incident a female survivor told a group of DPs on a crowded train that she had never had the satisfaction of "[doing] something to the Germans to compensate

[64] Margarete Myers Feinstein, "Absent Fathers, Present Mothers: Images of Parenthood in Holocaust Survivor Narratives," *Nashim: A Journal of Jewish Women's Studies and Gender Issues* 13 (Spring 2007): pp. 161–166.

[65] Dagmar Herzog, *Sex after Fascism: Memory and Morality in Twentieth-Century Germany* (Princeton, NJ: Princeton University Press, 2005), p. 140.

[66] Simon Schochet used this phrase. I adopt it as a homage to him and because it reflects the youth, childlessness, and usually unmarried status of many of the women who adopted this model of femininity.

[67] Gershon C. Bacon, *The Politics of Tradition: Agudat Yisrael in Poland, 1916–1939* (Jerusalem: The Magnes Press, The Hebrew University, 1996), pp. 155–158; Paula E. Hyman, *Gender and Assimilation in Modern Jewish History: The Roles and Representation of Women* (Seattle: University of Washington Press, 1995), pp. 146–150.

[68] Melman, "Re-Generation Nation and Construction of Gender," p. 126.

[69] Harmatz, *From the Wings*, pp. 115–140.

FIGURE 5. Members of hachshara Kibbutz Hathiya stand in formation during a procession at the Foehrenwald DP camp, 1945–1946. *Credit*: USHMM, courtesy of Samuel (Rakowski) Ron

for what they did to us." The group then offered to make room for a German, pulled him onto the train through a window, beat him, and then threw him off the train. Asked if she felt better, the female survivor replied, "even that couldn't make me feel better." As she recounted the incident, the survivor was laughing, seemingly out of embarrassment at not feeling remorse but also out of Schadenfreude. The beating of one German could not compensate for the suffering inflicted by the Nazis.[70] Another female survivor attempted to use her position as a military court translator to help free two Poles charged with murdering a German. She did not care whether or not they were guilty, only that no one should be convicted of killing a German.[71] While few Jewish women other than former partisans personally took physical action against Germans, many women DPs desired revenge and took satisfaction in German suffering.

Like the men, those women survivors who did not act on the overwhelming hatred they felt for their tormentors attributed their lack of violent revenge to their determination to maintain their moral dignity. In refraining from violence, the DPs sought to assert their moral superiority to the Germans. Esther Brunstein, observing the German soldiers forced to clear away corpses at Bergen-Belsen, noted, "There was murder in all of us and it scared me. I remember praying silently. I did not really know to whom to pray but I never prayed so fervently in all my life. I prayed not to be consumed by hatred and destroyed for the rest of my days."[72] As an interpreter for the British in occupied Germany,

---

[70] Helen Goldring, "Videotaped interview," VHA, IC 5590, Seg. 135.

[71] After differences with the British defense lawyer, she quit the case. The Poles received a 15-year sentence. Zula Schibuk, "Videotaped interview," VHA, IC37065, Segs. 189–192.

[72] Esther Brunstein, quoted in *Belsen in History and Memory*, eds. Jo Reilly et al. (London: Frank Cass, 1997), p. 214. Pearl Benisch watched the same scene and found it bittersweet revenge. "We

Lucille Eichengreen participated in the interrogation of an SS concentration camp guard. At the conclusion of the interrogation the British officer presented her with a pistol. This survivor recalled, "All during the war I had wished for a gun. I had wanted to kill one German – just one – before I died. ... I put the revolver down ... I was confronted with a cruel irony: somehow I still could not justify killing another human being; somehow, I had retained my faith in a just system of courts and juries."[73] Pearl Benisch observed German children at play and was overcome by a "lust for revenge." She realized that she was not capable of hurting "an innocent child, even the child of murderers. Neither, though, could I hug one."[74] She noted matter-of-factly that she felt no tenderness for German children. Although she imagines that their fathers had murdered innocent Jewish children, Benisch would not lower herself to their level. The children were spared, not because of a feminine affection for children, but because of her Jewish moral superiority. These survivors struggled successfully against blind hatred and maintained faith in either divine or earthly justice. At the same time, they could feel intense hatred without jeopardizing their sense of femininity because of the partisan-girl model. Hatred and revenge might not sit well with their notions of justice but were compatible with their perception of appropriate sentiment for Jewish women.

While Jewish men sought revenge through sexual contact with German women, it seemed unthinkable that Jewish women would consort with German men once they were no longer under the threat of death. None of the authorities attempted to prohibit such contact as they did in the case of Jewish men. In postwar Kovno, Rabbi Ephraim Oshry offered his responsa concerning whether a married man could reunite with his wife who had been forced into a brothel serving the German army. Rabbi Oshry declared it permissible since the wife had been under a death threat, and "there is not the slightest shadow of suspicion that she might have been seduced into voluntary intercourse with the Germans, since she herself saw what they had done to her fellow Jews. ... Certainly these oppressors were so disgusting, abominable, and detestable in her eyes that it is inconceivable they could have seduced her."[75] German men had been perpetrators, and it was unthinkable that a Jewish woman would voluntarily enter a relationship with one. If a Jewish woman were seen with a German man, other Jews quickly informed her that while Jewish men were free to fraternize, she was not.[76] While it was rare for a Jewish woman

---

saw them being degraded and humiliated. But the corpses they dealt with were not German. It was not their people, their dear ones, who had died of starvation, thirst, and disease. ... There is, in fact, no form of retribution we can exercise on them. We shall never be able to exact revenge; nor have we tried to. The Eternal Judge Himself must avenge our millions." Pearl Benisch, *To Vanquish the Dragon* (New York: Feldheim Publishers, 1991), p. 405.

[73] Lucille Eichengreen, *From Ashes to Life: My Memories of the Holocaust* (San Francisco: Mercury House, 1994), pp. 149–150.

[74] Benisch, *To Vanquish*, p. 411.

[75] Quoted in Irving J. Rosenbaum, *The Holocaust and Halakhah* (New York: KTAV Publishing, 1976), p. 146.

[76] Ruth Kluger, *Still Alive: A Holocaust Girlhood Remembered* (New York: The Feminist Press at the City University of New York, 2001), p. 166.

to associate with a German man, DP leaders in Belsen did recognize fraternization between Jewish young women and British soldiers as a problem.[77]

In reality partisan women had been subjected to sexual exploitation, loss of sex drive, and exclusion from more valued military duties.[78] The postwar image, however, was of valiant self-sacrifice and sexual control. At holiday celebrations and in newspapers survivors recounted the exploits of partisans, including those of the paratrooper Hannah Senesch, who was executed by Hungary's collaborationist regime.[79] DP theaters celebrated the partisan woman: On stage cabaret singers seduced German officers and stole their weapons to pass along to resistance fighters; a devoted fiancée and member of the underground killed a ghetto commandant and escaped to join the partisans.[80] These women were no longer sheltered innocents of traditional Jewish or bourgeois homes. In these plays female sexuality was accepted and even lauded as a weapon. The woman who used her sexuality to dupe the Nazis was just as valiant and honorable as the innocent who repressed her sexuality to further the underground's goals. The essential point was that the women did not succumb to sexual desire but disciplined it.[81] Each woman controlled her sexuality as the situation and needs of the partisans dictated.

Off stage, some women in the Zionist movement deliberately restricted their fertility at least for the near term, in order to ensure their preparedness for mobilization to Palestine.[82] Other women physically assaulted Germans who threatened them, whether a landlady who spoke fondly of Hitler or German police raiding the Stuttgart DP center.[83] A few young women assumed leadership roles in Zionist activities from Brichah, the organization for illegal migration, to various kibbutz movements and other political organizations.[84] They published magazines and acquired weapons for the Jewish community in Palestine.[85] At a Zionist demonstration in Hanover on November 16, 1945, British military police arrested three young women and seven men for "promoting a public political

[77] Benisch, *To Vanquish*, p. 415; Eryl Hall Williams, quoted in *Belsen in History and Memory*, eds. Reilly et al., p. 224.

[78] Tec, *Resilience*, pp. 282, 306, 325, and 328.

[79] "Hannah Senesch – The heroic daughter of the Jewish People" (in Yiddish), *Undzer Hofenung* 31 January 1947; "A Purim-ownt in kibuc haszomer hacair," *Bamidbar* 20 March 1946, p. 7.

[80] Sami Feder, *Farzeichenishn zum Tag-Buch fun "Kazet-teater" in Bergen-Belsen*, p. 9, YV O-70/31; Sender, *To Life*, p. 148; M. Pinezevski, "I am living," YV M-1/P-85.

[81] On the importance of sexual discipline for defining the "good" woman, see Sara R. Horowitz, "The Gender of Good and Evil: Women and Holocaust Memory," in *Gray Zones: Ambiguity and Compromise in the Holocaust and its Aftermath*, eds. Jonathan Petropoulos and John K. Roth (New York: Berghahn Books, 2005) pp. 166–170.

[82] Baumel, *Kibbutz Buchenwald*, p. 107.

[83] Sara Hauptman, "Videotaped interview," VHA, IC 28669, Seg. 33; Lillian Le Bental, "Videotaped interview," VHA, IC 3710, Segs. 61–62.

[84] Gabor, *Destiny*, pp. 216–235; Appleman-Jurman, *Alicia*, pp. 296 and 329; Baumel, "DPs, Mothers, and Pioneers," pp. 104–107.

[85] Faye Schulman, *A Partisan's Memoir: Woman of the Holocaust* (Toronto: Second Story Press, 1995), pp. 221–222.

meeting, and of having disturbed the public security."[86] A British military court
sentenced two of the women to one month's imprisonment and the third, who
was convicted of kicking an M.P., to three month's. Clearly some women were
willing to put their bodies on the line, participating in demonstrations. At one
protest against the American authorities in Landsberg, "Women with newborn
babies sat down on the streets and didn't let the Americans pass."[87] In their
defiance of outside authorities on behalf of the Jewish community and their
willingness to engage in physical confrontation, these women demonstrated the
partisan-girl spirit.

ADVOCATES FOR A GENTLER FEMININITY

The new femininity of the partisan girl did not go unchallenged. Allied officials
and some DPs sought to create a softer, domesticated woman. Social workers
encouraged women to engage in handicrafts, such as embroidery and knitting,
for decorative purposes and took the use of cosmetics as a sign of rehabilitation.[88] The supervising UNRRA nurse at Belsen also identified a renewed interest
in personal appearance as a sign of rehabilitation, but she refrained from making such gender-specific observations.[89] British military chaplain Rabbi Isaac
Levy told officers, "I want these women to be given the facilities to look like
women. I'd like them to have needle and cotton, knitting needles and wool,
lipstick, mirrors, combs; anything that makes a woman feel she's a woman."[90]
Secular women welcomed the opportunity to attempt to attain Allied standards
of beauty and femininity. Women from traditional Jewish homes had not worn
cosmetics before the war, although some had their interest piqued in the DP
camps through the examples of Anglo-American women working among DPs
and of American cinema.[91]

American films shown in DP and German theaters, selected by American
Information Control Officers "for the amount and subtlety of Americana they
could impart,"[92] promoted their own ideals of gendered appearance and behavior. Concerned about reeducating Germans, information officers decided against
films that were too militaristic, but gangster movies and westerns still presented
a virulent and violent version of masculinity. In addition to biographical films

---

[86] Norbert Wollheim, untitled report, no date, YV O-70/64. The chairman of the committee in
   Hanover received six months' imprisonment, four men were sentenced to three months (although
   two had their sentences commuted to twelve months of probation in view of their youth), and two
   men were acquitted.
[87] Julius Spokojny, "Zionist Activist in the DP Camp," in Brenner, *After the Holocaust*, p. 89.
[88] J. Weingreen, "Survey of Educational Work in Bergen-Belsen, July 30th to September 10th, 1946,"
   p. 5, YV O-70/28. Becky Althoff, "Observations on the Psychology of Children in a D.P. Camp"
   Journal of Social Casework 21 (January 1948): 21.
[89] Doherty, letter dated August 1945, *Letters from Belsen*, p. 75.
[90] Levy, "Videotaped interview," VHA, IC 8610, Seg. 42.
[91] Haddasah Bimko received her first ever tube of lipstick in January 1946 when Josef Rosensaft
   brought it as a gift upon his return from a trip to the States. *Yesterday*, p. 101.
[92] Jay E. Gordon, "Operation Celluloid," *Hollywood Quarterly* 2:4 (July 1947): 417.

of famous scientists and movies about the American military, showings included musicals, romantic comedies, and JDC-provided American Yiddish features such as *The Cantor's Son* (1937).[93] Spunky heroines who learn to play by the rules and strong, well-dressed men starred onscreen. For example, one favorite movie for DPs was *Sun Valley Serenade*, with Sonja Henie's character arriving in the United States as a DP orphan and skating her way into an urbane band-leader's heart.[94] Henie's (and her character's) charm and quick adaptability to American ways brought her success. DPs valued light entertainment as a way to find respite from their burdensome memories, and the images of Americana helped shape their definition of normal living. Schochet recalled the fairytale images in the films: "Everyone is dressed so elegantly, faces and figures glow with health and vitality and throbbing downbeats fill the air with an irresistible *joie de vivre* that makes worshipful converts immediately."[95] Their identification with their liberators that had promoted military dress now also encouraged the adoption of Hollywood's version of civilian fashions.

While in the Deggendorf DP camp, a young German-Jewish survivor of Theresienstadt and Auschwitz avidly attended concerts and films. An amateur musician herself, she enjoyed *There's Magic in Music* (1941), about a burlesque singer who reforms herself at the children's music camp of Interlochen.[96] The story of a rebellious, uncultured girl who learns to live by camp rules and then becomes successful enough to save the day (and the camp) may have resonated with her as much as the musical score. Although not fond of the film adaptation of the play *Heaven Can Wait*, she pasted in her diary the program for *Here Comes Mr. Jordan* (1941). Smiling from the cover are the attractive leads, Robert Montgomery and Evelyn Keyes. Inside, the German-language synopsis explains how a boxer prematurely taken to heaven is returned to Earth to live out his allotted years in the body of another man. Given a second chance, he performs good deeds and meets his romantic interest, the lovely daughter of a financier.[97] The back page featured glamour shots of Evelyn Keyes, whose beautifully coiffed and elegantly dressed image undoubtedly appealed to the imagination of a twenty-five-year-old woman, whose upper middle-class prewar life had been shattered.

The healthy glows and luxuriously clothed figures of Hollywood movies were ideals the DPs could not attain in their present state, but their desire to emulate those standards could be aroused. In Feldafing a DP photographer provided props, such as linen tablecloths, vases, silk kerchiefs, jackets, and American

[93] For more on American films and German audiences, see Heide Fehrenbach, *Cinema in Democratizing Germany: Reconstructing National Identity After Hitler* (Chapel Hill: University of North Carolina Press, 1995), Chapter 2. Lists of U.S. films approved for screening in the American Zone are in Appendixes A and B.

[94] Schochet, *Feldafing*, p. 93.

[95] Schochet, *Feldafing*, p. 93.

[96] This film was also very popular with German POWs. Gordon, "Operation Celluloid," p. 418.

[97] Sylva Loewenstein, "Tagebuch Diary I," 15 July 1945–20 September 1946, USHMM, Gertrud Lowenstein Collection, 1995.56. The program appears after the entry for 13 July 1946.

neckties, for portraits that mimicked middle-class furnishings and American fashions. His assistant retouched photographs to give the subjects a healthy appearance.[98] In another camp, a photographer posed the female students of a knitting class around their teacher, who was femininely dressed wearing a brooch and holding a puppy on her lap.[99] The image was one of middle-class respectability.

Along with assumptions about appearances, aid workers and middle-class DPs believed needlework to be an appropriate feminine pastime. Knitting, embroidery, and sewing were popular trades for girls in the vocational schools; girls were discouraged from taking courses in mechanics and other "masculine" trades.[100] The military and UNRRA employed women in traditionally female positions as laundresses, cooks, seamstresses, and office support staff.[101] The conditions in the DP camps also reinforced the traditional labor of women in the domestic trades, teaching, and nursing. Most of those women DPs who had practiced a trade prior to the war were seamstresses, and the dependence of ORT (Organization for Rehabilitation through Training) trade schools on DP instructors tended to reinforce the participation of women in the needle trades. With the assistance of ORT, the DPs also established a training program for nurses.[102]

Some DPs participated in constructing this domestic version of womanhood. One DP urged women "to assist actively in solving the educational problem. ... With every word, with every gesture and each interaction, they must instill aesthetic behavior in the youth."[103] Women still had a civilizing mission to perform in the DP camps. Also promoting domestic activities and the restoration of prewar gender roles were the Orthodox Beth Jacob schools for girls. The survivor teachers saw their mission in terms of national work and public education.[104] Intent on educating female survivors in Orthodox ways and on providing a more wholesome environment for them, the Beth Jacob teachers combined activism with traditional female assistance to men. "The crowning glory of our work is the care for the laundry of the Yeshiva; our work for the religious scholars will count as a holy deed for

[98] Schochet, *Feldafing*, pp. 80–81.

[99] Photograph in William Goldfarb collection, USHMM 1998.A.0278.

[100] Eleanor Barbag, "Videotaped interview," VHA, IC 44369, Seg. 36.

[101] Jo Reilly, "Writing Women Back into the Liberation of Bergen-Belsen," in *Belsen in History and Memory*, p. 157.

[102] A. G. Brotman and Harry Viteles, "Survey on Conditions of Jews in the British Zone of Germany in March 1946," page 2, YV O-70/6; Juliane Wetzel, *Jüdisches Leben in München 1945–1951: Durchgangsstation oder Wiederaufbau?* (Munich: Neue Schriftenreihe des Stadtarchivs München, 1987), p. 186.

[103] Pauline Fischer-Sztajer, *Iber die ojfgabn fun der Schejrts Haplejte-froj: Zum Ojfboj*, 11 December 1946, page 3, quoted in Jacqueline Dewell Giere, "Wir sind unterwegs, aber nicht in der Wüste: Erziehung und Kultur in den jüdischen Displaced Persons-Lagern der amerikanischen Zone im Nachkriegsdeutschland 1945–1949," (Ph.D. diss., Johann Wolfgang Goethe-Universität, Frankfurt a.M., 1993), p. 157.

[104] Beth Jacob Center in Bergen-Belsen, "Report on Our Work" (in Yiddish), 1945, p. 2, YV O-70/29.

us."[105] Their students sewed ritual objects for the Orthodox men and decorated their holiday tables. At the same time, their teachers encouraged them to learn sewing as a trade that would enable them to financially support their future scholar-husbands.

SEXUAL MORALITY

During the Holocaust some Jewish women (and, to a lesser extent, men) had learned to trade on their sexuality. In order to support themselves, they exchanged sexual favors for food, clothing, and transportation. Those recently liberated from the Nazi camps frequently found themselves caught between the illusion of freedom and the reality of powerlessness. Under such circumstances, survivors justified actions that would ensure their survival, whether they were theft of clothing, consumption of non-kosher foods, or bartering sex.[106] While survivors accepted such behavior when it was necessary, tolerance appears to have disappeared once circumstances became more stable.[107]

Within the DP community sexual innocence was not expected of Jewish women. It was understood that survival had often required the trading of sexual favors or that Jewish women had been victims of rape (during the war and after). A woman's lack of virginity or sexual innocence did not necessarily taint her as Rabbi Oshry's responsa (above) on the woman forced to become a sex worker indicated. Orthodox men willingly married sexually experienced women, even those who had engaged in sex with their wartime protectors.[108] A Jewish woman did not need to be sexually untouched, but she was expected to find a stable relationship with a Jewish man. DPs in Feldafing denounced an unwed Jewish mother for consorting with Americans and "with a mixture of anger, jealousy and pity, condemn her for not having found a husband amongst us instead of running about with the American soldiers."[109] Her sexual past did not trouble them whereas her lack of interest in Jewish DP men did. Not all Jewish men accepted the sexually compromised woman, however, even when they had been complicit in her violation. For example, the unwed mother at Feldafing had traded sex for the protection of her family and fiancé. Impregnated by their protector, she was abandoned by her fiancé after the war. We cannot know

---

[105] Beth Jacob Bergen-Belsen, "Report," p. 2.

[106] When it came to matters of survival, concentration camp inmates had learned that the morality of the normal world had no place in decision-making. Lawrence Langer refers to "choiceless choice" to describe these decisions made within a context of powerlessness that negates the meaning of moral categories. Choiceless choice also applies to the immediate postwar situation of survivors. Lawrence Langer, *Holocaust Testimonies: The Ruins of Memory* (New Haven, CT: Yale University Press, 1991), p. 26.

[107] Rubinstein, *After the Holocaust*, p. 35.

[108] Heller, *Strange and Unexpected Love*, p. 278. This immediate postwar understanding of survivors did not protect Heller from censure when she published her memoir in 1990. See Horowitz, "Gender of Good and Evil," pp. 173–175.

[109] Schochet, *Feldafing*, p. 158.

whether he was motivated by disgust at her violation or at himself and his own inability to protect her.

The poor sex ratio among DPs in the American Zone exacerbated DP men's frustration over Jewish women consorting with Allied soldiers. In 1945, two-thirds of Jewish DPs between the ages of 18 and 45 were male.[110] In Regensburg there were 703 Jewish men and only 480 Jewish women. Of these women, 67 were pregnant and 59 were breastfeeding. In Neunburg vorm Wald, there were 114 men and 49 women. Nine of the women were pregnant and another 10 were nursing infants.[111] Under these circumstances many Jewish men were left without the possibility of a Jewish female companion.

Given the squalid conditions and lack of privacy in the camps, sexual encounters between DPs could not meet the romantic expectations of normal society. Yet, the DPs did manage to find opportunities for sexual intercourse. For some, sexual contact represented a physical manifestation of freedom and an affirmation of life. One female survivor recalled a friend's explanation of her sexual experience: "For one precious moment she felt free. ... Today she felt the urge to do it, to feel free at last. ... There was a greater meaning to the intercourse than just sex. Gita knew that she shared her feelings with another person. She also experienced an exhilarating emotional high and a release of feelings she had kept tied in knots for so many years."[112] Sexual activity could serve as an emotional catharsis and as a way to feel connected to another human being.

Similar feelings of sexual awakening are reflected in the diary of Kibbutz Buchenwald: "We are always cheerful. We have become romantic. Everything is in flower, not just outside, but within. We are beginning to understand what it means to be a free person."[113] Certainly it is understandable that young adults seeking affection and the warmth of human contact after years of deprivation would express themselves sexually. It is also likely that the novelty of experiencing physical pleasure from one's body that for years had only felt pain would have been irresistible. The immediate postliberation period was a time of experimentation. The Nazis were defeated; their laws no longer applied. Freed from community and family restraints, some survivors seized the opportunity to make their own rules. While many sought to live by their parents' values,[114] young men and women delighted in their healing bodies. Heterosexual desire was something to be enjoyed and acted upon.

---

[110] Mankowitz, *Life between Memory and Hope*, p. 19.

[111] "Population in Oberpfalz," YIVO, RG 294.2, MK 483, Microfilm reel 63, Folder 888.

[112] Rubinstein, *After the Holocaust*, p. 63. See also Lala Fishman and Steven Weingartner, *Lala's Story: A Memoir of the Holocaust* (Evanston, IL: Northwestern University Press, 1997), p. 318.

[113] *Geringshof Diary: December 1945-July 1946*, quoted in Baumel, *Kibbutz Buchenwald*, p. 107.

[114] Sara Tuvel Bernstein, *The Seamstress: A Memoir of Survival* (New York: Berkley Books, 1997), p. 305.

Homosexuality is rarely mentioned in survivor accounts, and then only as a problem among boys. This absence is most likely due to the hostility of traditional Jewish society to homosexuality and its illegality in Germany. Homosexuals would have felt it necessary to hide their orientation, either through passing as heterosexual or through a secret life outside of the over-crowded confines of the DP camps. Relief workers noted that boys had been sexually abused by men during the Nazi period.[115] One open reference to homosexuality comes from Simon Schochet in Feldafing, who described it as a "problem" among young boys who had survived the camps because of their physical strength and the "special attention" they had received from kapos and other privileged prisoners.[116] Schochet attributes the postwar sexual transgressions of the boys to their wartime exploitation. Here the Nazi belief that homosexuality was a Jewish disease is stood on its head: The Nazi regime infected Jewish boys with homosexuality. As for the activities of adult homosexuals, military court cases may reveal more, but it is difficult to search the records. One case that I stumbled upon reveals two Jewish DPs convicted of sodomy placed in solitary confinement for fourteen days on a diet of bread and water.[117] If this is representative of treatment meted out to homosexuals, then it is clear why they would remain underground.

Soon advocates of restraint reigned in the sexually free. Aid workers sought to discourage sex outside of marriage. For example, a group of young Jewish women residing in the village where they were liberated began to discover their sexuality while in the proximity of British soldiers. Helen Bamber, an office worker with the JRU, visited these teenage women to educate them about menstruation and to caution them to restrain their sexual impulses, "because there was a wildness in them that was not going to be helped by going to bed with every British soldier. We were trying to give them some sort of pride."[118] The sexual activity of women survivors, however, was due to more than a lack of pride. It could be an expression of freedom and a discovery of physical pleasure. It could also be a means of acquiring cigarettes and other tradable goods.[119] The relief workers tended to impose their values and ideas of gender onto the DPs. The generally excitable and occasionally lawless behavior of the survivors led

[115] Ralph Segalman, "The Psychology of Jewish Displaced Persons," *Jewish Social Services Quarterly* 24 (June 1947): 364.

[116] Schochet, *Feldafing*, p. 24.

[117] Arthur A. Thue, Prison Officer, 1st US Infantry Division, to Summary Court Officer, Company D, 3rd Military Government Regiment, "Offense of Sodomy of Jewish DP Prisoners," 14 November 1946; Correspondence – General – 1946–47; General Records of Weiden-Neustadt Resident Liaison and Security Office 1945–49; Records of the Field Operations Division; Records of United States Occupation Headquarters, World War II (OMGUS), Record Group (RG) 260, Entry: Bavaria; National Archives at College Park, MD (NACP).

[118] Helen Bamber, quoted in Belton, *Good Listener*, p. 107.

[119] On relations between British soldiers and Belsen women DPs, see Erna Hilfstein, "Videotaped interview," VHA, IC 9995, Segs. 119–123.

many relief workers to believe that the victims of Nazism had become savages who needed to be re-civilized.[120]

Although DPs did engage in premarital sex, it seems to have been mostly confined to established couples. In Landsberg, the U.S. military camp commander Irving Heymont observed that many couples lived together without the benefit of marriage, but he was told that if a child resulted from the union, then marriage would follow.[121] Indeed, illegitimacy was virtually unknown among the Jewish DPs.[122] Some DPs simply wanted to be certain they were sexually functioning and fertile couples before getting married.[123] In the rare instance that a man did not marry his pregnant partner, she was likely to seek out an abortion. In Belsen, it was mostly DP women impregnated by married British soldiers having abortions.[124] Since abortion was illegal except for medical reasons, a DP would need to find a doctor willing to perform the procedure for a black market fee. Without connections or funds, women often resorted to self-induced abortions.[125] Many survivors seemed all too willing to embrace marriage, not as a means of having socially acceptable sex, but as a way to forge a familial bond, when they had no other family. The pain and fear of being alone in the world encouraged many to enter what they believed to be permanent bonds of matrimony.[126]

JEWISH MARRIAGES

Representing the forces of prewar society, religious leaders of the DP community also encouraged couples to legitimate their relationships in Jewish marriages.[127] Most DPs chose to create Jewish marriages and homes. Even secular Jews wanted a religious wedding ceremony as a means of forming links with the past and to ensure family continuity.[128] Erna Rubinstein's sister had lost

---

[120] "Inevitably the survivors' steps back to civilization will be faltering and confused, with many mistakes and setbacks." Friedman, "The Road Back for the DPs," p. 507. Another observer attributed the DPs' behavior to "psychological regression." Edward A. Shils, "Displacement and Repatriation," *Journal of Social Issues* (August 1946): 5.

[121] Heymont, *Among the Survivors,* p. 45.

[122] Rabbi Philip S. Bernstein, "Status of Jewish Displaced Persons," in U.S. Department of State, *The Displaced-Persons Problem: A Collection of Recent Official Statements* (Washington, DC: U.S. Government Printing Office, 1947), p. 1309.

[123] Biber, *Risen from Ashes,* pp. 37–38.

[124] Laurie A. Whitcomb, "Life Behind the Baby Carriage: Reassessing the Life Reborn Narrative of Jewish Displaced Persons through Survivor Testimony" (paper presented at the annual meeting of the German Studies Association, San Diego, CA, October 2007), p. 12.

[125] The number of abortions caught the attention of DP religious leaders. A tragic case of an unmarried Jewish DP dying from complications after an abortion is reported in Joseph Soski, "Memories of a Vanished World," (1992), p. 95, USHMM, RG 02.072.

[126] Hannah Modenstein, telephone interview with the author, tape recording, 18 July 1995. Also, Baumel writes, "marriages were inspired more by the desire to escape loneliness and to have children than by love and emotional intimacy." Baumel, *Kibbutz Buchenwald,* p. 106.

[127] Faye Doctrow, telephone interview with author, tape recording, 5 March 1996.

[128] Lavsky, *New Beginnings,* p. 149.

her faith during the war, but as she prepared to marry she told Rubinstein, "although it was sometimes difficult to believe in God after all we had been through, she and Dolek [her fiancé] felt very strongly that they must forever continue the Jewish tradition that the Nazis had tried to destroy. Pola said that to celebrate her marriage without our parents and without our little brother was very sad, but she and Dolek felt they had to go on, to hold onto their Jewish heritage and to build a better future for themselves and for their children."[129] The urgency for rebuilding Jewish life and transmitting it to the next generation was great, if only to rob the Nazis of a belated victory. The legacy of their prewar upbringings continued to influence the DPs even as they struggled with questions of faith raised by the Shoah. While their faith in God may have been shaken, they retained their Jewish identity and their prewar level of adherence to the performance of Jewish ritual.

Marriage and sexual relations raised the issue of family purity laws. While in some Orthodox communities men may have had the custom of visiting the ritual bath, or *mikvah*, on Friday afternoon before the Sabbath and before the start of holidays, the mikvah was expressly the legal obligation of married women. Observant, married Jewish women were required to ritually purify themselves in the mikvah after menstruation before marital relations could take place. Since no functioning mikvah had survived Nazi rule, the building of the mikvah was a top priority for religious DPs. The efforts undertaken in communities to construct a mikvah were also a sign of community regeneration.[130]

Determined Orthodox DPs were successful in enlisting the aid of Jewish chaplains and relief workers in obtaining the property and materials necessary for the construction of ritual baths, although not without controversy. A British rabbi serving Belsen DPs convinced authorities to build a mikvah for prospective brides;[131] however, secular DP leaders questioned the priorities of this rabbi since the wood used for the mikvah construction could have served as heating fuel in the bitter winter of 1945/46.[132] By Passover 1946, the Föhrenwald DP camp had a mikvah that was open daily for women's ritual purification and for men on mornings before the Sabbath and the beginning of holidays.[133] At Landsberg, DPs built a mikvah on their own initiative. When the military commander discovered it, it was declared a health hazard. A compromise was reached that permitted women to use the mikvah provided that they shower afterwards. DPs had hired German laborers to dig the mikvah.[134] One can only imagine the satisfaction, the sense of retribution, Jewish DPs felt at ordering Germans to do manual labor in order that Jewish family life could flourish.

[129] Rubinstein, *After the Holocaust*, p. 98.
[130] On the purpose of the mikvah, see Michael Asheri, *Living Jewish: The Lore and Law of the Practicing Jew*, 2nd edition (New York: Everest House, 1978), pp. 90–93.
[131] Isaac Levy, "Belsen Testimonies," in *Belsen in History and Memory*, eds. Reilly, et. al., p. 240.
[132] Lavsky, *New Beginnings*, p. 114.
[133] Rabinat in Fernwald, "Ojfruf cu Pejsach," 1946, YV M-1/P-121.
[134] Heymont, *Among the Survivors*, p. 83.

With sexual activity on the rise, the religious leaders sought to educate young couples in proper Jewish relations. Despite the severe paper shortage, a rabbi in the Föhrenwald DP camp managed to publish a volume on Jewish marital law, instructing women and men about such things as the proper timing of marital relations and use of the mikvah after menstruation. Exhorting young couples to observe the traditions, the author pulled no punches: "Whoever does not observe them puts his health in danger and corrupts the Jewish youth, the remainder that is left to us after the bloody deluge, the seed from which the Jewish future will sprout, the roots from which the Jewish people will branch out. ... Whoever honors and values his parents – and who among us is not filled with reverence for our martyrs – will observe completely the Jewish marital laws."[135] The Feldafing-based Agudat Israel used similar language in an appeal to Jewish wives and mothers: "Do not break the Jewish future! Sacred is the memory of your parents! Should the above words show you the path to your people, the attached booklet [on Jewish marital law] shall be your guide for how to build a pure, Jewish life."[136] These heavy-handed attempts to persuade Jewish DPs, the women in particular, to follow religious law indicated the religious leaders' concern that young survivors were ignorant of the traditions and not particularly interested in learning about them. Indeed, the majority of survivors came from nonobservant backgrounds. But it was not only secular Jews who ignored the directives of the religious authorities. Even more traditional Jews occasionally found it difficult to abide by the policies of Orthodox rabbis.

In the absence of a mikvah, traditional women could use a river for the purpose of immersion, so marriages could and did take place. At the Belsen DP camp, the initial absence of a mikvah led to a mini-revolt against rabbinic authority. A couple engaged before the war found themselves reunited as DPs. A British rabbi had agreed to officiate at the Sunday wedding in June 1945. On Friday afternoon, however, the rabbi informed a camp leader, Hadassah Bimko (later Rosensaft), that the marriage could not take place because there was no mikvah available for the bride. Bimko, a widow of Orthodox upbringing, informed the rabbi that Jewish law permitted any Jew to perform a marriage ceremony and that the wedding would go on with or without him. In the end the rabbi presided over the nuptials. As Rosensaft recalled, "it turned out to be an anti-mikvah wedding that took place on Freedom Square in Belsen, under a blue sky. It was the beginning of life."[137] The difficult material conditions of the early months following liberation required religiously observant survivors to make compromises and innovations in their adherence to Jewish law and tradition. As Bimko correctly observed, it is possible to follow Jewish law and tradition even without a presiding rabbi. The DPs' determination to marry and create Jewish families often overrode obedience to rabbinic decisions. It also points to

---

[135] N. Z. Friedmann, *Taharat Hamischpacha: Von di jidische Ehe-Gesetze* (Föhrenwald, Germany: 1945/46), YV M-1/P-65.

[136] Agudat Israel, "Jewish Wife! Jewish Mother!" (in Yiddish), YV M-1/P-65.

[137] Rosensaft, *Yesterday*, p. 79.

the loss of rabbinic authority brought about by the dissolution of established communities and the wartime struggle for survival that often forced individuals to rely on their own judgments.

The resolve of DPs to marry and the sympathy of Jewish chaplains meant that rules were often bent. Approached by young couples seeking to wed, Rabbi Levy wrote to the London Beth Din (religious court) for guidance. The response, "No marriages may be solemnised until a complete list of survivors is obtained," was out of touch with the reality of the situation. Levy writes, "To [the Beth Din's decision] my reaction was 'How long, O Lord, how long' would we have to wait for this to be achieved. It was obvious to us that those who wished to marry or, what was more probable, to cohabit, would not wait indefinitely."[138] While the Beth Din undoubtedly had wanted to verify the status of purported widows and widowers before authorizing a second marriage, a complete list of survivors would not be compiled within any reasonable amount of time. Many Jewish chaplains responded kindly to the urgency of DP couples.

Problems arose for those DPs who could not prove the death of a spouse before remarriage. Since the Nazis did not issue death certificates for the vast majority of their victims in the ghettos and concentration camps, many widows and widowers had to rely on eyewitness accounts and rumors for information on the fates of their spouses. When rabbis demanded further proof before solemnizing a second marriage, survivors searched for authorities who were willing to accept their testimony as proof. Frequently non-Orthodox Jewish military chaplains would take pity on these people. Some survivors in postwar Europe would not examine too closely the credentials of a man claiming to be a rabbi, if he consented to officiate the wedding.[139] The inability of DPs to procure official documents, combined with their drive to create new families, led them to disregard the strictures of rabbis. This resulted in ceremonies of questionable validity in Jewish law and in conflict between various rabbinical movements.[140] If no accommodating rabbi were to be found, some DPs would proclaim their intent to marry before witnesses and enter into a common law marriage.[141] Other DPs chose to live with their new partners without the benefit of marriage while they awaited further evidence of their spouses' fates.[142]

Rabbis had established the strict standards for proof of death for a reason, especially in the instance of a previously married woman. Without sufficient evidence of a husband's death, a woman was traditionally considered abandoned

---

[138] Levy, "Belsen Testimonies," in *Belsen in Memory*, pp. 239–40. See also Rabbi Yehezkel Abramski, responsum on permission for marriage (in Bergen-Belsen DP Camp), whether assignment in the direction of the crematoria is sufficient proof of death, whether ghetto expediency marriages are valid, in *Rabbinic Responsa of the Holocaust Era*, ed. Robert Kirschner (New York: Schocken Books, 1985), pp. 137–138.

[139] Ferderber-Salz, *Sun Kept Shining*, p. 213.

[140] Yehuda Bauer, *Out of the Ashes: The Impact of American Jews on Post-Holocaust European Jewry* (New York: Pergamon, 1989), p. 96.

[141] Levy, "Belsen Testimonies," in *Belsen in Memory*, p. 240.

[142] Rosensaft, *Yesterday*, p. 109.

and ineligible for remarriage. The standards of proof were less stringent for men since the consequences of their remarriage were not as severe. The rabbis wanted to avoid the possibility of sanctioning a bigamous relationship: If a previous husband should in fact be alive, not only would there be emotional distress to the various spouses, but the children of the second marriage would be deemed *mamzerim* (illegitimate). This would mean that although the children were legally Jewish, they would not be allowed to marry Jews unless they themselves were also mamzerim.[143] In turn, offspring from a *mamzer* couple would continue to be mamzer. One religious scholar noted that after the Holocaust "there were thousands of cases of *agunot* [abandoned wives], and the importance of marriage to the Jew can be seen in the fact that many of the world's most famous and prominent rabbis dedicated most of their time to finding legal ways through which such women could be freed for marriage again."[144]

This question of agunot was such an important issue that one of the first acts of the DP rabbinate in the American Zone was to send a request for guidance on the issue to Palestine.[145] In August 1946, the Rabbinic Council created a committee dedicated to the problem of agunot. It resolved that only a rabbi who was part of a beth din of three rabbis or a rabbi appointed by the agunot committee could hear evidence in such cases.[146] Trying to accommodate DP demands, camp religious offices published lists of engaged couples with the request that anyone with a reason to oppose the marriage inform the office.[147] In 1948 a rabbinic responsum from Palestine, recognizing the unusual circumstances of the Shoah, eased the requirements of proof in order to allow more remarriages. On the question of whether to accept testimony from witnesses who may be repeating rumor or may have profaned the Sabbath, Rabbi Shlomo David Kahana wrote, "But in our time, a time of general annihilation, a time when many of the martyrs submitted to death for the sanctification of God's name ... we should not worry about such suspicions."[148] Despite the care of the rabbis, the system was not infallible. One survivor reported a case in which DP newlyweds were faced with the return of a surviving spouse. Both marriages were dissolved, and the survivor was allowed to choose which former spouse to remarry.[149] Traditionally both former spouses would have been prohibited to the adulteress.

Like all weddings, DP weddings were emotional occasions, but unlike most, DP weddings were always accompanied by sorrow. In 1946 dozens of weddings

[143] Asheri, *Living Jewish*, p. 71.
[144] Asheri, *Living Jewish*, p. 72.
[145] "Council Meeting of Jews in Bavaria" (in Yiddish), *Unzer Weg*, 19 October 1946, p. 4.
[146] Alex Grobman, *Battling for Souls: The Vaad Hatzala Rescue Committee in Post-War Europe* (Jersey City, NJ: KTAV Publishing House, 2004), p. 168.
[147] See, for example, Landsberg Religiezer Amt, "Meldung fun Religiezn Amt," 6 September 1946, YV M-1/P-65; Eschwege Religiezer-Amt, "Meldung," 1 August 1946 (a second such document is undated), YV M-1/P-65.
[148] Rabbi Shlomo David Kahana, responsum on permission for *agunot* to remarry (after the war), in *Rabbinic Responsa of the Holocaust Era*, pp. 139–147, esp. 144f.
[149] Modenstein, interview.

took place on Lag B'Omer in the Belsen DP camp.[150] One Orthodox woman recalled, "The souls of parents who had not survived to lead their children beneath the wedding canopy hovered in the air of the camp. ... After the ceremony each couple went to their own corner, to commune with their sorrow, and there was no sound of rejoicing, singing or dancing, as is customary."[151] A similar mood prevailed at Sam Halpern's wedding to Gladys Landau: "Although we were not officially in mourning, our mood of loss remained with us. ... We celebrated this enormously important moment in our lives with a small meal and no music."[152] The usual joy surrounding the ceremony was marred by the absence of parents and extended family, and yet it was in this setting that past generations were remembered and a future generation was anticipated.

Marriages were an important step in recreating the family life that had been destroyed by Nazi persecution. Jewish ceremonies indicated the survivors' determination to continue their traditions. That these rituals necessitated building mikvaot on German soil, sometimes with German labor, highlighted the significance of survival and Jewish marital relations as a defeat of Nazism. The memories of the dead were vivid at these occasions that linked past and present and held the promise of future offspring. The tensions between DPs and rabbis over family purity laws reflected a loss of rabbinic authority but also the creativity of the survivors in adapting religious ritual and law to their unusual circumstances.

REPRODUCTION AND NAZI MEDICINE

Pregnancy demonstrated the recovery of sexed Jewish bodies. Women ovulated and men ejaculated. Many survivors' fears of infertility proved unfounded, but pregnancy brought new fears of its own. Memories of Nazi brutality toward mothers and children surfaced at the same time women DPs became dependent on German medical personnel for their care. Through their reproductive role, women DPs simultaneously signified the strength of Jewish survival and the continuing vulnerability of DPs to Germans.

Often young DPs were unaware of how babies were made and did not know that contraception was an option.[153] With the DP leadership pursuing a pronatalist policy, they were unlikely to learn otherwise. Reproduction had great social and political significance. At Landsberg German employees frequently asked the U.S. commander for contraceptives, but not the DPs: "I discussed this individually with several members of the camp committee. Each told me that the use of contraceptives is highly frowned upon by the camp people. They believe

---

[150] During the seven weeks between Passover and Shavuot, traditional Jews observe a period of semi-mourning. No marriages are performed during this time except on Lag B'Omer, which occurs on the thirty-third day of this period. Many couples wanting a spring wedding will choose this date.

[151] Ferderber-Salz, *Sun Kept Shining*, p. 226.

[152] Sam Halpern, *Darkness and Hope* (New York: Shengold, 1996), pp. 176–7.

[153] Mantelmacher, interview.

it is everyone's duty to have as many children as possible in order to increase the numbers of the Jewish community."[154] Reproduction was a civic responsibility for the survivors. DPs viewed children as essential to the revival of the Jewish people; thus, children were more than the products of private relationships.[155] As one DP recollected, "The young adults who survived ... had great hopes of building a new and better world. To accomplish this goal they had to produce a new generation, and so having children was one of their immediate goals."[156] Jewish births were a sign of the vitality of the survivors and their triumph over their oppressors. The birth of a new Jewish generation in the land of Nazism served as "biological revenge."[157] One woman DP recalled, "We all wanted to have families again. The feeling inside us was to show the Germans that they had not eliminated us all."[158] A parade of Jewish mothers pushing baby carriages down a German street clearly demonstrated Jewish triumph and Nazi defeat.

Pregnancy and childbirth posed significant challenges to women DPs. Suffering from malnutrition, pregnancy placed an added burden on the women's physical health. For example, Hilda Mantelmacher was hospitalized for three months after delivering her daughter because excruciating pain made it nearly impossible for her to walk. In addition to the physical pain, she was subjected to months in a German hospital under the care of mostly unsympathetic nuns who accused her of malingering. Finally diagnosed with osteomalacia, a weakening of her bones caused by a vitamin D deficiency, she was treated successfully with vitamin injections.[159] The fear of the medical profession learned in the concentration camps made such an extended hospital stay emotionally tortuous. This fear also kept many pregnant Jewish DPs from seeking prenatal care.[160]

Haunted by images of mothers murdered with their children, Jewish women survivors were aware of the vulnerability of mothers and of their ultimate inability to protect their children. One DP, upon seeing her newborn child, reacted with fear and guilt, "I didn't want to take [the baby] in my arms. In my mind babies had to be killed. No Jewish baby had the right to live. I couldn't imagine that I could keep this baby. ... My nightmares came back, and I started thinking again about Mother being taken away from us at Auschwitz, about how I had always thought we could have saved her."[161] Both mothers and children died at the hands of the Nazis, and the survivors feared that the same could happen to them. Testimonies by women survivors reiterate this association

---

[154] Heymont, *Among the Survivors*, p. 45.

[155] DPs recalled the community-wide celebration of the first children born in the DP camps. Biber, *Risen from Ashes*, p. 47; Millie B., "Videotaped interview," VHA, IC 35208, Seg. 42.

[156] Rubinstein, *After the Holocaust*, p. 61.

[157] Atina Grossmann, "Trauma, Memory and Motherhood: Germans and Jewish Displaced Persons in Post-Nazi Germany, 1945–1949," *Archiv für Sozialgeschichte* 38 (1998): 215–239.

[158] Modenstein, interview. Another DP wrote, "Giving birth to a Jewish child was a form of retaliation against the brutal cruelty of the recent past." Samuel Bak, "Landsberg Revisited," *Dimensions* 13 (1999): 33.

[159] Mantelmacher, interview.

[160] Modenstein, interview.

[161] Rubinstein's sister, quoted in Rubinstein, *After the Holocaust*, p. 167.

of children with death and the fear that Jewish children would not survive.[162] The complicity of German doctors in the brutality of the concentration camps heightened women's terror in seeking medical care.

The lack of early medical advice from professionals or from experienced mothers increased maternal anxiety. Nazi extermination policies had selected older women and women with young children for the gas chambers, leaving very few women survivors who had first-hand knowledge of childbirth. This lack of female elders meant that Jewish DPs went through pregnancy with little information about what to expect and about what was normal, increasing their fear. Many pregnant DPs did not understand what was happening to them when their labor began.[163] Mira Trocki entered the hospital screaming with fear. She thought that the baby would emerge from her belly button. The woman in the neighboring bed told her what would really happen, which seemed to reassure Mira.[164]

UNRRA hospitals were often staffed with non-Jewish DP doctors. Some DP women preferred to take their chances in German clinics rather than place themselves in the care of Ukrainian or Polish physicians.[165] Certainly there were DP women who were well treated by German doctors, nurses, and midwives.[166] A number of survivors credit German doctors with restoring their fertility and saving their sick children.[167] Some recall unexpectedly kind treatment from German medical personnel, such as Dora Sawicki, whose German doctor drove her home. She made him a package of soap and other rationed items as a thank you.[168] Some medical personnel hoped to get certificates to prove their good behavior toward Jews for denazification purposes. Others were never infected with Nazi ideology and treated Jewish patients with care. The remarkable birth-rate and acceptable infant mortality rate in the DP camps attests to the overall sufficient medical care mothers and children received.

Of the sixty-one testimonies concerning medical care during abortion, pregnancy, and birth that I viewed at the University of Southern California Shoah Foundation Institute for Visual History and Education, most were neutral in their attitude toward the medical care they received. Whether the survivors who

---

[162] See, for example, Gerda Weissmann Klein, *All but My Life* (New York: Hill and Wang, 1995), p. 227; H. Farkas, *Remember the Holocaust*, p. 150; Rubinstein, *After the Holocaust*, p.106; Sender, *To Life*, p. 164.

[163] Modenstein, interview; Mantelmacher, interview.

[164] Mira Trocki, "Videotaped interview," VHA, IC 43685, Seg. 195.

[165] Halina Biderman, "Videotaped interview," VHA, IC 23694, Seg. 42.

[166] Sonia Fruhman, "Videotaped interview," VHA, IC 43557, Segs. 136–137; Mira Trocki, "Videotaped interview," VHA, IC 43685, Seg. 195.

[167] See, for example, Bronia Waksbaum, "Videotaped interview," VHA, IC 7363, Segs. 107–109; Fela Leader, "Videotaped interview," VHA, IC 601, Seg. 103; Helena Silberman, "Videotaped interview," VHA, IC 24075, Seg. 56–59.

[168] Most likely her gift confirmed the stereotype of the well-off DPs in the doctor's mind, even though Dora only had a blanket and small pillow for her daughter until her husband acquired used baby clothes from the JDC. Dora Sawicki, "Videotaped interview," VHA, IC 32905, Segs. 90–92.

chose not to discuss the medical care they received had good or bad experiences cannot be determined. Of those sixty-one who did mention their medical care, many expressed fear at being treated by Germans and described callous treatment but had successful outcomes. Although the use of pain medication was not standard at the time, DP mothers remembered the lack of relief as a deliberate withholding by antisemitic health care workers. These memories intensified as they contrasted their experiences with those of their daughters, who gave birth during a time that favored the use of anesthesia. Thus even when they received standard care, they perceived their experience as one of continued persecution by hostile Germans.

At the same time, there is disturbing evidence that DP women and children were not infrequently victims of medical negligence, malpractice, and possibly even murder. Sixteen of the sixty-one patients described questionable care by German and other non-Jewish medical personnel. That is 26 percent of those oral histories, a significant number of cases. I determined that these sixteen cases had credibility because of the details provided and the overall reliability of the survivor's memories. A few additional testimonies mentioned rumors about mistreatment of women and babies by German medical personnel or personal experiences that either did not seem credible or lacked specifics. These are not included in the sixteen cases; thus the percentage of DPs who experienced mal-treatment may be higher. UNRRA workers tended to dismiss DP complaints of maltreatment as exaggerations and later scholars have not sought to correct this judgment.[169] In the following discussion of those sixteen, I test the experiences of the DP mothers against German medical standards of the time.

The most common complaints in all of the interviews were of perineal tears and extended labor (sometimes for three to four days) without medical intervention or sympathetic care.[170] While some instances certainly violated medical standards, the outcomes of the deliveries were not jeopardized.[171] More serious were infant deaths during labor and delivery. Many of these resulted from insufficient monitoring of the fetal heartbeat or misuse of forceps.[172] Only one of these cases appears to have met malpractice criteria

---

[169] See, for example, Atina Grossmann in *Jews, Germans, and Allies: Close Encounters in Occupied Germany* (Princeton, NJ: Princeton University Press, 2007), p. 214.

[170] Deborah Zweig, "Videotaped interview," VHA, IC 32066, Segs. 161–166; Ethel Kleinman, "Videotaped interview," VHA, IC 36783, Segs. 103–105; Nathan Nowak, "Videotaped interview," VHA, IC 29993, Seg. 67.

[171] V. Müller-Heß, "Gerichtsärtzliche Fragen in der Geburtshilfe," in *Lehrbuch der Geburtshilfe*, ed. W. Stoeckel, 8th ed. (Jena: Verlag von Gustav Fischer, 1945), pp. 893–896. Although pub-lished in 1945, this edition is a reprint of a 1942 edition. A study of East Prussian doctors found that they administered episiotomies in only 5.9% of their forceps deliveries even though it was recommended. W. Stoeckel, "Geburtshilfliche Operationen," in *Lehrbuch der Geburtshilfe*, p. 906. On the normal duration of labor, see W. Stoeckel, "Die normale Geburt," in *Lehrbuch der Geburtshilfe*, p. 197. On intervention in extended labor, see Stoeckel, "Geburtshilfliche Operationen," in *Lehrbuch der Geburtshilfe*, pp. 871–874.

[172] Ruth's son died from a botched forceps delivery. After immigrating to the United States, Ruth gave birth to a daughter and then a son. Ruth Zachary, "Videotaped interview," VHA, IC 20416,

of the day – an attending physician left the clinic before the baby had been delivered.[173]

Jewish women were in poor health after liberation, recovering from malnutrition, typhus, tuberculosis, and other ailments. Their general health may have made them more likely to suffer complications such as miscarriages and stillbirths.[174] Perhaps it was for these reasons that German physicians recommended abortions to some pregnant DPs in violation of standard German medical practice. I viewed six Holocaust survivor interviews in the Shoah Foundation Visual History Archives that discuss abortion in the DP camps. Of these, only one, a German Jewish survivor, actually had an abortion in postwar Germany.[175] The second suffered a miscarriage that required a dilation and curettage that she mistakenly referred to as an abortion.[176] In the third interview, the DP contemplated an abortion but chose not to risk an illegal procedure. Tragically her son died when his skull was crushed during a forceps delivery.[177] A fourth DP hospitalized for her entire pregnancy due to bleeding did not identify the nationality of the doctor who offered to perform an abortion that she refused.[178]

Two remaining testimonies about abortion reveal that their German doctors recommended that the women terminate their pregnancies. The outcomes of these two pregnancies raise questions about whether the doctors were genuinely concerned about the mothers' health or whether they were using the excuse of maternal risk to encourage DPs to terminate viable pregnancies. German medical standards required treatment of a complication, such as appendicitis or even lung disease, in order to allow a pregnancy to continue. A physician was required to consult with a specialist in the area of the complication and could undertake a

---

Seg. 106–107. During labor, Gina Freiden's child died in utero, "Videotaped interview," VHI, IC 24815, Segs. 102–104.

173 On forceps deliveries, see Stoeckel, "Geburtshilfliche Operationen," in *Lehrbuch der Geburtshilfe*, p. 913. On the monitoring of the fetal heartbeat during labor and the requirement to resuscitate in cases of asphyxiation, see Stoeckel, "Geburtshilfliche Operationen," in *Lehrbuch der Geburtshilfe*, pp. 871–874. Once engaged in a labor case, a physician was not allowed to leave even if a midwife were present. See Stoeckel, "Geburtshilfliche Operationen," in *Lehrbuch der Geburtshilfe*, pp. 871–874.

174 Survivors often attributed these tragedies to their concentration camp experiences. Luba Moskowitz, "Videotaped interview," VHA, IC 7784, Segs. 72–73; Mania Lederman, "Videotaped interview," VHA, IC 12556, Segs. 115–117; Regina Gaska, "Videotaped interview," VHA, IC 7188, Seg. 96.

175 At the time she was a German-Jewish teenager who became pregnant as the result of rape by the judge hearing her parents' restitution case. Although she hid the identity of the man from her parents, she told her rapist about the baby and subsequent abortion. He accused her of cheating on him with another man. Her parents' restitution case dragged on for years. This girl was sexually assaulted and then victimized a second time by being made to feel responsible for the delay in her parents' legal claim and their resultant financial hardship. Gerda Gottfried, "Videotaped interview," VHA, IC 34683, Seg. 20–22.

176 Lucyna Berkowicz, "Videotaped interview," VHA, IC 22640.

177 Ruth Zachary, "Videotaped interview," VHA, IC 20416, Seg. 106–107.

178 Mary Balzam, "Videotaped interview," VHA, IC 37216, Seg. 82.

medical abortion only with the concurrence of at least one other physician.[179] The following two cases involved physicians who fell short of the standards.

Esther Cane was being treated for tuberculosis and anemia when she became pregnant in Traunstein, Germany. The German doctor recommended that she abort the pregnancy, but Cane's father insisted on taking her for a second opinion to a female German doctor. Given that Jewish women had been forced to undergo abortions during the German occupation, it is not surprising that some hesitated to follow their German doctors' advice. The second doctor not only indicated that TB was not sufficient reason to terminate the pregnancy, she also warned that blood loss from an abortion could hurt Cane because of her anemia. After the birth of her daughter, Amy, Cane received a visit from the second doctor, who ordered a chest x-ray. Cane's lungs were clear, and she was allowed to breastfeed.[180] It is not clear from the videotaped interview whether the x-ray showed that the TB was no longer active or that Cane had never had TB. German physicians at the time often misdiagnosed tuberculosis.[181] In Cane's case, maintaining the pregnancy resulted in a healthy mother and child, leaving us to wonder about the medical advice dispensed by the first doctor.

Cane's first doctor failed her on two counts. First, he recommended an abortion without consulting a specialist to treat her TB with the intent of sustaining the pregnancy. Second, he did not get a second opinion concerning whether or not to terminate her pregnancy. It is possible that the first doctor had not kept up-to-date with the medical literature and was unaware of the relatively recent changes in attitudes toward tuberculosis and pregnancy.[182] It is also possible that he had such a high regard for his own ability to treat TB that he felt it unnecessary to consult a specialist in Cane's case. It is less likely, however, that he would have been unaware of the ethical need to consult a second doctor when

---

[179] Stoeckel, "Fehlgeburt (Abortus)," in *Lehrbuch der Geburtshilfe*, p. 691.

[180] Esther Cane, "Videotaped interview," VHA, IC 23633, Segs. 150–153.

[181] Dr. E. Ross Tenney, WD Civilian Chief Public Health Branch, to Director, Office of Military Government for Bavaria (OMGBy), Attn: Intelligence Branch, "Semi-Monthly OMG Report," 15 September 1947, p. 2; Public Health Reports; General Records of the Public Health Branch (Pub. H Br.), 1947–49; Records of the Civil Administration Division (CAD); OMGUS, RG 260, Entry A2 B3 C1; NACP; OMGUS Functional Report "Public Health," p. 1, attached to memo from Herbert B. Lupescu, Executive Officer Office of Military Government for Bavaria Civil Administration Division, to Chief, Public Health Branch, "Situation Report for the Period 1 Sept 48 to 1 March 49," 24 August 1948; Miscellaneous Reports (Continued) II; Pub. H Br., 1947–49; CAD; OMGUS, RG 260, Entry A2 B3 C1; NACP; Chas H. Moseley, Senior Public Health Officer, "Summary of Public Health Activities in Land Hesse for January 1949," 2 February 1949, p. 3; Miscellaneous Reports (Continued) II; Pub. H Br., 1947–49; CAD; OMGUS, RG 260, Entry A2 B3 C1; NACP; Chas. H. Moseley, "Summary of Public Health Activities in Land Hesse for May 1949," 4 June 1949, p. 2; Miscellaneous Reports (Continued) II; Pub. H Br., 1947–49; CAD; OMGUS, RG 260, Entry A2 B3 C1; NACP.

[182] A leading German pathologist reported, "our view of the influence of pregnancy on the course of tuberculosis of the lungs has undergone a great transformation in the last 10–15 years. ... While previously tuberculosis was the most common indication for the termination of a pregnancy, today it is only very seldom and in exceptional cases that a termination is necessary."

deciding on an abortion. Whether through malice, hubris, or incompetence, Cane's doctor did not provide her with acceptable care.

In a similar case, Rose Herskowitz's doctor recommended that she abort her third pregnancy. Her first pregnancy resulted in a dead baby (see below) and the second required a cesarean section. When Herskowitz became pregnant for a third time, her doctor wanted her to abort the pregnancy. Her husband and brother were both concerned for her health and deferred to the doctor's opinion. Herskowitz ran away until her male relations accepted her decision to carry the pregnancy to term. Herskowitz was determined to maintain the pregnancy, because her parents had always said she would have children – plural. In the end, she gave birth to a healthy daughter. Since cesarean sections carried their own risk, it may have been reasonable for the doctor to advise a medical abortion. However, Herskowitz does not say that she was sent for a second opinion or that there was any medical condition, other than a prior cesarean section, that would indicate the need for a medical abortion. Again, a doctor violated the standard that the possibility of a future complication was insufficient reason to terminate a pregnancy. The successful outcome of the pregnancy raises the question of how much the doctor's concern was for the health of the mother, and how much it was to discourage the birth of Jewish children. Herskowitz certainly came to believe that she and her child had nearly been postwar victims of German antisemitism.

Additional DPs recall German medical personnel who were too willing to accept the death of their Jewish patients. Rose Huppert and her baby almost died in childbirth. The baby was breech. The doctor, whom Huppert described as an SS-man responsible for the deaths of Jewish babies and his own midwife, gave Huppert's husband Morris a choice: Should the wife or the baby live? Morris said, "I want them both alive, or you're going to be dead." When neighbors got word to the Deggendorf DP camp about Rose Huppert's situation, DPs arrived at the hospital on bicycles as a show of force. The doctor became frightened. As he gave Huppert anesthesia, he yelled, "May you have a living child!" Her daughter was born healthy and Huppert suffered no complications from the emergency cesarean section.[183]

When he asked Morris to decide which life to save, Rose Huppert's doctor violated German medical standards, which specify that the life of the mother takes precedence when only one can be saved.[184] Thus, if there really had been an "either–or" choice to make in Huppert's case, the doctor already should have known the answer. Perhaps his question to Morris was simply a matter of cruelty, an attempt to enjoy the suffering of a Jewish man torn between his roles as father and husband, a male "Sophie's Choice." Since Huppert was in a hospital,

L. Seitz, "Die pathologischen Vorgänge im Organismus der Mutter während Schwangerschaft und Geburt (pathologische Biologie)," in *Lehrbuch der Geburtshilfe*, pp. 562–563.

[183] Rose Huppert, "Videotaped interview," VHA, IC 24268, Segs. 106–108.

[184] "When the mother's and child's lives are in competition," advised Stoeckel, "so that only one of them can be saved, the other must be sacrificed, then he [the doctor] must put a higher value on the mother's life than on that of the child and may not pull back from the hard and gruesome

the recommended action was a cesarean, which is what the doctor ultimately performed with success.

In this case the doctor had been willing to accept that either the mother or the baby would die in childbirth. It was the threat of violence to his own person that inspired the physician to use all means at his disposal to try to save both.[185] The happy outcome for Huppert convinced her and her friends among the Deggendorf DPs that Nazi physicians continued to practice a different sort of medicine for Jewish patients even after the defeat of the Third Reich. Indeed, in March 1946, Deggendorf physician Egon Weist was arrested on charges of being an SS-man.[186] In June 1946, the mayor of Deggendorf and the local Landrat were removed from office and convicted of acting against the interests of the Allied forces and disobeying an order of the military government.[187] Clearly, Deggendorf's leading citizens were not particularly hospitable to Allied nationals in 1946, lending credibility to the Hupperts' version of events.

Despite the mother having paid coffee to the midwife in advance, the German medical staff made no effort to revive Marion Samuel's infant when she was born blue and presumed dead. This lack of action ran counter to recommendations concerning treatment of asphyxiated infants. The nurse put the infant in the hallway with the dirty surgical tray. When Samuel's husband arrived, he was told that the baby was stillborn. Shortly thereafter, a nun who worked in another ward of the hospital and who had found the baby alive in the hallway brought her to the parents, clean and with a bow on her head.[188] The delivery team had been too quick to declare the baby dead. While it is impossible to say that they had hoped the Jewish baby was dead, it is also clear that they did little, if anything, to revive her.

Like many DP women, Samuel contracted an infection from improperly sterilized equipment. Because the hospital was unable to supply her with necessary nutrition and medicine, her husband traded alcohol on the black market to get her food and a Jewish doctor from their kibbutz managed to acquire some penicillin. Later, the hospital asked Samuel to sign a certificate that she had been well

---

necessity, to kill a still living child in the womb." Stoeckel, "Geburtshilfliche Operationen," in *Lehrbuch der Geburtshilfe*, p. 895.

[185] Cesarean sections were not without risk. Maternal mortality, mostly from postoperative infections, averaged 4–5 percent, although good surgeons had a mortality rate of 1–2 percent. Norbert Moissl, "Aspekte der Geburtshilfe in der Zeit des Nationalsozialismus 1933 bis 1945 am Beispiel der I. Frauenklinik der Universität München (Dr. med. diss., Ludwigs-Maximilians-Universität zu München, 2005), p. 33.

[186] Wolfgang Eibl, Kreiskommandant, to Dr. Vrabel, CIC, "Wochenbericht zum Donnerstag," 7 March 1946; Police Reports – 1946; Public Safety Reports – Deggendorf Res Liaison and Security Office 1945–48; Records of the Field Operations Division; OMGUS, RG 260, Entry Bavaria; NACP.

[187] Stadtpolizei Deggendorf to Kolb, Counter Intelligence Corps Deggendorf, "Lagebericht," 27 June 1946; Police Reports – 1946; Public Safety Reports – Deggendorf Res Liaison and Security Office 1945–48; Records of the Field Operations Division; OMGUS, RG 260, Entry Bavaria; NACP.

[188] Marion Samuel, "Videotaped interview," VHA, IC 40972, Segs. 210–219.

treated there. Samuel believed they needed non-Germans to vouch for them. Certainly, an affidavit from a Jewish DP would help a doctor or nurse called before a denazification tribunal. By contrast, Judith Ginsburg received penicillin and a blood transfusion for her postpartum infection. She remembered that the Hungarian DP doctors would not use Jewish blood since it was "aggravated," but her blood was a match with a German physician who told her not to worry "I have sweet and healthy blood." Ginsburg remained in the hospital for three months. Later the Hungarian doctors who had treated her so kindly were arrested as Nazi collaborators. With hindsight, she reflected that the doctors had befriended her out of fear of discovery.[189] Ironically the blood of the German physician saved her life, and the DP doctors turned out to be Nazis. If Jewish DPs did receive acceptable treatment from Germans or their former collaborators, they wondered if the physicians were truly decent or simply trying to escape detection as Nazi sympathizers. Jewish DPs found it difficult to determine who might be friend or foe.

A few women suspected German doctors of trying to induce miscarriages. Leah Binstock went to a German hospital because she felt unwell during her pregnancy. At the hospital she was given an enema. She says of the Germans, "they wanted me to lose the baby. ... I don't know how I got through this one."[190] When Tauba Friedlich was seven and a half months pregnant she went to a German doctor in Pocking for her first prenatal exam. During the exam, the doctor pushed so hard on her abdomen that she began bleeding. The doctor ran away and she was taken to the hospital, where she delivered her baby. The baby lived for two days. Later, Friedlich was told that the doctor was a Nazi and had killed many women.[191] We do not know if the doctors were indeed Nazis, but Friedlich and Binstock certainly experienced what happened to them as a continuation of the Nazi genocide against the Jews.

Other DP parents suspected German doctors of infanticide. There is a desire to blame doctors for tragic outcomes that are in reality beyond their control, but these cases suggest incompetence at best and malice at worst. Rose Herskowitz's first pregnancy ended in tragedy. The delivering doctor told Herskowitz that the baby had died of asphyxiation; the cord was wrapped around her neck. The nurse told her that the baby had been a beautiful girl and that the doctor's mistake had resulted in the death. The nurse urged her to lodge a complaint. In her interview Herskowitz commented, "I remember what they did. How should I sue for a baby when they took babies and threw them in the fire? I didn't say nothing. I lost my baby. I felt sick again. I was crying again."[192] Mourning her daughter, Herskowitz connected the child's death to those of Jewish children murdered in the Holocaust and relived the helplessness of those years. The nurse wanted the doctor charged for his incompetence (or worse), but Herskowitz was too lost in grief to act. She also accepted that Germans murder Jewish babies.

---

[189] Judith Ginsburg, "Videotaped interview," VHA, IC 24132, Segs. 134–137.
[190] Leah Binstock, "Videotaped interview," VHA, IC 21767, Seg. 102.
[191] Tauba Friedlich, "Videotaped interview," VHA IC 35575, Seg. 76–78.
[192] Rose Herskowitz, "Videotaped interview," VHA, IC 18630, Seg. 39.

In Föhrenwald, Renee Stern gave birth to a baby boy. He was strong enough to come home and undergo ritual circumcision. But a German doctor told the parents that the baby needed surgery to cut his breasts. It is not possible to determine the doctor's actual diagnosis, but German medical texts explained that under the influence of the mother's hormones, it was not uncommon for a newborn to experience swelling of the breast tissue three or four days after birth that decreased only after many weeks, even months. No mention was made of any sort of intervention being necessary, certainly not surgery.[193] Naively, the parents accepted the doctor's recommendation. The boy died from the procedure. With hindsight, Stern says, "If he was a doctor like they say, a Dr. Shoemaker, he would know this wasn't necessary, but he felt there was going to be another Jew less. And the baby died."[194] If they had been more sophisticated, Stern and her husband could have gone for a second opinion. Most DP parents were young and without elders to guide them. Devious physicians could take advantage of them, whether to receive payment for unnecessary procedures or to inflict harm on Jews.

The following case of Lucy Berger's daughter suggests that Stern may be right about the doctor's hidden motives. Berger's daughter was a sickly baby. The parents consulted a German expert in Munich who informed them that the baby would die any day from a heart defect. He advised, "Don't nurse her, let her starve, she'll die anyway." Berger recalled being confused by the advice and that her husband had to explain it to her. When Berger protested to the doctor that she could not just replace this child with another, the doctor laughed. Berger continued to breastfeed her daughter and a few months later went to another specialist, "a Nazi like the one before." This second physician confirmed the heart defect but told the parents that if she lived to her first birthday, then the child would survive. Twice that year Berger's daughter suddenly went limp but was revived by an injection to the chest at the Föhrenwald clinic. Berger's daughter survived to adulthood. Of the second doctor, Berger said "I think he got a heart of gold even being a Nazi."[195]

The advice of the first expert to stop breastfeeding and to allow the baby to starve is difficult to explain away. It is unlikely that it was an attempt at humor. Certainly the baby's condition was grave and there was no medical treatment available in Germany at the time, but the suggestion to starve the child makes no sense, unless we consider that starvation was one of the methods used in the Nazi euthanasia program to eliminate undesirable children, such as those with hereditary illnesses or mental deficiencies. Perhaps this physician similarly wanted to hasten the death of a Jewish child.

It is difficult to verify the details of these testimonies. Survivors no longer remember the names of the physicians or of the clinics. Medical records, even if available, will not show the intent of the doctors or nurses and will most likely ignore or minimize any action by medical personnel that could

---

[193] Gg. Bessau, "Physiologie, Pflege und Ernährung der Neugeborenen," in *Lehrbuch der Geburtshilfe*, p. 314.
[194] Renee Stern, "Videotaped interview," VHA, IC 25239, Segs. 99–100.
[195] Lucy Berger, "Videotaped interview," VHA, IC 11681, Segs. 50–54.

constitute malpractice or murder. None of the DPs say that they reported these events to military government authorities. UNRRA officials tended to dismiss Jewish accusations of mistreatment as exaggeration.[196] Perhaps they were too immobilized by grief, physical illness, or simply did not believe that Germans would be brought to justice for harming Jews. In any rate, such cases would have been tried in German courts, and Jewish survivors had no respect for German justice and wanted to limit their contact with German authorities.[197]

The prevalence of these stories suggests a disturbing pattern of cruelty at the hands of former Nazi physicians and midwives. One scholar of the medical profession has observed, "The record of medicine under the Nazis is largely one of eager and active cooperation; and neither resistance nor indifference was able to offset the enthusiasm of the profession for the regime and its policies."[198] Obviously, Nazi doctors did not become democracy-loving egalitarians overnight. It seems reasonable to assume that they would have continued to practice their racially biased medicine, especially if they found ways that would go undetected. Because babies and women die in childbirth, it would be difficult to prove deliberate homicide if it were a complicated delivery. If Morris Huppert had not frightened the doctor into saving both mother and child, it is unlikely there would have been an inquest if one of them had died. If Cane had terminated her pregnancy for medical reasons but then died or suffered other complications from her anemia, it is doubtful that the doctor would have been investigated for wrongdoing. If Berger had listened to the Munich expert and stopped breast-feeding her gravely ill baby, the child would have died but the doctor would not have faced repercussions. Failure to denazify the medical profession lends credence to these reports.

German nurses and midwives had been indoctrinated under the Nazis. The Nazis had promoted the role of the midwife in childbirth, seeking to make home deliveries the norm, and midwives had undergone training in Nazi racial doctrine. Muriel Doherty, the supervising UNRRA nurse at Belsen, wrote of the German women working in her hospital:

The young nurses have known nothing but the Master Race doctrine. They were trained to accept the shocking treatment meted out to foreign slave workers imported by the Nazis as part of this policy. Their bedside nursing on the whole is poor, but as we organize

---

[196] Grossmann, *Jews, Germans, and Allies*, p. 214.

[197] There may yet be confirmation of these or similar cases to be found in military government records. One survivor recalls an investigation of a clinic near Salzburg, Austria, that found a Nazi doctor responsible for the deaths of Jewish women. Rumors of Nazi doctors practicing medicine could have led to unrest that the military would have wanted to prevent and could have led to investigations. Israel Scharf, "Videotaped interview," VHA, IC 17120, Seg. 119. Martin Gross mentions a rumor of Jewish babies being killed in the Salzburg area, "Videotaped interview," VHA, IC 3450, Segs. 112.

[198] Robert N. Proctor, *Racial Hygiene: Medicine under the Nazis* (Cambridge, MA: Harvard University Press, 1988), p. 280. See also Henry Friedlander, *The Origins of Nazi Genocide: From Euthanasia to the Final Solution* (Chapel Hill: University of North Carolina Press, 1995); Michael H. Kater, *Doctors under Hitler* (Chapel Hill: University of North Carolina Press, 1989).

ward duties we hope to improve that. The older ones who trained in pre-Nazi days seem a little better, but with a few exceptions I would say from my observations that the general standard is well below our own.[199]

In a letter dated only two weeks later, Doherty expressed her distrust of the German surgeon on staff and the need for UNRRA medical personnel to constantly supervise his surgeries. She also noted of the German nurses, "it is difficult enough now to improve their bedside nursing, which is becoming worse and is probably a manifestation of passive resistance."[200] Later Doherty records the arrests of the German dentist and of a supervising nurse and her sister as Nazis.[201] She also charged that German nurses "frequently neglect the DPs and pilfer their food on a large scale."[202] DP women reported receiving uncaring treatment from German nurses and midwives, and their perceptions were likely accurate.

Denazification of the medical profession faced tremendous obstacles and led to many Nazi doctors remaining in medical practice.[203] German authorities argued against the removal of tainted doctors on the grounds of public health needs. Physicians in the lower categories of political suspicion were allowed to practice medicine as long as they did not employ more than two people and did not hold public office until cleared by a tribunal with the verdict acknowledged by the military government.[204] Tribunals were overloaded with cases and were subjected to pressure to exonerate "upstanding" citizens. Public perception was that the tribunals treated the upper classes (lawyers, doctors, businessmen) more leniently than the working classes. On December 9, 1946, the Doctors' Trial began at Nuremberg, charging twenty-three physicians for crimes against humanity, including participants in the Nazi "Euthanasia" program and medical experiments on concentration camp inmates. Despite the sensational case that resulted in the conviction of sixteen defendants with seven sentenced to death, little was done to remove Nazi ideologues from the practice of medicine.[205]

It is also likely that poorly skilled physicians were the ones available to DPs, while the better ones filled their practices with German patients. A study of

[199] Doherty, letter dated 25 August 1945, in *Letters from Belsen*, p. 99.
[200] Doherty, letter dated 5 September 1945, in *Letters from Belsen*, pp. 114 and 119.
[201] Doherty, letters dated 24 October 1945 and 6 December 1945, in *Letters from Belsen*, pp. 168 and 201.
[202] Doherty, letter dated 6 December 1945, in *Letters from Belsen*, p. 201.
[203] The Jewish Physicians Association represented the 350 surviving Polish Jewish doctors, most of whom worked with the Central Committee in the U.S. Zone and protested this state of affairs by refusing to participate in the elections of the Bavarian physicians professional association on the grounds that German doctors were guilty of crimes and that Nazi doctors were assuming leadership positions. Drs. Berman, Goldman, and Abend, "Ofener briw an das Staatskomissariat für rassisch, religiös und politisch Verfolgte, Herrn Staatskommissar Dr. Ph. Auerbach," *Ibergang* [December 1946?], YV M-1/P-85.
[204] Office of Military Government for Bavaria, Internal Affairs Division, Public Health Branch, "Cumulative Quarterly Report 1 January to 31 March 1947," p. 2; Annual History Reports; Pub. H Br., 1947–49; CAD; OMGUS, RG 260, Entry A2 B3 C1; NACP.
[205] Proctor, *Racial Hygiene*, pp. 298–312.

the University of Munich's Women's Clinic from 1933 to 1945 demonstrated that private patients were somewhat, but not significantly, more likely to have cesarean sections and other interventions in delivery.[206] This difference of treatment between private and general patients may have been more exaggerated outside of the university setting. Thus, the poverty of DPs may have influenced the physicians' decisions concerning treatment options.

The disarray of the German medical profession after the war contributed to the poor treatment of DPs as well as Germans. American public health officers observed that German doctors trained during the war years provided substandard care and often did not cooperate with military government laws and directives.[207] Most of the above-mentioned cases occurred in small towns and villages that were underserved by doctors in the immediate postwar era. The Bavarian *Ärztekammer* attempted to regulate competition among physicians by issuing settlement licenses that designated where a physician could practice. This was designed to prevent overcompetition for social insurance patients in the cities and to ensure that underserved areas would have access to doctors.[208] Despite this system, there were districts in which there was only one physician for 4,000 inhabitants whereas Munich had one physician for every 300 residents.[209] Physicians preferred to work in the cities where communications and access to medical supplies were better. Given the needs of the rural population and the absence of experts able to identify frauds, it is not surprising that a 1948 investigation of medical licenses found that individuals were representing themselves as physicians or taking the title "Doctor" without authorization.[210] With records destroyed during the war, it was difficult to verify an individual's credentials. Even DPs occasionally misrepresented their training. These factors affected not only the care provided to DPs but to the German population as well. Infant mortality rates reached an unprecedented high until German health departments instituted maternal and child welfare programs that brought the mortality rate back down to prewar levels.[211] In the DP camps, UNRRA and the JDC provided educational and welfare programs for DP mothers and children that most likely contributed to the generally acceptable mortality rates. Nevertheless, the encounters with German and collaborator medical personnel during pregnancy and childbirth left many Jewish women feeling victimized once again.

[206] Moissl, "Aspekte der Geburtshilfe," p. 68.

[207] Office of Military Government for Bavaria, Internal Affairs Division, Public Health Branch, "Cumulative Quarterly Report 1 January to 31 March 1947," p. 5.

[208] Office of Military Government for Bavaria, Internal Affairs Division, Public Health Branch, to Director, Office of Military Government for Bavaria, Attn: Chief, Intelligence Branch, "Cumulative Quarterly Report 1 January to 31 March 1947," 14 April 1947, pp. 1–2; Annual History Reports; Pub. H Br., 1947–49; CAD; OMGUS, RG 260, Entry A2 B3 C1; NACP.

[209] Office of Military Government for Bavaria, Internal Affairs Division, Public Health Branch, "Cumulative Quarterly Report 1 January to 31 March 1947," p. 5.

[210] "Public Health," p. 2, attachment to letter from James H. Kelly to OMBy Public Health Branch, "City of Munich Weekly Report," 16 September 1948; Weekly Health Report Munich City; Pub. H Br., 1947–49; CAD; OMGUS, RG 260, Entry A2 B3 C1; NACP.

[211] OMGUS Functional Report "Public Health," p. 1, attached to memo from Herbert B. Lupescu.

ENTERING THE COVENANT

As the guarantors of the Jewish people's survival, DP children aroused the interest of the religious leadership. Some religious authorities, such as the religious committee of the Eschwege DP camp, required that all births be registered at their office.[212] In late summer 1946, UNRRA clerks at the Landsberg DP hospital were kept busy reporting births to the religious office.[213] This was part of the rabbis' efforts to regulate who belonged to the Jewish community. In 1947, the Central Rabbinate of the British Zone reaffirmed matrilineal descent (that is, the inclusion of only children of Jewish mothers in the Jewish community) and reserved for itself the right to decide whether or not Jewish children introduced to another faith could be considered members of the Jewish community. This question was of concern for children who had spent the war years passing as Gentiles as well as those of mixed marriages, which included many surviving German Jews. In the same document the Central Rabbinate mandated that camp committees and communal organizations forward to the Rabbinate the names of all uncircumcised Jewish children.[214]

Just as with officiation at weddings, the rabbis found themselves in conflict with maverick DPs and German Jews over circumcision. Jewish male infants are circumcised as evidence of God's covenant with Abraham, marking their membership in the Jewish community on their bodies (*Brit Milah*). The vast majority of DPs circumcised their sons, as we will see below; however, some DPs may have chosen not to circumcise their sons, perhaps in order to increase their chances of "passing" as a Gentile should antisemitic violence once again become a threat. One mother claimed that had her child been a boy, she would have run away to prevent his circumcision, "because this is why my brothers were killed."[215] Intermarried DPs and German Jews also may have decided against circumcision as part of a resolution not to rear their children as Jews. The Rabbinate would want to know which families were no longer to be included on Jewish membership lists; however, the Central Rabbinate was also concerned about unauthorized circumcisions.

In guarding rabbinic prerogative and stemming the tide of assimilation, the Central Rabbinate of the British Zone decreed that circumcisions performed by unauthorized individuals were not religiously valid and called for the "strongest measures" to be taken against the offender.[216] Uncircumcised sons of Jewish women are legally Jewish but with restricted rights in the community; however, prewar Jewish communities frequently required circumcision before

[212] Eschwege Religious Committee, "Meldung," undated, YV M-1/P-65.
[213] M. Fratkin, multiple memos from Landsberg DP Hospital to Religious Office, August–September 1946, YV M-1/P-73.
[214] "Resolution of the Central Rabbinate to the 2nd Congress of the She'erit Hapletah in the British Zone" (in Yiddish), 22 July 1947, YV O-70/29.
[215] See Lynn Rapaport, *Jews in Germany after the Holocaust: Memory, Identity, and Jewish-German relations* (Cambridge: Cambridge University Press, 1997), pp. 92 and 182.
[216] Rat der Rabbiner in der Britschen Zone Deutschlands, letter to Zentralkomitee der Befreiten Juden in der Britischen Zone, 10 August 1948, YV O-70/29.

registering a boy as a member of the community.[217] DP rabbis were apparently concerned that intermarried Jews not misinterpret unsanctioned circumcision as automatically granting the baby membership in the Jewish community.[218] Given the low numbers of qualified religious leaders, these rabbinic orders must have seemed unrealistic and controlling to DPs and German Jews, who were content to have lay leaders perform the ritual. Despite these divisions between Jews over levels of observance, most parents affirmed their commitment to Jewish tradition by circumcising their sons.

The gathering of friends and dignitaries to witness the ceremony and to celebrate the entry of a new Jewish male into the covenant forged social bonds of community and signified Jewish renewal. As with other life-cycle events, the absence of the older generation was intensely felt upon the birth of a child. The parents of the first Jewish boy born in Belsen after liberation kept the assembled friends and UNRRA dignitaries waiting at the circumcision, because they did not know what to name the boy. Tradition was to name the first-born male after the mother's father, but only if he were deceased. The couple finally decided that since they did not know for certain the grandfather's fate, they would choose another name.[219] As time passed other couples gave up hope of their parents' survival and gave their names to the newborn generation.[220] DP Ruth Sender recalled trying to decide on a name for her second child, "Names. That is all we have left. Names. No visible traces of their lives. No pictures to show our children. Only memories of faces that fade in and out. How do I pass on the memories without falling apart each time the names are spoken? Will I ever have the strength to speak of them to my children?"[221] Ordinarily one named a child for an individual who died after a lengthy life and who left behind objects by which one could remember him or her and whose gravesite could be visited. The survivors' deceased loved ones left behind no such traces, making their names their sole legacy. The pain that came from having too many names to choose among and from knowing that their loved ones' lives had been ended so very brutally overshadowed the joy survivors felt at welcoming a new generation.

Often Jewish UNRRA and military personnel filled the gaps created by dead family members. In Leipheim, Jana Werner was still in the hospital when her son was circumcised. Since there were no surviving female family members present, an "UNRRA lady" held the baby.[222] The inclusion of UNRRA personnel

[217] Robin Judd, *Contested Rituals: Circumcision, Kosher Butchering, and Jewish Political Life in Germany, 1843–1933* (Ithaca, NY: Cornell University Press, 2007), p. 4.

[218] Beth Din London, "To the Jewish Communities of Great Britain and the Dominions," Rosh Chodesh Nisan, 5705 (15 March 1945), Lady Rose L. Henriques Archive, Wiener Library, London (Microfilm reel 41, USHMM).

[219] Doherty, letter dated 6/14 December 1945 in *Letters from Belsen*, p. 199.

[220] Rachela and Sam Walshaw, *From Out of the Firestorm: A Memoir of the Holocaust* (New York: Shapolsky Publishers, 1991), p. 139.

[221] Sender, *To Life*, p. 182.

[222] Jana Werner, "Videotaped interview," VHA, IC 29362, Seg. 124.

FIGURE 6. A blessing is recited during a circumcision ceremony in the Schlachtensee DP camp. *Credit*: USHMM, courtesy of Mayer and Rachel Abramowitz

in these celebrations also turned them into state occasions, linking the DPs to Allied authorities and symbolizing official sanction of Jewish life (Figure 6).

Despite the devastation of the Holocaust, Jewish couples strove to continue their family traditions and enter their children into the Covenant. In the Vilseck DP camp Jews who had survived the war in the Soviet Union were finally able to perform their religious rituals. Forty of the boys born in the Soviet Union had not been circumcised, and now their parents wanted it done.[223] Marking their Jewish identity on the bodies of their sons, the survivors embraced the heritage that the Nazis (and communists) had attempted to eradicate and proclaimed their determination to build a Jewish future. The celebrations were bright spots in an otherwise often bleak existence. DP parents took great care to provide special foods to their guests and to create as festive an atmosphere as possible. For example, Rachel Luchfeld's husband smuggled oranges into Belsen and she cooked fish for the celebration. They invited everyone who lived in their block to join them.[224] The ritual and accompanying festivities expressed the Jewish identity of the parents and forged Jewish community through the participation of neighbors and friends. The baby boys' bodies marked as Jews represented the continuity of Jewish manhood between the generations.

DOMESTICITY

The arrival of children encouraged the reestablishment of prewar gender roles. Women assumed household duties of diapering, laundry, cleaning, and procuring and preparing food. Fears that Jewish children would not be allowed to

[223] Harry Lerner, letter to his parents, 30 October 1946, USHMM, Harry and Clare Lerner Papers, RG 19.029*01.
[224] Rachel Luchfeld, "Videotaped interview," VHA, IC 50721, Seg. 112.

survive heightened natural maternal concern, putting great pressure on Jewish women to protect their children. Although some women managed to continue their employment or schooling, most gave up these activities when their children were born. Men worked (either for the Allies, in DP vocational schools and workshops, or on the black market) and dealt with emigration issues and the authorities. This division of labor was encouraged both by the conditions of camp life and by attempts to recreate the "normalcy" of their prewar homes.

Concern for their children's safety meant that DP mothers were constantly on guard. Hannah Modenstein recalled, "We were so afraid for our children. We wouldn't let our children out of our sight when they were going down to play or something."[225] During the Holocaust mothers had been forced to choose whether to remain with their children or to separate from them in the hopes that either the mother or children would survive. Their awareness that their own mothers, and perhaps they themselves, had not been able to maintain the ideal of protective motherhood under the conditions of German occupation made them exceptionally vigilant.[226] In their mothering, the survivors were reviving the prewar ideal of mother as constant protector in times of danger. This constant guarding of the children was the mother's responsibility. While mothers in the same building usually worked together to keep an eye on the children, there were no grandmothers or other trusted women to relieve them. The demands on the mothers' time and energy were great.[227]

Fathers, too, shared these feelings of inadequacy, guilt, and fear.[228] The inability of fathers to safeguard their families during the war led those who survived to suffer feelings of inadequacy and vulnerability. Aaron Hass, the interviewer of one such father, reported, "David Himmelstein feels guilty about *replacing* his first- and second-born, who were taken from him. ... Furthermore, to *enjoy* his post-Holocaust children ... would feel like another betrayal of the two daughters he was unable to protect."[229] The memories of the deceased children complicated the father's ability to relate to his new children. Those who had been fathers before the war and had outlived their children feared not being able to protect their new families. First-time fathers imagined that they could not do any better than their own fathers, who had been unable to shield them from harm.[230] Other men postponed or avoided fatherhood for these reasons.

[225] Modenstein, interview.

[226] On the crisis of motherhood, see Fodor, "The Impact of the Nazi Occupation," pp. 270–285.

[227] By 1947 the American Joint Distribution Committee had recognized that DP women bore the burden of dealing with poor living conditions and childrearing and assigned some women workers to train the women DPs to cope with the situation. Bauer, *Out of the Ashes*, p. 223.

[228] See Elie Wiesel, quoted in Judith Hemmendinger, *Survivors: Children of the Holocaust* (Bethesda, MD: National Press Books, 1986), p. 136; Zolan Farkas, interview with author, tape recording, Palo Alto, CA, 10 February 1997. See also Feinstein, "Absent Fathers, Present Mothers."

[229] Aaron Hass, *The Aftermath: Living with the Holocaust* (Cambridge: Cambridge University Press, 1995), p. 29.

[230] On the psychological impact of children experiencing the helplessness of their parents, see Davidson, "Surviving During the Holocaust and Afterwards," p. 69.

The tasks of daily life in the DP camps occupied much of the mothers' time, limiting their role to the domestic sphere. Many camps had inadequate water and power supplies. Keeping children in clean diapers frequently meant hauling water from a communal location and heating it on a stove in a crowded room. Without laundry facilities, dryers, or clotheslines, diaper washing could be an all-night process.[231] The demands of childrearing frequently meant that the mothers abandoned other activities; for example, both Hannah Modenstein and Hilda Mantelmacher gave up attending school. Only a few were able to combine motherhood with outside employment, such as Rubinstein, who worked for UNRRA and could afford to hire a nanny, and Mantelmacher, who could bring her daughter to the knitting room where she worked.

To help their wives, Jewish men hired Germans to do cleaning, laundry, and other work. Single men also engaged German domestic help. This activity frustrated camp officials, who tried to limit German entry into the camps in efforts to control the black market and prostitution. A report by the JDC and JRU explained that the DPs and others attributed these economic relations to "an act of what might be called retribution on the Germans for whom the Jews have been forced to labour." Being in a position to order Germans to perform menial labor could have satisfied a desire for revenge even though the Germans' working conditions were in no way comparable to the sufferings of slave laborers. The authors also noted that such employment was "a manifestation of normality – once more enjoying the normal and equal right with others of employing people and having things done for one by others."[232]

Domestic servants restored a sense of normalcy for survivors who had grown up in middle-class homes. Being relieved of the need to perform manual labor on their own behalf could help restore one's sense of one's own humanity and dignified status. And finally, the large number of single men explained the demand for domestic help since "How many unmarried men in normal society do all their own house work?"[233] Men of the time typically relied on female labor, whether that of mothers, wives, or housekeepers, to manage domestic chores. Orphaned and without wives, single Jewish men would look to hire domestic help. Married men employed domestic help to ease the burden on their wives and to demonstrate a standard of living comparable to that of normal society.

Without their mothers and other female relatives to assist them, DP women often turned to German women for assistance with childcare.[234] The health problems facing postpartum DP women often made it difficult for them to

---

[231] Mantelmacher, interview.

[232] Brotman and Viteles, "Survey on Conditions," pp. 5–6, YV O-70/6.

[233] Brotman and Viteles, "Survey on Conditions," pp. 5–6.

[234] I first proposed this avenue of inquiry in Margarete Myers Feinstein, "Domestic Life in Transit: Jewish DPs," (paper presented at the Conference on Birth of a Refugee Nation: Displaced Persons in Post-War Europe, 1945–1951, at the Remarque Institute, New York University, April 20, 2001), pp. 14–15. This topic was developed further by Atina Grossmann in *Jews, Germans, and Allies*, pp. 208–212.

care for their children.[235] If they were able to convince German physicians to document their need for assistance, then UNRRA would pay for the help and grant the German women entry permits to the camps.[236] Other DP women worked and arranged their own childcare. The access DPs had to goods that were valuable on the black market and to employment with the Allies helped to finance these relationships. For example, Erna Rubinstein was the sole wage earner for her family and had to return to work for UNRRA shortly after the birth of her daughter. "So I set about looking for a nurse to take care of my little one. I interviewed many women, and finally found a young German nurse who was very eager to work for me. I had a difficult time with this at first, but I convinced myself that the war was over, and that there were some people who were human beings even though they had been born German."[237] She writes no more about this woman to whom she entrusted her daughter, so we can only assume that the relationship was satisfactory. Perhaps she also felt some satisfaction in the role reversal of being the employer of a German.

Many survivors had themselves grown up in homes with non-Jewish governesses and domestic servants. Some of these non-Jewish women remained loyal to their employers even when the Nazis made it dangerous for them.[238] Historian and child survivor Saul Friedländer found his memories of his mother less vivid than those of his Czech governess, Vlasta. He wrote, "The influence of the Vlastas of all nationalities on the rapid assimilation of the Jewish bourgeoisie of Europe merits study. The Vlastas formed, quite naturally, the essential link between the Jewish child and the world around him."[239] Non-Jewish domestic servants had great influence in many prewar Jewish homes. Thus, for some DPs, hiring non-Jewish nannies represented a form of normalcy and the restoration of familiar patterns of interaction.[240]

The sharing of domestic tasks had provided an opportunity for Jewish and German women to form friendships that crossed the lines of persecutor and victim. After firing her first nanny for "going with boys," Sabina Cuker hired a young woman to whom she felt close enough to call "Tante Friede" and allowed the nanny to take the child to her home in Hamburg for Christmas.[241] Another DP recalled friendship with a German woman who organized his wedding and was *tate-mame* (father and mother) to his child. She became upset when the family emigrated.[242] The use of familial terms to describe these women suggests

---

[235] At the same time that her 18-month-old son was diagnosed with polio, a pregnant DP was put on bed rest. When the baby was born, the father paid a German family to care for it. Two and a half years later, they reclaimed the younger child when they immigrated to the States. The German couple had wanted to keep the child. Paula Warman, "Videotaped interview," VHA, IC 17437, Segs. 82–86.

[236] Grossmann, *Jews, Germans, and Allies*, pp. 208–210.

[237] Rubinstein, *After the Holocaust*, p. 108.

[238] Klein, *All But My Life*, pp. 34–35, 76–77; Kaplan, *Between Dignity and Despair*, p. 40.

[239] Saul Friedländer, *When Memory Comes* (New York: Farrar, Straus and Giroux, 1979), p. 16.

[240] I thank Doris L. Bergen for this insight.

[241] Sabina Cuker, "Videotaped interview," VHA, IC 27276, Segs. 96–97.

[242] Shlomo Szlamkowicz, "Videotaped interview," VHA, IC 1637, Segs. 51–52.

the closeness of the relationships but also the desire of DPs to create intimate bonds to replace the ones destroyed in the Holocaust.

The ties between DPs and German childcare givers did not, however, lessen the survivors' overall suspicion of Germans and their own desire to emigrate. Despite her friendship with a German widow who helped care for her son, Sara Bernstein remained convinced that "the Germans" looked upon her and her family as the enemy. Determined to raise her son in a place where he would not see "hatred in the eyes of every passing stranger," Bernstein and her husband pursued emigration possibilities.[243] Living in German rooms in Frankfurt with her young family, Regina Tauber hired a German woman she met in a shop and "lived like a person."[244] She recalled that the nanny became so attached to the family that she wanted to go with them with they left Germany for the United States. Tauber did not express regret that the nanny could not join them. One is left with the impression that she felt satisfaction that a German had become dependent upon and even fond of a Jewish family, while she herself remained detached.[245]

Certainly the German nannies benefited materially from these relationships, but many seem to have developed genuine feelings of affection for their employers and their young charges. DPs, on the other hand, often appeared less emotionally invested, perhaps because of their awareness of their dominant role as employer. These relationships also allowed survivors to feel morally superior to Germans, since the DPs demonstrated through them their ability to acknowledge that there could be good Germans in a way that Nazi Germany had not been able to accept the existence of good Jews. Despite the close domestic ties, these DPs still harbored general suspicions of Germans and viewed Germans as a whole as hostile antisemites.

Even though they were aware that domestic servants would be out of their reach once they emigrated, most DPs wanted to leave Germany as soon as possible. According to one woman DP, "I had a nanny and I had a maid, but I said 'I don't want their nannies and I don't want their maid. I want to get out. So whatever will come first, there we will go.'"[246] DPs and Germans engaged in relationships with the expectation that they would be temporary.

THE ZIONIST MAMELE

For six months in 1946, the Jewish DP birthrate was the highest of any Jewish population.[247] Nearly 1,000 babies were born each month to Jewish DPs by the

---

[243] See, for example, Sara Tuvel Bernstein, *The Seamstress: A Memoir of Survival* (New York: Berkley Books, 1997), p. 316.

[244] Regina Tauber, "Videotaped interview," VHA, IC 26587, Seg. 148.

[245] Regina Tauber, interview by the author, audio recording, Los Angeles, Calif., 4 June 2007.

[246] Rose Frochewajg Mellender, quoted in Rochelle G. Saidel, *The Jewish Women of Ravensbrück* (Madison: University of Wisconsin Press, 2004), p. 199.

[247] Kurt R. Grossman, *The Jewish DP Problem: Its Origin, Scope and Liquidation* (New York: Institute of Jewish Affairs, World Jewish Congress, 1951), p. 19.

FIGURE 7. Women sew by hand and by machine in an ORT training workshop in the Landsberg DP camp. On the wall are portraits of Theodore Herzl and other Zionist leaders. Date: 1945–1947. *Credit*: USHMM, courtesy of George Kadish/Zvi Kadushin

end of 1946.[248] At the same time, Polish Jews who had survived the war years in the Soviet Union made their way into Germany, bringing more children.[249] The births of children and the arrival of infiltrees who had not directly experienced the concentration camps coincided with the triumph of the more traditional image of the Jewish woman as self-sacrificing mother. In the DP camps, however, the prewar *Yiddishe mamele* acquired a Zionist consciousness (Figure 7).

With the baby boom, sexual experimentation and the partisan-girl ideal of the early months after liberation gave way to a more domestic model of the Jewish mother as protector of the young, manager of the home, and transmitter of Jewish culture. The Yiddishe mame of interwar Poland had been the incarnation of goodness and self-sacrifice. She was portrayed positively even by secularized Jewish youth.[250] In the DP camps, the desire to restore their now rosy childhood years encouraged adulation of the good Jewish mother. While the material conditions of the DP camps made self-sacrificing motherhood a necessity for survival, the desire to valorize the Jewish mothers who accompanied their children to the gas chambers also contributed to this model of Jewish motherhood. Self-sacrifice, however, was to be combined with a national consciousness.

The increasing numbers of young families benefited the Zionist leadership by helping to keep pressure on the Allies to solve the DP problem. A delegation from Palestine encouraged Landsberg DPs to procreate.[251] The Zionist leadership

[248] Abram L. Sachar, *The Redemption of the Unwanted: From the Liberation of the Death Camps to the Founding of Israel* (New York: St. Martin's/MAREK, 1983), p. 166.

[249] Mankowitz, *Life between Memory and Hope*, p.19.

[250] Celia S. Heller, *On the Edge of Destruction: Jews of Poland Between the Two World Wars* (New York: Columbia University Press, 1977), p. 242.

[251] William Eisen, "Videotaped interview," VHA, IC 20139, Seg. 22.

insisted that unrestricted immigration to Palestine was the only option for Jewish survivors.[252] Young families could promote the image of Jewish DPs as a healthy community unjustly confined to the land of their persecutors. At the same time Zionists were organizing the illegal immigration of Jewish women and men into Palestine, but pregnant women and families with young children were generally not eligible for this activity. Ironically, many young Zionist families would immigrate to the United States.

DP newspapers helped to promulgate the image of the new Jewish mother. For Hanukkah 1945, an editor of the Feldafing newspaper reflected on the biblical Hannah, who encouraged her seven sons to withstand Syrian-Greek pressure to apostatize and watched them martyred before taking her own life:

On this Jewish national holiday, when we celebrate our heroes and the heroic Jewish Hannah, we should also not forget the *mames* who didn't want to pay the price of apostasy to save the lives of their children and went together with them to a martyr's death. And our future mothers should know that they must not dishonor the holy glory of these mother-heroes. Their death may carry fruit and that is a new Jewish generation without diaspora-psychology, with a free and honest Jewish view on life. The future Jewish mothers who are far from Yiddishkeit should leave their Polish-Hungarian or other "cultures" by the wayside, remedy it a little with Jewish culture, history, moral teachings, etc. and prepare themselves to be worthy of the name: *jidisze mame.*[253]

The culturally assimilated mother of the prewar period was to be replaced with a mother educated in Jewish history and culture who would raise her children to be strong Jews free of the ghetto. Although she did not take up arms herself like the partisan-girl, this Jewish woman would raise her sons to be warriors and educate her daughters in Jewish heritage and pride.

DP artist Samuel Bak's mother is an example of the nationally minded woman. A nonreligious woman, she adopted Zionism as a result of her wartime experiences. Although she failed to convince her son to become bar mitzvah, she compelled him to forfeit a scholarship to study art in Paris in favor of immigration to Israel. She instructed him, "you will serve in the army and carry a rifle and no non-Jew will dare to tell you what you can or cannot do. And later, my child, if you decide to study in Paris, you will go to Paris with a Jewish passport. A passport displaying the proud blue and white Jewish Star of David that will have restored the broken world of the yellow star."[254] Although a newcomer to Zionism, Bak's mother assisted in the creation of this new Jewish mother, the mother who raised her son to be the strong, fighting, virile, new Jewish man.

Theater and cinema instructed women on how to be good Jewish mothers. For example, the first major professional Yiddish theatrical production in the

---

[252] The DP leadership successfully opposed relief workers' attempts to resettle Jewish orphans to places other than Palestine. They insisted that the survivors were the ones responsible for the children's future and that future would be in Palestine. Pinson, "Jewish Life in Liberated Germany," pp. 116–117; Mankowitz, *Life between Memory and Hope,* pp. 103–105.

[253] M. Gawronsky, "Chane un ihre 7 kinder," *Feldafinger Magazin* 7 December 1945, p. 4.

[254] Bak, "Landsberg Revisited," p. 35.

American Zone of occupied Germany was the Musical Yiddish Cabaret Theater's (MIKT, later MIT) performances of Sholem Aleichem's "Der blutiker Szpas." Reviews in the Yiddish-language press praised the lead actress for her portrayal of the prewar ideal Jewish mother, "showing motherly grace to the children, experiencing deeply the sorrows that swirl around the house," and highlighted the domestic scene of Sabbath candle lighting as particularly moving.[255] Survivors saw their idealized mothers on stage and were moved to tears and perhaps to emulation.

The artistic director and lead actor of MIKT/MIT, Israel Beker, co-wrote and starred in the 1948 film *Lang ist der Weg* (*Long Is the Road*) that portrayed the new Jewish family. A joint DP and German production, the film attempted to tell the story of the Holocaust and its aftermath through the fate of a Polish Jewish family.[256] The son, David, escapes to join the partisans and survives the war; the father dies in a concentration camp; the mother survives the concentration camps only to lose her mind when she is unable to find her son. During the search for his mother, David romances a German-Jewish survivor, expresses compassion for ethnic German expellees,[257] and rejects ideas of revenge in favor of planning for a future in Palestine. Ultimately, mother and son are reunited in Germany, whereupon the mother's sanity is restored. In the final scene, David's mother, wife, and son sit under a tree, while he plows a field on a DP kibbutz as the family awaits a future in Palestine. Each woman's raison d'etre is her son. The older mother is lost to the world until her son breaks through her isolation. The younger mother's only purpose in the movie is to comfort her husband and to ensure the future Jewish generation. The gender roles are those of prewar Zionism: the strong man willing to fight and to engage in productive labor on a training farm and the maternal, nationally minded woman.

The plot and characters in the movie were generally acceptable to the DPs, but the selection of a German actress for the role of the young woman survivor created controversy among DPs. Many objected to hearing the German language spoken by someone who was supposed to be one of them. Samuel Bak objected to the film's conciliatory note toward Germans and noted that the DPs "were a disturbing and uncomfortable 'merchandise' that was trying to sell itself and longed to be acquired. The DP camp was supposed to be a place for brief stays only, but the world did not want us and so we had nowhere to go."[258] In this light, the film served as propaganda, demonstrating the

---

[255] "'Der blutiker Szpas,' fun Sholem Aleichem," *Undzer Welt* (23 August 1946), YV M-1/P-85. David Pergament, "Szolom Elejchem's 'Der blutiker Szpas' in prinz regentn teater," *D.P. Express* (18 August 1946), YV M-1/P-85.

[256] Cilly Kugelman, "Lang ist der Weg: Eine jüdisch-deutsche Film-Kooperation," in *Fritz Bauer Institut Jahrbuch 1996 zur Geschichte und Wirkung des Holocaust. Auschwitz: Geschichte Rezeption und Wirkung* (Frankfurt a.M.: Campus Verlag, 1996), pp. 353–370.

[257] About this scene, Beker said, "We waited until the film was almost done to do this scene. It felt right to include such a scene, and every member of the crew agreed. It was not easy but it was the right thing to do." Quoted in Ira Konigsberg, "Our Children and the Limits of Cinema: Early Jewish Responses to the Holocaust," *Film Quarterly* 52 (Fall 1998): 10.

[258] Bak, "Landsberg Revisited," p. 34.

humanity and worthiness of the DPs. It was shown in German cinemas and in the United States. American military government officials worried that the film's emphasis on Jewish emigration from Europe would reinforce German antisemitic attitudes that Jews did not belong in Europe.[259] Meanwhile, a former DP leader reported from New York that the American Jewish community did not want to know about the DPs' sufferings and that *LongIs the Road* had played to empty theaters.[260]

Although it did not succeed in finding its audience, the movie did have a propagandistic intent, making more comprehensible the selection of a German actress for the romantic lead. The actress radiated healthy good looks. Her fairness, her "whiteness," could also serve the interests of the DPs who were hoping to persuade the United States to relax its antisemitic immigration quotas.[261] Earlier immigration debates in the United States had centered on the racial character of Eastern European Jews, questioning their whiteness.[262] The gender roles depicted in the film would be reassuring to an American audience. Jewish men were heroic partisans who eschewed revenge, and the women were passive, innocent concentration camp victims. Through the depiction of DP gender roles, the film could establish the DPs' respectability in the wider world.

The DP audience, however, was not happy with the conciliatory message, despite its compatibility with Zionist politics. David's sympathetic comments toward Germans fit with the Yishuv leadership's concern that Zionists focus on the fight in Palestine. Former partisans had had their plots for revenge foiled by Yishuv leaders who wanted to conserve resources and energy for the fight for an independent Jewish state. DPs, however, were not entirely prepared to displace all of their anger at Germans onto the British in Palestine. They still preferred the rhetoric of revenge even when they did not act on it. While DPs might be willing to forgo acts of revenge in favor of fighting contemporary enemies, they were not willing to express compassion or forgiveness.

CONCLUSION

In the DP camps of occupied Germany, survivors struggled to redefine what it meant to be a Jewish man and a Jewish woman. The values of the prewar era were modified to include revenge and national consciousness as Jewish male and female traits. No longer defined by the quiet dignity of the yeshiva *bocher* (boy) who, confident in his spiritual superiority to his tormentors,

[259] Jennifer Fay, "'That's Jazz Made in Germany': *Hallo, Fräulein!* and the Limits of Democratic Pedagogy," *Cinema Journal* 44 (Fall 2004): 23, n. 39.
[260] Abraham J. Peck, "'Our Eyes Have Seen Eternity': Memory and Self-Identity Among the She'erith Hapletah," *Modern Judaism* 17 (1997): 70.
[261] On gender and race in Hollywood films, see Diane Negra, *Off-White Hollywood: American Culture and Ethnic Female Stardom* (New York: Routledge, 2001), esp. chapter on Sonja Henie.
[262] Howard M. Sachar, *A History of the Jews in America* (New York: Vintage Books, 1993), p. 182.

would tolerate abuse, the new Zionist man fought back, sought revenge, and prepared for battle and productive labor in Palestine. The partisan-girl, sexually disciplined, childless, and dedicated to the national cause, formed one-third of the DP conscripts of *giyus* (the 1948 recruitment for the Haganah).[263] The Zionist mobilization for Israeli independence ensured that not all women would be encouraged to reestablish domesticity, at least not immediately.[264] At the same time, the high birthrate meant that most DP women assumed the role of mother. Jewish DP motherhood had political significance beyond the domestic model of womanhood promoted by the international relief workers and American movies. The Zionist mamele pushed her baby carriage in demonstrations on behalf of a Jewish state in Palestine and dedicated herself, physically and mentally, to the renewal of the Jewish people. Unlike violent retribution that only looked to what lay behind them, reproduction as a form of revenge permitted the DPs to avenge the crimes of the past while looking forward to the future.

The reality of life in Germany, however, continued to raise fears of persecution and victimization. Women experienced sexual assault by their liberators. Later, their pregnancies reminded them of the fate of Jewish mothers and children during the Holocaust, leaving them terrified for their safety and that of their unborn children. Jewish women interpreted the lack of pain medication during labor and delivery and their callous treatment by German medical personnel as continuations of antisemitic persecution. Their complaints of medical maltreatment suggested that some Germans and their former collaborators continued to practice Nazi medicine. Even in cases when there was no objective evidence of malpractice, DPs experienced it as such.

Jewish men feared for their fertility and virility in the immediate aftermath of the war. DPs displaced concerns about the inability of Jewish men to prevent the annihilation of the Jewish community onto sexual relations with German women. Their DP status restricted the ability of Jewish men to control their future. Camp conditions and international politics restricted their options for providing for their families and establishing a permanent home for them.

Within the context of the DPs' intense fears and feelings of continuing victimization, DPs struggled to make the ideals of the new Zionist man, partisan-girl, and Zionist mother their own. Their ability to live out these ideals often depended on outsiders. The new Jewish man could be confident in his dealings with Germans because, despite the antisemitism of individual officers, Jewish

---

[263] William Haber, "Report from Adviser on Jewish Affairs in American Zone of Germany to Meir Grossman, American Jewish Conference, New York, 10 June 1948," in *American Jewish Archives, Cincinnati: The Papers of the World Jewish Congress, 1945–1950*, Archives of the Holocaust, volume 9, ed. Abraham J. Peck (New York: Garland Publishing, 1990), p. 318.

[264] This delay is in contrast to the rapid "reconversion" of women workers to the domestic sphere and the return to sex segregation in the labor market in the United States after World War II. See Susan M. Hartmann, *The Home Front and Beyond: American Women in the 1940s* (Boston: Twayne Publishers, 1982), p. 24; Nancy F. Gabin, *Feminism in the Labor Movement: Women and the United Auto Workers, 1935–1975* (Ithaca, NY: Cornell University Press, 1990), p. 113.

DPs could trust the Allies to protect them from major harm. However, once the British began interning illegal immigrants to Palestine on Cyprus, a number of Zionist mameles (many of them former partisan-girls), fearful for the well-being of their husbands and children, abandoned thoughts of Palestine and registered for immigration to safer destinations.

The experiences of parenthood highlighted the courage survivors needed to rebuild their lives while living among Germans. Both mothers and fathers feared that they would be no less able to protect their children than their own parents had been. Surprisingly, given their distrust of Germans, DPs often depended on German childcare givers. This reflected not only the strains on DPs' physical and emotional well-being, but also their desire to attain a more normal standard of living and to restore familiar relationship patterns from their prewar homes.

Continuity with the past also encouraged the decision to circumcise their sons. This choice required courage for survivors still on German soil since it meant marking their Jewish identity on their sons' bodies and leaving them potentially vulnerable to antisemitic attack. The vast majority of DP parents engaged in the ritual, demonstrating their commitment to transmit Jewish traditions to a new generation. We now turn our attention to the children in the DP community.

4

Guarantors of the Future

DP Children

Approximately 1.5 million Jewish children were murdered in the Holocaust. In the ghettos children succumbed to disease and starvation. Sadistic German troops tormented parents with the mutilation and murder of their children. In hiding places, children died of suffocation, accidental or deliberate, to prevent their cries from revealing the hiding place. In the death camps Nazis sent children directly to the gas chambers. All survivors mourned children: their own, younger siblings, nieces, and nephews. It is small wonder that those few children who did survive were greatly cherished by the DPs. DPs had their own ideas concerning the best interests of the children and stood up to pressure from Allied personnel and representatives of world Jewry in order to protect the children as they saw fit. DP policies toward the children grew out of the DPs' fervent belief that the Shoah had proven the dangers of the Diaspora and that only in a Jewish homeland could Jewish children be free.

Child survivors of the concentration camps were usually those who could pass as older teenagers and somehow managed to endure the horrifying conditions. Some younger boys survived the camps as mascots of kapos and camp guards. Other children were hidden in Catholic institutions and with non-Jewish families. Some of them returned to their families or Jewish communities, but it is not known how many of them retained their assumed identities after the war, either withheld from their parents or with no surviving family members returning for them. Traumatized by feelings of abandonment and tremendous loss, hungry to make up for lost years of experiences and education, desperate for the comfort of family, and yet often fiercely independent, child survivors represented a tremendous challenge to the adults who would care for them and seek to ease their transition to life in normalcy.

The plight of child survivors greatly concerned international relief workers and adult survivors alike. As in other areas, Allied personnel and DPs came into conflict over the wisest course of action. Each group was convinced that it was in the best position to determine appropriate care for the children. Wary of the condition of adult survivors whom they viewed as emotionally unstable and criminally inclined, UNRRA and even Jewish aid workers believed they needed to protect children from the larger DP community and to remove them as quickly as possible from the DP camps and from Germany. For their part, Jewish survivors insisted that they understood the children as no one else could and knew best how to prepare them for the future. Having helplessly witnessed the mass murder of Jewish children during the Shoah, Jewish adult survivors dedicated themselves to protecting the children who remained and to strengthening their Jewish identity. The DP leadership insisted that unaccompanied children be prepared for new Jewish homes in Palestine.

CHILD SURVIVORS

Some Jewish children managed to survive the concentration camps. In Buchenwald, men with Zionist organizational experience protected boys in the camp.[1] Five hundred children were liberated in Bergen-Belsen. A future DP leader in the British Zone, Hadassah Bimko (later Rosensaft), along with a few other women, had personally supervised 150 Jewish children in Block 211 in the Bergen-Belsen concentration camp. A dentist by training, Bimko had used her medical knowledge and steady nerves to keep the children alive.[2] Older children, like Elie Wiesel, had pretended to be older than their years in order to escape selection to the gas chambers and survived as slave laborers, often aided by older relatives or prisoners. Some children managed to survive through the protection and extra food they received from sexual predators among the prisoners and staff in the camps. These camp survivors had often relied on instinct and cunning to survive.

During the war some parents had managed to find Christian families in Germany and in Nazi-occupied Europe willing to take their children, either for payment or out of friendship. Young girls were the easiest to place because, unlike circumcised Jewish boys, their bodies did not betray their Jewishness, and they could be useful as household help. Foster families also accepted infants and toddlers, since they did not yet speak and could not betray themselves and their rescuers by using Yiddish. The youngest children also aroused the most sympathy because of their tender age.

After the war some of these children were reclaimed by their Jewish parents or the Jewish community and brought to the DP camps in Germany. These situations were often traumatic for all involved. Frequently the young children had limited or no memory of their Jewish families. To make matters worse, many foster parents had raised the children as Christians in homes infused with antisemitism. When a surviving parent arrived, many children refused to go with him or her.

---

[1] Judith Tydor Baumel, "Kibbutz Buchenwald and Kibbutz Hafetz Hayyim: Two Experiments in the Rehabilitation of Jewish Survivors in Germany," *Holocaust and Genocide Studies* 9:2 (Fall 1995): 234.
[2] Hadassah Rosensaft, *Yesterday: My Story* (Washington, DC: United States Holocaust Memorial Museum, 2004), pp. 43–45.

Occasionally the foster parents would not relinquish the children. Jewish mothers who tried to press their claims in Polish courts often lost the legal battle for their children. Some were permanently deprived of their children. Others snatched the children themselves or with the help of Jewish Brigade soldiers whose mission was to return hidden children to the Jewish community.[3] Reunions of parents and children did occur, sometimes with the help of newspaper advertisements and lists of survivors. Occasionally desperate parents believed that a child was theirs when it most likely was not. And sometimes relief workers would allow the fiction to go unchallenged so that an orphan could find a loving parent.[4]

In the case of Edzia Mer, a DP arbitration court had to pass judgment similar to that of the biblical King Solomon. After the liquidation of the Lemberg ghetto, Ida-Wanda Mer fled to the Aryan side and gave her daughter to a Polish woman. Alone and on Aryan papers, Wanda was sent with a transport of Polish workers to Germany. In 1945 a Jew named Bezalel Mer returned to Poland from the Soviet Union. In Lemberg he sought his wife and their two-year-old daughter. The Lemberg Jewish Committee had been working to recover hidden Jewish children and had found a girl, Edzia Mer. The committee gave her to Bezalel as his child, and together they went to a DP camp in the American Zone of Germany. Shortly thereafter a notice appeared in the DP newspaper *Unzer Weg* from a Jewish woman seeking her daughter Edzia Mer. Certain that this woman was his wife, Bezalel wrote to her but was bitterly disappointed. The woman was not his wife, but she was the mother of the little girl for whom he had been caring. Edzia recognized her mother but did not want to leave the man she now loved and called father.

The chairman of the DP camp convened an arbitration court of four respectable men, including himself. The court decided that Edzia would be given over to Wanda Mer, and it consulted with all committees in the area to cover Bezalel's costs in the amount of 10,000 marks for caring for the child.[5] It was not uncommon for parents to reimburse their children's caregivers, and occasionally caregivers held the children for ransom.[6] In this case the Jewish community assumed the burden, since it (through its representative, the Lemberg Jewish committee) had mistakenly given the child to Bezalel. The tragedy of the case is heart wrenching. Bazalel went from believing that he had found his daughter and then his wife to being alone in the world. Edzia fortunately remembered her mother, but she still had to leave the father who had cared for her after the war.

---

[3] Rosensaft, *Yesterday*, p. 80; Bertha Ferderber-Salz, *And the Sun Kept Shining* (New York: Holocaust Library, 1980), pp. 187–188.

[4] Katie Louchheim, "The D.P. Summer," *Virginia Quarterly Review* 61:4 (Autumn 1985): 706.

[5] "A muter derkent ir kind baj a fremdn foter," *Undzer Hofenung*, 18 March 1947, p. 5.

[6] In one such case, the paternal aunt and uncle refused to hand over a boy to his Jewish father unless they were reimbursed for his care. Edith Dosmar, Comité Israélite des Refugiés Victimes des Lois Raciales to 92 Jewish Relief Unit, "Your ref.: Mr. Erich MOSES, Cologne," 17 April, 1947, Lady Rose L. Henriques Archive from the Wiener Library, London (Microfilm reel 41, United States Holocaust Memorial Museum).

The trauma did not end once the children were in the care of relatives or Jewish children's organizations (orphanages or kibbutzim). They often missed their foster families, and some rejected Judaism. They frequently had forgotten whatever Yiddish they had known and initially were at a loss in the DP camps and schools. In one such case, a young girl of two-and-a-half years in 1939 was hidden for three years in a convent and then with various Christian foster families. The mother and older sister survived on Aryan papers, but the nuns told the girl that her mother had died and at the age of six she received Communion. When the mother returned for her, the child did not believe she was her mother. The girl maintained that she was Polish and insisted that she have holy pictures and a crucifix in her room, even in Föhrenwald.

The psychiatric consultant provided by the JDC and a German psychologist interviewed the girl and determined that she was normal but needed additional help adjusting to her changed circumstances. They encouraged her mother to foster the relationship between the girl and her older sister. The school found a Polish-speaking teacher and that seemed to help put the girl at ease. The mother reported that the child had now asked for the removal of the holy pictures from her room and appeared to be more accepting of her Jewish heritage. The psychiatric consultant, Becky Althoff, observed that the case was "typical of many other situations where the child has been separated from the mother. ... Because most of these children are quite young, we feel that the prognosis is good provided understanding and insight is given to parents and instructors."[7] In fact, the early separation from key family members traumatized many hidden children, making it more difficult for them to establish trusting relationships later in life, and contributing to developmental and emotional impairment.[8]

Many recovered children could not be reunited with their parents. In Poland and Hungary, Zionist youth leaders organized unaccompanied children, those who were orphaned or whose parents' fates were unknown, into kibbutzim (communal living groups affiliated with political parties in Palestine) with the goal of immigration to Palestine. Some parents who were unable to care for their children or who wanted them to go to Palestine also sent children to the kibbutzim. Brichah led these groups to Germany in preparation for their move to Palestine.[9]

---

[7] Becky Althoff, "Report on Camela R.," pp. 1–4, attached to "Semi-monthly Report," June 21, 1946, United States Holocaust Memorial Museum Archive (USHMM), Henry Holland Collection, RG-10.146*01.

[8] Shamai Davidson, "Surviving During the Holocaust and Afterwards: The Post-Liberation Experience," in *Holding on to Humanity – The Message of Holocaust Survivors: The Shamai Davidson Papers*, ed. Israel W. Charny (New York: New York University Press, 1992), pp. 67–68.

[9] In early January 1946, two such kibbutzim arrived in Munich with a total of 150 young people. Eighty were under 16 years of age, fifty were between 16 and 20, and the remaining 20 were over 20 years of age. Susan Pettis, Deputy Director, UNRRA, Team 108, to Sam Zisman, UNRRA Regional Director, "Infiltree Group," 11 January 1946, USHMM, Samuel Zisman Papers, RG-19.047.02*08.

The transitions that hidden children experienced often inflicted great pain. They went from a familiar environment and family situation to people who were often strangers, speaking strange languages, and living a precarious existence as displaced persons. The children had learned that it was not safe or good to be a Jew. The trauma suffered by individual children, the youngest of whom could not remember their birth families and only knew their foster families, cannot be underestimated. Yet, leaving the children where they were, denying them knowledge of their heritage and further decimating European Jewry, were not options survivors or the leadership in the Yishuv were willing to entertain.

Most child survivors of the ghettos and camps were in their teens. They had been adolescents at the time of the Holocaust. Although DP youth felt themselves to be adults because of their wartime experiences, they had not been able to complete their educations and had missed some crucial developmental experiences of adolescence. The impact of experiencing their parents' helplessness to protect them left them predisposed to difficulties controlling aggressive impulses.[10] They tended to focus on physical needs and pleasures, such as eating, sexual acting out, and sleeping.[11] They often resented adults who wanted them to control their urges. They were child-adults who did not completely fit in with adults but for whom it was difficult to go back to recover what they had missed. In addition, they suffered from apathy and from a sense of having worked so very hard under the Nazis that they were now entitled to rest.

In 1946, large numbers of children who had survived in Soviet exile began to infiltrate into Germany. Some had endured Soviet labor camps; others had experienced harsh conditions in the Asiatic regions of the Soviet Union. Many lost family members, even parents, to disease, exposure, and starvation. Although most of the children had attended school, they were often functionally illiterate. After the war, these orphans returned to Poland from the Soviet Union and readily joined kibbutzim organized by former partisans and youth activists where they received food, clothing, and shelter. Some repatriated parents sent their children to join the kibbutzim both for the care they could receive there and for the promise of a speedy departure from Poland to Palestine. Hungarian children who had survived the war, mostly in hiding, also organized into kibbutzim and made the journey to Germany. UNRRA estimated that 13,878 children, of whom 2,458 were unaccompanied, entered the American Zone from June 15, 1946 to November 1, 1946. By December 5, 1946, there were 5,703 unaccompanied children under UNRRA care out of a total of 26,506 children in the American Zone.[12] The constant movement of children into Germany, between DP camps, and then out of Germany complicated matters for those adults engaged in their welfare.

---

[10] Davidson, "Surviving during the Holocaust," pp. 68–69.
[11] Davidson, "Surviving during the Holocaust," p. 71.
[12] Susan Pettiss, "Report on Jewish Infiltree Children," 22 January 1947, pp. 1–2 and 8, United Nations Archive (UN) S-0425, Box 64, File 11.

FIRST ATTEMPTS TO REHABILITATE THE CHILDREN

DPs and UNRRA officials alike recognized the need to organize unaccompanied children and to provide them with adult supervision. Initially this involved creating youth barracks within the DP camps where the children could live collectively with a foster mother or father. Children who had survived ghettos and concentration camps by cunning and instincts now needed to be socialized and taught self-discipline. The adults who tried to provide structure for these children confronted apathy, rebelliousness, and a host of other problems.

In the first months after liberation DP adults in Belsen, Feldafing, Landsberg, and Föhrenwald attempted to supervise hundreds of surviving children, most of them adolescents between the ages of fourteen and eighteen. All of these children had suffered traumatic experiences, and many enjoyed living according to their impulses. DP adults assumed responsibility for surviving children as if they were their own.[13] They attempted to supervise these children, but the children often ignored their efforts.[14] Bill Gluck was fourteen and a half years old when he moved into the youth barracks in Feldafing. He recalls that the children did not trust adults, but only each other. They ran around in "packs" and only listened to American MPs.[15] A twenty-four-year-old survivor whose younger brother worked in the Föhrenwald youth block observed that "a major problem was that [the youth] were considered and treated like children, when their experiences in the fight for survival had been in many respects more extensive than the experiences of most adults."[16] The desire of DP adults to impose structure met with resistance. In addition, DPs lacked training and sometimes the necessary instincts to work well with children,[17] and they initially received inadequate supplies for educational and recreational activities.

A JDC worker criticized the situation in the Feldafing youth block, reporting that nobody looked after the children, few of the advertised classes took place, and the children could be found in Munich or along Lake Starnberg or hanging around.[18] She recommended removing the children from the camp and putting

[13] On the phenomenon of foster parents among Holocaust survivors, see Margarete Myers Feinstein, "Absent Fathers, Present Mothers: Images of Parenthood in Holocaust Survivor Narratives," *Nashim: A Journal of Jewish Women's Studies and Gender Issues* (Spring 2007): esp. pp. 168–172.

[14] Simon Schochet, *Feldafing* (Vancouver: November House, 1983), pp. 24–25.

[15] Bill Gluck, "Videotaped interview, by the University of Southern California Shoah Foundation Institute for Visual History and Education," Interview Code (IC) 29159, Segment 172, Visual History Archive (VHA) [on-line at subscribing institutions]; www.usc.edu/vhi.VHA.

[16] Henry Holland, "Second Chance," (1988), p. 248, Holland Collection, RG-10.146*02.

[17] In Föhrenwald the foster mother "seems to be a rather rigid person, with limited understanding of the problems of this age group. She appeared prejudiced against certain groups because of their so-called communistic affiliations." Becky Althoff to Ethel Ostry, "Semi-monthly Report," 26 April 1946, p. 3, Holland Collection, RG-10.146*01.

[18] While "Papa Batchi," the 54-year-old DP supervising the Feldafing youth block, did not impress the JDC, another DP noted his hard work. Simon Schochet praised Batchi's dedication to the

them under the supervision of "competent persons, not internees, who like children and who understand their problems and their difficulties."[19] Many UNRRA and JDC workers feared that DP adults were not able to detach themselves enough from the children to consider their needs nor, did they believe, that adult survivors had the emotional and psychological strength to deal with the children successfully.

Group living, whether in a youth block or a kibbutz (see section on kibbutzim), provided many children with familial relationships that facilitated their transition to life in freedom. These bonds allowed many of them to gain social skills and reduced their anxiety, allowing them to regain emotional health. For others, group living reinforced their regressive tendencies.[20] Some children did not want to abide by the rules of the youth blocks and left the DP camp for the excitement of life on the black market.[21] Indeed, relief workers feared that the poor morale and black market activities of adult DPs as well as the adults' overidentification with the children were having negative effects on the children. In September 1945, JDC worker Miriam Warburg wrote, "They should be taken away from the grown-ups amongst whom they live, and who are terribly demoralized. Stealing, people of both sexes sleeping together (married couples sleeping with two or three friends is a common thing), unwillingness of three-fourths of all inmates to work; bad habits, etc., create a poisonous surrounding for children."[22] UNRRA and JDC officials sought to limit contact between children and adult camp life.

Radical measures were taken in Föhrenwald: Relief workers encouraged the separation of children from their relatives in an effort to protect the children from the traumatized adults. It is unquestionable that some survivors had odd behaviors and were subject to emotional outbursts, just as it is unquestionable that the social workers were motivated by what they believed to be the children's best interests. Yet, with hindsight, we can imagine the trauma done to many of these children as they were removed from the only adults left from their prewar lives. The children had either survived because of the adults from whom they were taken, or had suffered alone and were only recently reunited with a loved one – before being removed from them once again.

In a June 7, 1946 report, Becky Althoff admitted that she had come to question the usefulness of the Föhrenwald camp *Kinderheim* (children's home) since it did not have adequate facilities and staff to treat accompanied children within the camp:

The purpose has been somewhat misused, in that the family situation instead of being strengthened, has been weakened by the needless separation, and dissolution of family ties.

children he was able to reach, his willingness to step on UNRRA workers' toes by writing numerous letters abroad to find sponsors for the children, and his success when a Swiss boarding school offered one of the girls a two-year scholarship. Schochet, *Feldafing*, pp. 112–114.

19 Ruth Lambert, "Report," 8 September 1945, p. 2, UN S-0437, Box 12, File 16.
20 Davidson, "Surviving during the Holocaust," pp. 68 and 72.
21 Samuel Pisar, *Of Blood and Hope* (New York: Macmillan Publishing, 1980), p. 97.
22 Miriam Warburg quoted in Solomon Goldman, "Education Among Jewish Displaced Persons: The Sheerit Hapletah in Germany, 1945–1950" (Ph.D. diss., The Dropsie University, 1978), p. 74.

It has served to alienate children from responsible relatives, needlessly, without giving the child substitute relationships which would be constructive for growth and development. It has relieved the parent of the care and companionship of the child without purpose, and has been used as a boarding home for those who wish to continue hold of the child, for visiting purposes only.[23]

The relief workers found their presumption that separating children from responsible relatives would facilitate their rehabilitation to be in error. Althoff proceeded to move the remaining thirteen children from the Kinderheim.

The availability of a female caregiver facilitated the reunification of children with their families. Both DPs and relief workers affirmed women's responsibility for young children. Fathers and brothers assured Althoff that female relatives would help care for the children. The case of one DP father who could not rely on a female relative proved to be one of the most difficult to resolve. Mothers, however, did not need to demonstrate that they had additional assistance available to them. The first families to reunite were two children with their mother and one boy with his two brothers and sister-in-law. The sister-in-law reported that after the move the boy became less antisocial and happier.[24] The fact that the sister-in-law spoke on the boy's behalf reinforces the impression that women assumed the burden of childrearing. The restoration of family life appeared to have positive effects on the well-being of the children.

Most of the relatives were eager to be reunited with the children, although they had a number of concerns that needed to be addressed first. Parents feared that removal from the Kinderheim or an international children's center would jeopardize the children's chances of receiving certificates for immigration to Palestine. In their desire to facilitate their children's emigration, some parents gave aid workers the impression that they had abandoned their children, endangering their parental rights.[25] DP parents faced difficult decisions when trying to guarantee their children's future. Often they willingly endured separation when they believed it would benefit their children's emigration opportunities. Relief workers could interpret the apparent ease with which parents separated from their children as evidence of neglect, whereas parents viewed it as a sacrifice to speed their children's departure from Europe.

In Föhrenwald, Althoff first assured parents that reuniting with their children would not impede their emigration status and then tackled logistical problems,

---

[23] Becky Althoff to Ethel Ostrey, "Semi-monthly Report," June 7, 1946, p. 3, Holland Collection, RG-10.146*01.

[24] Becky Althoff to Ethel Ostrey, "Semi-monthly Report," June 21, 1946, p. 2, Holland Collection, RG-10.146*01.

[25] In one such case, a Jewish Relief Unit worker apparently informed the Jewish Agency for Palestine office in Munich that Mrs. Gutfreund had abandoned her then 9-year-old son. It was revealed to have been a misunderstanding. P. I. R. Hart, JRCA, to Marie Malachowski, letter dated 7 November 1947, Henriques Archive, Microfilm reel 41; P. I. R. Hart, "Interview with Mrs. Gutfreund," 5 November 1947, Henriques Archive, Microfilm reel 41; P.I.R. Hart, "Interview with Miss Rita Reinmann," 23 January 1948, Henriques Archive, Microfilm reel 41.

such as housing and childcare.[26] Although the mothers were willing to take their children and to arrange their work hours so that they could care for the children when they were not in school or attending after-school activities, the situation was different for Lutca H.'s widowed father, who worked as a bookkeeper in the camp and worried about his ability to care for her without female assistance. He hoped that Lutka would immigrate to Palestine before the Kinderheim disbanded, demonstrating his trust in the Jewish Agency to care for unaccompanied children once they arrived in Palestine.[27] Althoff's somewhat ready acceptance of the father's assertion that he could not be expected to care for a child without female assistance demonstrates a shared model of gendered responsibilities toward children. The father's lack of childcare options also speaks to the difficulties facing parents uprooted from their communities and without extended family or established social networks on which to depend.

When a biological parent was not present, social workers had to decide which relatives were legitimate guardians for the children. UNRRA feared that some relatives sought to claim children only to further their chances for speedy emigration as a family. UNRRA's policy of working to reunite families had to be balanced with caution and cases had to be handled on an individual basis.[28] Biological relationships and morality played decisive roles in Althoff's decisions. In the case of Zosia F., both a stepfather and an aunt by marriage claimed responsibility for the child. Althoff believed the aunt to be the better guardian but decided to consult with the camp rabbi.[29] The rabbi denied the stepfather's claim to the child. He also questioned whether the twenty-eight-year-old aunt-in-law, who was newly remarried and likely to start her own family, would make Zosia a true member of the family. Althoff shared the concern. The rabbi recommended that Zosia be transferred to the Children's Camp at Ansbach since she was "a full orphan whose care and responsibility should rightly be assumed by the Community, and as such, sent to a Children's Camp, where the child will obtain such training and supervision, as will be of greatest benefit to her."[30] Without a blood relation, Zosia was sent to Ansbach as an unaccompanied child.

In another case, Althoff had suspicions regarding Basia F.'s "putative aunt" and the unusual affluence she possessed. Her concerns hinted at extramarital sex and black market activities, an unwholesome environment for a young girl. Basia's father and "aunt" lived in Munich. The father was newly arrived from Poland and reportedly ill. The aunt visited often, bringing clothing and food, suggesting an interest in the child but no desire to assume full responsibility. Clearly unwilling to allow the "aunt," a woman of questionable familial and moral status, to decide the girl's fate, Althoff resolved to redouble her efforts to

[26] Althoff, "Semi-monthly Report," June 21, 1946, p. 2.
[27] Althoff, "Semi-monthly Report," June 21, 1946, p. 2.
[28] Pettiss, "Report on Jewish Infiltree Children," pp. 9–10.
[29] Althoff, "Semi-monthly Report," June 7, 1946, pp. 1–2.
[30] Althoff, "Semi-monthly Report," June 21, 1946, pp. 1–2.

find the father within a set period of time. Failing that, she would send Basia to Ansbach.[31]

These were not cases in which children faced imminent danger from the relatives. Social workers had decided that survivors as a whole were too unstable to be trusted with the care of children. Some adult relatives welcomed the intervention of the Kinderheim because it freed them of childcare worries while they worked and they believed that children in a Kinderheim would emigrate sooner. The fact that UNRRA and the military government employed many of these adults suggests that they were relatively well adjusted and not threats to their children. It also points out how the lack of extended families limited the availability of childcare and posed an obstacle to DP employment and/or family life.

MOVING OUT OF THE CAMPS

Conditions in the DP camps, particularly in the early months following liberation, were squalid and cramped. With few activities available, DPs were listless, apathetic, and bored when they were not agitated or engaged in black market activities. Both DP leaders and aid workers believed unaccompanied children would be better off separated from the demoralizing conditions of the camps. UNRRA and JDC workers encouraged the formation of separate children's centers, while DP youth organizers founded kibbutzim. All who worked with the children struggled to supply them with adequate living conditions and decent learning environments. The goal of Allied personnel was to secure the speedy emigration of the children, while DP leaders wanted the children kept in Germany until their immigration to Palestine.

In setting up international children's centers, UNRRA teams had to navigate relations not only with survivors but also with the armies, military governments, and Germans. Supplies were an ongoing problem for agencies caring for DPs, and the children's centers were no exception. Clothing, light bulbs, furniture, and linens were often in short supply. One UNRRA worker recalled that, desperate for spare parts and essential supplies, "sometimes the rule of not taking from the Germans was broken, at the risk of being reprimanded."[32] Responsibility for the supply program went back and forth between the military government and the Army, often leaving UNRRA caught in the middle. Not allowed to buy locally, the teams had to make do.

A sympathetic military officer had requisitioned glass "potties" for the first International D.P. Children's Center at Kloster Indersdorf. When these broke and the submitted requisition was returned "not available," the UNRRA workers improvised using dried milk containers inserted into wooden boxes manufactured in the village. Having villagers work for the center was not in

---

[31] Althoff, "Semi-monthly Report," June 21, 1946, p. 1.
[32] Greta Fischer, "D.P. Children's Center, Kloster Indersdorf Kreis Dachau," p. 10, USHMM, Greta Fischer Papers, RG-19.034*01.

accordance with military directives, but the need was urgent.[33] When the team requested that local craftsmen make nursery equipment, the Germans protested, "that they were not Nazis and should not be asked, *even if the order was paid for.* (emphasis added)."[34] Since the UNRRA team had offered to pay the craftsmen, their refusal cannot be attributed to their own economic plight but to an unwillingness to assist the Allies and victims of Nazism. To refuse to provide toddlers with furniture and necessary items indicates a high level of hostility toward the survivors and occupying forces. The suggestion that the craftsmen should not be required to do the work since they were not Nazis indicates their unwillingness to assume any responsibility for Nazi crimes or for redressing them. In the end, however, the villagers did accept work from UNRRA and relations improved.

Supply problems continued to plague children's centers as the numbers of unaccompanied children increased with the influx of infiltrees into Germany. At the Rosenheim Children's Center in autumn 1946, classes could not stay late because there were no light bulbs, and the theater did not have heating fuel. The center had received cloth for a sewing workshop but no thread. U.S. soldiers furnished barracks for a playroom and some came daily to supervise recreation.[35] The active involvement of local U.S. soldiers helped the center to meet the children's needs without depending on the local German population, but the lack of equipment interfered with educational projects and programs for the children's rehabilitation.

UNRRA often chose hotels, country estates, and cloisters to house the orphaned children, giving the children more pleasant surroundings than the squalid assembly centers. Kloster Indersdorf was a former monastery that served as an orphanage when it was requisitioned at the end of June 1945. According to one of the founding UNRRA workers, it looked like a typical German orphanage: "clean on the surface, the children – sad-looking, well disciplined, – doing most of the work, total lack of any play material, laughter or warmth."[36] The village of Markt Indersdorf was well kempt and gave the "impression that the war had bypassed Kloster Indersdorf."[37] In early 1947, after a diphtheria epidemic took the lives of four children at the center, the remaining children and part of the team moved to a more suitable but equally idyllic location in Prien am Chiemsee. Fresh air, natural surroundings, and locations free from rubble and other reminders of war were ideal for the recovery of child survivors.

The center at Indersdorf housed between 300 and 350 children. There were two distinct age groups: those under three years of age who had been kidnapped or hidden with German families and those over twelve years of age, most between fourteen and eighteen years old, who had come to Germany as slave

[33] Fischer, "D.P. Children's Center," p. 10.
[34] Fischer, "D.P. Children's Center," p. 34.
[35] Glenn O. Ratcliff, "Field Inspection Report," 9 November 1946, Zisman Papers, RG-19. 047.02*26.
[36] Fischer, "D.P. Children's Center," p. 7.
[37] Fischer, "D.P. Children's Center," p. 8.

laborers, or survived concentration camps, or hid in the woods and caves of
Eastern Europe. It was hard to determine the children's identities. Younger ones
had forgotten their origins and older ones had learned to adjust their age and
nationality to get the most benefit from their present situation. Teenagers who
had presented themselves as older than their years to the Nazis in order to avoid
selection for the gas chambers now claimed to be younger in order to be eligible
for special children's visas.[38]

The diversity of the children led to conflicts between groups, the most severe
between Polish Catholic and Jewish children. The UNRRA workers believed
that this experiment of having all the children live together fostered tolerance
and respect.[39] Early Allied policy avoided distinguishing between nationalities
and religions so as not to appear to endorse the racial thought of the Nazis.
The result forced Jews to live among antisemitic groups, continuing their wartime victimization. Later children's homes established to accommodate infiltrees allowed Jewish children to live apart from their potential tormentors. In
summer 1946, one such home was the Kinderheim Schwebda near Eschwege.
It had 200 children between the ages of 2 and 17, all orphans and most of them
returned from Russian exile, with 30 young adult supervisors (*madrichim*). The
madrichim had completed a six-week course before taking over their young
charges. The home was divided into Zionist youth groups: socialist Hashomer
Hatzair and Dror, labor-oriented Gordonia, and pluralistic Noar Hatzion. The
location in a castle allowed the children fresh air and activity on the wooded
grounds.[40] The Eschwege DP newspaper gloated over Jewish children playing in
the home of the antisemitic baron.[41]

At Kloster Indersdorf, the UNRRA team marveled that the children had high
ethical standards, despite their cravings for material goods and food. The team
agreed that even after their health was restored, the children would continue
to receive more than normal rations for the psychological benefit it afforded
them.[42] Children were encouraged to practice the manners of an upper-class
household and to participate in the running of the center. They helped remake
donated clothing into new clothes. The new attire seemed to "change the entire
personality of a child."[43] Older children also assisted with the care of younger
children, with great benefits for all. UNRRA headquarters considered separating
the age groups into two centers in order to simplify management, but the team
considered the benefits of mixed living and the family atmosphere it created to
outweigh the problems.[44]

---

[38] Fischer, "D.P. Children's Center," p. 13.
[39] Fischer, "D.P. Children's Center," p. 15.
[40] "Dos jidisze kinder-sanatorim in Szwebde," *Undzer Hofenung*, 11 July 1946, p. 3.
[41] "Dort wu s'hot geherszt der baron," *Undzer Hofenung*, 11 July 1946, p. 3.
[42] Fischer, "D.P. Children's Center," p. 25. The desire for material and physical satisfactions was
   common in adolescent survivors in an attempt to numb their grief. See Davidson, "Surviving during the Holocaust and Afterwards," p. 71.
[43] Fischer, "D.P. Children's Center," p.26.
[44] Fischer, "D.P. Children's Center," p. 39.

The need for family was great. Many children had left the center in unsuccessful searches for relatives before returning to its shelter. Those children without biological relatives created their own familial relationships. UNRRA worker Greta Fischer observed, "Next to the desire to find relatives was the need for remaining with friends especially those who had experienced similar hardships in the same ghettos or camps. Child after child asked to be allowed to sleep in the same room with his friends and that no movement plans be made unless they were moved, too."[45] Many of these friendships were as deep and strong as sibling relationships. This need was not limited to children. Survivors of all ages created surrogate families in the immediate postwar period. Unfortunately, authorities did not always understand the significance of these bonds.

Often emigration schemes would separate these friends, particularly if one of them had passed his or her sixteenth birthday. Teenagers sixteen and older were ineligible for visas as unaccompanied children and would be left behind as their younger friends departed for new countries. Early on a JDC official realized that there were children who could not be removed from a camp because they had a sibling who was too old to be considered a child and for whom "it is necessary to organize a convenient life till we will be able to give them the possibility to emigrate."[46] Without blood ties, surrogate siblings could be separated. UNRRA workers at Indersdorf appeared to be sensitive to these close friendships, but not all Allied personnel were as considerate.

Shortly after liberation, twenty-six-year-old Benjamin Jacobs befriended two teenage survivors in Germany. Jacobs became the authority figure of the group, and he worried about the boys' education and future. The boys thought of him as an older brother, and for him they were "my boys." While at a hotel in Frankfurt used as a DP center, Jacobs was approached by a Jewish chaplain who asked him to bring the two boys to the airport. When Jacobs and the boys arrived, the chaplain surprised them with another chaplain and a female UNRRA worker. After a brief discussion among the three Allied personnel, the woman told Jacobs to leave the boys there and they would soon go to the States. "Though I realized that this course of action was in the boys' best interests, it was difficult for me to think of losing them. I had gotten so used to them that we had grown into a family. Akiva and Yaakow looked at me as if to accuse me of abandoning them."[47] Jacobs asked if he could come, too, but was told that he was too old and needed a sponsor. Everyday Jacobs visited the boys. "One day, however, I was told that they had been sent to America. That was the last I saw of Akiva and Yaakow."[48] His heartbreak is palpable. One can only imagine the feelings of two boys denied the chance to say goodbye to yet another loved one and separated from the young man they had come to rely on as a family member. In

45 Fischer, "D.P. Children's Center," p. 31.
46 Lambert, "Report," p. 2.
47 Benjamin Jacobs, *The Dentist of Auschwitz* (Lexington: University Press of Kentucky, 1995), p. 209.
48 Jacobs, *Dentist of Auschwitz*, p. 209.

their eagerness to facilitate the emigration of children, relief workers sometimes demonstrated callousness toward the relationships that were torn asunder.

Hadassah Bimko, vice chairwoman of the Central Jewish Committee in the British Zone, intervened twice on behalf of DP children who were about to be taken from those close to them. In the spring of 1946, Bimko accompanied ninety-eight orphans to Palestine. Upon their arrival, representatives of various political parties attempted to determine the affiliations of the children in order to send them to appropriate kibbutzim, even though this meant separating friends, causing an uproar among the children. Bimko offered the solution: The children divided themselves into three groups of their choosing so that friends would go together to their new kibbutz.[49] One year later a Jewish women's organization in Switzerland offered vacation homes for Belsen children. When they arrived in June 1947, the children were told that only one child could go to each family. A sister and brother attempted to run away rather than be separated. In the end, all of the children were kept together and vacationed at a Zionist camp in the Alps.[50] Some Allied personnel and nonsurvivor Jewish leaders did not understand or value the strength of the bonds formed in these surrogate families.

BRITISH VISAS FOR JEWISH ORPHANS

The good intentions of Jewish relief agencies to remove orphans from the depredations of DP camp life ran afoul of survivor sentiments in the case of visas for orphaned children. The British Jewish community had been able to save thousands of German, Austrian, and Czech children with the Kindertransport of the 1930s, and it sought to do something similar for child survivors. In 1945, British Jewish agencies successfully lobbied for 1,000 entry visas to England for Jewish child survivors. The stay in England would be temporary until they could secure immigration certificates to Palestine. The Jewish agencies were caught off guard when the DP leadership rejected the plan.

The Central Committee of Liberated Jews in Bavaria met on October 14, 1945 to discuss the plan. Representatives of the JDC and of the Jewish Brigade were also present. Although some DP leaders in Feldafing had expressed reservations about the plan months earlier, it had not generated concern at the level of the Central Committee until a Jewish Brigade soldier at the October 14 meeting suggested that the transfer of children to Britain at a time of increasing tensions in Palestine would give the British a moral victory.[51] Although one member of the committee expressed concern for the well-being of the children if they stayed in the DP centers, the committee overwhelmingly rejected the notion that

---

[49] Rosensaft, *Yesterday*, p. 106f.

[50] Rosensaft, *Yesterday*, p. 116.

[51] Zeev Mankowitz, *Life between Memory and Hope: The Survivors of the Holocaust in Occupied Germany* (Cambridge: Cambridge University Press, 2002), pp. 103–104.

the children would be better off in England. The Central Committee passed the following resolution:

In view of the events in Palestine, where the British Administration did not hesitate to use arms and imprisonment against Jews who tried to find a refuge in Palestine, against the last remnant of the so-brutally persecuted European Jewry who did not wish for more than to find safety in one corner of the globe – in Palestine – where they hoped to return to a normal and peaceful life; the representatives of the Jews in Bavaria state that they have no confidence in the intentions and hospitality of the public in Great Britain who wish to accept Jewish children from the camps, and that they protest strongly against sending the children to England. The meeting instructs the Central Committee to ensure that no one single child should, under any circumstances, be allowed to emigrate to any other country than to the only possible haven for them – Palestine.[52]

The suggestion that the British people could not be trusted to welcome Jewish children because of British policies in Palestine seemed a bit hyperbolic, and the decision generated criticism of the Central Committee.

Some observers and scholars have accused the DP leaders of allowing their political objectives to cloud their judgment. For example, Koppel Pinson, a history professor who organized educational programs for DPs on behalf of the JDC, wrote, "The leadership was in the hands of radical Zionists and not even a trace of skepticism regarding Palestine was tolerated. ... Perhaps the fiercest and most fanatical demonstration of the denial of the diaspora was the refusal of the camp committees to allow orphaned Jewish children to be evacuated to more adequately equipped homes in Britain and France."[53] Some aid workers feared that adult DPs overidentified with the children and were thus unable to detach themselves enough to make the best decisions in the children's interests. For example, Feldafing DP leaders, concerned about how the children would be housed in Britain and what their long-term situation would be, already expressed reservations about the British plan at the end of July 1945, prompting an UNRRA report suggesting overidentification with the children to be a factor.[54] Certainly adult survivors felt a special obligation and connection to Jewish children. There were, however, legitimate reasons to question the reception that child survivors would receive and to suggest that the children would be better remaining in Germany until emigration to a permanent home.

The reception in the late 1930s of Jewish children who arrived in England on the Kindertransport from Germany and Austria can suggest what awaited orphaned DPs. The Kindertransport children had not experienced the ghettos, the

---

52 English translation quoted in S. Adler-Rudel, report to UNRRA Headquarters, Germany, Relief Services, "Evacuation of Jewish Children from D.P. Camps in Germany to England," 21 December 1945, p. 1, Central Zionist Archives (CZA), Shalom Adler-Rudel Papers, A/140/674.
53 Koppel S. Pinson, "Jewish Life in Liberated Germany: A Study of the Jewish DP's," *Jewish Social Studies* 9:2 (April 1947): 116–117.
54 [Cornelia D. Heise], "Field Report – Child Welfare Problems – Munich Area," 31 July to 3 August 1945, p. 1, UN S-0437, Box 12, File 16. See also, Lotte Lotheim, Principal Welfare Officer, UNRRA Team 1068, "Mental Hygiene Program in Purten I and Anschau: Monthly Report Feb. 8th to Feb. 20th 1947," 19 February 1947, p. 2, UN S-0425, Box 64, File 8.

concentration camps, or years hiding in bunkers. Even so, they found adjustment to life in Britain difficult. Language barriers frustrated them. No one seemed to understand their homesickness or their fear for their parents. Some children were initially housed in boarding schools or group homes with inadequate facilities.[55] Other children found themselves in host families that wanted them as cheap domestic help or abused them.[56] Children with relatives in England often fared no better. Their own relations did not want them or expected them to contribute significantly to the household income.[57] These were children without the emotional and behavioral problems of child survivors. How much less prepared to handle DP children were the British families willing to open their homes?

The visas were for temporary stays. The British did not offer these DP children permanent homes. On October 21, 1945, the Central Jewish Committee in the British Zone (the Belsen Committee) passed its own resolution prohibiting the transfer of the children to England:

> It is impossible for us to allow the children who have been with us from the very first, in ghettoes and concentration camps, and who have suffered with us, to go wandering from exile to exile. The children must stay with us until their emigration to Palestine. ... We demand that the first certificates for Palestine shall be given to our children so as to enable them to emigrate there as soon as possible.[58]

The emphasis on the connection between the children and adult survivors reflected the close relationship of the committee to the children in Belsen. The Belsen Committee believed that the children needed to be kept together with others of like backgrounds who understood them. A temporary residence in England exchanged one diaspora for another and kept the children in limbo, still unable to put down roots and to establish permanent bonds.

There is evidence to support the Belsen Committee's beliefs. In her book on the reception of Holocaust survivors in the United States, Beth Cohen demonstrates that the best situations for unaccompanied children had been a group home in Boston and a summer camp experience that drew child survivors together.[59] One of the more memorable camp events was a play that the children created and performed about their Holocaust experiences. These children had the benefit of working through their experiences with people who could understand and who were willing to listen. Social workers in the United States and in the DP camps often emphasized repressing memories of the traumatic past and

55 Max Bodenheimer, "Videotaped interview," VHA, IC 11739, Seg. 60; Naomi Alkalay, "Videotaped interview," VHA, IC 6665, Segs. 50–55.
56 Eva Abraham-Podietz, "Videotaped interview," VHA, IC 321, Segs. 41–42; Georges Kovacs, "Videotaped interview," VHA, IC 26094, Seg. 17.
57 Marion Alflen, "Videotaped interview," VHA, IC 42176, Segs. 48–50; Lorraine Allard, "Videotaped interview," VHA, IC 39689, Segs. 68–70; Ester Friedman, "Videotaped interview," VHA, IC 18331, Segs. 70–71.
58 English translation quoted in Adler-Rudel, "Evacuation of Jewish Children," p. 1.
59 Beth B. Cohen, *Case Closed: Holocaust Survivors in Postwar America* (New Bruswick, NJ: Rutgers University Press, 2007), pp. 108–112.

moving on. They did not allow survivors to process their experiences, leaving them frustrated and hurting.

Greta Fischer came to believe that DP children benefited from the extended stay in the children's homes. She initially believed that staying on German soil slowed the children's rehabilitation, since the children harbored intense hatred toward Germans and their confinement in Germany prevented its alleviation.[60] Later, however, Fischer reflected that "more time at the Center gave the team a chance to use the time in a constructive way to deal with the many symptoms of anti-social behaviour which could not have been corrected if there had been no time to build up deeper, more meaningful relationships and to get to know the youngsters more intimately and not only their distrustful façade."[61] In the end, the children's transition to life in freedom was eased by the time in the center, partly through the relationships built with the staff, but also through the time the children spent with one another.

Remaining with other survivors provided the children with opportunities to work through their past experiences. They did not stand out as oddities as they would in a normal environment. In the DP camps survivors talked about their experiences almost incessantly, and they wrote and performed plays about the ghettos, the partisans, and the concentration camps. DP poetry, music, and art worked through the horrors of the Holocaust. In DP schools they were not the only children who were too old for their grade level, and survivor teachers understood their outbursts, their silences, their difference. Group bonding between child survivors facilitated their adaptation to postwar life.[62] The Belsen Committee wisely recognized that the children could best work through their issues not isolated in a comfortable British home, but in the difficult conditions of postwar Germany, where they were together with others who shared their background and their language.

The British Jews who had worked so hard to secure the visas could not accept the view that the children would be better off in Germany. They and the Youth Aliyah emissary in Paris attempted to persuade DP leaders to change their minds.[63] Officially touring the DP camps as a representative of the Jewish Refugees Committee, a British organization, Salomon (aka Shalom) Adler-Rudel visited Germany and met with the Central Committees. It was in his capacity, however, as the Jewish Agency's representative in London that Adler-Rudel attempted to persuade the DP leadership that the children would benefit from staying in Britain until they could leave for Palestine. He assured the Central Committee of Liberated Jews in Bavaria that relocation to England would not interfere with the children's ultimate emigration to Palestine. He urged that children with relatives in England or the United States be allowed to go on the transports and promised

---

[60] Fischer, "D.P. Children's Center," p. 22.

[61] Fischer, "D.P. Children's Center," p. 46.

[62] Davidson cites a study of six child survivors, ages three to four, who survived Theresienstadt together. Their group bonding, maintained by staying together in an English nursery for one year, facilitated their adaptation to life in England. "Surviving during the Holocaust and Afterwards," p. 68.

[63] Lavsky, *New Beginnings*, p. 112.

that no further proposals for the removal of children would be made.[64] The Central Committee decided it would be willing to permit children to go to England to reunite with members of their immediate family (i.e., parents or siblings, but not aunts or uncles), but they refused to allow any other children to go.[65]

During his tour of the American Zone, Adler-Rudel met with forty-five children at Kloster Indersdorf. They were committed to going to Palestine but did not want to wait in the DP camps. The children wanted to make progress in their education and vocational training and agreed that temporary residence in England would be preferable to the camps. That Kloster Indersdorf was an international center where tensions ran high between Jews and non-Jewish Poles may have increased the children's desire to leave their current residence. Adler-Rudel noted the children's acceptance of the Central Committee's authority to decide the matter for them. In conversations with UNRRA and camp committee members at other DP camps, Adler-Rudel learned that conditions for the children had been improving with the establishment of schools and training centers. Adler-Rudel, however, remained distressed by the lack of privacy in the camps and the ways in which children participated in adult life.[66] The reality, however, was that the children had been forced to mature rapidly during the Holocaust, and they resented being treated as children even as they longed to be relieved of adult responsibilities.

Adler-Rudel arrived at Belsen at a time when relations between DPs and the British were highly strained. Military authorities threatened not to permit the chairman of the committee, Josef Rosensaft, to return to Germany if he attended a United Jewish Appeal conference in the United States.[67] Also, the Central Jewish Committee was absorbed by its efforts to defend ten members of the Jewish Committee in Hanover who were being tried in a British military court over events related to a protest meeting against British policies in Palestine. During his stay in Belsen, the Hamburg leaders were given heavy sentences of two to six months' imprisonment.[68] Not surprisingly, Adler-Rudel also failed to persuade the Central Jewish Committee to change its position.

In a draft of his report to UNRRA, Adler-Rudel conceded that the DP leadership in Belsen was not simply motivated by political concerns: "The relations between the members of the Camp Committee in Belsen and the children are more intimate than in the Bavarian Zone. There is genuine affection for the children and the Committee has the children's welfare at heart. To care for the children is one of the few bright spots in the misery of camp life."[69] Adler-Rudel was able to see what others, including Pinson, did not – that DP leaders

[64] S. Adler-Rudel, letter to the Central Committee of Liberated Jews in Bavaria (in Yiddish), 2 December 1945, YIVO RG 294.2, MK 483, Microfilm reel 2, Folder 16.

[62] Adler-Rudel, "Evacuation of Jewish Children," p. 4.

[66] Adler-Rudel, "Evacuation of Jewish Children," p. 3.

[67] Adler-Rudel, "Evacuation of Jewish Children," p. 4; Rosensaft, *Yesterday*, p. 99.

[68] Adler-Rudel, "Evacuation of Jewish Children," p. 5.

[69] S. Adler-Rudel, Draft of report to UNRRA HQS Germany, Relief Services, "Evacuation of Jewish Children from DP Camps in Germany to England," 21 December 1945, p. 6, Adler-Rudel Papers, A140/164.

did demonstrate concern for the children's welfare, but that concern did not necessarily translate into sending them to England.

Concerned by the conditions in which the children lived, Adler-Rudel enlisted the support of the JDC medical officer in Belsen. Rosensaft left for the U.S. conference, so Adler-Rudel and the doctor approached the acting chairman of the Belsen Committee, Hadassah Bimko. He was impressed by her concern for the children and suggested that if the children did not come to Britain, they should have a more suitable environment than what Belsen could provide. Bimko agreed to participate in medical examinations of the children and to work to find ways to remove them from the camp. The options they agreed upon were evacuation of the children to the American Zone with its better living conditions, the conversion of the Warburg Estate at Blankensee from a rest home for German soldiers into a large children's home, or, in the last resort, transfer of the children to England.[70] On December 17 the committee voted its approval of these options and decided to permit children to join relatives in England and the United States. Adler-Rudel believed the Central Jewish Committee in the British Zone had been more receptive to his ideas because conditions there were worse than in the American Zone and that enabled him to persuade the Belsen leadership that it was dangerous for the children to remain where they were.[71]

In his report to the Jewish Agency, Adler-Rudel urged Yishuv leaders to order the DP Central Committees to accept the immigration to England scheme. He said that only an order from Palestine would sway the DP leadership. If the Jewish Agency did not endorse the plan, he echoed the Belsen Committee's resolution, requesting that the orphans be given priority for certificates. Failing that, he suggested that resources dedicated to the children be sent to the DP camps. David Ben-Gurion, head of the Jewish Agency, informed the Belsen committee that the children would not be given priority for certificates but they would be sent additional resources. For its part, the Central Jewish Committee in the British Zone worked with the JDC to acquire the Warburg Estate as a children's home, giving the children more pleasant and normal surroundings while keeping them together with comrades of similar backgrounds as they awaited emigration. Children who had immediate family members in England were permitted to immigrate there.[72]

"New historians" in Israel have used the incident of the 1,000 visas as evidence that the Zionist leadership in the DP camps and in Palestine worked together, putting their ideological goals before the needs of the children.[73] That

---

[70] Adler-Rudel, "Evacuation of Jewish Children," p. 5.

[71] Adler-Rudel, "Evacuation of Jewish Children," p. 6.

[72] Two orphans in the U.S. Zone asked the JDC to help them accept England's offer so that they might reunite with relatives in England. Gerson Pasanowsky and Bronia Kasz to American Committee for Jewish Children (Joint), "Re: Placing of Jewish Orphans," 23 November 1945, YIVO, RG 294.2, MK 483, Microfilm reel 2, Folder 16.

[73] Yosef Grodzinsky, *In the Shadow of the Holocaust* (Monroe, ME: Common Courage Press, 2004), pp. 86–95; Idith Zertal, "Refugees for a State: History, Memory, and Politics" (paper presented at the Conference on Birth of a Refugee Nation: Displaced Persons in Post-War Europe, 1945–1951, at the Remarque Institute, New York University, April 21, 2001).

approach ignores the independent thinking of the DP leadership, particularly the Belsen Committee, which ultimately succeeded in pressuring the Jewish Agency into earmarking immigration certificates for the children. It fails to take into account that Jewish Agency representatives in London and Paris supported the British plan, indicating a plurality of opinions within the Zionist movement. It also confuses what was in the best interests of the children: staying with their new surrogate families or temporary residence in England.

Conditions in the DP camps had improved by autumn 1945, particularly in the American Zone. Although there was a harsh winter ahead, most of the children were not in imminent danger. The visas to England were intended for temporary stays. Imposing the emotional difficulty of adjustment to a foreign country, torn from the people who comforted them and understood what they had gone through, only to uproot them again was not necessarily the best solution for traumatized children. By remaining in Germany, these child survivors could openly talk about their experiences, express grief and anger, act out without being labeled as incorrigible, or told to put their past behind them. Undoubtedly there was an element of self-interest in the Central Committees' positions. They wanted to protect those children as some survivors had been unable to guard their own. Many adult survivors, including Hadassah Bimko, had suffered the murder of their own children, and all survivors had known children who were killed. To have children in their midst provided them comfort and reassurance that there was a future for the Jewish community. Their Zionism led them to the conclusion that the children's welfare was bound up in Palestine. For the DP leadership there was no conflict between the children's best interests and waiting for immigration to Palestine.

In the end the British allowed the conversion of the Warburg Estate into the Blankensee Children's Home and ninety-eight Belsen children moved there. In March 1946, the Jewish Agency finally allocated the immigration certificates demanded by the Central Jewish Committee to the ninety-eight children and three teachers. Hadassah Bimko accompanied the transport and saw the children settled into three kibbutzim. She reported with satisfaction, "There was no problem of absorption, as our children had been prepared for Palestine in our Belsen school. They knew Hebrew very well and easily became part of the Yishuv."[74] While there were undoubtedly difficult times ahead for the children, they knew the language and culture and had been able to remain with friends, all of which would bolster them as they made the transition to a new life in a new homeland. Blankensee continued to receive orphans and to send them on to Palestine.

DP SCHOOLS

While all involved in the care of child survivors wanted to promote their emotional and psychological health, Jewish DPs were vitally concerned with the

[74] Rosensaft, *Yesterday*, p. 107.

children's Jewish identity. Education became a means of strengthening Jewish identity in child survivors. The war years had interrupted the children's formal education, and separation from families had disrupted the transmission of family cultural and religious knowledge and values. DP educators focused on creating safe environments in which the children could discuss their wartime experiences and could learn to trust others once again. Within those safe spaces, they taught children about their Jewish heritage and about Zionism.

DPs with academic experience founded the first schools, and many of the teachers were survivors. They were aided by Jewish Brigade soldiers, particularly in Belsen, and later by teachers from Palestine. In the British Zone a number of qualified people resided in Belsen. The centralization of DP life in the British Zone facilitated the creation of an education committee under the control of the Central Jewish Committee. This board of education consisted of a member of the committee's cultural department, a representative of the JRU, the headmistresses of the elementary school and of the Hebrew high school, the director of the ORT vocational school, and soldiers from the Jewish Brigade. The inclusion of educators on the committee facilitated relations between teachers and agencies.[75] The Zionist curriculum received support from the Belsen Committee, Zionists among the JRU workers, DP instructors, and Jewish Brigade soldiers.

In the American Zone the situation was more contentious. The geographic distances in the American Zone isolated DP educators in the early phase of development and resources were spread out. Finally, in January 1947, UNRRA called together representatives of Jewish agencies interested in education to create a Board of Education that would coordinate resources and develop a standardized curriculum. The representative of the American Orthodox organization Vaad Hatzalah did not differentiate between secular and religious instruction and was discontent with the secular orientation of the proposed board. He wanted Vaad Hatzalah to have equal representation with the other agencies, but Rabbi Snieg, the head of the DP Central Rabbinate, stated that organizational representation was less important than the aim of providing education to all Jewish children.[76] In its final form the Board consisted of representatives from the Jewish Agency for Palestine, the JDC, and the Central Committee of Liberated Jews. The Jewish Agency selected the chairman of the Board and the JDC designated the administrator.[77] The Board sanctioned a Jewish nationalist curriculum that avoided partisan politics.

Many difficulties confronted DP teachers: lack of books and supplies, no common language among students and teachers (Hungarians who knew no Yiddish, children recovered from Polish gentile families who needed to be convinced they were Jews, children arriving from the USSR who spoke only Russian, and Lithuanian children who spoke fluent Yiddish), and mixed age groups as a

---

[75] Lavsky, *New Beginnings*, pp. 180–181.
[76] Susan Pettiss, "Meeting of Representatives of Jewish Agencies on Education," 28 January 1947, p. 4, UN S-0425, Box 64, File 6.
[77] Goldman, "Education among Jewish Displaced Persons," p. 42.

result of interrupted educations.[78] Though DP teachers were often untrained (with only slightly more education than their students), their commitment to the children was invaluable. One DP newspaper noted, "The children who, with only a few exceptions, have no one in the world, find in the school a home and from the teacher fatherly love."[79] Children yearning for familial affection could find it in the classroom. Later, infiltrees from the East brought more children and also experienced teachers to the DP camps. Emissaries from Palestine taught in DP schools during the 1947–1948 academic year, bringing pedagogical skills and knowledge of Hebrew. In the American Zone they contributed to political infighting among Zionists, while in the British Zone they had little impact on the Zionist unity dominant there.

DP teachers organized to promote their professional development and to demand improvements in working conditions. In November 1946, teachers in the American Zone organized, and 600 of them answered the call to strike.[80] The Eschwege Hebrew School teachers responded in support of the "demands for improvement of their situation and for a more appropriate attitude on the part of the higher authorities to their difficult and responsible work."[81] The teachers protested the lack of supplies and the deaf ears on which their pleas for assistance fell. They reiterated the difficulties they faced – children with different languages and of different ages all in one class, shortages of paper, lack of books – and proudly reported that despite everything the children still learned.[82] American Zionist educator Marie Syrkin noted that Allied personnel accused the DP teachers of avarice, even though UNRRA workers were well paid for their efforts. She accused UNRRA employees of hypocrisy for denying that DP teachers deserved economic remuneration for their efforts. It should also be emphasized that a main thrust of the teachers' demands was for improved classroom conditions, benefiting not only themselves but their pupils.

After liberation ultra-Orthodox DPs quickly established *Talmud Torahs* (Jewish primary schools for boys) and *yeshivot* (academies for Talmudic study) for boys, and Beth Jacob schools for girls. In the British Zone, Rabbi Israel Moshe Olevsky organized an elementary school in June 1945 and Yeshivat "She'erit Israel" in Belsen opened in November 1945 under Rabbi Zvi Meisels. Two Beth Jacob schools for girls operated in Belsen, and in 1946 a Beth Jacob

---

[78] Teachers in the ghettos of Nazi-occupied Europe had faced similar conditions. Most children had been taught in the language of their place of residence, but in some ghettos teachers were required to use Yiddish or Hebrew. In the Warsaw ghetto in 1941 there were 4 schools with instruction in Polish, 3 Tsisho, 3 Tarbut, and 5 Orthodox schools. See Isaiah Trunk, "Religious, Educational and Cultural Problems in the East European Ghettos under German Occupation," in *Eastern European Jews in Two Worlds: Studies from the YIVO Annual*, ed. Deborah Dash Moore (Evanston, IL: Northwestern University Press, 1990), pp. 166–170.

[79] "Unzer szule," *Feldafinger Magazin*, 12 February 1946.

[80] Pinson, "Jewish Life in Liberated Germany," p. 122.

[81] "Eszweger lerer in sztrajk," *Undzer Hofenung*, 29 November 1946, p. 8.

[82] "A sof cu der kalter baciung cum jidiszn lerer," *Undzer Hofenung*, 6 December 1946, p. 3.

seminar to train teachers opened.[83] By October 1945, the Rabbinic Council of the American Zone had established yeshivot in Föhrenwald, Landsberg, and other DP camps. From the Feldafing DP camp, Rabbi Yekusiel Halberstam, the Klausenberger Rebbe, established eight yeshivot. Vaad Hatzalah founded religious schools, including Talmud Torahs and yeshivot, in thirty-four DP camps in the U.S. Zone, reaching more than 3,000 students. At the high point, Vaad Hatzalah maintained approximately fourteen yeshivot and fifty-nine Talmud Torahs for boys and seven Beth Jacob schools for girls.[84] In May 1948, the JDC provided support to sixty-two Talmud Torahs and twelve yeshivot, serving 4,170 students in the American Zone.[85]

Becky Althoff completed her random sampling of yeshiva boys in Föhrenwald in June 1946. All were Hungarian and did not manifest the health problems that the Polish and Russian boys in the youth blocks did. Not one complained of insufficient food or clothing since they received significant supplementation from Agudat Israel. They were satisfied with their situation and had no complaints about their supervisor. They had all completed at least six years of elementary school and spent eight hours per day in the Yeshiva, although not all of that time in study.

Like adult ultra-Orthodox Hungarians, the boys isolated themselves from secular camp life.[86] They did not participate in the social and cultural activities of the camp and relied on matchmakers for introductions to girls. Many of them planned to go to the United States or Palestine but were not learning English or modern Hebrew. They neither worked nor expressed interest in learning a trade. "They are willing to continue on in the Camp, and wait for God or his emissary, Rabbi Halbertstein [sic?] to provide for them."[87] Althoff noted that the living arrangements were not different from those of the youth blocks or kibbutzim but that the better food and clothing "represents an unfair distribution and an unequal weighting in favor of the Orthodox Religious in contrast to other groups."[88] The distribution of resources led to many conflicts in the DP

---

[83] Lavsky, *New Beginnings*, p. 171.

[84] The number of schools supported by Vaad Hatzalah is approximate due to the organization's irregular accounting practices and disagreements among yeshiva directors as to which organization provided their essential needs. Alex Grobman, *Battling for Souls: The Vaad Hatzala Rescue Committee in Post-War Europe* (Jersey City, NJ: KTAV, 2004), pp. 163–164 and 250–252; Goldman, "Education among Jewish Displaced Persons," p. 105.

[85] Some of the JDC-supported schools also received some minimal aid from Vaad Hatzala and may have been included in their statistics. Solomon, "Education among Jewish Displaced Persons," p. 104.

[86] Ultra-Orthodox Polish Jews affiliated with Agudat Israel participated more readily in general DP camp life than did the Hungarians. Also, Hungarians proved more willing to consider repatriation than Polish or Lithuanian Jews. Hannah Modenstein, telephone interview by the author, tape recording, 7 July 1995; James E. King, Jr. to Georg Kohn, UNRRA Team 1047 (Pocking), 9 July 1947; PW & DP Branch; (National Archives Microfiche 3/174–1/20, 2 of 3); Civil Affairs Division (CAD); OMGUS, RG 260; National Archives at College Park, MD (NACP).

[87] Althoff, "Semi-monthly Report," June 21, 1946, p. 5.

[88] Althoff, "Semi-monthly Report," June 21, 1946, p. 5.

camps. Aid from Orthodox communities in Britain and the United States was earmarked for Orthodox DPs, but military officials, fearing the goods would land on the black market, ordered their distribution to the general population. DP rabbis objected to the appropriation of their property, pointing out that the religious needs of Orthodox Jews were not being met. Meanwhile broad-based organizations, such as the JDC and the JCRA, spread their resources to all Jewish DPs, including Orthodox, and believed Orthodox organizations should do the same.

One of the most important Beth Jacob schools was in the Belsen DP camp. Intent on educating female survivors in Orthodox ways and on providing a more wholesome environment for them, the Beth Jacob teachers combined activism with traditional female support for men. They saw their mission in terms of national work and public education; their educational goals were similar to those of the secular authorities. "We want to offer extra-religious instruction. Like Judaism, Bible, History, Palestinography. We teach English, Mathematics, and Geography. The road leads to the Land of Israel, and therefore naturally Hebrew is the language on which one most strongly focuses."[89] This focus on a future in Palestine/Israel led the Beth Jacob teachers to become intrinsically involved in the kibbutz movement to establish *hachsharot* (training farms) in Germany as preparation for immigration to Palestine.[90]

Beth Jacob teachers instructed their students to be activists for the observance of Jewish laws and tradition, while at the same time emphasizing that Jewish women were to find satisfaction in freeing Orthodox men from worldly concerns so that they might concentrate on prayer and study. Believing that the girls needed a trade to help support their future husband-scholars, the teachers founded a sewing workshop, "which should make it possible to clothe themselves and instruct them in the basics of tailoring, which is important for a woman."[91] These skills were put at the service of the religious men of the camp, who were provided with *kitteln* (white prayer garments), shirts, and slippers by the Beth Jacob seamstresses. Not confined to caring for the men's clothing, the women also sought to decorate the spaces in which the men wore the clothing, providing festive table settings for the holidays. In addition to traditional feminine housekeeping activities, the Beth Jacob women performed charitable acts. "The commandment to visit the sick occupies a prominent place in our work."[92] The goals of the Beth Jacob curriculum were to educate Jewish women and to place that education at the service of the religious community. The Beth Jacob movement assisted in the transmission of Jewish tradition and in the preparation for an Orthodox Jewish future in Palestine.

[89] Beth Jacob Center in Bergen-Belsen, "Report on Our Work" (in Yiddish), 1945, p. 2, Yad Vashem (YV), O-70/29.
[90] Judith Tydor Baumel, *Kibbutz Buchenwald: Survivors and Pioneers* (New Brunswick, NJ: Rutgers University Press, 1997), pp. 55 and 110–112.
[91] Beth Jacob Bergen-Belsen, "Report," p. 2.
[92] Beth Jacob Bergen-Belsen, "Report," p. 3.

FIGURE 8. Children put on a Hanukkah play in front of a portrait of Theodore Herzl in the Feldafing DP camp, 1946–1947. *Credit*: USHMM, courtesy of Rita Lifschitz Rubinstein

Secular school curricula usually included Hebrew, mathematics, geography of Palestine, Jewish history, the history of Zionism, music, and gymnastics. In some camps Orthodox Jews won the addition of one or two hours per week of religious instruction. In all schools, religious or secular, the calendar revolved around Jewish holidays, and school children presented pageants in celebration of Hanukkah and Purim (Figure 8). Children learned about Jewish heroes of old and of the recent past, connecting their experiences to the cycles of Jewish history. In general, DP schools reflected the ideological approach of the prewar Tarbut schools in Poland.[93] Those schools emphasized secular Zionism, teaching Jewish history and culture, but using Hebrew as the language of instruction, rejecting the Bundists' preference for Polish or Russian and the Yiddishist agenda of the prewar Tsisho schools.[94]

Jacob Biber founded Föhrenwald's Tarbut school: "I was determined to teach the children in Hebrew, hoping for a future for all of us in Israel, and knowing the need for some common language they could use to communicate with each other."[95] The multilingual nature of the student body made it imperative to find a common language of instruction. Yiddish and Hebrew were the two Jewish languages, but Hebrew was the politically preferred

---

[93] Pinson, "Jewish Life in Liberated Germany," p. 122; Goldman, "Education among Jewish Displaced Persons," p. 77.

[94] Most Jewish children attended public schools in the interwar period. Of the private Jewish schools in Poland, those run by ultra-Orthodox Agudat Israel were the most popular, followed by the Tarbut schools. In Lithuania Tarbut was more popular. On trends in interwar Jewish education, see Ezra Mendelsohn, *The Jews of East Central Europe Between the World Wars* (Bloomington: Indiana University Press, 1983), pp. 64–67, 233.

[95] Jacob Biber, *Risen from the Ashes: A Story of the Jewish Displaced Persons in the Aftermath of World War II* (San Bernardino, CA: Borgo Press, 1990), p. 20.

language since it indicated a Jewish future outside of Europe. Hidden children and those from Soviet exile frequently knew neither language. Because many teachers did not speak Hebrew, Yiddish was often the language of instruction until 1947, when books and teachers from Palestine arrived to improve Hebrew language skills.

In the international children's centers, teachers did their best to educate the child survivors according to their nationality. In Kloster Indersdorf children were divided into groups according to previous education and language ability. Instruction was given in many languages, including Hebrew and Yiddish. Social studies were tailored to the nationalities of the groups.[96] The team made vocational training available but had difficulty planning appropriate classes since they did not know the children's ultimate destination. Also, language often presented a barrier between the instructors and their apprentices.[97] Later, all-Jewish children's homes used survivor teachers who faced challenges similar to teachers in the DP camp schools.

The Zionist emphasis of DP education concerned some JDC and UNRRA workers, who maintained an ideal of apolitical education. UNRRA workers organized training courses for madrichim and teachers with the determination that "no political issues would be interjected into the course."[98] At Purten I children's home, an UNRRA welfare officer, disturbed by the political emphasis of teachers and madrichim, spoke with camp leaders "in order to help them to see the 'dangers' in their nationalistic education."[99] She also expressed concern that leaders used their traumatic experiences to motivate their charges to cling to Zionism.

In March 1947, Marie Syrkin attended a meeting of teachers from across the American Zone. Concerned about raising false hopes of a future in Palestine, she asked the teachers if it were pedagogically wise to indoctrinate children, even in what she agreed was the worthy cause of Zionism. The teachers acknowledged that the pedagogy was not ideal, but they defended the practice as their only option in the world of DP camps. One young woman responded, "The children have nothing, nothing. What should we talk about – the blessings of Poland? They know them. Or the visas for America? They can't get them. The map of *Eretz* is their salvation." A middle-aged man answered, "I have been a teacher all my life, and I also know about modern methods. Indoctrination may not be good for normal children in normal surroundings. But what is normal here? How can you make the same demands of us in the DP camps in Mariendorf as you do of your colleagues in a free American highschool? *Auf a krumme fuss passt a krumme shuh.* (A crooked foot needs a crooked shoe.)"[100] The Zionist

[96] Fischer, "D.P. Children's Center," p. 36.
[97] Fischer, "D.P. Children's Center," p. 37.
[98] Susan Pettiss, "Training of Madrichim and Personnel in Jewish Children's Centers," 25 November 1946, UN S-0425, Box 64, File 7.
[99] Lotte Lotheim, "Mental Hygiene Program at the Children's Center, Purten I," 8 February 1947, p. 2, UN S-0425, Box 64, File 8.
[100] Marie Syrkin, *The State of the Jews* (Washington, DC: New Republic Books, 1980), pp. 26–27.

curriculum helped the children to create a common identity and provided them with a vision for the future. The emphasis on Hebrew served the practical need for a common language of instruction, but it also symbolized the rejection of the Diaspora in favor of a new Jewish home in Palestine. Courses in Jewish history and the history of Palestine provided them with an ethnic identity that included their European heritage and that of their hoped-for future place of residence.

Other observers were shocked by schoolroom discussions about wartime experiences. JDC's Pinson wrote, "In their entertainments and in the education of their youth there is this constant preoccupation with their experiences under the Nazis, – gruesome recapitulation of concentration camp incidents combined with vows of undying loyalty to these memories and hopes for vengeance. It is especially depressing to see young boys and girls of 8–12 years of age, whose rehabilitation to normal childhood should emphasize obliteration of these memories, participate in and be encouraged to share in such demonstrations of emotional reliving of the past."[101] Even Jewish representatives from abroad thought that repression of memories was necessary for rehabilitation, but this ran counter to the survivors' instinctive need to retell and rework the past.

The teachers did not force the children to remember and discuss their terrible pasts. Evidence of the children's desire to talk about their experiences comes from UNRRA workers at Indersdorf. "When the children first arrived at Kloster Indersdorf, they talked and talked – about their experiences in the concentration camps and as slave laborers. Horror stories were intermingled with ordinary events, with little show of emotion. It took time for them to relax or play. Nearly all of the first creative plays presented by the children included scenes from the concentration camps, punctuated with wry bits of humour that did not seem funny to the UNRRA workers."[102]

One evening the staff at Kloster Indersdorf decided to hold a roll call in the children's bedrooms. The boys appeared dressed in their old concentration camp uniforms, and a "Stormtrooper" at the head of the line called out names and beat or "shot" those who did not answer quickly enough. The UNRRA team got the message that the children wanted "to be treated as individuals and trusted."[103] The children acted out a scene from their past in order to have themselves understood by the staff. With DP teachers who had shared their pasts such demonstrations were not necessary.

The children and their DP teachers instinctively realized what recent scientific studies have now confirmed. Converting intense emotions into narratives through writing or talking for several days about a traumatic experience can result in improved health and a reduction in the effects of post-traumatic stress syndrome.[104] While dull, monotonous, repetitive play might not aid children's

---

101 Pinson, "Jewish Life in Liberated Germany," p. 109.
102 Fischer, "D.P. Children's Center," pp. 37–38.
103 Fischer, "D.P. Children's Center," p. 38.
104 Daniel L. Schacter, *The Seven Sins of Memory: How the Mind Forgets and Remembers* (Boston: Houghton Mifflin, 2001), p. 171.

recovery, frequent retelling of traumatic experiences did not necessarily hinder their rehabilitation. In fact, contrary to the assumptions of postwar psychologists and educators, reenactments and creative expressions of the trauma could facilitate their recovery.[105] In fact, repression of traumatic memories in the immediate aftermath of the experiences leads to increased problems of post-traumatic stress syndrome, such as intrusive memories.

KIBBUTZIM

A DP alternative to the children's centers was the kibbutz. Many unaccompanied teenagers and young adults organized into kibbutzim following liberation, living communally within the camps or on property outside the camps acquired for their use. The hope of organizers was that kibbutzim would safeguard the moral fiber and morale of Jewish youth while preparing them for productive labor in Palestine. Kibbutzim provided education, activities, and comradeship. In some instances they provided leadership within the camps, while in others their elitism led to their isolation from the DP masses. Because of their ideological orientation, youth, and training, kibbutz members received priority for both legal and illegal immigration to Palestine.

Fearing the destructive influence of DP camp life on young people, DP leaders in Buchenwald approached American chaplain Rabbi Herschel Schacter, asking him if it would be possible to remove the Zionist youth from the demoralizing camp life by acquiring land for a training farm (*hachshara*) to prepare for immigration to Palestine.[106] Led by Arthur Poznansky and Yechezkel Tydor, this group acquired a German farm on June 3, 1945. Other DP kibbutzim followed, often established on farmland adjacent to the assembly centers. In late 1945, a Hashomer Hatzair kibbutz took over the land at Ahlem in the British Zone that had been a Jewish gardening school belonging to the Hanover Jewish community during the Weimar Republic. Unresolved issues concerning restitution of Jewish property prevented them from firmly establishing the hachshara until August 1946.[107] Sometimes the JDC leased German farmland for hachsharot; sometimes the military requisitioned the land, even though the Allies were concerned about the economic cost of turning productive land over to amateurs who would not maximize productivity and who did not intend to sell their produce to Germans. Often requisitioned land had belonged to former Nazis, such as the antisemitic publisher Julius Streicher, and Jewish DPs experienced a

---

[105] Creative processing of traumatic experiences within the context of group therapy can be helpful for children. Child psychiatrist Lenore Terr cautions, however, that a psychotherapist is needed to help the children move beyond repetitive play by enunciating the children's feelings and adding new endings and new coping possibilities for their reenactments of trauma. *Too Scared to Cry: Psychic Trauma in Childhood* (New York: Harper & Row, 1990), pp. 296, 299 and 301.

[106] Baumel, "Kibbutz Buchenwald and Kibbutz Hafetz Hayyim," p. 235.

[107] Lavsky, *New Beginnings*, p. 175.

sense of satisfaction at creating Jewish life on the land of those who had sought to murder them.

Few survivors had prior agricultural experience. By autumn 1945, *shlichim* (literally, messengers) from the Yishuv and JDC-sponsored instructors from the United States arrived to help with training, but they were too few to help all of the kibbutzim. One kibbutz suffered the repeated loss of cows during calving until it received help from a Jewish DP who had grown up on a prosperous farm. In exchange for fresh milk for his infant daughter, this survivor played the role of veterinarian.[108] Often the kibbutzim were forced to rely on assistance from German farmers. The ultra-Orthodox Kibbutz Haftez Hayyim took over farmland requisitioned from an ethnic German and suspected Nazi sympathizer named Schmidt. In 1946, Schmidt offered to help the inexperienced farmers for free, in an attempt to maintain his claim to the land. Initially the kibbutzniks refused but relented after a disastrous potato harvest. When the last of the Orthodox pioneers left in 1948 (most to the United States), Schmidt listed himself as the estate's original owner and local authorities turned the fields over to him.[109] Jewish revenge of this sort lasted only as long as they remained on German soil. It was the presence of Jews in places where people had sought to eradicate them that spoke to vengeance. When the Jews left, the places lost their retributive meaning and reverted to Germans.

For some DPs, kibbutzim represented continuity with the prewar years. Kibbutz Buchenwald's founding leaders had been Zionists with organizational experience before the Nazi onslaught.[110] These men organized youth within Buchenwald even before liberation. According to the Jewish Agency representative in Munich, Kibbutz Maapilim in Hospital Elisabeth (Feldafing) had 100 members, "mostly orphans till 18 years," who "got a Zionist education before the war and continued their Zionist work even under the German occupation. ... After the war they assembled first in the Hospital St. Ottilien and from there they were transferred to Landsberg as an organized group."[111] Because of poor health they were transferred to Hospital Elisabeth and became involved in the cultural life of the Feldafing DP camp. For these DPs, kibbutz life connected them to their prewar childhood and signified their ability to live freely as Jews.

While long-held political beliefs attracted some DPs to the kibbutzim, others joined out of opportunism or loneliness. Kibbutz members received priority for immigration certificates to Palestine as well as priority for illegal immigration. Kibbutz leaders successfully acquired better than average living space, kitchens, workshops, and supplies. In addition to agricultural kibbutzim, there were those inside the camps providing training in a variety of trades, from hairstyling

---

[108] Abe Tauber, interview with the author, audio recording, Los Angeles, Calif., 4 June 2007.

[109] Baumel, "Kibbutz Buchenwald and Kibbutz Hafetz Hayyim," p. 248, fn. 37.

[110] Baumel, "Kibbutz Buchenwald and Kibbutz Hafetz Hayyim," p. 234.

[111] Max Munk, "Report about Kibuc Maapilim in Hospital Elisabeth," [no date], Zisman Papers, RG-19.047.02*09.

FIGURE 9. Boys dressed in Betar Zionist youth uniforms in the dining room of the Schlachtensee DP camp, 1945–1948. *Credit*: USHMM, courtesy of Francoise Bielinski Sitzer

to radio technology. In Föhrenwald the initial postwar spirit of unity brought kibbutzim of different political movements into an inter-kibbutz committee, elected by the respective organizations, handling the problems of kibbutz life in both the camp and its agricultural center at Hochland. Together they petitioned UNRRA for improved living conditions.[112] The success of the kibbutzim in winning better accommodations and distribution of resources encouraged some young DPs to join them for these benefits but also led to resentment among those who chose not to join them.

With recruitment from among infiltrees and the arrival of organized groups from Eastern Europe, DP kibbutzim multiplied quickly. They represented a wide political spectrum from the socialist Hashomer Hatzair to the right-wing Betar (Figure 9). The religious Zionists (Mizrahi) and Agudat Israel organized kibbutzim as well.[113] In spring 1947 there were thirty-nine hachsharot in the American Zone with a population of 3,600, or 2.5 percent of the Jewish DP population. There were kibbutzim at fourteen children's centers with a population of 4,100, or 2.8 percent of the total population.[114]

Kibbutzim often became subunits in the children's centers. For example, in autumn 1946, UNRRA established the Rosenheim Children's Center to process

---

[112] Biber, *Risen from Ashes*, p. 98; Joseph Kolkolski to Missis Lewi, 20 January 1946, Zisman Papers, RG-19.047.02 *07 (1 of 3).

[113] In January 1946 in Bavaria: 862 DPs organized into 9 kibbutzim of left-wing Hashomer Hatzair, 947 joined 6 kibbutzim of the labor pioneering movement Dror, 446 were in 8 kibbutzim of Revisionist Betar, 327 DPs formed the 5 kibbutzim of Agudat Israel, and 1,731 were in Nocham kibbutzim (incl. Gordonia, Hanoar Haziyyoni, and Orthodox former Bnai Akiva). Another 705 DPs were members in kibbutzim of unaffiliated "plain pioneers," and 853 in kibbutzim of former partisans who had not belonged to Zionist youth movements before the war. Baumel, "Kibbutz Buchenwald and Kibbutz Hafetz Hayyim," p. 248, fn. 33.

[114] Philip S. Bernstein, "Displaced Persons," *American Jewish Year Book* 49 (1947–1948): 523.

infiltree children. After a minimum stay of three weeks the children would be transferred to another children's center. By early November 1946, Rosenheim cared for 972 children under 18 years old; it had 382 workers and leaders, including 5 UNRRA personnel and 3 voluntary agency personnel. Children were organized into kibbutzim, each with leaders and teachers, many of whom had traveled together from Poland to Germany. The organization of the children facilitated the administration of the children's center, although UNRRA workers wanted to deemphasize the role of kibbutzim that they viewed as interfering with child care.[115] Despite differences in religious observance and political ideology, the five kibbutzim at Rosenheim cooperated well on education and other issues.[116]

Like the Tarbut schools, kibbutz educational programs focused on Jewish history, Hebrew, the geography of Palestine, and Jewish culture. In addition, the kibbutz children also learned about the history of the Zionist movement, the ideals of their particular youth movement, and their connection to wartime heroism through the resistance fighters of their movement. Since kibbutz members were preparing for life in Palestine, their political affiliation had implications for the future of the Yishuv. The madrichim intended to win their allegiance not only to Zionism in general but especially to their particular movement within Zionism.

Jewish holidays provided additional opportunities to teach the children about the distant and recent Jewish pasts and their links to the present. In secular, socialist kibbutzim, holidays reinforced Jewish ethnic identity and forged an ethos of the heroic Zionist Jew. Kibbutz Hashomer Hatzair in Föhrenwald celebrated Purim by recalling the heroes of the recent past. The madricha (female youth leader), Miriam, spoke of "the heroes of today's Purim – the fighters of the Warsaw, Vilna, Bialystok, and Czenstochow ghettos, as well as the partisans and front soldiers who with their blood defended the honor of the Jewish people just as at the time of King Ahashuerus, Mordechai and Esther defended Jewish honor."[117] Significantly, Miriam and her brother had survived the war in the Soviet Union. They returned to Poland after the war and continued their Zionist youth work, eventually leading the kibbutz to Föhrenwald.[118] The linkage of ghetto fighters and partisans to the heroes of old created a new framework for both the madrichim and the child survivors with which to understand their past, present, and future as Jews, regardless of their personal experiences during the Holocaust. By recounting the stories of Hashomer Hatzair martyrs, the leaders intended to forge the children's allegiance to the

---

[115] Pettiss, "Report on Jewish Infiltree Children," p. 11.
[116] Glenn O. Ratcliff, "Field Inspection Report," 9 November 1946, Zisman Papers, RG-19.047.02*26.
[117] "A Purim-ownt in kibuc haszomer hacair," *Bamidbar*, 20 March 1946, p. 7.
[118] Avinoam Patt, "Living in Landsberg, Dreaming of Deganiah: Jewish DP Youth and Zionism after the Holocaust," in *We Are Here: New Approaches to the Study of Jewish Displaced Persons in Postwar Germany*, eds. Avinoam Patt and Michael Berkowitz (Detroit, MI: Wayne State University Press, forthcoming), m.s.p. 25.

movement. The emphasis on heroic action and honor reflected the gender roles of the new Zionist man and the partisan-girl that the youth movement leadership expected the children to adopt.

One former kibbutz member and resident of the Rosenheim Children's Center remembered it as a place with good food and educational opportunities. Having survived the war in exile in the Soviet Union, Uri returned to Poland with his father and siblings. There, partisans organized children into kibbutzim for immigration to Palestine. Uri was ten years old when his father placed him in the kibbutz, where he learned about Palestine and studied Hebrew. He remembered that the children's poor condition necessitated two teachers for every seven children. They collected clothing from abandoned ethnic German homes, likely vacated either during the Soviet Army's advance in 1945 or during the 1946 expulsions of ethnic Germans from Poland. The teachers and children crossed the border into Germany and took up residence at the Rosenheim Children's Center, where Uri initially became ill from the too rich food. The housemother was a survivor of the Warsaw ghetto, and the housefather had been a Jewish partisan.[119] Although Uri had survived in the Soviet Union, he was now in the care of those who had directly experienced the Holocaust and would now educate him and bring him into the memory community of Holocaust survivors.

Like many of the parents who took advantage of the Kinderheim in Föhrenwald, Uri's father told his children that he had placed them in the kibbutz so that they could get papers to Palestine, since he, the father, already had his papers. The father followed them to Rosenheim and found employment working in food distribution. Despite the father's efforts to stay close to the children, Uri did not believe his father's story. Uri suspected that his stepmother might have influenced the decision to put the children in the kibbutz.[120] It may have been that the father was too overwhelmed to provide adequate care for his children and that his new wife was unwilling to fill the void. However, the parents of the Föhrenwald children had also expressed the desire to facilitate their children's emigration. They still felt that Europe was a dangerous place for Jewish children. The quest to provide their children with the opportunity to leave Europe and to find a safe, Jewish home was a vital enough reason for them to temporarily separate from their children. Despite their efforts to safeguard their children's futures, the parents' actions had unintended emotional consequences for the children. Uri's feelings of abandonment and distrust are similar to those of the children documented by Althoff and to those of children hidden during the war.

Those kibbutzim located outside of assembly centers were vulnerable to antisemitic vandalism that reinforced the determination of children and their leaders to leave Europe for a Jewish home in Palestine. To ease the crowding at the Landsberg DP camp, UNRRA workers transferred 300 children ranging in age from 14 to 20 to a former girls' boarding school in nearby Greifenberg in

---

[119] Uri Urmacher, "Videotaped interview," VHA, IC 43456, Segs. 8–9.
[120] Uri Urmacher, "Videotaped interview," VHA, IC 43456, Segs. 8–9.

November 1945. The children had already organized into a kibbutz and eagerly tackled dirty jobs to prepare themselves for life in Palestine. The tightly knit group had refused relocation to Föhrenwald but accepted the opportunity for more independence that Greifenberg represented.[121] It was in February 1946 that an antisemitic picture was posted on the gate to Greifenberg, indicating the rising tensions between DPs and Germans. The picture depicted a dagger stabbing a Star of David with blood dripping down into flames.[122] Like at Indersdorf, local German resentment did not exempt DP children.

Later that year another kibbutz suffered antisemitic vandalism. A kibbutz of fifty-two children ranging in age from twelve to seventeen years old along with one man and one woman (referred to as the Kibbutz-Mother) had fled Hungary for Germany in spring 1946. Unable to register in a DP camp, the children had been working on a German-operated farm in the hamlet of Eisolzried, about 8 km west of Dachau and 17 km southeast of Markt Indersdorf, where they received German rations. In June 1946 someone scrawled antisemitic graffiti on the barns and fences and attempted to poison the animals. When MPs investigating the incident were unsympathetic, the fearful leaders secured transportation from a kibbutz at Deggendorf, 150 km to the northeast. Hearing the tale, the Deggendorf UNRRA team director acknowledged that the story might have been exaggerated but the needs of the children were undeniable. He requested that the kibbutz be incorporated into one of the Deggendorf camp farms.[123]

Despite aid from Jewish relief organizations, infiltrees faced tremendous difficulties. Often DP camps were overcrowded and infiltrees were denied the opportunity to register officially in the camps. The summer of 1946 saw rising tensions in the German countryside as Jewish infiltrees and German expellees from the East put a strain on local resources and local tempers. The influx of outsiders that the Allies forced upon them contributed to the German sentiment of victimization in the aftermath of military defeat. At the same time, many Allied soldiers fraternized with Germans and accepted their perspective that DPs, particularly Jewish DPs, were responsible for disorder and criminality. Although the UNRRA team director hesitated to accept all of what he had been told by the kibbutz leaders, he recognized that the children had suffered from their postwar experiences. The antisemitic attack on the kibbutz and the unsympathetic response of the military police were entirely plausible.

Outside observers differed in their assessments of the role of kibbutzim in rehabilitating survivors. At Föhrenwald Becky Althoff criticized the

[121] Susan Pettiss, Regional Child Welfare Officer, to Eileen Davidson, District Child Welfare Officer, "Greifenberg accommodations for children from Landsberg," 24 November 1945, UN, S-0436, Box 42, File 6.

[122] A. C. Glassgold, Director, UNRRA, Team 311, to Captain Toms, Commanding Officer, 3rd Battalion, 5th Infantry 9th Division Landsberg, "Acts against Security," 20 February 1946, Zisman Papers, RG-19.047.02*16.

[123] W. V. Buckhantz to UNRRA District Director, District 3 Hq, 12 June 1946, Zisman Papers, RG-19.047.02*02.

narrowness of education at the kibbutzim of Hochland Lager: "Their education is extremely limited, with little opportunity to explore other fields than Palestine Geography, History and Language. They are not taught English, world geography, history, or any of the cultural subjects, other than the traditional dances and songs of Palestine."[124] Althoff's ideal for DP education was probably not realizable because of lack of books, materials, and teachers trained in general subjects. At the same time, DP educators, particularly in kibbutzim, were concerned with preparing the children for immigration to Palestine and absorption there. The focus on Jewish and Yishuv culture not only prepared them for life in Palestine but also helped transmit Jewish culture to a new generation that no longer had parents and families to teach them about their heritage.

In addition to concerns about Zionist indoctrination, some were leery of the anti-individualistic aspects of kibbutz life. Althoff, for example, found the Hochland Lager kibbutzim to be comprised of the weak. She found one epilepsy case, several cases of heart disease, and one case of shell shock. A large number of her interviewees had nervous tics. She concluded:

While I am aware that most generalities are not sound, upon investigation, my overall impression points to a frightful retardation of individuality and self-expression. It would appear that the Kibbutz, attracts the dependent, immature type of personality who seek protection in an institution, which will provide them with maintenance, and direction; and with few exceptions to a few who are idealists enough to wish to sublimate their own individual egos, for the group ideal.[125]

Several of the individuals with whom she spoke expressed conflicted feelings about the kibbutz. On the one hand, they were grateful to the kibbutz for taking them in when there was no other refuge. Many had been recruited from transports arriving from Poland or could not be registered in the camp because it was over capacity. On the other hand, they wanted to live individually.[126] Many survivors of the concentration camps longed for the privacy and "normalcy" of smaller family units, similar to their prewar situation. Large communal groups and mess halls reminded them too much of the concentration camps.[127]

Other social workers, such as UNRRA field supervisor Helen Matouskova, reported enthusiastically about the rehabilitative success of kibbutzim. At Greifenberg kibbutz children engaged in study, agricultural work, and animal husbandry, as well as ran supporting operations such as a laundry, sewing shop, and hairdresser's. She did, however, express concern that the community spirit "goes a little too far. For instance, no one owns his own underwear. The underwear is owned collectively, washed collectively, and then given out as needed. I discussed the sanitary aspects of this unusual procedure … but

124 Althoff, "Semi-monthly Report," June 7, 1946, p. 4.
125 Althoff, "Semi-monthly Report," June 7, 1946, p. 4.
126 Althoff, "Semi-monthly Report," June 7, 1946, p. 5.
127 Becky Althoff, "Composite Interview – Boys," p. 3.

I am not confident that the youngsters will agree to change because it is an essential part of their political convictions."[128] She found a more positive manifestation of the collective spirit in the fifteen children who were on the local German mayor's payroll putting their money in a collective fund to finance improvements.

Similarly, at Kloster Indersdorf, Greta Fischer found that those children who affiliated themselves with national movements, whether Polish Scouts or Zionist groups, were more purposeful than unaffiliated children. "The Zionist groups showed evidence of social, as well as political motivation. ... The Zionists were concerned with promoting good living habits and ethics. They prohibited lying, stealing, smoking or at least attempted to do this. They emphasized physical activity, too, but more through folk dancing, games and work activities. Education was stressed strongly; cooperative and collective living was promoted. There was conscious development of leadership through organizational practices."[129] Fischer believed the kibbutzim successfully raised the morale of DP children. Israeli psychiatrist Shamai Davidson argued that in Israel the kibbutz provided social support to survivors and had a therapeutic effect.[130] This appears to hold true for kibbutzim in Germany as well.

DPs emphasized the positive influence the kibbutzim had on their members and on the larger community. One Föhrenwald DP noted that the non-Zionists in the youth blocks languished in comparison to the children whom he believed benefited from the capable leadership of the Zionists in the kibbutzim.[131] A DP journalist reported favorably on the efforts of kibbutz leaders to ease members back into productive living: "The madrichim strive to pull out the melancholy and replace it with work, sport, teaching and science, but all of the melancholy will disappear only when their holy ideal to come to the Land of Israel has been achieved."[132] According to this view, activity could alleviate the grief and despair while in Germany, but only immigration to Palestine would remove it completely. Certainly the madrichim believed that the solution to the children's problems was resettlement in Palestine.

Zionist leaders argued that the kibbutzim had a beneficial influence on general DP life. Kibbutz Maapilim of Feldafing became involved in the camp cultural life (arranging shows for Hannukah and Tu B'Shevat for the entire camp, and participating in meetings, shows, and concerts during their four months at Hospital Elisabeth). The Jewish Agency representative in Munich argued "from the standpoint of the Zionist Movement and of the Jews as a whole in Feldafing, it is of utmost importance that these people [Kibbutz

128 Helen Matouskova to S. B. Zisman, UNRRA District Director, "Report on Visit to Greifenberg, Team 311," UN S-0436, Box 42, File 6.
129 Fischer, "D.P. Children's Center ," p. 42.
130 Shamai Davidson, "The Transmission of Psychopathology in Families of Concentration Camp Survivors," in *Holding on to Humanity*, p. 119.
131 Holland, "Second Chance," p. 249.
132 "Haapejl! Naapejla!" *Bamidbar* 15 April 1946, p. 13.

Maapilim] who are an integral part of the Camp and who are devoted to the common ideal of the Jews, Palestine, and whose sole occupation is spiritual and vocational training for Palestine – without any contact with the black market – that these people should live in Feldafing and I am sure that is the will of all the different groups of the Camp."[133] In some camps the kibbutzim played prominent public roles intended to inspire emulation among the general public.

Not all camps benefited from the active involvement of kibbutzim. The new commander of the Landsberg DP camp agreed that kibbutzniks were productive but lamented their separateness from general camp life: "I learned today that the young and best elements in the camp are organized into Kibbutzim. It appears that a Kibbutz is a closely knit, self-disciplined group with an intense desire to emigrate to Palestine. ... Each Kibbutz is very clannish and little interested in the camp life."[134] The commander's complaint was that the kibbutzim were not assuming a leadership role in the camp. Although the kibbutzniks viewed themselves as setting an example for the wider community, their elitism, their intense focus on Palestine, and their anticipation of quick emigration could leave them relatively indifferent to general concerns.[135]

Although kibbutz membership was not for everyone, for some it promised purposeful activity in an environment that was characterized by boredom and aimlessness. Kibbutzniks lived separately from other camp residents, preparing and eating their own food, and organizing their own social events. At the same time they sought to provide inspiration to the camp community through their example and through cultural activities.[136] They studied Hebrew, Jewish history, and culture. The communal living experience and the cohesive forces of both a shared past and a shared dream for the future helped these groups to develop strong bonds of allegiance, creating surrogate families for the orphaned members.

The madrichim often presented themselves as surrogate fathers and mothers. In a report on the kibbutzim in Föhrenwald, the author wrote about the young Polish and Lithuanian Jews in Kibbutz Lematara who chose their "new kibbutz daddy and mommy."[137] At a kibbutz for survivors that originated in Hungary before making the journey to Germany, a teenaged survivor assumed what she refers to as a "mothering" role: "I was all: a big sister, a wise friend, counselor, negotiator, teacher, nurse, 'to each his own.' It was nice to be wanted, but it drained me. I hungered for parental love – to be liked for what I was, not just for what I could give. I needed to have a mother, not to be one."[138] Though

---

[133] Munk, "Report about Kibuc Maapilim."
[134] Irving Heymont, *Among the Survivors of the Holocaust – 1945: The Landsberg DP Camp Letters of Major Irving Heymont, United States Army* (Cincinnati, OH: American Jewish Archives, 1982), p. 21.
[135] Pinson, "Jewish Life in Liberated Germany," p. 119.
[136] "Di arbet fun Waad-Bejn-Kibuci," *Bamidbar*, 20 March 1946, p. 6.
[137] "Haapejl! Naapejla!" *Bamidbar*, 15 April 1946, p. 13.
[138] Georgia M. Gabor, *My Destiny: Survivor of the Holocaust* (Arcadia, CA: Amen Publishing, 1981), p. 207.

not suited to the maternal role with her own youth and emotional needs, the teen became a mother figure.

UNRRA and JDC workers expressed concern about the intensity of these bonds. They questioned the power that the madrichim and group leaders held over their charges, troubled that it was unhealthy for teenagers to be led by individuals scarcely older than themselves. At Purten I, the madrichim ranged in age from eighteen to twenty-two. An UNRRA welfare officer commented, "some of the young leaders have not gained enough 'emotional distance' regarding the problems they are dealing with – that often there is such 'a passion' to help which may lead to overprotection of the children and to overidentification."[139] UNRRA training classes were designed to help the madrichim develop a more clinical approach. DPs also organized training courses for madrichim,[140] but inevitably the personalities and qualifications of these group leaders varied.

UNRRA workers were also concerned about the emotional consequences to children who were pressured to go to Palestine or who were subjected to proselytizing from other youth movements.[141] Certainly some leaders abused their positions in their competition with other youth movements. Georgia Gabor discovered that the leaders of her Hanoar Hazioni Kibbutz were taking items intended for the children to trade on the black market. Her friends in the Betar Kibbutz claimed that the General Zionist kibbutzim leaders traded to get the money they needed to finance underground activities to smuggle people out of countries and into Palestine. They persuaded her that Betar did not resort to those tactics because of generous donor financing and greater respect for personal property. Disillusioned with her kibbutz leaders and attracted by the Revisionists' more militant stand on Palestine, Gabor joined Betar.[142] Eventually she was assigned to a hachshara at which she was the only Hungarian speaker and uninterested in agriculture. Although she made herself useful as a seamstress, the kibbutz leaders never truly accepted her. Twice the leader of the group arranged that she would miss her transport to Palestine so that he could send some of his favorites instead. The leader was probably aware of her political fickleness and unsuitability to kibbutz life in Palestine and put ideological considerations before ones of "fairness." Leaders had little tolerance for divided loyalties or ambivalence. Gabor decided to take up the offer of an American "UNRRA lady" to help her immigrate to the United States.[143] As kibbutz leaders from Eastern Europe and shlichim from Palestine arrived as representatives of particular movements, the initial unity of the DPs in the American Zone fractured. The competition between movements

[139] Lotheim, "Mental Hygiene Program," p. 2.
[140] For example, Kibbutz Poel-Hadatt in Eschwege thanked the religious Zionist party Mizrachi for sponsoring a course for Kibbutz madrichim in Feldafing. "Dankzogungen," *Undzer Hofenung,* 25 September 1946, p. 8.
[141] Pettiss, "Report on Jewish Infiltree Children," pp. 4 and 10.
[142] Gabor, *My Destiny,* pp. 218–221.
[143] Gabor, *My Destiny,* pp. 232–235.

dismayed many DPs and, in the case of Gabor, led some to disenchantment with Zionism.

CONCLUSION

In their quest to care for child survivors, DPs and Allied officials occasionally had conflicting visions of the children's future and the methods to achieve it. Allied personnel, whether Jewish or non-Jewish, wanted the children to repress their past and sought their speedy emigration from the DP camps. They worried that the children were too often treated as adults and could be harmed by the Zionist curriculum in the schools. In the children's centers, UNRRA workers attempted to educate children in their heritage while preparing them for a future in an unknown host country. In contrast, adult DPs allowed the children to rework their past through narratives, art, and performances. They argued that the Zionist school curriculum best fit the needs of a stateless population with no other chance for immigration than Palestine. The curriculum also fit the needs of a decimated Jewish community attempting to reclaim children who had been deprived of their cultural heritage during the war years and to instill in them a national, Zionist identity.

In their resolve to protect DP children and to determine their future, survivors demonstrated their newfound agency. They resisted pressure from international aid organizations and even from trusted Jewish Agency personnel and refused to remove 1,000 orphans to Britain on temporary visas. They pursued their own educational agenda even when confronted with the doubts and concerns of American Jewish leaders. They insisted that they best understood the needs of child survivors and used whatever means they could to meet them. Children also played a vital role in the survivors' efforts to restore Jewish community after the Shoah.

In many respects the DPs were proven right in their assessment of the children's needs. The ability to talk about their traumatic experiences was therapeutic for the children. Surrogate families and peer groups helped DP children to navigate their transition to normal life. Kibbutzim provided structure and community apart from the more sordid aspects of DP existence, often facilitating the children's rehabilitation. Those children who did immigrate to Palestine benefited from the language, cultural, and vocational instruction they received in DP schools and kibbutzim.

Moreover, with Jewish children still under threat of antisemitism, it is no wonder that DP parents were willing to do whatever was necessary to secure their children's immediate emigration from Europe. Many parents wanted their children to go to Palestine, where they would be among other Jews, and were willing to separate from them in order to speed their departure. Zionist leaders sought to protect unaccompanied children but also to mobilize them for the Zionist cause through the kibbutzim, believing that only in a Jewish homeland would Jewish security be assured.

Genocide is not only about the physical murder of a people; it is also about a people's destruction through the kidnapping or removal of children from their community and the eradication of their cultural identity so that there is no social memory to be shared with a new generation. Nazi persecution ruptured the generational transmission of Jewish religious and cultural values and knowledge. Many children who had survived in hiding or with Christian families lacked knowledge of their parents' heritage. For them to live as Jews, they needed to be taught about Jewish history, religion, and culture. Such an education would shape their identity and secure their membership in the Jewish community. Child survivors were an important link between the Jewish community's past and future.

5

Performing Identity and Building Community

Jewish DPs came from a variety of national, linguistic, religious, and socio-economic backgrounds. Even their wartime experiences varied. Some suffered in ghettos and concentration camps while others passed on Aryan papers, hid in the woods, or fought with the partisans. Many had survived the war in the Soviet Union and entered Germany as "infiltrees" after their repatriation to Poland in 1946. Out of this disparate group of people grew a DP community with a sense of shared destiny. In this "imagined community," Jewish survivors felt connected to individuals they would never meet and who did not necessarily speak the same language or engage in similar levels of religious observance. Despite their differences, the Jewish DPs formed a community out of a sense of a common past, shared cultural and religious traditions, and the desire to leave Germany. They identified themselves as Jews even though they understood being Jewish in different ways. Determined to live their lives as cultured people, these survivors observed their religious traditions, published newspapers, formed theaters, and established courts of law. The rhythms of the Jewish calendar united survivors even while religious observance often led to conflict. DP cultural and social activities also helped to forge an ethnic identity that united many of these survivors and led them to create a narrative of their lives that encompassed the prewar, wartime, and postwar periods.

ASSUMED IDENTITIES

The chaos of the postwar era created an opportunity for individuals to reinvent themselves, to adopt new identities. War had destroyed vast sums of documentation, from birth certificates to university diplomas. Additionally, wartime experiences had led individuals to adopt new personas. Those Jews hiding on Aryan papers acquired new names and invented family and personal histories to help them survive. Concentration camp inmates would give the title "Doctor" or "Dentist" to someone who had some medical knowledge or call someone "Rabbi" who had provided spiritual guidance. After the war, most individuals reclaimed their prewar identities, while a few attempted to carry their wartime personas into the liberated world.

Jewish physicians were scarce in postwar Germany, and their skills were greatly in demand. When a Jewish DP presented himself at a DP camp clinic and offered his services, there were few ways to check his credentials. No survivors had papers to verify their identity or their professional qualifications. Often there was only testimony from survivors from the same town or one's reputation from the ghettos and concentration camps to vouch for an individual. One man claiming to be Dr. Schwartz from Warsaw arrived at Föhrenwald and demanded to take over the hospital. The Camp Committee chairman sent him to the camp cultural director, Jacob Biber, to make arrangements. The doctor's youthful appearance made Biber suspicious and Biber gently probed the young man's knowledge of Warsaw's intellectual community. When asked if he had visited Ida Kaminski's theater, Dr. Schwartz betrayed himself, referring to the grande dame of Yiddish theater as "a no-good prostitute." Biber yelled, "You are no more Dr. Schwartz from Warsaw than I am!" Dr. Schwartz ran out, not to be seen again.[1] While Biber suspects that the incident was an example of one survivor's psychological reaction to the horrors of the Holocaust, Simon Schochet provided a more sympathetic interpretation of these pretenders.

Dr. Gwint worked at the Feldafing hospital. He had a spotless record as an inmate doctor in many concentration camps, but UNRRA learned that he did not have a medical degree. In prewar Poland unlicensed medical practitioners had commonly treated minor ailments, and Gwint had been one of these. In the concentration camps his skills were so valuable that inmates called him "Doctor," and after the war he found it difficult to leave that persona behind. Denounced, Gwint disappeared from Feldafing, as did other exposed professionals. DPs rejected these pretenders as cheats, but Schochet writes, "I have only respect and compassion for these so-called 'quacks and phonies.' In reality, they are not pretenders. They have simply not left off living the roles assigned them either by their fellow prisoners or their jailers. There are a few vain creatures who need the masquerade to feel important, but not many."[2] Schochet tells the reader of the great sacrifices inmate doctors made to serve their fellow prisoners and contrasts their valor to the well-respected German doctors who performed experiments on concentration camp inmates. He suggests that the DP pseudo-doctors should be rewarded with scholarships so that they can receive the training necessary to continue their professional pursuits.[3]

In the concentration camps those who retained their faith and were able to encourage and give hope to their fellow prisoners earned the title "Rabbi." Sara Bernstein was shocked when her previously anti-religious uncle appeared in Feldafing as a Hassidic rabbi.[4] He was apparently among the 6 percent of

[1] Jacob Biber, *Risen from the Ashes: A Story of the Jewish Displaced Persons in the Aftermath of World War II* (San Bernardino, CA: The Borgo Press, 1990), pp. 19–20.

[2] Simon Schochet, *Feldafing* (Vancouver: November House, 1983), p. 70.

[3] Schochet, *Feldafing*, p. 74.

[4] Sara Tuvel Bernstein, *The Seamstress: A Memoir of Survival* (New York: Berkley Books, 1997), pp. 297–298.

formerly nonobservant survivors who became observant after the war. Bernstein found him uneducated and hypocritical, yet she did not denounce him as an imposter; she believed the tragedy of his wife's and two little daughters' deaths at Auschwitz had altered him. His ability to inspire disciples speaks to the need for spiritual leadership among the survivors. Although Bernstein did not expose her uncle, often DPs turned on those who were revealed as imposters after liberation.

Postwar conditions encouraged the use of false identities. After the war, the illegal movement of Jews through the DP camps to Palestine depended on the use of false identity cards. To hide the movements in and out of the camps from Allied officials, illegal immigrants to Palestine would leave behind their identity cards to be used by incoming infiltrees from Eastern Europe. Even though these cards carried Jewish names, they were not the names of the bearer. It was often difficult for survivors to give up the use of their real names. Occasionally, sympathetic officials were able to substitute new identity cards with the real name of the DP for the old card, but this was a risky and illegal practice.[5] Sometimes because of overcrowding, DP camp directors would limit the registration of new DPs to relatives of those already in the camp. This could lead to DPs "adopting" a brother or sister in order that they might enter the camp. Sometimes the new sibling would decide to keep his or her new name.[6]

Nazi persecution had often forced Jews to adopt false identities, and now they sought to reclaim their religion and their names. Some German Jews in mixed marriages had converted to Christianity to ease the burden on their non-Jewish spouses in the Nazi period and now sought readmission to the Jewish community.[7] Others who had converted for opportunistic reasons and then suffered as Jews in the concentration camps also petitioned to return to Judaism. The rabbinate welcomed the return of such Jews as long as they were no longer in mixed marriages or raising non-Jewish children.[8] In one such case, the Hanover rabbinate decided to permit the return to Judaism of a sixty-three-year-old German woman, born Jewish, who had converted to Christianity in order to marry a man who would care for her and her illegitimate child. Now a widow and survivor of Theresienstadt, the woman insisted that she had always remained Jewish in her heart and pleaded "[I] stand at the end of my life and

---

[5] Lala Fishman's future husband, Morris, was the JDC director in the Kassel area and was able to help Czech Jews enter camps with reused identity cards and later secured blank identity cards to be used to give the Czechs their names back in exchange for the old cards. Lala Fishman and Steven Weingartner, *Lala's Story: A Memoir of the Holocaust* (Evanston, IL: Northwestern University Press, 1997), pp. 319–321.

[6] Isaac Marmor, "Videotaped interview, by the University of Southern California Shoah Foundation Institute for Visual History and Education," Interview Code (IC) 11303, Segments (Segs.) 79–80, Visual History Archive (VHA) [on-line at subscribing institutions]; www.usc.edu/vhi.

[7] Mimi Jeglinger to the legal editor of the *Jüdisches Gemeindeblatt* [Düsseldorf], letter dated 13 December 1948, Lady Rose L. Henriques Archive, Wiener Library, London (Microfilm reel 41, United States Holocaust Memorial Museum).

[8] "Richtlinien fuer die Wiederaufnahme in das Judentum," November 1946, p. 1, Henriques Archive, Microfilm reel 41.

need my spiritual peace. ... I urgently need my inner calm. Please open the way for my return."[9] Since she was no longer in a mixed marriage, this woman was eligible for return and to reclaim her Jewish identity. The rabbis tried to distinguish between sincere returnees to Judaism and those Germans who simply sought improved rations and assistance with emigration. Although the Nazis had defined Jews by their parentage regardless of religious belief, those Jews who had apostatized were not recognized as Jews by the DPs, unless they formally returned to Judaism.

Many Eastern European survivors who had assumed false identities to survive the Holocaust now wanted to reclaim their former names and life histories. During the war, some Jews attempted to evade the Nazis by posing as Christians, assuming completely new identities. For some recovering their name was as simple as registering at a DP camp. After liberation, Lala Fishman continued to use her assumed name, partly for the sense of security it provided and partly because her own family name reminded her that she was the sole survivor of her family.[10] In late 1945 she burned her false identity papers before entering the U.S. Zone of occupied Germany, since she had been told that the Americans repatriated anyone with false papers. Upon arrival in the Hasenecke DP camp, she signed her given name and listed the names of her parents and siblings on the registration papers. "In doing so I felt as if I were reclaiming not only my identity, but my family as well."[11] With the initial, intense period of grief behind her, Fishman was able to find comfort once again in identifying with her family name.

The security of the assumed names led some DPs to retain them even after registration in a DP camp. Some of these DPs permanently kept their adopted names. Those who wanted to reclaim their birth names after already registering under a false identity needed to prove their identities to officials. The Central Committee in Munich had a judicial branch that worked to provide survivors with replacement papers, such as birth certificates and marriage licenses. It was not always easy to satisfy the need for evidence.

After she arrived in a DP camp, Wanda Mehr decided it was an insult to her family to continue using her assumed identity. She traveled to Munich and found herself facing skeptical Hungarian Jews. Wanda's looks were not particularly Semitic and she spoke Polish, but no Yiddish. These attributes had helped her pass on the Aryan side during the German occupation. Now all of that worked against her efforts to establish her Jewish identity. She also had no witnesses to verify her prewar identity. In Munich she attempted to speak Yiddish, but it was so Germanized that it convinced the Hungarians that she was a German non-Jew trying to masquerade as a Jew in order to get a visa to America. They suspected that she had a Jewish boyfriend who had taught her some Yiddish. When she began to

---

[9] Rabbi Munk forwarded the letter in November 1946 to the JRCA. In January 1947 the Hanover rabbinate made its decision. Elfriede Grotefendt to Rabbi Munk, letter dated 21 January 1946; P.I.R. Hart to Rabbi Dr. Munk, letter dated 13 January 1947, Henriques Archive, Microfilm reel 41.

[10] Fishman, *Lala's Story*, p. 274.

[11] Fishman, *Lala's Story*, p. 306.

cry, an emissary from Palestine who was present said in Hebrew, "Perhaps she's really Jewish." Wanda had been in the Zionist youth group Hashomer Hatzair and understood enough to reply in Hebrew. Her knowledge of Hebrew satisfied them that she was Jewish, since they believed a German girl might learn some Yiddish but not Hebrew.[12] Wanda's questioners were not wrong to be suspicious of an undocumented individual wanting to claim Jewish identity. There were non-Jewish Germans who sought recognition as Jewish DPs in order to acquire better rations, improve their emigration possibilities, or identify themselves with Nazi victims. Others simply represented themselves as Jews in black market transactions, hoping to evade capture by police or military government authorities or, if captured, to win their sympathy and a quick release.[13]

Rabbinic authorities were often called upon to determine who was eligible for membership in the Jewish community. Their standards needed to be met for membership in the official community (*Gemeinde*) organizations and to be counted for minyan. Jewish law recognized only individuals born to a Jewish mother and reared as Jews to be eligible for membership in the Jewish community. However, some Jewish aid organizations had more flexible definitions when it came to providing nonmaterial assistance. To stretch its limited resources, the JDC restricted aid packages to Jews living outside of DP camps to those who were members of the Gemeinde[14] but provided emigration and family reunification assistance to individuals who had been persecuted as Jews. In a similar fashion, the JCRA exerted itself to reunite a father with his son, despite the fact that the father's mother was a non-Jew, as was his former wife, the boy's mother.[15] However, a woman who had twice left the Jewish community did not receive JDC packages distributed by the local Jewish community. JRU workers had provided her with occasional packages until they discovered that the local community did not consider her Jewish. The Belsen rabbinate had determined that she must undergo a waiting period before she could be readmitted to the Jewish faith.[16] In such a case, the JRU chose to abide by the decision of the local Jewish authorities.

RELIGIOUS LIFE

Jewish DPs resided on a broad spectrum of religious observances and beliefs, from secular to ultra-Orthodox. Among scholars there has been an assumption

[12] Wanda Mehr, "Videotaped interview," VHA, IC 26609, Segs. 519–527.

[13] A certain Hannes Opitz, for example, was falsely posing as a Jew and was wanted by the police. Di jidisze gemajnde in Coburg, "Cu der ojfmerkzamkajt fun der jidiszer Bafelkerung in Dajczland," *Landsberger Lager Cajtung*, 30 August 1946, p. 13.

[14] Atina Grossmann, *Jews, Germans, and Allies: Close Encounters in Occupied Germany* (Princeton, NJ: Princeton University Press, 2007), p. 97.

[15] "Memorandum: Betr. Erich Moses," 13 March 1947; E.G. Lowenthal, JRU, to Edith Dosmar, Comité Israélite des Refugiés, letter dated 24 March 1947; E.G. Lowenthal to Edith Dosmar, letter dated 8 July 1947, Henriques Archive, Microfilm reel 41.

[16] Mia Fisher, JCRA, to E. G. Lowenthal, "Subject: Neustadt Community," 30 January 1948; Y. Greenberg, JRU, to Mia Fisher, letter dated 22 January 1948; E. G. Lowenthal to Mia Fisher, "Subject: Frau Else Gerland," 13 February 1948, Henriques Archive, Microfilm reel 41.

that religion played a small role in the survivors' lives, since most DPs were non-Orthodox, and some appeared to have lost at least part of their faith in the ghettos and concentration camps. In fact, DPs strove to recreate a sense of normalcy in their lives. Asserting their values and rebuilding Jewish community was part of that process, and religious ritual played an important role. Some appeals for religious observance were more suited to Orthodox than secular Jews, but almost all chose to commemorate Jewish holidays in ways that were meaningful to them. The Orthodox found community through holiday religious services, while secular Jews were more inclined to literary and musical evenings. As we have seen, nearly all came together for memorial prayers to commemorate their dead. The Jewish calendar organized the rhythm of DP life and fostered ethnic as well as religious identity.

Rabbinic Politics

DP rabbis organized to supervise the legal aspects of Jewish religious life, regulating membership in the community, certifying weddings and circumcisions, and overseeing kosher kitchens and ritual baths. The rabbinic councils of the Central Committees in the American and British Zones acted as the supreme religious courts in Germany. Rabbis in the American Zone turned to the Chief Rabbi of Palestine when they needed further guidance, as in the case of agunot discussed in Chapter 3. Representatives of the Agudat-Israel–oriented Vaad Hatzalah also sought to influence DP rabbis in the American Zone. In the British Zone, the London Beth Din advised the British chaplains and the civilian rabbis sent by the Chief Rabbi's Religious Emergency Council (CRREC). Initially, the CRREC worked only with Agudat-Israel rabbis among the DPs.

The impact of outside influences on the DP rabbinate was most strongly felt in the British Zone, where CRREC rabbis refused to recognize the head of the religious committee in Belsen, Rabbi Hermann Helfgott. Helfgott was a modern Orthodox Zionist who had served as an army chaplain for the Yugoslav forces and was imprisoned in 1941 as a prisoner of war, not as a Jew. Liberated near Celle, Germany, he arrived in Belsen on April 30, 1945 and assumed the role of chaplain and joined the nascent Jewish committee.[17] As a modern Orthodox rabbi, he did not meet with the approval of the Agudat-Israel–oriented CRREC. In fact, with the separate financial assistance of the CRREC assured, Agudat Israel left the Belsen Camp Committee. In practice, however, Helfgott was in charge of religious issues in Belsen, and the rabbis of Celle and Hanover consulted him as the supreme religious authority in the British Zone. In 1947 an agreement between all Belsen Orthodox groups, including Agudat Israel, led

---

[17] During the Israeli War of Independence he made aliyah and joined the Israel Defense Forces. Later he returned to Germany as the rabbi of Cologne and Hanover. Hagit Lavsky, *New Beginnings: Holocaust Survivors in Bergen-Belsen and the British Zone in Germany, 1945–1950* (Detroit, MI: Wayne State University Press, 2002), p. 68; Hadassah Rosensaft, *Yesterday: My Story* (Washington, DC: United States Holocaust Memorial Museum, 2004), p. 56.

to CRREC recognition, and British authorities in July 1947 finally recognized Helfgott as Chief Rabbi of the British Zone.[18]

Under the guidance of the London rabbinic court, chaplains and DP rabbis discouraged the conversion of non-Jews to Judaism.[19] A rabbinic court could convert the non-Jewish spouse of a Jew, but in July 1947 a Munich conference of rabbis residing in Germany decided to suspend conversions of non-Jews who were not married to Jews.[20] JRU rabbi A. Carlebach expressed concern about the London Beth Din's insistence that intermarried Jews should be denied membership in the Jewish communities and that such Jews who were already members should not be allowed to assume leadership positions. Most of the German-Jewish leadership was married to non-Jews.

The pressure on Orthodox DPs to live up to the expectations of their coreligionists from abroad manifested itself in a young DP rabbi's choice to grow his beard in order to meet with the approval of American Orthodox rabbis.[21] Relief workers assumed that Orthodox Jews would want to be separated from secular Jews. In Belsen, sixteen Orthodox children pleaded in stilted English with relief workers not to separate them from their secular friends:

Although some of our comrades are not orthodox, they always respected our feelings and definitely *could not have any demoralizing influence upon us.* After long years of suffering we went through together and trying continuously not to be separated!!! We can not justify a slightly different attitude towards religion as a reason to part us from our friends. We expect this problem to be considered with understanding of our situation and we shall regard *ANY ATTEMPT OF PARTITION AS AN INTERFERENCE OF OUR FREEDOM!!!*[22]

Unity between Orthodox and secular DPs was possible in the immediate aftermath of the war, but as allegiances to prewar organizations returned, encouraged by the efforts of American and British Orthodox agencies, this unity often fragmented.[23]

Faith, Doubt, and Ethnicity

The emergence of religious differences among DPs revealed the continuing influence of prewar practices and trends. Interwar Jewish communities had been divided between traditionalist (ultra-) Orthodox and modern, liberal Orthodox,

---

[18] Lavsky, *New Beginnings*, pp. 117–118.

[19] Rev. A. Carlebach to Court of the Chief Rabbi, letter dated 29 November 1946, Henriques Archive, Microfilm reel 41.

[20] "Richtlinien fuer die Wiederaufnahme in das Judentum," p. 1.

[21] Samuel Bak, "Landsberg Revisited," *Dimensions: A Journal of Holocaust Studies* 13:2 (1999): 36.

[22] Shoshannah Fine, letter to Judy, dated May 1983 and accompanying petition, USHMM, Documents relating to Shoshannah Fine's work with Displaced Persons, RG-19.041.08.

[23] Judith Tydor Baumel, *Kibbutz Buchenwald: Survivors and Pioneers* (New Brunswick, NJ: Rutgers University Press, 1997), p. 112.

between religious and secular. Even among the secular Jews there were divisions between those who identified themselves culturally and politically as Jews, Zionists, or Bundists and those who advocated assimilationism. During the war these religious and political differences were occasionally put aside in recognition of the need to cooperate in facing a shared enemy. The ideal of political unity persisted into the immediate post-liberation era, but religious differences reasserted themselves almost immediately. Debates over Sabbath observance and *kashrut* (Jewish dietary laws) continued prewar controversies that were now heightened by the decline of rabbinic authority during the war years. Yet, even as they argued about levels of observance, rituals and holiday celebrations allowed DPs to express their Jewish identity and to join in community building.

In his study of Holocaust survivors living in Israel, Reeve Brenner measured the survivors' level of observance by the number and types of rituals they practiced. His statistics demonstrated that a total of 55 percent of survivors had been at least moderately observant prior to the war. The remaining 45 percent Brenner defined as unobservant, although this category included those who practiced a limited number of Jewish traditions as well as those who observed none at all. "Nonobservance," therefore, should not be interpreted as a rejection of Jewish identity, peoplehood, or as evidence of atheism. In the immediate postwar period 66 percent of survivors could be characterized under Brenner's schema as nonobservant, an increase of 21 percent over the prewar era.[24] This change likely reflected a continuation of prewar trends toward secularization and the difficult conditions of life in postwar Germany. Although Orthodox observance may have declined, religion and ritual still played an important role in the DP communities.

Secularization had been a trend among Eastern European Jews prior to the Shoah. Children of Orthodox parents had been joining secular Zionist youth movements, attending public schools, migrating to cities, and moving away from their families' traditional observances in the interwar period. One scholar estimates that the majority of the prewar older generation was Orthodox, but only 30 percent of the younger generation was,[25] and most DPs were from that younger generation. In one prewar example, an Orthodox family moved from their shtetl to a city, and contact with secular and liberal Jews along with the attractions of Yiddish theater facilitated change in the religious and social lives of the younger generation.[26] In families with strained relations between parents and children, this secularizing trend could be viewed as rebellion against parental values, but, by the same token, the willingness of parents to tolerate experimentation and questioning could allow adolescents with strong family ties to

---

[24] Reeve Robert Brenner, *The Faith and Doubt of Holocaust Survivors* (New York: Free Press, 1980), p. 37.

[25] Alex Grobman, *Battling for Souls: The Vaad Hatzala Rescue Committee in Post-War Europe* (Jersey City, NJ: KTAV, 2004), p. 23.

[26] Nathan Katz, *Teach Us to Count Our Days: A Story of Survival, Sacrifice and Success* (Cranbury, NJ: Cornwall Books, 1999), pp. 41–43. In postwar St. Louis, Katz joined an Orthodox synagogue

move away from the practices of their childhood home.[27] One survivor recalled his childhood of wearing *payes* (side locks) and growing up surrounded by ultra-Orthodox relatives, while his parents befriended Christians and occasionally ate nonkosher foods: "And so the days and years passed, torn between my family's secretive tries to break away from tradition and their need to still get along with my ultra-Orthodox relatives, all living under the same roof."[28] In such a case, the parents had sown the seeds of secularization. Most survivors were adolescents during the war years, and after the war they sought to engage in religious practices in keeping with their parents' values. DPs tended to continue the rituals of their family homes even as some of them struggled with religious doubt.

Ritual practice and faith can be treated as two distinct categories. Orthodox Jews may be motivated by their God belief and/or family heritage to fulfill religious rituals, but secular Jews may also perform religious observances for reasons of ethnic identity.[29] Brenner found that some survivors retained their faith after the Shoah but restricted their ritual observance because they had gotten out of the habit and it was too difficult to return to their previously intense level of observance.[30] In the DP camps, the lack of ritual objects, such as mikvaot and tefillin, as well as difficulties procuring kosher food, made religious observance difficult. The decline in immediate postwar observance that Brenner documented may have had as much to do with such obstacles to practice as with lack of desire.

On the question of faith, Alexander Groth's survey of survivors in North America and Israel discovered that 56 percent expressed faith in God. The remaining 44 percent described themselves as nonbelievers or doubters.[31] This split is remarkably similar to Brenner's findings of prewar observant and nonobservant

but observed Conservative Jewish practices in his home, unless his more observant father was visiting (p. 180).

[27] In a study of Catholic, Protestant, and Jewish adolescents, the author noted that Jewish adolescents were least likely to exhibit change. Since none of these subjects had experienced anything remotely comparable to the Holocaust, it is not possible to ascertain how such a traumatic event might have influenced the results. Still, the findings of parental influence are consistent with those of Brenner, Groth, and this work. It is interesting to consider how age and developmental factors affected the DPs. See Elizabeth Weiss Ozorak, "Social and Cognitive Influences on the Development of Religious Beliefs and Commitment in Adolescence," *Journal for the Scientific Study of Religion* 28 (December 1989): 460 and 461.

[28] Thomas Toivi Blatt, *From the Ashes of Sobibor: A Story of Survival* (Evanston, IL: Northwestern University Press, 1997), p. 9.

[29] A study of contemporary Jews in Israel found that traditional (nonaffiliated) and Orthodox Jews participate in rituals primarily for motives concerning religion and continuity with past family practices. Secular Jews also performed rituals but were motivated by ethnic feelings and desire for family gatherings. See Aryeh Lazar, Shlomo Kravetz, and Peri Frederich-Kedem, "The Multidimensionality of Motivation for Jewish Religious Behavior: Content, Structure, and Relationship to Religious Identity," *Journal for the Scientific Study of Religion* 41:3 (2002): 509–519.

[30] Brenner, *Faith and Doubt*, pp. 78–80.

[31] Alexander J. Groth, *Holocaust Voices: An Attitudinal Survey of Survivors* (Amherst, NY: Humanity Books, 2003), p. 94.

Jews. Groth further notes that those from religious and nonassimilated prewar homes were more likely to be believers, and those from assimilated, nonreligious backgrounds were significantly less likely to be believers. Groth concludes, "What the surviving remnant 'learned' [from the Holocaust] was substantially conditioned by the legacy of their past. There were dramatic crossovers, but most of the religious kept their faith; most of the secular Jews remained within the realm of their earlier agnosticism or atheism."[32] The continuity of faith, or lack thereof, from the prewar era to the postliberation period is striking. Brenner also found that 68 percent of his respondents "retained unwaveringly the religious or irreligious conviction of their childhood and youth."[33] Family upbringing and religious education influenced the survivors more than their Holocaust experiences. Thus, while Brenner's statistics certainly indicate that a significant minority of the DP population became less observant, we need to be careful not to attribute the change solely to the Holocaust. Moreover, these statistics also do not tell us the role that religious ritual played in creating social bonds between the survivors or in shaping their identity.

The Jewish Calendar

Sabbath observance both united and divided Jewish DPs. Philip S. Bernstein, adviser to the U.S. Military Governor, remembered, "I attended the first *Yizkor* service on Shavuot in a Bavarian displaced persons camp. Instead of comforting the survivors over their losses, the rabbi, himself bereaved said, 'Observe the Sabbath.' I thought at first how unfeeling, and then I began to sense the wisdom of an ancient therapy."[34] Placing the emphasis on the return to religious practice, the DP rabbi rooted the Shoah in the context of Jewish history and called on the survivors to perpetuate the Jewish community. The renewed observance of the Sabbath became central to the perseverance of Jewish communal and religious life.

Most DPs did engage in at least some rituals of Sabbath observance. On Friday nights DPs welcomed the Sabbath by lighting candles, blessing the wine, and singing songs. Even secular kibbutzim performed these rituals. For the Orthodox these were rituals expressing their faith and fulfilling their obligations to God, and on Saturday they would observe a day of rest and study. For secular Jews, the motives had more to do with connecting to tradition and to lost family.[35] The DP rabbinate was aware of the connection between observance and family and, in its efforts to combat secularization, issued calls to prayer that appealed to the memories of the parents and of the dead millions.[36]

---

[32] Groth, *Holocaust Voices*, p. 94.

[33] Brenner, *Faith and Doubt*, p. 122.

[34] Philip S. Bernstein, "The Role and Functions of the Modern Rabbi," *Central Conference of American Rabbis Annual* 79 (1969): 227.

[35] Lavsky, *New Beginnings*, pp. 161–162.

[36] See, for example, Bergen-Belsen Rabbinate, "An Appeal to All Jews" (in Yiddish), June/July 1947, Yad Vashem (YV), O-70/29; Hanover Rabbinate, "Call to the Jewish Population!" (in Yiddish), no date, YV O-70/29.

With each camp population containing a cross section of Jewish society, there were many differing traditions that came into conflict. The secular-dominated camp committees attempted to respect the sanctity of the Sabbath by restricting automobile traffic and secular entertainments on the Sabbath.[37] These restrictions grated against secular Jews who had been accustomed to living in urban areas before the war, but they were not enough to satisfy ultra-Orthodox Jews who wanted to recreate the Sabbath peace of the shtetl. At Belsen Hassidic Jews attacked a bus carrying secular Jews out of the camp for a cultural excursion on the Sabbath. The tour organizer defended the practice, "What right do the Hassidim have to force Jews not to enjoy the pleasure that one can find in the Sabbath? ... What can be a greater pleasure than to drive in a comfortable omnibus, to see the beautiful landscape, to hear the most beautiful music, opera, etc. ... The Torah was given to all Jews, not only those people who use it for their personal material purposes."[38] Secular Jews resented the interference with what for them was their Sabbath observance. Before the war, Orthodox and secular Jews had been able to separate themselves geographically. Within the DP camps this spatial distance disappeared and conflict resulted.

Offended by the activities of the less observant Jews on the Sabbath, some Orthodox sought to isolate themselves. Hungarian survivors, many of them Hassidim, were the largest group that maintained a distance from the rest of camp life. Another group was the Beth Jacob teachers from Bergen-Belsen. A group of Beth Jacob women had joined Kibbutz Buchenwald in the hopes of earning certificates for immigration to Israel. Although the Beth Jacob leadership was concerned about exposing "their girls" to the secular Jews, they were more worried about losing their followers to secular Zionist groups that were having greater success in acquiring the coveted immigration certificates. At the kibbutz unity was initially maintained through the keeping of a kosher kitchen and religious observance of the Sabbath in public spaces. This cooperation gave way by autumn 1945, when some secular Jews smoked in the dining hall and new arrivals from Belsen added musical entertainment on the Sabbath. These developments distressed the Beth Jacob leader, who eagerly seized the opportunity to begin an ultra-Orthodox kibbutz elsewhere, away from the Sabbath-desecrators.[39] Interestingly, the Orthodox Zionists affiliated with Mizrahi decided to stay at Kibbutz Buchenwald, demonstrating the continuation of prewar divisions among Orthodox Jews.

Even among observant Jews there were willful instances of Sabbath desecration. Since the kindling of flame is prohibited on the Sabbath, smoking is also not allowed. However, one moderately observant Jew chose to smoke cigars on

[37] Religious Office, Kassel to Jewish Committees, 1 June 1948, YIVO Institute for Jewish Research (YIVO), RG 294.2, MK 483, Microfilm reel 64, Folder 928.
[38] Josef Butterman, "Nider mit dem Fanatism!!" [May 1947?], YV O-70/30. On the reverse is the advertisement for the next Sabbath outing to the Hanover opera on June 7, 1947.
[39] Baumel, *Kibbutz Buchenwald*, pp. 110–112.

the Sabbath as his means of rebelling against God's silence during the Shoah.[40] Brenner recorded additional instances of even highly observant Jews stopping their observance of one practice or another, such as the daily use of phylacteries, because of their Holocaust experiences. Yet other survivors took on religious obligations for the same reasons. This is a reminder that individuals come to terms with their religious needs in their own way. Even as the meaning attributed to various practices varied by the individual, the shared recognition of Jewish holidays helped to shape an ethnic identity.

While Sabbath observance was a cause for tension, other holidays on the Jewish calendar promoted a sense of community. Orthodox and secular Jews observed Hanukkah and Purim without rancor. In both the Book of Maccabees (the source for Hanukkah) and the Scroll of Esther (the story of Purim), the focus is on human action. Thus, secular Jews could observe these minor holidays, not included in the Five Books of Moses, as expressions of ethnicity rather than religious faith. The historical themes of the holidays – Hanukkah, celebrating the triumph of the Maccabees over the Syrian Greek desecrators of the Temple, and Purim, celebrating the rescue of Jews from the genocidal plans of the Persian vizier Haman – easily connected to the liberation from Nazi bondage and to the national struggle of the Zionists. The entire Jewish DP community perceived the contemporary relevance of these holidays.

Hanukkah celebrations frequently took place in DP schools with children performing songs and plays.[41] At the first Hanukkah concert in Belsen, the junior class did a dance of the candles and Lola Kuschenblatt performed "the Dance of Liberation." The evening concluded with the singing of the Zionist anthem, "Hatikvah." An UNRRA nurse found the concert well presented but "rather tragic."[42] At Föhrenwald, 750 kibbutz children, their leaders, and a couple of hundred other children formed a torch-lit parade to celebrate the liberation from the Syrian Greeks. They left the camp and impulsively marched into the Wolfratshausen town square intending to go to the military government headquarters to express their gratitude for their own liberation. Although they returned to camp without incident, two trucks of armed American soldiers confronted the group. The military government feared not only the fire danger represented by the torches but also the possible reactions of the German public to what could have appeared to be a looting raid. A few days earlier, "a military formation of D.P.s" had marched to the local military government detachment without permission, likely increasing the concerns of the local authorities.[43] The friendly impulse of the children in celebration of both the ancient and their own

---

[40] Brenner, *Faith and Doubt*, p. 53.

[41] "Fajerlecher chanuke-ownt," *Undzer Hofenung*, December 1946, YV M-1/P-85.

[42] Muriel Knox Doherty, letter dated 6 December 1945 in *Letters from Belsen 1945: An Australian Nurse's Experiences with the Survivors of War*, eds. Judith Cornell and R. Lynette Russell (St. Leonards, NSW Australia: Allen & Unwin, 2000), p. 198.

[43] Lieutenant David S. Buttler, CAC Supply Branch, to Lieutenant Colonel Bender, Chief of Supply Section E-201, "D.P. Camp Landsberg/Lech," 29 November 1945, p. 3, United Nations Archives (UN) S-0425, Box 43, File 6.

liberation had ominous undertones to Germans and Americans who distrusted large demonstrations by Jews.[44] Hanukkah gave the survivors the opportunity to teach Jewish tradition to the few remaining children and to understand their present circumstances within the context of Jewish history. At Föhrenwald they also learned the limits to their self-expression.

Purim festivities involve a carnivalesque turning of the world on its head, mocking authority, and reveling in jokes and satire. One young DP child remembered wearing her coat inside out and singing Yiddish songs for her neighbors to celebrate Purim.[45] Newspaper photographs from 1946 show happy children from the Feldafing Purim play and, at the Purim carnival in Landsberg, a DP dressed as Hitler surrounded by DP police and a child in a striped concentration camp uniform.[46] At Landsberg a man in a concentration camp uniform read the story of Esther, and Hitler was hung in effigy. To complete the demonstration of victory over Nazism, DPs burned Hitler's *Mein Kampf* in the city where it had been written.[47] The survivors joyously celebrated their freedom. In the DP camps costumed survivors depicted their triumph over the Nazis by parading around as Hitlers and Nazis. The ancient triumph over Haman easily transferred onto present circumstances (Figure 10).

In 1947 Purim also became a time to demonstrate bonds to the Jewish community in Palestine. At camp Fritzlar, Purim was an occasion for raising money for the Yishuv. A children's performance included dances, montages, and recitations. The highlight was a Purim comedy, *In the Days of Yore*. A traditional Purim ball began with greetings from all of the Zionist organizations with the wish that next Purim be celebrated in Palestine. A representative from Hashomer Hatzair spoke briefly about the Jewish National Fund (JNF), the organization for the reclamation of land in Palestine. For entertainment the Fritzlar drama circle performed, an orchestra played, and a buffet dinner was served. The proceeds from the children's performance and from the ball were donated to the JNF.[48] At Hasenecke-Münchberg children performed Hebrew songs and created pictures of Palestine, and an evening ball raised money for the JNF.[49] The ability of aid recipients to raise funds for Palestine indicated an improvement in material conditions by 1947. It also demonstrated an attempt to connect the successful resistance against Haman's, and Hitler's, genocidal plans to a future in Palestine.

---

[44] R. Rachmen, kibbutz leader, to Mrs. Henshaw, UNRRA, 1 December 1945 USHMM, Samuel Zisman Papers, RG-19.047.02*07; M. Jean Henshaw, Acting Director, UNRRA, Team 106, to Helen Matouskova, UNRRA Supervisor, "Chanukah Festivities on November 29th," 3 December 1945, Zisman Papers, RG-19.047.02*07.

[45] Faye Doctrow, telephone interview by author, tape recording, 25 March 1996.

[46] *Unterwegs (Feldafinger Magazin)*, 15 April 1946.

[47] Toby Blum-Dobkin, "Rituals of Transition: An Ethnographic Approach to Life in a Displaced Persons Camp," *The Netherlands and Nazi Genocide: Papers of the 21st Annual Scholars' Conference*, eds. G. Jan Colijn and Marcia S. Littell, vol. 32 (Lewiston, NY: The Edwin Mellen Press, 1992): p. 493.

[48] "Di purim-fajerungen in lager Fritzlar," *Undzer Hofenung*, 18 March 1947, p. 5.

[49] "Di purim fajerungen in Hasenheke-Minchberg," *Undzer Hofenung*, 18 March 1947, p. 5.

FIGURE 10. Jewish DPs dress up one of their own as Adolf Hitler and capture him for a Purim masquerade at the Landsberg DP camp, March 24, 1946. *Credit*: USHMM, courtesy of Herbert Friedman

Secular and observant Jews alike celebrated Passover, the great Jewish festival of liberation. The defeat of Pharaoh and the exodus from Egypt had special meaning for the survivors of Nazi tyranny. Traditional observance involves participation in a seder on the first and second nights of Passover. During the seder, the Haggadah is read, establishing the order of the service and narrating the story of the Jews' exodus from Egypt. Symbols on a seder plate represent various aspects of the story. A cup of wine is poured for the Prophet Elijah, whom tradition maintains visits each seder and who will bring the Messiah when it is time. In honor of the first Passover seder following liberation, Jews in the British and American Zones wrote new Haggadot.[50] In Belsen, the Haggadah compared the exodus from Egypt with the survivors' hopes for an exodus from Europe and the creation of a Jewish state in Palestine.[51] The holiday coincided with the first anniversary of Belsen's liberation, making the parallel between the Israelites' flight to freedom and the survivors' own liberation especially vivid. The Nazis had frequently scheduled their actions to coincide with Jewish holidays. It was at the beginning of Passover 1943 that the Nazis entered the Warsaw ghetto to liquidate it but encountered stiff resistance. Thus, Passover in the DP camps was connected to mourning academies for communities murdered at that time of year, to the heroic resistance fighters of the Warsaw ghetto, and to the liberation from the Nazis in spring 1945.

In Munich the United Zionist Organization and its youth group Nocham published a "Supplement to the Haggadah" that American chaplain Rabbi Abraham Klausner used to lead seders for free-living Jews in Munich during Passover 1946. Although calling itself a supplement, perhaps so as not to offend Orthodox Jews with its innovations, this book had all of the elements of a Haggadah, and, like the Belsen Haggadah, this one connected the slavery in Egypt to the horrors of Nazi persecution. Instead of God liberating the Jews, it is the Allies who free the survivors from Nazi bondage. Their trials are not ended, however, as the Jews are forced to flee for their own safety: "[T]hey saved their lives, and they went to Bavaria in order to go up to our Holy Land."[52] The story continues with the Jews of Palestine fighting to bring the survivors to Israel. But when the emissaries of Palestinian Jewry encounter the survivors, they ask to which group the survivors belong. Here the author proclaims the message of the United Zionists: "The remnants answer: But was not all of Israel slaughtered together? Is not all of Israel to rebuild the land together? ... We all belong to one group, we are Israel, all of us, and we have no interest in factions."[53] The emissaries respond that rivalry breeds strength. The dream of Zionist unity collides with the reality of Yishuv politics.

Perhaps the most heart-wrenching aspect of this Haggadah is the *Dayenu* (We would have been content). Traditionally, this song recites all of the blessings God bestowed on the Israelites, but here rather than blessings are a list of afflictions. "Had He scattered us among the nations but had not given us the First Crusade, we would have been content. Had He given us the First Crusade but not the Second, we would have been content. Had He given us the Second Crusade but not the Blood Libel, we would have been content." This litany continues through

---

[50] The Landsberg *Haggadah* linked ancient oppression to the Holocaust. On its cover pyramids were juxtaposed with concentration camps. She'erit Hapletah b'Landsberg, "Haggadah shel Pesach," YIVO, RG 294.2, MK 483, Microfilm reel 113, Folder 1554.

[51] Lavsky, *New Beginnings*, p. 161.

[52] Saul Touster, ed., *A Survivors' Haggadah: Written, Designed, and Illustrated by Yosef Dov Sheinson with Woodcuts by Miklós Adler* (Philadelphia: Jewish Publication Society, 2000), p. 31. This is a facsimile edition of the 1946 Sheinson *Haggadah* with commentary and an English translation.

[53] Touster, ed., *Survivors' Haggadah*, p. 35.

FIGURE 11. Passover seder in the Traunstein DP camp, 1948–1949. *Credit*: USHMM, courtesy of Lucy Gliklich Breitbart

the bondage, hunger, disease, and torture of recent times. The survivors' *Dayenu* concludes, "All the more so, since these have befallen us, we must make *Aliyah*, even if illegally, wipe out the Diaspora, build the chosen land, and make a home for ourselves and our children for eternity."[54] Just as God did not liberate the Jews of Europe, the Jews cannot wait for Him to create a homeland in Palestine. The survivors' Haggadah taught it was the task of the survivors to move to and build up the Jewish homeland.

The first seder was particularly emotional for survivors. They were homeless and without their families. At many seder tables there was no child to ask the Four Questions, reminding the DPs of their truncated communities and family trees. Tears were common on this night celebrating freedom. The concluding words to the seder, "Next Year in Jerusalem" took on deeper significance in the DP camps. Instead of the traditional religious hope that the messianic age would arrive to bring the Jews to Jerusalem, it became the call of nationally minded DPs to work for the creation of a Jewish state. At the community seder in Traunstein (Figure 11), "In great voice the public sang 'next year' with the fullest hopes that this is the last Seder night in the Diaspora."[55] Also connecting the holiday with Zionist aspirations was the "outdoor Palestinian Passover service" at Hochland Lager, the agricultural training center for Föhrenwald. The evening concluded with Palestinian folk dancing around a campfire.[56] Within the DP camps the Jewish calendar provided opportunities for connecting DPs to a shared ancient history to the recent Nazi past and to a future in the Jewish homeland.

[54] Translation adapted from Touster, ed., *Survivors' Haggadah*, p. 63.
[55] A. Fersztman, "Di Seder-fajerung in Traunstein," *Landsberger Lager Cajtung*, 3 May 1946, p. 7.
[56] Henry Cohen, Director, UNRRA, Team 106, to Samuel Zisman, UNRRA, District 5 Headquarters, letter dated 10 April 1946, Zisman Papers, RG-19.047.02*07.

Passover unified Jewish DPs in their common celebration of liberation and exodus. However, the demand for kosher matzah revealed differences. Relief workers were overwhelmed by demands for sufficiently kosher matzah. Certain groups insisted that only matzah that they themselves had prepared could be eaten. This required the acquisition of flour and the availability of suitable ovens. In 1947 rumors circulated that the JDC matzah had been prepared with ritually impure flour, until the head of the Rabbinic Council of the American Zone, Rabbi Snieg, conceded that the JDC matzah was strictly kosher.[57] To meet demand for kosher wine, the JDC arranged production at a German factory using raisins.

Although Jews are to celebrate Passover joyously, the eight days could bring hunger to observant DPs. Passover observance requires avoiding all leavening agents. Ashkenazi Jews also do not eat foods that swell, such as rice and legumes. Passover desserts, such as sponge cake or meringue, require many eggs to make up for the lack of leavening. Thus, Passover cuisine required an adjustment in rations allocated to DPs. In 1946, UNRRA officials in the Heidelberg area sought approval from the military government to provide Jewish DPs with one egg per person per day for the duration of the holiday along with other foodstuffs. The request was denied, but the UNRRA director for the American Zone advised the Heidelberg Liaison Office that the Army, military government, and JDC "are co-ordinating the matter of providing eggs, onions, butter, sugar and raisins requested for the Jewish Easter holidays."[58] The lack of cultural awareness, that one could confuse Passover with Easter, was a major obstacle for Jewish DPs and Jewish relief agencies when trying to make their needs understood to the higher authorities.

Jewish Dietary Laws

The ability to obtain kosher food was of great significance to the Orthodox, although even less observant Jews would prefer kosher food if it were available. Haskel Tydor recalled, "Only in Munich or in other places with remnants of a Jewish community, could Jews afford the luxury of being scrupulously observant. For the rest of us, there was no question of obtaining kosher; it was enough to try not to eat *treif* [ritually unfit foods]."[59] Most difficult for those DPs who wanted to keep kosher were obtaining fats and meat. Kosher meat had to be ritually slaughtered. Lard, a pork product, was unacceptable, and most German bread was prepared with lard. Butter and margarine containing dairy products could not be used in meals featuring meat. The struggle for kosher food demonstrated the determination of Jewish DPs to return to familiar religious practices and their refusal to bow meekly to Allied authorities, Germans, and relief workers.

[57] Judith Tydor Baumel, "The Politics of Spiritual Rehabilitation in the DP Camps," *Simon Wiesenthal Center Annual* 6 (1989): 62.
[58] Pearl Morris, UNRRA Liaison Officer, to Captain Carl, Special Projects, "Rations for Jews for Passover Holidays," 11 April 1946, UN, S-0437, Box 21, File 22.
[59] Quoted in Baumel, "Politics of Spiritual Rehabilitation," p. 65.

Frustrated with the apparent lack of will among the British officials and the Belsen Camp Committee to provide a kosher kitchen, ultra-Orthodox Beth Jacob teachers decided to take action. On the occasion of a camp gathering on a Sabbath four months after liberation, the leader of the Beth Jacob School announced to the assembled throng that "our girls will not touch any cooked food of any kind until we are provided with kosher food – so help us God!"[60] For three days following, pots sent from the camp kitchen to the girls' barracks were returned untouched. At the end of the third day, one of the DP rabbis arrived and attempted to persuade the women leaders that their still weakened physical condition made it imperative under Jewish law for them to eat the food, whether or not it was kosher. The Beth Jacob leaders remained firm, and at least one of them believed the rabbi was secretly pleased with their obstinacy. Perhaps the rabbis had requested permission to bring the kitchen into compliance with Jewish dietary laws and had met with resistance from the British or secular DP leaders who may have claimed that there was no popular demand or that other needs took priority. With the public declaration of the Beth Jacob women and girls, the rabbis made great efforts and finally won the grudging permission of the Jewish Committee and British authorities – provided that they supply a petition with 100 signatures. The Beth Jacob girls gathered 800 names, some of which probably belonged to Jews who did not necessarily intend to keep kosher but who wanted to express Jewish solidarity.

Told by the British that they must get permission from the German authorities to use their slaughterhouse for kosher butchering, the DPs were once again at the mercy of Germans. The Germans refused to grant the permit on the grounds that kosher slaughter was an inhumane method of butchering.[61] Also, the 1933 law prohibiting kosher slaughter was still technically in effect until the Allies repealed Nazi legislation in 1946.[62] After a number of meetings with British and German authorities and the distribution of cigarettes, the currency of the black market, the rabbis were victorious. Nearly a month after the Beth Jacob girls began their boycott of the camp kitchen, they were served their first postliberation kosher meal on August 21, 1945.[63] In March 1946, 5,500 Jews in the British Zone were able to obtain kosher meat.[64]

[60] Pearl Benisch, *To Vanquish the Dragon* (New York: Feldheim Publishers, 1991), p. 426.

[61] Ritual slaughter required the butcher to quickly and cleanly slit the throat of the conscious animal. Rabbis rejected stunning the animal first because it could cause bruising or involuntary movement resulting in an improper cut that could injure the animal. Only after the carcass had been examined and found without flaw could it be hung upside down (to promote drainage of blood) and prepared for consumption.

[62] For an interesting discussion of pre-1933 debates over kosher slaughter and their significance for German and Jewish relations, see Robin Judd, *Contested Rituals: Circumcision, Kosher Butchering, and Jewish Political Life in Germany, 1843–1933* (Ithaca, NY: Cornell University Press, 2007).

[63] Benisch, *Vanquish the Dragon*, pp. 426–427.

[64] A. G. Brotman and Harry Viteles, "Survey on Conditions of Jews in the British Zone of Germany in March 1946," p. 9, YV O-70/6.

Not all communities had the facilities for kosher slaughter, so rabbis worked to ensure that kosher meat was widely distributed. In 1945, DP Rabbi Solomon Weider traveled from the Windesheim DP camp in the U.S. Zone to other DP camps to help those who observed the dietary laws. "I was also active to procure Kosher Meat for many other Camps by going myself every week to the City of Nuremberg, where the slaughtering of cattles were under my personal supervision, where from the Kosher Meat was distributed to the other camps."[65] In November 1945, American officials banned kosher slaughter in order to protect German livestock supplies. Kosher slaughter continued under black market conditions while advocates for DPs lobbied U.S. military government officials. In late December 1945, Landsberg DP Rabbi David Horowitz accompanied Rabbi Alexander Rosenberg, the new director of JDC religious activities in the American Zone, to a meeting with General Bedell Smith, resulting in the legalization of kosher slaughter.[66]

The U.S. Army ordered that German sources be used to provide Orthodox DPs living inside of DP camps and centers with fresh kosher meat at the rate of 3 ounces per person per day. Only one central slaughtering point was to be established in each military district. The military government assumed responsibility for supervising the slaughtering and distribution points and for the supply of animals from German sources.[67] Orthodox Jews turned over the meat from their Red Cross packages in exchange for the kosher meat. If the fresh meat allotted exceeded the amount in the Red Cross packages, DPs were told that they had to exchange their fish and cheese rations as well to make up the difference.[68]

It was not until August 1946 that Landsberg DPs were permitted to resume kosher slaughter. Rabbi Horowitz, who had met with General Smith the previous December, and another DP leader, Berysz Erlich, intervened with the military government authorities in Landsberg and Munich to convince them to allow a facility at Landsberg. The resumption of kosher slaughter became an official occasion with American, German, and Jewish DP representatives in attendance.[69] The presence of secular DP leaders demonstrated that kosher slaughtering had significance to all Jews as a symbol of the survival of the Jewish people and their customs. The participation of a German mayor highlighted the symbolism. The DPs likely invited him so a German could witness this Jewish ritual performed on German soil and know that Jewish life continued. The mayor would have accepted the invitation since his attendance

---

[65] Weider to AJDC, 25 June 1951, quoted in Gerd Korman, "Survivors' Talmud and the U.S. Army," *American Jewish History* 73 (1984): 263.

[66] Grobman, *Battling for Souls*, pp. 174–176.

[67] USFET Main to CG East Mil Dist, "Supply of Kosher Meat to Jewish DP's in Approved Camps and Centers," UN S-0437, Box 21, File 22.

[68] Pearl Morris to Colonel Roffe, "Exchange of Canned for Kosher Meat," 8 March 1946; Norma MacDonald to Pearl Morris, "Kosher Food," 25 March 1946, UN S-0437, Box 21, File 22. Handwritten notes at the bottom of the page provide the answer to the question posed in the memo.

[69] "Banajt di koszere szchite in landsberger centr," *Landsberger Lager Cajtung*, 30 August 1946, p. 13.

would demonstrate to the American officers present that he understood the importance of German–Jewish relations in the new German democracy under construction.

The need for kosher butchers in the DP camps and in Palestine led some Orthodox men to study for such a career. The JDC published a training manual and provided ritual knives manufactured in Germany to ritual slaughterers.[70] In the British Zone, CRREC representatives believed that ritual slaughterers could be trained in Germany if there were salaries for them. The CRREC was prepared to provide ritual knives.[71] Faye Doctrow's father trained in the DP camp to become a kosher butcher primarily because he thought it would be a useful trade in Palestine. However, when confronted with a live chicken for his final exam, he found himself unable to go through with it.[72] The training of kosher butchers in the DP camps was a necessary response to the determination of those who continued to observe Jewish dietary laws as well as those who sought to prepare themselves for a useful life in a Jewish homeland.

Disputes over the distribution of supplies arose between Orthodox and non-Orthodox Jews, and even between Orthodox and ultra-Orthodox DPs. Competition for the control of relief supplies led to destructive conflicts within the rebuilding German Jewish communities as well.[73] Orthodox organizations abroad, such as the CRREC and Vaad Hatzalah, earmarked their aid for Orthodox Jews only, primarily those ultra-Orthodox affiliated with Agudat Israel. The CRREC, for example, wanted to distribute kosher meat to DPs who ate only kosher meat, whereas the JCRA planned to give priority to those who ate only kosher meat but then distribute the remainder of the meat to other Jewish DPs.[74] Josef Rosensaft, chairman of the Belsen Committee, protested that all Jews needed food and that non-Orthodox Jews also wanted religious items.[75] Once again the Jewish DPs found the principle of unity running aground on points of practice. This demonstrated the persistence of prewar allegiances and identity into the postwar era. Despite

[70] Baumel, "Politics of Spiritual Rehabilitation," p. 77, fn. 22.

[71] Henry Pels, Secretary of CRREC, to Leonard Cohen, Vice-Chairman of JCRA, letter dated 5 December 1946, Henriques Archive, Microfilm reel 43.

[72] Doctrow, interview.

[73] For example, in Hamburg a survivor attempted to found an association of Theresienstadt survivors with the apparent intent of taking over the local Jewish community organizations. Many of those involved in the plan were baptized Jews, and the leader had publicly stated that he did not believe in the Jewish faith and was suspected of apostasy. The illustrious Reform Rabbi Dr. Leo Baeck, formerly of Berlin and a survivor of Theresienstadt, was dragged into the situation from his residence in England. See Jüdische Gemeinde in Hamburg [signature illegible] to Rabbi Dr. A. Carlebach, letter dated 4 April 1947; Rabbi Leo Baeck to Rabbi A. Carlebach, letter dated 11 April 1947; Rabbi A. Carlebach, JRU to Rabbi Dr. L. Baeck, letter dated 16 April 1947, Henriques Archive, Microfilm reel 41.

[74] M. Stephany, Secretary Central British Fund (CBF), to Leonard Cohen, JCRA, letter dated 26 November 1948; A. C. Jacobs, JCRA, to M. Stephany, CBF, letter dated 29 November 1946, Henriques Archive, Microfilm reel 43.

[75] Lavsky, *New Beginnings*, p. 114.

their hope for unity, DPs discovered that in many ways they still retained the expectations and prejudices of their prewar religious, national, social, and political backgrounds.

Religious Space and Ritual Objects

Building shortages interfered with the restoration of Jewish life and overcoming them required determination from the DPs and the assistance of local military government officers and German officials. The acquisition of buildings for use as synagogues was a relatively simple matter in the larger DP camps. Confined in what was essentially an independent village from the surrounding German communities, the DPs used whatever large halls were available to them. The theater or mess hall frequently doubled as a house of worship. For Jews who chose to live outside of the camps, securing a place of worship would depend on the goodwill of the military and German authorities.

In the American Zone, military commanders frequently assisted survivors by giving them priority in the allotment of building materials and by requisitioning space from Germans. In the British Zone, DP leaders frequently complained of mistreatment by British military government officials. The anti-Zionist policies of the British government as well as the officers' own sense of loyalty to their beleaguered counterparts in rebellious Palestine may have encouraged officials to treat the requests of Jewish leaders with little respect. The British also had a less rigorous policy of denazification and may have been less zealous than the Americans in overseeing the decision-making process of German authorities concerning space allocation. Whatever the motive, representatives of the JDC and the JCRA reported to UNRRA in March of 1946 that there was a lack of synagogues throughout the British Zone, including in major cities such as Hanover or Düsseldorf. In München-Gladbach the permit for building materials needed for the proposed synagogue had been revoked "because it was not considered of sufficiently high priority by the present Building Officer of Mil.Gov."[76] This situation helps to explain why religious survivors envied their counterparts in the American Zone and why so many of the infiltrees from the east preferred to enter the American Zone of occupation.

DPs were forced to rely on the occupying military governments and on relief workers for other ritual objects. The Nazis had stripped the survivors and much of Europe bare of Torah scrolls, prayer books, prayer shawls, tefillin, and other items. Torah scrolls and phylacteries were perhaps the most difficult to replace since they are handwritten on special parchment by scribes under strict conditions. The lack of paper combined with the Nazi destruction of Hebrew typesetting equipment meant that the reproduction of prayer books was only slightly less problematic. It was necessary to acquire these items through donations from Jewish communities abroad.

---

[76] Brotman and Viteles, "Conditions of Jews in the British Zone," p. 14.

Occasionally DPs were able to issue appeals for private aid from abroad. Rivkah Horowitz published an article on the Belsen Beth Jacob's activities in the June 29, 1945 issue of the British newspaper, *Jewish Weekly*. In response to the article, a London rabbi's wife sent them packages containing sewing needles, thread, and scissors. With these items, the Beth Jacob students began sewing religious garments for Orthodox men.[77] Even so, in March 1946, British Jewish representatives reported, "religious organisations in Britain and the USA are providing religious books and other requisites, but the quantities particularly of phylacteries and prayer shawls are insufficient to meet the demand."[78] When the JDC discovered that half of the phylacteries it imported to Germany were not kosher, it went ahead with plans to manufacture them in Germany despite difficulties obtaining materials and finding qualified scribes.[79] While the materials may have been in short supply, the determination of observant Jews to restore Jewish practices was great. The demand for ritual objects increased with the arrival of Orthodox Jews from Eastern Europe and with normalization of life in the DP camps.

In the American Zone, Information Control Division (ICD) officials were initially generous in allocating resources to the publication of religious works that had been banned by the Nazis. Later, however, officials balanced the needs of the various DP populations and, while sympathetic to the demands of the Jewish DPs, frequently decided that fairness to the other religious denominations meant limiting the amount of paper available to the Jewish DPs on the assumption that American Jews would supply their coreligionists to cover the shortfall.[80] Unlike the books of other DP religious groups, Jewish religious books had been destroyed throughout Europe and Jewish libraries were virtually bare; thus, this ostensibly fair policy in effect put the Jewish DPs at a disadvantage. Nevertheless, by February 1946, the ICD had begun to respond to the requests of DP rabbis and their American allies, the Union of Orthodox Rabbis and the JDC, and had published or was preparing to publish some much-needed books. These included a prayer book, a Haggadah for the Passover seder, a book of Esther for Purim celebrations, and a guide to family purity for religious marriages.[81]

Although Sabbath observance frequently highlighted differences between Jews, life-cycle events, such as weddings, births, and circumcisions, provided DPs with less volatile opportunities to affirm their commitment to Jewish tradition. Even secular Jews dreamed of standing beneath the marriage canopy, passing on their deceased parents' names to a new generation, circumcising their sons, and seeing their sons become *bnai mitzvah*. While the rituals had different meanings for observant and secular Jews, most embraced them as signs of continuity with

[77] Benisch, *Vanquish the Dragon*, pp. 418f.
[78] Brotman and Viteles, "Conditions of Jews in the British Zone," p. 10.
[79] Baumel, "Politics of Spiritual Rehabilitation," p. 68.
[80] See, Korman, "Survivors' Talmud," esp. pp. 269–70.
[81] Korman, "Survivors' Talmud," pp. 262–263.

the world they had lost and as the heart of the new Jewish community they were creating. Regardless of their motivation, Jewish DPs participated in rituals that affirmed Jewish community and values.[82] Where Orthodox DPs found spiritual meaning, secular Jews sought to maintain an ethnic or cultural identity. These differences occasionally led to tensions, such as in the case of circumcisions performed by unauthorized *mohalim*. Yet ritual could also create solidarity, even among those of differing beliefs and rationalizations.

By engaging in Jewish ritual practices, the DPs were performing Jewish community.[83] Anthropologist David Kertzer's observation that "solidarity is produced by people acting together, not by people thinking together"[84] is instructive here. The power of ritual lies in its ability to form community out of autonomous individuals. The performance of Jewish funeral rites, weddings, and circumcisions facilitated the creation of community and solidarity despite differences over levels of observance and questions about God. Communal celebrations of minor holidays, such as Hanukkah and Purim, also highlighted a shared Jewish history and use of a common calendar. This unity was channeled into the political arena with the emphasis on Jewish nationhood and Zionist politics. Secular and religious Jews alike believed that they shared a common history of persecution, the tribulations of displacement, and the goal of emigration from Germany. For most DPs, the exodus from Germany should lead to a Jewish home in Palestine.

TOWARD A NATIONAL LANGUAGE

Although the DPs accepted a shared history and calendar, they did not necessarily speak a common language. Yiddish and Hebrew were the two Jewish languages, and yet there were many survivors who spoke neither fluently. Within the DP camps cultural leaders waged a campaign to promote Yiddish and Hebrew over the national languages of the countries of origin. Polish, Hungarian, Czech, and other non-Jewish languages represented the threat of assimilation and a lack of Jewish national consciousness. Yiddish was the national language promoted by the Bundists in their quest for Jewish autonomy within the Diaspora. It also had been the spoken language of the East European shtetl and the language of a flourishing literary culture beginning in the late-nineteenth century. Hebrew, traditionally the sacred language of text

---

[82] Lynn Rapaport notes that in the predominantly secular postwar Frankfurt Jewish community, religious ritual benefits "the maintenance of Jewish identity and the vitality of the community." High Holy Day observance establishes and reinforces group solidarity and serves as a sign of ethnic identity, a public demonstration of Jewishness as opposed to Germanness. Lynn Rapaport, *Jews in Germany after the Holocaust: Memory, identity, and Jewish-German relations* (Cambridge: Cambridge University Press, 1997), p. 106.

[83] For an interesting empirical study of the relationship between ritual and social bonds, see Richard Sosis and Bradley J. Ruffle, "Religious Ritual and Cooperation: Testing for a Relationship on Israeli Religious and Secular Kibbutzim," *Current Anthropology* 44 (December 2003): 713–721.

[84] David I. Kertzer, *Ritual, Politics & Power* (New Haven, CT: Yale University Press, 1988), p. 76.

and prayer, had become the language of the Zionists and their movement for a Jewish homeland in Palestine.

Language shift in bilingual communities usually takes place over generations as the prestige of one language grows and changing social networks encourage its use in an increasing number of social settings.[85] Unlike most bilingual communities, Jewish DPs were not simply motivated to give preference to a language they already spoke fluently. They were attempting to adopt a new language as a mother tongue. Jewish DPs attempted to accelerate the process of language shift for ideological and practical reasons. Survivors in the DP camps were those Jews who rejected returning to Eastern Europe and labeled their former neighbors murderers. Polish, Lithuanian, and even Russian fell into disfavor as the languages of antisemitism and persecution. The two Jewish languages of Yiddish and Hebrew grew in stature. Yiddish served a practical function of permitting communication between Jews of different national origins. Despite regional variations in Yiddish, Yiddish-speaking Jews could still understand one another. Even assimilated Jews with knowledge of German could read transliterated Yiddish newspapers and learn to make themselves understood to Yiddish-speakers. The prestige of Hebrew grew during the war and afterward as the language of Jewish strength and independence. The Sephardic Hebrew of the Yishuv represented the Jewish future and Zionist values, not the Yiddish of the Diaspora or the Ashkenazi Hebrew of the yeshiva.[86]

The minority Lithuanian Jews tended to speak Yiddish almost exclusively. They were also overrepresented among the DP leadership in the American Zone. Polish Jews were in the majority, with the Hungarians making up a significant minority of DPs. These two groups were less likely to speak Yiddish. Reacting against an article in the *Landsberger Lager Cajtung* defending the use of Polish, L. Rudnick pointed out the preposterousness of Jews speaking Polish when none intend to return to Poland. "I accuse! I accuse the Jewish intelligentsia from Poland there in the camps of a backward and anti-national attitude! In the speaking of Polish I see weakness of character and lack of consciousness! Speak in our mother tongue ... – the rich and pleasant sounding Hebrew language that will help the further development and cementation of the Szejris-Haplejto and for which each has a responsibility. If it is not hard to learn English that is foreign to us – then certainly it is not too hard to learn our own [language], with which each one of us is more or less familiar."[87] Since Yiddish was commonly referred to as the *mameloshen* (mother tongue), the exhortation to speak "our mother tongue ... Hebrew" would have come as a surprise to readers. Survivors were encouraged to imagine Israel as their motherland and Hebrew as their native language. The use of Yiddish to make this plea is telling. Assimilated Jews

[85] Susan Gal, *Language Shift: Social Determinants of Linguistic Change in Bilingual Austria* (New York: Academic Press, 1979), p. 17.

[86] Languages can represent value systems, and a shift in values can influence language choices in bilingual communities. See Gal, *Language Shift*, p. 63.

[87] L. Rudnick, "Fraje tribune: Noch wegn der frage pojlisz-rejdn," *Jidisze Cajtung*, 22 November 1946, p. 9.

would often recognize and understand Yiddish as the language of their parents or grandparents, but Hebrew and the Hebrew alphabet would be less familiar to them. Yiddish could serve as a bridge between the Polish of the past and the Hebrew of the future.

In 1946 the Landsberg *Jidisze Cajtung* ran a debate over DP use of Polish, but favored the Yiddish of the newspaper and of the Lithuanian leadership of the camp. An author in the Polish-Jewish paper tried to out-Yiddish the Lithuanians by calling on Poles, Hungarians, and Lithuanians to "Forget the languages of your yesterday to which you will never return, and in the diaspora of Germany speak the language of today, your language, the language of Jews – Yiddish, and teach your children and learn yourself the language of tomorrow – Hebrew."[88] DP cultural leaders shared this attitude toward the Jewish national languages.

The majority of Jewish DP publications were written in Yiddish. The lack of Yiddish type, however, meant that Latin letters were used in the early period following liberation. Assimilated Jews who may have had a familiarity with spoken Yiddish or German could read these transliterated texts. It also meant that interested Germans could read DP newspapers. When the U.S. military government decided to restrict the licenses to newspapers in the U.S. Zone, the Central Committee used the occasion to demand that the remaining Jewish newspapers be printed in Hebrew type. There were two motives. The first was ideological. The DP leadership hoped to force Jewish DPs to learn the Hebrew alphabet that it viewed as the key to Jewish cultural and national values. The change in type was to inspire the Jewish national spirit of the DP youth. The second was economic. The official newspaper had switched over to Hebrew type, and competition from the more cheaply produced Latin text newspapers, such as the Polish-Jewish *Ibergang*, was cutting into its circulation.[89]

In most DP schools Yiddish was the language of instruction, with Hebrew-language classes included in the curriculum. Yiddish was the predominant language of DP theaters, although occasionally school performances demonstrated the growing Hebrew language skills of the students.[90] Yiddish was the language that bound the majority of DPs together linguistically, even though their dialects differed. Even secular Jews with no Yiddish background could enter somewhat into the conversation if they had some knowledge of German. Yiddish was the language of the mourning academies. It was the language of the DP courts.[91]

Although we will examine the DP courts in more detail later in this chapter, one case deserves attention here for the significance of Yiddish in expressing and forging Jewish national identity. Dr. Samuel Gringauz wrote of his experience as

[88] Hirsch Altruski, "Rejd jidisz – lern hebrejisz," *Ibergang* [December 1946?], YV M-1/P85.
[89] Tamar Lewinsky, "Displaced Writers? Zum kulturellen Selbstverständnis jiddischer DP-Schriftsteller," in *Zwischen Erinnerung und Neubeginn: zur deutsch-jüdischen Geschichte nach 1945*, ed. Susanne Schönborn (Munich: Meidenbauer, 2006), pp. 200–201.
[90] "In Fernwalder Tarbut," *Ibergang* [December 1946?], YV M-1/P-85.
[91] Some courts only chose Yiddish as their official language later. The Eschwege court decided in 1947 that all of its proceedings would be conducted in Yiddish. "Onerkenung," *Undzer Hofenung*, 18 March 1947, page number illegible.

a judge in the case of Bartzion, the Salonika boxer who terrorized the Salonika ghetto and later was a block-elder in Auschwitz. For Gringauz the trial demonstrated the national unity forged in the concentration camps. The Greek Jews did not speak Yiddish and appeared exotic to the Polish and Lithuanian Jews. At the trial, however, all of these Jewish groups expressed common values. The Greek DP policeman who acted as the court translator had learned Yiddish while on the police force. The courtroom spectators, Greeks, Poles, Germans, Lithuanians, and Americans, all reacted with outrage to the defendant's assertion that he would like to immigrate to Palestine. "A unified cry of outrage, a cry in various languages but filled with the same sentiment that was: 'In our land we won't have you.'" Gringauz asked the leader of the Greeks what sentence he would like to see passed on Bartzion. The response, "I want to send him where the six million are!" created a storm of applause. Gringauz writes: "All applauded – the Greek and the Polish Jews, the Lithuanian and the American, he had spoken for everyone, he had spoken in the language of unified national-moral sentiment. He had spoken … Yiddish! On November 23rd I saw in the Landsberg courtroom how from the socially and nationally amorphous masses of Salonikan Jews, how a Jewish national community had built itself out of the fires of the concentration camps."[92] The Greek Jewish leader's choice to speak in Yiddish rather than go through the translator carried great symbolic significance. In the context of the court proceeding Yiddish reflected the values of Jewish nationhood and solidarity. Reflecting the importance of a unifying Jewish language, the Eschwege court decided in 1947 that all of its proceedings would be conducted in Yiddish.[93]

The choice of language in the DP camps had political implications, but language also had personal meaning. Samuel Bak resisted his mother's demand that he become bar mitzvah. For his mother a bar mitzvah was a social rite of passage without religious significance. Bak wanted to protest against God for the Holocaust by not becoming bar mitzvah. When Bak's more observant stepfather supported the boy in his decision, Bak's respect for the man grew. After that point, Bak no longer spoke to his mother in their native Polish, but spoke to her in Yiddish out of deference to his Lithuanian stepfather.[94] Although Bak had no use for institutionalized religion, he identified as a cultural Jew. Zionist leaders encouraged DPs to learn Hebrew, but Yiddish was the language that most often enabled communication across boundaries of national origin. One survivor from a German-speaking Czech family told me that it was in the DP camps, not the concentration camps, that she learned Yiddish as a means of communicating with fellow Jews.[95] Within the DP camps, survivors created a linguistic community based on Yiddish. This was the last hurrah of Yiddish language and culture. While Yiddish was a unifying language in the DP camps, it would soon be nearly

[92] Szmuel Gringauz, "Fal Barcion," *Landsberger Lager Cajtung*, 2 December 1945, p. 7.

[93] "Onerkenung," *Undzer Hofenung*, 18 March 1947.

[94] Bak, "Landsberg Revisited," p. 36.

[95] Hilda Mantelmacher, interview with the author, tape-recording, Harrisburg, PA, 31 March 1996.

forgotten. Hebrew would be the language of the future Jewish state, and Yiddish would be a relic from the Diaspora.

Of male Holocaust survivors immigrating to Israel in 1948–1954, more than 97 percent were literate in their first language and 72.9 percent demonstrated Hebrew literacy. Nearly 95 percent of women immigrating from Europe and America were literate in their first language, but only 55.8 percent had knowledge of Hebrew.[96] The gender differences most likely reflected the greater emphasis on men's religious education in Hebrew. Orthodox Jewish men used Hebrew for prayers and study, and although their pronunciation differed from the Sephardic usage in Israel, they were literate in Hebrew. Prewar Zionist activists had also studied Hebrew for political reasons. Within the DP camps, schools, kibbutzim, and adult education programs offered Hebrew language instruction. Newspapers encouraged DPs to learn Hebrew as the language of the Jewish future. The familiarity with Hebrew, often gained within the DP camps, aided the DPs' integration into Israeli society.

WRITING ABOUT THE RECENT PAST

In addition to their role in the linguistic debates, DP newspapers greatly shaped the collective memory and identity of the Jewish survivors by providing forums for commemoration of the recent past, expression of DP concerns and activities, and debates about the future. Newspapers helped to spread the work of the Central Historical Commission that created local historical commissions seeking to collect survivors' testimonies both to preserve the history of the Holocaust and to find useful witnesses against war criminals.[97] Although relatively few survivors chose to respond to the historical commissions' requests for materials, their work reached a wide audience through articles published in the newspapers both commemorating Jewish martyrdom and celebrating heroic resistance. For example, the Eschwege DP newspaper published material from the historical commission about the uprising in Treblinka.[98] In the issue of the newspaper reporting Hanukkah celebrations, the historical commission provided two stories of recent Jewish heroism: the partisans in the Polish woods and the Treblinka uprising. Also in that issue was a story about the wartime heroine Hannah Senesh.[99]

---

[96] Dalia Ofer, "Holocaust Survivors as Immigrants: The Case of Israel and the Cyprus Detainees," *Modern Judaism* 16 (February 1996): 17.

[97] Eastern European Jews began documenting their persecution as a response to pogroms beginning in the early twentieth century. The work of the DP historical commissions can thus be seen as a form of continuity with the pre-Holocaust world. Laura Jockusch, "Chronicles of Catastrophe: History Writing as a Jewish Response to Persecution Before and After the Holocaust," in *Holocaust Historiography in Context: Emergence, Challenges, Polemics and Achievements*, eds. David Bankier and Dan Michman (Jerusalem: Yad Vashem, 2008), p. 162.

[98] J. Miler, "Der ojfsztand in Treblinke," *Undzer Hofenung*, 22 November 1946, p. 6.

[99] Mieter, "Di kamfn fun jidisze partizaner in di Garbower welder," *Undzer Hofenung*, 31 January 1947; J. Miler, "Pruwn fun an ojfsztand in Treblinke," *Undzer Hofenung*, 31 January 1947; "Hannah Senesch – The heroic daughter of the Jewish People," *Undzer Hofenung*, 31 January 1947.

The historical commissions provided material to the newspapers concerning wartime events.[100] Newspapers published photos of Nazi atrocities, giving survivors graphic evidence of what had happened to their families and communities.[101] Through the newspapers, survivors could learn about the variety of Jewish experiences during the war. The *Landsberger Lager Cajtung*, for example, published side-by-side articles about Jewish resistance in Buchenwald and about eleven young women passing on Aryan papers in Poland. Both authors demonstrated familiarity with accounts of the death camps and sought to demonstrate the comparability of their experiences. In the account of Buchenwald, Gustaw Schiller mentioned that much had been written already about the death camps of Auschwitz, Maidanek, Treblinka, among others. In what appears to be an attempt to demonstrate that Buchenwald was not much better, Schiller points out that of the 2,000 Jews interned in Buchenwald in 1937, only 3 survived the camp. He then described the harsh conditions in the camp, conditions that were more extreme for the Jewish inmates. His account of the Jewish resistance group in the camp, emphasizing the harsh justice the group meted out to kapos and others who assisted the Nazis and the group's efforts to rescue children, added more heroes to the DP pantheon of Jewish resistance fighters.[102] Buchenwald was not a death camp, but its survivors, he implied, deserved recognition from the DP community for their physical toughness and for their courage.

The tale of Lea Blum and her ten co-survivors started almost apologetically. Blum acknowledged that they did not see the flames of the crematoria or smell the burning bodies. But the next line was filled with bitter sarcasm: "'We had it good.' It was the Garden of Eden on earth." Undoubtedly concentration camp survivors had expressed the opinion that those living on the outside had had an easier time. Blum went on to describe the women's constant fear of discovery, their awareness that a death sentence was on their heads, their need to act appropriately in every instant, to be aware of their gestures, their gazes. "We began to wait for death. We worked, laughed, slept, but not as people, but like machines, automatons." The girls contemplated suicide should they be captured. Blum seemed to be seeking understanding from the concentration camp survivors that she and others on false papers had been forced to confront death, forced to live

---

[100] Although DP newspapers publicized the work of the historical commissions, they also inadvertently hindered their collection activities by providing an alternate site for the recording of memories. Newspapers also tended to focus on stories of heroism in contrast to the commissions' attempts to record all experiences. Ada Schein, "'Everyone Can Hold a Pen': The Documentation Project in the DP Camps in Germany," in *Holocaust Historiography in Context*, pp. 127 and 133. See also Laura Jockusch, "A 'Folk Monument for Our Destruction and Heroism': Jewish Historical Commissions in Displaced Persons Camps in Germany, Austria, and Italy," in *"We Are Here": New Approaches to Jewish Displaced Persons in Postwar Germany*, eds. Avinoam J. Patt and Michael Berkowitz (Detroit, MI: Wayne State University Press, forthcoming).

[101] "From the recent past" (in Yiddish), *Bamidbar*, 7 July 1946, p. 4.

[102] Gustaw Schiller, "Jidisze kamfs-grupe in Buchenwald," *Landsberger Lager Cajtung*, 21 June 1946, p. 6.

by their instincts with the awareness that one false step could lead to disaster.[103] Their experiences, she implied, were not so very different after all.

It is likely that concentration camp inmates would have found Schiller's argument more convincing than Blum's. No one can imagine the horrors of the death camps, but a prison camp like Buchenwald had its own share of executions, deaths, and sadism. At the same time, Blum may have increased awareness that living on false papers had its own psychological terror and was its own form of suffering in the struggle for survival. These articles and others like them helped survivors identify their common sufferings and struggles. Those who had not experienced the death camps clearly had learned about them and had found ways to make connections among the varied experiences of the DPs.

PERFORMANCE AND REWORKING THE PAST

Like newspapers, DP theaters linked survivors to their distant and recent pasts and offered opportunities for shared experiences. Theater served a variety of needs for both performers and their audiences. Yiddish was the predominant language in DP theaters, and the shows facilitated the creation of a linguistic community. Through the performances of familiar standards of the prewar Yiddish theater, DP productions provided continuity with the survivors' destroyed communities and former ways of life. At the same time, theatrical groups included in their repertoire revues reminiscent of the ghetto cabarets as well as new dramas based on wartime experiences. These productions enabled DPs to rework their immediate past, to interpret it, and to assert some control over it. Within the context of the limited resources of the DP camps, staging theatrical productions with their requirements of costumes, make-up, scripts, and sets expressed the DPs' defiance of the restrictions imposed by their immediate circumstances.[104] Thus, DP theaters allowed the survivors to reassert themselves as civilized beings, to demonstrate their connection to their prewar past, to create social memories of the Holocaust, and to imagine a future in Palestine.

The Performers

As soon as their physical condition permitted, survivors organized performances for one another. Some were professionals but most were amateurs. Some had performed in school or youth group productions before the war. Some had performed secretly in ghettos and concentration camps. Others had spent the war years with no outlet for their creative urges and now hurried to join drama circles and theatrical troupes.

---

[103] Lea Blum, "Mir zajnen in kacet nyt gewen," *Landsberger Lager Cajtung*, 21 June 1946, p. 6.

[104] A production of Sholem Aleichem's *Hard to be a Jew* in the Deggendorf DP camp required 20 complete sets of actor's make-up, 2 kilograms of make-up removal (Vaseline), 100 square meters of fabric for scenery, 60 meters of rubber hose, 2 projectors, furniture, household items (tablecloth, books, vase, etc.), and costumes. Jidisz Naj Teater (Deggendorf), Program for "Szwer cu zein a Jid," YV M-1/P-85.

The demographics of the survivors meant that many had limited experience with prewar theatrical life. Most of the DPs' cultural education ended abruptly when their lives were disrupted by the war. Most were between the ages of twelve and twenty when they were deprived of the opportunity to attend professional performances or to participate in school plays. In addition to the limitations imposed by the war, those survivors reared in traditional Jewish homes often had only been exposed to Purim plays. Traditional parents sheltered their children from the theater that permitted the mixing of men and women and that tempted young minds to think of frivolous, worldly things. Thus, the initial number of survivors who had the knowledge and skills to stage productions was small, and they tended to be older than the average age of DPs. Later, as those who had survived the war years in the Soviet Union or who had hidden in the woods or fought with the partisans fled the postwar pogroms of Eastern Europe, the Jewish DP population came to include more culturally knowledgeable individuals.

Upon his arrival at Föhrenwald in July 1945, Jacob Biber found himself deeply impressed by the camp's theater building that during the Nazi regime had been used for political training classes. He became determined to direct productions there. Biber was the sole survivor of a traditional Ukranian family. Except for Purim plays and his mother's knowledge of popular Yiddish show tunes, theater was forbidden to him as a child. His first exposure was when, as a young boy, he snuck into a theater. When he was fifteen he founded a group that staged monthly performances of classic Yiddish theater at the headquarters of a local Zionist organization.[105] At thirty years of age when he arrived at Föhrenwald, Biber had more familiarity with Anski and Sholom Aleichem than most survivors. Within five weeks of his arrival in the camp, Biber's students performed a talent show and he was already writing a play called *In Storm*.[106]

At the Belsen DP camp in the British Zone of occupied Germany, Sami Feder began his professional troupe, KZ-teater, immediately after liberation. A prewar director of Yiddish theater, Feder contacted surviving professional Polish actors and theater technicians throughout liberated Germany and brought them to Belsen. Their biological families lost to them, the reunions of these prewar colleagues took on tremendous significance. They came together not only to practice their craft in freedom but also for companionship. In 1947, a workers' group formed in Belsen to produce Yiddish plays with a social message. Even the Orthodox community created an amateur theater group.[107]

In other camps small groups came together bound by their interest in theater. Lacking such basics as scripts, music, make-up, and costumes, these drama circles initially staged revues drawing on their memories of childhood songs, school-learned poetry, and ghetto cabarets. Using the experiences of the concentration camps, which had emphasized resourcefulness, "organizing," and making do, these early groups managed to revive cultural life against tremendous odds.

[105] Biber, *Risen from Ashes*, pp. 12–13.
[106] Biber, *Risen from Ashes*, p. 27.
[107] Lavsky, *New Beginnings*, pp. 158–159.

The precariousness of life in postwar Poland and the promise of eager Yiddish-speaking audiences in the American Zone of Germany brought the professional Musical Yiddish Cabaret Theater (MIKT) to Munich in spring 1946.[108] DP audiences and the press liked their revues and their staging of Sholem Aleichem's comedy *The Jackpot.* On June 12, 1946, the Central Committee's plenary session granted MIKT official status and promised to subsidize the theater. Later, breakaway actors using the same name forced the theater to change its name to the Munich Yiddish Art Theater (MIT). The arrival of professional actors raised the standards of DP productions and invigorated cultural life.

DP troupes viewed their mission as waging a battle to reclaim the Jewish heritage, to revive the Jewish soul, and to imagine the Jewish future. H. Perlmutter, the so-called Showman of Auschwitz and later director of the Feldafing DP camp's "Amcho" troupe, was struck by the tremendous responsibility he had to rebuild Jewish cultural life.[109] Ruth Minsky Sender's brother-in-law founded a Yiddish theater in the Leipheim DP camp. She recalls his excitement about the audiences' reception of the performances: "We bring them the voices of the past, the good and the evil. We remind them that we, the remnants of our people, must carry on. … It is up to us to rise from the ashes and build a new life."[110] For these former victims of Nazi persecution, survival meant more than physical existence; it meant the revival of Jewish cultural life.

Even the struggle to overcome the material deprivations of the DP camps took on significance in this battle for Jewish culture. At Belsen, Feder "organized" drapery from a British officer's room to be used for his heroine's costume. In concentration camp parlance, "organizing" involved stealthily acquiring needed items from the oppressive authorities, and it had a moral quality that ordinary theft did not. For Feder, the British stood between the survivors and Palestine, and the removal of the drapes represented a blow for Jewish culture and for Jewish freedom. Costumes and supplies were often organized. At Leipheim, the clothing committee received a crate of evening dresses. Not at all useful as everyday clothing, some of those dresses became theater costumes.[111] All sorts of materials, including a piano at Föhrenwald,[112] were secured on the black market, bringing the DPs into contact with the German population. Such black market activities fed the German prejudice against Jewish DPs and, if caught by the authorities, the DPs could forfeit their right to emigration. Thus, the willingness of the DPs to engage in black market activities to support their art speaks to the importance they attached to their work. Jewish theaters also depended on assistance from the American and

---

[108] In Poland on March 30, 1946, a group of Yiddish actors and community leaders founded MIKT to perform revues and concerts, but the troupe transformed the theater's mission to reforge the links to the vast Yiddish theater culture with a classical repertoire.
[109] H. Perlmutter, *Bine-Maskes Bay Katsetlekh* (Tel Aviv: Hamenorah, 1974), p. 28.
[110] Ruth Minsky Sender, *To Life* (New York: Macmillan Publishing, 1988), p. 143.
[111] Sender, *To Life*, p. 147.
[112] Biber, *Risen from Ashes*, p. 51.

British Jewish communities. Belsen's theater received cosmetics from colleagues in Britain. The Jewish Professional Actors' Union in the American Zone depended on the typewriter presented to it by their counterpart in New York. Later, funds from the JDC administered by the Cultural Office of the Committee of Liberated Jews in the American Zone permitted DP theaters to purchase materials from legitimate businesses, decreasing their reliance on the black market.

Reenacting the Holocaust

The repertoire of the initial theater productions is at first glance surprising. DPs frequently performed songs and plays dramatizing the horrors of the Shoah, tapping into their memories and emotions. Rather than suppress the memories of their ordeal, the survivors sought to recreate them. The first concert of Belsen's Central Jewish Committee's Cultural Department took place on September 15, 1945 as part of the Jewish New Year festivities. Most scenes in the revue depicted life during the Holocaust.[113] One depicted a Jew hiding in a cellar. Dolly Katz's *The Mother's Dance* showed a mother in a concentration camp after her child's death. The artist performed in a striped dress reminiscent of concentration camp uniforms in front of a swastika flag.[114] Another piece depicted concentration camp inmates keeping up morale with music after guards left them without food or light. Later Belsen performances included the play *In Auschwitz* and Sonia Boczkowska's recital of the poem "Shoes from Majdanek" (Figure 12). Boczkowska wore a stylized concentration camp uniform and stood before a mountain of shoes for the performance. The first revue at Föhrenwald included a song about the emotional suffering of mother and child separated when the mother leaves the child with a Christian family for safekeeping. Theatrical evenings often included songs or skits from the Holocaust period, songs from the wartime exile in the Soviet Union, Hebrew songs, and folk songs.[115] A favorite song performed by the Ex-Concentration Camp Orchestra from St. Ottilien, "ein, zwei, drei," was about the selections in the concentration camps. One performer remembered, "They loved it; we were expressing what they felt."[116] Survivors were drawn to artistic expressions of their suffering that enabled them to work through their traumatic past.

Yiddish theater traditionally incorporated songs, and folk songs and dance music were popular in the DP camps. These musical forms were easily accessible for an audience that had suffered interrupted educations and often did not have the background or concentration skills necessary to enjoy classical music.[117] DP musicians often had difficulty finding suitable instruments and sheet music. The

---

113 Doherty, letter dated 18 September 1945 in *Letters from Belsen 1945*, eds. Cornell and Russell, p. 121.
114 Photo, "The Mother" (in Yiddish), no date, YV O-70/31b.
115 "Program von 'Bunten Abend,'" 28 October 1945, YIVO, RG 294.2, MK 483, Microfilm reel 2, Folder 16.
116 Henny Gurko, "Videotaped interview," VHA, IC 13811, Segs. 105–106.
117 Lavsky, *New Beginnings*, p. 160.

FIGURE 12. Sonia Boczkowska reciting the poem "Shoes from Majdanek" at the Belsen DP camp. *Credit*: Yad Vashem, courtesy of Hadassah Rosensaft

founding members of the jazz band Happy Boys traveled to Poland to retrieve instruments from where they had been hidden during the war,[118] but some musicians managed to acquire the necessary equipment with the assistance of military and UNRRA personnel and established ensembles and the famous DP orchestra from St. Ottilien. In deference to the audience's tastes, concerts often combined a few classical pieces with folk songs, ghetto and DP compositions, as well as songs from the Yishuv.[119] Those DPs who had an interest in full-scale

---

[118] Michael Brenner, "Impressionen jüdischen Lebens in der Oberpfalz nach 1945," in *Die Juden in der Oberpfalz*, eds. Michael Brenner and Renate Höpfinger (Munich: Oldenbourg Wissenschaftsverlag, 2009), p. 238.

[119] See, for example, "Programme of the Concert of the Jewish Orchestra in Bavaria," 14 November 1945, YIVO RG 294.2, MK 483, Microfilm reel 113, Folder 1564; Gurko, "Videotaped interview," Segs. 100–107.

FIGURE 13. Scene from the Katzet-Theater play *Partisans* at the Belsen DP camp.
Credit: Yad Vashem, courtesy of Hadassah Rosensaft

orchestral or operatic performances had to satisfy their cultural thirst in German recital halls.[120] DP camps were more likely to have dance bands playing on Saturday night, such as Daniel Grossman's quintet that played waltzes and Polish dance music for 500 people each week in Föhrenwald.[121] While Grossman occasionally hired German musicians and played for Germans, the Happy Boys refused to have contact with Germans.[122] Music filled the survivors' need for entertainment, but it was secondary to DP interest in theatrical performances.

The need to rework the past led to dramatic productions written by survivors and drawing on the immediate past. At Belsen, Sami Feder wrote and directed a play called *Partisans* (Figure 13). In one scene, a cabaret singer, her costume made from that heroically obtained curtain, seduced German officers and stole their weapons to pass along to resistance fighters.[123] (In Leipheim, Sender's brother-in-law had a similar plot in mind for a skit.[124]) Plays in Feldafing and Föhrenwald continued the storyline into the postliberation era, emphasizing the survivors' ties to Palestine.

Blood and Fire, the first play produced by the Feldafing amateur ensemble that would become the acclaimed Amcho troupe, began in prewar Poland in the home of a bourgeois Jewish family. One of the sons, a member of a kibbutz, urges his

---

[120] Posters announcing cultural excursions from Bergen-Belsen, YV O-70/29.

[121] The DPs paid the musicians with profits from "making business" with Germans. Occasionally, DP bands hired German musicians to complete the ensemble, making the arts another place where Germans and Jews met in the postwar period. Daniel Grossman, "Videotaped interview," VHA, IC 17126, Segs. 112–114.

[122] Brenner, "Impressionen jüdischen Lebens," p. 238.

[123] Sami Feder, *Farzeichenishn zum Tag-Buch fun "Kazet-teater" in Bergen-Belsen*, p. 9, YV O-70/31.

[124] Sender, *To Life*, p. 148.

parents to sell their possessions and move the family from the burning earth of Poland to Palestine. The parents laughingly dismiss their son's advice and he journeys alone to Palestine. With the arrival of the Nazis, the parents meet their end in the gas chamber. After the war, the Zionist son, now an officer in the Haganah, returns to Poland in an effort to find his family. He does not encounter a single family member, but he hears a rumor that his youngest sister is alive and in a DP camp in Germany. In Germany, the officer locates his sister and then takes her with him to Palestine. This play affirmed the foresight of prewar Zionists and drew a connection between the sufferings of the Shoah and the need for a home in Palestine. It also held out the comforting dream that somehow the survivors would be reunited with a family member who will rescue them from the DP camp.

The Föhrenwald play was more graphic and melodramatic. It used the Shoah as a prologue to the main action, illegal immigration to Palestine. The curtain opened on one part of the stage to show pious Jews in prayer shawls at prayer in Jerusalem. The audience's attention is then directed to the other side of the stage, where a mother and child stand before the crematorium in a concentration camp. A camp guard grabs the child and throws it into the flames of the crematorium. As the guard continues to slaughter inmates, on the other side of the stage British soldiers enter the Palestine scene and begin beating the praying Jews. The Jews in the concentration camp cry, "They kill us here and beat us there! Where shall we go?" while the Jews in Palestine scream, "They kill us there and beat us here! What shall we do?" The ensuing play focuses on bands of illegal immigrants to Palestine who meet and join forces. They are caught by a British border patrol and taken to court, where a young Zionist defendant passionately explains why these survivors are determined to enter Palestine. One of the British judges recognizes two elderly defendants as his parents. The play concludes with the family's reconciliation and the judge's promise to serve the Jewish people.[125] In this drama, the horrors of the Shoah were juxtaposed and even equated with the brutality of the British occupation of Palestine. Here, Jews were seen as paralyzed by their persecution at the time of the Shoah, but in its aftermath they were filled by determination and Zionist purpose. It was the survivors who awaken the judge, and the rest of the world, to the need for unity and for a homeland in Palestine. The survivors were urged to recognize their kinship with one another and with Jews in Palestine. They were called on to devote themselves to the Zionist cause of resettlement in Palestine. The fantasy of a reunion with lost parents and children must have resonated with many in the audience.

However, just as some outsiders were disturbed by the survivors' preoccupation with their recent past, so too did the graphic staging of such material unsettle some survivors. Jonas Turkow, a professional actor and director in prewar Poland and active in Warsaw ghetto theatrical life, wrote of the theater in Föhrenwald:

---

[125] "Di Ensztejung fun Dramkrajz 'Maapilim' in Föhrenwald," YV M-1/P-81.

(As many as two theater groups are there competing with one another not, God forbid, in theatrical ambition and artistic quests, but only in tastelessness and boorishness.) During such a performance one saw on the stage … a crematorium, how a Jewish child, torn from its mother, was thrown into the oven … I could barely remain seated. How dare one offer such a profanity?! Our bloody wounds are still too fresh to allow them, in such a brutal form no less, to be exposed on the stage. Even veteran, talented artists must be careful when touching such painful problems that are so holy and dear to us. If one had simply alluded to the crematorium and not shown it in such a brutally realistic form, the effect would have been stronger. It is simply enough to talk about a crematorium to send a shudder through our limbs.[126]

Turkow did not object to dealing with Holocaust experiences in the theater but felt the staging required greater restraint. His sophisticated sensibilities were also offended by the connection the play made between the Shoah and illegal immigration to Palestine. Certainly from the dramatic point of view the Föhrenwald production went over the top, battering the audience's emotions. Perhaps it was unnecessarily "brutally realistic" for legitimate theater; however, it served to rework the immediate past and give it some connection to the present, by interpreting the Nazi persecution as a phase in Jewish history and as a precursor to a new homeland in Palestine. Of the theater in Leiphcim, Sender wrote, "Under Yosef's direction, the theater brightens our lives with new plays, concerts. We laugh, cry, dream of a place that we can call home."[127] At least for her, the theater represented a place in which to explore emotions and to imagine a new home.

While amateur theaters in the American Zone from the time of their formation had attempted to portray Holocaust experiences, MIT's production created controversy that probably contributed to its demotion from official status. On November 6, 1946, MIT premiered Moshe Pintschewski's *Ich leb*, in which ghetto leaders are intellectuals who comply with the Gestapo, while a young man seeks to organize an underground movement. He is captured but later freed by partisans. His devoted fiancée, Miriam, disguises herself as an old woman to escape lecherous Ukrainian police, but she reveals herself when the ghetto commandant takes hostage her scholarly father and others. She pretends to assist the Gestapo in order to save her father. Ultimately, Miriam kills the commandant and escapes with the assistance of a maid who is also a liaison to the partisans. Meanwhile, a German officer, despairing of the bad news from the front and hoping to win their gratitude, releases Miriam's father and a violinist. The two intellectuals then join the partisans and are reunited with Miriam and her fiancé.[128] The emphasis in this play, as in the Belsen play *Partisans*, is on heroic action and self-sacrifice, not on passive victimhood. These plays enabled the audiences to feel that they, too, had participated in the victorious battle against the Nazis. The reenactment of the traumatic past with

[126] Jonas Turkow, "Dram-Krajzn un zajere Aufgabn," [no date], p. 18, YV M-1/P-81. Also printed as Jonas Turkow, "Dram=krajzn un zejere ojfgabn," *Undzer Hofenung*, 1 November 1946, p. 4.
[127] Sender, *To Life*, p. 168.
[128] M. Pinezevski, "I Am Living," YV M-1/P-85.

new coping strategies and new endings had therapeutic value for the survivors' recovery, aiding the integration of Holocaust experiences into the survivors' life stories.[129] Through the characters on stage, they, both men and women, became heroes rather than victims.

Some DP theater critics viewed Pintschewski's emphasis on resistance as a lack of respect for Kiddush ha-Shem – the term for traditional Jewry's willingness to accept martyrdom. This complaint was part of a larger dialogue taking place in the DP newspapers in 1946, attempting to reconcile the Zionist valorization of resistance with the reality of mass death in shooting actions and gas chambers.[130] One critic wrote, "Against the backdrop of our gruesome past, the author set himself the goal of bringing to light a host of problems from our recent martyrology; for example, passive Kiddush ha-Shem or heroic resistance against our hangmen, the role of Jewish leaders in our bloody survival, the victory of the simple Jewish people's healthy national instincts over the reticent and cautious intellectuals, etc."[131] But he goes on to accuse the author of cheap effects and suggests that Pintschewski, who had written the play in exile in Argentina and then the Soviet Union, did not have the experience necessary to write a successful play. Other critics emphasized that the play lacked perspective that the passage of time would allow.[132]

The MIT directors anticipated the reaction of the critics. In the program the artistic director, Israel Segall, acknowledged that there were those who opposed treatment of the recent past:

"One may not touch on recent events," it is said, because the wound is too fresh, there's no perspective, no artistic forms to express it. If we could only forget. Even if we did forget after awhile? Then let us remember that in the darkness, bright lights often flickered, figures and events that threw light on the darkness could also today exalt us to decisive action in our fate. ... We impatiently await a work that will reflect not only the recent past but also the present and our attempt [Ich leb] should encourage the creation of such a work.[133]

In justifying his choice of material, Segall emphasized the didactic function of the theater. The troupe was portraying behaviors from the past that could inspire action in the present. The bright lights of resisters and partisans were to inspire the survivors to heroic action in the postwar era. The stage director, Israel Beker, argued that the survivors had a responsibility to tell about the "gruesome tragedy" and not permit it to be forgotten.[134] Later, Beker and

---

[129] See Lenore Terr, *Too Scared to Cry: Psychic Trauma in Childhood* (New York: Harper & Row, 1990), p. 301.

[130] See Chapter 2.

[131] *Ich leb* (in Yiddish), 15 November 1946, M-1/P-85. Another reviewer noted the absence of Kiddush Ha-Shem and the inaccuracies from an author who had not experienced the Nazi terror, B. H. "Ich leb," *Jidisze Cajtung*, November 1946, YV M-1/P-85.

[132] Awrohom Gurwicz, "Ojfn weg fun kinsterliszn jidiszn teater," *Undzer Hofenung*, YV M-1/P-85; M. D. Ejlihaw, "Ich leb," *Ibergang*, 17 November 1946, YV M-1/P-85; B. H., "Ich leb," *Jidisze Cajtung*, November 1946, YV M-1/P-85.

[133] Israel Segall, "Repertoire" (in Yiddish), in program of *Ich leb*, November 1946, YV M-1/P-85.

[134] Israel Beker, "Our New Production" (in Yiddish), in program of *Ich leb*, November 1946, YV M-1/P-85.

other key figures from MIT would create the film *Lang ist der Weg*, in which the protagonist also joined the partisans and then after the war prepared for a life in Palestine, completing the link of the recent past to the present that they had awaited. In this way, MIT participated in rewriting the Holocaust experience from one of victimization into one of heroic resistance and a legitimation of Zionist goals.

Yiddish Classics

The professionalization of DP theater as well as improved material conditions enabled theaters to stage Yiddish classics. These productions encouraged the identification of recent sufferings with those of previous generations. The Bamberg drama studio put on a performance of Sholem Asch's *Kiddush ha-Shem*. A reviewer for the Föhrenwald newspaper found the play quite appropriate for the stage of the Sheerit Hapletah: "When we remember today Kiddush ha-Shem from the book or when we see the shadow of Asch's masterwork on the camp stage, we are as if elevated and it seems to us as if we are organically bound together with the martyrs of our people from Chmielnicki's time. That is the long, holy, golden chain, in which we are bound and put into the context of the generations."[135] The chain did not stop with the Shoah but continued to a future in Palestine, when the next night the same troupe performed a revue, *Tel-Aviv*. In the skit *Haganah* illegal immigrants swam to shore just as described in the newspapers, and, for added drama, an old mother recognized her son on shore. In all of the scenes the ensemble tried to portray the essence of the Yishuv. The inclusion of Palestinian songs and melodies aided the effect.[136]

On August 3, 1946, MIKT premiered *Der blutiker Szpas* (*The Bloody Hoax*), its version of Sholem Aleichem's novel by the same name. The story was a Yiddish version of *The Prince and the Pauper*: A Russian nobleman trades places with a Jewish classmate, David Shapiro, and learns about the daily discrimination Jews faced in Czarist Russia. When the disguised nobleman is put on trial for blood libel charges, Shapiro returns to rescue him and to reclaim his Jewish identity. The play won accolades in the DP press for the professional production and for the psychological depth of the treatment.[137] One critic wrote that the play had a "powerful effect, the audience applauded approvingly and spontaneously (like at a rally) in the middle of a scene and were transported, together with David Shapiro, in the moment when he emphasizes his national

---

[135] ",Kidusz Haszem' Ojsgefirt fun Bamberger dramatiszer studje," *Bamidbar*, 4 June 1946, p. 7.

[136] "Tel-Awiw," *Bamidbar*, 4 June 1946, p. 7.

[137] Joseph Gar, "Der blutiker szpas," *Unzer Weg*, 9 August 1946, YV M-1/P-85; Ewen-Adin, "Der blutiker szpas," *A heim* (Leipheim), 25 September 1946, YV M-1/P-85; David Pergament, "Szolom Elejchem's ,Der blutiker Szpas' in prinz regentn teater," *D.P. Express*, 18 August 1946, YV M-1/P-85. One reviewer noted the appropriateness of the material and the audience's positive reaction but complained that the actors had played too much for comedy. Shlomo Frank, "Der blutiker szpas," *Unzer Weg*, 16 August 1946, YV M-1/P-85.

dignity and consciousness of belonging to a persecuted people."[138] Another reviewer used the opportunity to profess Zionist goals: "Never has our heart been so heavy, alone and mournful as now when we the Saving Remnant stand with eyes open and see the big world that should open the doors of the Land of Israel and let us in there so that we should be able to live our lives culturally and nationally as do all peoples on this earth."[139] Sholem Aleichem's national consciousness made his texts relevant to Holocaust survivors and his loving treatment of the characters of the shtetl, even as he criticized some aspects of Orthodoxy, appealed to the nostalgic among the DPs. The domestic scenes of Sabbath candle lighting and the Passover seder were particularly poignant, as well as the depiction of the Jewish mother.[140] To emphasize the national-ist implications of the performances they concluded with the Zionist anthem, "Hatikvah." When DP theaters performed classic Yiddish works, they empha-sized the connections to the persecution the DPs had experienced and to the importance of Jewish ethnic identity.

The Audience

Theater reached many survivors in the DP camps, and audience reception points to the popularity of the artistic visions presented. The JDC sponsored free performances by international Jewish stars, such as conductor Leonard Bernstein and American Yiddish actor Herman Yablokoff. DP professional troupes, although often subsidized by the Central Committee, needed to gen-erate some revenues, and their attendance figures tell us a few things. First, the Jewish DPs had access to money that they could spend on theater tickets. Many DPs set up small businesses in their rooms, ranging from restaurants to tailor shops to photography studios, while others worked for either the occupation forces, the JDC, or UNRRA and still others profited from trad-ing with Germans. Second, the high rate of attendance speaks to the value the DPs placed on such entertainment. In 1946, MIKT/MIT toured DP camps and Jewish communities in Germany, staging 3 premiers and 66 performances, and reaching 50,000 viewers. Frequently more than 400 patrons attended a single performance in the larger camps, and MIT reported total attendance figures of 180,000 during the first two years of its existence. DPs clearly valued their experiences at the theater.

At a time when UNRRA workers and other international observers discour-aged survivors from discussing their recent past, accusing them of an unhealthy obsession with it, these productions acknowledged the survivors' experiences in

[138] "'Der blutiker szpas' fun Sholem Aleychem," *Undzer Welt*, 23 August 1946, YV M-1/P-85.

[139] Frank, "Der blutiker szpas," *Unzer Weg*, 16 August 1946.

[140] "'Der blutiker szpas' fun Sholem Aleychem," *Unzer Welt*, 23 August 1946; Pergament, "Szolom Elejchem's 'Der blutiker Szpas' in prinz regentn teater," *D.P. Express*, 18 August 1946. In the Ulm area 1,000 children attended a free performance. Quiet and attentive, the seder scene moved them to tears. "Theater 'MIT' Plays for Children" (in Yiddish), *Unzer Weg*, p. 4, YV M-1/P-85.

the concentration camps and validated their preoccupation. Through the plays, performers and audiences alike were able to experiment with new roles and to relearn the rules of social interaction.[141] Research on trauma survivors has demonstrated that imaginational therapy plays an important role in recovery and in reducing the symptoms of post-traumatic stress syndrome.[142] Audience reactions to the graphic portrayal of Holocaust experiences within the relative safety of the DP community suggest that DP theater functioned as a form of therapy.

DP performances allowed survivors to reexperience their suffering in a safe environment. Biber reports, "The lengthy applause [following this song] showed our need to cry, to demonstrate our collective pain."[143] Sender comments on the catharsis that survivor audiences experienced when they saw their lives depicted on stage:

I watch Mala, dressed in black and sitting on the darkened stage amid rubble. I know it is my sister, but on that stage she is every one of us who returned to the ruins of our homes, found rubble or strangers where our families once lived. Her pain-filled voice is the voice of all who survived and found only ashes. ... She cries bitterly. We all cry with her. The score is too big.[144]

Denied the luxury of expressing, or even of feeling, emotion during the Shoah, the performances permitted survivors to weep and grieve. Revues and plays also helped to shape social memory of the Holocaust by putting experiences into narrative form and allowing individuals of disparate backgrounds to learn about what had happened to each other. Mala, for example, had survived the war in exile in the Soviet Union, yet through her performances she portrayed the collective experience of loss.

Performers and audiences were engaged in creating social memories and in becoming a community based on these shared memories. Through the performances of Holocaust-themed plays, actors and audiences came together to remember the past and to weave together the individual stories of suffering and survival into a coherent master narrative.[145] The narrative emphasized

---

[141] Shamai Davidson, "Encounter," in *Holding on to Humanity – The Message of Holocaust Survivors: The Shamai Davidson Papers*, ed. Israel W. Charny (New York: New York University Press, 1992), p. 213.

[142] Neuroscientist Daniel Schacter reports, "Repeated reexperiencing of a traumatic memory in a safe setting can dampen the initial psychological response to trauma." The most effective therapies for the reduction of intrusive memories, flashbacks, and related symptoms of post-traumatic stress disorder are "imaginal exposure therapies" that repeatedly expose patients to stimuli associated with the trauma, prompting them to recall and reexperience vivid images of the experience. Daniel L. Schacter, *The Seven Sins of Memory: How the Mind Forgets and Remembers* (Boston: Houghton Mifflin, 2001), p. 177.

[143] Biber, *Risen from Ashes*, p. 27.

[144] Sender, *To Life*, pp. 143–144.

[145] Child psychiatrist Lenore Terr described post-traumatic play and reenactments among children as "contagious" since even nontraumatized children came to participate. *Too Scared to Cry*, p. 279.

the suffering of mothers and children alongside heroic resistance. These themes were reinforced by newspaper articles and holiday celebrations.

Theater could alleviate the monotony of life in the camps, transporting the audience from Germany to one of three places: the world of their childhood, the Shoah itself, and their future in Palestine. The first offered the comfort of the prewar past and a momentary connection with parents and community. The second expressed the torment of loss but also rewrote the immediate past into a story of partisan resistance to Nazi power, giving the former victims a sense of control over their destiny. The third enacted the Zionist dream of redemption in Palestine. Sender recalled watching her brother-in-law perform in Leipheim: "The people around me cry and laugh. Shout their anger. Burst into song as they wander with him from yesterday to today, to tomorrow."[146]

"JUSTICE, JUSTICE SHALL YOU PURSUE"

Jewish national life was played out not only on the stage but also in the law courts established by DPs. After liberation, Jewish Holocaust survivors struggled to rebuild their lives in a world that viewed them with suspicion. Some Allied personnel and Germans held antisemitic stereotypes of Jewish criminality that they believed were confirmed by the existence of the black market and Jewish acts of retribution. Even leaders of the Jewish communities in Palestine, the United States, and Britain initially believed that only criminal elements and the morally bankrupt could have survived the Nazi onslaught. Within this context, Jewish DPs created courts of honor as part of their effort to reclaim agency over their lives and to assert their dignity. In the process they differentiated themselves from Germans, whom they viewed as criminal, and from the Allies, whom they considered potentially hostile or naïvely susceptible to German influences. Through the workings of the courts, DPs sought to articulate their communal values and their adherence to civilized codes of justice.

The DP judicial system was in many ways reminiscent of the police and courts established in the ghettos of Nazi-occupied Eastern Europe. The maintenance of law and order had been an urgent matter for the Jewish Councils, which created ghetto police forces and courts to facilitate communal life. In some ghettos the courts came into being through the public initiative of legal professionals. The harsh conditions of ghetto life were reflected in the types of cases handled: shirking of work, housing and sanitary infractions, and economic exploitation of the weak. Sanctions varied from warnings, to fines, to imprisonment.[147]

Within the concentration camps a sort of vigilante justice had prevailed. Kapos who abused their power or other prisoners who stole from fellow inmates could be subjected to reprisals.[148] This sort of vigilantism continued after liberation,

---

[146] Sender, *To Life*, p. 143.

[147] Dina Porat, "The Justice System and Courts of Law in the Ghettos of Lithuania," *Holocaust and Genocide Studies* 12:1 (1998): 49–65.

[148] In Buchenwald, where a Socialist/Communist underground operated, a Jewish prisoner denounced a brutal kapo from Auschwitz who had arrived in a transport. The underground executed him by drowning. David Boruchowicz, "Videotaped interview," VHA, IC 317, Seg. 21.

spurring the creation of DP courts.[149] It was necessary to put former kapos and ghetto policemen on trial to prevent mob attacks against them that disrupted public order and threatened to reinforce an image of DPs as violent and uncivilized. The promise that justice could be achieved in a Jewish court could deter such assaults. Moreover, maintaining justice fulfilled a pillar of traditional Jewish values.

DPs wanted to form their own communal standards of justice. One DP commentator wrote:

We are building a small society that is bound with general laws that can be broken by some of us, and it is desirable that such cases should be decided by us alone and not through foreigners. ... The citizens' court also has the task of resolving conflicts with an educational goal. In its decisions, one often finds an indication of how to conduct oneself rightly and morally; in pointing out bad deeds, it points simultaneously to the right way. We must acknowledge that under the influence of the demoralizing power of the last world war, people became culturally and ethically backward; mainly the youth that grew up without proper educators finds itself deadlocked now, when life returns to normalcy. They don't know where to turn or on which path to go, they are naturally good people perpetrating crimes on account of only that they did not receive the proper education. Our citizen's court will not punish or, as I have already said, frighten; it will simply resolve conflicts and simultaneously point out bad deeds.[150]

These courts indicated that the Jews were a separate community from the surrounding Germans and the liberating Allies. DPs did not want "foreigners," neither friend nor foe, to decide their cases, implying that Jews were their own nationality. The author explains DP crime as being the result of the war years that disrupted normal development and education. Offenders were basically good people by nature but had lacked "proper" up-bringing, and the court could help in their education. DPs had a sense that they best understood the context in which the crimes had occurred and were best suited to decide the consequences.[151]

The creation of Jewish DP camps furthered the development of Jewish self-government, and in fall 1945 Jewish DP camp courts were functioning in Deggendorf, Landsberg, and Föhrenwald. In Belsen a court briefly operated in the spring and summer of 1946.[152] It was not until fall 1946 that Jews in Poland

---

[149] Isaiah Trunk, *Judenrat: The Jewish Councils in Eastern Europe under Nazi Occupation* (Briarcliff Manor, NY: Stein and Day Publishers, 1972), p. 552.

[150] M. Cukerfajn, "Undzer lager-gericht," *Undzer Hofenung*, 25 September 1946, p. 7.

[151] Germans made similar arguments in advocating local indigenous control of denazification tribunals.

[152] The Belsen court's founding statutes and related documents are in YV O-70/30. Disputes between the court and the DP police led to the judges' resignations and the court's dissolution. The presiding judge destroyed most of the court documents rather than turn them over to police. See L. Wagenaar, Presiding Judge of the Jewish Court, "Cum Efentlechen Onklager baj Jidiszen Gericht un cu di Jidisze Lager Policaj," 21 June 1946, YV O-70/30; Ari' Wagenaar, Fridman, and [illegible, presumably Szmul Grünpeter], "Jidiszes Gericht," Ow TSZW 3 [date is equivalent to 31 July 1946], YIVO,

would create their own court of honor despite having been liberated a year before the Jews in Germany.[153] There are a few possible reasons for this difference in timing. In Germany, the confinement of Jews in DP camps separated from the outside world created a need for local police and courts just as the wartime ghettos had. Under the military occupation of Germany, DPs were subjected to military government courts for criminal matters but to German courts in civil matters. While Jews in Poland might consider going before a Polish court, no Jewish survivor would willingly stand before a German one. Also, the sheer number of survivors in the DP camps increased the odds that former ghetto police and kapos would encounter survivors familiar with their wartime deeds who might seek retribution.

In February 1946 the Central Committee of Liberated Jews in the American Zone created its Judicial Division to assist with drafting administrative regulations, handling cases involving commercial law and discrimination against Jews, gathering materials for the Central Court of Honor, collecting documentation against war criminals, cooperating with all agencies engaged in the capture and prosecution of war criminals, and issuing certificates and replacement personal papers, such as birth and marriage certificates.[154] By June 1946 all major Jewish DP camps had courts, and in the American Zone the Central Committee had established regional appellate courts and a Central Court of Honor in Munich.[155] UNRRA officials welcomed the courts and DP police forces as means both to regulate and maintain order in the camps and to promote the survivors' rehabilitation.

In the British Zone, DPs did not develop a court system like that of the American Zone. The Belsen court and DP police fought over jurisdiction. Three of five judges resigned from the Belsen court claiming, "it is not morally possible to fulfill what the Jewish Central Committee and the Jewish Police expect of the activities of a court in the police-state Bergen-Belsen."[156] The Belsen court ceased to exist. One judge later recanted the negative comments about the police, blaming Presiding Judge Wagenaar for telling him that the letter was simply for the dissolution of the court, which he welcomed since he had not enjoyed serving on the bench.[157] The chief of police then complained that Wagenaar was refusing to turn over the court archives.[158] On August 1,

---

RG 294.2, MK 483, Microfilm reel 114, Folder 1583; "Statement of Dr. Wagenaar" (in Yiddish), 7 August 1946, YIVO, RG 294.2, MK 483, Microfilm reel 114, Folder 1583.

[153] Gabriel N. Finder, "The Trial of Shepsl Rotholc and the Politics of Retribution in the Aftermath of the Holocaust," *Gal-Ed: On the History and Culture of Polish Jewry* 20 (2006): 63–89.

[154] "Organizacjoneler statut fun der Juridiszer Optejlung bajm C.K.," YIVO, RG 294.2, MK 483, Microfilm reel 4, Folder 44.

[155] "Tätigkeitsbericht der Juridischen Abteilung der Zentralkomitees für die Zeit von 22/6 – 22/8 1946, YIVO, RG 294.2, MK 483, Microfilm feel 4, Folder 44.

[156] Arje Wagenaar, Arje Fridman, and Szmuel Grinpeter, "Jidiszes Gericht," YIVO, RG 294.2, MK 483, Microfilm reel 114, Folder 1583.

[157] Szmul Grünpeter to the Central Comite u. die Jüdische Polizei, YIVO, RG 294.2, MK 483, Microfilm reel 114, Folder 1583.

[158] Policaj Szef to Jidiszn Komitet in Bergen-Belsen, 31 July 1946, YIVO, RG 294.2, MK 483, Microfilm reel 114, Folder 1583.

1946, DP police arrested Wagenaar for destroying the court archives,[159] and Wagenaar subsequently acknowledged that he burned the records on July 30.[160] While Wagenaar may have been a particularly difficult individual,[161] another DP accused Belsen police of abuse, saying, "The [DP] police is worse than the Gestapo."[162] Some Belsen police were apprehended for taking bribes and thievery.[163] Others beat suspected kapos in order to gain confessions. Perhaps influenced by the former partisans within the police force, Belsen police administered their own form of justice. When it came to the everyday petty crimes within the DP camps, minor thefts and civil disturbances, Belsen police adjudicated the cases. In the American Zone, many of these cases would have been forwarded to DP courts.

During the war ghetto police had often administered justice instead of courts, and in many ways DP police and courts dealt with crimes similar to those in the ghettos. Disputes over housing, property, and infractions of DP camp regulations came before the courts. Violations of sanitation regulations resulted in warnings, fines, and even brief imprisonment for incorrigible repeat offenders. The camp newspaper would publish the sentences to serve as a warning to others.[164] The pedagogical role of the courts was evident. For example, three Landsberg residents accused of stealing two cans of gasoline from American cars from which Red Cross packages were being unloaded were set free since the court could not determine whether they had had criminal intent. The court did note that in the future such cases would be punished, indicating that the judges felt that DPs accustomed to "organizing" in the ghettos and concentration camps needed instruction in the new rules before sentences should be handed down.[165] Others convicted of theft received fourteen-day jail sentences and were ordered to pay restitution to the victims.[166]

If the example of the Eschwege DP camp is any indication, agitated DPs frequently vented their frustration on DP officials. The Eschwege court heard a

---

[159] Jewish Police Bergen Belsen, report (in Yiddish), 1 August 1946, YIVO, RG 294.2, MK 483, Microfilm reel 114, Folder 1583.

[160] Statement of Dr. Wagenaar (in Yiddish), 7 August 1946, YIVO, RG 294.2, MK 483, Microfilm reel 114, Folder 1583.

[161] In summer 1946 Wagenaar had been discontent. He complained to the Central Committee that his rations were not enough for his family of four and a week later he complained to the school that his daughter should not have been expelled for not participating in an after-school event. Wagenaar to dos Prezidjum fun 'm Jidiszen Central Komitet, 26 June 1946, and Wagenaar to alle Lerers fun di Jidisze Szul in Belsen, 5 July 1946, YIVO, RG 294.2, MK 483, Microfilm reel 114, Folder 1583.

[162] "Hollenberg," YIVO, RG 294.2, MK 483, Microfilm reel 114, Folder 1594.

[163] "Haberfeld: Accepting bribes," 24 February 1946, YIVO, RG 294.2, MK 483, Microfilm reel 114, Folder 1594; "P.C. Sabo. No. 53: Stealing food from L 5. Food Store," YIVO, RG 294.2, MK 483, Microfilm reel 114, Folder 1594.

[164] Helen Matouskova, Field Supervisor to S. B. Zisman, District Director, UNRRA, District 5, "Field Supervisor's Monthly Report, Team 311 Landsberg," 14 March 1946, p. 2, UN S-0436, Box 42, File 6.

[165] "Fun gerichts-zal," *Landsberger Lager Cajtung*, 15 April 1946, p. 2.

[166] "Di ferte sicung fun lager-gericht," *Landsberger Lager Cajtung*, 12 November 1945, p. 6.

slander case between the head of the Jewish Committee and Mr. Gartenkraut. The accused Mr. Gartenkraut asked the chairman and the entire Jewish Committee for forgiveness, explaining that it had been a moment of great agitation for him. On September 4, 1946, the court heard another slander case between the DP police and Mrs. Roza Rabunska. Mrs. Rabunska explained that she had been in a hurry to go to the doctor and was very unnerved, and she had great remorse for her untactful treatment of the camp police and apologized.[167] At the bottom of the same newspaper page, Szlojme Kaplanski apologized to the police for his poor behavior and promised that it would not happen again.[168] The emphasis on public apology served an educational purpose as well as one of reconciliation. The court instructed DPs in civil behavior.

The courts also heard corruption charges against DP officials,[169] and the disposition of these cases was important not only to the efficient running of DP camp administrations but also to demonstrating the trustworthiness of the DP leadership to DPs and relief organizations alike. DP police investigated theft and black marketeering that occurred within the camps and the courts tried such cases; however, similar to the ghetto courts, the DP legal system was more concerned with the economic exploitation of the weaker members of the Jewish community than with the black market per se. DPs most closely watched those trials involving former ghetto police, kapos, and block leaders in the concentration camps.

The composition of DP courts may have encouraged leniency. The courts generally assigned three to five judges to sit on a trial. The presiding judge was usually an experienced jurist. In the larger camps, the panel might consist of all attorneys, but frequently at least one judge was a layperson of good reputation. In disputes between DPs, the courts favored reconciliation rather than punishment. One former lay judge in Föhrenwald commented, "They chose from the survivors three people. Someone who was like a judge before, someone who was a lawyer, and me. We listened to people, and decided what to do. I was the easiest of them all. I always told them, 'Try to look at it through his eyes. Try to see what he did with his thoughts and reasons.' I always wanted to let them go."[170] Perhaps lay judges encouraged the tendency toward reconciliation. Frequently sentences for violation of camp regulations were warnings or loss of cigarette rations for a brief period. Possession of black market goods might lead to a sentence of three days in the camp jail. As we saw in Chapter 1, DPs had a very different view of economic crimes from the Allies. The value DPs placed on community harmony was demonstrated in a case about theft between friends. A DP

---

[167] "Fun Eszweger lager-gericht," *Undzer Hofenung*, 25 September 1946, p. 10.

[168] "Antszuldikung," *Undzer Hofenung*, 25 September 1946, p. 10.

[169] See, for example, the dossier concerning Hermann Aftergut, YIVO, RG 294.2, MK 483, Microfilm reel 18, Folder 196, and the cases against Motija Soroka and against four Föhrenwald officials, YIVO, RG 294.2, MK 483, Microfilm reel 18, Folder 197. The short-lived Belsen court convicted canteen workers for skimming rations and trading them on the black market, "Judgment in the Name of the Sheerit Hapletah," 23 March 1946, YIVO, RG 294.2, MK 483, Microfim reel 114, Folder 1591.

[170] Simon Sterling, "A Survivor's Story," p. 128, USHMM, RG 02.156.

court resolved the dispute with a handshake between the parties while the court spectators applauded their approval. However, while property violations could be treated with leniency, betrayal of the Jewish community invoked serious consequences.

Collaboration with the Germans during the Holocaust constituted treason, especially if the accused had been unnecessarily brutal toward fellow Jews. Survivors believed that most Jews had behaved decently even under dehumanizing conditions and condemned people who had beaten and denounced Jews in the ghettos and concentration camps.[171] By sentencing those former ghetto policemen and kapos who had abused their power, the courts attempted to demonstrate that the majority of survivors had remained decent people even under extreme circumstances.

Like DP police across Germany, the Belsen police attempted to confront the crimes of the past by apprehending former kapos and Nazi collaborators.[172] An investigation into a former kapo, Chazciel Jungster, living near Kassel led to conflicting testimony. Many men repeated that the kapo had used his position in the kitchen to keep his men fed and that he had looked out for the young boys. Jungster acknowledged, "sometimes they made him so angry that he had to slap their faces. They were jealous of him too."[173] The nearly identical statements in support of Jungster raised suspicion, especially since other witnesses mentioned Jungster beating Jews to death and stealing food from others. One witness accused those who spoke well of the kapo of having been bribed.[174] Without a DP court, police forwarded their dossiers to the British military government when their investigations were complete.[175]

Public opinion demanded harsh sentences for those convicted of assisting the Nazis (Figure 14). On November 12, 1945, the *Landsberger Lager Cajtung* reported the convictions of a block elder who brutally beat prisoners in the Kaufering concentration camp and of a Krakow ghetto policeman who zealously rounded up Jews for transport, telling one family "you have lived long enough."[176] The author considered too lenient the ghetto policeman's sentence of four months' imprisonment and loss of communal rights: "It is noticeable that the public is not satisfied with the judgments against kapos, demanding harsher sentences. And rightfully so. If the court finds such a kapo guilty, he must then sit for as long as the camp exists. And concerning the removal of rights, one should perhaps instead impose simple, Jewish excommunication." On the same page of the newspaper, camp officials issued an appeal, in Yiddish and English,

[171] Charles Sternbach, "Videotaped interview," VHA, IC 8981, Seg. 100.
[172] Michael Berkowitz, *The Crime of My Very Existence: Nazism and the Myth of Jewish Criminality* (Berkeley: University of California, 2007), p. 216.
[173] "Jungster Chazciel," YIVO, RG 294.2, MK 483, Microfilm reel 114, Folder 1594.
[174] "The evidence of Rotenberg Hirsch," YIVO, RG 294.2, MK 483, Microfilm reel 114, Folder 1594.
[175] "RIBNER Selig to Mil. Gov. 618," 8 March 1946, YIVO, RG 294.2, MK 483, Microfilm reel 114, Folder 1594.
[176] "Harbere sztrofn far kapos!" *Landsberger Lager Cajtung*, 12 November 1945, p. 6.

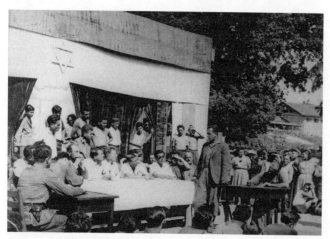

FIGURE 14. Jewish DP lawyers (in the white shirts) in the Feldafing DP camp serve as judges in a trial involving a fellow DP, who is accused of having sold his identification card to a former Nazi, 1945. *Credit*: USHMM, courtesy of Allen Rezak

to camp residents to refrain from attacking suspected kapos.[177] Another commentator called for the removal of former kapos from positions of power:

The Jewish community forcefully fights kapos in general and Jewish kapos in particular. It is enough to mention that the congress of liberated Jews in the American Zone that occurred on the 27, 28, and 29 January 1946 in Munich decided that kapos may hold no public office. The meeting of partisans and front fighters "Pachach" held in Leipheim on the 8 and 9 May 1946 decided in the political resolution point 9 the following: "We demand of the higher authorities the cleansing and removal of all kapos from communal life." Together with bankruptcy of national socialism, fascism and Hitlerism the common criminals along with their servants must disappear from the horizon.[178]

Since kapos had been in better physical health at the end of the war because of their privileged status, they often had taken on organizational responsibilities in the early days after liberation. Unlike the above author, who did not allow for the rehabilitation or innocence of individual kapos, the courts carefully weighed the evidence against the accused and made their decisions accordingly.

The care with which the courts proceeded, occasionally dismissing cases for lack of evidence, testified to the respect leading DPs had for the rule of law. Having held the office of ghetto policeman or of kapo was not proof of guilt. Specific crimes supported by evidence needed to be demonstrated to the court's satisfaction before a guilty verdict would be handed down.[179] Sentences depended on the circumstances of the case. On October 2, 1945, the Landsberg DP court convicted

[177] "Appeal to Residents of the Landsberg Jewish Center" (in Yiddish) and "Ojfruf cu ale bawojner fun Landsberger Centr.," *Landsberger Lager Cajtung*, 12 November 1945, p. 6.
[178] B. Orenstein, "Wos iz azojns kapo?" *Jidisze Cajtung*, 6 December 1946, p. 6.
[179] Dr. Szlojme Orensztajn, "Majne baobachtungen fun gerichts-zal," *Landsberger Lager Cajtung*, 15 April 1945, p. 2; Trunk, *Judenrat*, p. 549.

Maier Rubin of stealing from, denouncing, and beating fellow Jews in a labor camp. He was sentenced to four months in the Landsberg camp jail and lifelong banishment from the Jewish community.[180] On March 22, 1946, the same court acquitted a man accused of beating and killing Jews in Gleiwitz V for lack of evidence.[181] In a spring 1946 case, an accused kapo was convicted of collaborating with the Germans and maltreating Jewish inmates. Sentenced to two years' imprisonment, the kapo, in a rare move, was reportedly handed over to German authorities, who enforced the sentence.[182] On September 6, 1946, in camp Herzog, the court found twenty-three-year-old Jakow Flajszhecker guilty of beating Jews, particularly women, during his disinfection work in a concentration camp from 1942 through 1943. He was sentenced to three months in jail and immediate removal from the camp. He had the possibility of appearing before the Jewish court after one year and could be forgiven if he could prove that since his expulsion he had worked for the good of the Jewish community and had earned recognition as a full citizen.[183] This court offered the convicted kapo a path to rehabilitation and return to the community. Historian Isaiah Trunk examined twenty-seven verdicts against former ghetto policemen and/or kapos. Of these, nine defendants were acquitted or rehabilitated, thirteen were forbidden to hold any office in the Jewish community, and five were banished from the community.[184] The sentences speak to the restraint and professionalism of the DP courts.

The resentment survivors felt toward collaborators united Jews of disparate backgrounds. Trials provided an opportunity for DPs to forge a community ethic, emphasizing what behavior the community would tolerate and who could belong. Presiding judge of the Landsberg court and member of the Central Committee, Dr. Samuel Gringauz, reported approvingly of the uniform sentiments of the public as a sign of Jewish national consciousness.[185] The first prosecutor of the Landsberg DP court wrote about the relationship between the court and the public: "Simultaneously [the public] holds the court in high esteem and yet allows itself a certain freedom in its behavior. That is the awareness that they find themselves in their own court, that the judges are their brothers. In no other court can many Jews feel that way."[186] This was a court of their peers, and it inspired Jewish national pride.

It was the trial of a kapo that first brought the DP courts into open conflict with the U.S. military government. On September 19, 1946, while visiting Föhrenwald, Salomon Schulsinger was denounced as a kapo who had beaten fellow Jews in the Görlitz concentration camp. The DP police arrested him. In a proposed plea deal,

[180] "Bekanntmachung," *Unzer Welt*, 19 October 1945.
[181] "Fun gerichts-zal," *Landsberger Lager Cajtung*, 15 April 1946, p. 2.
[182] The former kapo later immigrated to the United States and became a prosperous member of the Jewish community. Solomon Fromer, VHA, IC 4650, Segs. 137–138.
[183] "Urteil fun lager-gericht N. 146," *Undzer Hofenung*, 25 September 1946, p. 7.
[184] Overall, Trunk found 42 trials mentioned in his sources but only 27 verdicts. Trunk, *Judenrat*, p. 555.
[185] Gringauz, "Fal Barcion," *Landberger Lager Cajtung*, 2 December 1945, p. 7.
[186] Orensztajn, "Majne baobachtungen."

the camp court offered Schulsinger his freedom in exchange for a $600 fine, payable to his accusers. Unable to raise the money, Schulsinger stood trial. Convicted and sentenced to six months' imprisonment in the camp jail, he had the right to appeal his conviction to the Jewish court in Munich. At this point, his wife violated the DP code of honor and appealed to military authorities. The investigating officer found the convicted kapo sympathetic and doubted the character of his accusers. The officer recommended the arrest of the camp court and of an UNRRA official, Carl Atkin, whom he believed had perjured himself during the investigation.[187] UNRRA ordered the suspension of all camp courts as the military contemplated further action. Both UNRRA officials and the Army's Advisor on Jewish Affairs office argued that the court had operated in good faith.

In the end Schulsinger was turned over to military authorities and the Apprehension Section of the War Crimes Commission examined his case. In a later interview given by a survivor other than the ones who accused him in Föhrenwald, Schulsinger is described as the only fat child in Görlitz because of his work assisting the head kapo,[188] suggesting that Schulsinger may have been guilty. No charges were brought against any UNRRA worker, although upon the military's recommendation UNRRA fired Edouard Frum, the camp director who had championed the court. The DP court was exonerated of any wrongdoing in Schulsinger's trial.[189]

Military authorities decreed that only military courts had the power to fine or imprison defendants. In cases that merited such sentences, defendants were to be handed over to military courts for prosecution. DP courts under firm UNRRA supervision could impose administrative penalties, such as withholding supplemental rations or imposing labor requirements. In late October 1946, while the Föhrenwald investigation was underway, General McBride of the 9th Army ordered that DP courts could only hear cases concerning crimes committed in the DP camps. Cases against kapos would need to be turned over to the general courts.[190] In defiance DP courts continued to sit and hear cases against kapos, and apparently the military remained unaware of or did not enforce McBride's order.

---

[187] Paul Winter, Acting Legal Adviser, UNRRA U.S. Zone Headquarters, to R. W. Collins, Deputy US Zone Director, Division of Field Operations, "Mr. Carl Atkin, Deputy Director, UNRRA Dist. No. 5. – Request by G-5 TUSA for Investigation and Disciplinary Action," 10 December 1946, UN S-0425–0018-12.

[188] Nathan Freund, "Videotaped interview," VHA, IC 31262, Seg. 169

[189] The only DP official charged with a crime was Josef Schawinski, a judge who, upon advice of the Central Committee Judicial Division in Munich, initially refused to hand over Schulsinger to the military. After serving his sentence, the judge won a lawsuit for moral and material damages against the Central Committee in the Munich Court of Honor. Angelika Königseder and Juliane Wetzel, *Lebensmut im Wartesaal: Die jüdischen DPs (Displaced Persons) im Nachkriegsdeutschland* (Frankfurt a.M.: Fischer Taschenbuch Verlag, 1994), pp. 144–145.

[190] General McBride contacted the Landsberg chairman to apologize for military police breaking up a religious service of Lithuanian Jews on October 28, 1946. He took the opportunity to inform Gringauz of the decision to restrict the DP courts. "Wegn farbot fun der ceremonje ojfn jidiszn bejs-olom un wegen di jidisze gerichtn in di lagern," *Jidisze Cajtung*, 1 November 1946, p. 2. The written order followed: Louis Zuckerman, Lieutenant Colonel, Assistant Adjutant General,

Despite the U.S. Army's insistence that accused kapos be turned over to it for trial, the DPs did not trust the Allies' interest in prosecuting kapos. The Nuremberg Trials had disappointed Jewish DPs:

We Jews, like all nations, we may examine the verdict from our standpoint. We may examine the sentence from the standpoint of 6 million dead of our people and from that standpoint look at the results of the work of the international tribunal. The 6 million did not have their representative at the prosecutors' dais, did not have their representative among the judges. ... Yes, we the living do not have the right to criticize but they, the tortured, the gassed, the shot, the thousands of brother martyrs, they have the right to scream! They cannot be forbidden by anyone! If there in Nuremberg at the court of the major defendants a just verdict cannot come down, then what will happen in the day-to-day cases of little crimes?[191]

The Jewish dead had not been heard in the court, and the verdicts did not meet Jewish DP standards of justice. The Nuremberg Trials had focused on war crimes and not the murder of the Jews, allowing Germans to misinterpret crimes against Jews as war crimes rather than part of a criminal system of Nazi racial politics.[192] Allied justice was not Jewish justice. As the Cold War intensified and the Western Allies began to build a new German state, Allied interest in the crimes of the recent past waned. In addition, what DPs considered to be unacceptable behavior did not necessarily rise to the criminal standards of an American military court. And there was no substitute for Jews standing before Jews in their own court of law.

The potential penalties and the desire to clear one's name led individuals to request rehabilitation trials. In 1947 Wladyslaw Friedham requested a rehabilitation trial after one survivor appealed to the Jewish Agency to revoke Friedham's immigration certificate on the grounds that his brutal past as a kapo should make him ineligible for legal entry to Palestine. At trial Friedham submitted in his defense a newspaper article in which he was affectionately ridiculed for his sensitivity: "What kind of kapo are you? You don't have a stick; you don't hit, you don't scream ... a schlimazel for a kapo."[193] Numerous witnesses testified to the fact that Friedham had been a gentle kapo, securing light labor for his details. Friedham had been a community leader in Feldafing during the early days after liberation and later on the Central Committee. Given his visibility "at the same time people were beating the kapos they found in Feldafing," one witness testified, the charges should have surfaced sooner had they been true.[194]

Headquarters, Ninth Infantry Division, "Maintenance of Law and Order among United Nations Displaced Persons," 6 November 1946, UN S-0425, Box 18, File 12.

[191] "Der ‚gerechter' urtejl," *Undzer Hofenung*, 9 October 1946, p. 3; "The Führer is Gone, the Party Remains ..." (in Yiddish), *Unzer Weg*, 30 August 1946, p. 6; Zeev Mankowitz, *Life between Memory and Hope: The Survivors of the Holocaust in Occupied Germany* (Cambridge: Cambridge University Press, 2002), p. 250.

[192] Peter Reichel, *Vergangenheitsbewältigung in Deutschland* (Munich: Verlag C.H. Beck, 2001), p. 44.

[193] "Ojscug fun artikel, welcher iz farefentlicht geworn durch Dr. Dowid Wdowinski untern titl: ‚Wi mir hobn durchgemacht a Pejsach in koncentracje-lager' in der Amerikaner cajtung ‚Der Tog' Montik dem 7 April 1947 in Nr. 11.765." YIVO, RG 294.2, MK 483, Microfilm reel 18, Folder 195.

[194] Testimony of Hersc Schwimmer, "Protokoll," 22 August 1947, YIVO, RG 294.2, MK 483, Microfilm reel 18, Folder 195.

The Central Court of Honor determined that the accusations were baseless. The accuser appeared to have been motivated by the misapprehension that Friedham had been responsible for the release from U.S. custody of a notorious kapo.[195] Just as in postwar retribution trials throughout Europe, so, too, among the DPs the danger existed of personal scores being settled under the guise of punishing collaborators. The DP courts were up to the challenge.

The symbolic significance of Jews on German soil trying their fellow Jews cannot be underestimated. The cases tried and the sentences meted out reflected the values of the Jewish community. Leniency and reconciliation were the focus in cases concerning infractions of camp regulations. The DP judicial system struggled to limit black marketeering to improve the image of Jews with Allies and Germans but at the same time sought to take into consideration the needs of the DPs and their motives.

In trying and convicting wartime collaborators, the survivors distinguished themselves from the Germans whose courts cleared many individuals with the blood of innocents on their hands. In this regard the uniqueness of the DP community, with its members drawn from many places of origin and bound to many different destinations, made it easier to censure its members. For denazi-fication tribunals, Germans were put in the position of denouncing and sitting in judgment on lifelong neighbors and colleagues amongst whom they would continue to live afterward. That social reality, along with whatever political proclivities influenced the tribunals, prevented a thorough political cleans-ing.[196] DPs viewed the weaknesses of German denazification tribunals, how-ever, simply as a sign of Nazi sympathies. Although civil cases were under the jurisdiction of German courts, DPs held all Germans to be criminals, which disqualified them from sitting in judgment on Jews. The legal punishment, or at least the threat of it, for those Jewish men who would consort with German women reinforced the chasm between Jews and Germans. Survivors con-structed an identity that placed the morally superior Jew opposite the impure German.[197]

Whether hearing cases about wartime crimes or about corruption and sanitation violations in the DP camps, the courts helped construct a national consciousness as Jews of differing countries of origin came together to forge communal standards of justice. That Jews could stand before other Jews in the pursuit of Jewish justice filled DPs with pride. The DP courts revealed the deter-mination of survivors to pursue justice, to reclaim control over their lives, and to build a new community.

---

[195] American MPs had detained that kapo on suspicion of black market activity and released him when he could prove his innocence. "Protokoll," 22 August 1947, YIVO, RG 294.2, MK 483, Microfilm reel 18, Folder 195.

[196] Reichel, *Vergangenheitsbewältigung*, p. 35.

[197] Lynn Rapaport has shown that Jews in postwar Germany contrasted morally pure Jews with impure Germans when constructing their ethnic identity. Rapaport, *Jews in Germany*, pp. 18 and 45.

CONCLUSION

First and foremost, Jewish DPs identified themselves as Jews. While their understanding of what it meant to be Jewish ranged from Orthodox religious observance to ethnic or cultural affinity, they all acknowledged their membership in the Jewish people. Divisions between Orthodox and ultra-Orthodox and between observant and secular Jews remained even though the Nazis had persecuted all of them as Jews. Despite the conflicts over ritual supplies and levels of observance, Jewish DPs were united by the cycle of holidays, particularly the ones that emphasized Jewish triumph over historical oppressors. The Sabbath and Passover led to friction over differences in observance and traditions, but for the most part these can be seen as age-old conflicts within the Jewish community, comparable to the divisions within prewar communities. The participation of the religious parties in the camp committees and the Central Committees demonstrated their awareness that they were part of a larger DP community. Many of the secular leaders came from Orthodox backgrounds and had some respect for the position of the rabbis even as they disagreed on priorities. Even observant DPs occasionally came into conflict with rabbinic authorities over how to practice Judaism given the restrictive conditions in postwar Germany. Overall, life-cycle events tended to emphasize commonality since secular and observant Jews alike participated in them.

The babble of languages gradually gave way to Yiddish. Yiddish was the predominant language of DP culture. Survivors who had gone through the concentration camps speaking a different language found it easier to navigate the DP camps by learning Yiddish. Newspapers and theatrical productions presented themselves in Yiddish. Both served to help survivors create a coherent narrative of their past, present, and future. The past was one of tragedy as well as heroism, the present was the fight for autonomy and emigration, and the future was a Jewish home in Palestine. Cultural life permitted the reworking of the past in ways that most likely benefited the survivors' mental health. It also promoted the formation of collective memories that helped DPs who had not experienced the concentration camps to integrate into the community of survivors.

DP courts played their part in coming to terms with the recent past. Proceedings against kapos and ghetto police allowed DPs to examine Jewish actions during German occupation and to determine which behaviors were excusable and which were not. Aware that years of living under Nazi oppression had skewed the ethical compass of Jewish youth, DP leaders used the courts as a pedagogical tool. More important than punishment, particularly for property offenses, the courts instructed DPs in Jewish standards of behavior. Although DPs might acknowledge the need for such remedial education, they asserted their moral authority over the Germans. DPs defined themselves as naturally good and attributed any misdeeds they might commit to the disruptive and corrupting influence of the Nazis. Germans, the DPs believed, had no such excuse for the crimes they had perpetrated against the Jews. The Jewish DP code of justice helped express a sense of ethnic identity that distinguished Jews from other nationalities.

In building community, DPs had to rely on material aid from Jewish relief organizations, Allied military governments, and German officials. Frequently, DPs encountered opposition to their efforts, but it did not deter them. Despite the building shortage, Jewish communities found space for prayer services. They persevered in their quest for kosher meat. Theatrical troupes could "organize" costumes and materials for set construction or purchase them on the black market. DP courts heard cases against accused kapos despite the American directives that ordered them to turn over such cases to the military authorities. This unwillingness to be limited by material shortages or opposition of outsiders led Germans and Allies to view the DPs as troublemakers. For the DPs, obstinacy was the only course possible. They were fighting to reclaim their cultural and religious heritage and to pass it along to a new generation. They were also waging a battle for the right to a Jewish homeland in Palestine.

6

Out of the Wilderness

Contemporaries often dismissed the survivors as a people without an elite, unruly and unfit.[1] UNRRA and military government personnel, as well as some Jewish relief agency workers, were often annoyed by Jewish DP demands for better living conditions, their frequent demonstrations, and their disregard for outside authority. They attributed the DPs' rowdy behavior to the dehumanization of the concentration camps rather than recognizing it as their political reawakening and reassertion of autonomy. Lengthy internment left its mark on the DPs. The seemingly endless stay in DP camps led to their political radicalization and encouraged many to emigrate at the first opportunity. Zionism permeated DP politics as the expression of Jewish national will. Regardless of their destination, most DPs left Germany while holding on to their dreams of a Jewish homeland.

Although most of the highest ranking DP leaders had held public offices before and during the war, many of the DPs who came forward to organize the political and cultural camp life of the survivors were new to these roles. At the same time, DP leaders were not completely lacking in skills or experience. Lawyers acted as judges and drafted bylaws for the various committees, experienced teachers became founding directors of schools, and partisans organized police forces. Despite their lack of official credentials, DP leaders were determined to represent the interests of their community. Their accomplishments in establishing political and cultural institutions were demonstrable.

In the initial postwar period DP leaders and organizations centered their activities on security and locating surviving family members. When survivors' expectations that the world would open its arms to them were not met, emigration became a top priority. A majority of DPs focused their hopes on immigration to Palestine, and DP political and cultural life soon revolved around Zionist aspirations. Bundists on the socialist left and Agudists on the religious right put

---

[1] One official for the JDC noted that "the Jewish DP's are a marvelous example of a society without an elite. ... The present leadership of Jewish DP's is, but for a few exceptions, made up of people who have little experience in social planning or social responsibilities." Koppel S. Pinson, "Jewish Life in Liberated Germany: A Study of the Jewish DPs," *Jewish Social Science* 9 (April 1947): 126.

aside prewar hostility to Zionism and worked toward immigration to Palestine. With limited emigration possibilities, the DPs became increasingly frustrated by conditions in the camps; demonstrations about opening the doors to Palestine were frequently accompanied by demands for better food, and vice versa. The lengthening stay in the DP camps increased tensions not only among DPs, Germans, and Allies, but among DPs as well. In the American Zone the initial emphasis survivors had placed on political unity gave way to factionalism and polarization, while DPs in the British Zone successfully fought to maintain unity. Even as they continued to demand entrance to Palestine, however, fatigue with camp life led many DPs to find emigration opportunities wherever they could. In the end, nearly 60 percent of DPs made their way to *Eretz-Yisrael* (the Land of Israel). The remainder found new homes in the United States, Australia, Canada, and South America, even as the majority of these survivors remained devoted to the goal of a Jewish homeland in Palestine.

EARLY DP ORGANIZATIONS

DP leadership emerged from members of the concentration camp undergrounds, Zionist movements, religious groups, and partisan units. Preparations for political organization began even before liberation.[2] DP leaders established mutual aid societies to provide for the medical and nutritional needs of the survivors. They struggled to win recognition for Jews as a group with distinct needs from other DPs. Dedication to the communal good characterized the individuals who would gain the respect of fellow DPs and assume leadership in the DP camps.

The survivors who founded DP organizations had frequently served as leaders in the wartime ghettos, concentration camps, and underground movements. The emerging leadership in the American Zone tended to consist of men from the Lithuanian educated middle classes, such as the physician and former head of the Kovno ghetto hospital Zalman Grinberg, who organized a hospital staffed by Jewish DPs and later served as chairman of the Central Committee of Liberated Jews in Bavaria, and the former judge Samuel Gringauz, who had been part of the Zionist underground in the Kaufering concentration camp and acted as the head of the Landsberg Camp Committee and chairman of the Central Committee's policy-making arm, the Council of Liberated Jews. Another member of the Central Committee and the first managing editor of the *Landsberger Lager Cajtung* was Rudolf Volsonok, who had been head of the Kovno ghetto Population Department and one of the leaders of the Communist underground.

In the British Zone, DP leaders tended to be from the Polish petit bourgeoisie. The director of the Culture Department of the Central Jewish Committee,

---

[2] For an excellent discussion of the origin of DP organizations in the spring and summer months of 1945, see Yehuda Bauer, "Initial Organization of Holocaust Survivors in Bavaria," *Yad Vashem Studies* 8 (1970): 127–157; Zeev Mankowitz, "The Formation of She'erit Hapletah," in *She'erit Hapletah, 1944–1948: Rehabilitation and Political Struggle*, eds. Yisrael Gutman and Avital Saf (Jerusalem: Yad Vashem, 1990), pp. 337–370.

Paul Trepman, was a former teacher and member of the underground in wartime Poland. Other committee members Berl (Dov) Laufer, Rafael Olevsky, and Norbert Wollheim had all been active in Zionist or Jewish community organizations before the war. Josef Rosensaft and Hadassah Bimko (later Rosensaft) demonstrated their leadership in the concentration camps. Bimko was one of the few politically active DP women. Women rarely held elected office, although many women worked on behalf of cultural and religious organizations and served as leaders within kibbutzim.[3]

In spring and summer 1945 some survivors formed camp committees to protect Jewish interests and to lobby for separate Jewish camps. These activities were especially important in camps with minority Jewish populations. With non-Jewish Polish or Baltic DPs in charge of distributing rations, Jewish DPs frequently received less than their allotted share. Security concerns also ran high; in Belsen Polish DPs attacked Jews, and at Feldafing DPs feared belligerent Germans. DP leaders agitated for the formation of Jewish police forces and for military government and UNRRA recognition of Jewish camp committees. This movement to organize began weeks before the first emissaries of Palestinian Jewry, members of the Jewish Brigade of the British Army, arrived in German-area DP camps and months before agents of American and British Jewish relief organizations entered Germany. Throughout the DP camps, survivors established communal organizations on their own initiative despite severe logistical problems created by the postwar chaos. Sympathetic Jewish chaplains and soldiers assisted them in their efforts.

In the British Zone most Jewish DPs were located in Belsen, facilitating the creation of a centralized Jewish committee there. A provisional committee formed by elected leaders from three housing blocks met on April 25, 1945. The first two chairmen quickly repatriated to their homes, leading to the election of Josef Rosensaft, who would remain chairman until the closure of the DP camps in the British Zone. The Central Jewish Committee advocated on behalf of Jewish DPs not only in Belsen but throughout the British Zone. In June 1945, German-Jewish survivor Norbert Wollheim joined the provisional committee. He served as an important liaison between German Jews in the Gemeinden and the DPs, resisting efforts by British and World Jewish Congress officials to separate the German Jewish communities from the Central Jewish Committee. Relations between the DP leadership and the Gemeinden were remarkably close in comparison to the situation in the American Zone, where the DP leadership claimed to speak on behalf of all Jews but essentially ignored the voices of German Jews.[4]

DP leaders had attempted to create a committee that would represent both the American and British Zones, but logistical problems and the development

---

[3] This absence of women from political leadership reflected the gendered distribution of domestic labor in the DP camps. See Margarete Myers Feinstein, "Jewish Women Survivors in the Displaced Persons Camps of Postwar Germany: Transmitters of the Past, Caretakers of the Present, and Builders of the Future," *Shofar: An Interdisciplinary Journal of Jewish Studies* 24:4 (Summer 2006): 67–89.

[4] Jay Geller, *Jews in Post-Holocaust Germany, 1945–1953* (Cambridge: Cambridge University Press, 2004), pp. 45–52.

of parallel structures in the two zones prevented it from coming to fruition.[5] American observers blamed Rosensaft for fearing that the Central Committee in the American Zone would dominate such a joint effort, but it may also have been the result of longstanding divisions between Polish and Lithuanian Jews. In her memoirs, Hadassah Rosensaft characterized the American Zone leaders as aloof and accused them of being detached from the DP masses because of their residence outside of the camps in Munich. Her charges of elitism against the predominantly Lithuanian leadership in Munich are reminiscent of pre-war tensions stemming from non-Hassidic Lithuanian Jews considering themselves more intellectual and stoic than what they saw as the irrational and uneducated (Hassidic) Polish Jews. For their part, Polish Jews considered the Lithuanians to be cold fish. Despite prewar cultural, political, and religious tensions, however, survivors found community in their shared experiences of persecution.

In the American Zone geographic distance separated DPs, but already less than a month after the end of the war, survivors in the Feldafing DP camp organized a Committee of the Jews from Poland and sought contact with other Polish Jews in Munich for the purposes of organization.[6] With the assistance of Rabbi Abraham J. Klausner, on July 1, 1945 Jewish DPs created a federation of camp organizations to represent Jewish interests before the Army and UNRRA and, later, Jewish welfare organizations. They held the first Congress of the *She'erit Hapletah* (Surviving Remnant) of European Jews in the American Zone of Germany on January 27–29, 1946. Camp committees sent delegates who elected members to the administrative body, the Central Committee of Liberated Jews, and to its executive, the Council of Liberated Jews. Later congresses would elect members of the Central Court of Honor that heard cases involving Central Committee officials and employees, as well as appeals from the camp courts.[7] The Jewish DPs were establishing self-government.[8]

In autumn 1945, the U.S. Army and UNRRA permitted a measure of autonomous administration in the DP camps. This was partly in response to lobbying by DP leaders as well as to the inability of Army and UNRRA personnel to meet the administrative needs of the camps. The camp committees assumed responsibility for, among other things, police work, fire fighting, and educational activities. Initially UNRRA personnel appointed some of the camp leaders, but the DPs sought to create a democratic system. Soon DPs elected their

---

[5] See Hagit Lavsky, *New Beginnings: Holocaust Survivors in Bergen-Belsen and the British Zone in Germany, 1945–1950* (Detroit, MI: Wayne State University Press, 2002), pp. 71–72 and 75.

[6] "Protokoll Nr. 2 der Sitzung des Praesidium des Hauptkomitees der Juden aus Polen vom 6. Juni 1945," YIVO Institute for Jewish Research (YIVO), microfilm read at Yad Vashem (YV) JM/10297, Folder 477.

[7] "Regulamin fun Centralen Erengericht bajm farband di bafrejte Jidn in der amerikaner Zone in Dajczland," YIVO at YV, JM/10263, Folder 44.

[8] The organizing efforts of Jewish DPs stood in contrast to that of non-Jewish DPs. See Zorach Warhaftig, *Refugee and Survivor: Rescue Efforts during the Holocaust* (Jerusalem: Yad Vashem, 1988), p. 280.

camp committee members, increasing their sense of their own human value and power.[9]

Resentment grew against the patronizing attitude of Jewish representatives from abroad. After one such visit, Zalman Grinberg proclaimed, "although they are men from the free world, we can describe them as ghetto Jews. We, the former ghetto Jews, have a free view and a free approach to all of our problems. We don't want a protectorate. We want to be co-workers who have the necessary intellectual equipment."[10] The DP leadership believed that it had learned important political lessons during the Holocaust that made them valuable partners in the governance of Jewish survivors. They rejected outsiders' depictions of DPs as broken and demoralized.[11]

Greater DP autonomy meant that more DPs needed to become involved in the daily functioning of the camps. Some individuals took on governmental responsibilities out of a sense of obligation to the Jewish community.[12] Some DPs responded to the payments of cigarettes and cosmetics, both currencies in the black market, offered to encourage participation in camp administration.[13] Camp committees eventually won the right to distribute supplies, including the payments of supplements to committee members, although this presented opportunities for corruption. The Central Committee established guidelines, and camp internal audit committees as well as the Central Audit Commission of the Central Committee worked to ensure that the guidelines were followed and that violators were brought before courts of honor.[14]

Political demonstrations established the Central Committee's power to mobilize DPs, reinforcing its claims to represent them. To illustrate their strength but also their respectability, DP organizers carefully orchestrated protests with parade routes and speakers' platforms. DP police maintained order and demonstrated DP respect for law and order. Strike committees frequently proclaimed

[9] Jacob Biber, *Risen from the Ashes: A Story of the Jewish Displaced Persons in the Aftermath of World War II* (San Bernardino, CA: Borgo Press, 1990), p. 34.

[10] "Council Meeting of the Jew in Bavaria" (in Yiddish), *Unzer Weg*, 19 October 1945, p. 4.

[11] Zalman Grinberg, speech, YIVO, RG 294.2, MK 483, Microfilm reel 113, Folder 1564.

[12] Faye Doctrow reported that her father's Orthodox beliefs led him to work as an assistant to a Feldafing rabbi and an aide to a camp judge. Telephone interview by author, tape recording, 25 March 1996.

[13] Kurt R. Grossman, *The Jewish DP Problem: Its Origin, Scope and Liquidation* (New York: Institute of Jewish Affairs, World Jewish Congress, 1951), p. 14; *Landsberger Lager Cajtung*, 8 October 1945, p. 1.

[14] Cases included officials charged for misappropriation of vouchers for apples, abusing one's office to profit from clothing intended for passengers of the ship *Exodus*, and improperly distributing or taking extra JDC rations. In Belsen DP police also sought to root out corruption, such as a major case against canteen workers stealing food rations to run black market operations. See "Fun ern-gericht bajm C.K.," *Jidisze Cajtung*, 15 November 1945, p. 8; Decision of Central Court of Honor in case against four Landsberg officials, YIVO, RG 294.2, MK 483, Microfilm reel 18, Folder 197; Decision of Central Court of Honor in case of Motija Soroka, YIVO, RG 294.2, MK 483, Microfilm reel 18, Folder 197; documents concerning case of Aftergut, RG 294.2, MK 483, Microfilm reel 18, Folder 196; Jewish Committee in Belsen to Jewish police, 27 August 1947, YIVO, RG 294.2, MK 483, Microfilm reel 114, Folder 1582.

hunger strikes and rabbinic authorities occasionally supplemented this by pro-
nouncing a fast day.[15] Official protests coordinated out of Munich targeted
British policy in Palestine, but the question of emigration was often bound up
with demands for improved conditions, particularly food, in the camps.[16] The
mass arrest of Yishuv leaders on June 29, 1946 spurred the Central Committee
to proclaim a day of protest. The threat to emigration that these arrests represented resulted in widespread DP participation in the protest. Local communities
and camp committees also organized demonstrations against living conditions.
In August 1946, seven Jewish communities under the jurisdiction of UNRRA
Team 558 declared a hunger strike claiming that their food rations were dwin-
dling as a result of the team appointing non-Jewish DPs as camp officials.[17] All
of these demonstrations were sanctioned and organized by DP leaders. All of
them proceeded in an orderly fashion.

The Central Committee viewed its mission as one of overseeing the reconstruction of Jewish life in the DP camps and communities while agitating for
unrestricted immigration to Palestine. From March to December 1946 the
Central Committee expanded its operations to support the activities of thirty-
three Jewish camps, seventy-two communities, four children's homes, thirty-
eight kibbutzim, and three convalescent hospitals. The committee financed
these projects with funds from Jewish agencies, primarily the JDC, and from
German government sources.[18] The Central Committee had nineteen administrative divisions with responsibilities ranging from a tracing bureau to health
to labor and industry. Its cultural office sought to facilitate the founding of DP
schools, the acquisition of materials, and the recruitment of teachers. By May
1948 the Central Committee supported 3,397 individuals in 60 departments,
camp administrations, and external organizations.[19] Impressive as its accomplishments were, its ambitions to provide a strong representative voice on
behalf of the Jewish DPs exceeded its powers. Ultimate authority rested with the
American forces, and financial dependence on international aid weakened DP
autonomy as well.

---

[15] M. Jean Henshaw, Acting Director, UNRRA, Team 106, "Progress Report Camp Foehrenwald,"
15 November 1945, United States Holocaust Memorial Museum Archive (USHMM), Samuel
Zisman Papers, RG-19.047.02*07 (1 of 3); G.C. Brooke, Field Supervisor, to S. B. Zisman,
Director, UNRRA District 5, "Team 165 – Leipheim Camp – DP's Hunger Strike," 5 February
1946, Zisman Papers, RG-19.047.02*09.

[16] "Resolution at [Föhrenwald] protest-meeting held on 15.11.45," YIVO, RG 294.2, MK 483,
Microfilm reel 113, Folder 1564; "Protest-Mitingen in ale jid. jiszuwim in golus-Dajczland,"
Jidisze Cajtung, 10 April 1947, p. 7.

[17] *Landsberger Lager Cajtung,* 9 August 1946, p. 8; G. C. Brooke, Field Supervisor, to S. B. Zisman,
Director, UNRRA District 5, "Team 165 – Leipheim Camp – DP's Hunger Strike," 5 February
1946, Zisman Papers, RG-19.047.02*09.

[18] A. Blumowitsch, "Baricht fun der Tetikajt fun Central Komitet Farn Kadenc-Jor 1946," p. 11,
YIVO at YV, JM/10262, Folder 3.

[19] "Liste fun Perzonen wos zajnen batrojt durch di Inere Farzorgung Optejlungen bajm C.K.," 13 May
1948, YIVO at YV, JM/10262, Folder 39.

In dealings with the military government, German officials, and with Jewish welfare organizations, especially the JDC, the Central Committee sought to assert its authority to represent Jewish DPs and to administer Jewish life in the DP camps. These efforts became more urgent in the summer of 1946 since conditions in the DP camps were deteriorating as DP frustration over lack of emigration possibilities increased and tensions mounted between Germans and DPs and U.S. troops and DPs. One positive piece of news came in June 1946, when the Judicial Section of the Central Committee reported that the State Commission for the Care of Jews in Bavaria recognized the right of DP authorities to issue replacement documents (e.g., birth certificates, identity papers, marriage licenses) to Jewish survivors, although it was not allowed to issue marriage certificates for new couples.[20] These documents were vital for DPs dealing with bureaucracies, particularly in the quest for visas. The granting of this official function to the Central Committee bolstered its claims as sole representative for Jews in the American Zone.

Relations with the JDC, strained by the survivors' criticism of the late arrival of JDC aid, became increasingly tense by the summer of 1946, as the Central Committee pressed for greater autonomy. DPs in general did not want to feel like charity cases, and the DP leadership in particular resented the controls the JDC insisted on maintaining. Needing to justify its expenditures to donors in the United States, the JDC hesitated to grant DPs a free hand in allocating JDC assets. Also, the JDC, as a welfare organization, needed to keep its distance publicly from the political activities of the Central Committee. The DP leadership resented any implication from the JDC (aka the Joint) that it needed American political tutelage, since survivors had known a strong tradition of self-government in prewar Poland and Lithuania. The Central Committee made its point in a scathing letter from Grinberg to the JDC director:

The men who have undertaken leadership in our many fields of endeavor are men far superior and far more capable than those sent in to assist us. It must also be said that these same individuals during their days of peace and security and thereafter in ghetto life held positions far more responsible than those now being held by themselves or by Joint workers. Any program instituted by the Joint can be executed by these people to a greater advantage for those concerned. It is our feeling that the Directors of the American Joint look upon us as DPs. ... an individual not only displaced in terms of a home but also in terms of vision and responsibility. ... The story of the Central Committee continues to be one of the great accomplishments whether it be in its Tracing Bureau, its newspaper, its hospitals, its clinics – all these created by the DPs with practically no assistance from any outside organization.[21]

While circumstances dictated that DPs rely on financial assistance from the American Jewish community, the DPs insisted that they were qualified to manage

---

[20] "Tätigkeitsbericht der juridischen Abteilung beim Zentralkomitee," 9 June 1946, YIVO at YV, JM/10263, Folder 44.

[21] Zalman Grinberg and David Treger, letter to Edward M. Warburg, 5 July 1946, YIVO at YV, JM/10262, Folder 36.

the distribution of those resources. Some of the members of the Central Committee had prewar experiences as Zionist or Jewish community leaders, and most had played leadership roles in the ghetto administrations and underground movements of wartime Europe. They viewed the JDC workers as pampered, inexperienced, and out of touch with the experiences and needs of European Jewry. DP leaders greatly resented implications that they were neither talented nor trustworthy.

Once the Central Committee understood the JDC's need to be accountable to donors, relations improved. One former JDC official who worked with the Central Committee recalled that as social workers JDC workers were happy to see the survivors standing up for their rights and their goals. "The only trouble is it went into two in the morning and they had better Sitzfleisch [ability to sit for a long time] than we did. Many decisions came at a point when we would say it's time to go home."[22] This tenacity paid off when the Central Committee was able to announce in August 1946 that "control of the economic office and all Joint warehouses has been transferred to the Central Audit Commission."[23] The reality of dependence on JDC funds still hampered the Central Committee's ability to carry out its most ambitious plans, but the victory on the principle of self-determination helped satisfy the survivors' demands for agency and for recognition as human beings equal to all others.

The Central Committee's next victory came on September 7, 1946, when U.S. General Joseph McNarney gave official recognition to the Central Committee of Liberated Jews in Germany. This recognition sanctioned many of the activities of the Central Committee and its role as mediator between Jewish DPs and the military authorities. Colonel Scithers became the liaison officer with whom the Central Committee then communicated and he was sympathetic to the aspirations of Jewish DPs, as we will see later. The Central Committee welcomed the move as an affirmation of its legitimacy and accomplishment. But when the Central Committee attempted to act on what it perceived to be its newfound authority, it discovered that the real power still lay in the hands of the military and UNRRA. Even so, the Central Committee's relations with the American forces were more cordial than those between the Central Jewish Committee in the British Zone and British authorities; the situation in Palestine heightened British suspicion of Jewish political leaders and DP distrust of the occupiers.

In April 1947 the British finally gave official recognition to Josef Rosensaft as "spokesman of the Jewish committee in Hohne Camp." This change in status was connected to the agreement of Belsen leaders to prevent the entry of infiltrees into the camp and came seven months after the U.S. military recognized the Central Committee of Liberated Jews in the American Zone.[24] The

---

[22] Theodore Feder, "Videotaped interview, by the University of Southern California Shoah Foundation Institute for Visual History and Education," Interview Code (IC) 10080, Segments (Segs.) 83–84, Visual History Archive (VHA) [on-line at subscribing institutions]; www.usc.edu/vhi.VHA.

[23] Blumowitsch, "Baricht Kadenc-Jor 1946," p. 11.

[24] British authorities had considered granting recognition in summer 1946 but feared the committee would lose incentive to help curb infiltration. Crawford, Control Office to BERCOMB, 8 August 1946, Public Record Office (PRO), Foreign Office (FO) 945/723 (microfilm, USHMM).

British also made it clear, however, that they would not recognize any committee representing Jews throughout the zone.[25] The British insisted that the DPs and German Jews should be treated separately on the supposition that DPs were mobile while German Jews were static. This argument was used to deny the Belsen committee the right to represent all Jews in the British Zone, but it also served British policymakers' desire to separate the question of DPs from that of Palestine. If German Jews could be encouraged to stay in Germany, it would demonstrate that Palestine was not the only answer to the Jewish refugee problem. The British also asserted that a Central Committee would increase antisemitism among the German population.[26] Official recognition had great symbolic significance for DPs but little real effect on their power.

THE MESSAGE OF ICHUD (UNITY)

Jewish DPs were determined to leave Europe. Many longed for a Jewish homeland where they would achieve a sense of belonging and of family. In their memorial ceremonies, DPs repeatedly expressed the belief that the dead wanted them to build a Jewish home in Eretz-Yisrael. Holiday observances and theatrical productions often emphasized the connection between the recent past and a future in Palestine. For a variety of reasons, DPs embraced what Mankowitz has called an "almost intuitive Zionism."[27] Zionism offered an explanation of the past and hope for the future. In a world of continued antisemitic violence, the need for a Jewish homeland seemed clear to many. As historian Avinoam Patt writes, "Zionism in the DP camps was thus not merely a monolithic Zionism geared solely to the requirements of the Yishuv; it filled the needs of many groups, productively, therapeutically, and diplomatically."[28] The survivors' determination to help create a Jewish state in Palestine stemmed both from political, ideological commitment and from psychological, emotional, and pragmatic impulses.

Older survivors often had prewar political experience, and a number of the emerging leadership had been active in the Zionist movement. Kibbutz Buchenwald leaders wrote to the Jewish Agency that "Most of us are Zionists of old; the rest, through prison and suffering have come to the realization that the only place for us is our own national home."[29] Veteran Zionists found their ideas falling on fertile soil. The lessons that DPs drew from the Holocaust led them to

[25] J. W. L. Ivimy, Foreign Office (German Section) to Berlin, 24 April 1947, PRO, FO 945/723.

[26] "Minutes of a meeting held on 18th June to discuss Jewish problems in the British Zone of Germany," p. 1, PRO, FO 945/723.

[27] Zeev Mankowitz, *Life between Memory and Hope: The Survivors of the Holocaust in Occupied Germany* (Cambridge: Cambridge University Press, 2002), p. 69.

[28] Avinoam J. Patt, "Living in Landsberg, Dreaming of Deganiah: Jewish DP Youth and Zionism after the Holocaust," in *We Are Here: New Approaches to the Study of Jewish Displaced Persons in Postwar Germany*, eds. Avinoam J. Patt and Michael Berkowitz (Detroit, MI: Wayne State University Press, forthcoming), ms. p. 33.

[29] "Homecoming in Israel: Journal of Kibbutz Buchenwald," in *The Root and Bough: The Epic of an Enduring People*, ed. Leo W. Schwarz (New York: Rinehart, 1949), p. 319.

FIGURE 15. Jewish DPs in the Neu Freimann DP camp protest British immigration policy to Palestine. The Yiddish banner reads, "We want to go back to our home in the Land of Israel." *Credit*: USHMM, courtesy of Jack Sutin

find in Zionism a coherent explanation for their past suffering and a program that led to an autonomous, secure Jewish future. In 1945 most DPs were adolescents and young adults searching for ways to forge a new sense of home and psychic nourishment (Figure 15). Israeli psychiatrist Shamai Davidson pointed out, "The Zionist ideology and the longing to go to Palestine was widespread [among this group] as an expression of fidelity to their family and people, as a reaching back into the destroyed pre-Holocaust life and its family and community ethos, as a means of realizing themselves as human beings again, as a transcendental triumph after years of struggle for physical survival."[30] They understood Zionism as a way of connecting to their lost families and of restoring Jewish values and community. Normal adolescent involvement in ideological issues and a desire for peer group bonding reinforced their attraction to the Zionist youth movements and kibbutzim.[31] If a survivor's parents or older siblings had been politically active, s/he was likely to connect with their political movement. Otherwise, social bonds drew individuals to particular youth groups and kibbutzim. Zionism was an expression of survivors' longing for family and for belonging to a Jewish community.[32]

The survivors experienced great disappointment at the failure of the democratic world to open their doors to them immediately after liberation. Only the Jews of the Yishuv appeared to want them. The DPs were needed to increase

---

[30] Shamai Davidson, "Surviving During the Holocaust and Afterwards: The Post-Liberation Experience," in *Holding on to Humanity – The Message of Holocaust Survivors: The Shamai Davidson Papers*, ed. Israel W. Charny (New York: New York University Press, 1992), p. 73.

[31] Davidson, "Surviving During the Holocaust," pp. 70–71.

[32] On the connection between social life, the search for surrogate family, and politics, see also Lavsky, *New Beginnings*, pp. 164–165.

the number of Jews in Palestine and to pressure world opinion to support the creation of a Jewish state. Recalling a visit by Jewish Agency officials to Föhrenwald, a former DP remarked, "They did not want for us to disappear here, there, and everywhere. Palestine was the place to go. They needed us, too. They needed us over there."[33] For some survivors, the indifference of the world community contrasted starkly with the active concern of the Yishuv. In the Zionist cause, survivors found purpose and significance. These developments convinced many survivors that a Jewish homeland in Palestine was the only answer to the DPs' emigration needs.[34] Reports of pogroms in postwar Poland persuaded those survivors who had hoped that a new order would permit Jewish–Christian coexistence that Jewish life could only be guaranteed in a Jewish homeland.[35]

Zionism promised self-determination. After years of being at the mercy of their persecutors' whims, survivors wanted to determine their own future. They were not interested in accommodating themselves to the world. The world now needed to respond and adapt to the demands of the Jews. They demanded equality with the nations of the world and that meant a state of their own own. Within this context the activities of the Jewish armed resistance movements grew in stature. Survivors valorized the ghetto fighters and partisans, emphasizing the role of Zionists in the wartime underground movements. Their demands for a Jewish homeland frequently referred to the part Jewish soldiers, ghetto fighters, and partisans had played in the Allied victory against Nazism.[36] In Belsen, the Central Jewish Committee proclaimed, "The Jews fought on various fronts on the side of the Allies against the Nazis ... and should enjoy the same rights as the Allies."[37] The desire to identify with Jewish resistance to Nazism and to assert Jewish dignity and self-determination in the present further fostered DP identification with Zionist goals.

There were few alternatives to Zionism in the DP camps. Of those survivors who had remained steadfast in their Communist or Bundist beliefs, many had repatriated to the East to participate in the building of socialism there. Bundism had advocated building Jewish life in the communities where Jews found themselves, viewing the solution of Jewish concerns as inseparable from that of the international proletariat; however, many Bundists had their hopes of Jewish coexistence in Eastern Europe dashed by the events of the war and postwar

---

[33] Hannah Modenstein, telephone interview by author, tape recording, 18 July 1995. Alicia Appleman-Jurman expresses a similar sentiment in her memoir, *Alicia: My Story* (New York: Bantam Books, 1988), p. 329.

[34] Biber, *Risen from Ashes*, p. 55.

[35] For an interesting discussion of how two leading DPs came to embrace Zionism, see Mankowitz, *Life between Memory and Hope*, Chapter 8.

[36] See, for example, "Landsberg Jewish Center," 15 November 1945, YIVO RG 294.2, MK 483, Reel 113, Folder 1564; Pachach, "Declaration" (in Yiddish), [June 1946?], YIVO RG 294.2, MK 483, Reel 113, Folder 1555.

[37] Dov Laufer, Central Jewish Committee Sekratariat, "Rundschreiben Nr. 25/10: An alle Gemeinden und Committees in der brit. Zone," 17 April 1947, YV O-70/13.

pogroms. Those who had experienced abandonment by the Communist under-ground movements in Nazi-occupied Europe or Soviet oppression either rejected Bundism or decided its future lay in the West.[38] The Bundists who remained in the DP camps joined with the Zionist majority in calling for the opening of the gates to Palestine even as they retained their belief that Jewish life in the Diaspora was possible in Western Europe and the United States.

A relatively large group of Polish Bundists was active in the camp administra-tion in Feldafing. Bundists found some common ground with left-wing Zionists just as in the prewar period they had occasionally formed alliances for self-defense. The vice-chairman of the Eschwege Camp Committee was a prewar Bundist, and other Bundists served the camp population through educational and medical work.[39] Bundist representatives attended the first Congress held in Belsen on September 25–27, 1945. Foreign dignitaries were also present, includ-ing Professor Selig Brodetsky, a member of the World Zionist Executive and the first Zionist to be elected president of the Board of Deputies of British Jews. One Bundist recalled, "One of the most eloquent speeches at the conference was by my friend Chawcia Rosenfarb. Although Brodetsky did not agree with some of her arguments and demands, he was so impressed with her speech, that he pub-licly acknowledged this and congratulated her."[40] The urgent desire for speedy emigration from Germany allowed ideological opponents to find common ground and to demonstrate a modicum of respect for one another.

The ultra-Orthodox Agudat Israel had been the dominant party of prewar Polish Jewish communal politics, rejecting Zionism and secular movements, such as the Bund. Yet the desire of Orthodox youth for certificates to Palestine in the last years before the war had led Agudat Israel to modify its positions some-what. It permitted male-only *hachsharah* (agricultural training farm), secured some immigration certificates from the Jewish Agency, and supported invest-ment in Palestine so that Orthodox Jews could lead religious lives in the Yishuv. It advocated for Jewish rights in Palestine but separately from other Jewish groups, including the Orthodox Zionist party, Mizrahi.[41] The postwar situation, however, led to an amazing amount of cooperation between these previously feuding groups.

Orthodox DP thinkers elaborated an understanding of the Holocaust as a familiar form of catastrophe (*hurban*). They emphasized that after each destruc-tion the Jewish people had been renewed. In the post-Holocaust era that renewal

---

[38] Biber, *Risen From Ashes*, pp. 57–59.

[39] Joseph Soski, "Memories of a Vanished World" (1991), pp. 88, 90–92, USHMM, 02.072.

[40] Soski, "Memories," p. 86. This recollection is in contrast to a fictional scene in Chava Rosenfarb's novel *Brif zu Abrashn*, in which the Zionists at the conference shout down her Bundist protagonist Miriam. Quoted in Yosef Grodzinsky, *In the Shadow of the Holocaust* (Monroe, ME: Common Courage Press, 2004), p. 77.

[41] Gershon C. Bacon, *The Politics of Tradition: Agudat Yisrael in Poland, 1916–1939* (Jerusalem: The Magnes Press, The Hebrew University, 1996), pp. 71, 77, 88–89, and 94; Celia S. Heller, *On the Edge of Destruction: Jews of Poland between the Two World Wars* (New York: Columbia University Press, 1977), pp. 167, 180.

was to be the return to the Land of Israel and the creation of a Jewish state. The lesson of the Holocaust was to be that the state and the Torah were intrinsically intertwined. As one scholar has noted, "The urge for *aliyah* was inseparable in the Orthodox mind from going to the only place where Torah could be properly and purely advanced and where the people could be filled with its living source. Only in the Holy Land could that pattern of assimilation which catalyzed God's release of Amalek be decisively ended. For the Orthodox survivors, Torah and state were inseparable."[42] The Shoah was understood as belonging to the flow of history in its similarity to earlier destructions but as unique in providing the opportunity to break the cycle. Orthodoxy and Zionism were reconciled in the call for a Jewish state based on the Torah.

Most survivors initially emphasized unity in their political life. Although some contemporary observers viewed the emphasis on unity as an unhealthy identification with the Nazis and remnants of totalitarianism,[43] there was little difference between Jewish survivor aspirations for national unity and those throughout postwar Europe. Just as the underground fight against Nazism in occupied Europe had led to the hopes of national unity governments, especially in France and Italy, the wartime cooperation of Jewish groups in the ghetto resistance movements and partisans led to a belief in the necessity for a united front. The lesson of the Holocaust, then, was that Jewish survival depended on unity of action. This was the message that the survivors wanted to bring to the Yishuv.[44] It also accounted for the initial cooperation of a wide spectrum of political groups in the DP camps.

The first shlichim of the Yishuv to reach the survivors were Jewish Brigade soldiers, who were sympathetic to the call for unity. Brigade soldiers had retained their individual ideological orientations, but service in the Brigade had taught them how to cooperate with those from differing movements. As a result, they were able to respect the DP desire for unity. Later shlichim, chosen after political wrangling between the Yishuv parties, were party loyalists intent on recruiting DPs for their movement since they would have an influence on Yishuv politics after their immigration. The arrival of shlichim in the DP camps in 1947 would contribute to political fragmentation in the American Zone.[45]

In 1945 the dominant political movement in the DP camps was the United Zionist Organization (UZO or *Ichud*). Under this banner a coalition of labor and Zionist parties presented a single list of candidates for DP camp elections.

[42] Gershon Greenberg, "From *Hurban* to Redemption: Orthodox Jewish Thought in the Munich Area, 1945–1948," *Simon Wiesenthal Center Annual* 6 (1989): 102.

[43] Pinson, "Jewish Life," pp. 113–114; Meir Ya'ari quoted in Anita Shapira, "Yishuv's Encounter with the Survivors," in *She'erit Hapletah*, p. 87.

[44] "Homecoming in Israel: Journal of Kibbutz Buchenwald," p. 323; Mankowitz, "Formation of She'erit Hapleita," p. 361. On the incompatibility of the survivors' lesson of unity and the political situation in the Yishuv, see Benjamin Bender, *Glimpses: Through Holocaust and Liberation* (Berkeley, CA: North Atlantic Books, 1995), pp. 220–221.

[45] Irit Keynan, "The Yishuv's Mission in Germany, August 1945–May 1946," in *She'erit Hapletah 1944–1948*, p. 239.

Most of these parties had their roots in prewar Poland, but their previous factional strife was temporarily suppressed by their common goals of advocating for survivor rights and a Jewish homeland in Eretz-Yisrael. In the first election for the Landsberg Camp Committee, the Ichud list won 81 percent of the vote on a platform promoting the preparation of agricultural workers for immigration to Palestine.[46]

The statements of two DP political parties, Agudat Israel and the Revisionist Zionists, exemplified the atmosphere of compromise. In the prewar period, Agudat Israel represented Orthodox Jewry and had refused to work with secular Jewish parties. In the face of an Ichud-dominated Central Committee in early 1946, Agudat Israel's leaders resolved that they would accept the single seat offered to them on the Executive Council and announced that "in view of the responsibility of the hour ... they are willing to work together on behalf of united Israel, for the honor of the Jewish people and their redemption."[47] The willingness to work side-by-side with secular Jewish parties represented a fundamental shift for Agudat Israel.

At the second congress of Agudat Israel in Germany in September 1946, leaders of the party addressed three concerns: the Land of Israel, the education of the youth, and the unity of Orthodox Jews. The president of the organization in Germany, Jicchok Zemba, proclaimed that his party "felt itself to be an integral part of the builders of the Land of Israel" and offered a blessing to the fighting Jewish Yishuv because "you fight for truth and righteousness."[48] In addition to this unprecedented support for secular Zionists in Palestine, these Orthodox survivors proclaimed their unequivocal desire for aliyah. "We have declared to Agudat Israel World Union that the Agudists of the She'erit Hapletah see for themselves nothing other than the Land of Israel and we continue to hold that position."[49] Frustration with the American Agudat Israel's emphasis on bringing DP Agudists to the States was evident, and there was also a meeting of the minds with Poale Agudat Israel in Palestine, a wartime Zionist offshoot of Agudat Israel.[50] DP Orthodox thinkers now viewed aliyah as facilitating the redemption of the Jewish people and the arrival of the messiah.[51]

On the question of youth education, the leaders noted the important work of their kibbutzim and decided to approach Mizrahi, the religious Zionist party,

---

[46] The opposition was headed by the camp police and street-cleaning department representing younger Polish Jews. Irving Heymont, letter of 20 October 1945, *Among the Survivors of the Holocaust – 1945: The Landsberg DP Camp Letters of Major Irving Heymont, United States Army* (Cincinnati, OH: American Jewish Archives, 1982), p. 62; "Noch di waln," *Landsberger Lager Cajtung*, 28 October 1945, p. 2.

[47] "Declaration from Agudat Israel" (in Yiddish), *Landsberger Lager Cajtung*, 5 February 1946, p. 8.

[48] Mosze Fridenzon, "2-te landes-konferenc fun Agudas-Jisroel in Dajczland," *Landsberger Lager Cajtung*, 25 September 1946, no page number.

[49] Fridenzon, "2-te landes-konferenc."

[50] In Belsen, Poale Agudat Israel had a large following among Orthodox DPs. Lavsky, *New Beginnings*, p. 163.

[51] Greenberg, "From Hurban to Redemption," pp. 103–105.

about creating a joint educational program. The conference noted that Agudat Israel had a voice in DP politics and had won the confidence of other political parties. Reflecting the general desire for unity among the survivors and their almost universal quest for a Jewish homeland, Agudat Israel in Germany's political agenda became more like that of Mizrahi. The lesson drawn from the Shoah was that Jewish life was no longer possible in the Diaspora. Only a Jewish homeland could secure the future of the Jewish people and the Torah. DPs from across the political spectrum called for unity.

The Revisionist party was a right-wing, antisocialist, secular Zionist organization that believed a Jewish state could be founded only through military victory and should include the territory of all of Palestine and Transjordan. It stood outside the mainstream of Yishuv politics.[52] Initially its DP leaders also opted for cooperation with the majority socialist Zionist parties within UZO. At an April 1946 meeting of 2,000 party members, the Revisionists declared: "In view of the Jewish condition in the Diaspora and in light of the heroic fighters in Zion, it is resolved to secure a united Jewish front. ... The holy duty to secure a Jewish government of national unity shall be a goal of the struggle and lead the people Israel to victory."[53] The willingness of left- and right-wing Zionists to work together was a remarkable development, as was the mutual tolerance of Agudists, Zionists, and Bundists in the initial postwar period.

FRAGMENTATION AND POLARIZATION

As the stay in the DP camps lengthened, factionalism reemerged. Frustrated by the lack of emigration opportunities and the failure of DP leaders to secure certificates to Palestine, DPs became increasingly restive, leading to the fragmentation of Ichud and the polarization of DP politics. By the summer of 1946, Jewish DP leaders had to acknowledge the hardening of the DP situation. Of the 1,000 certificates to Palestine issued for European Jews in February 1946, only 450 were assigned to Germany and Austria. British policy remained unchanged even in the face of increasing international pressure and illegal immigration. The April 1946 incident of the ship *La Fede*, during which illegal immigrants threatened suicide if they were not permitted entrance to Palestine, succeeded in its immediate goals of immigration for the passengers, but in the long run it strengthened British resolve in opposing immigrants and led to the far different conclusion of the *Exodus 1947* affair.[54] The refusal in late summer 1946 of the British government to issue 100,000 certificates as recommended by the Anglo-American Committee of Inquiry further contributed to the growing despair and

---

[52] On the history of Revisionsim and Betar, see Walter Laqueur, *A History of Zionism* (New York: Schocken Books, 1972), Chapter 7.

[53] "Erszte konferenc fun Rewizjonistn in der amerikaner zone," *Landsberger Lager Cajtung* 10 May 1946, pp. 6 and 7.

[54] Abram L. Sachar, *The Redemption of the Unwanted: From the Liberation of the Death Camps to the Founding of Israel* (New York: St. Martin's/MAREK, 1983), pp. 182–186.

frustration among DPs. As the DP camps began to seem less temporary, conflict with the German population and the military governments increased, and the united front became strained.

In addition to concerns about emigration, ideological differences that DPs had been willing to overlook initially became more irritating as time went by. In May 1946 the influential and Ichud-oriented *Landsberger Lager Cajtung* declared it incomprehensible that Bundists should have a following in Feldafing.[55] Competition for scarce resources and ideological differences over property aggravated divisions between various Zionist groups in the DP camps.[56] Although on the anniversary of the Bolshevik revolution in October 1945 the Marxist workers in Landsberg had proclaimed their willingness to fight for a Jewish homeland before joining the world proletariat, only eight months later the Poale Zion Left (PZL) seceded from Ichud. The left-wing Zionist party acknowledged that after liberation it had seemed promising to unite with other parties when immigration to Palestine was the only goal, but now faced with a long stay on the "bloody soil" of Germany, such unity was no longer justified. The PZL specifically denounced the destructive effects of "reactionary religious elements" fostered by Ichud.[57] Going forward, the PZL would advocate workers' interests, joining with other left-wing labor movements, such as Vaad Hapoalim (Workers' Council) and Dror, with the support of the Bund.[58] For many, this meant agitating for immigration to any country outside Europe, not only Palestine. Thus cracks in the united front were already present when Eastern European infiltrees and shlichim from Palestine arrived.

In December 1946, the first world Zionist conference following the war concluded with the decision to dissolve the unity that had been achieved in Poland between the Hashomer Hatzair and Dror youth movements. Even though many denounced the conference for undermining unity, young kibbutz members soon proclaimed loyalty to their own particular movement. Many of these young people had been members of the movements before the war, and their close bonds had often aided their wartime survival. With the movement of these groups into Germany, the factionalism spread from within the DP community as well as from the outside influence of shlichim. Those survivors who first joined a youth movement after the war also felt fierce loyalty to the organization that had provided them with a semblance of family and hope for the future. Their loyalty to the movements, though, had more to do with social ties than ideological ones.[59]

[55] "Cijonistisze noticn," *Landsberger Lager Cajtung*, 10 May 1946, p. 5.
[56] See Georgia M. Gabor, *My Destiny: Survivor of the Holocaust* (Arcadia, CA: Amen Publishing, 1981), p. 220; Shapira, "Yishuv's Encounter," p. 97.
[57] "Statement of the Central Committee of the Jewish Workers' Party" (in Yiddish), *Landsberger Lager Cajtung*, 14 June 1946, p. 7.
[58] Announcement of meeting of labor organizations in *Landsberger Lager Cajtung*, 12 July 1946, p. 5; Executive of the Bund groups in Germany, "Bulletin no. 1/48," February 1948, YIVO RG 294.2, MK 483, Microfilm reel 113, Folder 1552.
[59] Keynan, "The Yishuv's Mission in Germany," pp. 234–235.

There was also a pragmatic side to kibbutz membership. Membership in a kibbutz improved a survivor's chances of receiving a certificate for legal immigration to Palestine. Even those who were not committed Zionists might join a kibbutz to increase their opportunity for rapid emigration. For example, every member of Kibbutz Buchenwald hoped that being part of the kibbutz would expedite emigration from Germany. Only a minority "had Zionist leanings." Most wanted to escape the idleness in the assembly centers.[60]

The Jewish Agency for Palestine distributed certificates based on a key that reflected the proportional representation of political parties in the Yishuv. The kibbutzim affiliated with the dominant political parties in Palestine, therefore, received more certificates than, say, the Revisionist kibbutzim. Thus, DPs seeking entry to Palestine would be encouraged to join the favored kibbutzim, regardless of their personal political views. The distribution of certificates contributed to the growing factionalism among DPs that reflected the divisions within the Jewish community in Palestine. In Kibbutz Buchenwald, DPs argued over whether prewar Zionists should receive priority for certificates or whether it should be first come, first served.[61] As we will see at the end of this section, DPs in the British Zone rejected the Jewish Agency's key and based the distribution of certificates on the proportion of followers within the British Zone rather than within the Yishuv.

Fissures became publicly visible. Once DP leaders had prided themselves on the orderliness of their demonstrations, but as tensions mounted, both spontaneous and organized demonstrations against the camp committees took place. These unauthorized protests threatened the stature of the committees and their efforts to promote an image of DP unity and discipline. In May 1946, the Landsberg Camp Committee denounced unsanctioned demonstrations as counterproductive and "shaming the name" of the community.[62] Increasingly demonstrations took place in opposition to the DP leadership when Revisionists decried its moderate stance on Palestine and workers condemned employment practices.[63]

The political polarization of the DPs realized itself in the electoral successes of the Revisionsists and leftist labor parties. In July 1946, voters in Landsberg had a choice between two competing lists: UZO (representing moderate labor-Zionist organizations, Revisionists, a partisan organization, and a local kibbutz)

---

[60] Baumel, "Kibbutz Buchenwald and Kibbutz Hafetz Hayyim," p. 236.

[61] Baumel, "Kibbutz Buchenwald and Kibbutz Hafetz Hayyim," p. 238.

[62] *Landsberger Lager Cajtung*, 10 May 1946, p. 2. Interestingly, although most of the newspaper was printed in Latin type, this statement appeared in Hebrew lettering perhaps in an attempt to keep non-Jews from reading the message and taking delight in Jewish disunity.

[63] On April 17, 1947, free-living Jews in Munich demonstrated against the Central Committee for denying permission to demonstrate against the British hanging of four Irgun terrorists in Palestine. In Stuttgart, Revisionists called for a similar demonstration. In September 1947, the Stuttgart Committee came under attack from Jewish workers who accused the committee of improperly distributing rations and maintaining fictitious workers on the payroll. Report dated 18 April 1947; Jewish Affairs in U.S. Zone; PW & DP Branch (National Archives Microfiche 3/174–1/20); Civil Affairs Division (CAD); Office of Military Government United States (OMGUS), RG 260;

against the Progressives (representing the PZL, Vaad Hapoalim, and Dror). The Ichud-oriented camp newspaper called on its readers to vote for "nationally aware people for whom the interests of nation and land stand higher than personal and lesser interests."[64] The unpleasant nature of the campaign over emigration and the future of Palestine resulted in an unprecedented appeal from the Jewish members of the Landsberg UNRRA team to the DPs to vote based on the merit of the individuals and not along political lines.[65] In the end Ichud retained seven out of eight seats on the Camp Committee. The following month the Jewish community of Schwarzenfeld voted on two lists, and UZO again won a large majority. The Progressives had a respectable following but at first could not outweigh the combined weight of the moderate and right-wing parties joined in UZO.

Only a few months later, in the elections for the Twenty-Second Zionist Congress, both Progressives and Revisionists would demonstrate great gains. UZO, representing Mapai (the moderate labor movement in Palestine associated with David Ben-Gurion), Mizrahi, and General Zionists, received 33 percent of the vote. Close behind was the Workers' Bloc (Poale Zion, Hashomer Hatzair, Dror, partisans organized in Pachach, and Haoved), with 32 percent. The United Revisionist Party claimed 26 percent of the vote.[66] The Workers' Bloc had the prestige of resistance fighters and partisans from Pachach and the mobilized youth in the kibbutzim. The Revisionists had a militant, nonsocialist platform that appealed to the increasingly restive DPs. A majority of DPs had voted for the solutions offered by the far left and far right.

The leadership of the Central Committee faced its next election in January 1947. The United Zionists' list, now clearly affiliated with Mapai, won the highly contested election through a split of the extremist votes. The Revisionists, who frequently cooperated with UZO, garnered 18 percent of the vote, while the Progressive Left received just over 30 percent. The split allowed the center parties to dominate leadership positions, and an Army observer at the Bad Reichenhall Conference in February 1947 described Jewish leaders as "Zionists and usually fairly conservative middle class individuals."[67] Nevertheless, the Central Committee was at the head of a fragmented and increasingly polarized population.

Some smaller communities attempted to fight the trend toward polarization. In elections for the local committee, sometimes the political parties agreed to a unified list or surprising alliances occurred.[68] Most likely personal loyalties took

National Archives at College Park, MD (NACP); Jidiszer Komitet in Sztutgart, "Cu der Jidisz efntlechkajt!" [no date], YIVO RG 294.2, MK 483, Microfilm reel 70, Folder 1010; Sztrajk-komitet fun jid. Arbeter in Sztutgart-west un Degerloch to Jidiszn komitet Sztutgart, 1 September 1947, YIVO 294.2, MK 483, Microfilm reel 70, Folder 1010.

[64] J. Olejski, "Gedenkt!" *Landsberger Lager Cajtung*, 23 July 1946, p. 2.

[65] "Ofener briw cu der landsberger jid. bafelkerung," *Landsberger Lager Cajtung*, 23 July 1946, p. 2.

[66] See "Report of the Central Election Committee in the American Zone" (in Yiddish), *Unzer Weg*, 15 November 1946, p. 11.

[67] George S. Wheeler, Chief, Manpower Allocation Branch to Director, Manpower Division, "Report of Conference at Bad Reichenhall," 6 March 1947, Jewish DP Conferences; PW & DP Br. (Microfiche 3/173–1/21); CAD; OMGUS, RG 260; NACP.

[68] Yisroel Elenczajg, "Noch di waln," *Jidisze Cajtung*, 7 February 1947, p. 3.

precedence over politics in these areas, and those survivors with strong political differences would have moved on to a community more accepting of their views. In the January 1947 local elections, a new phenomenon of "the impartial" (*umpartejisze*) and "the independents" appeared on ballots. Although one DP journalist feared the susceptibility of this group to demagoguery,[69] it appears to have been an unsuccessful protest against the growing fragmentation of DP politics. The independent lists fared poorly at the polls. The progressive left and their opponents on the other extreme, the Revisionists, frequently in alliance with Agudat Israel, tended to draw the largest shares of votes.[70]

Survivors impatient with the apparent disinterest of the major powers in their cause turned to the Revisionists and their ideology of action. In Feldafing, Asher Schorr joined the Revisionist youth group Betar and received military training. On a visit to Landsberg, someone from Hashomer Hatzair, a leftist kibbutz, offered him a watch to join them, telling him "Betar are fascists; they want to fight for the Jewish state." Schorr replied, "So what! I want to also!"[71] The competition for members drove some shlichim to bribe potential members, but in this case the ideology of Betar proved more attractive to the DP. As a Föhrenwald leader of Betar told an old acquaintance, "The only reprieve is when daylight comes and I rush to participate in the morning training of the young pioneers. They give me the will to go on living. I will go and fight for a homeland for the Jews."[72] For this man, preparations for the fight for Israel alleviated the suffering of lonely, pain-filled, dark nights. The militant position of the Revisionists represented a way to reject the role of victim dictated to Jews by the Nazis and to overcome the indignities of the DP camps.

The workers' parties attacked the Revisionists for claiming to monopolize action. The League for a Laboring Eretz-Israel argued that the Revisionists "talk as though they are the leading fighters ... you see though that the English government sees its primary enemy in the worker communities, kibbutzim; there they search for weapons, there they arrest thousands of workers. They know that the primary force is the 'Haganah' – and not the 'Etzel' or 'Stern Group.' Yes, and the Revisionists don't even have a single kibbutz of their own."[73] In addition to Revisionists not being the dominant threat to British forces, the implication was that without a kibbutz the Revisionists did not have a positive program for the building of Jewish Palestine.

To make clear the danger of the Revisionists to the working class, campaign literature denounced them as strikebreakers. To make clear the threat they presented to all responsible Zionists, a poster for the Zionist-Socialist Workers Bloc displayed photographs of pioneers in Palestine over which loomed the outline of a hand plunging a dagger into their hearts. The text explained, "Revisionism – a

[69] Elenczajg, "Noch di waln."

[70] "Wajterdike rezultatn fun di komitet-waln," *Jidisze Cajtung*, 24 January 1947, p. 2; "Wajterdike rezultatn fun di komitet-waln," *Jidisze Cajtung*, 7 February 1947, p.2.

[71] Asher Schorr, "Videotaped interview," VHA, IC 16141, Segs. 81–84.

[72] Quoted in Biber, *Risen from Ashes*, p. 90.

[73] Etzel is another name for the Irgun. Campaign poster, YIVO at YV, JM/10260, Folder 10.

danger for our national independence and future. Not one vote for those who would tear down what we are building."[74] Here the British are absent and the true threat is Revisionist Zionism.

Meanwhile, Revisionists presented themselves as a party of unity with solutions to the DPs' problems. Running on List 4 as the United Zionists-Revisionists in the January 1947 Eschwege DP camp election, they rejected the class-based ideology of the workers' parties:

The only Jewish party that represents the entire people and that without exception does not make a distinction between Jews is the Revisionist Party. ... Give your vote to the list of the United Zionist-Revisionist Party that will continue the fight against the demoralization of the She'erit Hapletah. Protect the everyday interests of every camp resident. Vote for a traditional and national education of the youth. For substantially productive youth and elders until the final solution of the She'erit Hapletah problem through a full evacuation to Eretz-Israel.[75]

To further their claim to being the party of unity, the Revisionists posters for the 1947–1948 winter campaign equated their own success to that of the Jewish people and included the warning, "With the Revisionists' defeat comes your defeat."[76]

Although there were a few references to the need to improve life in the DP camps, all of the political parties emphasized that the future of Israel was at stake in the March 1948 election. Religious parties appealed to the memory of parents and the need to defend tradition against the secular parties. The middle-class General Zionists had characterized their supporter as a "national worker who places the nation's interest above his class interests ... who is for changing the situation of the She'erit Hapletah not just with words but with deeds."[77] The electoral results confirmed the decline of the centrist UZO and the sustained appeal of the Labor Bloc and the Revisionists. In the election a majority of DPs voted for the extremes. The Labor Bloc garnered 30 percent of the vote, while the Revisionists polled 21 percent. UZO came in third with 20 percent of the vote. Agudat Israel and the General Zionists each received 10 percent, and Mizrahi collected 9 percent of the vote.[78]

The results reflected DP dissatisfaction with the Central Committee, particularly in its failure to facilitate emigration.[79] The low voter turnout most likely stemmed in part from the perception that the Central Committee was unable to deliver on that most crucial issue. At the same time, the United Nations had already voted for the partition of Palestine and the United States Congress was

---

[74] Campaign poster, YIVO at YV, JM/10260, Folder 10.
[75] Campaign poster, YIVO at YV, JM/10231, Folder 252.
[76] Campaign posters, YIVO at YV, JM/10260, Folder 9.
[77] Campaign posters, YIVO at YV, JM/10260, Folder 7.
[78] Abraham S. Hyman, "Displaced Persons," *American Jewish Yearbook, 1948–1949* 50 (1949): 471.
[79] Angelika Königseder and Juliane Wetzel, *Lebensmut im Wartesaal* (Frankfurt a.M.: Fischer Taschenbuch Verlag, 1994), pp. 91–92.

debating the DP Act of 1948, and DPs could reasonably anticipate the imminent opening of immigration opportunities. Under this changed circumstance, control of the Central Committee did not interest the majority of DPs. In the end the election changed little. The Revisionists were excluded from power by the cooperation of the other Zionist parties and Agudat Israel. For the most part, UZO leaders remained in their positions. For example, David Treger, who had been chairman of the Central Committee, retained that position until his immigration to Israel in November 1948.

The Bund encouraged its members to vote for the left-wing labor parties, and the intrusion of American Bundists into DP political life further aggravated tensions. Initially DP Bundists had supported the Zionist program of immigration to Palestine, but the American Representation of the Bund in Poland, comprised of wartime refugees, rejected this cooperation. The most extreme of the Bund parties in its rejection of any cooperation with Zionists or the Yishuv, the American Representation strenuously opposed the decision of its parent organization, the Jewish Labor Committee (JLC), to aid immigrants to Palestine. The American Representation opposed the establishment of the State of Israel while the Bund in Poland offered its congratulations to the Yishuv.[80] The divergence in opinion between the Bund in Central Europe and the American Representation appears traceable to the differences in wartime experiences. One DP journalist noted, "The simple Bundist worker who on his own body endured the catastrophe has certainly learned much more than their leaders, theoreticians, and ideologues that sit content in their cabinets in America and sit comfortably away from the bloody soil of Diaspora-Europe."[81] Those Bundists who survived in exile in the States or in the Soviet Union did not necessarily internalize the sense of shared Jewish destiny felt by those who had suffered through German occupation until the war's end.

In 1947 there were 949 Bund members and their relatives in the German DP camps out of a total of over 200,000 Jewish DPs. Most of those who had participated in the early days of political unity had emigrated. Eighty percent of the remaining DP Bundists had survived in Soviet exile. Bund leaders in Poland and in the DP camps advocated that survivors be allowed to settle wherever they wanted, including Palestine; however, the American Representation rejected any accommodation to the Zionist position. American Bund publications began alleging Zionist intimidation and terrorization of Bundists in the DP camps. These charges were echoed in DP Bund publications. In a vigorous reply to the charges, a DP journalist blamed the accusations on paid party functionaries carrying out the policies of American and French Bundists.[82] Indeed, in 1947, the American Representation through the JLC had begun payments for personal relief to Bundists in the DP camps and to establish ten camp

---

[80] Daniel Blatman, *For Our Freedom and Yours: The Jewish Labour Bund in Poland 1939–1949* (London: Vallentine Mitchell, 2003), pp. 205–206.
[81] Mosze Leseny, "Di ofensiwe fun 'Bund' un zajne sibes," *Jidisze Cajtung*, 6 June 1947, p. 6.
[82] Leseny, "Di ofensiwe fun 'Bund.'"

organizations. Political violence in the DP camps occurred between all political factions, including Zionist on Zionist violence, but it is likely that the Bundist charges were exaggerated to encourage financial assistance from the American Representation.

A June 1947 emissary of the JLC investigated claims of Zionist intimidation in the DP camps. He found that Zionists were engaged in a campaign of persuasion and there was no coercion. His findings also confirmed reports from DP Bundists that Zionism had attracted a grassroots following among the DPs because of the Holocaust.[83] The American Representation, however, continued its invective against Zionists in the DP camps, contributing to the political fragmentation.

Given the inflammatory rhetoric of the Revisionists and the Workers' Bloc, it is not surprising that opponents frequently came to blows. As former DP Hannah Modenstein recalled, "The [leftist] Zionist organizations and the Revisionist organizations used to fight with each other. There were a lot of riots. ... Everybody was already saying how Palestine should be run and what should be done. There was a lot of controversy between a lot of people. It was good; it was healthy this way."[84] Although the rising conflict distressed those who had hoped the lesson of the Holocaust would forge a unified people with a single voice, for others the lively political debate marked a return to normalcy. DP child artist Samuel Bak noted the return of political, cultural, and class divisions among the DPs: "The healthy desire to re-create the familiarity of an imperfect society was an encouraging sign of normalcy."[85] Just as the dream of national unity was not sustained in the DP community, so, too, did the national unity governments of France and Italy fall to internal strife and international pressures during this time. While fragmentation may have been a sign of a return to normalcy, the polarization of the DPs and its accompanying violence suggested a reaction to the condition of long-term displacement.

JDC and UNRRA workers tended to view DP political agitation with suspicion, so it is perhaps not surprising that JDC psychiatrist Paul Friedman, who toured the DP camps in 1946 and worked with DPs detained on Cyprus in 1947, wrote warningly about the problems of long-term internment. Friedman noted that all survivors were predisposed to aggressive tendencies after years of persecution during which there was no outlet for their hostility. DPs who resettled recovered quickly, but "most survivors who have had to remain in the camps under continuous regimentation have grown more anxious and aggressive. Despite all that continues to be done for them, they see themselves betrayed and abandoned a second time."[86] Friedman's tone implies that the DPs were unreasonably ungrateful for "all that continues to be done for them." No aid from the JDC or UNRRA (or its successor organization, the International Refugee Organization) could replace independent living in a normal setting. The failure

[83] Blatman, *For Our Freedom and Yours*, pp. 202–203.
[84] Modenstein interview.
[85] Samuel Bak, "Landsberg Revisited," *Dimensions* 13 (1999): 33.
[86] Paul Friedman, "Road Back for DP's: Healing the Psychological Scars of Nazism," *Commentary* 6 (1948): 508.

of international organizations and governments to resettle the survivors quickly did constitute a form of abandonment. The DPs came to realize that failure when the hopes raised by the Anglo-American Committee of Inquiry came to naught in the fall of 1946, coinciding with the beginnings of political polarization.

Aid workers and scholars of other displaced populations have observed that the idleness of refugee camp life encourages fighting and political activism. The condition of homelessness and its accompanying feelings of powerlessness and despondency breed violence in refugee camps. This violence can take the form of fights between different political factions, recruitment for militant action against outside forces, as well as domestic violence.[87] Although DP sources are silent on the question of domestic violence, DP political aggression did increase as the perceived abandonment by the outside world encouraged DPs to take matters into their own hands. In 1946 and 1947, the shift of international attention away from the DPs and the lack of progress on the diplomatic front in winning immigration to Palestine made the Revisionist emphasis on military action more appealing.

Conflicts revolved around two key issues: meeting the present needs of the DPs (including employment and the possibility of immigration to countries other than Palestine) and Zionist debates concerning attainment and governance of a Jewish state. These conflicts had been present early on but were exacerbated "when various party partisans from Israel arrived."[88] Aware that the anticipated influx of DPs into Palestine could alter the political balance there, representatives of the Yishuv sought to recruit members for their own political parties. In the American Zone they had success in fragmenting the survivors' unity movement. Ichud became just another party on the electoral lists. While the promotion of party interests can be attributed to the Yishuv emissaries, they cannot be held responsible for the radicalization of the DPs. The Jewish Agency, dominated by Mapai in alliance with Mizrahi, sent shlichim according to a party key, meaning that they represented the political distribution of the Yishuv, which favored the centrist Mapai and its allies. The distribution of immigration certificates also depended on party affiliation. This policy had kept the number of Revisionist immigrants to Palestine in the prewar years small in relation to

[87] Dia Cha and Cathy A. Small, "Policy Lessons from Lao and Hmong Women in Thai Refugee Camps," *World Development* 22 (July 1994): 1055; Charles Foster, "The Palestinians in Lebanon: Singing Somebody's Song in a Strange Land," *Contemporary Review* 266 (1995): 282; Eva V. Huseby-Darvas, "'But Where Can We Go?' Refugee Women in Hungary from the Former Yugoslavia," in *Selected Papers on Refugee Issues: III*, eds. Jeffery L. MacDonald and Amy Zharlick (Arlington, VA: Committee on Refugee Issues of the General Anthropology Division of the American Anthropological Association, 1994), pp. 69–70, 73; Lynellen D. Long, *Ban Vinai: The Refugee Camp* (New York: Columbia University Press, 1993), p. 189; Emanuel Marx, "Palestinian Refugee Camps in the West Bank and the Gaza Strip," *Middle Eastern Studies* 28 (April 1992): 282; Elisabeth Mayer-Rieckh, *"Beyond Concrete and Steel": Power-Relations and Gender: The Case of Vietnamese Women in the Detention Centres in Hong Kong* (The Hague: Institute of Social Studies, Working Paper Series, 1993), pp. 58, 61.
[88] Biber, *Risen from Ashes*, p. 98.

their numbers in the Diaspora. Revisionists were at a disadvantage and yet they continued to attract DP support.

In the British Zone, however, survivors successfully resisted the factionalism sent from the Yishuv. Historian Hagit Lavsky has demonstrated that some Jewish Agency emissaries to the British Zone accepted the survivors' emphasis on unity, most importantly Kurt Lewin, the head of the Jewish Agency in the British Zone, who was accused of not keeping to party politics.[89] In addition to the personalities involved, British policy discouraged entrance of infiltrees into its zone of occupation, resulting in the majority of ideologically committed kibbutzim entering the American Zone. The Belsen leadership also demonstrated a remarkable unity of purpose that dealing with British, as opposed to American, authorities encouraged. The battle for Palestine took place in its own backyard. DPs' suspicions of British motives reinforced their determination to maintain a united front.[90]

Disillusioned by the party politics of the World Zionist Congress in December 1946, Belsen DPs turned their attention from Zionist internal politics to immigration to Palestine.[91] In January 1947 seven political parties had entered the election campaign in Belsen, but in the end the Central Jewish Committee reported with satisfaction, "Jewish Belsen, standing on the threshold of aliyah, understood the task for which it is responsible and put forward a unity list of all political parties to the satisfaction of the entire Jewish population of Belsen."[92] That same month British authorities announced that 350 of the 1,500 certificates for Palestine would be allocated to the British Zone of Germany. The Central Jewish Committee could claim some success in achieving emigration goals, whereas the DP leadership in the American Zone could not.[93] Remarkably, the Central Jewish Committee with the assistance of Kurt Lewin was able to modify the political key for the distribution of certificates so that Revisionists and Agudat Israel received numbers proportionate to their following in the British Zone and the Committee even allocated certificates to unaffiliated DPs.[94] The DP leadership in the British Zone remained committed to the postwar ideal of unity.

[89] Lavsky, *New Beginnings*, p. 201.

[90] Everything from British refusal to recognize Jews as a distinctive group until spring 1946, to the November 1946 closure of a DP fishery school, to the delayed recognition of the Belsen Committee in 1947 contributed to the perceived need to join against the British. The fishery school's kibbutz declared that "it understands this decision of the [Military Government] as a political attack." Norbert Wollheim, report on Jewish fishery school in Hamburg-Blankensee, 12 November 1946, YV O-70/13.

[91] Lavsky, *New Beginnings*, p. 197.

[92] Central Jewish Committee, "Rundschreiben Nr. 2/17," 23 January 1947, YV O-70/13; Central Jewish Committee, "Rundschreiben Nr. 23/8," 24 March 1947, YV O-70/13.

[93] British authorities rejected American military government requests to allot some of the certificates to Jewish orphans from the U.S. Zone. U.S. Military Governor General Clay first made inquiries in May 1947 and again in October 1947. General Lucius D. Clay to Lieutenant General Sir Brian H. Robertson, 3 October 1947, and Robertson to Clay, 21 October 1947, PRO, FO 1052/75.

[94] Lavsky, *New Beginnings*, pp. 205–206.

PREPARATION FOR PALESTINE

Anticipation of immigration to Palestine influenced camp life in many ways. The increasing conflict between Jews and British forces in Palestine encouraged clandestine military training. Vocational training programs featured instruction in skills geared toward the Palestinian economy. Cultural activities promoted familiarity with Yishuv language, politics, dance, and music. Fundraising campaigns by the Jewish National Fund also kept DPs engaged with life in Palestine. Whatever their personal plans for emigration, DPs could not escape the continuous activity on behalf of Zionist aspirations in Palestine.

Military preparation began immediately in the DP camps, led by former partisans and veterans.[95] Faye Schulman was one such former partisan. She volunteered to work for Brichah in Lodz before she and her husband themselves crossed the borders to Germany and entered Landsberg in 1945. There they joined other former partisans and engaged in Zionist work. They published a magazine called *Der Widerstand*, organized Zionist demonstrations, and purchased weapons on the black market for the Jewish community in Palestine.[96] Jewish Brigade soldiers aided in recruitment and training.[97] Betar ran a training camp led by Polish-Jewish veterans of the Soviet army and a Palestinian Jew.[98] DP police were also active in military activities. Police from Feldafing read German obituaries and then at night visited German widows and demanded their husbands' guns. These weapons were then prepared for transport and handed over to Haganah agents.[99] In Feldafing, Jewish police trained Irgun (Revisionist milita) recruits with wooden rifles.[100]

Survivors willing to attempt illegal immigration to Palestine were the primary recipients of training. Brichah agents organized unmarried young men and women in Eastern Europe and smuggled them into Germany, where they received weapons training. Other DPs recruited for illegal immigration in Germany were sent for one week of "self-defense" training.[101] Leo Silvers was a DP hired by UNRRA as a supply and transportation officer when a Brichah agent approached him requesting trucks for a nighttime operation. After consulting with a Jewish chaplain who promised to get him released should he be

---

[95] On Haganah activities in the DP camps and *giyus* (mobilization) see Avinoam J. Patt, *Finding Home and Homeland: Jewish Youth and Zionism in the Aftermath of the Holocaust* (Detroit, MI: Wayne State University Press, 2009), pp. 237–253.

[96] Faye Schulman, *Partisan's Memoir: Woman of the Holocaust* (Toronto: Second Story Press, 1995), pp. 221f. On the purchase of weapons, see Nathan Bram, "Videotaped interview," VHA, IC 34727, Seg. 41.

[97] Asher Schorr, "Videotaped interview," VHA, IC 16141, Segs. 80–81.

[98] Larry Reich, "Videotaped interview," VHA, IC 19145, Seg. 21; Samuel Silbiger Falsehaber, "Videotaped interview," VHA, IC 28336, Segs. 99–100.

[99] Frieda Reinstein, "Videotaped interview," VHA, IC 46129, Seg. 95.

[100] Schorr, "Videotaped interview," VHA, IC 16141, Seg. 81.

[101] David Boruchowicz, "Videotaped interview," VHA, IC 317, Segs. 25–29; Lea Finder, "Videotaped interview," VHA, IC 50787, Segs. 131–133; Julie Weingarten, "Videotaped interview," VHA, IC 27079, Seg. 158.

arrested, Silvers agreed. After the trucks were returned, the agent informed him that 400 infiltrees had been brought to Ulm, where they would be trained as soldiers before departing for Palestine. Later Silvers took a convoy of visiting dignitaries to Ulm. He was shocked when DP police initially refused them entry to the camp, until he realized that they had arrived during military training. Reflecting on his work for Brichah, Silvers proudly stated, "I was so glad I had a chance to contribute."[102] Silvers's experiences reflected the collaboration between DPs, agents from the Yishuv, and Allied personnel in the work of Brichah.[103] In 1947, with the arrival of infiltrees and the growing appeal of Revisionism and Betar, paramilitary training increased under the guise of physical exercise and agricultural work details.[104]

The British Foreign Office took notice of an UNRRA report that a group of Jews in Föhrenwald were selecting individual young people to be sent to Palestine. Those chosen joined the youth groups and "receive a certain discipline training, they have a kind of uniform and march round the camp with the Jewish Flag and Red Flags."[105] The leader of the movement came from Palestine and had resided in the camp for only two weeks. The British understood the significance of the mobilization for illegal immigration.

Drill formations and uniforms also disturbed some American officers, who viewed Jewish militancy as a threat to local calm and to their own authority. In April 1946 former partisans attempted to poison SS prisoners en masse in Nuremberg. The plot succeeded in killing a couple of hundred SS men, and the incident may have increased some American officers' suspicions that military activity in the DP camps could be directed at Germans. At Föhrenwald military officers abruptly cancelled the 1946 May Day demonstration, charging DPs of engaging in militaristic activity. UNRRA officials attempted to explain that UNRRA had distributed the clothing that appeared to be uniforms and that the marching, drills, and flags were similar to what occurred in scouting organizations in the United States.[106]

It is difficult to know whether the aid officials knew the extent of the military training. One former DP stated that an UNRRA officer at Feldafing trained DPs.[107] Henry Cohen, a former director of Föhrenwald, recalled that he had no "specific knowledge" of the Haganah activities that took place there, suggesting

[102] Leo L. Silvers, "Videotaped interview," VHA, IC 42476, Segs. 20–22.
[103] Not all Americans were sympathetic to Brichah. UNRRA drivers for Brichah caught crossing borders illegally could be arrested, although Jewish officers often secured their release. Charles Greenspan, "Videotaped interview," VHA, IC 3348, Segs. 192–198.
[104] Yehuda Bauer, *Flight and Rescue: Brichah* (New York: Random House, 1970), p. 94.
[105] "Extract from letter from Captain J.Y. Pembroke, UNRRA H.Q., American Zone," 6 May 1946, PRO, FO 945/655.
[106] Becky Althoff, JDC, to Henry Cohen, Director, UNRRA, Team 106, 3 May 1946, Zisman Papers, RG-19.047.02*07 (2 of 3); Abraham Zierer, Jewish Agency for Palestine, to Henry Cohen, "May Day Celebrations," 2 May 1946, Zisman Papers, RG-19.047.02*07 (2of 3); Henry Cohen to Sam Zisman, Director, UNRRA District No. 5, "Interference by military in May Day Celebration," 2 May 1946, Zisman Papers, RG-19.047.02*07 (2 of 3).
[107] Schorr, "Videotaped interview," VHA, IC 16141, Seg. 81.

that he had his own suspicions that he chose to keep to himself.[108] The JDC's Koppel Pinson claimed that the military drills, marching, demonstrations, and banners were the totalitarian legacy of Nazism.[109] Although this assessment appears to be consistent with his overall opinion of the survivors, there remains the possibility that Pinson was attempting to deflect attention from the actual purpose of military training.

While military training was essential for illegal immigrants who were intending to join the battle against the British in Palestine, DP leaders and relief organizations alike advocated vocational training for the DPs in the camps. All agreed that productive activity was essential for rehabilitation and protection against the demoralization of a long stay in the camps. A number of obstacles stood in the way. First, many survivors, exhausted after years of slave labor, wanted to rest. Second, DPs had no intention of contributing to the German economy. Third, DP camps lacked the necessary equipment and supplies for large-scale training. Fourth, those DPs who did receive training faced unemployment once they completed their course.

The Central Committee sent a delegation from the American Zone to Palestine in an effort to ensure that training matched the needs of the Yishuv and would smooth the absorption of new immigrants. DP leaders then waged a propaganda campaign to encourage DPs to prepare for immigration by learning a trade that was needed in Palestine. In the American Zone, the JDC and ORT had to guarantee military government authorities that equipment used in training courses and workshops would not come from the German economy. Workshops were established to provide employment for graduates, and a point system that allowed workers to buy items from JDC canteens made employment more attractive.[110] In the British Zone, aid workers and representatives from the Central Jewish Committee met to coordinate vocational training programs and decided to copy the payment system from the American Zone.[111]

Although vocational training programs did not reach optimal numbers of DPs, cultural ties to the Yishuv were apparent to all. Developments in Palestine made front-page news in DP newspapers. In addition to Jewish Brigade soldiers and shlichim who lived and worked among the DPs, political leaders and cultural figures from the Yishuv, such as David Ben-Gurion (Jewish Agency), Yaakov Zerubavel (Poale Zion and author) and Paula Padini (dancer), made well-publicized visits to the DP camps.[112] Concert programs included songs

[108] Henry Cohen, "The Anguish of the Holocaust Survivors: Talk at Conservative Synagogue of Fifth Avenue on Yom HaShoah," 13 April 1996, http://remember.org/witness/cohen.html, accessed 10 July 2008.

[109] Pinson, "Jewish Life," p. 113.

[110] Joseph J. Schwartz, "Europe's Jews Begin to Rebuild," *JDC Digest* 6/2 (March 1947): 2 and 12; "JDC News Month," *JDC Digest* 6/7 (December 1947): 13.

[111] Jewish Advisory Committee on Vocational Training, Minutes, 13 January 1948, PRO, FO 1052/80.

[112] Padini entertained 150,000 Jewish DPs in 20 camps in the U.S. Zone under the auspices of the JDC. "JDC News Month," *JDC Digest* 6/7 (December 1947): 13.

and dances from Palestine, and schools and kibbutzim taught them to young people.[113] Children performed plays in Hebrew, and newspapers urged DPs to learn Hebrew as the language of their future.[114]

The Jewish National Fund (JNF) also played a role in DP cultural life and in fostering connections between DPs and the Yishuv. Founded in 1901, the JNF raised funds for land acquisition and reclamation, community development, forestation, and agricultural research. Survivors organized on behalf of the JNF as a link to the dead and to a future in the Land of Israel. Organizers asserted that those who had opposed the JNF before the war "today they would be avid converts."[115] They proposed that the significance of the JNF for the She'erit Hapletah consisted of four factors: morally through a connection to the Land of Israel, educationally for Zionist work, politically to ensure that DPs would be a factor in Yishuv politics, and practically to acquire land for new immigrants.[116] At a meeting on January 30, 1947, JNF leaders resolved that camp committees would be required to contribute 10 percent of the proceeds from cultural events to the JNF.[117] In the DP camps the JNF organized "Blue and White" Purim balls both as fundraisers and as educational programs to raise awareness of JNF activities and their relevance to the survivors.[118]

For Rosh Hashanah (Jewish New Year) the JNF sold greeting cards that depicted the Land of Israel (Figure 16). Even on non-JNF cards, the themes of aliyah and Palestine were prevalent, depicting ships and planes headed toward Palestine (sometimes with the photographs of the senders positioned as passengers), scenes of Haganah forces, and locations in Palestine. Even a card with a more traditional motif, decorated with the Ten Commandments and a man blowing the shofar (ram's horn), contained the text "Gather our dispersed from the uttermost parts of the world." In this version, the shofar did not sound to awaken the penitent soul but to herald the return to Zion. These greeting cards differed greatly from prewar Rosh Hashanah cards that favored three themes: religious scenes related to the holiday, photographs of the senders, and scenes from the senders' hometown.[119] The holidays of the Jewish calendar

---

[113] See, for example, "Programme of the Concert of the Jewish Orchestra in Bavaria," 14 November 1945, YIVO RG 294.2, MK 483, Microfilm reel 113, Folder 1564.

[114] For example, the *Landsberger Lager Cajtung* ran many Yiddish-language slogans promoting Hebrew, such as "Your aliyah is at the threshold – do you know Hebrew?" (12 July 1946, p. 1), "one people – the Jewish people; one land – the Land of Israel; one language – Hebrew" (19 July 1946, p. 3), and "Hebrews: Speak Hebrew!" (9 August 1946, p. 4).

[115] Mosze Lestny, "Di banajung fun Keren-Kajemet-arbet in Dajczland," *Jidisze Cajtung*, 1 November 1946, p. 3.

[116] Lestny, "Di banajung."

[117] Hawad Hamkomi, l'K.K.L., to Komitet bajm D.P. Center in Stuttgart [February 1947?], YIVO, RG-294.2, MK 483, Microfilm reel 70, Folder 1010.

[118] "KKL-ball in Starnberg," *Jidisze Cajtung*, 24 January 1947, p. 11; "Impozante Keren-Kajemet-fajerung in Fürth," *Jidisze Cajtung*, 21 February 1947, p. 6; "Keren-Kajemet-tetikajt in Deggendorf," *Jidisze Cajtung*, 28 March 1947, p. 8.

[119] Assorted New Year's Cards, YIVO RG-294.2, MK 483, Reel 113, Folder 1565. See http://www1.yadvashem.org/exhibitions/from_our_photo_archive/data/rosh_hashana/home_rosh_hashana.html, accessed 12 July 2008.

FIGURE 16. Personalized Jewish New Year's card sent in September 1948 by a Jewish DP couple living in Stuttgart, Germany. The card is decorated with a map of Israel and a boat with the Hebrew word for Israel, a reference to the newly independent State of Israel. *Credit*: USHMM, courtesy of Fela and Natan Gipsman

provided opportunities to link Jewish DPs with a Jewish future in Palestine, through blending traditional cultural practices with the activities of the JNF. DPs could imagine their contributions to the JNF financing projects that would ultimately facilitate the DPs' absorption into the Yishuv.

EMIGRATION OR ALIYAH?

Zionist leaders contrasted the purposelessness of emigration and its limited ambition of simply leaving Germany with aliyah and its goal of building a Jewish state in the Land of Israel.[120] Although the vast majority of DPs participated in the Zionist culture of the DP camps and responded on questionnaires that their first choice for immigration was Palestine, approximately 40 percent of them relocated elsewhere. In making their immigration choices, personal considerations often outweighed political allegiances, although the survivors remained committed to furthering the ideal of a Jewish national homeland.

Just as the desire for a surrogate family encouraged many DPs to enter the embrace of kibbutzim and to dream of a Jewish state, those survivors who had relatives in other parts of the world were often eager to be reunited with them. When asked by an interviewer why he had chosen the United States, Berthold Zarwyn replied, "Of course that is where I wanted to go; that is where I had my family."[121] Larry Reich was preparing for aliyah with a Betar kibbutz when he discovered extended family in the United States. When he persisted in his decision to go to Palestine, his grandmother said, "Why don't

---

[120] Yaakov Zerubavel quoted in "3-te land-konferenc fun linke P.C. in Dajczland," *Jidisze Cajtung*, 18 February 1947, p. 5.
[121] Berthold Zarwyn, "Videotaped interview," VHA, IC 41186, Seg. 21.

you come see me first?" His kibbutz leaders let him go with his promise that he would never forget Israel.[122] Shortly after illness had delayed Freda Narev's departure on Aliyah Bet (illegal immigration to Palestine), she received a letter from a cousin in New Zealand and somewhat reluctantly decided to immigrate there.[123] Among the more public figures making the choice to join family was Samuel Gringauz, who in September 1947 immigrated with his son to the United States to join relatives there, perhaps explaining his unwillingness to head a DP Zionist organization despite his obvious Zionist sympathies.[124] The desire to be part of a family again took precedence. For many the decision to forego aliyah, even for the opportunity to join family elsewhere, came with great difficulty.

The fear of detention on Cyprus drove many young families to abandon thoughts of illegal immigration.[125] Unwilling to remain indefinitely on German soil, they looked for other possibilities. Joseph Biber had resisted his brother's entreaties to join him in Argentina, since he planned to make aliyah with his small family. A decisive moment for him came with the visit of Poale Zion-Left leader Yaakov Zerubavel from Palestine. Zerubavel told the DPs, "You need rest. You need comfort. I know how you are all ready to go immediately to Israel, to fight and to struggle again until we have an independent country. ... I think it is time for American Jews to help rebuild the land of Israel by coming from America. ... So let them come to Palestine and you go for a little rest to America. It is a fair exchange."[126] This permission from a Zionist leader allowed Biber to accept his brother's next suggestion: that they meet in the United States and together immigrate to Israel from there.

Other survivors found it easier to give up their plans of immigration to Palestine when they were advised to do so by an authority figure. Lucy Berger's daughter suffered from a heart defect. When she mentioned her plans of immigration to Palestine to the pediatric specialist, he told her that they needed to go

---

[122] Larry Reich, "Videotaped interview," VHA, IC 19146, Seg. 22. Other survivors made similar decisions to join family. See Abe Bobrow, "Videotaped interview," VHA, IC 7659, Seg. 10; Roman Kriegstein, "Videotaped interview," VHA, IC 10183, Seg. 67; Molly Preis, "Videotaped interview," VHA, IC 4582, Seg. 42; Max Silbernik, "Videotaped interview," VHA, IC 3067, Seg. 104.

[123] Freda Narev, "Videotaped interview," VHA, IC 38341, Seg. 16. Another DP received Betar military training but decided to join family members in the United States. Carl Kauman, "Videotaped interview," VHA, IC 14318, Seg. 12.

[124] Alex Gringauz, "Videotaped interview," VHA, IC 24880, Seg. 18; Mankowitz, *Life between Memory and Hope*, pp. 190–191.

[125] William Eisen, "Videotaped interview," VHA, IC 20139, Segs. 21–22; Regina Fields, "Videotaped interview," VHA, IC 22256, Seg. 162; Mira Trocki, "Videotaped interview," VHA, IC 43685, Seg. 198; Ruth Minsky Sender, *To Life* (New York: Macmillan Publishing, 1988), p. 77. Erna S. Rubinstein and her husband attempted illegal immigration but got caught trying to leave Germany. Feeling fortunate to have escaped back to the Erlangen DP camp and then expecting their first child, they decided to wait for immigration to the United States. *After the Holocaust: The Long Road to Freedom* (North Haven, CT: Archon Books, 1995), p. 105.

[126] Biber, *Risen from Ashes*, p. 67.

to the United States for her daughter's medical care.[127] Another couple whose young child had died in Germany told a rabbi of their plans to make aliyah and to rebury their child in the Land of Israel. The rabbi suggested that since legal immigration was not possible, they should go elsewhere and immigrate to Israel later.[128] These survivors needed the legitimating permission of an authority figure to allow them to abandon temporarily the Zionist goal of moving to Palestine. Many of them planned to immigrate to Israel at a later time.

Harsh conditions in Palestine also dissuaded some survivors from immigrating there immediately. Many received letters from friends and families who had preceded them to Palestine, advising them to go elsewhere at least until conditions in Palestine improved.[129] In the first three years following Israeli independence the country received more than 600,000 Jewish immigrants, doubling its Jewish population and exceeding its ability to absorb them. Josef Rosensaft visited Israel in April 1949 and discovered former Belseners living in squalid conditions. Upon his return to Belsen, Rosensaft gave a major speech informing the DPs that Israel was wonderful but difficult. He urged them to make aliyah as long as they were prepared for harsh conditions. Although the Rosensafts had already shipped Hadassah's dental equipment to Israel, they chose not to make aliyah.[130] Like most survivors who emigrated, the Rosensafts remained active in Zionists affairs and maintained close ties to Israel.

Generational differences over the question of aliyah created difficulties. In some families, the parents wanted to immigrate to Palestine but their children resisted. One boy felt his parents were old-fashioned because they wanted to go to Palestine and were too religious. "No longer certain that they were going to Palestine because of the lack of legal certificates [the parents] felt that they ought to learn English to keep abreast of their young son."[131] Later, the father heard from relatives in the United States and made plans to immigrate there as soon as possible.[132] The boy's intransigence and the lack of legal immigration opportunities had opened the parents to the possibility of moving to the States; the discovery of relatives decided the matter. For Wanda Mehr the question of Palestine was decided by her young daughter, who had survived the war hiding in a Polish family. The daughter was fearful of going into a war zone, and given

---

[127] Lucy Berger, "Videotaped interview," VHA, IC 11681, Segs. 53–54. Another physician told Rose Huppert that she would not survive in Palestine. Rose Huppert, "Videotaped interview," VHA, IC 24268, Segs. 103–104.

[128] Edda Birnbaum, "Videotaped interview," VHA, IC 983, Segs. 55–57.

[129] Sylvia Friedman, "Videotaped interview," VHA, IC 26955, Seg. 21; Judith Ginsburg, "Videotaped interview," VHA, IC 24132, Seg. 139; Anna Rozen, "Videotaped interview," VHA, IC 5256, Segs. 86–89; Rachela and Sam Walshaw, *From Out of the Firestorm: A Memoir of the Holocaust* (New York: Shapolsky Publishers, 1991), pp. 139–140.

[130] Hadassah Rosensaft, *Yesterday: My Story* (Washington, DC: United States Holocaust Memorial Museum, 2004), p. 120.

[131] Becky Althoff, "Report on Israel S.," pp. 1–2, attached to "Semi-monthly Report," June 21, 1946, USHMM, Henry Holland Collection, RG-10.146.01.

[132] Becky Althoff, "Report on Israel S.," p. 4.

the difficulties in readapting children to their Jewish families, it is not surprising that Mehr complied with her daughter's wishes. Since she would not be finding a surrogate family in the Jewish state, Mehr followed friends who had immigrated to Australia.[133]

Older children tended to be in favor of immigration to Palestine. One girl who had survived the war in hiding wanted to go to Israel. She thought "if I went to Israel I'd be like everybody else; I'd no longer be different."[134] Having lived in fear of being discovered to be Jewish, she longed to be safe as a Jew among other Jews. Roman Ferber joined Betar in Belsen and dreamed of being a rabbi in Israel.[135] In both cases, the children's parents chose to bring their families to the United States. Lila Millen wanted to go to Israel, but concern for her weak father led her to choose to rejoin her father's sister in New York.[136] The fear of entering a war zone and the potentially harmful health effects of an unfamiliar climate prevented many from choosing aliyah.

Like in prewar Germany, it often was women who determined whether or not the family immigrated to Israel. Husbands who were willing to fight for Israeli independence found themselves coming up against the opposition of their wives, who were unwilling to risk losing their husbands in combat.[137] The arrival of infants also influenced Jewish DP women to opt for immigration to places other than Palestine.[138] Despite the ideal of the Zionist mother, DP women often could not face endangering the lives of their husbands and children by moving to a war zone. As survivors of war and genocide, they could not harbor any romantic notions about combat. For many, illegal immigration to Palestine was too dangerous to attempt with an infant. Former partisan Faye Schluman was among those Zionist women who found that motherhood altered their priorities concerning emigration. Anxious to leave Germany as soon as possible, she and her husband applied for emigration and went to the first country that accepted them: Canada.[139] Determined to raise Jewish children outside of Germany and frustrated by British restrictions on immigration to Palestine, many DPs put their Zionist dreams on hold and resettled at the first opportunity.[140]

A few survivors were forced to leave Germany at the earliest opportunity or face legal consequences. Charged before a military court with blackmarketeering,

[133] Wanda Mehr, "Videotaped interview," VHA, IC 26609, Segs. 575–576.

[134] Anne Levy, "Videotaped interview," VHA, IC 28991, Seg. 19.

[135] Roman Ferber, "Videotaped interview," VHA, IC 43707, Segs. 115–116.

[136] Lila Millen, "Videotaped interview," VHA, IC 43507, Segs. 14–15.

[137] Ned Aron, "Videotaped interview," VHA, IC 7724, Segs. 180–181; Abe Tauber, interview with the author, audio recording, Los Angeles, CA, 4 June 2007.

[138] One DP wanted to raise her children in the United States and registered for U.S. visas despite her husband's refusal to go up until the last minute. Sara Hauptman, "Videotaped interview," VHA, IC 28669, Seg. 37.

[139] Schulman, *Partisan's Memoir*, pp. 222–223.

[140] See Sara Tuvel Bernstein, *The Seamstress: A Memoir of Survival* (New York: Berkley Books, 1997), pp. 315–316; Bertha Ferderber-Salz, *And the Sun Kept Shining* (New York: Holocaust Library, 1980), pp. 230–232. Also, Hilde Mantelmacher, interview by the author, tape recording, Harrisburg, PA, 31 March 1996 and Modenstein, interview.

Morris Berman was given three months to leave Germany or else go to jail. Using identity papers issued to him in his cousin's name, Berman was able to use his cousin's papers to emigrate.[141] In a similar case, Germans arrested Herschel Balter and charged him with smuggling since he was listed as co-owner on a truck that had been used in illicit activity. A friend came with a lawyer to get him released from jail and put his name on a list for immigration to Australia. He was called within seven days and accepted because of his experience as a mechanic.[142] His legal difficulties encouraged him to accept the first opportunity for emigration. It was her fear that her husband would murder the German doctor who delivered their stillborn child that led Gina Freiden to ask the JDC for help in emigrating. She registered for Palestine, Australia, and the United States and told her husband that they would go to whichever country came through first. It was the United States.[143] Personal considerations were frequently the primary determinant for the choice of destination.

Disillusionment with Brichah tactics also led some survivors to choose alternatives to Palestine. Leo Weber blamed Brichah couriers for not preventing his parents' death when their transport came under attack from Polish units. The Jewish Agency offered the surviving children immigration certificates. Although his sister accepted and immigrated to Palestine, Weber, however, viewed this offer as a bribe and admission of guilt. He immigrated to the United States.[144] Brichah agents took help wherever they could find it, and this alienated another DP. Zwi Rosenwein worked for Brichah from 1946 to 1948 and recalled that the shlichim had the attitude that "everything is allowed for the purpose of building Israel." For Rosenwein, staying away from the Germans and remembering what they had done to the Jews was more important. Although Palestine was his ideal, he immigrated to the United States in 1949. As he remarked, "it was a revolution in my way of thinking."[145]

Ideological concerns sometimes led DPs to destinations other than Palestine. Bundists were likely to join their friends and family in France, Belgium, or the United States. During the war Vaad Hatzalah had saved a number of prominent rabbis from Eastern Europe, and their ultra-Orthodox, anti-Zionist followers sought to join them in the United States. After the fledgling Israel Defense Forces (IDF) sank the ship *Altalena* in June 1948 to prevent its cargo of weapons from reaching the Irgun, some Revisionists decided to go elsewhere until the political climate in Israel changed.[146]

Yet for all of the difficulties involved in illegal immigration and in life in Palestine/Israel, the majority of DPs chose aliyah. Approximately 37,000 Jewish DPs from occupied Germany and Austria attempted illegal immigration in the

[141] Morris Berman, "Videotaped interview," VHA, IC 19960, Seg. 32.
[142] Herschel Balter, "Videotaped interview," VHA, IC 35851, Segs. 429–437.
[143] Gina Freiden, "Videotaped interview," VHA, IC 24815, Segs. 102–104.
[144] Leo Weber, "Videotaped interview," VHA, IC 7919, Segs. 127–128.
[145] Zwi Rosenwein, "Videotaped interview," VHA, IC 1598, Segs. 154–157.
[146] Yechiel Haberman, "Videotaped interview," VHA, IC 43122, Seg. 21.

years 1945 to 1948.[147] In the year 1946, nearly 10,000 DPs left the American Zone of Germany on illegal immigration to Palestine. That same year, 4,135 Jews left the American Zone for the United States, 1,217 to South America, 82 to Australia, and 310 to European countries.[148] The following year, the very real possibility of detention on Cyprus discouraged some DPs from attempting illegal immigration, and yet approximately 20,000 more attempted the journey from Germany. Another 7,450 legally immigrated to Palestine from 1947 until May 1948, 6,000 of them from the British Zone through Operation Grand National.[149] In that same period another 10,000 Jewish DPs entered the United States. Despite all of the hardships, DPs left for Palestine, legally and illegally, at a rate more than double that going to the United States. Sara Dembowski's husband wanted to go to the United States where she had family, but Dembowski wanted to join her other relatives in Palestine. She told him, "We were in camps; we suffered so much, at least in Israel we are in the Jewish state."[150] The desire to be at home, among one's own people, motivated many survivors in their quest for a Jewish state in Palestine.

THE BUSINESS OF EMIGRATION

Leaving the DP camps involved overcoming a number of bureaucratic hurdles and closing the European chapter of one's life while preparing for a new one in an unknown environment. With the creation of the State of Israel on May 14, 1948 and the passage of the DP Act of 1948 by the U.S. Congress, DPs finally had legal options for emigration. Other countries began offering immigration schemes to recruit workers for particular industries. In their desperation to leave Germany and the DP camps behind them, DPs found creative ways around the bureaucratic obstacles of documents and medical exams. Other DPs found new business opportunities in assisting emigrants. Emigration became quite a business.

JDC and the Hebrew Immigrant Aid Society (HIAS) offices assisted DPs with locating host countries for which DPs needed sponsors or special trades. They helped with preparing visa applications, arranging medical exams, and checking affidavits. The JDC's legal department in Germany also filed petitions with the

---

[147] The numbers of illegal immigrants provided by Arieh J. Kochavi, *Post-Holocaust Politics: Britain, the United States, and Jewish Refugees, 1945–1948* (Raleigh, NC: The University of North Carolina Press, 2000), p. 235. The number may have been higher. Abraham S. Hyman put the number of illegal immigrants who passed through Germany at 40,000. "Displaced Persons," *American Jewish Year Book* 50 (1948–1949): 471.

[148] Mankowitz, *Life between Memory and Hope*, pp. 272–273. Similar figures are found in "Reconstruction – JDC's Task for 1947," *JDC Digest* 6/1 (January–February 1947): 12.

[149] The Zionist priority on fighting men resulted in Jewish men from the U.S. Zone being smuggled into Belsen to receive certificates. Approximately half of the DPs leaving on Grand National were not originally from the British Zone. Lavsky, *New Beginnings*, pp. 208–209.

[150] They made the illegal journey and spent time in detention on Cyprus before reaching Israel. Sara Dembowski, "Videotaped interview," VHA, IC 1635, Segs. 26–28.

High Commissioner's Clemency Board to clear the records of minor offenders for their visa applications.[151] Even with this assistance, survivors had much bureaucracy to navigate on their own.

Legal emigrants needed documents to complete their visa applications. Survivors often did not have birth certificates, marriage licenses, or divorce decrees. Even if authorities in their former countries had been inclined to assist them, the war had destroyed many records. These documents were especially necessary for immigration to destinations other than Palestine. The United States agreed to accept a DP's sworn statement if it could be demonstrated that all attempts had been made to obtain the written records. HIAS advised DPs to request that their sponsoring relatives submit sworn affidavits attesting to the DPs' parents' names and their places and dates of birth.[152] German authorities granted the Central Committee in Munich the power to issue replacement documents, and this greatly assisted DPs in proving their identities to bureaucrats.

Married DPs who wished to emigrate as a family needed to provide marriage certificates. To their distress, DPs learned in 1946 that their postwar marriages performed by rabbis were not valid under German or international law. In prewar Poland marriages officiated by a rabbi were valid if the rabbi also was a designated registrar, but after January 1, 1946 a marriage had to be solemnized before a civil registrar independent of a clergyman.[153] This legal situation also affected Hungarian Jews in Germany because of similar laws in Hungary. DPs who wished to have the legitimacy of their marriages and their children recognized by civil authorities, therefore, needed to record their marriages before a German registrar. Approximately 2,500 marriages in the British Zone were affected by this legal state of affairs.[154] DP leaders at Belsen objected to the idea of going before German officials. The British arranged that Belsen would be its own *Standesamtsbezirk* (registration district) and that a German Jew would be the registrar.[155] In the American Zone UNRRA workers provided DPs with certificates attesting to their religious marriages and requesting that German registrars record them.

DPs immigrating to the United States under the DP Act of 1948 had to provide proof that they had been in Germany permanently since no later than December 22, 1945. This cutoff date meant that those survivors who had returned home in the search of family and did not return to Germany until after December 22, 1945 were not eligible. Also, the vast majority of Jewish DPs were infiltrees from

[151] Student thesis, "The Displaced Jews," p. 35, Central Zionist Archives (CZA), Shalom Adler-Rudel Papers, A140/161.

[152] M. Kraicer, Zone Director, HIAS HQ Hannover Region, "Bekanntmachung: Betreffs Ausreise nach U.S.A.," 15 December 1948, Lady Rose L. Henriques Archive, Wiener Library, London (Microfilm reel 35, United States Holocaust Memorial Museum).

[153] Dr. Weis, Jewish Relief Unit (JRU) Legal Advisor to All JRU Representatives, "Marriages of D.P.'s," 26 May 1946, Henriques Archive, Microfilm reel 31.

[154] H. Romberg, Legal Division Main HQ, Control Commission for Germany, "Marriage of Jewish DPs," 29 May 1946, Henriques Archive, Microfilm reel 31.

[155] Dr. G. Weis to R. L. Henriques, 12 December 1946, Henriques Archive, Microfilm reel 31.

Eastern Europe, primarily Poland, who entered Germany in 1946 and 1947. The need to prove earlier entry to Germany resulted in a mini-business for German registrars and their Jewish middlemen. In exchange for a fee, Germans made false log entries to backdate residency papers for DPs.[156]

Documents needed to be supplied in translation. Jewish DP businesses advertised their translation services for marriage and birth certificates and diplomas. They offered assistance in procuring travel papers and information regarding emigration. Photographers directed advertisements toward emigrants, not only for the requisite passport photo but also for photographs to give as mementoes to friends and as introductions to family abroad.[157] With all of their documents in order, DPs received their coveted visas.

The next hurdle was the dreaded medical exam. Rejection because of an x-ray showing a spot on the lung could be devastating for survivors so close to finally leaving Germany. Some emigrants were deferred for three months to see if the x-ray showed active tuberculosis or old scars. Anxiety over the exams was great.[158] Some DPs found their way around this requirement, however. When Erna Rubinstein's husband's x-ray came back positive for tuberculosis, Rubinstein appealed to her colleagues in the IRO for help. Two days later a second x-ray came back clear, after a conference of the German doctor and emigration officials. Rubinstein credited the IRO representative's intervention for getting them clearance.[159] Those DPs without such connections could get the desired result for a price. Sara Hauptman's husband finally agreed to join her in immigrating to the United States but failed his medical test. Another survivor told Hauptman that she needed to bribe the x-ray technician with $50. She gave the technician twice that amount and her husband passed his medical test.[160] For those who suspected in advance that they had lung problems, they could hire a DP stand-in.[161] Germans and Jews alike could make a profit from this aspect of emigration.

DPs leaving Germany could only take very little out of the country with them. Allied occupation laws prohibited them from possessing foreign currency, and German currency could not be exchanged outside of Germany.[162] Currency restrictions were enforced.[163] For example, a friend came to visit young Roslyn Lowy

---

[156] Zoltan Marek, "Videotaped interview," VHA, IC 1767, Segs. 115–116; Charles Sternbach, "Videotaped interview," VHA, IC 8981, Segs. 101–102.

[157] Business advertisements, YIVO RG 294.2, MK 483, Reel 113, Folder 1569.

[158] Mia Fisher, Jewish Committee for Relief Abroad (JCRA) Field Director, to Rose L. Henriques, Chairman Germany Department, "Wentorf Transient Camp to America," 27 June 1949, p. 2, Henriques Archive, Microfilm reel 35.

[159] Rubinstein, *After the Holocaust*, pp. 113–114.

[160] Hauptman, "Videotaped interview," VHA, IC 28669, Seg. 37.

[161] David Ackerman, "Videotaped interview," VHA, IC 2416, Seg. 91.

[162] Anne Steyn, JCRA Germany Department to Anne Casper, JRU, "Permission for Emigrants to Take Money Out of Germany," Henriques Archive, Microfilm reel 35; Lily Schwarzschild, JRU to Ruth Fellner Jewish Refugees Committee, "Transfer of Money," 9 September 1949, Henriques Archive, Microfilm reel 35.

[163] DPs visiting Britain were only allowed to take RM 20 out of Germany, and that sum was insufficient to purchase their train tickets to their final destination after their return to Hanover. JRU

while she awaited her ship at Bremerhaven. When he was searched, two ten-dollar bills were found on him. Thinking that she was safely on the way to the United States, Lowy claimed that they were hers. Arrested, she threatened suicide and spent four weeks watched by a German woman before being released to a boat.[164]

Immigrants needed to bring German currency to the transit centers to buy food to supplement the insufficient IRO rations,[165] but once they left Germany they only had what pocket money they were given for their voyage. Immigrants to the United States received $10 each, while those to Britain received £1 for incidental travel expenses. Those who spent that money in transit arrived at their final port with very little indeed. DPs could also only bring as much luggage as they could carry. Immigrants to Britain were advised that their luggage could not exceed 160 pounds per adult and 80 pounds per child. These restrictions meant that DPs had to leave behind items that had been hard to obtain and were likely to be difficult to replace in their receiving country, creating seemingly unnecessary hardship.[166] DPs gave away household items to friends and sold what they could. Because of the currency restrictions, they exchanged money and goods for small items that they could sell once they arrived at their destination. Told by relatives that cameras were in high demand in the United States, the Soskis invested in a Leica camera. They also had German silver coins melted down into silver spoons.[167] The Taubers packed Meissen porcelain in their suitcases to provide their seed money in America.[168]

Legal immigrants to Palestine/Israel were able to ship larger containers, since the Israeli economy welcomed the influx of goods. A Jewish packing company in Munich offered its services making crates and packing them with furniture, pianos, and equipment, and another firm sold crated living room sets suitable for the Israeli climate.[169] Despite Israel's willingness to receive DP possessions, the Western Allies hesitated to permit equipment and machinery to leave Germany as part of their program to rebuild the German economy. Artisans who used small tools could often avoid difficulty, but craftsmen who relied on large machines could find themselves caught up in bureaucratic red tape when they attempted to bring their equipment with them.[170]

workers devised a scheme that permitted DPs to leave money with a Hanover JRU worker to retrieve upon their return. Lily Holt, JRU, to Ruth Fellner, Jewish Refugees Committee, 28 May 1948, Henriques Archive, Microfilm reel 35.

[164] Roslyn Lowy, "Videotaped interview," VHA, IC 7310, Segs. 73–75.

[165] Fisher to Henriques, "Wentorf Transient Camp," p. 1. British regulations limited the allowed amount to 40 Marks. British Red Cross, "Instructions for Your Journey," [1946], Henriques Archive, Microfilm reel 35. On similar conditions at the Bremen transit camp, see Soski, "Memories of a Vanished World," p. 97.

[166] Dr. Ernst Portner to Mrs. Selby [JRU?], 17 October 1946, Henriques Archive, Microfilm reel 35.

[167] Soski, "Memories of a Vanished World," pp. 95–96.

[168] Abe and Regina Tauber, interview.

[169] Business advertisements, YIVO, RG 294.2, MK 483, Microfilm reel 113, Folder 1569.

[170] JRU officials were unable to assist a shoemaker who wanted to transport several machines that he had received under German reparations. Their only advice was to hand over the machines

Emigration reopened disputes between Germans whose homes had been requisitioned and the Jewish DPs who lived in them. Germans accused Jewish emigrants of removing household items that belonged to the Germans. In Weiden, the U.S. military government officer ordered the Jewish Committee to report to the Housing Office who was emigrating so that an inventory could be conducted to ensure that furniture and personal property were returned to the rightful owner. A second inventory would follow immediately after the emigrant's departure to assure that all property was disposed of properly.[171] In the British Zone, holders of exit permits were required to prepare a complete list of their baggage contents and submit one copy to the mayor. The mayor had to certify that all of the items belonged to the emigrant. For DPs living in camps, the camp leader could do this with the countersignature of a Control Commission for Germany (CCG) official.[172] DPs took offense at these requirements since they suggested dishonesty on the part of DPs and gave Germans the opportunity to make false claims of ownership to household items; however, some DPs did try to take the opportunity to damage or remove German property before their departure as a last act of vengence. Even the departure of Jewish DPs from Germany led to conflict with Germans.

Among Jews in the DP camps, arrangements had to be made for the disposal of property. As camps liquidated, their supplies needed to be inventoried and redistributed. In the U.S. Zone a central liquidation commission ordered that the contents of magazines were to be turned over to the regional committees' warehouses for redistribution. Supplies in the ORT schools that did not belong to ORT remained the property of the Central Committee.[173] Occasionally the line between private and public property became blurred. In the Rochelle DP camp, five disabled DPs claimed to own the piano in the camp theater. They said that they had loaned it to the camp until they were called for aliyah. Now that they had received word that it was their turn to go, they wanted to take the piano. The remaining disabled DPs and camp residents claimed that the piano was camp property. The camp court of honor was to decide the case.[174]

to the Jewish Agency for Palestine in the hopes that an official organization would have an easier time obtaining the necessary export license. Trudie Grossman, Palestine Transit Camp to Mr. Lipski, JRU Hanover, 25 January 1948, Henriques Archive, Microfilm reel 35; Lipski to G. Grossmann, 26 January 1948; Henriques Archive, Microfilm reel 35.

[171] Joseph P. Lanzano, Director Office of Military Government for Bavaria Area Amberg to Jewish Committee Weiden, 26 January 1949; Correspondence – General – 1949; General Records of Weiden-Neustadt Resident Liaison and Security Office 1945–49; Records of the Field Operations Division; Records of United States Occupation Headquarters, World War II (OMGUS), RG 260, Entry: Bavaria; NACP.

[172] W. Eveleigh, German Travel Section, Chief Public Health Officer, "Instructions to Exit Permit Holders," [no date], Henriques Archive, Microfilm reel 35.

[173] Central Likwidacje Komisje, "Aktn-Notic far der likwidacje-brigarde far di Lagern," 10 December 1948, YIVO, RG 294.2, MK 483, Reel 64, Folder 928.

[174] Jidiszer komitet in Rochelle to Ern Gericht in Rochelle, "Dringend!" 17 October 1948, YIVO, RG 294.2, MK 483, Reel 64, Folder 928.

Leaving Germany had its own difficulties. Documents had to be collected, translated, and submitted. Medical exams needed to be passed. Decisions regarding what to leave and what to take had to be made. In 1948 emigration opportunities opened up with the creation of the State of Israel and with the passage of the DP Act, but there were still obstacles to be overcome and conflict ahead.

MOBILIZATION FOR THE ISRAELI WAR FOR INDEPENDENCE

On November 29, 1947, the United Nations voted to partition Palestine into a Jewish state and an Arab state. The Declaration of the State of Israel on May 14, 1948 profoundly affected DPs and provided a boost to morale. DPs' hopes rose that aliyah was at hand. Hannah Modenstein recalled her response to the announcement:

We were all standing in the middle of the camp and singing "Hatikvah." It was wonderful. ... We were very proud, and we felt that we had something to hang on to. We are people like every other people. All of those years we had felt we were nothing. All those names we were called, even before the war, feeling like second-class citizens in Poland and in Lithuania. We never felt that we belonged there. So [the creation of the State of Israel] gave us a big boost, that's for sure.[175]

The founding of the state fulfilled the DP's longing for a home, for recognition of being a nation like all others. Even though the future of the new state remained uncertain with enemy armies amassed on its borders, Israel now provided a tangible goal for DPs. When the Jewish Agency representative in Germany created lists of those who would immigrate to Israel, 70 percent of DPs registered.

Alongside celebrations over partition and independence, the serious business of military mobilization took place. Potential soldiers received priority for legal immigration to Palestine and then Israel. Most of the ardent activists had already left Germany on illegal immigration transports. Those who remained often did not meet the Jewish Agency's criteria for mobilization. For them, the prospect of waiting their turn for aliyah was disheartening. For other survivors the prospect of another war was unbearable. Jewish DPs began registering for immigration to other countries to the dismay of the Zionists. Mobilization began to lose its voluntary character.

Volunteers for *giyus* (mobilization) received the accolades of the DP leadership and population. DP organizations hosted farewell banquets to send off their members. Camp committees, to the dismay of the JDC, issued special "farewell allocations" from JDC packages to immigrants to Palestine.[176] In Pocking DP dental technicians made false teeth for those going to Israel to fight.[177] The

---

[175] Modenstein, interview.
[176] Committees were not supposed to have any extra supplies to make such gifts. Abe Cohen, JDC Director District 2, to All Regional Committees in District 2, "Special rations for Workers Emigrating to Palestine," [no date], YIVO, RG 294.2, MK 483, Microfilm reel 64, Folder 928.
[177] Sam Goldofsky, "Videotaped interview," VHA, IC 29363, Segs. 86–88.

voluntary stage of the mobilization, however, received a lukewarm response from the DPs.

In February 1948, the DP leadership orchestrated a propaganda campaign on behalf of giyus. By April sanctions were being imposed on those who had failed to provide a legitimate reason for not registering for mobilization.[178] One commonly imposed sanction was loss of employment, and the supplemental rations to which it entitled a worker. The small groups of Bundists and non-Zionists were especially isolated and subject to harassment.[179] Shirkers received threatening letters, such as the form letter sent by the draft board in Stuttgart: "You have not supported the fighting Yishuv. With such behavior you close yourself off from the community of Israel, and the entire Jewish public rebukes such actions and will not tolerate it any longer."[180] The letter stated that the recipient had a few days to rectify the matter, and then the names of those "who do not want to support the Yishuv" would be published and the list given to Jewish emigration bureaus "who will draw the necessary consequences." The implied threat was that HIAS and the JDC would refuse assistance to those on the list. It was, in fact, a hollow threat. In the British Zone, the Jewish Agency had attempted to gain assistance from HIAS and the JDC to exclude applicants who double registered for emigration, but Jewish aid organizations continued to assist all Jews regardless of their destination.[181]

Even DP leaders received letters of rebuke. At the Belsen DP camp, the draft board made an example of Paul Trepman. In prewar Poland, Trepman had been an active Revisionist. He served in the Polish underground for most of the war. Liberated in Belsen, he helped publish *Unzer Sztyme* and was the founding editor of the Belsener *Wochenblatt*. In Belsen Trepman served on the Central Jewish Committee as one of the heads of the Culture Department. Because Trepman did not register for giyus, he was removed from his position at the newspaper.

Trepman appealed the decision to the Jewish Agency representatives in Europe, Chaim Hoffman (Yachil) in Munich and Shalom Adler-Rudel in London. Trepman argued that he was an ardent Zionist who was unable to make aliyah

---

[178] I have come across accounts by two former DPs who claimed to have participated in shanghaiing DPs for military service in Palestine/Israel. Both men immigrated elsewhere. I have not found corroborating evidence or accounts by anyone claiming to have been recruited forcibly. This remains an open question for further investigation. See Henry Friedman, *I'm No Hero: Journeys of a Holocaust Survivor* (Seattle: University of Washington Press, 2001), pp. 88–91; Nathan Bram, "Videotaped interview," VHA, IC 34727, Seg. 40.

[179] Arbeitsamt Lager Rochelle to the Religious Office Rochelle, 18 April 1948, YIVO, RG 294.2, MK 483, Microfilm reel 64, Folder 928; Executive of the Bund Groups in Germany, "Bulletin no. 48/2," April 1948, YIVO, RG 294.2, MK 483, Microfilm reel 113, Folder 1552.

[180] Di Sankcje Komisje bajm Birger komitet far Mas Am lochejm to Choszewer Chawer, 21 December 1948, YIVO, RG 294.2, MK 483, Microfilm reel 70, Folder 1010.

[181] In keeping with its claim to represent all Jews in the British Zone, the Central Jewish Committee made the decision not to discriminate against those immigrating to countries other than Israel. "Protokoll der Sitzung der Executive des Central Jewish Committee," 28 November 1948, p. 2, YV O-70/4; Lavsky, *New Beginnings*, pp. 208 and 211.

due to his wife's medical condition, which required advanced treatment in the United States. There his wife's family could also assist in her care. Since transportation from the British Zone to the United States was unavailable, he had received papers to travel to Montreal, Canada. From there they planned to join family in Pittsburgh, Pennsylvania. Trepman accused the chairman of the draft board, H. Chamsky, of waging a vendetta against him. Trepman had previously reported to the Jewish Agency that Chamsky looked out only for his own political party, and Trepman now believed that in retaliation Chamsky had blocked the board's consideration of his request for an exemption from mobilization.[182]

Adler-Rudel believed that Trepman's case warranted review and wrote to Josef Rosensaft for his opinion on the matter.[183] Rosensaft's reply confirmed the facts of Trepman's case: An illness had rendered his wife blind in one eye and she was in danger of losing sight in the other eye unless surgery not available in Germany could be done, Trepman had arranged papers to Canada but delays in the process had led to a prolonged stay in Belsen, resulting in the question about giyus, and there was no love lost between Chamsky and Trepman. At this point, Rosensaft distanced himself from Trepman's appeal. Rosensaft was a member of the draft board. He felt it was not possible to ascertain whether Chamsky's hostility toward Trepman had led to the denial of a hearing. Certainly Rosensaft and other friends of Trepman were aware of his situation. Rosensaft acknowledged that Trepman had consulted with the Belsen leadership before deciding to immigrate to North America, and Trepman had received their support in that decision. A formal hearing was not required to inform the board of Trepman's extenuating circumstances. Rosensaft also explained his concern to separate his friendship from his decisions regarding mobilization. Rosensaft wrote, "if I have made an error, I have made it by striving to strengthen the action for giyus and not allowing any personal factors into the case."[184] And this is the clue to the case of Trepman.

The draft board wanted to make an example of Trepman to promote giyus. Here was a well-known Zionist DP leader about to immigrate to Canada instead of registering for military service in Israel. Stripping Trepman of his office would signal to Belsen DPs the board's serious intent. But because Trepman's papers had already come through for Canada, he would not face any serious financial hardship through the loss of his position. Trepman's honor was grievously offended, but that was his only real hardship. Thus, even though the draft board demonstrated that high-ranking Zionists were subject to giyus and would not receive special favor, the case also showed the board's limited ability to enforce its policies on individuals who were eligible for immigration elsewhere. Those DPs who did not have immigration papers in their pockets could be adversely affected by their removal from their positions in the camps.

---

[182] Paul Trepman to S. Adler-Rudel and Haim Hoffman, [no date, but received by Adler-Rudel on 24 May 1948], Adler-Rudel Papers, A140/490.
[183] S. Adler-Rudel to Josef Rosensaft, 10 June 1948, Adler-Rudel Papers, A140/490.
[184] Josef Rosensaft to S Adler-Rudel, 14 June 1948, Adler-Rudel Papers A140/490.

Trepman had been a lifelong ardent Zionist. His reasons for not going to Israel were personal. His dilemma and his decision were similar to those faced by many other DPs. Health and family relationships frequently determined an individual's, or a family's, choice for immigration. For those people who demand complete consistency between beliefs and actions, the reasons given by the DPs for why they did not follow their Zionist passions to Israel may sound like excuses. Certainly health and family sound more honorable than cowardice and the desire for material comfort. The case of Trepman, however, demonstrates how heavily immigration decisions weighed on Zionists and their desire to be members in good standing in Zionist circles despite their personal choices.

Giyus succeeded in mobilizing 13,000 troops from DP camps in Europe between February and August 1948.[185] Approximately 8,000 came from Germany. Not surprisingly, given their educational work and close-knit social ties, the youth movements were more successful than the general camp population in meeting their mobilization quotas.[186] The majority of these DP soldiers came from the American Zone, partly because there was a larger pool of young people there from which to draw, but also because the United States permitted the departure of DPs for Israel, with the exception of the brief period from June to August 1948. The British initially refused to recognize the State of Israel and prohibited aliyah from its zone from May 1948 until November 1948.

When the British finally permitted Jewish DPs to leave for Israel, they exempted men between the ages of eighteen and forty-five because they were of military age. Josef Rosensaft protested to the Foreign Office that this amounted to preventing the DPs from leaving. Using himself as an example, Rosensaft said that he could not very well send his wife and nine-month-old son to Israel while he remained behind.[187] Rosensaft failed to persuade the British to ease the restriction so that married men could make the journey. In fact, at the time of Rosensaft's meeting, CCG officers in Berlin had just requested permission to ban military-aged Jewish women from receiving exit visas from the British Zone. The Foreign Office denied the request since "quite apart from giving fresh ammunition to Jewish propagandists (who are already making great play of the cancellation of 'journey's end'). Such a proposal would be out of line with the policy which we have adopted in Cyprus."[188] The British reassured themselves that their policy was in line with that pursued by the Americans and the French in their occupation zones. The CCG had a change of heart in late January 1949,

---

[185] "Displaced Persons," *American Jewish Year Book* 51 (1950): 320.
[186] Patt, *Finding Home and Homeland*, p. 251.
[187] "Notes of Meeting at Foreign Office, London," 8 January 1949, p. 2, USHMM, Hadassah Rosensaft Papers, RG-08.002*05.
[188] BERCOMB Berlin to Foreign Office, Telegram No. 46 Basic, 5 January 1949, PRO, FO 1052/82; M & M.C. to CONCOMB Lubbecke, Re: Foreign Office Telegram No. 139 Basic, 11 January 1949, PRO, FO 1052/82.

when the efficacy of the ban was called into question and the two other Allies indicated a desire to lift the ban.[189]

Indeed, U.S. policy did prohibit the travel of military-age men to Israel. However, DPs had found their way around that obstacle with the help of Colonel George Scithers, the liaison officer to the Central Committee. When Scithers first received orders to check all trains to ascertain that no military-age men were onboard, he approached Theodore Feder of the JDC. After consulting with the Central Committee and Chaim Yachil, head of the Jewish Agency mission in Germany and now Consul of Israel, Feder suggested a plan. If Scithers stood on one designated side of the train, he would see only women and children. According to Feder, that is what Scithers did with two officers in tow.[190] Under this arrangement, young men continued to leave the American Zone for Palestine. The bans were finally lifted in mid-February 1949.[191]

Despite the continuing hostilities in the Middle East, 86,356 DPs left Germany, Austria, and Italy (53,388 of them from Germany) for Israel in the period July 1, 1948 to June 30 1949. An additional 10,000 DPs who had been interned on Cyprus as illegal immigrants also arrived in Israel. During the same period, 15,322 Jewish DPs from Europe immigrated to the United States. A further 6,000 went to Canada, 2,287 to Australia, and 10,325 to other countries.[192] Thus, of the more than 120,000 DPs who left DP camps that year, 72 percent made aliyah. By mid-1949, however, news of difficult conditions in Israel slowed aliyah, and in 1950 revisions to the DP Act made immigration to the United States a bit easier.

Statistics concerning DP emigration are a bit messy. Governments had different ways of identifying people and did not always distinguish Jews from other DPs. Some statistics lump Jewish DPs together with other Jewish immigrants. Many available statistics for DPs are not broken down by country, so that DPs from Germany, Austria, and Italy are counted together. In addition, the constant flow of illegal immigrants through the DP camps using the identity and ration cards of those who had already left for Palestine, along with the existence of forged and stolen cards, meant that it was not possible to obtain an accurate accounting of the number of DPs.

Using demographic studies of the DP population by contemporaries and the best research available it is possible to create a general picture of Jewish DP migration from Europe. By 1952, approximately 96,000 Jewish DPs had left Germany, Austria, and Italy for the United States under the Truman Directive and the DP Acts of 1948 and 1950.[193] A few thousand more immigrated under existing U.S. immigration quotas. Another 16,000 immigrated to Canada, 8,200

[189] CCG Political Division to Foreign Office, Telegram No. 134, 27 January 1949, PRO, FO 1052/82.
[190] Theodore Feder, "Videotaped interview," VHA, IC 10080, Segs. 56–59.
[191] Louis G. Kelly, Chief, Displaced Persons Branch, OMGUS, to Logan Gray, Director, DP Branch CCG, 7 March 1949, PRO, FO 1052/82.
[192] "Displaced Persons," p. 319.
[193] Leonard Dinnerstein, *America and the Survivors of the Holocaust* (New York: Columbia University Press, 1982), p. 251.

to Australia, 6,600 to countries in South America, 4,387 to places in Europe, and 930 to other destinations.[194]

The largest number of Jewish DPs made their way to Palestine/Israel. Numbers concerning this immigration are significant because they can be used to demonstrate the sincerity of DPs and Zionist leaders in their demands for open immigration to Palestine as the solution to the DP situation.[195] From July 1, 1947 to December 31, 1951, the period of operation for UNRRA's successor organization, the IRO, Palestine/Israel accepted 132,109 DPs. This number refers to immigrants in possession of certificates, since only they received IRO assistance.[196] This figure did not include 15,000 illegal and legal DP immigrants who entered Palestine from 1945 until the IRO came into effect.[197] Jacques Vernant, in his work commissioned by the new U.N. High Commissioner for Refugees, reported that an additional 30,000 DPs immigrated illegally during the period of the IRO's existence and were not included in IRO statistics. This brings the total of DPs making aliyah from Germany, Austria, and Italy to 177,109.[198] This figure is consistent with that reported by other scholars when illegal immigration is taken into consideration.[199] In their immigration choices, nearly 60 percent of Jewish DPs made aliyah. The United States received the next largest group: approximately one-third of Jewish DPs.

An estimated 10,000 Jewish DPs remained in Germany along with 10,000 German Jews.[200] Some "stayers" had established businesses. Some had married

---

[194] Jacques Vernant, *The Refugee in the Post-War World* (New Haven, CT: Yale University Press, 1953), p. 65.

[195] Yosef Grodzinsky grossly underestimates immigration to Palestine by ignoring illegal immigration and overestimates DP out-migration from Israel. This slight of hand serves his argument that "the aftermath of the Holocaust, then, was not necessarily Zionist." *In the Shadow of the Holocaust*, pp. 223–224 and p. 271 n. 27.

[196] Of these, 6,585 came from the British Zone of Germany, 19 from the French Zone, and 63,447 from the U.S. Zone. Louise W. Holborn, *The International Refugee Organization: A Specialized Agency of the United Nations, Its History and Work 1946–1952* (London: Oxford University Press, 1956), pp. 415 and 434.

[197] Kurt R. Grossmann, *The Jewish DP Problem: Its Origin, Scope, and Liquidation* (New York: Institute of Jewish Affairs, World Jewish Congress, 1951), p. 23. In his work commissioned by the new U.N. High Commissioner for Refugees, Jacques Vernant accepted Grossmann's figures. *The Refugee in the Post-War World* (London: George Allen & Unwin, 1953), p. 65.

[198] Vernant also suspected that 50,000 Jews interned on Cyprus were not included in the IRO statistics. Since 60 percent of those interned on Cyprus came through the DP camps, this means that an additional 30,000 DPs may have immigrated to Israel, bringing the total to 207,109. Vernant, *Refugee in the Post-War World*, p. 446, fn. 1 and p. 65, fn. 4. On the number of DPs interned on Cyprus, see Dalia Ofer, "Holocaust Survivors as Immigrants: The Case of Israel and the Cyprus Detainees," *Modern Judaism* 16 (February 1996): 1.

[199] This figure is just slightly higher than the sum of Leonard Dinnerstein's estimate of 136,000 legal immigrants and the 37,000 illegal DP immigrants from the period 1945–1948 reported by Arieh J. Kochavi. That total is 173,000. Kochavi's numbers may be slightly low. A contemporary source put DP illegal immigration at 40,000, and Brichah scholar Yehuda Bauer estimated the total number of DP immigrants at 200,000. Dinnerstein, *America and the Survivors*, p. 285; Kochavi, *Post-Holocaust Politics*, p. 235; Hyman, "Displaced Persons," p. 471.

[200] Vernant, *Refugee in the Post-War World*, p. 65.

German women, many of whom would convert to Judaism. Some did not want to go to Israel and were not eligible for immigration elsewhere. Others were simply too tired to begin again. Lea Fleischmann's mother told her:

How could I live here, you ask? You should have seen me after the war. A wreck, a living wreck. In the entire world there was no one who belonged to me or to whom I belonged. No family, no friends, no acquaintances. And it was no different for your father. We were too weak to leave, to gain a firm footing in another country. And later I thought over why I should leave at all. That would have suited them. First they degrade us and then they [sic] disappear. So simple it is not. The Germans must hear from me what I think of them, and if it does not suit them, then they should exile me or lock me up. If they use a few Jews here to cleanse themselves of their past, then they must also endure my thoughts.[201]

For Fleischmann's mother, the inability to leave became the virtue, and burden, of being a living, accusatory reminder to the Germans.

By December 1951 only Föhrenwald remained as a Jewish DP camp in Germany. The IRO transferred the camp to German jurisdiction. German police took over responsibility for the camp from DP police. The JDC actively assisted in providing aid to the remaining DPs and sought their resettlement, offering grants to those DPs who would leave the camp.[202] The "hardcore" DPs who remained presented a great challenge. They were unwilling or unable to emigrate, yet they refused to integrate into the German economy and society. They had become camp Jews, comfortable among their own people in the little shtetl they had created.[203] Finally, Föhrenwald closed in 1957, bringing the DP era to an end.

RETURNEES

While the international Jewish community had a difficult enough time understanding the willingness of some German Jews to return to Germany, few could comprehend how Eastern European Jews could remain. To add to their dismay, approximately 3,500 former DPs returned to Germany looking for an easier time than they had found elsewhere.[204] Some returned from Western Europe and the United States. Most had left Israel. In their decisions to return to Germany, they were motivated by the desire to reunite with friends and family, to seek medical care, to improve their economic situation (including applying for restitution

201 Lea Fleischmann, *Dies ist nicht mein Land* (Hamburg: Hoffman und Campe Verlag, 1980), pp. 247–248.
202 American Jewish Joint Distribution Committee, "Annual Report," 1953, pp. 7–8; JDC, "Annual Report," 1954, p. 7; JDC, "Annual Report," 1957, p. 8. For more on Föhrenwald after 1951, see Ronald Webster, "American Relief and Jews in Germany, 1945–1960: Diverging Perspectives," *Leo Baeck Institute Year Book* 38 (1993): 295–321.
203 Hal Lehrman, "The Last Jews in the Last German Camp," *Rescue* (Fall 1953): 3–4.
204 Webster, "American Relief," p. 309, n. 67.

from West Germany), and to gain entry to North America.²⁰⁵ Rarely did their choices reflect political or ideological motives.

Europeans often found the conditions in Israel inhospitable. A JRU worker described a settlement for new immigrants in July 1949:

[The houses] are very primitive. They have no electric light and for some houses the water has to be fetched up the mountain. No lavatories, only holes in the ground. ... The conditions are extremely difficult, as the climate for the new immigrants is not easy to bear. There are millions of flies, mosquitos and vermin. The houses have hardly any furniture. ... The cooking of foreign vegetables and produce have to be taught ... The children suffer mostly in the heat from flies and mosquitos. ... Millions of flies and mosquitos – known and unknown insects – djukens, ants and bugs plague the people and children and have to be fought every day again and again. ... There are different sub-tropic diseases, skin diseases, food poisoning etc.²⁰⁶

This village was located in the more temperate area near Haifa and still conditions were intolerably uncomfortable.

In addition to the physical environment, the economy was insufficient to absorb the steady influx of immigrants. JRU workers estimated that social workers would be needed for the next few years, "until industrial capacity has expanded sufficiently to allow for full employment. While new olim [immigrants] arrive at the present rates, they have to undergo a period of unemployment/or underemployment (10–12 days a month) lasting many months."²⁰⁷ The DPs' desire to feel at home and to establish a sense of normalcy would not be immediately satisfied. Most were willing to make the adjustment. Others could not.

The decision to leave Israel rarely had any political impetus. Women frequently cited health reasons for leaving Israel. They returned to Germany for treatment and the hope of immigrating elsewhere. For example, Sara Dembowski had persuaded her husband to make the illegal journey to Palestine. After the birth of her son in Israel in 1949, she developed a condition that required surgery not available in Israel. She went back to Germany for medical treatment. From there she received help from HIAS to move her family to Canada. She did not explain her decision not to return to Israel except to note that life had been difficult there at the beginning and that her husband had struggled to earn a living, having tried his hand as a confectioner and plumber.²⁰⁸

Economic difficulties contributed to the decision to leave, particularly for men. Steady employment was hard to find in the Israeli economy overburdened by a flood of immigrants. Adam Goldman, a veteran of the Polish Army, had volunteered to fight in the Israeli War for Independence. After the war he was

---

²⁰⁵ Lynn Rapaport, *Jews in Germany after the Holocaust: Memory, Identity, and Jewish-German Relations* (Cambridge: Cambridge University Press, 1997), pp. 5, 9, and 163; Webster "American Relief," p. 306.

²⁰⁶ "Extracts from Ida Lieberfreund's Report to be Used for the Dominion Bulletin for August," [1949], pp. 1–2, Henriques Archive, Microfilm reel 35.

²⁰⁷ Sidney Kahan to Leonard Cohen, 22 June 1949, p. 2, Henriques Archive, Microfilm reel 35.

²⁰⁸ Dembowski, "Videotaped interview," Seg. 29. See also, Cela Rosenfeld, "Videotaped interview," VHA, IC 18069, Segs. 77–79; Rapaport, *Jews in Germany*, p. 9.

alone and finding it hard to make a living as a construction worker building settlements. When he saw in the newspaper that a cousin in the United States was searching for family, he decided to leave Israel.[209] After eight years in Israel, Eva Lehner's husband decided that they would out-migrate when he was denied permits for his planned chicken farm. Faced with limited economic prospects, they chose to join Eva's sister in Australia.[210] While economic factors made men consider leaving Israel, the attraction of family was also great and influenced the destination.

Siblings had a great influence on migration decisions. Even though Shlomo Szlamkowicz had convinced his brother to join him in illegal aliyah to Palestine over joining relatives in the United States, in 1955 his brother decided to immigrate to the United States after all. Szlamkowicz followed his brother in 1958.[211] David Ackerman had volunteered for the Haganah and spent one year in the elite Palmach. He recalled standing in uniform by the Israeli flag and taking his oath: "I had the same feeling as when I was liberated by the Russians. An electric shock went through my body." Ackerman received permission to return to Germany to retrieve his belongings from Frankfurt. It is not clear whether or not he intended to return to Israel, but when he arrived in Frankfurt, he discovered that his brother had immigrated to the United States. Wanting to follow his brother, he was initially told that he was ineligible under the DP quota because of his prior emigration. He received assistance from an attorney who successfully argued his case, and he immigrated to Chicago.[212] Family remained a crucial factor in deciding where to go or stay. Samuel Falsehaber had been imprisoned briefly by the Palmach after the Altalena Affair. In 1951 his father, sick in Germany, sent for him. There he met a German woman whom he married. He and his bride decided to join his sister who had immigrated to the United States. Since he had already emigrated once, he had to finance his travel himself.[213] Falsehaber did not explain his decision not to return to Israel. Was it because he had a German wife, or did he miss his sister, or did he resent the treatment of Revisionists in Israel?

[209] Adam Goldman, "Videotaped interview," VHA, IC 15582, Segs. 97–102, 104–106. Alex Balkowski also fought in the War for Independence. He could not find steady work and encouraged his wife to contact her American relatives, because he was certain that he would be able to find work in the United States. "Videotaped interview," VHA, IC 24970, Segs. 55–62.

[210] Eva Lehner, "Videotaped interview," VHA, IC 30032, Seg. 28. Sometimes women left for similar reasons. A woman who had arrived on Aliyah Bet fell on hard times and left Israel in 1959 to join her uncle in the United States. Roza Chlewicki, "Videotaped interview," VHA, IC 22059, Seg. 69.

[211] Shlomo Szlamkowicz, "Videotaped interview," VHA, IC 1637, Segs. 49, 63–64. In another case of sibling following sibling, Joel Berkovc served in the Haganah and found a job in a glass factory after his discharge, but when his sister immigrated from Austria to Canada in 1953, he accepted her request to join her. Joel Berkovc, "Videotaped interview," VHA, IC 35686, Segs. 162–163.

[212] David Ackerman, "Videotaped interview," VHA, IC 2416, Segs. 79–84, 87–88, 94.

[213] Samuel Silbiger Falsehaber, "Videotaped interview," VHA, IC 28336, Segs. 113–114, 122–124.

In the case of Asher Schorr, his departure from Israel most definitely had to do with politics. Schorr had joined Betar in the DP camps and strongly identified with the Revisionist position. He knew he wanted to leave Israel in 1960 when a taxi driver, referring to the Altalena incident, said that he would fire again on an Irgun ship. Schorr deplored the discrimination against the employment of Revisionists and left for the United States.

The vast majority of DPs who made aliyah remained in Israel. Significantly, returnees and others who left Israel did so primarily for personal reasons. Conditions in the early years of the State of Israel were difficult, and some survivors did not have the stamina any longer to hold out for better times. The pull of biological family was sometimes stronger than the ideological family of the nation. Their stories are not about Zionist trickery or their disillusionment with Israel. It is about survivors of genocide struggling to find a place where they could create a sense of normalcy for themselves. Some survivors would find it where they were with family, had adequate health care, and could have economic security. Others would search for home their entire lives.

CONCLUSION

As their stay in the DP camps lengthened and as new Jewish refugees from Eastern Europe flooded the camps, Jewish DPs created political institutions to administer and regulate camp life and to represent DP interests to the military and international organizations. In the summer of 1946, with hopes for speedy immigration dashed, Jewish DPs increasingly disagreed over how to achieve their goals. Immigration to Palestine remained the common purpose of DP camp committees and political parties, but the Jewish DP electorate was increasingly voting for the radical parties of the right and left. Political radicalization and violence was more a response to the condition of displacement than to the influence of outside political activists from the Yishuv.

In 1947 DPs became more assertive in trying to realize their goal of emigration. Some DPs, desperate to raise their children outside of Germany and the DP camps, abandoned their dreams of a new life in a Jewish homeland and accepted entry to another country. While most survivors supported the creation of a Jewish state, not all wanted to immigrate there. Family, health, and personal security often decided emigration questions. As the stay in Germany lengthened, even some Zionist leaders began to encourage their followers to take their first opportunity for emigration. Other DPs entered vocational and agricultural training programs to improve their chances for legal, as well as illegal, immigration to Palestine. Some DPs risked imprisonment and even death to reach Palestine by illegal means. Still other DPs engaged in political demonstrations to draw the attention of the international community and to pressure the DP leadership itself.

In 1948 the creation of the State of Israel and the relaxation of U.S. immigration laws helped empty the DP camps. The majority of DPs built new lives for themselves in Israel, while a significant minority went to the United States. Life in Israel was difficult. The country was at war with its neighbors, the economy struggled to absorb hundreds of thousands of immigrants, and no one had time for the remnants of European Jewry and their tales of the Holocaust. A small fraction of the DPs who originally immigrated to Israel left to find family or better economic opportunities elsewhere. Most of those who left still professed Zionism even as their personal needs took them to other countries. At the same time there were former DPs who immigrated to Israel when the situation was more stable. For example, Sami Feder, director of Belsen's Katzet Theater, initially settled in Paris and made aliyah in 1962; Livia Bitton-Jackson, Beth Jacob teacher and DP translator, and her elderly mother immigrated to Israel from the United States in 1977.

In the DP camps, 80 to 90 percent of respondents insisted that Palestine was their first choice for immigration, and yet only 57 percent or so actually made their home in Israel. Did the Zionist leadership cleverly manipulate the DPs, as some post-Zionists suggest? Or is there a way to reconcile Zionist beliefs with personal decisions that led to other countries? Survivors emerged from the Holocaust with an intense desire for Jewish unity. Even if a DP planned to join family elsewhere, s/he would demonstrate unity with other Jews and their desire for Palestine. Samuel Gringauz fell into this category as a fervent advocate of Zionist causes even as he chose to reunite with family in the United States. Changed circumstances also explains the seeming contradiction between many DPs' professed intention to immigrate to Palestine and the later move elsewhere. The arrival of children and developing health concerns encouraged choices based on personal needs rather than ideological convictions.

Israeli "new historians" have suggested that Zionist emissaries from the Yishuv manipulated DPs, coercing them into accepting the Zionist agenda.[214] Yosef Grodzinsky argued that Zionism failed to make a significant impact on DP identity because in his accounting so few of the DPs actually made their homes in Israel.[215] The assumption, to paraphrase Lenin, is that the DPs voted with their feet and they did not vote for Israel. And by not voting for Israel, they allegedly demonstrated weak identification with the Zionist political program and exposed the false premises of the Zionist agenda.[216] In reality, individuals consist of multiple identities and are in an ongoing negotiation with those identities. Public and private identities vie for primacy, as do gender, ethnic, familial, and religious identities. Often identities are in conflict with one another and the individual makes whatever accommodations s/he finds satisfying to keep

---

[214] Idith Zertal referred to the passengers of *Exodus 1947* as "captives" of the Zionist struggle and claimed that DPs listened to Zionist emissaries solely because they had no other options. *Israel's Holocaust and the Politics of Nationhood* (Cambridge: Cambridge University Press, 2005), pp. 45 and 49.

[215] Grodzinsky, *In the Shadow of the Holocaust*, p. 224.

[216] Grodzinsky, *In the Shadow of the Holocaust*, pp. 225–231. In her more careful and nuanced work, Idith Zertal argues that Zionists considered their own needs and did not mourn the destruction of the Diaspora but used it as a tool "in its national struggle." *From Catastrophe to Power* (Berkeley: University of California Press, 1998), pp. 10–11.

functioning. It is entirely plausible that a committed Zionist would not move to Israel, even as a non-Zionist might. Most former DPs describe themselves as Zionists. Their reasons for not going to Israel included the desire to reunite with family, health concerns, the intense desire to leave Germany but being ineligible at the time for immigration to Palestine, and the need to provide a safe environment for their children. Post-Zionists might argue that it is hypocritical to advocate an independent Jewish state without being willing to fight and die for it, but the survivors had already experienced a war and survived genocide. Their internment in the DP camps was their contribution to the fight for an independent Israel.

There are ways other than immigration to measure the place Israel held in DP hearts and minds. A number of survivor memoirs conclude with details about the survivors' activities on behalf of Israel: fundraising for the JNF, Haddasah, the United Jewish Appeal; purchasing Israel Bonds; and other methods of contributing to the construction of the Jewish state.[217] Through their charitable activities and social and political affiliations, many former DPs maintained their connection to Israel and Zionism.

In his survey of Holocaust survivors, Alexander J. Groth discovered an extraordinarily strong bond between survivors and Israel. The majority of survivors he surveyed resided in North America. Of these, 52 percent had seriously considered making aliyah, 16 percent were either permanent residents or long-time residents of Israel during their lives, and 9 percent had made short attempts to live in Israel. Only 21 percent had never considered moving to Israel as a personal option. Even more impressive is the comparison between visits to Israel made by American Jews and by survivors. Fewer than 16 percent of American Jews had visited Israel more than once, whereas 79 percent of survivors had. In fact, 16 percent of survivors had visited Israel ten times or more, while 43 percent had visited five times or more.[218] Considering that DPs arrived virtually destitute in their new countries, these visits represented a great expenditure of resources and time. Even without making aliyah, former DPs demonstrated the sincerity of their deeply held Zionist convictions.

The new historians' claim that DPs were pawns of the Zionist leadership appears greatly exaggerated in light of the evidence. Certainly corruption and intimidation did exist in the DP camps, but they could be between competing Zionist groups as well as between Zionists and non-Zionists. Most survivors would have preferred a life without war and economic turmoil. Some may have gone to Israel simply because of a lack of options. Some may have gone with

---

[217] See, for example, Biber, *Risen from Ashes*, p. 138; Joe Gelber, "Memoirs of a Survivor," (1980), p. 148, USHMM, Joe Gelber Collection RG 02.153; Sam Halpern, *Darkness and Hope* (New York: Shengold Publishers, 1996), pp. 208–211; Nathan Katz, *Teach Us to Count Our Days: A Story of Survival, Sacrifice, and Success* (Cranbury, NJ: Cornwall Books, 1999), p. 169 and back flap of book jacket; Gerda Weissmann Klein, *All but My Life* (New York: Hill and Wang, 1995), p. 250; Rosensaft, *Yesterday*, pp. 132, 135, and 145–146.

[218] Alexander J. Groth, *Holocaust Voices: An Attitudinal Survey of Survivors* (New York: Humanity Books, 2003), p. 116.

Zionist zeal only to be disappointed by their tepid welcome in Palestine and the lack of economic opportunities. In most cases, DPs made the best decisions for themselves that they could under the circumstances. In general, survivors of the Holocaust were a savvy bunch, not easily manipulated.

Zionism served a number of functions for survivors. It offered an explanation for the horrific events of the past and a program for the continuation of Jewish community. Even Orthodox thinkers found themselves linking the Holocaust to a call for rebuilding Jewish life in the Land of Israel. The experiences of the postwar period with continued antisemitic violence and the seeming disinterest of the international community for their plight convinced additional survivors that only a Jewish homeland would permit Jewish renewal. Zionist youth movements and kibbutzim offered young survivors a surrogate family and the ideological commitment and peer group experiences adolescents gravitate toward. For many, the idea of living among Jews promised a sense of home.

Conclusion

In 1980, the memoirs of a thirty-three-year-old Jewish woman became a best-seller in the Federal Republic of Germany. In *Dies ist nicht mein Land: Eine Jüdin verläßt die Bundesrepublik* (*This Is Not My Country: A Jewish Woman Leaves the Federal Republic*), Lea Fleischmann explained why after ten years in a DP camp and twenty years living among Germans she was leaving the country of her birth for a new life in Israel. She compared her early childhood in the Föhrenwald DP camp to life in an Eastern European shtetl, a world away from the German village just 2 kilometers down the road. The residents spoke Yiddish, telling unbelievable, fantastic stories of gas chambers and babies thrown into pits of fire. Children ran noisily through the synagogue and learned that the denunciation of a fellow Jew was a loathsome crime. These memories of the DP camp reflected the perspective of a child kept close to her immediate family, but in reality, the Föhrenwald of Fleischmann's childhood contained many Germans. In addition to German converts to Judaism who resided in the camp with their DP husbands, one-third of married women in Föhrenwald were non-Jewish Germans.[1] DP adults entered nearby Wolfratshausen for economic transactions with Germans and for entertainment. Before the mass emigration of Jews from 1948 to 1950, interactions between Jewish DPs and Germans had been even more frequent in small towns, where DP assembly centers consisted of requisitioned hotels or apartment buildings, and where DPs often lived in rooms in German homes. These contacts had significance for DPs and Germans alike, shaping collective memories of the war and attitudes toward the postwar condition.

In constant contact with the German environment, Jewish DPs could not avoid their tormented memories. For those liberated in Germany, the landscape served as a reminder of their sufferings and of those Jews who did not survive.

---

[1] Anthony D. Kauders, *Democratization and the Jews* (Lincoln: The University of Nebraska Press for the Vidal Sassoon International Center for the Study of Antisemitism, The Hebrew University of Jerusalem, 2004), pp. 61–62, n. 28.

The sight of Germans living in their own homes, fashionably dressed, eating fresh vegetables and meat reminded DPs of all that had been stolen from them. The fences surrounding DP camps, the monotonous food, and the regulations of camp living had enough similarities to Nazi labor camps to cause distress. During the day survivors could hold off their tortured memories, but at night they returned. Pregnancy increased the terrors for Jewish women, who could not imagine that they and their children would be allowed to live. Brought into contact with German medical personnel, many Jewish women and children received adequate care while a significant minority suffered negligence, malpractice, and possibly even murder at the hands of German and former collaborator physicians and nurses. The story of the physical rebirth of European Jewry was one of courage and continued experiences of victimization.

Surrounded by their former tormentors, DPs took an aggressive stand, ready to defend themselves from German aggression and to demand German contrition. The unwillingness of Germans to confront their responsibility for the war and genocide increased survivors' fears of German animosity. Despite efforts by DPs to force German acknowledgement of responsibility and expressions of remorse, most Germans defensively insisted on their personal innocence. Feeling themselves unjustly charged with collective guilt, Germans expressed solidarity with their beleaguered *Volksgemeinschaft* (national community).[2] Remarkably, the presence of Holocaust survivors in Germany facilitated German rejection of responsibility for wartime crimes. The Eastern European origins of the DPs made it easier for Germans to assert that they should not be required to provide aid to these outsiders. Germans believed that DPs should return to their countries of origin and did not feel responsible for them when they chose not to do so. In addition, many Germans forced to participate in reburials of death march victims believed themselves to have been absolved of responsibility for German crimes and, busy rebuilding their own lives, did not concern themselves with the legacy of Nazi racial policies. For their part, many Germans would have welcomed considerably more distance from the surviving Jews.

Multiple groups came into contact in postwar Germany, shaping the political and cultural landscape. Germans, Allied troops, Jews, non-Jewish DPs, and ethnic German expellees interacted in ways that influenced collective memories of the war and attitudes toward the postwar condition. Germans redirected their anger at defeat and occupation onto the DPs, who were safe targets as the weaker dependents of the Allied forces. Today Neunburg vorm Wald and other Bavarian communities credit the arrival of ethnic German expellees with reversing the prewar trends toward decline, but they often ignore their communities' experiences with Jewish DPs. With the restoration of German political life in 1949 and the departure of many DPs for Israel and other destinations, Germans began removing the remaining traces of Jews from their towns. Once again, death march victims were exhumed, this time from their graves in the various town cemeteries. Their remains were interred in special, regional,

---

[2] Norbert Frei, *1945 und Wir* (Munich: Verlag C.H. Beck, 2005), p. 33.

"concentration camp" cemeteries, where memories of the turbulent postwar years could be contained and forgotten. In the mid-1950s many of these cemeteries closed, and the remains were exhumed once again and transferred to memorial sites at the former concentration camps Dachau and Flossenbürg, moving them even further out of sight and out of mind.[3] The presence of these dead Jews was too accusatory, too discomforting, to Germans trying to minimize their feelings of shame.

At the same time that Jewish graves were being removed from sight, national events kept the question of Germans and Jews in the public eye, from the 1959 vandalism of the Cologne synagogue to the 1963 Auschwitz trials to the 1979 broadcast of the television miniseries *Holocaust*. In the 1970s, Floß rediscovered interest in the history of its German-Jewish community and restored its synagogue even though Jews no longer resided in the village. By the 1980s, Germans were engaged in a major reassessment of German responsibility for crimes against the Jews. Ironically, after twenty years of struggling to fit into German society, Fleischmann left Germany just as this transformation began to take place. As a testament to this change, Fleischmann's book became a bestseller, and she continues to publish in German and regularly makes speaking tours of Germany. The Federal Republic of Germany today is a vastly different place from the Germany of Fleischmann's childhood, when DPs were unwelcome reminders of crimes many Germans preferred not to acknowledge.

This is not to say that Germans in the immediate postwar period ignored or forgot the Nazi past entirely. In fact, they were engaged in trying to understand where things had gone wrong, and by the mid-1950s leading Germans were discussing the question of individual responsibility for Nazi crimes.[4] Still, the genocide against the Jews was not a focal point. Faced with their own wartime and postwar traumas (including bombings and mass rape), the continued imprisonment of thousands of German soldiers in the Soviet Union, the return of non-Jewish German concentration camp inmates (such as Social Democrats, Communists, homosexuals, and others labeled asocials), and the arrival of millions of ethnic German expellees from the East, many Germans believed the murder of the Jews to be one among many catastrophes.[5] The presence of non-Jewish German concentration camp survivors served as evidence that Germans also had been victims of the Nazis, at the same time that they reminded Germans of how neighbors had turned on neighbors in the

---

[3] The transfer to the larger cemeteries absolved the German towns of the costs of maintaining the graves. In Neunburg and Mallersdorf, the Jewish communities financed the completion of the enlarged cemeteries. The Bavarian agency for state castles, gardens, and lakes took over responsibility for maintaining the centralized cemeteries in 1953. Katrin Greiser, "Die Todesmärsche von Buchenwald: Räumung des Lagerkomplexes im Frühjahr 1945 und Spuren der Erinnerung" (Ph.D. diss., Universität Lüneburg, 2007), pp. 363–365, http://kirke.ub.uni-lueneburg.de/volltexte/2007/414/pdf/Dissertation.pdf, accessed 1 January 2008.

[4] Kauders, *Democratization and the Jews*, pp. 182–183.

[5] Peter Reichel, *Vergangenheitsbewältigung in Deutschland* (Munich: Verlag C.H. Beck, 2001), p. 69.

name of eliminating threats to the Volksgemeinschaft.[6] Even denazification trials tended to obscure Nazi crimes against Jews. German tribunals could only try cases of crimes committed by Germans against Germans, excluding crimes against non-German Jews in Nazi-occupied territories. Therefore, many of the crimes against European Jews lay outside of their purview. The Allies retained for themselves the right to try crimes against Allied nationals, but the focus of the widely publicized Nuremberg Trials was on war crimes and not on the mass murder of Jews. Thus, many Germans mistakenly categorized the treatment of the Jews as excesses of war rather than the result of deliberately implemented racial policies. Only with the passage of time and through heated public debates would many Germans come to appreciate the enormity of the Shoah.

While most Germans required distance before substantively grappling with the legacy of genocide, DPs were compelled to confront it immediately. Needing to talk about their trauma, survivors found a safe audience within the DP camps. The retelling of Holocaust experiences allowed many DPs to begin coping with their traumatic experiences. Neuroscience and psychiatry have demonstrated that creative expression and the writing of new endings and new coping strategies into narratives of traumatic experiences have therapeutic value. However, as Fleischmann's memories of Föhrenwald suggested, repetitive recounting of trauma can be detrimental and pass the trauma along to others. It would be interesting for mental health workers studying elderly Holocaust survivors to examine what influence, if any, a stay in the DP camps had on survivors' symptoms of post-traumatic stress syndrome. I suspect that there was a benefit to a short stay among those with whom one could safely reenact past trauma but that the benefits would have diminished from a protracted stay in the abnormal conditions of a DP camp, since political extremism and violence increased over time.[7]

The DP community formed out of an assortment of Jewish survivors who came from a variety of backgrounds. It was not a foregone conclusion that individuals from different social backgrounds, national origins, political affiliations, and levels of religious observance would form a cohesive community. Indeed, there was significant conflict between subgroups of the DP community. The Zionist leadership attempted to intimidate and bully its opponents, and inequities within the Zionist movement alienated some of its own followers. Linguistic debates over Yiddish, Hebrew, and the national languages of Eastern Europe revealed tensions between assimilated, religious, and Zionist DPs. Disagreements between Orthodox and secular Jews and between the religious movements within the Orthodox community were also divisive, often exacerbated by the

---

[6] The efforts of persecuted non-Jews to reintegrate into German society deserve scholarly attention. It would be instructive to compare their experiences to German Jews, expellees, and DPs to better understand postwar German mentalities and the legacy of the Volksgemeinschaft ideal.

[7] As I finish this book, there are news reports that militant and gang activity is rising to dangerous levels in camps for displaced Darfurians, where joblessness and despair are high. Protracted displacement continues to be a problem that the international community has not had the will to solve.

distribution of resources by international Jewish organizations. The length of internment encouraged not only despair and apathy but also political radicalization and aggression. The constant movement of people between DP camps as well as into and out of the DP camps made for a community that was, at one level, constantly in flux. At the same time, there was a significant constancy in leadership and in cultural, political, and social organization and expression that provided a coherent structure within the DP camps, facilitating a shared identity and recognition of a common fate. Ultimately, dissension and discord occurred within a communal framework that promoted a shared understanding of the past, present, and future. Some DPs even welcomed the political turbulence as a sign of recovery and a return to normalcy.

Their common suffering as Jews gave DPs a sense of connection to one another. The collective memories formed in mourning assemblies and theaters helped to supplant earlier differences with a shared past. In attempting to understand the recent catastrophe of European Jewry, they turned to biblical and historical metaphors. Hitler became the reincarnation of the biblical destroyer Amalek. The slavery of the Jews in ancient Egypt was a parallel for the suffering under the Nazis. Finding a common past in ancient and recent times, DPs could see themselves as members of a community that rose above differences of language or country of origin.

Unlike those survivors who remained in Eastern Europe, most DPs had emerged from the Holocaust with an awareness that assimilation had failed. They no longer believed that non-Jews would protect Jews. Jews needed to look out for one another. Antisemitic attacks by non-Jewish DPs reinforced those lessons. The Holocaust survivors who chose to become DPs had decided that Jewish life could not be secure in Europe, and they shared that rejection of Europe along with their common situation in the DP camps. The need to compete for Allied attention and resources further encouraged Jewish DPs to unite together for the protection of their common interests. Bound by their distrust of Germans, their belief in their own entitlement to Allied assistance, and their shared commitment to a Jewish future, Jewish DPs formed a community.

Religious rituals, cultural activities, and concepts of justice helped to shape social memories and a common DP identity. Most DPs performed and participated in religious rituals as a means of identifying themselves as members of the Jewish community. Survivors created a connection with their prewar lives and families when they recited *Kaddish*, married beneath the wedding canopy, circumcised their sons, and celebrated the Passover seder. Although DPs fought over levels of observance and the limits of rabbinic authority, religious observance served to underpin an ethnic identity for secular Jews as well as a religious one for Orthodox Jews. Through mourning academies survivors formed collective memories of their communities' destruction regardless of their personal wartime experiences. Newspapers and historical commissions educated survivors about different experiences of survival and integrated them into coherent narratives, helping to create a shared past out of a wide variety of experiences. Theatrical productions were especially suited to enabling DPs to rework their immediate past, to reinterpret it as one of resistance, and to imagine a Jewish future in Palestine. These cultural venues and DP courts of law were centers for the negotiation and articulation of what Jewish values and community meant after the Shoah.

By arguing for a shared identity, I do not presume that all DPs held every aspect of that identity to be true for themselves personally, merely that the majority found significant elements that spoke to them and that bound them together with other DPs. The majority of DPs were non-Orthodox and Zionist. A minority were Orthodox and non-Zionist, and some, such as the few Bundists, were secular and non-Zionist. Nevertheless, I argue that these survivors of differing beliefs, social and national origins, and Holocaust experiences forged a common identity as Jews and survivors of the great catastrophe. DP Bundists believed in the necessity of immigration to Palestine as one of the possible destinations for survivors and were much more cooperative with Zionists than their American counterparts. DP Bundists participated in the political and cultural life of the DP community. Polish ultra-Orthodox DPs of Agudat Israel also accommodated themselves to Zionism more than world Agudat-Israel organizations did, advocating that the future of the Jewish people lay in Palestine even while they decried the lack of religious observance among secular DPs. Jews who survived the war in the Soviet Union adopted a sense of having survived the Holocaust since they, too, had experienced the loss of family and home and shared the common experience of the DP camps and DP visions for the future.

Feeling abandoned by the Allies who seemed content to leave them in camps, DPs focused their hopes on a Jewish future in Palestine. These survivors remained on a wartime footing, both against the Germans and against the British rulers of Palestine. The need for Jewish fighters in both Germany and Palestine shaped gender roles for Jewish men and women, emphasizing physical resistance and revenge. The Zionist new man and the partisan-girl received military training in the DP camps, made the dangerous illegal voyage to Palestine, and fought for Israeli independence. At the same time, the desire for "normalcy" encouraged marriage and the re-creation of domestic life that they remembered from their prewar homes. The new Jewish mother had a national consciousness and raised her children to be new Jewish men and women dedicated to the Jewish people and a Zionist future.

Zionism played a major role in DP cultural and political life. DPs understood the lesson of the Holocaust to be that Jewish life could only be secure within a Jewish state. Contrary to the claims of Israeli "new historians," the DPs were not the passive victims of Zionist manipulation, nor was DP Zionism born out of desperation and a lack of opportunity. Those who survived the Nazi years were remarkably strong-willed and had clear ideas about their own self-interest. That not all of those who professed Zionist sympathies made aliyah had more to do with personal circumstances than with hypocrisy or coerced professions of Zionism. Desperate to rear their children away from the cemeteries of Europe, DPs often took the first country of immigration available to them but remained devoted to the idea of a Jewish homeland. Zionism played a healthy role in the rehabilitation of Holocaust survivors, providing purpose and meaning, creating surrogate families, and offering a new concept of home.

The DP camps were not the isolated communities a ten-year-old Fleischmann perceived them to be, but as she so vividly illustrated, they were vibrant and assertively Jewish communities. Jewish DPs exerted tremendous will to reclaim control over their lives. Despite their dependence on the Allies and international relief organizations and despite unimaginable trauma, Jewish DPs demanded the right to rebury their dead, observe Jewish dietary laws, and to develop their own political organizations. They agitated against British policies in Palestine, protested German police actions, and insisted that Allied personnel and leaders of international Jewish organizations treat them with respect. They repeatedly confronted Germans with the crimes of the past, hoping to generate acknowledgement and remorse. During their stay in the land of their former tormentors, in the shadow of Amalek, Jewish DPs transformed themselves from the victims of Nazism into the survivors of the Holocaust.

Bibliography

Archives

Archiv KZ-Gedenkstätte Flossenbürg
Central Zionist Archive, Jerusalem
Great Britain, Foreign Office, *Control Office for Germany and Austria and Foreign Office, German Section; General Department Public Records, 1945–1947* (microfilm USHMM)
Stadtarchiv Neunburg vorm Wald
United Nations Archive, New York
United States Holocaust Memorial Museum Archive, Washington, DC
United States National Archives II, College Park, MD
University of Rochester Archive
University of Southern California Shoah Visual History Foundation, Los Angeles
Yad Vashem, Jerusalem
YIVO Institute, New York

Eyewitness Accounts, Published Reports, and Document Collections

Bak, Samuel. "Landsberg Revisited." *Dimensions* 13 (1999): 31–36.
Bernstein, Philip S. " The Role and Functions of the Modern Rabbi." *Central Conference of American Rabbis Annual* 79 (1969): 225–227.
Cohen, Henry. "The Anguish of the Holocaust Surivors: Talk at Conservative Synagogue of Fifth Avenue on Yom HaShoah." 13 April 1996, http://remember.org/witness/cohen.html, accessed 10 July 2008.
Doherty, Muriel Knox. *Letters from Belsen 1945: An Australian Nurse's Experiences with the Survivors of War.* Eds. Judith Cornell and R. Lynette Russell. St. Leonards, NSW Australia: Allen & Unwin, 2000.
Friedman, Paul. "Road Back for DP's: Healing the Psychological Scars of Nazism." *Commentary* 6 (1948): 502–10.
Hemmendinger, Judith. *Survivors: Children of the Holocaust.* Bethesda, Maryland: National Press Books, 1986.
Heymont, Irving. *Among the Survivors of the Holocaust – 1945: The Landsberg DP Camp Letters of Major Irving Heymont, United States Army.* Cincinnati, OH: American Jewish Archives, 1982.

Hirschman, Ira A. *The Embers Still Burn.* New York: Simon and Schuster, 1949.

Hyman, Abraham S. "Displaced Persons." *American Jewish Year Book* 50 (1948–49): 455–472.

Kirschner, Robert, ed. *Rabbinic Responsa of the Holocaust Era.* New York: Schocken Books, 1985.

Kleiman, Yehudit and Nina Springer-Aharoni, eds. *The Anguish of Liberation: Testimonies from 1945.* Jerusalem: Yad Vashem, 1995.

Merritt, Anna J. and Richard L., eds. *Public Opinion in Occupied Germany.* Ubana: University of Illinois Press, 1970.

Peck, Abraham J., ed. *American Jewish Archives, Cincinnati: The Papers of the World Jewish Congress, 1945–1950.* Archives of the Holocaust, volume 9. New York: Garland Publishing, 1990.

Pinson, Koppel S. "Jewish Life in Liberated Germany: A Study of the Jewish DP's," *Jewish Social Studies* 9 (April 1947): 101–126.

Segalman, Ralph, "The Psychology of Jewish Displaced Persons," *Jewish Social Services Quarterly* 24 (June 1947): 361–369.

Shils, Edward A. "Social and Psychological Aspects of Displacement." *Journal of Social Issues* 2 (August 1946): 4–18.

Stoeckel, W., ed. *Lehrbuch der Geburtshilfe,* 8th ed. Jena: Verlag von Gustav Fischer, 1945.

Syrkin, Marie. *The State of the Jews.* Washington, DC: New Republic Books, 1980.

Touster, Saul, ed. *A Survivors' Haggadah: Written, Designed, and Illustrated by Yosef Dov Sheinson with Woodcuts by Miklós Adler.* Philadelphia: Jewish Publication Society, 2000.

Warhaftig, Zorach. *Refugee and Survivor: Rescue Efforts During the Holocaust.* Jerusalem: Yad Vashem, 1988.

Memoirs

Appleman-Jurman, Alicia. *Alicia: My Story.* New York: Bantam Books, 1988.

Bender, Benjamin. *Glimpses: Through Holocaust and Liberation.* Berkeley, CA: North Atlantic Books, 1995.

Benisch, Pearl. *To Vanquish the Dragon.* New York: Feldheim Publishers, 1991.

Bernstein, Sara Tuvel. *The Seamstress: A Memoir of Survival.* New York: Berkley Books, 1997.

Biber, Jacob. *Risen from the Ashes: A Story of the Jewish Displaced Persons in the Aftermath of World War II.* San Bernardino, CA: Borgo Press, 1990.

Bitton-Jackson, Livia. *My Bridges of Hope: Searching for Life and Love after Auschwitz.* New York: Simon & Schuster, 1999.

Blatt, Thomas Toivi. *From the Ashes of Sobibor: A Story of Survival.* Evanston, IL: Northwestern University Press, 1997.

Dawidowicz, Lucy S. *From that Place and Time: A Memoir, 1938–1947.* New York: W.W. Norton & Co., 1989.

Eichengreen, Lucille. *From Ashes to Life: My Memories of the Holocaust.* San Francisco: Mercury House, 1994.

Farkas, Helen. *Remember the Holocaust: A Memoir of Survival.* Santa Barbara, CA: Fithian Press, 1995.

Ferderber-Salz, Bertha. *And the Sun Kept Shining ...* New York: Holocaust Library, 1980.

Fishman, Lala and Steven Weingartner. *Lala's Story: A Memoir of the Holocaust.* Evanston, IL: Northwestern University Press, 1997.

Fleischmann, Lea. *Dies ist nicht mein Land: eine Jüdin verläßt die Bundesrepublik.* Hamburg: Wilhelm Heyne Verlag, 1980.

Friedman, Henry. *I'm No Hero: Journeys of a Holocaust Survivor.* Seattle: University of Washington Press, 2001.

Gabor, Georgia M. *My Destiny: Survivor of the Holocaust.* Arcadia, CA: Amen Publishing, 1981.

Halpern, Sam. *Darkness and Hope.* New York: Shengold Publishers, 1996.

Harmatz, Joseph. *From the Wings: A Long Journey, 1940–1960.* Sussex, England: The Book Guild, 1998.

Heller, Fanya Gottesfeld. *Strange and Unexpected Love: A Teenage Girl's Holocaust Memoirs.* Hoboken, NJ: KTAV Publishing, 1993.

Hulme, Kathryn. *The Wild Place.* Boston: Little, Brown and Company, 1953.

Jacobs, Benjamin. *The Dentist of Auschwitz: A Memoir.* Lexington: The University Press of Kentucky, 1995.

Katz, Nathan. *Teach Us to Count Our Days: A Story of Survival, Sacrifice and Success.* Cranbury, NJ: Cornwall Books, 1999.

Klausner, Abraham J. *A letter to My Children from the Edge of the Holocaust.* San Francisco: Holocaust Center of Northern California, 2002.

Klein, Gerda Weissmann. *All But My Life.* rev. ed. New York: Hill and Wang, 1995.

Kluger, Ruth. *Still Alive: A Holocaust Girlhood Remembered.* The Helen Rose Scheuer Jewish Women's Series. New York: The Feminist Press at the City University of New York, 2001.

Lasker-Wallfisch, Anita. *Inherit the Truth.* New York: St. Martin's Press, 1996.

Levy, Isaac. *Witness to Evil: Bergen-Belsen, 1945.* London: Peter Halban Publishers, 1995.

Linder, Bert. *Condemned without Judgment.* New York: S.P.I. Books, 1995.

Perlmutter, H. *Bine-Maskes Bay Katsetlekh.* Tel Aviv: Hamenorah, 1974.

Pisar, Samuel. *Of Blood and Hope.* New York: MacMillan Publishing, 1979.

Rosensaft, Hadassah. *Yesterday: My Story.* Washington, DC: United States Holocaust Memorial Museum, 2004.

Rubinstein, Erna F. *After the Holocaust: The Long Road to Freedom.* North Haven, CT: Archon Books, 1995.

Saaroni, Sarah. *Life Goes On Regardless....* Hawthorn, Australia: Hudson Publishing, 1989.

Schochet, Simon. *Feldafing.* Vancouver, Canada: November House, 1983.

Schulman, Faye. *A Partisan's Memoir: Woman of the Holocaust.* Toronto: Second Story Press, 1995.

Sender, Ruth Minsky. *To Life.* New York: Macmillan Publishing, 1988.

Vida, George. *From Doom to Dawn: A Jewish Chaplain's Story of Displaced Persons.* New York: Jonathan David, 1967.

Walshaw, Rachela and Sam. *From Out of the Firestorm: A Memoir of the Holocaust.* New York: Shapolsky Publishers, 1991.

Waterford, Helen. *Commitment to the Dead.* Frederick, Colorado: Renaissance House, 1987.

Weitz, Sonia Schreiber. *I Promised I Would Tell.* Brookline, MA: Facing History and Ourselves, 1993.

Wiesel, Elie. *All Rivers Run to the Sea: Memoirs.* New York: Alfred A. Knopf, 1995.

Un di velt hot geshvign. Buenos Aires: Tsentral-Farband fun Poylische Yidn in Argentine, 1956.

Zelman, Leon. *After Survival: One Man's Mission in the Cause of Memory*. New York: Holmes & Meier, 1998.

Zyskind, Sara. *Stolen Years*. Minneapolis: Lerner Publication Group, 1981.

Secondary Sources

Agar, Herbert. *The Saving Remnant*. New York: Viking Press, 1960.

Aschheim, Steven A. *Brothers and Strangers: The East European Jew in German and German Jewish Consciousness, 1800–1923*. Madison: University of Wisconsin Press, 1982.

Asheri, Michael. *Living Jewish: The Lore and Law of the Practicing Jew*. 2nd edition. New York: Everest House, 1978.

Bacon, Gershon C. *The Politics of Tradition: Agudat Yisrael in Poland, 1916–1939*. Jerusalem: The Magnes Press, The Hebrew University, 1996.

Baer, Elizabeth R. and Myrna Goldenberg, eds. *Experience and Expression: Women, the Nazis, and the Holocaust*. Detroit, MI: Wayne State University Press, 2003.

Barnouw, Dagmar. *The War in the Empty Air: Victims, Perpetrators, and Postwar Germans*. Bloomington: Indiana University Press, 2005.

Bauer, Yehuda. *Flight and Rescue: Brichah*. New York: Random House, 1970.

    Out of the Ashes: : The Impact of American Jews on Post-Holocaust European Jewry. New York: Pergamon Press, 1989.

Baumel, Judith Tydor. *Double Jeopardy: Gender and the Holocaust*. London: Vallentine Mitchell, 1998.

    Kibbutz Buchenwald: Survivors and Pioneers. New Brunswick, NJ: Rutgers University Press, 1997.

    "DPs, mothers and pioneers: Women in the She'erit Hapletah." *Jewish History* 11 (September 1997): 99–110.

    "Kibbutz Buchenwald and Kibbutz Hafetz Hayyim: Two Experiments in the Rehabilitation of Jewish Survivors in Germany." *Holocaust and Genocide Studies* 9 (Fall 1995): 231–249.

    "The Politics of Spiritual Rehabilitation in the DP Camps." *Simon Wiesenthal Center Annual* 6 (1989): 58–79.

Belton, Neil. *The Good Listener: Helen Bamber, A Life against Cruelty*. New York: Pantheon Books, 1998.

Berkowitz, Michael. *The Crime of My Very Existence: Nazism and the Myth of Jewish Criminality*. Berkeley: University of California Press, 2007.

Blatman, Daniel. *For Our Freedom and Yours: The Jewish Labour Bund in Poland 1939–1949*. London: Vallentine Mitchell, 2003.

Blum-Dobkin, Toby. "Rituals of Transition: An Ethnographic Approach to Life in a Displaced Persons Camp." In *The Netherlands and Nazi Genocide: Papers of the 21st Annual Scholars' Conference*, edited by G. Jan Colijn and Marcia S. Littell, vol. 32. Lewiston, NY: The Edwin Mellen Press, 1992.

Boyarin, Daniel. *Unheroic Conduct: The Rise of Heterosexuality and the Invention of the Jewish Male*. Berkeley: University of California Press, 1997.

Brenner, Michael. *After the Holocaust: Rebuilding Jewish Lives in Postwar Germany*. trans. Barbara Harshav. Princeton, NJ: Princeton University Press, 1997.

    Am Beispiel Weiden: jüdischer Alltag im Nationalsozialismus. Würzburg: Arena, 1983.

Brenner, Michael and Renate Höpfinger, eds. *Die Juden in der Oberpfalz*. Munich: Oldenbourg Wissenschaftsverlag, 2009.

Brenner, Reeve Robert. *The Faith and Doubt of Holocaust Survivors.* New York: Free Press, 1980.

Browning, Christoper. *Collected Memories: Holocaust History and Post-War Testimony.* Madison: University of Wisconsin Press, 2003.

Bush, Barbara. "Gender and Empire: The Twentieth Century." In *Gender and Empire,* edited by Philippa Levine, pp. 77–111. Oxford: Oxford University Press, 2004.

Cameron, Robert. "There and Back Again: Constabulary Training and Organization, 1946–1950." In *Armed Diplomacy: Two Centuries of American Campaigning.* Ft. Leavenworth, KS: Combat Studies Institute Press, 2003.

Carlebach, Julius and Andreas Brämer, "Flight into Action as a Method of Repression: American Military Rabbis and the Problem of Jewish Displaced Persons in Postwar Germany." *Jewish Studies Quarterly* 2 (1995): 59–76.

Cohen, Beth B. *Case Closed: Holocaust Survivors in Postwar America.* New Brunswick, NJ: Rutgers University Press, 2007.

Confino, Alon, Paul Betts, and Dirk Schumann, eds. *Between Mass Death and Individual Loss: The Place of the Dead in Twentieth-Century Germany.* New York: Berghahn Books, 2008.

Conway, Jill Ker. *When Memory Speaks: Reflections on Autobiography.* New York: Alfred A. Kopf, 1998.

Cullather, Nick. "The Foreign Policy of the Calorie." *American Historical Review* 112 (April 2007): 337–354.

Davidson, Shamai. *Holding on to Humanity – The Message of Holocaust Survivors: The Shamai Davidson Papers,* edited by Israel W. Charny. New York: New York University Press, 1992.

Des Pres, Terrence. *The Survivor: An Anatomy of Life in the Death Camps.* Oxford: Oxford University Press, 1976.

Dietrich, Susanne and Julia Schulze Wessel. *Zwischen Selbstorganisation und Stigmatisierung: Die Lebenswirklichkeit jüdischer Displaced Persons und die neue Gestalt des Antisemitismus in der deutschen Nachkriegsgesellschaft.* Stuttgart: Klett-Cotta, 1998.

Dinnerstein, Leonard. *America and the Survivors of the Holocaust.* New York: Columbia University Press, 1982.

Eder, Angelika. *Flüchtige Heimat: Jüdische Displaced Persons in Landsberg am Lech, 1945 bis 1950.* Miscellanea Bavarica Monacensia, vol. 170. Munich: UNI-Druck, 1998.

Elazar, Dahlia S. "'Engines of Acculturation': The Last Political Generation of Jewish Women in Interwar East Europe." *Journal of Historical Sociology* 15 (September 2002): 366–394.

Epstein, Louis M. *Sex Laws and Customs in Judaism.* New York: Ktav Publishing, 1948.

Fay, Jennifer. *Theaters of Occupation: Hollywood and the Reeducation of Postwar Germany.* Minneapolis: University of Minnesota Press, 2008.

"'That's Jazz Made in Germany': Hallo, Fräulein! and the Limits of Democratic Pedagogy," *Cinema Journal* 44 (Fall 2004): 3–24.

Fehrenbach, Heide. *Race after Hitler: Black Occupation Children in Postwar Germany and America.* Princeton, NJ: Princeton University Press, 2005.

Cinema in Democratizing Germany: Reconstructing National Identity after Hitler. Chapel Hill: University of North Carolina Press, 1995.

Feinstein, Margarete Myers. "Jewish Observance in Amalek's Shadow: Mourning, Marriage, and Birth Rituals among Displaced Persons in Germany." In *We Are*

Here: New Approaches to Jewish Displaced Persons in Postwar Germany, edited by Avinoam J. Patt and Michael Berkowitz. Detroit, MI: Wayne State University Press, forthcoming.

"Absent Fathers, Present Mothers: Images of Parenthood in Holocaust Survivor Narratives." _Nashim: A Journal of Jewish Women's Studies and Gender Issues_ 13 (Spring 2007): 155–182.

"Jewish Women Survivors in the Displaced Persons Camps of Postwar Germany: Transmitters of the Past, Caretakers of the Present, and Builders of the Future." _Shofar: An Interdisciplinary Journal of Jewish Studies_ 24:4 (Summer 2006): 67–89.

"Domestic Life in Transit: Jewish DPs." Paper presented at the Conference on Birth of a Refugee Nation: Displaced Persons in Post-War Europe, 1945–1951, at the Remarque Institute, New York University, April 20, 2001.

"Jewish Displaced Persons: Reconstructing the Individual and Community in the U.S. Zone of Occupied Germany." _Leo Baeck Institute Year Book_ 42 (Fall 1997): 303–324.

Finder, Gabriel N. "The Trial of Shepsl Rotholc and the Politics of Retribution in the Aftermath of the Holocaust." _Gal-Ed: On the History and Culture of Polish Jewry_ 20 (2006): 63–89.

Fodor, Renee. "The Impact of the Nazi Occupation of Poland on the Jewish Mother-Child Relationship." _YIVO Annual of Jewish Social Science_ 11 (1956/1957): 270–285.

Frei, Norbert, _1945 und Wir: Das Dritte Reich im Bewußtsein der Deutschen._ Munich: Verlag C.H. Beck, 2005.

Friedlander, Henry. _The Origins of Nazi Genocide: From Euthanasia to the Final Solution._ Chapel Hill: University of North Carolina Press, 1995.

Friedländer, Saul. _When Memory Comes._ New York: Farrar, Straus and Giroux, 1979.

Gal, Susan. _Language Shift: Social Determinants of Linguistic Change in Bilingual Austria._ New York: Academic Press, 1979.

Geller, Jay Howard. _Jews in Post-Holocaust Germany, 1945–1953._ Cambridge: Cambridge University Press, 2005.

Giere, Jacqueline Dewell. "Wir sind unterwegs, aber nicht in der Wüste: Erziehung und Kultur in den jüdischen Displaced Persons-Lagern der amerikanischen Zone im Nachkriegsdeutschland, 1945–1949." Ph.D. diss., Johann Wolfgang Goethe-Universität zu Frankfurt am Main, 1993.

Gilman, Sander. _The Jew's Body._ New York: Routledge, 1991.

Goldman, Solomon. "Education among Jewish Displaced Persons: The Sheerit Hapletah in Germany, 1945–1950." Ph.D. diss., The Dropsie University, 1978.

Goschler, Constantin. "The Attitude towards Jews in Bavaria after the Second World War." _Leo Baeck Institute Year Book_ 36 (1991): 443–458.

Gott, Kendall D. _Mobility, Vigilance, and Justice: The U.S. Army Constabulary in Germany, 1946–1953._ Ft. Leavenworth, KS: Combat Studies Institute Press, 2005.

Green, Nancy L. "Gender and Jobs in the Jewish Community: Europe at the Turn of the Twentieth Century." _Jewish Social Studies_ Ser. 2, vol. 8 (2002): 39–60.

Greenberg, Gershon. "Yehudah Leb Gerst's Religious 'Ascent' Through the Holocaust." _Holocaust and Genocide Studies_ 13 (Spring 1999): 62–89.

"From Hurban to Redemption: Orthodox Jewish Thought in the Munich Area, 1945–1948." _Simon Wiesenthal Center Annual_ 6 (1989): 81–112.

Greenspan, Henry. _On Listening to Holocaust Survivors: Recounting and Life History._ Westport, CT: Praeger Publishers, 1998.

Greiser, Katrin. "Die Todesmärsche von Buchenwald: Räumung des Lagerkomplexes im Frühjahr 1945 und Spuren der Erinnerung." Ph.D. diss., Universität Lüneburg, 2007. http://kirke.ub.uni-lueneburg.de/volltexte/2007/414/pdf/Dissertation.pdf, accessed 1 January 2008.

Grobman, Alex. *Battling for Souls: The Vaad Hatzala Rescue Committee in Post-War Europe.* Jersey City, NJ: KTAV Publishing, 2004.

Grodzinsky, Yosef. *In the Shadow of the Holocaust.* Monroe, ME: Common Courage Press, 2004.

Grossman, Kurt R. *The Jewish DP Problem: Its Origin, Scope and Liquidation.* New York: Institute of Jewish Affairs, World Jewish Congress, 1951.

Grossmann, Atina. *Jews, Germans, and Allies: Close Encounters in Occupied Germany.* Princeton, NJ: Princeton University Press, 2007.

"Victims, Villains, and Survivors: Gendered Perceptions and Self-Perceptions of Jewish Displaced Persons in Occupied Postwar Germany." *Journal of the History of Sexuality* 11 (January/April 2002): 291–318.

"Trauma, Memory and Motherhood: Germans and Jewish Displaced Persons in Post-Nazi Germany, 1945–1949," *Archiv für Sozialgeschichte* 38 (1998): 215–239.

Groth, Alexander J. *Holocaust Voices: An Attitudinal Survey of Survivors.* Amherst, NY: Humanity Books, 2003.

Gubar, Susan. "Dis/Identifications: Empathic Identification in Anne Michael's Fugitive Pieces: Masculinity and Poetry after Auschwitz." *Signs: Journal of Women in Culture and Society* 28 (2002): 249–276.

Gutman, Yisrael and Avital Saf, eds. *She'erit Hapletah 1944–1948: Rehabilitation and Political Struggle.* Jerusalem: Yad Vashem, 1990.

Hartman, Geoffrey H. "Learning from Survivors: The Yale Testimony Project." *Holocaust and Genocide Studies* 9 (Fall 1995): 192–207.

Hass, Aaron. *The Aftermath: Living with the Holocaust.* Cambridge: Cambridge University Press, 1995.

Heifetz, Julie. *Too Young to Remember.* Detroit, MI: Wayne State University Press, 1989.

Heineman, Elizabeth. "The Hour of the Woman," *American Historical Review* 101:2 (April 1996): 354–395.

Heinemann, Marlene E. *Gender and Destiny: Women Writers and the Holocaust.* New York: Greenwood Press, 1986.

Heller, Celia S. *On the Edge of Destruction: Jews of Poland between the Two World Wars.* New York: Columbia University Press, 1977.

Herzog, Dagmar. *Sex after Fascism: Memory and Morality in Twentieth-Century Germany.* Princeton, NJ: Princeton University Press, 2005.

Höhn, Maria. *GIs and Fräuleins: The German-American Encounter in 1950s West Germany.* Chapel Hill: The University of North Carolina Press, 2002.

Holborn, Louise W. *The International Refugee Organization: A Specialized Agency of the United Nations, Its History and Work 1946–1952.* London: Oxford University Press, 1956.

Horowitz, Sara R. "The Gender of Good and Evil: Women and Holocaust Memory." In *Gray Zones: Ambiguity and Compromise in the Holocaust and Its Aftermath,* edited by Jonathan Petropoulos and John K. Roth, pp. 165–184. New York: Berghahn Books, 2005.

"Gender, Genocide, and Jewish Memory," *Prooftexts: A Journal of Jewish Literary History* 20 (Winter/Spring 2000): 158–190.

"Memory and Testimony of Women Survivors of Nazi Genocide." In *Women of the Word: Jewish Women and Jewish Writing*, edited by Judith R. Baskin, pp. 259–282. Detroit, MI: Wayne State University Press, 1994.

Hyman, Paula E. "Gender and the Shaping of Modern Jewish Identities" *Jewish Social Studies* 8 (2002): 153–161.

Gender and Assimilation in Modern Jewish History: The Roles and Representation of Women. Seattle: University of Washington Press, 1995.

Isaacs, Miriam. "Historicizing Trauma, Rituals of Mourning: The Case of Jewish DPs." Paper presented at the Conference on Birth of a Refugee Nation: Displaced Persons in Post-War Europe, 1945–1951, at the Remarque Institute, New York University, April 20, 2001.

Jacobmeyer, Wolfgang. *Vom Zwangsarbeiter zum Heimatlosen Ausländer.* Göttingen: Vandenhoeck und Ruprecht, 1985.

Jacobs, Janet. "From the Profane to the Sacred: Ritual and Mourning at Sites of Terror and Violence." *Journal for the Scientific Study of Religion* 43 (2004): 311–315.

Jacobs, Margaret D. *Engendered Encounters: Feminism and Pueblo Cultures, 1879–1934.* Lincoln: University of Nebraska Press, 1999.

Jockusch, Laura. "Chronicles of Catastrophe: History Writing as a Jewish Response to Persecution Before and After the Holocaust." In *Holocaust Historiography In Context: Emergence, Challenges, Polemics and Achievements*, edited by David Bankier and Dan Michman. Jerusalem: Yad Vahem, 2008.

Judd, Robin. *Contested Rituals: Circumcision, Kosher Butchering, and Jewish Political Life in Germany, 1843–1933.* Ithaca, NY: Cornell University Press, 2007.

Kaplan, Marion. *Between Dignity and Despair.* New York: Oxford University Press, 1998.

Kater, Michael H. *Doctors under Hitler.* Chapel Hill: University of North Carolina Press, 1989.

Kauders, Anthony D. *Democratization and the Jews: Munich, 1945–1965.* Lincoln: The University of Nebraska Press for the Vidal Sassoon International Center for the Study of Antisemitism, the Hebrew University of Jerusalem, 2004.

Kertzer, David I. *Ritual, Politics, and Power.* New Haven, CT: Yale University Press, 1989.

Kochavi, Arieh J. *Post-Holocaust Politics: Britain, the United States, and Jewish Refugees, 1945–1948.* Chapel Hill: University of North Carolina Press, 2000.

"British Policy toward East European Refugees." *Simon Wiesenthal Center Annual* 7 (1990): 63–76.

"The Displaced Persons' Problem and the Formulation of British Policy in Palestine." *Studies in Zionism* 10 (1989): 31–48.

Konigsberg, Ira. "Our Children and the Limits of Cinema – Media Coverage of the Holocaust," *Film Quarterly* (Fall 1998): 7–19.

Königseder, Angelika and Juliane Wetzel. *Lebensmut im Wartesaal.* Frankfurt a.M.: Fischer Taschenbuch Verlag, 1994.

Korman, Gerd. "Survivors' Talmud and the U.S. Army." *American Jewish History* 73 (1984): 252–285.

Kugelman, Cilly. "Lang ist der Weg: Eine jüdisch-deutsche Film-Kooperation." In *Fritz Bauer Insistut Jahrbuch 1996 zur Geschichte und Wirkung des Holocaust. Auschwitz: Geschichte Rezeption und Wirkung*, pp. 353–370. Frankfurt a.M.: Campus Verlag, 1996.

Lamm, Maurice. *The Jewish Way in Death and Mourning.* New York: Jonathan David Publishers, 1969.

Lang, Berel. "Holocaust Memory and Revenge: The Presence of the Past." *Jewish Social Studies* Ser. 2, vol. 2 (1996): 1–20.

Langer, Lawrence. *Holocaust Testimonies: The Ruins of Memory*. New Haven, CT: Yale University Press, 1991.

Laqueur, Walter. *A History of Zionism*. New York: Schocken Books, 1972.

Lavsky, Hagit. *New Beginnings: Holocaust Survivors in Bergen-Belsen and the British zone in Germany, 1945–1950*. Detroit, MI: Wayne State University Press, 2002.

Lazar, Aryeh, Shlomo Kravetz, and Peri Frederich-Kedem. "The Multidimensionality of Motivation for Jewish Religious Behavior: Content, Structure, and Relationship to Religious Identity." *Journal for the Scientific Study of Religion* 41 (2002): 509–519.

Lewinsky, Tamar. "Displaced Writers? Zum kulturellen Selbstverständnis jiddischer DP-Schriftsteller." In *Zwischen Erinnerung und Neubeginn: zur deutsch-jüdischen Geschichte nach 1945*, edited by Susanne Schönborn. Munich: Meidenbauer, 2006.

Libby, Brian Arthur. "Policing Germany: the United States Constabulary." Ph.D. diss., Purdue University, 1977.

Linden, R. Ruth. *Making Stories, Making Selves: Feminist Reflections on the Holocaust*. Columbus: Ohio State University Press, 1993.

Mankowitz, Zeev. *Life Between Memory and Hope: The Survivors of the Holocaust in Occupied Germany*. Cambridge: Cambridge University Press, 2002.

Marcuse, Harold. *Legacies of Dachau: The Uses and Abuses of a Concentration Camp, 1933–2001*. Cambridge: Cambridge University Press, 2001.

"The Formation of the She'erit Hapleita," *Yad Vashem Studies* 20 (1990): 337–370.

Marrus, Michael. *The Unwanted*. New York: Oxford University Press, 1985.

Melman, Billie. "Re-Generation and the Construction of Gender in Peace and War – Palestine Jews, 1900–1918." In *Boderlines: Genders and Identities in War and Peace, 1870–1930*, edited by Billie Melman. New York: Routledge, 1998.

Mendelsohn, Ezra. *The Jews of East Central Europe between the World Wars*. Bloomington: Indiana University Press, 1983.

Moeller, Robert G. *War Stories: The Search for a Usable Past in the Federal Republic of Germany*. Berkeley: University of California Press, 2001.

Moissl, Norbert. "Aspekte der Geburtshilfe in der Zeit des Nationalsozialismus 1933 bis 1945 am Beispiel der I. Frauenklinik der Universität München." Dr. med. diss., Ludwigs-Maximilians-Universität zu München, 2005.

Morris, Benny. *Making Israel*. Ann Arbor: University of Michigan Press, 2007.

Müller, Ulrich. *Fremde in der Nachkriegszeit: Displaced Persons – zwangsverschleppte Personen – in Stuttgart und Württemberg-Baden, 1945–1951*. Stuttgart: Klett-Cotta, 1990.

"Displaced Persons (DPs) in der amerikanischen Zone Württembergs 1945–1950." *Geschichte in Wissenschaft und Unterricht* 40 (1989): 145–161.

Myers, Margarete L. "Jewish Displaced Persons: Reconstructing Individual and Community in the US Zone of Occupied Germany," *Leo Baeck Year Book* 42 (1997): 303–324.

Neumann, Klaus. *Shifting Memories: The Nazi Past in the New Germany*. Ann Arbor: University of Michigan Press, 2000.

Negra, Diane. *Off-White Hollywood: American Culture and Ethnic Female Stardom*. New York: Routledge, 2001.

Ofer, Dalia. "Holocaust Survivors as Immigrants: The Case of Israel and the Cyprus Detainees." *Modern Judaism* 16 (February 1996): 1–24.

Ofer, Dalia and Lenore J. Weitzman, eds. *Women in the Holocaust*. New Haven, CT: Yale University Press, 1998.

Olick, Jeffrey. *In the House of the Hangman: The Agonies of German Defeat, 1943–1949.* Chicago: University of Chicago Press, 2005.

"Collective Memory: The Two Cultures." *Sociological Theory* 17 (November 1999): 333–348.

Ozorak, Elizabeth Weiss. "Social and Cognitive Influences on the Development of Religious Beliefs and Commitment in Adolescence." *Journal for the Scientific Study of Religion* 28 (December 1989): 448–463.

Patt, Avinoam J. *Finding Home and Homeland: Jewish Youth and Zionism in the Aftermath of the Holocaust.* Detroit, MI: Wayne State University Press, 2009.

Patt, Avinoam J. and Michael Berkowitz, eds. *We Are Here: New Approaches to the Study of Jewish Displaced Persons in Postwar Germany.* Detroit, MI: Wayne State University Press, forthcoming December 2009.

Peck, Abraham J. " 'Our Eyes Have Seen Eternity' ": Memory and Self-Identity Among the She'erith Hapletah," *Modern Judaism* 17 (1997): 57–74.

"Jewish Survivors of the Holocaust in Germany: Revolutionary Vanguard or Remnants of a Destroyed People?" *Tel Aviver Jahrbuch für deutsche Geschichte* 19 (1990): 33–45.

Penslar, Derek J. *Israel in History: The Jewish State in Comparative Perspective.* London: Routledge, 2007.

Perry, Adelle. "From 'the hot-bed of vice' to the 'good and well-ordered Christian home': First Nations Housing and Reform in Nineteenth-Century British Columbia." *Ethnohistory* 50 (Fall 2003): 587–610.

Porat, Dina. "The Justice System and Courts of Law in the Ghettos of Lithuania." *Holocaust and Genocide Studies* 12:1 (1998): 49–65.

Proctor, Robert N. *Racial Hygiene: Medicine under the Nazis.* Cambridge, MA: Harvard University Press, 1988.

Rabinbach, Anson and Jack Zipes, eds. *Germans and Jews since the Holocaust: The Changing Situation in West Germany.* New York: Holmes and Meier, 1986.

Rapaport, Lynn. *Jews in Germany after the Holocaust: Memory, Identity, and Jewish-German Relations.* Cambridge: Cambridge University Press, 1997.

"The Cultural and Material Reconstruction of the Jewish Communities in the Federal Republic of Germany." *Jewish Social Studies* 49 (1987): 137–154.

Reichel, Peter. *Vergangenheitsbewältigung in Deutschland: Die Auseinandersetzung mit der NS-Diktatur von 1945 bis heute.* Munich: Verlag C.H. Beck, 2001.

Reilly, Jo, et. al., eds. *Belsen in History and Memory.* London: Frank Cass, 1997.

Rosenbaum, Irving J. *The Holocaust and Halakhah.* New York: KTAV Publishing, 1976.

Rosensaft, Menachem, ed. *Life Reborn: Jewish Displaced Persons 1945–1951, Conference Proceedings.* Washington, DC: United States Holocaust Memorial Museum, 2001.

Sachar, Abram L. *Redemption of the Unwanted.* New York: St. Martin's Press, 1983.

Sachar, Howard M. *A History of the Jews in America.* New York: Vintage Books, 1993.

Saidel, Rochelle G. *The Jewish Women of Ravensbrück Concentration Camp.* Madison: University of Wisconsin Press, 2004.

Schacter, Daniel L. *The Seven Sins of Memory.* Boston: Houghton Mifflin Company, 2001.

Searching for Memory: The Brain, the Mind, and the Past. New York: Basic Books, 1996.

Schein, Ada. "'Everyone Can Hold a Pen': The Documentation Project in the DP Camps in Germany." In *Holocaust Historiography In Context: Emergence, Challenges, Polemics and Achievements*, edited by David Bankier, and Dan Michman. Jerusalem: Yad Vahem, 2008.

Segev, Tom. *The Seventh Million: The Israelis and the Holocaust*. New York: Hill and Wang, 1993.

Seidman, Naomi. "Elie Wiesel and the Scandal of Jewish Rage." *Jewish Social Studies* Ser. 2, vol. 3 (1996): 1–19.

Sicher, Efraim, ed. *Breaking Crystal: Writing and Memory after Auschwitz*. Urbana: University of Illinois Press, 1998.

Sosis, Richard and Bradley J. Ruffle. "Religious Ritual and Cooperation: Testing for a Relationship on Israeli Religious and Secular Kibbutzim." *Current Anthropology* 44 (December 2003): 713–721.

Stern, Frank. *The Whitewashing of the Yellow Badge: Antisemitism and Philosemitism in Postwar Germany*, trans. by William Templer. Series: Studies in Antisemitism, Vidal Sassoon International Center for the Study of Antisemitism, The Hebrew University of Jerusalem. Oxford: Pergamon Press, 1992.

"The Historic Triangle: Occupiers, Germans and Jews in Postwar Germany," *Tel Avivier Jahrbuch für deutsche Geschichte* 19 (1990): pp. 47–76.

Tec, Nechama. *Resilience and Courage: Women, Men, and the Holocaust*. New Haven, CT: Yale University Press, 2003.

Terr, Lenore. *Too Scared to Cry: Psychic Trauma in Childhood*. New York: Harper & Row, 1990.

Trunk, Isaiah. "Religious, Educational and Cultural Problems in the East European Ghettos under German Occupation." In *Eastern European Jews in Two Worlds: Studies from the YIVO Annual*, edited by Deborah Dash Moore. Evanston, IL: Northwestern University Press, 1990.

Judenrat: The Jewish Councils in Eastern Europe under Nazi Occupation. Briarcliff Manor, NY: Stein and Day Publishers, 1972.

Tzahor, Zeev. "Holocaust Survivors as a Political Factor." *Middle Eastern Studies* 24 (1988): 432–444.

Verdery, Katherine. *The Political Lives of Dead Bodies: Reburial and Postsocialist Change*. New York: Columbia University Press, 1999.

Vernant, Jacques. *The Refugee in the Post-War World*. New Haven, CT: Yale University Press, 1953.

Webster, Ronald. "American Relief and Jews in Germany, 1945–1960: Diverging Perspectives." *Leo Baeck Institute Year Book* 38 (1993): 295–321.

Wetzel, Juliane. *Jüdisches Leben in München, 1945–1951: Durchgangsstation oder Wiederaufbau?* Munich: Kommissionsverlag UNI-Druck, 1987.

Woodbridge, George. *UNRRA: The History of the United Nations Relief and Rehabilitation Administration*, vol. 2. New York: Columbia University Press, 1950.

Wyman, Mark. *DPs: Europe's Displaced Persons, 1945–1951*. Ithaca, NY: Cornell University Press, 1998.

Young, James E. *Writing and Rewriting the Holocaust: Narrative and the Consequences of Interpretation*. Bloomington: Indiana University Press, 1990.

Zertal, Idith. *Israel's Holocaust and the Politics of Nationhood*. Cambridge: Cambridge University Press, 2005.

"Refugees for a State: History, Memory, and Politics." Paper presented at the Conference on Birth of a Refugee Nation: Displaced Persons in Post-War Europe, 1945–1951, at the Remarque Institute, New York University, April 21, 2001.

From Catastrophe to Power: Holocaust Survivors and the Emergence of Israel. Berkeley: University of California Press, 1998.

Zerubavel, Eviatar. "Social Memories: Steps to a Sociology of the Past." *Qualitative Sociology* 19 (1996): 283–299.

Index